Look up, Pennsylvania!

Walking Tours of 50 Towns in the Keystone State

DOUG GELBERT

D1214251

CRUDEN BAY BOOKS

About the author:

Doug Gelbert has written over 30 guidebooks on such diverse topics as public golf courses, the Civil War, movie filming locations and the best places to hike with your dog. For more information on this title visit the website *walkthetown.com*.

The towns...

How to use this book...

There is no better way to see Pennsylvania than on foot. And there is no better way to appreciate what you are looking at than with a walking tour. Whether you are visiting a new town or just out to look at your own town in a new way, a walking tour is ready to explore when you are.

Each of the 55 walking tours in Look Up, Pennsylvania! describes a mix of historical and architectural and ecclesiastical landmarks. A quick primer on identifying architectural styles seen on Pennsylvania streets can be found at the back of the book on page 436.

Where are the maps?

Let's face it, in today's world of GPS, Google Maps and Mapquest trying to squeeze a detailed map onto a 7" a 10" piece of paper can be a superfluous exercise. The best way to get a map of these towns is to pick an address from the tour and plug it into your favorite mapping program. Adjust the map to whatever size best suits your needs and print it out to carry with you.

These tours are designed to be followed and enjoyed without maps. Each entry includes a street address and step-by-step directions. Note that when following a tour, street crossings are omitted. Always continue walking on your current street until a turn is indicated. Whenever possible the tours complete a circular route but sometimes retracing your steps is required. The tour starting points have been selected to be near convenient parking.

Where are the pictures?

They are all online. You can see photos of all the tour stops included in the book at this website: http://www.flickr.com/photos/walkthetown/. Click on "sets" and choose the town you are touring.

One more thing. Consider tearing out the pages from this book when you take a tour - the book is created so that each tour can be pulled out without impugning another tour. You may find it easier to tour with just a few foldable pages in your hand than holding an entire book.

And, one really last thing. Look twice before crossing the street. So get out and look up, Pennsylvania!

Look Up,

Allentown

A Walking Tour of Allentown...

Allentown was originally named Northamptontown by its founder, Chief Justice of Colonial Pennsylvania's Supreme Court, William Allen. Allen, also a former Mayor of Philadelphia and successful businessman, drew up plans for the rural village in 1762. Despite its formal name, from the beginning, nearly everyone called it "Allen's town." Allen hoped his village on the banks of the Lehigh River would evolve into a thriving commercial center. It was not to be. The low water level most of the year made river trade impractical. Sometime in the early 1770s, William Allen gave the property to his son, James, who built a country home here called Trout Hall after his father's hunting and fishing lodge. Even by the time of the American Revolution, Allentown remained little more than a small hamlet of German, farmers and tradesmen.

By the 1850s, however, on the back of the local iron industry, this youngest of the three cities in the Lehigh Valley had become the largest, as it remains today. From its founding in 1762 until its incorporation as a city in 1859, Allentown's boundaries were 4th and 10th Streets, east to west, and Liberty and Union Streets, north to south. The Old Allentown Historic District comprises the northwest quadrant of the city's original plan, with the addition of the blocks west to 12th Street between Liberty and Linden, including the 14-acre Union and West End Cemetery in the District's northwest corner.

This area developed rapidly as a result of a series of speculative real-estate booms (and busts) during the period 1865–1910. Early frame houses were replaced by more substantial two-and three-story row houses that took advantage of all usable space on both the main streets and the half-streets and alleys to meet the housing needs of a growing and changing population. Though primarily a residential district, Old Allentown contains the typical 19th-century mix of housing with commercial buildings, factories, stables, churches, schools, and saloons. Some of these latter structures stand on the sites of former brickyards and sawmills, which supplied the materials used to construct the neighborhood's buildings.

While Old Allentown contains many individual buildings of great charm, its historic value and distinction lie in its ensemble character. Our walking tour of this dense, richly textured 19th-century urban environment will start in Allentown Arts Park, a greenspace just off the main thoroughfare of Hamilton Street...

1. Allentown Arts Park
N 5th, Linden and Court streets

The centerpiece of the City's Art District, the $2 million, half-acre park offers an inviting fountain, locust trees, sunken green lawn, towering street lamps and marble retaining walls. A massive mural painted on the back of Symphony Hall looms over the greenspace.

LOOK NORTH ACROSS LINDEN STREET.

2. Baum School of Art
510 Linden Street

The Baum School of Art began in the summer of 1926 when Mrs.Blanche Lucas recruited Walter Emerson Baum, the noted Sellersville artist, to provide art instruction for 22 Allentown teachers. The following year, classes resumed on the third floor of the old Franklin Fire House which became the first home for the school. This modern 15,000-square foot facility is the school's fifth location, built in 1987. The David E. Rodale Gallery, located inside the main entrance of the School, provides a venue for a wide variety of art exhibitions.

LOOK EAST ACROSS N 5TH STREET.

3. Allentown Art Museum
31 N Fifth Street

The older wing is a Neo-Roman temple with Corinthian columns, built as the First Presbyterian Church in 1902. The modern north wing, constructed in 1974-1975, was designed by Edgar Tafel, Frank Lloyd Wright's most famous student. The museum was incorporated in 1939 when its collection was housed in the stone house adjacent to the city's Rose Garden at Cedar Park. The then vacant church structure was purchased in 1956.

EXIT THE PARK ONTO LINDEN STREET AND TURN RIGHT, WALKING TOWARDS THE RIVER (THE ART MUSEUM WILL BE ON YOUR RIGHT).

4. Butz-Groff House
111 N 4th Street

Built in 1872 by attorney Samuel A. Butz, this handsome dark stone Victorian home was once the center of Allentown's most fashionable residential district. The home was built for Butz's first wife, Mary Albright, who died in 1901. Butz, a long time member of the board of Allentown College of Women, now Cedar Crest College, practiced law up to the day of his death in 1930. It was purchased in 1975 by Allentown entrepreneur Ray Holland and renovated to house his antique car memorabilia collection.

TURN RIGHT ON N 4TH STREET. CROSS HAMILTON STREET TO ALLEN PARK AT THE SOUTHWEST CORNER OF WALNUT STREET.

5. Trout Hall
411 W Walnut Street

The impressive Trout Hall was built in 1769-1770 as the summer estate of James Allen, then 28-year old son of Allentown's founder. James was William Allen's third son and as a wedding present his father, the richest man in Pennsylvania, gave him over 3,000 acres in the Lehigh Valley that included the rents from the surrounding farmers. It stands today as Allentown's oldest home.

The start of the American Revolution shattered Allen's tranquil life. At first he supported the Colonial cause, but when the time came to make the final break with England in 1776 he could not go that far. Allen gathered up his family and servants and went to Trout Hall, hoping to ride out the Revolution as a neutral observer. But when he entertained British officers who were then prisoners he was denounced as a Tory and a spy. Members of the militia even attacked the coach carrying his wife and daughters.

In 1778 Allen got a pass from his friend George Washington to take his family to British-occupied Philadelphia. His wife was about to have a baby and her family, who were in the city, wanted her to be with them. While there Allen, age 37, died of tuberculosis on September 19, 1778. In one of the last entries in his diary he wrote of longing for "my old situation at Trout Hall."

There was once another Trout Hall in Allentown. Sometime before 1755 William Allen, Allentown's founder, built a small hunting and fishing cabin or his friends near Jordan Creek, behind what is now Central Catholic High School. The last known reference to the first Trout Hall was in 1845 when its foundation was torn down to widen Jordan Street.

6. Lehigh Valley Heritage Museum
432 W Walnut Street

The Lehigh County Historical Society is one of the largest historical societies in America. Its 30,000 square foot headquarters museum is a state-of-the-art climate-controlled facility that houses one of the finest historical research libraries in Pennsylvania. The Heritage Museum includes four galleries with more than 10,000 square feet of exhibits.

TURN RIGHT ON PENN STREET.

7. Homeopathic Healing Art Plaque
31 S Penn Street

The Homeopathic Healing Art Plaque marks the location of the world's first medical college exclusively devoted to the practice of homeopathic medicine. Called "The North American Academy of Homeopathic Healing Art," it was founded on April 10, 1835. The technique of homeopathic medicine - the idea that a drug which will produce certain symptoms in a healthy person will cure a sick person with the same symptoms - was developed in Germany by Dr. Samuel Hahnemann and carried to America. The Academy flourished until 1843 when it was discovered that its treasurer, Allentown banker John Rice, had embezzled the school's funds. It then moved to Philadelphia and developed into what today is the city's Hahnemann Hospital.

8. Allentown City Hall
435 Hamilton Street

In need of a new building for city offices, the five-story City Hall, the three story Public Safety building, and a three level parking deck were built in 1964 as part of the Allentown Redevelopment civic center plan after clearing the area between 4th and 5th Streets of blighted and deteriorated buildings.

TURN LEFT ON HAMILTON STREET.

9. United States Post Office
southeast corner of Hamilton and 5th streets

Built in 1933-1934, the Art Deco design adds a touch of distinction to a rather simple building. On the interior is a series of murals produced in New York artist Gifford Reynolds Beal. Each deals with a theme from Allentown history. One of the most familiar is the parade of Allentown's militia units marching off to defend the Capitol building in Washington on April 14, 1861. They are known locally as the First Defenders. Another depicts the journey of the Liberty Bell to Allentown. Other scenes show Allentown industries from the past.

10. Old Lehigh County Courthouse
northwest corner of Hamilton Street and N 5th Street

Built between 1814 and 1817, the Old Lehigh County Courthouse is the oldest active courthouse in the Commonwealth of Pennsylvania. It was altered in 1841 to show a new style.

STEP DOWN N 5TH STREET TO THE REAR OF THE COURTHOUSE BEFORE CONTINUING UP HAMILTON STREET.

11. Old Lehigh County Courhtouse Annex
(rear of building)

An addition to the Courthouse in 1914 is an excellent example of the Beaux Arts style of architecture popular at that time for government buildings. It features a generous rusticated base, window pedestals and ornate cornice.

12. Breinig and Bachman Building
southeast corner of 6th and Hamilton streets

Breinig and Bachman was a men's clothing store that occupied the ground floor for many years. No one can say for sure why the animal heads were added. Perhaps it was to please one of the building's original long-time tenants, the wholesale grain and animal feed dealer George W. Eckert. Built in 1894, this yellow bricked structure replaced a building of a similar name built three years before. The first B & B building was destroyed along with the rest of the southeast side of the street in a fire on the night of Friday, October 13, 1893.

13. Americus Hotel
northeast corner of 6th and Hamilton streets

The Americus Hotel, built by Allentown businessman Albert "Bert" Gomery, was named for 15th century Italian explorer Amerigo Vespucci and the interior walls once had elaborate murals depicting the Spanish Empire. The guest list totaled 700 at the opening on September 13, 1928.

14. Liberty Bell Shrine
622 W Hamilton Street

In September of 1777 General George Washington was unable to keep the British out of the capital city of Philadelphia, having lost the Battle of Brandywine. During a war, metal becomes scarce, so it was feared that the British might melt down the city's church bells and the bells of the State House, including the bell we now know as the Liberty Bell. The Supreme Executive Council decided to remove the eleven bells from the city so they would not fall into enemy hands.

A train of 700 wagons was organized to carry military stores to Bethlehem. Camouflaged by hay and manure, the bells were transported on sturdy wagons and then hauled to Allentown where they were hidden under the floorboards of old Zion's Reformed Church. There, they remained in safety until the following July. By the end of June, 1778, the British had evacuated Philadelphia and the Liberty Bell and the church bells were restored to their rightful places.

15. Zion's Reformed United Church of Christ
622 W Hamilton Street

The Zion's Reformed Church was built in 1886 and is the fourth to bear that name. Its roots go back to a log structure that was built to the rear of the current site in 1762 that housed the two oldest congregations in Allentown. The church was shared with the Lutherans until the 1770s. In 1773 Zion's Reformed congregation built a brick church on the lot it occupies today. The Lutherans remained in the log church until 1794 when they moved to South 8th Street off Hamilton.

16. Lehigh Valley Bank and Trust Company
600 Block Hamilton Street

The Lehigh Valley Trust dates to 1886. With its ornate columns and Beaux Arts festoons of stone garlands, its 1911 bank building is everything a bank should be - solid, conservative, and respectable. Its front was clad in white marble from Vermont, its four Ionic columns supported a marble cornice and gable, and the lobby was entered through ornamental bronze doors.

17. Zollinger-Harned Company Building
605-613 Hamilton Street

Zollinger-Harned was one of three major downtown department stores, along with Hess's and Lehr's that made Allentown a premier shopping destination in the Northeast. All are gone now; Zollinger-Harned left Hamilton Street in 1978.

18. Center Square/Hamilton Mall
Hamilton Street and 7th Street

Center Square is the focal point of the community as it was conceived by William Allen in 1762. In the not-too-distant past, clothing stores were located on each corner. Today, banks have established themselves in the buildings making the Square the financial heart of Allentown.

19. *Soldiers and Sailors Monument*
Hamilton Street and 7th Street

This city landmark, was originally dedicated on October 19, 1899 to honor General Phillip

Sheridan's Civil War unit – the 47th Regiment of Pennsylvania Volunteers - who fought at the battle of Cedar Creek. Governor William Stone did oration duty and more than 1,000 schoolchildren sang the national anthem as the monument was unveiled. The 99-foot high Vermont granite was re-dedicated as a monument to veterans of all wars on May 30, 1964.

20. Lehigh County Government Center
southeast corner of Center Square

The former H. Lehr & Company Department Store property was recently renovated by Lehigh County to expand and create much needed additional office space.

21. First National Bank
northeast corner of Center Square

The First National Bank of Allentown was formed in 1954 by the merger of Allentown National Bank and Second National Bank. The bank's headquarters was built on the site of the landmark Hotel Allen in 1958 and once sported a giant "1st" looming over the Square from the top of the corner.

22. Allentown National Bank
northeast corner of Center Square

This was the site of Allentown's first financial institution, the Northampton Bank, chartered in 1814. When the Allentown National Bank opened its Beaux Arts style headquarters in 1905, the handsome white eight-story structure was the pride of the City. Designed by Allentown architects Jacoby, Weishampel & Biggin, it boasted "two smoothly running hydraulic elevators that were the ultimate in safety" and a spacious rotunda surmounted by a dome 32 feet in height supported by six onyx columns. It was the essence of magnificence. When the bank relocated it served other tenants until it was vacated in the 1990s. Taken over by the City of Allentown, the building is being adapted for housing.

23. Dime Savings and Trust Company
northwest corner of Center Square

The maroon brick, Art-Deco style building was the former Dime Savings Bank and Trust Company, which opened in 1929 just in time for the Great Depression, which killed it.

24. Merchants National Bank
southwest corner of Center Square

Merchants National Bank opened its doors for business in 1903. The building, currently twice as wide on Hamilton Street, was completed in the late 1920s. Prior to this time, the bank conducted business in the lower level of the YMCA building.

25. Portland Place
southeast corner of Hamilton Street and Hall Street

Portland Place was formerly known as the Lehigh Portland Cement Company. The building served as the company's headquarters. It was also known as the Young Building after one of the company's founders, Edward M. Young. Built in 1902, it was extensively remodeled in the late Art-Modern style in 1939-1940. Over the front door is a glass relief sculpture designed by the Italian-American artist Oronzio Maldarelli. At that time it was the largest glass mural panel in the world. Cast at the Pittsburgh Corning Company's glass works, its three stylized allegorical figures represent the strength, durability, and permanence of cement.

26. Farr Building
739 Hamilton Street

This was originally the site of one of four hospitals that operated during the Revolutionary War. Shoe magnate Harvey Farr set up the headquarters here for his footwear company. Since the 1860s, the Farr family business had flourished and this 32,000 square foot, 5-story structure was to be its crowning glory. No expense was spared to construct the masonry and steel edifice and, when completed in 1927, its classic Revival style dominated Hamilton Street.

After the Farr family sold the business in the

1980s the building went through a succession of forgettable retail uses and the upper four floors went unutilized. Ultimately the building contained loft apartments that have been occupied since 2006.

TURN RIGHT ON N 8TH STREET.

27. Strand Theatre
12-16 N 8th Street

Opened in 1917, the Strand Theatre featured an Austin organ. Later it became the Cinema, when in the 1940s and early-1950s it was listed with 1,000 seats. The marquee and auditorium are gone but the facade remains.

28. Merkle Company Store
243-247 N 8th Street

William Merkle emigrated from Stuttgart, Germany in the 1850s and opened the Merkle and Company Store in this small, stable-like building which today looks much as it did when the store opened. The doors and shutters are original. Small as it is, this building for a time housed the Merkle family, as well as the store (they later moved to 342 North 8th Street). Five generations of the Merkle family continued to own and operate the business until 1985.

The Merkle Building at 245-247 North 8th Street is an unusually grand structure—four stories with stone facing, bays, arched windows and a copper-clad cornice gracing the facade. Constructed around 1900 on the site of two former houses, it was built as an apartment building—the first of its kind in Allentown—with the spacious first floor housing, besides the retail grocery, a millinery shop, a whole-sale dairy business, and a warehouse.

TURN RIGHT ON CHEW STREET.

29. Liberty Engine House
711 Chew Street

This is the original Liberty Engine House, built by the city in 1871 and enlarged to its present three stories in 1902. A group of 32 volunteers founded the Liberty Hose Company in 1869 to provide fire protection to the rapidly expanding northern wards of Allentown. After moving to the Chew Street building, the company acquired a horse-drawn, steam-powered Silsby rotary-pump fire engine, state-of-the-art equipment at the time, at a price of $4,200. Besides fighting fires, the Liberty crew used their pumper to sprinkle water on the streets to keep the dust down in dry weather in the days before asphalt. The company moved out of the building in 1958.

TURN AROUND AND WALK WEST ON CHEW STREET. TURN LEFT ON FOUNTAIN STREET.

30. 929-937 Turner Street; northwest corner of Fountain Street

Among the earliest extant structures in Old Allentown are the row houses at 929–937 Turner Street, sometimes called the "The Five Sisters." These small, peaked-roof frame buildings probably date to the 1830s. The diminutive scale, the use of wood rather than brick as a siding material, and the central chimneys are indicative of pre-Civil-War construction. The steeply pitched roofs with gable ends facing the street are a unique feature of these row houses. This design peculiarity may be the reason for the row's survival. While most other frame dwellings were dismantled and/or moved to other locations to make way for larger brick structures in the 1870s and 1880s, no single unit in this row could be removed without destroying the structural integrity of the one next to it.

31. Allentown Cemetery Park
southwest corner of Turner Street and
Fountain Street

Allentown Cemetery Park was created by William Allen as the graveyard for his little community. The first person recorded as being buried in the cemetery was Mary Huber in 1765. The older stones have epitaphs written in ornate German Gothic script. A large plaque at the corner of 10th and Linden lists veterans of the American Revolution and War of 1812. Among the most famous interred here is Peter Rhoads Sr., a local storekeeper and member of the Revolutionary-era Committee for Public Safety.

TURN LEFT ON HAMILTON STREET.

32. Pennsylvania Power and Light Building
9th and Hamilton streets

Thanks partly to General Henry Trexler, one of the principal directors of Lehigh Valley Transit, Pennsylvania Power and Light, a young company in the new and expanding power industry, was persuaded to locate its headquarters in downtown Allentown. The building has reigned as Allentown's tallest since its completion in June 1928. This 322-foot skyscraper was designed by architect Harvey Corbett and became a prototype for Art Deco architecture in New York City; Corbett would be one of several architects who planned Rockefeller Center in the 1930s. At the time it opened the PP&L had the fastest elevators in the world. When illuminated at night the PP&L was visible from most parts of Lehigh County and was featured in the 1930 edition of the *Encyclopedia Britannica* as the best example of a modern office building.

Among the building's outstanding exterior features are bas-reliefs by the Ukrainian-born sculptor Alexander Archipenko, a pioneer of modern sculpture. Archipenko was one of the leading figures in the so-called "School of Paris" that flourished in that French city in the pre-World War I years. He came to America in 1923 and the PP&L may have been one of his first public commissions in this country. Relief sculptures over the doorway show two eels pouring water over cog wheels as symbols of the uses of hydroelectric power. Other reliefs combine a mixture of birds and flowers, reflecting Ukrainian folk themes.

TURN LEFT ON 6TH STREET.

33. Allentown Symphony
23 N 6th Street

The Allentown Symphony has the unique distinction of being the smallest symphony orchestra in America to own its own performance hall. The historic, 1,200-seat Allentown Symphony Hall was built around 1896 as the Central Market Hall. The structure was converted to a theater in 1899 by the architectural firm of J.B. McElfatrick and renamed the Lyric Theatre. Perhaps one of only a dozen of the famous McElfatrick designs still standing, for many years it was one of the leading burlesque halls in the eastern United States.

In 1953, with the help of a number of community leaders, the Allentown Symphony Association bought the hall as a permanent home for its symphony orchestra, and re-christened it Symphony Hall. The Allentown Symphony has had only three music directors throughout its history with Donald Voorhees, famed conductor of the "Bell Telephone Hour," serving as the first music director for over thirty years from 1951 to 1983. Under his direction, the orchestra collaborated with such music legends as Placido Domingo, Phyllis Curtin, Rudolf Serkin, John Corigliano, Benny Goodman, and many others.

34. *Morning Call*
101 N 6th Street; northeast corner of Linden Street

The *Critic*, an Allentown newspaper founded in 1883, was the direct ancestor of the *Morning Call*. The editor, owner and chief reporter of the *Critic* was Samuel S. Woolever. In 1894 Muhlenberg College senior David A. Miller came on board as its sole reporter. Later that year the newspaper ran a contest. A school boy or girl in Lehigh County would receive $5 in gold if he or she could guess the publication's new name. The identity of the lucky winner is lost to history, but on Jan. 1, 1895, Allentown City Treasurer A.L. Reichenbach, who had supervised the contest, read out the new name: "The Morning Call." Miller would remain in charge of the paper until he died in 1958 at the age of 88.

TURN RIGHT ON LINDEN STREET TO RETURN TO THE TOUR STARTING POINT IN ALLENTOWN ARTS PARK.

Look Up,

Altoona

A Walking Tour of Altoona...

Before the Pennsylvania Railroad (PRR) stretched between Philadelphia and Pittsburgh, a system of railroads, canals and inclined planes across the Alleghenies, known as the Main Line of Public Works, linked the eastern and western sections of the state. The system was time consuming and inefficient, if not entirely useless during the winter freeze and spring floods. Meanwhile, Pennsylvania was rapidly being usurped by New York state and its Erie Canal as America's pathway to the West.

The founders of the PRR approached the State legislature in 1846 to build a railroad using low grades over the majority of the route west with a single short, but steep climb over the mountains. The point at which the water grade ended and that mountain passage began was Robinson's Ridge, the present site of Altoona, located 117 miles east of Pittsburgh and 235 miles west of Philadelphia. Here, beginning in 1849, the PRR built a facility for housing and repairing the additional locomotive power required to make that passage — it also spurred the development of a city.

West of town the challenge of carrying the Pennsylvania Railroad Mainline over the rugged Allegheny Mountains was met with the design and construction of "The Horseshoe Curve" in 1854. The huge loop connects one side of the valley with the other and was carved from the rugged mountainside entirely by men using picks, shovels and horses. To this day, the curve is considered to be an engineering marvel. Spending so much time digging out the curve it was natural that Altoona would become the major supplying town to the railroad industry, and for several years Altoona was the greatest railroad town in America.

Altoona was incorporated as a borough on February 6, 1854, and as a city under legislation following the Civil War. The town grew rapidly in the late 19th century, its population approximately 2,000 in 1854, 10,000 in 1870, and 20,000 in 1880. In the early 20th century, the Pennsylvania Railroad's Altoona Works complex alone employed, at its peak, approximately 15,000 people and covered three miles in length, 218 acres of yards and 37 acres of indoor workshop floor space in 122 buildings.

Live by the railroad, die by the railroad; Altoona declined in tandem with the abandonment of rail passenger service in America after World War II. Our walking tour will concentrate on the downtown area and visit financial sites, cultural sites, residential sites, sacred sites and, of course, the remnants of the largest railroad shops America has ever seen...

1. Mishler Theater
1208 12th Avenue

Born in Lancaster in 1862, Isaac Charles Mishler was the son of a carriage builder-turned-businessman whose family, Swiss-German in origin, arrived in Pennsylvania more than a century before. Had young Isaac accomplished nothing else in what grew into a relatively long life, this alone would have warranted a footnote in the annals of commerce: as a teenager, Mishler became the first employee of the first Woolworth's when Frank Woolworth, who wasn't all that much older, hired him to work in his first 5-and-10-cent store, in downtown Lancaster. In time, that store grew into the nationwide chain that made Woolworth a retailing legend. Mishler didn't stay long, though, for he heard the whistle of opportunity blowing from the west - in Altoona.

Mishler quickly found work in one of the railroad's repair shops, but within a few years, barely in his twenties, he was operating a successful downtown cigar store. He next invested in local semi-professional and minor league baseball before becoming a partner in Altoona's Eleventh Avenue Opera House in 1893. A year later he took over two theaters in nearby Johnstown. Within a decade, his domain had spread to include theaters in Allentown, Trenton, and Paterson, New Jersey.

Its external façade was made of red brick and Indiana limestone balustrade, twelve doors, and four circular windows flanked by statues of two Muses: Terpsichore and Melpomone. The lavish interior, built of marble and ornamental plaster, boasted gilt ceilings and chandeliers, and a massive stage, eighty-four feet wide and forty-two feet deep. Seating 1,900 patrons on three levels, the Mishler also offered an early version of air conditioning to keep patrons cool in the summer, and modern safety features that included twenty exits, sprinklers, and a fire-proof curtain.

Despite these precautions, it burned down just nine months later, when high winds swept a fire from an adjacent building into the belly of the theater. Mishler was devastated - but rebuilt and for the next two decades, his theater, that could hold its head with any cousin from the flashier environs of Broadway, attracted top talent from vaudeville, the legitimate stage, opera, the concert hall, and the lecture circuit. Mishler's legacy

lives on in the theater that still carries his name. Through several incarnations - and one close call with the wrecking ball in the 1960s - it continues to thrive, under the auspices of the Blair Country Arts Federation and local cultural organizations. In 1973, the Mishler Theatre was entered onto the *National Register of Historic Places*.

WALK WEST TOWARDS
13TH STREET.

2. First Methodist Episcopal Church
1208 13th Street, at northeast corner
of 13th Street and 12th Avenue

Built of rough-faced Hummelstown brownstone with smooth-faced brownstone accents, the First Methodist Episcopal Church and its adjoining rectory were designed by M. R. Brown of New York City in 1905. The well-preserved building boasts more than seventy memorial windows and one of the largest congregations in the city that was first organized in 1851, with a membership of thirty-seven. Its first church, also on this site, was a two-story, Gothic Revival-style building constructed of red brick, the building material of choice for five other downtown churches. The massive stone church holds its corner stoutly, albeit without its 115-foot high steel steeple that was removed in 1940, due to leaks it developed when it was struck by lightning in 1936.

TURN LEFT ON 13TH STREET AND
WALK DOWN THE HILL TO 11TH
AVENUE. TURN RIGHT.

3. McCrory's
1306-10 11th Avenue

Built in 1937, this Art Moderne style department store was constructed on a steel frame faced with concrete. The upper floors are divided into three bays separated by streamlined pilasters.

TURN AND WALK EAST ON
11TH AVENUE.

15

4. Central Trust Company Building
1210-12 11th Avenue

The Pittsburgh architectural firm of Robinson & Winkler blended elements of Richardsonian Romanesque and Beaux Arts styles to create this white, glazed brick building with brownstone trim in 1906. It was constructed by P.W. Finn, one of Altoona's busiest contractors. The Central Trust Company traced its origins to the Altoona Bank, a private bank established in 1872. In 1875 the firm constructed a three-story brick bank on this site. In 1901 the Central Trust Company organized and operated as the clearing house for Altoona's seven banking institutions.

5. Brett Building
1214-1218 11th Avenue

Jacob Brett was born in Lithuania in 1876 and came to America at an early age. He arrived in Altoona in 1891 and could be seen peddling wares around the countryside. By 1898 he had accumulated enough capital to establish his own general merchandise store in Vintondale. In 1908 Brett made the move to Altoona and engaged in a wholesale clothing partnership. The firm dissolved in 1914 and Brett started his own store, specializing in women's ready-to-wear clothing.

In 1922 Brett purchased the former residence of the Pennsylvania Railroad's general superintendent here for $155,000. He demolished the house and built his store, the only example of pure Sullivanesque architecture in Altoona; that is, creating a high-rise in the form of a classical column with defined base, shaft and capital. Julian Millard, who began his practice in Hollidaysburg, just south of Altoona, in 1907, designed the Brett Building and it was one of his final commissions before being named supervising architect for the Commonwealth of Pennsylvania. Jacob Brett remained in daily control of his business until 1962 and died in 1964 at the age of 87.

6. First National Bank of Altoona
1206 11th Avenue

The second headquarters of a bank established in 1863, the First National Bank of Altoona was described as a "magnificent temple of finance" when it opened in 1926. Architect John A.

Dempwolf s monumental, temple-front design well suited Altoona's prosperous commercial streetscape of the 1920s. The bank's Neoclassical exterior is complemented by a virtually unaltered interior featuring two murals depicting a century of progress in the transportation industry.

7. Silverman Building
1200-1204 11th Avenue, at northwest corner of 12th Street

The Silverman Building is the most elaborate office building on 11th Avenue. Dating to 1924-25, the steel-framed structure is faced with white glazed terra-cotta in a Neoclassical design. The building, constructed for local real estate entrepreneurs Jacob and Isaac Silverman, was erected on a site that had been owned and occupied by the Pennsylvania Railroad Company since 1851. Later known as the Black and Yon Building, this is historically Altoona's most prestigious business address.

8. United States Post Office
1201 11th Avenue

The monumental, Neoclassical building, constructed on the site of the Logan House Hotel in 1931, exhibits the flat ornamentation and hard-edged, geometric lines of the Art Deco style. The oldest and most distinguished hotel in town, the four-story brick Logan House was heralded as a luxury hotel when it was constructed by the Pennsylvania Railroad in 1855. By the late 1910s, however, the hotel was considered less than first class because it lacked the conveniences of modern plumbing; it was finally demolished in 1931 to make way for the new post office.

TURN RIGHT ON 12TH STREET AND WALK DOWN TO THE RAILROAD YARD.

9. Railroaders Memorial Museum
1300 Ninth Avenue

For more than a century Altoona was one of the most important rail facilities in the United States. The city was home to the Altoona Pennsylvania Railroad's repair and maintenance shops, its locomotive construction facility, and its test

16

department. Altoona's location at the foot of the Allegheny front and its proximity to the Horseshoe Curve route over the mountains made the city a key location in the Altoona Pennsylvania Railroad's operations.

The Altoona Pennsylvania Railroad's contribution to the nation's transportation infrastructure, and to production standardization, marks it as one of the most important contributors to America's industrial revolution. By the 1920s, the Altoona railroad works employed 15,000 workers, and by 1945 the Pennsylvania Railroad's facilities at Altoona had become the world's largest rail shop complex.

The Railroaders Memorial Museum is dedicated to revealing, interpreting, commemorating and celebrating the significant contributions of Railroaders and their families to American life and industry.

RETRACE YOUR STEPS TO DOWNTOWN AND WALK UP 12TH STREET. TURN RIGHT ON 12TH AVENUE.

10. Altoona Trust Company
1128-1130 12th Avenue, at northeast corner of 12th Street

The city's fifth bank, Altoona Trust Company was founded in April 1901 by a group of prominent businessmen from Hollidaysburg, Altoona, and Pittsburgh. After leasing temporary offices in the Blumenthal Building at 1128 11th Avenue, this building, designed by Mowbray and Uffinger of New York, opened on New Year's Day, 1903. January 1, 1903. It was the first Classical Revival-style building in downtown Altoona.

The U-shaped, five-story building introduced new materials - gray brick, limestone and terra-cotta - to the predominantly red-brick cityscape and was the first downtown office building to boast an electric elevator. The offices were regarded as some of the most prestigious in the city; several major coal mining companies, that established headquarters here. The Altoona Trust Company was one of three local financial institutions to survive the Depression.

11. Texas Hot Dogs
1122 12th Avenue

When Peter George opened Texas Hot Wieners in 1918 buttermilk sold for a nickel a glass and a hot dog with everything -- chili, brown mustard and onions -- sold for just 10 cents. The location has changed a few times but the family business is in its third generation. Almost as famous as the tube steaks is the birch beer dispensed from an old barrel dating to the 1930s that maintains a perfect 38-degree temperature. Barack Obama stopped in for a Texas Hot Dog while campaigning for president in 2008.

12. Lincoln Deposit and Trust Company
1108-1110 12th Avenue

Built in 1917, this Neoclassical vault is fronted by four granite Ionic columns and topped by a cornice and tall parapet. The ornament in the door surround and cornice includes egg-and-dart, acanthus leaves and guilloche. It was later the home of the Royal Order of Moose, which installed four bowling alleys in the basement, and then the Frohsinn Singing Society.

13. 1115 12th Avenue

Altoona architects Louis Beezer and Michael J. Beezer were prolific apostles for the Queen Anne style around town until they moved to Pittsburgh in 1899. The house features contrasting limestone quoining and splayed lintels. A Flemish gable with paired Gothic windows is separated by a terra-cotta inset with its 1895 date plaque.

TURN LEFT ON 11TH STREET; TURN RIGHT ON LEXINGTON AVENUE

14. Lexington Avenue, from 11th Street to 8th Street

By the second decade of the twentieth century Lexington Avenue was counted among the finest residential neighborhoods in Altoona. While architect-designed Italianate and Second Empire mansions were interspersed all along the avenue, most of the houses were more modest frame and brick-veneered dwellings, the homes of artisans, mechanics, and clerks. The houses, mostly from the 1870s and 1880s, are in various states of repair.

TURN LEFT ON 8TH STREET.
TURN LEFT ON HOWARD AVENUE.

15. Howard Avenue Armory
1000 Howard Avenue

The brick veneered Howard Avenue Armory was completed in two stages; the first in 1922, the second in 1931. It features battlements, a canted corner entrance with cast stone caps and a keystone. The building was faced with a wrecking ball in 1983 before it was saved for a second life as an athletic club.

TURN LEFT ON 11TH STREET.
TURN RIGHT ON 14TH AVENUE.

16. 1108-1110 14th Avenue

This 2 1/2-story, four-bay brick double residence dates to around 1860. The Victorian first floor porch is constructed with chamfered posts and jig-sawn brackets.

17. 1109 14th Avenue

From 1870, this brick Gothic Revival house is dominated by a central cross gable. The Queen Anne porch has chamfered posts, turned balustrade, incised brackets and pendants.

18. Altoona Bible Institute
1111 14th Avenue

The Altoona Bible Institute began its teaching ministry in 1934. There is no tuition charged and no entrance requirements. After World War II the organization purchased this 1885 Queen Anne-style brick house. Constructed on a rusticated stone base the house is dominated by a corner turret with a slate-shingled roof. It is fronted by a porch with paired, fluted Ionic columns.

TURN LEFT ON 12TH STREET.

19. First United Presbyterian Church
southeast corner of 14th Avenue and 12th
Street

This Romanesque Revival-style church constructed of rock-faced sandstone ashlar quarried in southern Cambria County was built in 1898 on designs by Pittsburgh architect William J. East. It follows a Greek cross plan with transepts of equal length with a three-story lantern tower over the crossing.

TURN RIGHT ON 13TH AVENUE.

20. Altoona City Hall
1200 13th Avenue

The first building on this site was erected for the Vigilant Steam Fire Engine Company in 1870, two years after Altoona was chartered as a city. Funds for construction were raised through private subscriptions and contributions from members of the company. The engine house's 75-foot corner tower, which served as a hose lookout, was a landmark on the late nineteenth-century skyline.

When the building was razed in 1925 to make way for this Beaux Arts city hall, the old clock and the bell, which for years sounded the general fire alarm, were donated to the Blair County Historical Society, where they remain today.

Construction of the new city hall commenced with a ground-breaking ceremony on June 22, 1925, and the building was occupied on November 11, 1927. Altoona architects Frederic Shollar and Frank Hersh designed the building with a Rockport gray granite foundation, a rusticated Indiana limestone first floor and Flemish bond buff brick on the second and third floors. However, to cut expenses, they decided to continue incorporating the various municipal functions under one roof, in contrast with the nationwide trend toward more specialized structures for each branch of local government. To this day, the police department, jail, courts, city treasurer, and mayor share the building.

21. Tom and Joe's
1201 13th Avenue

Tom & Joe's was founded by Tom Batrus and brother Joe in December 1933. Joe sold out in the late 1940s and Tom continued to run the business under the name Tom & Joe's. With more than 75 years in Altoona, the diner is now in the third generation of the family. The one-story brick veneer diner sports brick lintels, limestone sill and metal awnings.

22. Cathedral of the Blessed Sacrament
1301 13th Avenue

Few towns can boast of as impressive a landmark as the Cathedral of the Blessed Sacrament at the peak of Gospel Hill. St. John's Roman Catholic Church was established on this site in 1854 with the founding parish including many families who were employed in the construction of the Allegheny Portage Railroad and the Staple Bend tunnel. The first church was a small frame building, which was replaced in 1871 by a Gothic Revival-style, two-story, brick structure with twin spires rising 200 feet.

Several private residences, as well as the landmark St. John's Convent building, had to be demolished to make way for the construction effort, which commenced September 17, 1924. The original plans calling for a $1 million structure were halted in 1931 due to the hardships of the Depression. Still, the unfinished building was dedicated on September 7, 1931, before a crowd of 5,000. Construction resumed again in 1959. As a result, the cathedral's exterior represents a stark, academic, interpretation of Italy's early Renaissance cathedrals, while its interior, embellished with a modern blend of aluminum, glass and marble, is clearly a product of 1959-60.

TURN LEFT ON 13TH STREET.
TURN LEFT ON 12TH AVENUE
AND WALK ONE BLOCK TO THE
TOUR STARTING POINT.

A Walking Tour of Bellefonte...

Bellefonte lies in a spot where an enormous mountain spring emits as much as 13.5-million gallons a day -- enough to supply a 17-foot-wide stream. In 1785, William Lamb used that water to power a flour mill. The community that developed around the mill was known as Lamb's Crossing.

Lamb sold his mill, the spring, and 800 acres in the 1790s to James Dunlop, an ironmaster from Cumberland Valley. Soon James Harris and James Dunlop, his father-in-law, laid out, block by block, a village they called "Big Spring." Tradition holds that the town was named "Bellefonte" by Nancy Harris, Dunlop's daughter and James' wife. It happened during a visit by the French diplomat Charles Maurice de Talleyrand. When Mrs. Harris showed him the massive spring, he exclaimed, "La belle font!" and that, she thought, was a most appropriate name for the town. Others believe the name sprouted from the Bell Fonte forge that was operating at the time.

Bellefonte, rich with iron-industry money, became the most influential town in Pennsylvania between Pittsburgh and Harrisburg. Its big-city trappings included six opera houses, and at one point, two daily and five weekly newspapers. The *Centre Democrat*, founded by General Philip Benner in 1827, was one of the oldest weekly newspapers in the United States

Early on Bellefonte battled then larger Milesburg for the county seat and a display of superior political muscle landed the Centre County government in Bellefonte in 1805. The first county court house, an unpretentious two story stone building, was erected on the site of the present court house. Bellefonte was to become a political breeding ground in the 19th century - five Pennsylvania governors hailed from the town in the 1800s.

The business district that developed about the Diamond (directly in front of the courthouse) is one of Pennsylvania's most eye-catching. Our walking tour will get there soon enough but we'll start near the historic Big Spring, one of the ten largest springs in the Commonwealth, that gave birth to the town...

1. Bellefonte Passenger Station
Talleyrand Park

The first depot on the site was built in 1864 and served trains from the Pennsylvania Railroad's newly constructed Bald Eagle Valley line that ran between Tyrone and Lock Haven. When a new railroad - to be known as the Bellefonte Central - was proposed twenty years later the wooden structure was derided as "a miserable old shed of a depot that would be a disgrace to a way-station on a coal road." The Pennsylvania Railroad concurred and the wooden station was relocated nearby to serve as a freight station, and its place taken by a new the current brick station that opened on February 11, 1889.

In its heyday the station hosted as many as twenty regularly scheduled arrivals and departures daily, and tracks were located on both sides of the building. The most prestigious train to use the station was the Penn Lehigh Express, which operated between Easton and Pittsburgh by way of Williamsport and Lock Haven. It catered to the travel requirements of steel company executives at both ends of the state. Passenger service in Bellefonte began to slide away in the 1930s and by 1949 the daily train to and from Lewisburg made its last run, soon after losing its milk and mail contracts. On August 23, 1950, the Pennsylvania Railroad withdrew the last pair of passenger trains on the Bald Eagle Valley line, the weary remnants of the Penn Lehigh. After a restoration in the 1970s, the station became home to the Chamber of Commerce, an office of the Centre County Convention and Visitors' Bureau, and the ticket office of the Bellefonte Historical Railroad Society.

LEAVE THE TRAIN STATION ON HIGH STREET AND TURN RIGHT, CROSSING SPRING CREEK.

2. Talleyrand Park

In the 1960s, Bellefonte Borough Council developed plans for a park at the site of the deteriorated McClain block. The Talleyrand Park Citizens Committee formed in 1974 and a coalition of volunteers, non-profit and public agencies set about building the gazebo and landscaping the grounds along Spring Creek. The George Grey Barnard Sculpture Garden in the park was formerly a gas station. In 1983, the Committee installed the bust of Abraham Lincoln, cast from the original plaster head sculpted in 1917 by the famous Bellefonte-born sculptor George Grey Barnard. The memorial to Bellefonte's seven governors (five Pennsylvania, one California and one Kansas Territory) stands along High Street.

3. Bush Arcade
212-220 1/2 High Street

Self-made businessman Daniel G. Bush was responsible for the erection of some 27 buildings in Bellefonte, including the massive Bush House Hotel and this ornate commercial block. The original Arcade was destroyed by fire in January of 1887 but was rebuilt almost immediately according to the design and under the supervision of P. A. Walsh, a Philadelphia architect. Still in use as a commercial arcade, the building is a fine example of the Queen Anne-eclectic mode.

4. Brisbin Home
southwest corner of High Street and
Spring Street

James Sanks Brisbin was born in 1837 at Boalsburg. He studied at the Boalsburg Academy and upon graduating began teaching. He later purchased and edited the *Centre Democrat* newspaper in Bellefonte and was later admitted to the bar of Pennsylvania. Brisbin was prominently known as an anti-slavery orator. and served as a general in the Union Army during the Civil War. After the war he remained in the military for the rest of his life and authored several works on a variety of subjects. The Brisbin Home was built in 1865, constructed of bricks that were hand-wrapped and shipped from Philadelphia. It is an excellent example of Italian revival architecture. Once the home of the Decker Motor Company, it today contains offices.

5. The Manse
201 West High Street

This was the site of the residence of Reverend James Linn, a vernacular two-story structure with pent roof and wooden porch. Linn was pastor of the Bellefonte Presbyterian Church and his son Samuel Linn became a prominent judge in Pennsylvania. Linn Street was named for him. The present picturesque building was once the First National Bank, a smorgasbord of Gothic, Romanesque, and Egyptian architecture.

6. First Courthouse
143 High Street

Dunlop House was built in 1795 by Lt. Col. James Dunlop, who with his son-in-law, James Harris, founded the town. The parlor of this stone structure housed the first courthouse from 1800 to 1806. In 1797 Dunlop built the house immediately to the east side for Alexander Diven. The architect for these houses, as well as many others built in that era, was John Lowery, who managed the Bell Font Forge for his cousin, Dunlop. The Diven House is a fine example of the Georgian style, favored by the early settlers. Four original fireplaces remain in the building; one still retains its original decorative style.

7. Reynolds House
southeast corner of West High Street and Spring Street

This midtown corner was the site of the popular McKee's Tavern around 1796. The current town house was built by Thomas R. Reynolds in 1880. The decorative iron railing is a product of local craftsmen.

8. Petrikin Hall
136 High Street

Petrikin Memorial Hall was built in 1901-1902 for the Women's Christian Temperance Union. The *Keystone Gazette* in July, 1901 reported that, "On the ground floor will be two large rooms and a large hallway running through to the auditorium, which will accommodate from 600 to 800 people, with a stage that will hold at least 150 people. Underneath the stage will be the dressing rooms. The room on the east facing High street will be occupied by the Women's Christian Temperance Union, and the one across the hall, on the west will be used as the public library. The second and third floors will have an entrance from the front and will be divided into six apartments, each having six rooms and a separate bathroom

with all other conveniences." It is the handiwork of local builder John Robert Cole. Cole was born in Houserville in 1850 and even though he had no more than a carpenter's training, his designs would dominate local architecture from the early 1890s until his death in 1916.

9. Plaza Theatre
124 West High Street

The Plaza Theater Building was designed by Anna Wagner Keichline. Keichline, a Bellefonte native and Cornell graduate, became the first woman registered as an architect by the state of Pennsylvania, in 1920. She designed numerous buildings, including the Plaza, the Juniata Colony Country Club in Mt. Union, and several Bellefonte homes. She was also an inventor, women's suffrage advocate, and Special Agent for Army Intelligence in WWII. The Anna Keichline Gallery, an exhibit of her life and career, is on the second floor of the Brockerhoff House on Allegheny Street.

The theater featured a 30 ft x 60 foot stage, orchestra pit, and pipe organ. A second, smaller theater showed silent movies. On opening night of the theater -- October 19, 1925 -- 2,500 people attended. Two showings were necessary to accommodate the throng. The theater also featured the "Cry Room," a glass-enclosed space on the balcony level where parents with young children could see the movies without disturbing other patrons. Today the Plaza is a cooperative of dealers in antiques and collectibles.

10. Curtin Residence
120 West High Street

Andrew Gregg Curtin was born in Bellefonte in 1817, the son of a prosperous iron manufacturer. After graduating from Dickinson College he became a lawyer and entered public service, becoming Governor of Pennsylvania during the Civil War from 1861 to 1867. He became a close friend and confidant of Abraham Lincoln, visiting the White House several times in order to converse about the status of the war effort and was active in the Gettysburg Campaign. After the war, Curtin was appointed Minister to Russia by President Ulysses S. Grant and later served as a Democratic Congressman from 1881 until 1887 in the United States House of Representatives. He died at his birthplace of Bellefonte and is buried in Union Cemetery. In World War II the United States liberty ship *SS Andrew G. Curtin* was named in his honor. The Curtin Residence, built in 1868 of limestone, is a superb example of Tuscan revival architecture with handsome bracketing. The front porch, constructed from the piers of a viaduct built over Spring Creek in 1895 by the Warner Company, was added in 1909 by the Elks, who purchased the property for $10,000.

TURN LEFT AND WALK UP THE WEST SIDE OF ALLEGHENY STREET.

11. First National Bank Building
137 North Allegheny Street

Formerly the site of the home of Pennsylvania Supreme Court Justice Thomas Burnside, the First National Bank Building was constructed in 1872. The present structure was rebuilt following a fire in 1888, along with the Crider Exchange Building next door on North Allegheny Street. Together these two buildings help anchor the Diamond, one of the most picturesque squares in Pennsylvania.

12. Crider Exchange
133 North Allegheny Street

In 1888 a block of stores owned by E.C. Humes was totally destroyed by fire. Fountain W. Crider, a shrewd businessman, bought the charred ruins and constructed the Crider Exchange Building. The Exchange, another creation of Robert Cole in the Queen Anne style, is notable for its unusual fish-scale tin facade.

13. Linn House
133 North Allegheny Street

This house was built in 1810 by Philip Benner, pioneer Centre County ironmaster. The house was later occupied by Judge Charles Huston and Governor James A Beaver. Beaver was a Brigadier General in the Civil War, wounded four times. He was a Republican governor of Pennsylvania from 1887 and 1891 and resided in Bellefonte until his death in 1914.

Historian John Blair Linn, who in 1883 wrote *Linn's History of Centre and Clinton Counties*, and who married Benner's granddaughter, moved into the house that her grandfather had built. The structure is of Trenton limestone, a high quality building stone that has given rise to one of the major industries of present-day Bellefonte. The Georgian-style building now houses The Bellefonte Museum for Centre County.

14. Potter House/Centre County Library
203 North Allegheny Street

Built at the edge of the sidewalk on the corner of Allegheny and Howard Streets in 1815 by John Miles, son of Colonel Samuel Miles, mayor of Philadelphia and founder of Milesburg, this building was jacked up and moved back twelve feet from its original site in 1896. It was then sold to W.W. Potter, lawyer and congressman. The house was bequeathed in 1935 to Bellefonte for use as the county library.

15. Thaddeus Brew Hamilton House
251 North Allegheny Street

Thaddeus Brew Hamilton once owned the land where Denver, Colorado is now located. He traded it for a mule which he needed for his prospecting ventures in the Colorado gold rush. Of the eight prospectors who, in 1858, first settled where Denver now is, four were from Bellefonte - Hamilton, John Rothrock, James Turner, and Sam Decker. In California, for $600, Hamilton was offered the land where the city of San Bernardino is now located, but rejected it. The eclectic house features elements of the Second Empire, Gothic and Queen Anne styles.

16. St. John's Episcopal Church
southwest corner of Lamb Street and
North Allegheny Street

St. John's Episcopal parish was established in 1837; the Gothic stone church was built in 1871.

17. Reynolds Mansion
northwest corner of Linn Street and North Allegheny Street

The Reynolds Mansion was built in 1884 for Major William F. Reynolds and later was the home of Colonel W. Fred Reynolds, who was instrumental in locating the Diamond wooden match company in Bellefonte. With its towers and asymmetrical massing the house is primarily of the Queen Anne style with Gothic influences in the use of stone, steeply-pitched roofs and gables, and also Italianate details in the tall, narrow windows and the prominent eave brackets. Its construction of red sandstone required twenty Italian stone-masons and an army of other artisans. A two-story carriage house was added in 1893.

TURN RIGHT ON LINN STREET.

18. Barnard House
113 East Linn Street

This 1858 Pennsylvania farmhouse was the birthplace of George Grey Barnard, famous American sculptor and son of a Bellefonte Presbyterian minister. Among his famous works were the Barnard groups of statuary flanking the main entrance of the State Capitol Building in Harrisburg and a Statue of Lincoln, a replica of which is located in Cincinnati, Ohio. He also collected medieval sculpture that formed the nucleus of the collection in The Cloisters museum in Manhattan. The frame siding on this house was scored to suggest masonry blocks with quoined corners.

RETRACE YOUR STEPS TO NORTH ALLEGHENY STREET AND TURN LEFT.

19. Hastings Mansion
254 North Allegheny Street

Daniel H. Hastings came to Bellefonte as principal of the high school in 1867. Later he edited the Bellefonte *Republican* and gained admittance to the Centre County Bar. He eventually served one term as Republican governor of Pennsylvania from 1895 to 1899. In the meantime he took possession of the former John Lane mansion in the 1890s and remodeled it by facing it in brick and adding the south wing and portico and windows fashioned after the old State Capitol Building in Harrisburg. The house is a polyglot of architectural ideas. It could be called mostly classical with dentils under eaves, bracketing, pilasters and pediments on dormers, pillars, leaded windows, large pane windows, and a mansard style roof. The Hastings Mansion, now apartments, sits on the site of the Red Lion Inn from the 1830s.

20. James T. Hale House
222 North Allegheny Street

James Tracy Hale was born in Towanda in 1810; he studied law, was admitted to the bar in 1832 and commenced practice in Bellefonte. Hale was elected as a Republican to three terms in the United States Congress. He died in Bellefonte in 1865. The core of this red brick house dates to 1843 before the Victorian decorations were added to the upper floors.

21. Joseph Ceader House
214 North Allegheny Street

Joseph Ceader was a baker, caterer and confectioner who operated a shop at 26 South Allegheny Street. His fine brick home dates to 1899.

22. Centre County Courthouse
208 North Washington Street

The Centre County courthouse was first constructed in 1805 and 1806, with a wing added in 1811. The Ionic columns on the porch were built in 1835. With the exception of this porch, the entire building was replaced in 1854 and 1855. The rear section was added in 1909 through 1911, and the new east wing was built in 1963-1964. The *Soldiers and Sailors War Memorial* and statue of Andrew Gregg Curtin were dedicated in 1906. The Memorial was designed by Joseph M Huston, the architect who designed the State Capitol Building in Harrisburg. The intersection of four streets in front of the Courthouse, known as The Diamond, has been the hub of all activity in Bellefonte since its founding and is representative of the Pennsylvania Diamond, characteristic of towns in Pennsylvania and nearby areas which were settled by Pennsylvanians.

23. Brockerhoff House
southwest corner of High Street and
Allegheny Street

In 1866, Henry Brockerhoff rebuilt the old Pennsylvania Hotel in this style. Today this building is dominated by its eclectic-style roof and attic story but betrayal of the original Italianate building is seen in the steady articulation of brick wall arches below and the surrounds on the narrow windows. This was once the site of a log cabin tavern owned by James Benner. It was redesigned by Robert Cole in the 1890s by adding a fourth floor and multi-tiered slate mansard roof.

24. Reynolds Bank
southwest corner of High Street and
Allegheny Street

Colonel W. F. Reynolds, who came to Bellefonte in 1841, established his bank on the Diamond in 1859 and amassed quite a sizable fortune through his financial transactions. When he died in 1893, he left an estate of $801,000. The Reynolds Bank was built in 1887 but experienced several fires and by 1889 was rebuilt and named the First National Bank. In 2005-2006 it was bought by the County, restored, and restructured as additional courtroom space. The third floor, formerly accessible by a ladder, had been the location of the Masonic Lodge and currently has been restored for use by the community.

TURN LEFT ON EAST HIGH STREET.

25. Garman House
110 East High Street

This hotel was purchased by Daniel Garman in 1861. It was remodeled around 1888 and was a gathering place for politicians, salesmen, attorneys and other leading lights of the town. It is currently operating as the Hotel Dode.

26. Garman Opera House
116 East High Street

Built in 1887 as an opera house, the Garman was converted in the 1930s to a movie house known as the State Theatre. It closed in the 1960s and became a warehouse. It became a movie house

again in July 2000 showing art, foreign, and first run films but the Garman Opera House closed once more in October 2008, and was put up for sale.

RETURN TO ALLEGHENY STREET AND TURN LEFT.

27. Temple Court Building
130 South Allegheny Street

Another creation by John Robert Cole, this time in thin, orange Roman brick. The Romanesque Temple Court Building, constructed in 1894, also carries a sunburst ornamentation theme throughout the facade.

28. 100 Block of South Allegheny Street

Most of this block, including the corner of East Bishop Street, was destroyed in the fire of 1885. The southwest corner, where the postal box now stands, was then called "strychnine corner" because of the notable number of bars and saloons located there.

TURN RIGHT ON BISHOP STREET.

29. Meyer House
140 West Bishop Street

This double house is the birthplace of Jacob H. Meyer, inventor of the voting machine, an appropriate claim to fame for a town that produced seven governors.

TURN RIGHT ON SPRING STREET.

30. Bush Residence/VFW Hall
123 South Spring Street

Daniel Bush was responsible for many of Bellefonte's finest buildings and his grand 1864 Victorian residence here certainly qualified for the list. The building lost much of its ornamentation when it was converted into the Markland Hotel. Now a VFW Hall, the building looks much as it did as the Markland Hotel, sans elaborate porch.

31. Bellefonte's First Hospital
113 South Spring Street

Bellefonte's first hospital began in 1902, housed in this building on a lot first owned by Thomas Burnside. The carriage house located directly behind it is one of the finest restored buildings in Bellefonte.

TURN LEFT ON HIGH STREET AND WALK ONE BLOCK BACK TO THE TOUR STARTING POINT IN TALLEYRAND PARK.

Look Up,

Bethlehem

A Walking Tour of Bethlehem...

In 1741 a small band of Moravian missionaries walked into the wilderness and began a settlement on the banks of the Lehigh River near the Monocacy Creek. From the start it was to be a planned community in which property, privacy and personal relationships were to be subordinated to a common effort to achieve a spiritual ideal. On Christmas Eve of that first year the Moravians' patron, Count Nicholas Ludwig von Zinzendorf of Saxony, Germany, visited the new settlement. The community was christened "Bethlehem" to commemorate the time of his visit.

To encourage communal living the Moravians built large Germanic-style structures of native limestone known as "choirs." Choirs were organized by gender and age and marital status so there were choirs for single men, married couples, little girls and so on. Some of these sturdy structures, among the most impressive buildings constructed in pre-Revolutionary America, have been in continuous use for over 250 years. The self-sufficient community wasted no time in building industry - more than three dozen trades and mills were in operation within five years. Goods from Bethlehem were known throughout the American colonies. This heritage of manufacturing braced Bethlehem perfectly for the oncoming Industrial Revolution. When the Lehigh Canal opened in 1829, quickly followed by the Lehigh Valley Railroad, Bethlehem became a nationally known center of heavy industry. The zinc industry was centered here and iron companies were established by the 1850s. Through the building of government ordnance the Bethlehem Iron Works and then Bethlehem Steel Company were supplying war efforts around the globe.

Much of the face of present-day Bethlehem dates back to 1904 and the arrival in town of 42-year old Charles Michael Schwab. At age 39 Schwab was president of the biggest company in the world, U.S. Steel. But after personality conflicts there, he left to take over and remake Bethlehem Steel Company and began pushing for a new type of wide-flange steel beam that required building an entire new mill. The H-beam and its descendent, the I-beam, would revolutionize the construction trade and make Bethlehem Steel the second largest steel company in the world.

Away from the office Schwab united the city from four fractious municipalities. He filled the surrounding neighborhoods with Bethlehem Steel employees and spurred the building of landmark neighborhoods such at Mt. Airy, where many of his executives set up camp. Our walking tour will focus on the streets and buildings of the Moravian community in historic central Bethlehem but, before that, we will start at one building that stands as a legacy to Charles M. Schwab and the halcyon days of Bethlehem Steel...

1. **Hotel Bethlehem**
   437 Main Street

The hotel rests on the site of the famous "First House of Bethlehem" built in 1741 by missioning Moravians. Here on December 24th of 1741, the Moravians' patron, Count Nicholas Von Zinzendorf, sang a hymn about Bethlehem, after which those gathered decided to name the town Bethlehem. The "Golden Eagle Hotel" operated here from 1794 until April of 1919; in it's last days it was used for soldiers returning from World War I as a convalescence home.

In 1922 Charles Schwab created the Hotel Bethlehem so his Bethlehem Steel clients could stay at a classier place than the Colonial-era Sun Inn. Military artist George Gray painted a series of murals for the hotel that depict the history of Bethlehem.

WALK SOUTH ON MAIN STREET AND TURN RIGHT ON OLD YORK ROAD NEXT TO THE HOTEL.

2. **Colonial Industrial Quarter**
   Old York Road, west of Main Street

Among the earliest of urban planners, the Moravians sited their heavy industry along the Monocacy Creek. By 1745 there were 35 industries humming in Bethlehem, the remains of several that are preserved in the Colonial Industrial Quarter. The oldest is the Tannery, from 1761, where over 3,000 animal hides were processed each year into leather for shoes, harnesses and belts for machinery. Also in the complex is the Luckenbach Mill, a descendent of a wooden 1743 flour mill. That mill was replaced with a limestone model in 1751 that was gutted by fire in 1869. The third mill was this brick one that operated well into the 1900s and was restored to working order in 1982.

Of particular note is a small limestone building that functioned as a waterworks for the community beginning in 1762. It was, in fact the first pumped municipal water system in the American colonies and would not be duplicated elsewhere for another 35 years. An undershot waterwheel powered three pumps, forcing spring water uphill into a collecting tower where Central Moravian Church now stands. From here it flowed into cisterns and then into individual houses and shops. The restored Waterworks is a National Historic Landmark.

3. **Central Moravian Church**
   73 West Church Street at Main Street

By 1802 there had been agitation for a larger church in the Moravian community for a good twenty years. Finally the church Council received a unanimous vote to proceed but then disagreement arose over the location. This location, which necessitated the clearing of two log buildings, was the compromise choice. Construction began with the building of massive six-foot thick foundation walls on April 16, 1803. This enabled the sanctuary to be completely free of interior pillars normally necessary to support the roof and belfry. When the building was completed in 1806 the Moravians had the biggest church in Pennsylvania. The final cost of $52,000 well exceeded the $11,000 estimated when the plans were approved. It was capable of seating 1,500 at a time when the total population of Bethlehem numbered 580, the better to reach out to the growing and expanding community.

4. **Brethren's House**
   south side of Church Street at Main Street

Believing that men and women had different religious needs, Count Nicholas Ludwig von Zinzendorf in 1736 organized the Moravian community around groups of members known as "Choirs." Age, gender, and marital status determined what Choir a person would live in, and each group provided spiritual and social guidance to its own. When children reached eighteen months of age, their parents sent them to the communal Nursery. At four they moved to either the Little Boys' or Little Girls' Choir. At age twelve, they joined the Older Boys' or Older' Girls' Choir and at nineteen they moved into either the Single Brothers' or Single Sisters' Choir. Married members became part of the Married People's Choir and when a spouse died, the surviving spouse joined the either Widows' or Widowers' Choir.

The "Brethren's House" housed the community's single men. Because of the variety of skills brought to the community by this group they required an unusually imposing building. The workshops of the tailor and shoemaker were located here as was the silkworm industry and bell foundry. The Moravian bakery operated in this 1748 building. Twice during the Revolutionary War, the building became an official hospital of the Continental Army. Casualties were brought to Bethlehem from both the New York and Philadelphia areas but few returned - the mortality rate was nearly 50 percent. General Washington was entertained here in 1782 in what is now called the Washington Room. Restored to its original appearance, without change to the original walls, Brethren's House is home to the Moravian College Music Department.

TURN LEFT ON CHURCH STREET.

5. **Main Hall**
   north side of Church Street, east of Brethren's House

This handsome four-story Greek Revival brick building was constructed in 1854 to house the growing number of students enrolled in the Moravian Female Seminary. It remains a a women's residence, featuring original double parlors with paintings by early College art master Gustavus Grunewald. It was one of the first Bethlehem buildings lighted by gas.

Organist, composer and conductor John Frederick Wolle was born in Main Hall in 1863 and raised here. He founded the Bethlehem Bach Festival and conducted the Bach Choir of Bethlehem. The choir sang the first complete American presentation of Bach's Mass in B Minor in the Central Moravian Church in 1900, an occasion that landed the church on the list of National Landmarks of Music.

6. **Moravian College President's House**
   north side of Church Street, east of Main Hall

This Federal brick home, a single story when built in 1819, was the home of John F. Frueauff, ninth principal of the Moravian Female Seminary. It received a Victorian second story but was lassoed back to its original appearance in 1961 and today is the residence of the college president.

TURN LEFT ON HECKEWELDER PLACE.

7. **Old Chapel**
   west side of Heckewelder Place

This was Bethlehem's second place of worship after the congregation outgrew the Gemeinhaus chapel in 1752. Services were held on the second floor and the ground floor contained a large tiled dining hall. The Marquis de Lafayette and George Washington bowed their heads here during the Revolutionary War. The stone structure was renovated to its present appearance back in the 1860s. Today it is used for special events.

8. **Nain-Schober House**
   429 Heckewelder Street

This is the last remaining home from the American Indian mission village of Nain which existed from 1758 to 1765 in the vicinity of 12th and 13th avenues in West Bethlehem. The house was originally built around 1758 by Moravian missionaries with the help of American Indians. It was a log structure with a wood-shingled roof. In 1765 the home was sold to Andreas Schober, a Bethlehem Moravian, who moved the house up the street. In 1906 it was moved to this location. The current metal panel siding is temporarily protecting the building as it is being restored.

John Heckewelder, famous Moravian missionary and writer, moved to this alley in 1810 at the age of 61. Heckewelder, who was appointed the first United States commissioner to the Indians in the Ohio territory by George Washington, traveled over 30,000 miles to spread the Moravian word. His house in the middle of the block still stands although it has been completely altered.

RETRACE YOUR STEPS TO CHURCH STREET AND TURN LEFT.

9. **Gemeinhaus**
   66 West Church Street

Erected in 1741, the Gemeinhaus is the oldest structure in Bethlehem. The massive building served as a school, house of worship (the Saal on the second floor was the place of earliest worship in Bethlehem), and a workspace for the growing

Moravian community. Inside the frame cladding the building is constructed of logs, probably the largest log structure in continuous use in the United States, today as the Moravian Museum of Bethlehem.

10. Bell House
north side of Church Street, set back, west of Gemeinhaus

When it was built in 1746 this was the residence for Bethlehem's married couples but was quickly expanded and turned over to the Moravian Seminary for Girls. The present bell, still in use, was cast in Bethlehem in 1776 by Matthias Tommerup. The turret housed the first town clock back in 1746; the weathervane is the church seal in metal.

11. Sisters' House
56 West Church Street

This stone building was originally erected in 1744 as the Brothers' House for single men but was changed to the single women in 1748. Here the sisters had dormitories, a chapel, a dining room and kitchen, and a workshop area for crafts. Buttresses were added in 1756 to support walls weakened by the weight of the original tile roof.

12. Widows' House
south side of Church Street, across from Bell House

This was the last of the choirs, or residence halls, built by the Moravians. It was erected on the site of a large congregational garden in 1768 for 30 widows who moved into the community from Nazareth.

13. Clewell Hall
southwest corner of Church Street and New Street

This brick Second Empire-influenced house was built in 1870 and eventually acquired the name of John H. Clewell, a college president in the early 1900s. The building is now a 21-room dormitory.

14. City Center
south side of Church Street at New Street

City Center was developed of granite and quartzite in 1967 and contains civic buildings, the Town Hall rotunda and town library. The *Symbol of Progress* is 60 feet high and weighs 12,000 pounds. Joseph Greenberg of Philadelphia designed the sculpture to be representative of the diversity of Bethlehem's people welded in the pursuit of progress. It is made of Bethlehem Mayari-R Steel. Also in the plaza, on the west side of the library, is a Japanese garden that was a gift to Bethlehem from its sister city in the Land of the Rising Sun, Tondabayashi.

TURN LEFT ON NORTH NEW STREET.

15. Kemerer Museum of Decorative Arts
427 North New Street

The Kemerer Museum of Decorative Arts uses period rooms to showcase nearly three-hundred years of folk art, furnishings and paintings. Its unique collection of cast-iron toys, maps, prints, and textiles open a window into the past. Incorporated in 1954, the museum set up in this stylish Federal brick home in 1969.

TURN LEFT ON MARKET STREET.

16. Bernard Lehman House
northwest corner of Market Street and New Street

This Italianate-flavored house was built by Bernard Lehman, whose father Ernest started a brass foundry in a building behind his house in 1832. When he moved the shop and foundry to South Bethlehem in 1864 it triggered the coming industrialization of the community.

17. Devey Building
11 West Market Street

These walls have seen a bit of everything since its construction in the 1850s. Charles Schwab purchased it to house the Bethlehem Steel company band. It later became the town library and for a short time housed the Bethlehem Chamber of Commerce. It now serves the Moravian Academy as their middle school.

18. God's Acre
south side of Market Street

The Moravian cemetery was laid out in 1742; the flat stones indicate that all were equal in death as they were in life. One of the 56 Indians buried here was a Mohican named Tschoop, popularly thought to have been the character of Uncas popularized in James Fenimore Cooper's *Last of the Mohicans*. The graves along the fence were known as Stranger's Row, reserved for non-Moravians.

19. Horsfield House
42 West Market Street

Timothy Horsfield constructed this stone house in 1749 and a few years later built an addition to the west end that was the first store in Bethlehem. The inventory included over 200 items, most of which were made by townsfolk. The store addition was demolished in 1890.

TURN RIGHT ON MAIN STREET.

20. Sun Inn
564 Main Street

John Adams called this hostelry, "the best Inn I ever saw." Opened in the Colonial crossroads town of Bethlehem in 1760, the Sun was the official "Gasthaus" for travelers to the Moravian community. With its widely established reputation for hospitality, superior accommodations and fine food the guest book at the Sun Inn reads like a *Who's Who* of of Founding Fathers.

A full second story was added in 1826 and the inn operated as the Sun Hotel into the middle of the 20th century. In 1975 the building was acquired by the Sun Inn Preservation Association, restored to its original interior and exterior appearance and opened for tours in 1982.

TURN AND WALK SOUTH ON MAIN STREET.

21. Goundie House
501 Main Street

Dating to 1810, this Federal-style house is considered the oldest brick structure in Bethlehem. John Sebastian Goundie was a brewmaster and businessman who served the community as mayor and fire-inspector.

22. Temperance Fountain
Main Street at head of Market Street

Water fountains like this one were donated to towns around America by temperance groups in the hope that access to cool drinking water would keep people from consuming alcohol.

CONTINUE A FEW MORE STEPS TO THE TOUR STARTING POINT.

Look Up,

Bloomsburg

A Walking Tour of Bloomsburg...

Bloomsburg's original town streets were laid out in 1802 by Ludwig and John Adam Eyer, confident that the location at a regional crossroads would guarantee growth. After a slow start the village grew rapidly in the latter half of the 19th century. A majority of the buildings in the Historic District date from that era, with a few earlier and a number of 20th-century buildings. Architectural styles are varied, from austere Federal to highly decorative Second Empire and Romanesque.

The "character" of the downtown is evoked chiefly by two- and three-story brick commercial buildings erected along Main Street before 1900. These buildings evidence a variety of 19th-century styles, but many of them have common features: narrow sash windows,ornamental brickwork, wrought-iron details, and prominent cornices (roof-line projections). The focal point of the downtown is the Market Square with its Civil War monument and Stroup Fountain.

The adjoining residential districts, particularly on Market Street and Fifth Street, display numerous attractive homes from the same era. Some of these are fairly grand but all were built as "livable" single-family homes. Several homes retain hitching-posts in front and/or small stables at the back, relics of the pre-automobile age when the homes were built.

In the 1980s the Town of Bloomsburg began a concerted effort to maintain and enhance its architectural heritage. The Town Council established a Historic District, roughly five blocks long and four wide. The Town also created a Historic Architectural Review Board to assess building-permit applications to ensure that the historic qualities of the District are preserved even in details such as the style of windows.

Our walking tour of Pennsylvania's only incorporated town (ther municipalities of this approximate size are generally boroughs) will begin at Market Square and radiate in every direction...

1. **Town Fountain**
   Market Square at intersection of
   Market Street and West Main Street

The town acquired the fountain from the J. L. Mott Company in New York City, and had it installed in the fall of 1892. The Bloomsburg Water Company informed Town Council it would supply free water for a fountain, and Town Council used money from the David Stroup estate to purchase the fountain. In the late 1960s the fountain was replaced; some twenty years later it was re-installed and then in 2002 refurbished to its original appearance.

WALK NORTH ON MARKET STREET TO THE END IN TWO BLOCKS.

2. **Woodward House**
   head of Market Street

This is the 1840s home of Judge Warren Woodward, who was the first elected judge of the 26th judicial district and later became a Justice of the Pennsylvania Supreme Court. Built in the Federal style with Greek Revival details in the porch, the cornice, and pilasters distinguish this structure that commands the vista down Market Street.

TURN AND WALK SOUTH ON MARKET STREET BACK TOWARDS MARKET SQUARE.

3. **Waller House**
   1 North Market Street

Reverend David J. Waller, a Presbyterian minister, purchased the property in 1847 and constructed an Italianate home in the style of the day, topped by a cupola and encircling verandah with its fanlike brackets. He lived here until he built a grander home on the southwest corner of Market and Fifth Streets (where Memorial Elementary School now stands). Retiring from the pulpit in 1871, Waller devoted his time to public affairs in Bloomsburg, including development of industries, a railroad, and extensive housing tracts. A later owner, William M. Reber engraved his surname on the carriage stepping stone at the front of the property.

4. **Thornton House**
   102 North Market Street

James Thornton, a blacksmith, owned this property at the time of the 1830 census. This post-and-beam Federal-style house is one of the oldest standing frame structures in Bloomsburg.

5. **St. Matthew Lutheran Church**
   123 North Market Street

St. Matthew's originated in St. Paul's Lutheran Church, founded in 1807; for fifty years it shared a building on First Street with the German Reformed congregation. In 1857 the Lutherans erected a church at this site and changed its name to St. Matthew. The current church, designed by Ritter & Shay of Philadelphia with random coursed rock-face and ashlar masonry (dressed stone). opened in 1925, and the education wing in the rear in 1957.

6. **Caldwell Consistory**
   150 North Market Street

The Ancient Accepted Scottish Rite of Freemasonry is a fraternal organization for master Masons founded in 1867 and named for John Caldwell, a prominent Philadelphia Mason. One million terra-cotta bricks were used in constructing the Victorian Eclectic/Modified Colonial Revival building in 1907. The double-headed eagle above the front door is the symbol for a consistory.

TURN RIGHT ON WEST MAIN STREET ON THE NORTH SIDE OF THE STREET.

7. *Morning Press* **Building**
   111 West Main Street

The building was designed to house the *Morning Press* newspaper, established in 1902 by Paul Eyerley and Charles Vanderslice. Indiana limestone and gray pressed brick with matching mortar provide a striking exterior contrast with the cast-iron trim. Needing more space, the newspaper, renamed the *Press Enterprise*, built a new plant in Scott Township in 1972.

8. Moose Lodge
203 West Main Street

The Bloomsburg Lodge, No. 623, Royal Order of Moose, was founded on January 18, 1920. Membership steadily increased over the years and the lodge decided to build its own home at this site in 1950, designed in the Art Deco-Miami Style by local architect John Schell. The Moose sold the building in June 1999 and moved to Scott Township.

9. 227 West Main Street

This excellent example of Second Empire/Victorian architecture features original fret work, mansard roof and a cupola.

10. Iddings Barkley House
259 Main Street

One of the oldest standing structures on Main Street and an excellent example of pure, early Federal style, this was the home of Iddings Barkley, a pioneer at Bloomsburg, where he developed a large business as a carpenter and cabinetmaker. The brickwork is traditional Flemish bond.

CROSS THE STREET AND TURN LEFT, WALKING BACK ON WEST MAIN STREET, ON THE SOUTH SIDE OF THE STREET.

11. Lutz Agency
246 West Main Street

This Second Empire Style house with mansard roof and twin pedimented dormers accented by semicircular windows was built for Lloyd T. Sharpless, a grocer. It later did time as the Kriner Funeral Home. The front entrance is not original.

12. Kleim's Drug Store
128 West Main Street

Christopher A. Kleim purchased the building in 1895; he raised his family and operated a drugstore here until 1944. The Queen Anne-style building features a roof with cross gable and turret. Look for interesting interplay of polychromatic brick and shingle surfaces on the second floor façade.

13. Peacock and Moyer Building
102-106 West Main Street

This Georgian Revival building with Neoclassical elements was built for entrepreneur Clinton C. Peacock and Lucas N. Moyer, president of Bloomsburg Silk Mills, to provide retail, office and residential space in 1894.

14. *Civil War Soldiers and Sailors Monument*
Market Square

Constructed in 1908 from seventeen blocks of granite, weighing 100 tons and rising sixty feet tall, the *Civil War Soldiers and Sailors Monument* was purchased by the County Commissioners from Worden Brothers, Batavia, NY. On the shaft are the names of Civil War battles in which Columbia County soldiers fought. Statues on the four corners represent the infantry, cavalry, artillery, and navy.

15. McKinney/Wirt Building
36 West Main Street

Paul E. Wirt purchased the Italianate-style building from the William McKinney estate in 1887. He used it as the office for the Wirt Fountain Pen Company and as a rental property; the post office was on the ground floor. When the Bloomsburg National Bank was established in 1899, it leased office space on the ground floor, replacing the post office. Wirt served as the bank's vice president. The bank was the predecessor of today's First Columbia Bank and Trust Company. The columns and entrance arches in Classical Revival Style were added later.

16. Former Exchange & Magee Hotels
20-24 West Main Street

Casper Chrisman built the original log and frame Exchange Hotel in 1810 which was replaced in the 1850s by a three-story brick Federalist Style building. Destroyed by fire in 1870 it was replaced in 1874 by an impressive four-story brick Second Empire building with mansard roof.

Bought in 1912 by James Magee II, the founder of the Magee Carpet Company, it was renamed after himself. Following fire damage in 1933, the present Neoclassical façade was constructed. The hotel ceased operation in 2003.

TURN RIGHT ON CENTER STREET.

17. Alvina Krause Theatre
226 Center Street

The Grand Opera House built here in 1874 was demolished in 1938 to make way for the Columbia Theatre, which opened in 1940. The Bloomsburg Theatre Ensemble (BTE) purchased the building in 1980, gutted it, and renovated the interior to make it suitable for live performance. Original Art Deco decorations were re-installed inside the theatre.

Alvina Krause was the founding artistic director of the BTE, which is the resident acting company of the Alvina Krause Theatre, named in her honor in 1983. She was born January 28, 1893 in New Lisbon, Wisconsin, and spent 34 years as a drama teacher at Northwestern University before moving to Bloomsburg in 1971.

RETURN TO MAIN STREET AND TURN RIGHT TO CONTINUE ONTO EAST MAIN STREET.

18. Phillips Building
10 East Main Street

In May 1886, Mary Gross Phillips, purchased the bilding at 10-12-14 East Main Street for $5,000. She opened Phillips Cafe and Phillips Boarding House. About 1920 she rented the commercial floor to F.W. Woolworth, which remained a fixture on Main Street until 1990. Still in the family, Phillips Emporium & Coffeehouse is now the sole commercial occupant. The original wood floors remain beneath the linoleum and carpeting and remnants of the pressed-tin ceiling are reminders of an era when building codes were less particular.

19. Crescent Building
56-64 East Main Street

The distinctive crescent of bricks, the floral terra-cotta embellishments, and the curved wrought-iron balconies are emblematic of the late Victorian Romanesque and Queen Anne styles.

20. WHLM Radio
124 East Main Street

In the fall of 1947, two brand new radio stations signed on the air in Bloomsburg. The *Morning Press* turned on AM 930 and a group of local business people fired up AM 690 WLTR. In September 1951, Harry L. Magee changed the call letters of WLTR to WHLM - Magee's initials. Two years later WHLM became Bloomsburg's first 24-hour radio station.

21. Sneidman's Jewelers
130 East Main Street

The street clock was erected by the A.B. Hess Jewelry Store and was re-lettered when the business was bought by Sneidman around 1924. A similar clock stood near Market Square at the former Roy's Jewelers, 40 West Main Street.

22. Housenick Ford Dealership
300 East Main Street

Housenick Motors Company on the ground floor was the second oldest Ford dealership in the country. Notable amongst second floor tenants was a dance hall known as the "Casino" and a training area for George Keller's circus animals. Keller, a former Bloomsburg University professor, had a successful career with a variety of shows including Ringling Brothers and Barnum & Bailey circus.

23. Robbins House
352 College Hill

In the blocks below Bloomsburg University are several homes in the Queen Anne style of the late 1800s. This one was built for Cortez B. Robbins in 1889. A wholesale liquor dealer and a lifelong bachelor, Robbins lived here until he died in 1937.

CONTINUE UP COLLEGE HILL TO
THE END OF THE STREET.

24. Carver Hall
Bloomsburg University at the head of College Hill

This signature academic building was erected in 1867 as Institute Hall - the first building on the present campus. It was later renamed in honor of Henry Carver, principal from 1866 to 1871. The center cupola of the Italianate/Georgian Revival tour de force was replaced by a projecting domed bell tower in 1900. Lights were added to the tower in 1954 as a memorial to students who died serving in World War II.

TURN AROUND AND WALK BACK
DOWN COLLEGE HILL TO EAST
MAIN STREET, USING THE
SIDEWALK ON THE NORTH SIDE
OF THE STREET.

25. Bloomsburg Town Hall
northeast corner of College Hill and East Main Street and East Street

The Romanesque town hall was home to the municipal government, a lock-up, public meeting rooms, and also the Friendship Fire Company station when it opened in 1890. The exterior walls of the Romanesque structure incorporated molded terra-cotta bricks (now painted).

26. St. Paul's Episcopal Church
105 East Main Street

St. Paul's, dating back to 1790, is the oldest continuous congregation in Columbia County. The one-acre site for the church was the original town burial ground (later moved to Rosemont Cemetery). The present church was preceded by three structures which stood to the right where the Rectory (built in 1876 in the Gothic Style) now stands. The current bell tower of the Victorian Gothic church was completed in 1891 and the attached parish house in 1892. The first pipe organ in Bloomsburg was installed here in 1874; Tiffany stained-glass windows can be found on either side of the nave, near the chancel.

27. Capitol Theatre
45 East Main Street

The theater began premiering major Hollywood movies in 1929, surviving into the 1990s.

28. Columbia Trust Company
northeast corner of Main Street and Center Street

The Columbia County Trust Company was formed in 1916 and moved into this corner building with Neoclassical details. In 1926, Bloomsburg National Bank merged with Columbia County Trust to become the Bloomsburg Bank-Columbia Trust Company. In 1990, the name of the Bank was changed to First Columbia Bank & Trust Co.

29. Columbia County Courthouse
35 West Main Street

When the county seat was moved from Danville to Bloomsburg in 1846, the town's citizens raised private funds to erect the courthouse and jail. The original small brick courthouse had a front portico with six Ionic columns, and a tower reaching eighty feet above the ground. The building has been enlarged three times: rear extension in 1868, expansion to the front in 1891 (with a new entrance and clock tower), and a second addition to the rear in 1938.

30. Farmer's National Bank
37 West Main Street

Originally the Farmer's National Bank opened for business in 1891 in an earlier building at this location. In 1909, the bank purchased and remodeled the building but demolished it in 1941 in order to erect the present bank. Art deco details mingle with Egyptian Revival motifs.

TURN LEFT ON MARKET STREET
AND WALK ON THE WEST SIDE OF
THE STREET.

31. U.S. Post Office
   230 South Market Street

From 1840 to 1847 J. R. Moyer operated the Post Office in his store on this site. Built as a project of the Depression-era Works Progress Administration, the Georgian Revival building uses Flemish bond veneer brickwork; of note in the lobby are low-relief sculptures depicting agricultural scenes.

32. Tustin Mansion
   240 South Market Street

Built for Edward B. Tustin, the cost totaled $200,000 ($100,000 for the building and $100,000 for the furnishings). The porch with its Ionic columns was constructed of ashlar masonry. Outstanding interior features include nine fireplaces and a Georgian Revival staircase of wooden pinned construction, purchased at the 1904 St. Louis Exposition. Tustin, a local entrepreneur and director of the Bloomsburg & Montour Electric Railway Company, lost his fortune shortly after occupying the house in 1906 and so resided here only briefly. Purchased by the Bloomsburg Elks in 1923 and expanded in 1942, it served as a lodge for almost eighty years. The Elks and the current owner, the Columbia Alliance for Economic Growth, both undertook significant restoration of the mansion.

33. Wesley United Methodist Christ
   300 South Market Street

Philadelphia, Architect Thomas P. Lonsdale designed this church in 1896 in the Victorian Gothic Revival Style. B.W. Jury built it with Elk Grove Graystone trimmed with Indiana limestone for $55,000, including furnishings. The slate roof was recently restored. An education wing and gymnasium were added in 1927. Two previous Methodist churches (1837 frame, 1857 brick) occupied the back of the present lot.

34. Gunton House
   414 South Market Street

This Queen Anne style home built upon an ashlar foundation sports a second-story recessed porch with Ionic columns. It was built for T.L. Gunton, proprietor of the Marble and Granite Works and known as the "Monument Man." Note the dragon gargoyles on the roof and the griffins guarding the front steps.

35. Law House
   434 South Marker Street

The current structure was built in the Georgian Revival style circa 1907 around the original narrow Victorian house from 1870. Note the side windows which differ from the front. This was the home of James Law, president of the Magee Carpet Company.

36. Gunter/Housenick House
   450 South Market Street

This unique Prairie Style home was built in 1925 for William F. Gunter, operator of Bloomsburg Silk Mills. Cubistic shapes and earthy organic colors were a rebellion against late Victorian grandeur. Purchased in 1929 by the Housenick family; the sisters Elizabeth and Helen resided here for their entire lives.

37. Funston House
   503 South Market Street

John A. Funston built this substantial Colonial Revival home when he moved from Jerseytown to Bloomsburg in 1867. He was actively involved in civic and business affairs, founded the Bloomsburg Banking Company, was president of the Bloomsburg Water Company, and served on the Bloomsburg State Normal School Board of Trustees.

HEAD EAST ON FIFTH STREET AND WALK ON THE SOUTH SIDE OF THE STREET.

38. Peacock House
   4 West Fifth Street

This Colonial Revival home belonged to C.C. Peacock, a town Councilman in the 1890s, Secretary of the Magee Carpet Company and Director of the Bloomsburg Industrial Building and Loan Association. The property originally had a balustraded deck above the porch.

41

39. Koons House
2 East Fifth Street

William B. Koons, one of the proprietors of the Exchange Hotel, purchased a lot here in 1868 and erected a two-story Gothic Revival style frame house by 1870.

40. Ikeler House
42 East Fifth Street

This 1895 house was designed in the Victorian Eclectic Style with a distinctly Byzantine influence, including an Onion dome and radially skewed slate roof. Note the giant owls placed on the gables to deter birds. Built for Fred T. Ikeler, a lawyer and later owned by his brother Frank Ikeler, Mayor of Bloomsburg.

41. Wirt House
60 East Fifth Street

Paul Wirt married Sara Funston on January 1, 1878; her parents, John and Elmira Funston, provided this home as a wedding gift. The classical porch was a later addition to the Queen Anne style building. Although Wirt was an attorney, his dominant interest was to develop a reliable and workable fountain pen. He began manufacturing pens in 1884 and by 1900 had sold two million fountain pens, making him a leader in the industry.

42. Ratti House
106 East Fifth Street

This is the former home of Joseph Ratti, founder of Bloomsburg Silk Mills in 1888 and benefactor of what is now the Bloomsburg Hospital. Ratti, a first cousin of Pope Pius XI, died while visiting Italy in 1906. The present porch with Corinthian columns replaced an earlier porch.

CROSS FIFTH STREET AND WALK BACK TOWARDS MARKET STREET ON THE NORTH SIDE OF THE STREET.

43. Lockard House
133 East Fifth Street

This Queen Anne-Victorian Eclectic style house was the home of early industrialist John Lockard, who manufactured railroad cars. The G.M. and J.K. Lockard Car Works, established in 1872, was later known as the Bloomsburg Car Co., and finally the American Car & Foundry Co. The interior contains the same type of lumber used in railroad cars.

44. Neal/Mears House
49 East Fifth Street

Robert Neal was former owner of the Bloomsburg Furnace Company and Treasurer and Secretary of the Tyrone Iron Co. Purchased in 1919 by H. Reber Mears, General Manager of Bloomsburg Brick Company, the Italianate home continues to remain in that family.

45. Van Tassel House
3 East Fifth Street

This Queen Anne house was built in 1880. It was the home of attorney Levi E. Waller on September 11, 1896 when the building was dynamited, destroying windows and the front porch, in an attempt to do mortal harm to the Waller family. Later it was the residence of Miss Sarah (Sadie) Van Tassel. She was a board member and benefactor of the Bloomsburg Public Library (where her portrait is installed) and owner of the first electric car in Bloomsburg. It is rumored that Sadie's ghost still resides here.

46. Vanderslice House
27 West Fifth Street

This Colonial Revival Style brick house was constructed in 1929 for C.T. Vanderslice, co-owner of the *Morning Press.*

TURN RIGHT ON MARKET STREET AND WALK DOWN THE EAST SIDE OF THE STREET.

47. Magee Store and Letterman Bakery
401 South Market Street

Owned by James Magee II, the former Snyder & Magee Co. Ltd. Store was a general store used by employees of the Magee Carpet Co. In 1895 it became the Leader Department Store. Another Leader store was located in the Exchange Hotel. In the 1920s the building housed the Letterman Baking Co. and to the right, on the site of present offices, was a shed used to store the bakery's delivery wagons. The Romanesque 1893 building is highlighted by rusticated masonry with decorative pointing with red mortar.

HEAD EAST ON FIFTH STREET AND WALK ON THE SOUTH SIDE OF THE STREET.

48. First Presbyterian Church
northeast corner of South Market Street and Fourth Street

The Victorian Gothic Style First Presbyterian Church features Hummelstown brownstone laid in random courses. C.W. Bolten, of Philadelphia, was the architect. Walk down Fourth Street and observe the carriage entrance. Note also the Sunday School addition to the right of the carriage entrance built in 1915. To the left of the sanctuary on Market Street is the Christian Education Building designed by the Bloomsburg architect John Schell and built in 1963.

49. Ikeler House
325 South Market Street

This Italianate Revival home with Moorish influence was built in 1890 utilizing cast cement. Note the amphorae with swags on the façade. Built for Judge Elijah R. Ikeler, it was later the residence of his son Fred. Additions at the rear accommodated a succession of funeral homes.

50. Christian Science Church/Reading Room
317 South Market Street

This is a Sears & Roebuck house, built from a mail order kit delivered by train and truck in 1920. The bungalow is in the popular Arts & Crafts style.

51. John Jordan Brown House
311 South Market Street

This Queen Anne style house shows interesting fishhook ornamentation and circular patterned shingles around the third story window. John Jordan Brown, a physician, began his medical practice in Bloomsburg in the late 1880s; after his death the home was gifted to the Methodist Church and became the church's parsonage.

52. Yorks Mansion
249 South Market Street

This is the original home of Frederick G. Yorks, who was a director of the Bloomsburg Silk Mills, founded in 1888 and employing 350 people. It was the site of the second Presbyterian Church building, a Georgian Style chapel which later became the Cummings & Verdy Co., a chewing gum manufacturer.

53. Bloomsburg Public Library
225 South Market Street

The engaged stone façade and pedimented gable roof mark the High Georgian Revival Style. Note the stone relief depicting the shield from the Pennsylvania coat of arms in the triangular pediment. An outcome of Bloomsburg's centennial celebration in 1902 was the establishment of a free public library. It began in rented rooms until this building was erected at a cost of $100,000.

54. *Man, Dog and Beast* Fountain
in front of the Public Library

This cast iron fountain was erected on the southeast corner of Market and Main Streets in 1892 after 66 citizens petitioned Town Council for a drinking fountain at Market Square; it was restored and relocated to this site in 1991. The name represents the three basins - for people, horses, and dogs.

CONTINUE WALKING TO THE TOUR STARTING POINT.

Look Up,

Carbondale

A Walking Tour of Carbondale...

Despite its relative nearness to New York City and Philadelphia, settlers did not penetrate these mountains and put down roots until 1802. Originally the city was called Ragged Island, then Barrendale. The true pioneers of the upper Lackawanna River Valley were brothers from Philadelphia, William and Maurice Wurts, who believed the anthracite (hard) coal they found in the region could produce cheap energy as successfully as the popular bituminous (soft) coal of the day. They staged a demonstration in New York City and found enough subscribers in their enterprise proposing to send "Black Gold" out of the Moosic Mountains to New York to form America's first private million-dollar corporation.

By 1828 the Wurts' Delaware and Hudson Canal Company had hand-dug and blasted a 108-mile canal from Honesdale to Kingston, New York, an engineering marvel that would ignite the growth of the region. In June 1831, the first underground Anthracite Coal mine in the United States was opened near the base of Seventh Avenue. Washington Irving, the famous author, and Philip Hone, founder of Honesdale, have been credited by many with choosing the name of Carbondale, "carbon" meaning coal discovered here and "dale" meaning valley.

Still the coal had to be moved from Carbondale over the Moosic Mountains to the head of the canal in Honesdale. The Delaware & Hudson solved this problem by means of a "gravity railroad." Cars loaded with coal were hauled up on tracks on a series of planes, or inclines, to the top of Farview by stationary steam engines, then lowered by gravity down planes on the other side to the town of Waymart, finally coasting on a steady downgrade into Honesdale. Empty cars were brought back to Waymart by horse or mule.

The city boomed. By 1851 Carbondale had over 5,000 citizens and was incorporated on March 15, 1851, making it the oldest (the "Pioneer") city in Lackawanna County, and the fourth oldest city (after Philadelphia, Lancaster, and York) in the Commonwealth of Pennsylvania. Carbondale grew and prospered from the mining industry. Many Europeans from different backgrounds traveled to the New World in search of great opportunities and found it all here in Carbondale. Mining remained the chief economic source in the city until the late 1940s and early 1950s when light manufacturing became the new economic lifeblood of the community.

Our walking tour will begin at the site of a former grand train station near the world's first underground anthracite coal mine where there is abundant parking...

1. **Carbondale Train Station**
   behind River Street at Seventh Avenue

In its glory days Carbondale hosted six train stations - a grand one built in 1895 stood on this site. Passenger service to Carbondale ended on January 4, 1952 and the station burned to the ground on July 3, 1970. Lackawanna Heritage Valley constructed the present platform to greet tourists traveling from Steamtown National Historic Site.

FOLLOW THE TRACKS OVER TO SEVENTH AVENUE AND TURN RIGHT.

2. **Coal Mine Monument**
   north side of Seventh Avenue

This monument marks the site of America's first underground coal mine. The city founders, the Wurt brothers, opened the mine in June of 1831.

RETURN TO THE PARKING LOT AND WALK OUT TO RIVER STREET. TURN LEFT.

3. **Trinity Episcopal Church**
   58 River Street

The first service at this location took place on July 17, 1842. The present stone church replaced the original wooden structure in 1901. Several of the stained glass windows are from the initial church. Four of the windows were signed by Louis Comfort Tiffany and three others were made by John LaFarge, a Tiffany protege.

CROSS THE LACKAWANNA RIVER ON SIXTH AVENUE. TURN LEFT ON MAIN STREET.

4. **Carbondale City Hall**
   1 North Main Street

Listed on the *National Register of Historic Places*, this Romanesque Revival red-brick municipal building was designed by Truman I. Lacey around the original two-story structure to the rear by changing the roof, adding the three-story wing and incorporating the signature clock tower. The home for city government offices opened in 1894.

5. **Miners & Mechanics Savings Bank**
   Building
   19 North Main Street

The Miners & Mechanics Savings Bank opened for business in 1871 and moved into this Neoclassical vault, designed by Edward Langley, in 1914. The bank failed in 1931 after a run through the Ionic columns. Today the building, also listed on the *National Register of Historic Places*, is the home of Adams Cable Television.

6. **Pioneer Dime Bank Building**
   27 North Main Street

This ornate Beaux Arts bank operated from 1904 until the 1970s. The building stands out of the Carbondale streetscape for its intricate detailing and stone carvings. During its life as a bank, large decorative coins embellished each side of the facade at the first floor. The Carbondale Chamber of Commerce now occupies the building.

7. **Pennstar Bank Building**
   41 North Main Street

This fine example of Art Deco architecture has been in use as a bank since 1928. The building sports large stone eagles on the exterior facing Main Street and its meticulously restored lobby featuring marble floors, large windows and intricate chandelier.

8. **Hotel American**
   55 North Main Street

The first visitors signed the Hotel American guest book in 1893. The four-story structure is made of Pocono sandstone, quarried near Forest City. The building features intricate decorative carvings in the facade.

9. Carbondale Post Office
   69 North Main Street

The handsome Beaux Arts United States post office was built in 1911. It features an elaborate entranceway between Ionic columns and beneath a pair of carved eagles.

10. Ben Mar Restaurant
   89 North Main Street

The Ben Mar Restaurant is the last remaining building from the Delaware & Hudson Canal Company Gravity Railroad. To the rear of the white-washed restaurant resided the Gravity Shops. The first facility was built in 1832. In 1857, a 14,000-square foot building was constructed here at the base of the railroad's Plane 1 to provide machine and blacksmith work on rolling stock and other equipment. the facility served the D & H until 1955. Attempts at restoration were unsuccessful and the building was demolished in 1988.

11. Carbondale YMCA
   82 North Main Street

In 1912, Catherine and Anna Alexander, daughters of a prominent Carbondale businessman, donated $10,000 for the establishment of the YMCA. Boyd & Stewart, architects from Pittsburgh, won the commission and delivered this eight-bay Colonial Revival headquarters. Today the exterior of the building looks much as did when it was completed in 1914.

TURN LEFT ON CHURCH STREET.

12. Gravity Park
   southeast corner of Garfield and Church streets

This monument was placed in 1923 to mark the beginning of the Delaware & Hudson Canal Company Gravity Railroad in its centennial year. The park stands at the foot of the Gravity Railroad's Plane 1.

TURN AND WALK BACK INTO TOWN ON CHURCH STREET.

13. First Presbyterian Church
   33 Lincoln Avenue on northwest corner of Church Street

The church was dedicated on April 1, 1889, built on the site of the town's first foundry that was established in 1833 by Abiran Gurney and Alanson Reed. The building was devastated by fire on August 21, 1968 and was rebuilt over a two-year period.

14. First Presbyterian Church
   76 Salem Avenue at southeast corner of Church Street

Founded in 1829, this was the first organized church in Carbondale and the oldest Presbyterian congregation in Lackawanna County. Four church buildings have stood on this site; the first appeared in 1834. The current Gothic-inspired structure dates to June 3, 1951.

15. First United Methodist Church
   20 North Church Street

A single-story wood structure built in 1832 served as the first Methodist church on the site. In 1892 Edward Langley designed a new church that was soon destroyed by fire. The congregation rebuilt using the identical plans and incorporating bits and pieces salvaged from the rubble of the former building. The church was dedicated on March 8, 1903.

16. Saint Rose of Lima Roman Catholic Church
   6 North Church Street

This is the third church to be built on this location. The first was constructed in 1832, the second a decade later. The present church, that serves one of the largest parishes in the Scranton diocese, was built in 1872.

TURN RIGHT AND WALK INTO MEMORIAL PARK.

17. Memorial Park
between 6th and Park avenues

In the 1880s, under the leadership of William H. Davies Post 187 of the Grand Army of the Republic (G.A.R.) Memorial Park was established on the former Carbondale militia parade ground and a monument and fountain were erected to honor the veterans of the Civil War. Over the years, monuments were added to honor the memory of veterans of the Spanish American War, World War I and II, the Korean War and Vietnam conflict, along with plaques recognizing Patrick De Lacey and Lieutenant Joseph R. Sarnoski, both recipients of the Congressional Medal of Honor.

CONTINUE WALKING STRAIGHT ON 6TH AVENUE BACK TO THE TOUR STARTING POINT.

Look Up,

Carlisle

A Walking Tour of Carlisle...

With ties to George Washington, Molly Pitcher, the Civil War and even "America's Greatest Athlete," Jim Thorpe, for many years Carlisle billed itself as "America's Most Historic Town." The Carlisle Barracks, built in 1751, were George Washington's choice for his army's first arsenal and school. This Colonial ammunition plant was called Washingtonburg when it was constructed in 1776, the first place in America named for the general.

The Town of Carlisle was laid out and settled by Scotch-Irish immigrants in 1751 and became the center of their settlement in the Cumberland Valley. It was named after its sister town in Carlisle, England, and even built its former jailhouse to resemble Carlisle Citadel. The town was well-known at one time for the Carlisle Indian Industrial School, which trained Native Americans from all over the United States; one of its notable graduates was Thorpe, hero of the 1912 Olympics.

During the first half of the 20th century, the Carlisle Historic District was the hub of activity in the agricultural region located west of the Susquehanna River. Carlisle remained the largest town in Cumberland County during this period, with its population of 9,626 persons in 1900 swelling to 16,812 by 1950. It was a market town and legal and service center for the surrounding Cumberland Valley throughout the 20th century, as it had been in the past. Before 1930, two trolley lines and a passenger railroad, and after 1930, an extensive network of public roads connected the Carlisle Historic District with other communities in the region.

This walking tour will begin on Courthouse Square, an area known to George Washington when he worshipped here...

1. **First Presbyterian Church**
   northwest corner of Carlisle Square

This is the oldest public building in Carlisle. Many Revolutionary War officers were members of this congregation. President George Washington attended service here on Oct. 5, 1794 before marching to western Pennsylvania to quell the Whiskey Rebellion.

The 1769 building contract for the church stipulated that the stonework should be massive at the base, building up to stones of a smaller size. The chapel and tower were added to the west end of the church in 1872, and in 1952, an educational-social annex was built.

WALK NORTH ON NORTH HANOVER STREET.

2. **Carlisle Deposit Bank & Trust**
   3 North Hanover Street

The former Carlisle Deposit Bank & Trust Company building is a fine example of Neoclassical architecture highlighted by engaged Doric columns.

3. **Blaine House**
   4 North Hanover Street

Col. Ephraim Blaine, Commissary General during the Revolutionary War, began construction on this house in 1794. Note the brick water table running below the first floor windows and the stringcourses with their flat arches and keystones above the first and second story windows. The elaborate cornice and the large door with its delicate fanlight add to the beauty of the exterior. The house retains much of its original interior and is the best-preserved 18th century house in Carlisle.

TURN LEFT ON LOUTHER STREET.

4. **Union Fire Company #1**
   35 West Louther Street

The Union Fire Company boasts a proud history of over 215 years. The Company was organized in 1789 and later became incorporated by a special act of Pennsylvania legislature in 1840. It still operates today under the same name and charter as when the Company was established.

The Union Firehouse, built in 1888, has not only been meticulously repaired and maintained, but has a particularly well designed and appropriate hand painted sign.

RETURN TO NORTH HANOVER STREET AND TURN RIGHT, HEAD BACK TOWARDS THE SQUARE.

5. **St. John's Episcopal Church**
   northeast corner of the Square

St. John's still occupies the original site on the town square that was reserved for the "English Church." The first celebration of the Eucharist took place on Trinity Sunday 1752. The first church to meet in Carlisle, the parish is named in honor of St. John, evangelist and apostle, also know as the "Beloved Disciple."

The church building is the third to serve this congregation. A rustic log structure was first erected in the 1750s and did double duty for a time as the county courthouse as well as a church. A modest stone colonial church was built in the 1760s. Both of these early church buildings were located adjacent to East High Street, in the area now occupied by the Parish Hall. Work on the present church began in 1826 and concluded the following year, making use of stone from the dismantled colonial building. An original tower on the east end of the church was removed during a large renovation in 1861 and the present tower and steeple were erected.

6. **Cumberland County Courthouse**
   1 Courthouse Square

In their 1751 plan for Carlisle, the Penn family designated a portion of the Square to be used as a market. At least three market buildings stood here over the years. A 1760s map depicts an open-air building facing High Street. It was destroyed by a violent windstorm in 1836, and a similar structure replaced it the following year. The last Market House, a grandiose Victorian structure, was built in 1878. Market business took place on the open first floor, while the second floor housed various Borough offices. Despite a valiant preservation effort by a group of townspeople and farmers, the building was demolished in 1952 ending two centuries of tradition. This classically-themed courthouse was erected in 1962.

TURN LEFT ON EAST HIGH STREET.

7. Stephen Duncan House
4 East High Street

Stephen Duncan, a merchant who came to Carlisle in the 1750s, built this stone house. Duncan was a Justice of the Peace, a member of the Pennsylvania Assembly, and a trustee of Dickinson College. Duncan's son John was killed in a duel in 1793, and his widow became the second wife of Col. Ephraim Blaine.

8. Duncan-Stiles House
52 East High Street, southwest corner of Bedford Street

This grand three-story Federal-style house "was by far the most expensive private house ever built in Carlisle," wrote James Hamilton, Jr. in the 1870s. It was planned and built in 1811, by Judge Thomas Duncan's wife as a dwelling for her son Stephen and his bride Miss Margaretta Stiles.

Marble stairs and a delicate iron railing lead up to the front door. Fluted pillars and a vaulted ceiling in the entry set off the curving staircase that leads to the third floor. A Robert Welford mantel that stood in one of the parlors is now in the American Wing of the Metropolitan Museum of Art.

Sadly, Stephen Duncan's bride died less than three years after their marriage. Duncan moved to Philadelphia and sold the house to his brother-in-law, attorney Benjamin Stiles. Stiles sold the house in 1840 to Rev. J.V.E. Thorn, an eccentric minister, and his equally eccentric wife Susan Hamilton, daughter of Judge James Hamilton. Mrs. Thorn often said that one of her expressed ambitions was "to see the devil just long enough to get his daguerreotype." The Thorns were childless, and when Mrs. Thorn died in 1867 she bequeathed her fortune to religious and educational institutions.

9. Cumberland County Prison
37 East High Street, northwest corner of Bedford Street

When this English-looking castle was constructed in 1854 it represented the latest fashion in Pennsylvania prison architecture made popular by architect John Haviland. An earlier prison was erected at this location in 1754, and even though it was deemed unfit for human incarceration as early as the 1770s, it remained in use for another 80 years. Escapes were a common occurrence and for years the people of Carlisle pleaded for a new and stronger jail. This prison was built, but determined inmates still managed to regularly break out. Some inmates chipped the plaster and mortar from the walls, removed the stones and crawled through the holes. Then lowering themselves from the cell block to the ground with blankets, they scaled the outer wall and fled. Others escaped by filing through the iron bars of their cells, and one prisoner even set fire to his flooring planks hoping to escape through the smoke screen. He failed.

The brownstone used in the construction of the prison was quarried in York County and stones from the first prison were most likely used to make the prison yard walls. While the prison yard was used mainly for exercise, the last hanging in the county took place there in 1894 when Charles Salyards was hanged for the murder of policeman Charles E. Martin. In 1984, a larger modern facility was built on Claremont Road, and the "old" prison has been readapted for county use.

10. First Lutheran Church
21 South Bedford Street, southeast corner of East High Street

This church, which evolved from the German Lutherans, is one of Carlisle's foremost examples of Romanesque Revival architecture.

11. Lyon House
119 East High Street

William Lyon, born in Ireland in 1729, built this house in 1788, according to notations in his business record. Lyon served as a First Lieutenant in the Pennsylvania Regiment during the French and Indian War, was a prosperous shopkeeper, and held several offices in county government. It is likely that he used the one-story portion of the house as his office.

12. "Sign of the Turk"
137 East High Street

Tavern keeper John Pollock built the house in the 1760s. The tavern was described in a 1773 newspaper advertisement as a 33-foot square stone house with a 25 foot square stone addition that housed a kitchen and bar room on the first floor and lodging rooms on the second floor. Both buildings are still standing. The tavern had its own brewery and a still in the cellar, and the stone-lined well can still be seen today. This elegant tavern was favored by traveling dancing masters who gave lessons and held candlelight balls here in the 18th and early 19th centuries.

The house was updated in the 1870s when a mansard roof and a new cornice were added. Although the windows and doors have been altered, the original stone arches can still be seen at the window and cellar openings.

13. Lydia Baird Home and Hospital
East High Street

In the early 1890s the community launched a movement to establish a hospital in Carlisle. Their vision was to offer an avenue through which the poor would receive medical treatment through a charitable institution. In April 1893, The Hospital Wards of the Lydia Baird Home and Hospital were opened. It had one private room. When the doors opened, no rush for treatment occurred. In fact, April gave way to May without anyone venturing to cross the hospital's threshold for treatment. So when the first patients actually did arrive, they were "greeted with much acclaim". This came about when the Barnum and Bailey Circus came to town. An accident occurred and injured circus employees became the first patients on May 12. Hospital officials were so excited they forgot to call a doctor. The Baird Hospital lasted three years, setting a precedent for the need of such an institution in the community. The doors only closed to make way for a new and better hospital.

TURN LEFT ON NORTH EAST STREET.

14. Trent House
7 North East Street

This is one of the few surviving houses in Carlisle built before the Revolutionary War. Note the arched stone lintels over the windows on the first floor. Original windows can be seen in the rear. The house may have been built by William Trent who mortgaged it in 1769 to his partner George Croghan, known as the "King of the Indian Traders." Trent, son of the founder of Trenton, New Jersey, was an Indian trader, land speculator, soldier, and guide for General Forbes's army during the French and Indian War.

15. Dwen Cottage
22 North East Street

Built in 1857, this house is an outstanding example of the Gothic Revival style. Inspired by the work of Andrew Jackson Downing, full-blown Gothic Revival houses such as this are somewhat rare in Pennsylvania.

TURN LEFT ON MULBERRY STREET.

16. Log House
157 Mulberry Alley

Although the location of all the doors and windows were altered in the 19th century, this log house most likely dates to the Revolutionary War era. Note the half dovetailed construction at the corners of the house.

RETURN TO NORTH EAST STREET AND TURN LEFT.

17. Alexander House
60 North East Street, southwest corner of Louther Street

John and Jacob Crever of York County, bought this property in 1774 and built a brewery and a malt house. The brew house fronted on Louther Street while the tavern fronted on East Street.

TURN RIGHT ON
LOUTHER STREET.

18. Pollock House
229 East Louther Street

This 18th century stone house was owned by John Pollock, maltster and tavern keeper. In 1792 the property included the present two-story stone house with two kitchens, a brew house, and a back building of log. Except for the addition of a porch, there have been few alterations made to the house.

RETURN TO NORTH EAST STREET
AND TURN RIGHT.

19. McManus House
131 North East Street

This classic 5-bay Georgian-style house with a center hall was built in 1803 by tavernkeeper Charles McManus. McManus also built and operated a distillery at the lower end of the lot adjoining the LeTort stream. This end of town was considered rough, and McManus's rowdy Irish tavern, named the "Sign of the Eagle and Harp," was the scene of many fights during his reign as tavernkeeper. McManus died in 1817, and the tavern and distillery were sold in 1824.

TURN AROUND AND WALK SOUTH
ON EAST STREET TO POMFRET
STREET.

20. Sign of the Cross Keys
176 East Pomfret Street

This large stone house was built between 1788-1798. Robert Taylor, a freemason, operated the "Sign of the Cross Keys" here from 1806-1822.

TURN RIGHT ON
POMFRET STREET.

21. Saint Katharine Hall
140 East Pomfret Street

Built by Saint M. Katharine Drexel, a Philadelphia heiress who conducted a "select free colored school" for black children and served the Carlisle Indian School. She vowed to be "mother and servant of the Indian and Negro races." She was declared a saint on October 1, 2000.

22. Bethel A.M.E. Church
131 East Pomfret Street

Established in 1820, this is among the earliest African American congregations located west of the Susquehanna River. It was the site of Underground Railroad activity.

23. Captain William Armstrong House
109 East Pomfret Street

This 1 1/2-story stone house, with later additions, is the oldest documented stone house still standing in Carlisle. It was built in the summer of 1759 by stone mason Stephen Foulk who came to Carlisle from Chester County, Pennsylvania. Records show that workmen were paid eight gallons of whiskey for digging the cellar. The 27' x 25' house was built for Captain William Armstrong, brother of Colonel John Armstrong of Carlisle, the "Hero of Kittanning."

24. Sign of the White Horse
54 East Pomfret Street

Lewis Lewis, a surveyor and father of the infamous "Lewis the Robber," operated the "Sign of the White Horse" tavern in this house from 1784-1787. The 2 1/2-story log house was built around 1780 and stuccoed in the 1840s. The house has corner fireplaces on the first and second floors and a cooking fireplace in the cellar.

TURN LEFT ON SOUTH HANOVER
STREET AND WALK DOWN THE
EAST SIDE OF THE STREET.

25. Farabelli Building
115 South Hanover Street

Many late 19th century Victorian and Italianate decorative elements are widely present on buildings dating from the first few years of the 20th century, as new innovative styles were slow to reach the Carlisle Historic District. Common elements of commercial buildings with Italianate architectural elements include either cast iron or wooden cornices on both the upper cornice and storefront windows. Many windows also have decorative architraves also common to the period.

26. Major Andre Detention Site
northeast corner of South Hanover Street and East Chapel Avenue

As early as June 1775, local citizens who favored independence had organized a militia. They sent troops under Colonel William Thompson to Boston, where the Virginia militia officer who had experienced defeat with Braddock 20 years earlier in western Pennsylvania was forming the Continental Army. As the war broadened and Washington's Army captured British soldiers, places of confinement for the enemy parolees were sought away from centers of mischief and intrigue. Carlisle was one of those sites. Among the prisoners was Major John Andre, a key figure in Benedict Arnold's plot to betray the Continentals. Major Andre was detained in a tavern that stood on this site and several years later, after exchange and recapture in New York, he was executed.

CROSS THE STREET, TURN RIGHT AND WALK BACK UP THE WEST SIDE OF SOUTH HANOVER STREET, TOWARDS POMFRET STREET.

27. Beetem House
110 South Hanover Street

This exuberant example of the Queen Anne style of architecture was constructed in 1896. A member of the Beetem family, William Luther, was the first man from Carlisle killed during the Civil War. This was the home of Charles Gilbert Beetem, a rug manufacturer, local historian and genealogist, amateur artist, and omnivorous collector. His longtime interest in United States island possessions is the subject of his large collection of publications and books housed in the Dickinson College library.

28. Musselman House
102 South Hanover Street

Jacob Musselman built this large brick house in the 1790s. On the exterior the flat marble lintels with keystones above the windows are of particular note; inside the interior paneling and staircase remain intact.

The house was rented in 1793 by Charles Steineke who practiced medicine in Carlisle for several years before moving to Baltimore. The doctor's daughter, Maria Steineke, was poisoned in 1869 by Dr. Paul Schoeppe of Carlisle after he was made the beneficiary of her considerable fortune. She was buried in Baltimore, but the growing supposition in Carlisle that her death was not accidental led to her body being exhumed 13 days after her death. Upon examination, the doctors concluded that she had been poisoned. Schoeppe was tried and found guilty of murder.

TURN LEFT ON POMFRET STREET.

29. Empire Hook and Ladder Company
38-40 West Pomfret Street

The Carlisle Fire Department originally consisted of five companies: Union, Cumberland, Goodwill, Friendship, and Empire. This firehouse was built in 1859 for the Empire Hook and Ladder volunteer force. The companies were forced to merge for financial and political reasons leaving only three: Union, Cumberland-Goodwill, and Empire-Friendship. After two notable downtown fires in the 1920s, the first on North Hanover Street taking the Woolworth, Haverstick, and Berg stores in 1924 and another in 1929 that burned down Kronenberg's, a clothing store that replaced the space left by these businesses, the building received an Art Deco face lift. it is, along with the Carlisle Theater, one of only two Art Deco buildings in town.

30. The Barber Shop
42 West Pomfret Street

This 30' x 30' two-story stone house was built before 1798 and was home to several blacksmiths in the 18th century. Note the elegant cornice and stone lintels above the windows. In the past 200 years it has been adapted for many business uses.

31. First Baptist Church
51 Third Street

This is a good example of how houses were enlarged and remodeled over the years. Originally a one-story log house, the second story and fashionable peaked gable were added in the 19th century when the exterior was covered with frame. Portions of the original structure can be seen behind a Plexiglass wall inside.

CROSS PITT STREET AND TURN RIGHT ON WEST STREET.

32. Dickinson College President's House
southwest corner of West Street and High Street

Much changed from its origins as a Colonial Revival villa, the house's original owner was Cumberland County Judge James Reed (Class of 1806), who opened a law school out of his basement in 1834. What started as a informal series of lectures for $75 a year eventually became the Dickinson School of Law; and in 2000, the Penn State Dickinson College School of Law.

33. Old West
beyond the gate on the north side of West High Street, opposite President's House

Dickinson College was America's first college chartered after the end of the Revolutionary War. Benjamin Rush, a prominent Philadelphia physician, prepared the charter in 1783 and asked that John Dickinson--known widely as the "Penman of the Revolution" and the governor of Pennsylvania--to lend his support and his name to the college that was being established in the western frontier of his state. So on September 9, 1783, a struggling grammar school in Carlisle was transformed into Dickinson College.

As the college grew in population and prominence a new "edifice" was needed to allow Dickinson to move out of the old grammar school that had been its home since its founding. Called "New College," the building was constructed slowly, over a period of four years. In 1803, as the college prepared to settle into New College, a blustery snowstorm pushed through the Cumberland Valley, stirring some smoldering ashes

in the building's basement. The ashes began to flame, and before long the building had burned to the ground. Quickly rebuilt, Old West, as it is commonly called, hosted its first classes in November 1805.

RETURN TO HIGH STREET AND TURN LEFT, HEADING BACK TOWARDS THE SQUARE.

34. Denny Memorial Hall
173 West High Street, northeast corner of West Street

The Denny family, early pioneers and prominent settlers in Carlisle and Pittsburgh donated the lot at the corner of what is now High and West streets to the College with the reservation that any building erected there be christened with the Denny name. First raised in 1897, the hoped for purpose of the edifice was to alleviate the crowded conditions students faced in recitation halls on campus, as well as to provide "two elegant and commodious" halls for the Dickinson's thriving intellectual Societies: the Union Philosophical and Belles Lettres Literary Society. Scarred by a major fire only eight years after completion, the Romanesque Revival building is the more grandiose design of Miller Kast, finished in 1905, and the product of extensive renovations in the mid-1980s. On this site in 1794 President George Washington reviewed militia from Pennsylvania and New Jersey.

35. Bellaire House
141 West High Street

This early Greek Revival-style mansion began life in 1820 as the Parker House. Converted into a public house, the Bellaire became a long-time statement of elegant dining in Carlisle. Today the double curving stairway leads to office space.

36. Centenary Building
54 West High Street

In 1827, a German Reformed congregation built a stone church at this location. At the time, a Methodist congregation was housed in a church on Church Alley. The location was not ideal due to boisterous behavior in the alley during church services and "offensive" odors coming from nearby stables. In 1833, the Methodist congregation decided to find a more suitable building and purchased the stone church. In 1875, the two Methodist congregations decided to reunify. They tore down the stone church and replaced it with a two story brick church. Completed in 1877, it became known as the Centenary Church in recognition of the centenary of American Independence. The reunified Methodist congregation worshiped here for twelve more years until they decided to move closer to the Dickinson College campus. In 1889 the building was sold, and for the next 110 years it housed a variety of businesses.

37. Carlisle Theatre
40 West High Street

The Carlisle Theatre, originally called The Comerford, opened its doors in May of 1939. It was by far the grandest of three movie "palaces" all within a block of one another and was the first centrally air conditioned building in Carlisle. The Theatre was built in the Art Deco style known as "streamlined moderne." From the razzle-dazzle modernistic marquee with its bold Deco lettering, to the richly designed interior, Art Deco styling abounds.

During its early years, the Theatre offered daily continuous shows from 2:30 until 11:30 p.m. The matinee price for adults was 25 cents and the evening price 40 cents. The Theatre flourished through the 1960s, acting as the "hub" of a vibrant downtown. With the advent of cineplexes, the Theatre entered a state of decline in the 1970s, eventually closing in 1986.

A fundraising effort was launched and the Theatre was purchased in 1991. After thousands of hours donated by a skilled volunteer workforce, the Theatre was restored to its 1930's Art Deco brilliance and reopened for independent films and the performing arts in 1993.

38. Human Services Building
16 West High Street

This Neoclassical building was erected for the Cumberland Valley Savings and Loan Association that was founded in 1906. The building is now home to a variety of social agencies, including the Offices for Children and Youth, Aging, Community Services, Mental Health/Mental Retardation, and the Drug and Alcohol Commission.

39. Farmers' Trust Company
1 West High Street

The Farmers' Trust Company was chartered in 1902, absorbing the assets of the Farmers' Bank and occupying this prominent location in town.

40. Civil War Monument
Courthouse Square, southwest corner

The monument honors Cumberland County's Civil War dead. Confederate troops, on their way to Gettysburg, shot up the town.

41. Old Cumberland County Courthouse
Courthouse Square, southwest corner

The original courthouse rose on this spot in 1766. After an arsonist burned it in 1845 this building, fronted by sandstone columns, replaced it. On June 27, 1863, a dusty column of 15,000 rebels led by General Richard Ewell marched up the road from Shippensburg into Carlisle. Foraging for supplies, they camped here until Tuesday, June 30. They departed that day, headed towards Mount Holley Springs. Other than the ample provisions they had taken, they left the community unscathed. The next day, July 1, the townspeople cheered the arrival of Major General William Smith's four regiments of Federal militiamen, but their joy was short-lived. Late that afternoon, Major General J.E.B. Stuart and 3,500 rebel cavalrymen appeared at the intersection of York and Trindle roads.

The rebels unlimbered their artillery, demanded the surrender of the town, and threatened to burn it. General Smith refused, the artillerymen let fly, and townspeople and militiamen alike scattered for shelter. Over the next few hours, shells struck the columns of the courthouse, blew holes in the Presbyterian and Episcopal churches, damaged numerous other properties, and wounded a few unlucky souls near the square, including twelve militiamen. After setting fire to the U.S. Army's Carlisle Barracks, Stuart's men disappeared to the south, ordered to Gettysburg. The threat had ended. Although most of the damage done by the rebel shells was long ago repaired, scars can still be seen here on the facade of the Old Court House. You can still see where a pillar was chipped and bricks were broken by flying shrapnel.

YOU HAVE REACHED THE
BEGINNING OF THE TOUR.

Look Up,

Clarion

A Walking Tour of Clarion...

Clarion County was created as the 54th of Pennsylvania's 67 counties on March 11, 1839, from parts of Venango and Armstrong counties. The Clarion River was the dividing line between the two mother counties was in early times known as Stump Creek and Toby's Creek. In 1817, the legislature passed an Act, authorizing the survey of a state road from Indiana to Franklin. The surveyors selected were David Lawson and Daniel Stannard. While lying in their tent one night, along Toby Creek, which was heavily fringed by a wall of close and massive timber, they noticed this wall condensed and reflected the murmur of the stream, giving it a silvery mellowness. Stannard remarked, "The water sounds like a distant clarion." And so Pennsylvania got a name for a river, a county, and, a town.

Sometime in the fall of 1839, the town plot containing 200 acres, was surveyed by John Sloan, Jr. There were 275 in-lots and 50 out-lots. The public sale of the lots began October 30, 1839 and continued for three days. The highest price for a lot was $757.50 and the next in value was sold for $560.00.

The community was incorporated as a borough in 1841 and lay along the historic overland Susquehanna and Waterford Turnpike (later known as the Lakes-to-Sea Highway and now U.S. Route 322). Large stands of virgin timber provided the impetus for the first industry; later, local sand reserves helped make Clarion known as a producer of glass bottles. Clarion also prospered during the region's oil boom f the 1860s and 1870s. Around that time the Carrier Seminary was established in Clarion; it eventually became Clarion University of Pennsylvania, and continues to be among the leading economic forces in the community.

Our walking tour will begin in a small park dedicated to America's veterans, opposite the town's most obvious landmark...

1. **Clarion County Veterans Memorial Park bounded by Main Street, Grant Street, 4th Avenue and Jefferson Place**

Clarion County Veterans Memorial Park includes a large gazebo and memorials to conflicts through America's history. The POW/MIA monument that was placed here in July 2001 contains the ashes of a "watch fire," a symbolic fire that is burned until the last patrol returns to base camp, signifying all of those who are missing in action or are prisoners of war. This monument was dedicated during a visit of the "moving wall" a traveling version of the Vietnam Veterans Memorial.

CROSS MAIN STREET TO THE COURTHOUSE.

2. **Clarion County Courthouse**
   421 Main Street

This is the third courthouse that has graced the county seat of Clarion. The first Clarion County Courthouse, completed in 1842 at the cost of $10,636.16, was brick, two stories, and divided by a slight offset — from which there were two narrow recesses into two longitudinal wings. In 1859 fire erupted in a faulty flue and destroyed the building. It was replaced by a substantial brick building with, unfortunately, a wooden roof approximately 65 feet high. About one o'clock on the morning of September 12, 1882, fire which had been smoldering in the loft, burst through the roof. The water pressure was not enough to force the stream to the top. The building was gutted in a few hours, leaving the walls standing comparatively intact for a new courthouse.

The current Victorian courthouse was completed shortly afterwards. It is dominated by a 25-foot square tower, 213 feet high. It rises 139 feet above the roof. The walls of the main part are 22 inches thick. This roof is of tin and slate. The clock dial, nine feet in diameter, and the bell, weighing 1,313 pounds, were furnished by the Howard Clock Company from New York. The interior of the clock loft is fitted with gas pipes for illumination. Todays' appearance reflects a complete exterior renovation undertaken in 1981.

WALK BEHIND THE COURTHOUSE, ON THE WEST SIDE.

3. **Grace Lutheran Church**
   421 Madison Street

This Gothic Revival brick church with stone trim was completed in 1844, originally for the Methodist congregation in town.

TURN RIGHT, WALKING BEHIND THE COURTHOUSE.

4. **Clarion County Jail**
   421 Main Street

This imposing brick and stone structure with a square battlement was built in the 1870s and is the second jail on this site. The first jail was a plain structure of square cut sandstone with a small yard surrounded by a stone wall in the rear. In 1847 the building was remodeled and a new front put on. After the completion of the new prison, it was finally torn down in 1883 and its stones used in the foundation of the courthouse. The old jail stood just west of the present one. It is 97 feet in height from the ground and 18 feet square at the base and 10 feet at the top. The outside walls of the prison proper are of ashlar rough dressed sandstone 2 feet in thickness. It contains 20 cells at 81/2 x 14' each, arranged in two tiers on each side of the interior court.

On June 11, 1911 the only execution in the history of the county took place here. Vincent Voycheck of Rimersburg, an immigrant coal miner, stabbed his landlord Andrew Stupka to death and was convicted of murder. It was said that a woman, Zoe Himes, secretary in a courthouse office, pulled the cord that released the trap on the gallows.

RETURN TO MAIN STREET AND TURN LEFT, WALKING EAST.

5. **Orpheum Theatre**
   511 Main Street

Clarion's first nickelodeon, owned by Finkbeiner and O'Brien, opened at Wood Street and Sixth Avenue in 1908. The Orpheum Theatre, with its Art Deco facade, opened in the days of silent films in 1925. A movie house managed to stay in business here until 1998 before going the way of most downtown theaters - out of business.

6. Crooks Clothing
539 Main Street

Crooks Clothing Co., Inc. was founded in 1905 by F.L. Crooks at the same location it is today. The two-story building with large display cases and a neon sign, once housed Weaver Hardware and the Clarion Restaurant in the basement. Murals depicting scenes of Clarion grace the walls.

7. Kaufman Building
southeast corner of Main Street and Sixth Avenue

Charles Kaufman built this two-story brick structure to serve as a clothing store and family home in 1853. It remained in the Kaufman family as it was rented out; a long-time tenant was Widman's Store.

8. Cherico Building
606 Main Street

These Main Street fixtures were built between 1840 and 1860. At 606 Main Street Sam Cherico opened the Modern Store, the first self-serve grocery store in northwestern Pennsylvania in 1938.

9. United States Post Office
626 Main Street

In the first half of the 20th century the federal government set out to provide small towns with significant architecture, usually in the form of a post office that was most people's only connection to the United States government until the Great Depression. In Clarion, the post office received an Art Deco treatment on dark brick.

10. Ross Memorial Library/Clarion Free Library
644 Main Street

The Clarion Free Library opened its doors in a gymnasium on Fourth Avenue with 225 books. in 1914. in 1920, the will of the late John D. Ross, member of a prominent Clarion family and son of a former mayor, provided for the erection of a memorial library and auditorium, to be known as the Ross Memorial Library and to be built in Clarion to perpetuate the memory of his late mother, Mrs. Mary Ann Wilson Ross. Completed in 1929, it is an excellent example of Carnegiesque influence in civic architecture of the period. The roof edge is balustraded and the pediment features an open book motif framed by leafy vines. The pediment is supported by Doric columns and the doorway has a bracketed cornice with dentils and a transom.

11. Newspaper Building
645 Main Street

The *Clarion News* was first published in 1840, the same year Clarion County was formed. It was then the *Clarion Democrat* and was the only paper in the county until 1843 when the *Clarion Republican* made its debut. The two papers were published separately for 122 years until they merged in November 1965 and became the *Clarion News*. With one brief exception - during the oil excitement days when the Edenburg *Daily Herald* was founded in Knox - all the papers that have served Clarion County have been weeklies. The *Clarion News* publishes each Tuesday and Thursday.

The brick newspaper building, sporting an elaborate cornice with finials and corner quoins, dates to 1876. The windows have caved hood moldings and stone sills.

12. First Baptist Church
northwest corner of Main Street and Seventh Avenue

The First Baptist Church earned the designation in its name by appearing on the Clarion streetscape in 1877.

TURN RIGHT ON SEVENTH AVENUE.

13. First Presbyterian Church
   700 Wood Street on the southeast corner of Seventh Avenue

The first church meetings of the Clarion Presbyterians were held in the loft of the old jail in 1841. The first church building was located nearby on Grant Street. This Romanesque stone church began serving the congregation in 1896.

TURN RIGHT ON WOOD STREET.

14. First United Methodist Church
   600 Wood Street on southeast corner of Sixth Avenue

The First United Methodist Church of Clarion has its roots in 1840 when Methodists first began to hold services here. The Erie Conference of the Methodist Episcopal Church appointed its first minister in 1841. The early meetings were held in a schoolhouse and then in the jail. In 1843, the congregation decided to build a meeting place that was completed in 1844 (the present Lutheran Church). After fire destroyed the Clarion County courthouse in 1882, the Methodist Church was used for holding court until the present courthouse was completed in 1885. The present Romanesque building of native stone was erected and dedicated in 1887-1889.

TURN RIGHT ON 5TH AVENUE. TURN LEFT ON GRANT STREET AT VETERANS PARK.

15. Chase and Stewart Block
   west side of Franklin Street between Spring and Central streets

Listed on the *National Register of Historic Places*, the three-bay Greek Revival style Sutton-Ditz house was constructed when Clarion was still in its infancy. Thomas Sutton, a native of Indiana County and Deputy Attorney General of the county, came to Clarion in 1846 and built a small brick law office opposite the courthouse and, a year later, this brick house as well. Tragedy struck the Suttons in Clarion when Thomas died in 1853 of typhoid fever at the age of 37 and two days later Thomas, Jr. passed away from scarlet fever. Widow Anne remained in the house until 1862 when she left for Philadelphia to oversee a girls' school. She sold the property for $2,000.

A succession of private owners followed until John Ditz, a prosperous hardware dealer in town, purchased the property in 1908. Ditz tore down the former law office and gave his new home a major remodeling in the then-popular Neoclassical style with a new domineering Ionic portico. Ditz suffered financial reversals in Florida land speculation in the 1920s and the house was converted into "tourist rooms" while the family remained in the house. Minnie Ditz lived here until she died in 1972 at the age of ninety-nine. In 1975 the house was acquired by the Clarion County Historical Society.

YOU HAVE NOW RETURNED TO THE TOUR STARTING POINT IN VETERANS PARK.

Look Up,

Connellsville

A Walking Tour of Connellsville...

Zachariah Connell was already 65 years old when he laid out the town that would be his namesake in 1806. Connell was born in Virginia in 1741 and came to Fayette County after 1770 as a surveyor and land agent. Seeing this area as a natural stopping place for travelers who wanted to build rafts and float them down the river, Connell surveyed a tract of land on the east bank of the Youghiogheny River for himself containing 147 acres which he called "Mud Island." Connellsville was incorporated on March 1, 1806 and the founder died in 1813; he is buried on a hill overlooking East Francis Avenue.

For fifty years, Pennsylvania's steel industry depended to an amazing extent on a skinny strip of land, scarcely two or three miles wide and about 50 miles long, called the Connellsville Coalfield. Here, a seven-foot-thick seam of the finest metallurgical coal in the world lay exposed and ready to burn. Connellsville coal was eighty-nine percent composed of carbon, a major source of heat, and sulphur, undesirable, made up only one percent. Actual coking of the coal, a process whereby the raw material was baked into a valuable industrial fuel in a beehive oven, was first tried near Connellsville in the 1840s. The first successful beehive oven was built only 300 feet from the old stone house erected by Zachariah Connell. After the Civil War a beehive coke industry gained a foothold in the region.

One of the biggest players in the game was Henry Clay Frick, who would parlay the 200 beehive ovens he owned by the age of 24 in 1873 into one of the world's greatest fortunes. In fact for a spell during the heyday of the coke days from the 1880s to the 1920s, Connellsville was said to have more millionaires per capita than any other place in the country. At its peak in 1913, the Connellsville district's 38,000 ovens provided fully half the entire nation's supply of metallurgical coke. It took 2,000 railcars each day to haul it away. Most of the coke was used in blast furnaces to smelt iron ore into molten pig iron, the raw material for steel.

The demand for coke pushed many other emerging industries out, making the city along with Fayette County almost entirely dependent on both coal and coke. When better heating processes were developed, Connellsville coke was no longer needed and the industry went bust — along with the economy of Fayette County. A few ovens remain in operation at spots throughout the region, but the industry no longer belongs to Connellsville. The coal today goes into by-product ovens where every ingredient is captured and used.

Our walking tour will begin at the Carnegie Free Library, a gift from the man whose fantastic wealth sprang from what Connellsville gave him...

1. **Connellsville Free Library**
   304 South Pittsburgh Street

The Carnegie Free Library was built in 1903 with funds donated by philanthropist Andrew Carnegie. The Italian Renaissance building of Ohio Buff stone opened with only 2,000 books. The auditorium on the second floor has hosted many cultural activities including William Jennings Bryan, celebrated orator and oft-frustrated Presidential candidate. His speech raised such a ruckus that the library's trustees declared that politicians would no longer be invited to speak.

CROSS THE STREET, DOWN THE HILL.

2. **First Christian Church**
   212 South Pittsburgh Street

This is the third home for the First Christian congregation that was founded in 1832. Their first was located at the St. John's German Lutheran Church on South Street and later moved to North Pittsburgh Street. This handsome Romanesque church of orange brick has served the congregation for more than a century; the dedication took place on June 26, 1898.

WALK SOUTH ON PITTSBURGH STREET, UP THE HILL (THE LIBRARY WILL BE ON YOUR LEFT).

3. **Masonic Temple**
   302 South Pittsburgh Street

This four-story brick and granite building was built in the early 1900s as a Masonic temple for King Solomon's Lodge No. 346. It was constructed in a Beaux Arts style by the Connellsville Construction Company, a busy firm at the turn of the 20th century.

4. **First Baptist Church**
   301 South Pittsburgh Street

This is the oldest ecclesiastical organization in Connellsville and the fourth oldest Baptist Church in Fayette County, organizing on June 26, 1796. This fine stone structure of massive columns and symmetrical arches was designed in the English Gothic style in 1900. Including all furnishings and the organ, the building cost an estimated $40,000.

CROSS OVER QUEEN STREET AND KING STREET TO CONTINUE AROUND PENN SQUARE.

5. **Wesley United Methodist Church**
   417 South Pittsburgh Street

The origin of this Church dates back into the 18th century when a Methodist class was formed in the home of town founder Zachariah Connell. In the 1790s it was a preaching stop on the Pittsburgh Circuit; the first church was a stone building dedicated in 1808 when it was only partially finished. This is the congregation's fourth home, occupied since 1925. In 1968 First Methodist changed its name to Wesley United Methodist.

6. **P.S. Newmyer House**
   507 South Pittsburgh Street

Porter S. Newmyer was a long-time attorney in town, a vice-president of the First National Bank and the owner of Connellsville's opera house. His brick Queen Anne home on a hill was completed in 1893 and is chock full of hand-carved wood. The house now survives as a bed-and-breakfast.

7. **First Presbyterian Church**
   701 South Pittsburgh Street

This church and manse were built at a cost of $18,500 in 1913. The congregation, that had organized in 1831, moved here from Main Street.

TURN RIGHT ON WASHINGTON AVENUE.

8. **Pennsylvania National Guard Armory**
   108 West Washington Avenue

The Connellsville Armory, built in 1907, blends elements of the Tudor Revival and Late Gothic styles. Covered by a gambrel roof, the armory exterior features a coursed ashlar stone foundation, decorative brick and stone work and brick courses that form common window lintels. The armory represents the common function to serve the Pennsylvania National Guard for storage, meeting, and training.

Detour: To see a rare living tree that was presented to Olympic gold medal winners at the 1936 Berlin Olympic Games, turn left on South Arch Street. If not turn right. If you go to visit the tree, retrace your steps on South Arch Street to pickup the tour again.

9. **Olympic Oak**
   South Arch Street

Connellsville is the only city in the United States to produce a Heisman Trophy winner as the nation's top college football player (Johnny Lujack, Notre Dame University, 1947) and an Olympic gold medal winner (John Woodruff, 1936). Woodruff won the 800-meter run in Berlin, Germany and, in addition to his gold medal, was awarded a young tree which he presented to his hometown.

The Olympic Oak was originally planted in the flower bed at the east side of the library. After Campbell Stadium, named for the family that owned the land, was completed as a Depression-era Workers Progress Administration project in 1938, the tree was replanted at the south corner near the track where John Woodruff started his career.

The tree flourishes today at the re-named Falcon Stadium, John Woodruff Track/John Lujack Field and stands 78 feet tall with a trunk nearly 13 feet in diameter. It is one of only a few Olympic trees that survived.

10. **Emory Hungarian Catholic Church**
    425 South Arch Street

This one-story brick structure with a spire surmounted by a cut-glass mosaic cross was built in 1905 for a congregation originally composed of about 130 Hungarian families living in Fayette and Westmoreland Counties.

11. **United States Post Office**
    115 North Arch Street

The Neoclassical post office, constrcuted of marble and decorative brick, was dedicated on January 5, 1913. It is now listed on the *National Register of Historical Places.*

RETURN TO CRAWFORD AVENUE AND TURN LEFT.

12. **Trevor Store**
    172 West Crawford Avenue at northeast corner of Arch Street

Brothers Samuel and Caleb Trevor, the first successful merchants of the town, used this building as a store room and dwelling. The boys wouldn't recognize the old store today - it has been altered, currently carrying remnants of an Italianate remodeling in the late 1800s, and the street regraded.

13. **Atkins Building**
    166 West Crawford Avenue

This two-bay Romanesque commercial building with an elaborate cornice was built in 1892. The Atkins Music Store has been in the space for a half-century.

14. **Yough National Bank**
    124 West Crawford Avenue

The Yough National Bank is the oldest existing banking institution in Connellsville, chartered by the Commonwealth of Pennsylvania on May 9, 1871. Its first banking office was in the Snyder Building on Water Street. This little Neoclassical vault with Ionic pilasters was home until a 1920s merger with Western Title and Trust.

15. Leche Building
104 West Crawford Avenue

This building was built in 1893 to house the W.N. Leche Dry Goods store. The facade is a pressed metal front, a popular affectation for downtown stores in the late 1800s. It is one of only six buildings remaining in Western Pennsylvania with such a facade.

16. Title and Trust Building
northeast corner of Pittsburgh Street and Crawford Avenue

This building was first occupied on May 1, 1901. It is constructed of Pompeian brick and Native sandstone.

TURN RIGHT ON PITTSBURGH STREET.

17. Colonial National Bank
101 South Pittsburgh Street at Crawford Avenue

This exuberant Beaux Arts bank building, with Ionic columns on both street elevations, was built in 1906 of white marble and pink Milford granite.

18. Odd Fellows Hall
107 South Pittsburgh Street

This brick temple was constructed in the early 1870s for the General Worth Lodge No. 386, International Order of Odd Fellows. It sports a particularly decorative cornice.

TURN LEFT ON EAST FAIRVIEW AVENUE.

19. Trinity Lutheran Church
126 East Fairview Avenue

The cornerstone for this church was laid on 1910 to replace a previous brick house of worship on Apple Street. It is built of hard, white silica stone from a quarry in South Connellsville. The outside walls are 18" thick, and the entire building is trimmed in Indiana Limestone. This congregation was organized on September 16, 1884.

20. Connellsville High School
201 East Fairview Avenue at Prospect Street

This school was built in 1916 to replace Cameron High School. In 1970, with the new construction again and consolidation of Connellsville Area High School, the aging school was left empty for a couple of years until the city stepped in and made it the Greater Connellsville Community Center. The building has a full-size gymnasium, pool, and auditorium.

TURN RIGHT ON PROSPECT STREET. TURN RIGHT ON SOUTH STREET.

21. St. John's Evangelical Lutheran Church
144 East South Street

This German-English congregation was organized in the spring of 1871. It continued that way until 1884 when the English Lutherans formed their own church. In the spring of 1901, the cornerstone was laid for this Gothic style church built of red and yellow brick. The windows were of imported stained glass, highly decorative and depicting biblical scenes. Around 1905, the original cross was replaced with a large electric frosted cross. However, it was blown down by high winds in 1946. The spire was then removed, and the tower was finished in brick.

CONTINUE ON SOUTH STREET TO THE TOUR STARTING POINT.

Look Up,

Doylestown

A Walking Tour of Doylestown...

Doylestown is practically unique among prominent Pennsylvania towns. There is no water here to power industries; not even a mill. There is not a wealth of natural resources nearby. The railroad never rolled through town with the promise of progress. No important school was founded here to attract new residents. There were no great personal fortunes made here to kick-start economic growth.

The reason Doylestown is here today is because it was the exact spot where the Colonial road from the Schuylkill River at Swede's Ford to the Delaware River at Coryell's Ferry crossed the main road linking Philadelphia to Easton. In 20th century automobile-speak, it is where Route 202 crosses Route 611. To the Delaware Valley traveler of the early 1700s, it was simply "the crossroads." They met here to arrange transport of their goods; while they waited for the ferrymen they slept in their wagons and hoped for good weather.

In 1745 William Doyle obtained a license to build a tavern on the crossroads. Now weary road warriors could at least share a hot meal and a pint or two with other tradesmen and merchants before settling into their wagons for the night. Doyle's Tavern was situated at what is presently the northwest corner of Main and State streets and the second Doyle's Tavern still stands at the crossroads.

A friendly tavern does not a town make. While a smattering of establishments grew up around the crossroads the village's success was assured in 1813 when discontent with the location of the Bucks County seat in Newtown led to the selection of the more centrally located Doylestown as the county seat. Inns, public houses and shops followed and Doylestown evolved into the professional and residential character it retains today. The lawyers set up shop in existing houses or built new houses that doubled as offices. Even the buildings erected in downtown Doylestown as office buildings often don't look like office buildings.

In the early 20th century, Doylestown became best known to the outside world through the museum of the Bucks County Historical Society, following Henry Mercer's construction of the unusual reinforced concrete building in 1916 to house his collection of mechanical tools and utensils. Upon his death in 1930, Mercer also left his home, Fonthill, to be operated as a tile museum, which reinforced the community as a center for cultural attractions. Our walking tour will start at one, head for the other and take in Doylestown in between...

1. Moravian Tile Works
East Court Street and Swamp Road

Henry Chapman Mercer came from a privileged American background, growing up on a Bucks County estate. After a trip to Europe in 1870 at the age of 14, Mercer attended a military boarding school in New York, and then went on to Harvard. After his return home he helped found the Bucks County Historical Society and spent much of the next decade on houseboats sailing around Europe. During his travels Mercer continued his historical studies, published several books, and collected artifacts and art works for his private collection.

After a stint as a manager of the newly created Museum of Science and Art at the University of Pennsylvania, Mercer set out to revive the native Bucks County craft of pottery-making in the late 1800s. His attempts failed, but he turned his attention to hand-crafted tiles instead and became a leader of the Arts and Crafts movement of the early 20th century. The Moravian Pottery and Tile Works, completed in 1912, produced tiles and mosaics for floors, walls and ceilings. Mercer's artistry and abilities produced floor tiles for the rotunda and halls of the Pennsylvania State Capitol, depicting 400 scenes in the Commonwealth's history. His tiles adorn buildings throughout the United States and the world.

2. Fonthill
East Court Street and Swamp Road

In 1907 Henry Mercer inherited a large amount of money and bought 70 acres of land in Bucks County. He spent the next three years building Fonthill, an eccentric masterpiece. He used concrete, but in an unusual fashion. He and his workmen formed the structure a room at a time, building an interior frame from earth and wood. Decorative tiles, furniture, and other architectural elements were then placed on the surface, and concrete poured around and over them. Once the concrete hardened, the supporting earth was dug out, leaving a solid structure with inset decorations. Mercer eventually encased an adjacent farmhouse (original to the property) with concrete as well.

Built entirely of hand mixed concrete, Fonthill has 44 rooms, 18 fireplaces, 32 stairwells and more than 200 windows of varying size and shape. The National Historic Landmark contains more than 900 prints and other objects that Mercer gathered throughout the world, creating an intensely personal statement of his genius. The lavishly embellished interior surfaces show an incredible array of Mercer's original decorative tiles.

EXIT FONTHILL ONTO COURT STREET AND TURN RIGHT.

3. Salem United Church of Christ
186 East Court Street

Salem congregation was formally organized in March, 1861 with a membership of twenty. Services, first held in the public school building and later in the Masonic Hall, were in both English and German. A lot was purchased in 1863, located on the south side of East Court Street between Broad and Church streets; a brick church building was erected there and dedicated in July of 1865. By this time there were thirty three members and a Sunday school of eighty.

The year 1897 marked the completion of the new church building (the front portion of the present church) which took care of the congregation's needs until 1928, when a large addition was undertaken. In the chancel of the newly remodeled church were placed the Biblical tiles presented to the church by Henry Chapman Mercer, who personally supervised their installation.

4. Doylestown Presbyterian Church
127 East Court Street

The Presbyterian Congregation of Doylestown started when the Reverend Uriah DuBois came to Doylestown to found Union Academy in 1804, at what is now the corner of East Court and Broad streets. The building was razed in 1889 to make way for the Doylestown Borough School which was destroyed by fire in 1973. In 1871, the old church building was torn down and a new edifice was constructed facing East Court Street.

TURN LEFT ON CHURCH STREET AND TURN RIGHT ON EAST OAKLAND STREET.

5. Doylestown Friends Meeting
95 East Oakland Avenue

Friends met regularly in Doylestown by 1806, and the present meetinghouse was built in 1836. The meeting was indulged under Buckingham until 1951, when Doylestown Monthly Meeting was established. The basement expansion was done largely by the members in 1955.

6. Saint Paul's Church
84 East Oakland Avenue

Saint Paul's owes its birth to one woman - Elizabeth Pawling Ross - who in the 1840s was the only Episcopalian in Doylestown and who rode by horseback to Germantown once each month to receive Holy Communion. Perhaps at her encouragement, the Reverend George P. Hopkins journeyed to Doylestown from Philadelphia to see if he could stir any interest in founding a congregation here. For two years Hopkins "commuted" by stagecoach from Philadelphia to conduct a weekly service. In April, 1846, the parish was formally organized and shorlty thereafter land purchased and money raised to build a church building. The first services in the church were held on April 23, 1848.

TURN LEFT ON PINE STREET.

7. James A. Michener Art Museum
138 South Pine Street

In 1988, with the support of many dedicated citizens, the James A. Michener Art Museum opened as an independent, non-profit cultural institution dedicated to preserving, interpreting and exhibiting the art and cultural heritage of the Bucks County region. The Museum is named for Doylestown's most famous son, the Pulitzer-Prize winning writer and supporter of the arts who had first dreamed of a regional art museum in the early 1960s. The massive stone walls and warden's house that make up the core of the Michener Art Museum today began as the Bucks County prison in 1884. After a century of use, the abandoned and antiquated buildings were being torn down when the County Commissioners agreed to preserve the historic landmark and lease the land and buildings to house the museum.

8. Mercer Museum
84 South Pine Street

In 1916, Henry Mercer erected this utterly unique 6-story concrete castle to house his collection of some 40,000 objects that document the lives of everyday Americans through the Industrial Revolution. The towering central atrium of the Museum was used to hang the largest objects such as a whale boat, stage coach and Conestoga wagon. On each level surrounding the court, smaller exhibits were installed in a warren of alcoves, niches and rooms according to Mercer's classifications -- healing arts, tinsmithing, dairying, illumination and so on.

RETURN TO THE CORNER OF PINE STREET AND ASHLAND STREET AND TURN LEFT. TURN RIGHT ON DONALDSON STREET AND FOLLOW IT TO THE END. TURN LEFT ON STATE STREET.

9. Masonic Temple
55 East State Street

Beneficial Hall, as it was known in the early 1800s, is now known as the Masonic Temple and has been occupied continuously by the Doylestown Freemasons since 1857. The Doylestown Free and Accepted Masons, York Rite, and Order of Eastern Star meet here. There have been a few renovations and additions, but the building would be recognizable to those first, long-ago congregants.

10. County Theater
20 East State Street

Moving pictures in Doylestown began in 1907 when Hellyer's Movie House opened on South Main Street in the back of what is now County Linen. In 1909 Hellyer's moved across the street to Lenape Hall where it operated until 1925. That year the Strand Theatre became Doylestown's first "real" movie theater. In 1938 the Strand was replaced by the Art Deco County Theater, which rose up in its place. The County featured that most modern of conveniences - air-conditioning. Designed by the Philadelphia architectural firm of Silverman and Levy the theater had seating for 715 patrons.

After several successful decades the County staggered to its 50th birthday before closing in 1992. It re-opened a year later as a non-profit house for art films, which it remains today.

11. Lenape Hall
1 South Main Street and East State Street

Philadelphia architect Addison Hutton collaborated with Thomas Cernea to create this picturesque pile of over half a million bricks; storefronts, offices and an 800-seat theatre were all housed behind a trio of unified Victorian facades. The round Romanesque Revival arch is repeated in the tall windows and accented by belt courses. Classic Greek overtones are present in the roof pediments and the suggestion of supporting columns.

12. Doylestown Inn
18 West State Street

The Inn began life as three separate commercial buildings: a shoe store, a hat shop, and a bookbinding business. All three were incorporated in a hostelry beginning in 1902. The Doylestown Inn was a favorite stopover for stage and literary celebrities on their frequent visits to Doylestown.

RETRACE YOUR STEPS TO MAIN STREET AND TURN LEFT.

13. Fountain House
West State and North Main streets

This building occupies the approximate site of William Doyle's second colonial roadhouse circa 1758; it marks the wilderness crossroads from which Doylestown grew. The inn and stagecoach stop was advertised in 1817 as being close to its present dimensions. The building was redesigned in the Second Empire style with a prominent mansard roof. The namesake fountain made its appearance in 1872 and thereafter the Doylestown Hotel, as it was called from 1770 to 1873, was renamed the Fountain House Hotel. Over the years the hotel was used as a furniture store, then a bank; it is presently a coffeehouse.

14. Hart Building
423 Chestnut Street

This 1900 structure is one of the town's earliest office buildings. The emphasis on massed and massive round arches, hallmarks of the Romanesque Revival, as well as the vertical pilasters banded by belt courses link these buildings to Lenape Hall, a predecessor in both form and function.

BEAR LEFT ON SHEWELL STREET.

15. Doylestown Fire House
68 Shewell Avenue

Doylestown Fire Company No. 1 was organized on August 4, 1879 with 25 charter members. The land for the firehouse on Shewell was purchased in 1900, only two years after the street opened. Oscar Martin, a Doylestown architect, drew the plans. The cornerstone was laid on Aug. 20, 1902. The project cost just over $8000 including plumbing, heating, gaslights, and a fire bell, which is still in serviceable condition. The three new engine bays on the right and the single bay on the left were added in 2001.

RETRACE YOUR STEPS TO THE INTERSECTION ON COURT STREET AND MAIN STREET.

16. Civil War Monument
Courthouse Lawn at Court and Main streets

The surviving members of Bucks County's 104th Volunteer Regiment raised $1,600 of the $2,500 cost of this monument through a bakery they inherited from another regiment during the Civil War; the bread they baked was sold to the Union Army.

The monument is constructed of White American marble and is between 32 and 35 feet high above the base; it was designed to be as high as the three story buildings surrounding it. It was completed in time to be dedicated on the first official Memorial Day in 1868.

WALK A FEW STEPS UP
EAST COURT STREET.

17. *Intelligencer* Building
10 East Court Street

The Second Empire design of this building by architect Thomas Cernea was the fanciful former office of Bucks County's oldest existing newspaper, dating to 1876. It was built at head of Printers Alley and features carved keystones, balconies, and elaborate ornamentation.

RETURN TO MAIN STREET
AND TURN RIGHT.

18. Josiah Hart Bank
21 North Main Street

This is one of Doylestown Borough's only definitive Greek Revival buildings. It was probably designed by Thomas Cernea, however, the documentation is confusing and so no one is certain. It was built for Josiah Hart and Company Bankers in 1858. The Greek Revival style is obvious in the projecting pediment and large supporting columns.

19. Nathan James House
110 North Main Street

Nathan James was district attorney of Bucks County from 1853 to 1859 and a one-time President of the Bucks County Bar Association who spent his spare time as an apprentice under a clockmaker in Doylestown. This massive stone house was completed in 1888 and shows influences of the Queen Anne style (corner turret and tall, corbelled chimneys) and the Shingle Style (broad gambrel roof and the shingled upper floor exterior.) Like many of the Victorian homes around Doylestown it was modeled after the second courthouse that was built in 1877 and razed in 1960.

20. The James-Lorah House
132 Main Street

This plot of land was the original site of the Zerick Titus Harness and Saddle Shop which was demolished in 1844 by Judge Henry Chapman, the grandfather of the Henry Mercer. After 25 years he sold it to Oliver James for $10,000, a town doctor who then lived here until he and his wife died in 1894. After that, his daughter, Sarah, who had married the Reverend Doctor George Lorah, and her sister Martha used the home as a summer vacation house.

The house exhibits three main architectural styles: Federal, Greek, and Italianate. The earlier Federal style can be found in the flat front elevation, symmetrical shape of the main structure, the connected double chimneys, and the fanlight found atop the side entrance door. The Greek Revival style is seen in the small third floor "eyebrow" windows (named this for their positioning above the other windows as an eybrow is to an eye). The Italianate style is evident in the window hood moldings found over top of the first, second, and third floor windows.

TURN RIGHT ON
NORTH BROAD STREET.

21. W.H. Kirk House
87-89 North Broad Street

This house was built in 1888 with a combination of two Victorian styles, the Shingle style and the Queen Anne style. It was designed as a duplex home with one side for William Kirk and his wife and the other side for William's mother. The Shingle style can be seen in the upper floor where shingles are used as siding. The Queen Anne style is evident in the tall decorative chimneys, gingerbread on the porch columns, and other decorative detail such as the elaborate cornice treatment. The pediment over the front entrance is a feature of the Greek Revival style. Over 100,000 bricks were used to construct this home which is now used as law offices.

TURN RIGHT ON
EAST COURT STREET.

22. **Home of Civil War General W.W.H.**
     Davis
     60 East Court Street

William Watts Hart Davis was 41 when the Civil War erupted. He was wounded in the left elbow in Richmond and lost a finger on his right hand in Charleston during a rise to the rank of general. After the war he served as acting governor of the Territory of New Mexico. In a life that spanned 90 years, Davis was also a lawyer and historian, author of ten books and founding member of the Bucks County Historical Society in 1880. He lived in this house, built in the 1830s, from 1859 until his death in 1910.

TURN AND WALK EAST ON
COURT STREET, AWAY FROM
THE COURTHOUSE.

23. **Lawyers Row**
     East Court Street from Broad Street to
     Church Street

It was common for law offices to cluster in the immediate vicinity of a county courthouse and in Doylestown this block functioned historically as Lawyers Row. Though most of these buildings show evidence of later Victorian remodeling, this block of stately brick structures with decorative fanlights and double connecting chimneys epitomizes the conservative late Federal style architecture of the county seat's first buildings.

CONTINUE WALKING ON EAST
COURT STREET, PAST THE
CEMETERY, TO THE TOUR
STARTING POINT AT FONTHILL.

Look Up,

Easton

A Walking Tour of Easton...

In 1736 Thomas Penn, son of William Penn, and Benjamin Eastburn, surveyor general, selected and surveyed the "Thousand Acre Tract" of land at the confluence of the Delaware and Lehigh Rivers. William Parsons and Nicholas Scull began their survey for a town in the 1750s at a spot called by the Indians "Lechanwitauk" or "the Place at the Forks." The new town was to be called "Easton" in the new county of "Northampton." The Great Square (now known as Centre Square) was, and remains, a gathering place for residents and travelers. In fact, on July 8, 1776, the square was the site for one of only three readings of the Declaration of Independence. This historic event is celebrated each year on Heritage Day, when thousands gather to join in reenactments of the reading and to revel in entertainment, good food, and fireworks over the Delaware and Lehigh Rivers.

With the completion of the Lehigh Canal in 1829, the lands along the Lehigh River attracted great industrial development. The movement of the coal brought capital & investment to Easton. All along Canal Street was built one of the largest industrial manufacturing centers of America during the 1830s and 40s. Easton continued to prosper as a center for industry, manufacturing, commerce, and culture at the Forks of the Delaware and along the great rail lines.

The Easton Historic District is an example of a relatively intact Victorian commercial center. Although the District contains historically and architecturally significant buildings from almost all periods of its development, edifices completed between 1830 and 1910 dominate its streetscapes. This period saw Easton's prosperity at its height, due to its position at the junction of three major canals and five important railroads.

The Easton Historic District is situated on a peninsula that is generally bounded by the Bushkill Creek to the north, the Delaware River to the east and the Lehigh River to the south. The western limits of the District are marked by the crest of a series of hills. The integrity of the Easton Historic District is highlighted by the fact that only twenty of its 425 buildings can be considered to be intrusions.

Our walking tour will start in Centre Square, laid out in a grid pattern by William Parsons at the center of the city. The square has been the site of a courthouse for over 100 years, the place of that historic public airing of the Declaration of Independence, the location of important Indian Councils during the French and Indian War and a farmers' market that has been operating since 1791...

1. *Soldiers' and Sailors' Monument*
   Centre Square, 3rd and Northampton streets

The tall 75-foot shaft, erected in 1899 and dedicated a year later on the site of Northampton County's first courthouse, was dedicated to the area's Civil War dead.

WALK WEST ON NORTHAMPTON STREET (AWAY FROM THE DELAWARE RIVER).

2. **Alpha Building**
   1 S 3rd Street

The Beaux Arts-style Alpha Building was built by and named for the Alpha Portland Cement Company. The company vacated the nine-story building in the late 1970s and the building stood vacant for many years. In the early 1990s the City entered into a partnership with Roberts & Co. to rehabilitate the structure and re-located City Hall offices from 650 Ferry Street in 1995.

3. **Bixler's Jewelers**
   24 Centre Square

Bixler's Jewelers has the distinction of being America's oldest jewelers. Revolutionary War veteran Christian Bixler III opened what would ultimately become the first Bixler's Jewelers, a jewelry store in Easton back in 1785. The business remains in the family today.

4. **Easton National Bank**
   316 Northampton Street

The Easton National Bank and Trust Company was chartered back in 1814; this Art Deco-influenced building dates to 1929.

TURN LEFT ON BANK STREET. TURN RIGHT ON PINE STREET.

5. **Pomfret Club**
   33 S 4th Street, corner of Pine Street

John O. Wagner was born in 1832 into a prominent family of mill owners. His great-grandfather, Judge David Wagner, established a mill on Bushkill Creek in 1776 and became one of Easton's largest landowners. John Wagner operated two 3-story mills on Bushkill Creek. These were first built in 1870 to make paint but in 1882 were converted to producing soapstone (for paper), talc, and asbestos pulp.

He inherited this property and erected a proper Second Empire mansion in the late 1860s. In 1895, the Pomfret Club purchased the Wagner Mansion. The Pomfret Club is the oldest private club in the Lehigh Valley. It was first organized as "The Crypt" (or the "Crypt Club") on 13 March 1885, meeting in the basement to the annex building to the United States Hotel then located on North Third Street. It was "a purely social club for Easton's gentlemen," devoted primarily to whist and conversation, with 35 members.

6. **Pine Street, between 4th and 8th streets**

During the Prohibition Era of the 1920s Pine Street was lined with brothels and had a reputation in the United States Navy that stretched from coast to coast. Enough partygoers came to Easton from New York City that it was known as the "Little Apple."

TURN LEFT (SOUTH) ON 4TH STREET AND WALK TO FERRY STREET.

7. *George Taylor House*
   northeast corner of 4th Street and Ferry Street

Born in 1716, probably in northern Ireland, George Taylor came to Pennsylvania as an indentured servant in 1736. He was put to work as a clerk at the Warwick Iron Furnace and Coventry Forge in Chester County, and by 1739 had become manager of this 1796-acre plantation. In 1742 he married Anne Taylor Savage, widow of the ironmaster for whom Taylor had been working. About 1757 Taylor moved to the Durham Furnace in Bucks County, which he and a partner leased. From 1757 to 1778 Taylor's business interests were to be largely centered on the 8,511-acre Durham plantation, which was located about 10 miles south of Easton.

After 1763, however, Taylor lived much of the time at or near Easton which became the scene of his political activities. Sent to the Pennsylvania Assembly in October 1775, Taylor served with distinction on important committees and helped draft instructions to delegates to the Continental Congress in November. On July 20, 1776, Taylor was appointed to the Continental Congress to replace the Pennsylvania delegates who refused to sign the Declaration of Independence. Taylor signed the engrossed copy of that document on August 2 but took no other part in the activities of Congress, except to represent it, with George Walton, at a conference with Indians at Easton in January 1777. Taylor evidently quit Congress soon afterward. He died in this house in 1781, as had William Parsons, a founder of Easton, 24 years earlier.

8. **Our Lady of Lebanon Maronite Catholic Church**
    55 South Fourth Street, southeast corner of Ferry Street

The Our Lady of Lebanon congregation began in 1901 and until 1916, they attended Mass at St. Bernard's, St. Joseph's, and St. Anthony's, which was a small chapel located above Gazzetta's garage on South Bank Street. It's priest, Father John Dario, was sent by the Archdiocese of Philadelphia to administer to the Italian people and to build a church. They purchased an old Jewish synagogue at 321 Lehigh Street and demolished it in 1915. With the help of the parishioners, the new St. Anthony's church was completed in 1916. Three years after the mortgage on the church on Lehigh street was retired in 1966 the redevelopment authority destroyed it. Our Lady of Lebanon was relocated to 4th and Ferry streets, and the rectory to 54 South 4th street.

9. **Northampton County Historical Society (Ilick House/Mixsell House)**
    107 S 4th Street, northwest corner of Ferry Street

This Federal style building was constructed for Jacob Mixsell in 1833. A cast iron grape-sculpted fence borders the property. A granddaughter was married to Colonel Charles A. Wickoff, who was killed during the assault on San Juan Hill

in Cuba. He was the highest ranking American officer to die in the Spanish American War. The family donated the house to the Northampton County Historical & Genealogical Society in 1928.

TURN RIGHT ON FERRY STREET.

10. **Jacob Nicholas House**
    southeast corner of Ferry Street and 5th Street

The Jacob Nicholas House is named for its first resident, who lived there from 1807 until 1832. Nicholas was a wood turner when he purchased the property, but later became a Durham boat captain. Durham boats carried freight between Easton and Philadelphia on the Delaware River. They were put out of business in the 1830s by the new canals. The house was occupied until 1961.

TURN LEFT ON 5TH STREET.

11. **St. Bernard's Church**
    132 S 5th Street

St. Bernard's Church, founded in 1829 with 100 members, is the oldest Catholic parish in the Lehigh Valley. Members first met at 151 South Fifth Street until the dedication of the church and adjoining cemetery on Gallows Hill in 1836. The first church was re-built after a fire in 1867. North of church is the rectory, a Second Empire-style townhouse built in 1847.

TURN AROUND AND WALK NORTH ON 5TH STREET TO NORTHAMPTON STREET.

12. **Boyer Building**
    southwest corner of 5th Street and Northampton Street

Named for Harry J. Boyer, who operated a firm of hatters here in the 1880s, the building has also been used as the offices of Easton's Mayor and Treasurer, and during the 1870s as a newspaper office. Note the ornate roof cornice and stone corner quoins, trademarks of the Italianate style, popular with commercial buildings at that time.

13. Hooper House
northwest corner of 5th Street and Northampton Street

This was the home of Col. Robert L. Hooper, Jr., one of three superintendents of the Continental Army magazines during the Revolutionary War. He also served as the Deputy Commissary of Transportation for General Sullivan's 1779 expedition that marked the demise of the Iroquois Confederacy in America. Although not generally regarded to be true, some local tradition holds this stone building, partially encased in brickote, is the oldest in Easton, predating the Bachmann Publick House down the street.

14. Rock Church of Easton
20 N 5th Street

Built in 1852 for the First Reformed Dutch Church, the clock tower is out of proportion to the rest of the building because the City gave funds to house the town clock. It was also rumored that the plans were in inches but the tower was constructed using the metric system. In 1868, it became the Zion Evangelical Lutheran Church and later the Easton Bible Church, the Eastern Star Temple and the Easton Assembly of God Church. Since 1981, it has been the home of the nondenominational Rock Church.

15. Easton Area Public Library
515 Church Street at the northwest corner of N 5th Street

The library was one of hundreds of libraries funded across the nation by industrialist Andrew Carnegie in the early 1900s. The Beaux Arts-style building was constructed with a $50,000 grant from Carnegie's foundation that also funded a 1913 addition. The library was built atop a graveyard of the German Reformed and Lutheran Church. Most of the bodies were removed but 30 were not claimed by family members and were placed in a burial vault on the site. The two most noted figures interred in the burial ground were William Parsons, surveyor general of Pennsylvania, and Elizabeth Bell 'Mammy' Morgan, a folk healer, from Williams Township. The library displays the American flag from when Declaration of Independence read in Easton.

RETURN TO NORTHAMPTON STREET AND TURN LEFT.

16. Heckman's Oyster Bar
southeast corner of 5th Street and Northampton Street

Now covered in modern brickote facing, this building was Heckman's Oyster Bar during the Civil War.

17. Phyl's Theatre Vue Antiques
466 Northampton Street

This building was once the Boas Beer Saloon and German Emigrant Boarding House, which pretty much says it all.

18. Golden Swan Hotel
460 Northampton Street

The 4-1/2 story red brick building with cream decorative window trim (third from the corner) is the Golden Swan Hotel, opened at the time of the Revolutionary War, and operated through the 19th Century as simply The Swan. It was extensively remodeled in 1906 as the Hotel Stirling.

19. State Theatre
453 Northampton Street

While the granite facade and foyer are original, the rest of the building was demolished in 1910 for construction of the Neumeyer Theater, presenting vaudeville shows and silent films. In 1914 it was renamed the Colonial Theatre and began running silent films accompanied only by an orchestra. Noted theater architect William H. Lee redesigned the now State Theatre as a vaudeville palace, drawing upon the architecture of old Spain and the Davanzanti Place in Florence, Italy. The State hosted Milton Berle, Fatty Arbuckel, Eddie Foy, magician Harry Blackstone, and ventriloquist Edgar Bergen.

It was remodeled again in 1929 to showcase first run movies, sometimes run in connection with big bands or revues. Bing Crosby and Frank Sinatra both sang at the State. The building was restored by a citizens group in 1985–1990, and continues to hold a full theatrical season each year.

20. Lawall Drugstore Building
437 Northampton Street

Cyrus Lawall started business in 1851 next to William Lawall's Store and moved into this building in 1871. He ultimately became the President of the Northampton County National Bank. During his funeral in 1892, local merchants closed all of the business buildings on the 400 block as a mark of their respect.

21. Clemens House
433 Northampton Street

The Clemens House is named after physician B. Clemens who practiced in Easton at the time of the Civil War. Maurice Clemens became a "musician of Easton," a choral leader, and in 1902 was elected the Captain of Company I of the 13th Regiment, Pennsylvania National Guard.

22. Werner Building
432 Northampton Street

The 3-story white brick Victorian with elaborate buttressed roof cornice is the Werner Building, built in the early 1900s for watchmaker William Werner. William ultimately branched out into jewelry, luxury goods, and specially designed pianos, as well as becoming the nation's first wholesaler for Thomas Edison's new phonograph machines. The Werner business continued in this location until 1970.

23. Odenwelder Building
404 Northampton Street

Odenwelder's Drug Store was begun under a prior owner's name in 1824 and acquired by Asher J. Odenwelder, Sr. in 1871. It later moved to a small frame house at this location. The present ornate building was built by Asher J. Odenwelder, Jr. after 1905.

24. Latino Heat
411 Northampton Street

At age 13 Larry Holmes quit school to help support his family and worked as a shoe shine boy, learning to box at a local Easton gym. At age 23, Holmes beat Rodell Dupree in his first professional bout. He went on to compile a record of 68-5, including 41 knockouts while reigning as Heavyweight Champion of the World from 1978 to 1985. This location is where he began his club in Easton.

25. Rosenbaum Building
407 Northampton Street

The striking 6-1/2-story building was named for milliner Levi Rosenbaum, who established his business here in the 1870s.

26. Old Newspaper Building
403 Northampton Street

The 6-story cream brick building is the Old Newspaper Building. In the late 1850s the first floor held the office of the *Northampton Correspondent*; the second floor housed the *Easton Argus*; and on the third floor were briefly located the offices of the fledgling Easton *Daily Express*. A mural in the upper windows of this building reflects the Northampton National Bank Building across the street. The mural was painted by Easton artists Donna Thatcher and Kim Hogan.

27. Pomp/Bixler Building
401 Northampton Street

The Pomp/Bixler Building is a small 4-story brick building with a dental cornice. Peter Pomp operated the P. Pomp "Pure Drugs" store there by the 1850s. The Bixlers acquired the building from the Pomp family in 1919, and briefly used it for their "oldest jewelry store in America," which moved to Centre Square in 1925. After their brief tenure, the The "Bixler Building" legend was placed above the Fourth Street entrance.

28. Northampton National Bank
400 Northampton Street

This 7-story, Beaux-Arts building, with a mural of *Labor* in the foyer, now houses The *Morning Call* Easton Bureau and other businesses. It was opened in 1909, when the Bank moved to this address from the building that has now become the State Theatre.

TURN LEFT ON N 4TH STREET.

29. Easton Daily Express
30 N 4th Street

First printed 1855 as *The Easton Daily Express*, the name changed to *The Easton Express* in 1917 and was abbreviated to *The Express* in 1973.

30. Bell Telephone Building
47 N 4th Street

This was the site of the former White Horse Hotel; the Art Deco-style building dates to 1929 and was used as a telephone switch exchange.

RETURN TO NORTHAMPTON STREET AND TURN LEFT, HEADING TOWARDS CENTRE SQUARE.

31. Hotel Lafayette
northeast corner of 4th Street and Northampton Street

This somewhat faded hotel stands on property that once was the location of a frontier home and tavern, owned by Jacob Hoffman, that may have occupied the north part of this site as early as 1728, well before the town of Easton was founded. The first well in Easton was built on this site in 1752. A stone house and tavern was built on the site in 1754.

This tavern became Jacob Opp's Inn during the Revolutionary War, and was the residence of Continental Army officers during the time of General Sullivan's campaign. A hostelry has operated on the site ever since that time, although the building may have been remodeled.

32. Lafayette Ambassador Bank
southeast corner of 4th Street and Northampton Street

The Lafayette Ambassador Bank was founded in 1922 and this Neoclassical building went up in 1933 during the Great Depression when many banks were closing across the country. It is still in operation today.

33. Dauphin Deposit Trust Company
62 Centre Square

The main floor of this historic building houses the famous Carmelcorn Shop, open since 1931. The third floor of this building was seriously damaged by a fire on October 18, 2006. The fire was started by workmen removing paint with a blowtorch. It was estimated the fire caused about $500,000 in damages to the historic structure.

34. Detweiler Building
52 Centre Square

The Detweiler Building dates back to 1824. The building houses retail shops on the main floor and apartments above. The Victorian style house was constructed for Henry Detwiller, born in Switzerland, who was a doctor and advocate of preventive medicine. He lived in this house, later enlarged and modified, until 1887.

TURN LEFT ON N 3RD STREET.

35. The Huntington
58 Centre Square

This commercial building and apartment house, formerly a hotel was renovated in 1910 by architect William Michler. He was born and raised on College Hill and attended Lafayette College and the University of Pennsylvania. Known for eclectic style, he masterfully incorporated Victorian and American Arts and Crafts elements into his designs. Michler built or renovated over 60 residences, primarily on College Hill. He also designed approximately 20 public buildings in Easton and the surrounding area.

36. Quadrant Bookshop
20 N 3rd Street

This house dates to the mid-1800s when it was constructed by the Ennis family and later subdivided for small businesses. In 1976, when the building was slated for demolition. Opposition spawned the creation of Historic Easton, Inc., now known as the Easton Heritage Alliance.

37. First United Church of Christ
27 N 3rd Street

The First United Church of Christ, formerly the German Reformed Church, was built in 1775. During the Revolutionary War, this church served as a hospital and was visited by George Washington. It was also the site of the Indian Treaty Conference of 1777. The church has a Star of David in honor of Meyer Hart, Easton's first Jewish citizen and a contributor to the original church building fund.

38. Simon Mansion
41 N 3d Street

The mansion was built in the early 1900s, at a cost of $250,000, for Herman Simon, a wealthy silk manufacturer. The Simon mansion was designed by William Michler in the High Renaissance French Chateau style. The exterior is graced with Indiana limestone, granite base, and a red Vermont Slate roof with cooper ornamentation. Directly adjacent, Simon built a home for his daughter. Massive cast iron gates remain, which once led to the formal gardens. Carved images of Simon's wife and daughter are still distinguishable on pillars outside the mansion.

39. YMCA
northeast corner of N 3rd Street and
Spring Garden Street

The original Easton brick YMCA has been restored and converted to apartments.

TURN LEFT (WEST) ON
SPRING GARDEN STREET.

40. First Presbyterian Church
333 Spring Garden Street

The First Presbyterian Church is the "mother" church from which all other Presbyterian Churches in Easton and Phillipsburg are descended, either directly or indirectly. The congregation traces its roots back to 1811 when 43 citizens petitioned the Presbytery of New Brunswick, New Jersey for the establishment of a Presbyterian Church in the Borough of Easton.

TURN AROUND AND FOLLOW
SPRING GARDEN STREET ACROSS
N 3RD STREET.

41. Trinity Episcopal Church
234 Spring Garden Street

Episcopalian church services were held in congregants' homes until 1798, when Samuel Sitgreaves donated the land for the construction of a church on this site. The existing building, dates to 1876, replaced the original church which was destroyed by fire. Designed by William Haight, the Stone Gothic Revival architecture is graced with a battlemented bell tower, rose window, and other stained glass by Nicholas D'Ascenzo of Philadelphia. The floor is Mercer tile from the Moravian Tile works in Doylestown.

42. St. Michael's Lithuanian Roman Catholic Church
219 Spring Garden Street

Founded in 1916 by immigrants from Lithuania, St. Michael's and St. Bernard's (132 South Fifth Street) congregations have shared a pastor since 1964. The building, built in 1852, was originally home to the Brainerd Presbyterian Church. After a merger of Brainerd Presbyterian with First Presbyterian Churches, the building was converted to a club for Civil War Veterans called Heptasoph Hall that had a bowling alley and billiard parlor on the first floor.

43. 217 Spring Garden Street

This Federal-style house from 1830 with Victorian alterations was reportedly home for Woodrow Wilson's father while he was a Presbyterian minister at the adjacent Brainerd Presbyterian Church.

44. Howard Riegel House
214 Spring Garden Street

Benjamin and Barbara Riegel built this house for their son Howard and his wife. The communities of Riegelsville, New Jersey and Pennsylvania, were named for the family that founded the Riegel Paper Company with several mills near the Delaware River south of Easton. The Federal Revival style building was built in 1909 by William Michler and has two Tiffany sky light windows and a Tiffany window in a bathroom that faces Spring Garden Street.

45. 208 Spring Garden Street

In 1880, M. McCartney and her sister L.D. Maxwell lived here.

46. Floyd Bixler House
206 Spring Garden Street

Floyd S. Bixler, resident here in the 1880s until after 1920, was the great-grandson of jeweler Christian Bixler III, who founded the Easton Bixler dynasty, grandson of jeweler William Bixler, and son of jeweler J. Elwood Bixler. Unlike his forebearers, however, Floyd S. Bixler's firm, Bixler & Correll, was in the wholesale dry goods trade. Floyd Bixler was also an Easton historian, writing (among other things) a history of Easton's early taverns, and a history of the Bixler family.

47. 204 Spring Garden Street

This Victorian Romanesque style house (built circa 1900) was constructed for the Bixler/Laubauch family. There are Fatur stained glass bay windows on west side.

TURN RIGHT ON N 2ND STREET.

48. Dr. Florence Seibert birthplace
73 N 2nd Street

This was the birthplace of scientist Florence Seibert in 1897, who, in a long list of achievements, developed a reliable test for tuberculosis that is still in use today.

49. Governor Wolf School Building
45 North 2nd Street

Until the mid 1800s, Easton's children were taught at home or at church. Built in 1893, the Governor Wolf School building has elaborate yellow Roman brickwork, stained glass windows, a bell tower and a spiral staircase in the left tower. The stone entry, called Penny Arch, is topped by a marble globe of the world paid for by school children's pennies. The Wolf Building now houses Northampton County Human Services.

The former school on North Second Street was named for Governor Wolf of Easton, founder of the Pennsylvania Free Public School System and proponent of the 1834 School Act. The Act was zealously supported by Wolf but was met with great resentment by the local German population, who feared that formal instruction would be in English. The farming population also opposed the act because adults needed the children at home for chores. The loss of church-based education added hostility. Had it not been for Wolf's determination, the act may have been repealed. It did, however, cost him his bid for re-election.

50. Benjamin Riegel Mansion
44 N 2nd Street

This Flemish Revival-style house was built in 1902, reportedly from the pen of architect Stanford White of the fabled firm of McKim, Mead & White of New York. Benjamin and Barbara Riegel had a house built for their son and his wife around the corner at 214 Spring Garden Street.

51. Library Hall
32 N 2nd Street

Philadelphia Federal Style architecture with late Victorian bracketed cornices proudly announces Library Hall, site of Easton's first library. Located at the northwest corner of Second and Church Streets, Library Hall was built in 1811, and like most of the city's older buildings, is fully functional and in commercial use.

TURN LEFT ON NORTHAMPTON STREET AND WALK DOWN TOWARDS THE DELAWARE RIVER.

52. Bachmann Tavern
northeast corner of Northampton and
Second streets

The Bachmann Tavern is the oldest building remaining in the City. The land deed was secured from the Penns on November 17, 1754 by John Bachmann, its builder. The building served as a tavern and long time residence of George Taylor, a signer of the Declaration of Independence. The tavern was visited by George Washington and Ben Franklin. It was, like many taverns, a social center of colonial times, and often served as a courtroom until the original courthouse was completed in 1765. Some 70% of the building's original fabric is intact. The upper windows are original, as is the interior. In 1991 the stucco was removed from the exterior, revealing the date marker of 1753.

53. Hotel Easton
140 Northampton Street

Built in 1926, "The Hotel Easton," featured some of the day's most contemporary architectural designs. Abandoned in 1989, the hotel remained closed for nearly a generation with significant damage on the interior and upper levels. In 2004, the building was acquired and renovated as a condominium with great care for the surviving historic features, while combining the upper levels' 170 hotel rooms into 30 apartments.

54. Northampton Street Bridge

The first wooden bridge at this location was built in 1805. Celebrating its 100th birthday in 1996, the "free bridge" (there is no toll to cross), with its Gothic detail, is the last of its type in the United States and is a National Civil Engineering landmark.

TURN AROUND AND WALK BACK UP NORTHAMPTON STREET, AWAY FROM THE RIVER AND TURN LEFT ON 2ND STREET.

55. First United Methodist Church
34 S 2nd Street

The current brick church was built in the 1850s to replace an earlier one that was destroyed by fire.

56. United States Post Office
201 Ferry Street, northwest corner of S 2nd Street

The 1910 Neoclassical Post Office was the site of a terrorist bombing on December 30, 1931, when a postal clerk became suspicious that a group of six packages contained liquor in viola-tion of Prohibition. Upon opening one of the packages two postal clerks were killed when the package exploded. The packages were being sent to representatives of Mussolini's fascist Italian government in the United States. No one was ever convicted of the crime.

TURN RIGHT ON FERRY STREET.

57. Phoenix Hose Company
219 Ferry Street

In 1858 this building was constructed to house the Engine House No. 1 of the Phoenix Hose Company. The company acquired a house at 48 Sitgreaves as a fire engine driver's residence. The property was bought by George Hellick Coffee in 1927 and converted to industrial use. It was converted into a restaurant in 1991.

TURN RIGHT ON SITGREAVES STREET. TURN LEFT ON NORTHAMPTON STREET.

58. Sitgreaves' Folly (East and West)
237-241 Northampton Street

Samuel Sitgreaves was a lawyer; a Federalist Congressman from Pennsylvania; and from 1798 a Commissioner to Great Britain regarding British claims under the Jay Treaty. In addition, he was the first President of The Easton Bank, a leader of the campaign to build the Delaware River Bridge in 1806, and made crucial donations to found Easton's Library Hall and the Easton Trinity Episcopal Church. The "Folly" took some five years to build standing three stories high with an "imposing central entrance of an old English design." Sitgreaves lived here beginning in 1817 and died here in 1827.

59. Jacob Mayer Building
1 Centre Square

This vintage Art Deco style building in marvelous shape was originally a men's clothing store.

YOU HAVE NOW RETURNED TO THE TOUR STARTING POINT IN CENTRE SQUARE.

Look Up,

Erie

A Walking Tour of Erie...

Erie was named after the Eriez tribe, which was destroyed by a combination of pestilence and the Seneca nation under Chief Cornplanter in the middle 1600s. The first European settlers in the area were the French, who built Fort Presque Isle on the city's site in 1753. The French abandoned the fort to the English, who lost it in 1763 at the start of Pontiac's Rebellion. When General "Mad" Anthony Wayne induced the native tribes to make peace in 1794, the area was opened to settlement. The city was laid out in 1795 and became a port, engaged principally in the salt trade, in 1801. Erie became a borough in 1805, and was granted a city charter in 1851. The village of South Erie was incorporated as a borough in 1866, and was consolidated with Erie in 1870.

The city's history throughout the nineteenth century was dominated by activity on the lake. During the War of 1812 Commodore Oliver Hazard Perry used a harbor on the east side of Presque Isle as a base of operations for the critical Battle of Lake Erie on September 10, 1813. Most of the victorious Perry's ships were built in Erie. The fishing industry, which later gave Erie the honor of being the largest fresh water fishing port in the world, began with the establishment of the Shaw Fish Company in 1821. The opening of the Erie and Pittsburgh Canal in 1844 brought a boom to business in the section; the canal did a profitable business for thirty years and lapsed quietly, despite the protests of the canal men, when the Erie and Pittsburgh Railroad bought it to eliminate competition.

Erie grew into the third largest third city in Pennsylvania (it is now fourth). The last decades of the 1800s brought a golden age; in 1885 Erie adopted the electric trolley system, being the second city in the United States to do so. By 1900 Erie had become nationally known for the manufacture of its engines and boilers, which were shipped to all parts of the world.

But the importance of the city and its port gradually diminished throughout the twentieth century as the development of automobiles, the railroad, and airplanes eroded the lake trade. In recent decades Erie has been the site of considerable renewal, developing the waterfront for resort activities, clearing buildings for parking lots to serve health care facilities and other projects.

Our walking tour will ignore the Great Lake that gives the city purpose altogether, starting six blocks away in the city's central park that is dedicated to the hero of the Battle of Lake Erie...

1. Perry Square
State Street and 6th Street

Perry Square carves out two city blocks of greenspace, roughly in the center of downtown. The open-air plaza has been transformed in recent years with the clearing of many maple trees and in the warm weather now hosts the Erie Farmers' Market. A statue of the namesake Oliver Hazard Perry, commander of the United States Naval Fleet in the Battle of Lake Erie and hero of the War of 1812, stands at the east end of the park. It was erected on August 23, 1985, the bicentennial of Perry's birth. Other statues an memorials remember Revolutionary War hero Anthony Wayne (he died in Erie on December 15, 1796), the Civil War, and the various conflicts of the 20th century.

IN THE CENTER OF THE SQUARE START BY FACING LAKE ERIE, ON THE EAST SIDE OF THE SQUARE. WALK CLOCKWISE AROUND PERRY SQUARE.

2. Ford Hotel/Richford Arms
515 State Street

Now a residential high-rise, the 10-story Renaissance Revival brick building opened as a distinguished 400-room hotel. The Ford Hotels chain had guest houses in Rochester, Erie, Toronto and Montreal and Buffalo.

3. Erie Public Library
southwest corner of French Street and South Park Row, opposite Perry Square

Completed in 1899, the Erie Public Library was designed by the firm of Alden & Harlow of Pittsburgh. It combines elements of the Beaux Arts Classicism and Second Renaissance Revival styles of architecture, clad in Pompeian red brick. The building features arched openings, a prominent cornice, swag and garland decorations, and a roofline balustrade. The original facade is dominated by a marble portico, which was removed and stored by previous owners. The library rotunda is one of the most significant interior spaces in Erie and has been meticulously restored. Mahogany paneling and marble floors serve as a backdrop for a decorative paint scheme. Spectacular allegorical murals on each side of the coffered skylight refer to literature, art, science, and poetry. They were completed by Elmer Ellsworth Garnsey, who also rendered murals in the New York Stock Exchange and the Library of Congress. The building, no longer serving as a library, was listed in the *National Register of Historic Places* in 1979.

4. Federal Courthouse
southeast corner of State Street and South Park Row, opposite Perry Square

The 1938 courthouse was designed in the Stripped Classical style, which was commonly used for Federal buildings constructed during the Depression era. The building has the monumental scale and form of earlier classically inspired Federal architecture, but lavish ornamentation commonly found in previous eras is missing. The building is clad in Indiana limestone with polished black granite accenting the building base and entrance area. Carved soapstone panels with a Greek key motif are on the second level.

TURN LEFT AND WALK SOUTH, AWAY FROM LAKE ERIE, ON STATE STREET. STAY ON THE EAST SIDE OF THE STREET.

5. Isaac Baker Building
northeast corner of State and Seventh streets

The 1947 Baker Building was originally a clothing emprium. Isaac Baker and Son established its first store in the 1850s at another downtown location that was destroyed by fire. Erie architect Walter Monahan created a Moderne style building, rare in Erie. Its massing is horizontal and rectangular, with a juxtaposed rounded corner containing the sign "BAKER'S" at the top of the parapet, and the recessed entrance doors at street level. The plan of the shop utilizes strategically-placed curved partitions to draw the shopper's eye deep into the store. Mezzanines, balconies, and two-story spaces are also positioned to break up the uniformity of the space and provide transition from a room on one level to other rooms on other levels. In addition, balcony railings are long and curving, and subtlely evoke a nautical image. The building has been adapted for use as part of the United States courthouse next door.

6. Warner Theatre
811 State Street

Designed by architects Rapp & Rapp, a Chicago architectural firm responsible for some of America's most ornate theaters, Warner Brothers spent $1.5 million Depression-era dollars to create Erie's first and only deluxe downtown picture palace. When the Warner opened its doors April 10, 1931, more than 8,000 colored lights illuminated the 10-ton marquee that announced the feature film of the opening evening, *The Millionaire* starring George Arliss with James Cagney. The 2,506-seat theater closed in 1976, when it was sold to the City of Erie which converted the theater to a performing arts center, a centerpiece of a downtown revival. The theater features a 65-foot-by-28-foot proscenium stage and is complemented by crushed velour, gold and silver leaf, and gold-backed French mirrors. Today it hosts concerts and Broadway theatre performances and is home to the Erie Philharmonic and the Lake Erie Ballet.

CROSS THE STREET AND WALK NORTH ON STATE STREET, ON THE WEST SIDE OF THE STREET, TOWARDS LAKE ERIE.

7. Boston Store
718 State Street at southwest corner of West 8th Street

In 1885 Elisha Mack purchased a bankrupt retail emporium called the Erie Dry Goods Company at 1604 Peach Street and renamed it "The Boston Store." A year later he moved to larger quarters on this block of State Street. Mack was still going strong when his six-story, Art Deco-inspired flagship store was opened in 1931; he would pass away in 1952.

The Boston Store was Erie's premier department store and its favorite place to shop. Perhaps no other feature is as well-remembered as the tra-

dition of the large bronze clock centrally located on the Boston Store's ground floor. The familiar Erie phrase, "I'll meet you under the clock" was used when friends would gather downtown. Like so many of its downtown cousins across America, the Boston Store could not withstand the rise of suburban malls and closed in the summer of 1979.

8. City Hall
626 State Street

On July 31, 1884 this cornerstone for a new City Hall was laid here that would become a 3-story building of red pressed brick, trimmed in sandstone, with a square tower rising from its northwest corner. In the basement were police headquarters and the dungeon-like city jail. The bell of the Queen Charlotte, the British flagship captured by Commodore Oliver Hazard Perry in the Battle of Lake Erie, was suspended from the ceiling of the first floor corridor, at the foot of the wide oaken stairway. That building was razed in 1964 after 80 years of service to make room for the current, more modern city office building.

WHEN YOU REACH PERRY SQUARE, CROSS OVER TO NORTH PARK ROW, ON THE WEST SIDE OF THE SQUARE.

9. West Park Place
west side of Perry Square along North Park Row

West Park Place - bounded by historic Perry Square to the south, and by two leading thoroughfares, Peach Street on the west and State Street on the east - was the heart of Erie's business district during most of the latter half of the 19th century. During the early decades of the century Erie's commercial district gradually shifted from the bayfront to the periphery of the central park. This complex of commercial and professional buildings came into existence following a major fire in the winter of 1857 which destroyed all the wooden structures extending from the corner of Fifth and State Streets to the middle of North Park Row. In rapid succession substantial three-story brick buildings were erected in their space, and by 1865 all vacant space along North Park Row and Peach and State Streets had been filled. All of the original 13 main buildings that were erected along North Park Row, and along State and Peach Streets as far as Fifth, remain with one exception. That exception is the Park Opera House which was demolished in 1939.

EXIT PERRY SQUARE ON THE NORTHWEST CORNER, ONTO PEACH STREET.

10. Mary, Seat of Wisdom Chapel
512 Peach Street

In 1860 Erie Presbyterians dedicated a brick church, marking the rise of a congregation that had come from an old military barracks at Third and Sassafras Streets in 1815. When constructed, this church was considered the largest building in Erie County, and its spire was visible for miles. The building was partially destroyed by fire some twenty years later and not fully restored until 1940. A second fire then completely destroyed the building four years later. The only part of the original complex which remains today is the Seldon Chapel annex, dedicated in 1892. The present church was built in 1950. Gannon University purchased the property and its buildings in 1981 as the University Chapel and other buildings of the complex for Student Services; it was renovated in 1989.

TURN AND WALK BACK TOWARDS 6TH STREET.

11. Erie Club
524 Peach Street

The present Erie Clubhouse was originally the home of General Charles Manning Reed, one of Erie's wealthiest and most influential citizens of the mid-1800s. General Reed, a Brigadier General in the Pennsylvania Militia, was born in 1803, the only child of Rufus Seth Reed, one of Erie's first settlers in 1795. Seth Reed established a number of business enterprises, among them a store, a trading post and a hotel. Charles Reed continued in his father's business footsteps, with interests in trading posts, grist mills, distilleries, banks, stage coaches, railroads, the Erie Canal, ship building and shipping lines. When Charles Reed died in 1871, he was rumored to be the wealthiest man West of New York City. He chose a site for his home "up and away from the center of town" on a tree shaded rise overlooking the "diamond" (what is now Perry Square). Construction began on plans drawn up by Edward Smith of Buffalo in 1846 and was completed in 1848. Reed chose the "boss carpenter" of his shipping lines to be the carpenter for the mansion; the beautiful wood carvings throughout the building attest to the wisdom of this choice. Architecturally, the mansion is Greek Revival, as evidenced by its classic columns and the two welcoming "goddesses" near the Peach Street entrance, both holding symbolic torches.

The Erie Club evolved from two organizations in the early 1880s, the Undine Boat Club and the McClane Light Guard. Its list of charter members reads like the pages of *Who's Who* in the business and industry of that day. After meeting in a house on West 7th Street the Erie Club purchased the Reed mansion in 1905 and the building has housed the Club ever since.

TURN RIGHT ON WEST 6TH STREET.

12. Erie County Courthouse
140 West 6th Street

The first court house, a small brick building that stood in the West Park was completed in 1808. In the early hours of Sunday morning, March 23, 1823, the court house was destroyed by fire, taking with it all the county records up to that time. The west wing of the current Erie County Court House dates to 1855, originally of late Greek Revival design. In 1929 the structure was entirely rebuilt and enlarged by Walter T. Monahan, Erie architect, to its present "U" plan, the west wing retaining the wall structure of the early building. Faced with gray, cut cast stone, its two similar Corinthian porticos with their tall fluted columns are monumentally impressive.

TURN AND WALK WEST ON GOLDSBOROUGH STREET.

13. Strong Mansion/Gannon University Old Main
southwest corner of Peach Street and West 6th Street

The marriage of Anna Wainwright Scott and Charles Hamot Strong in 1896 also wed the two largest family fortunes in the history of Erie. William L. Scott, who amassed more money than just about any Pennsylvanian in the 1800s through his investments in coal mining, steel-making, railroading and land development personally supervised construction of the house he built for his daughter. Since the tab for the massive 10-bay building was an estimated $500,000 who was to say otherwise. The result was the showiest house ever built in Erie, an English town house design, with considerable French chateau influence. It contains 40 rooms.

Anna Strong was perhaps the most significant individual in the history of the district, and her home was the social hub of Erie well into the twentieth century. She was profiled in a November 1934 article in *Fortune* magazine as Erie's "social dictator." Strong Mansion was acquired in 1941 by Archbishop John Mark Gannon as the main building for Gannon University. During that time it contained classrooms, the library, cafeteria, offices, and some student housing.

TURN RIGHT ON WEST 6TH STREET.

14. The Episcopal Cathedral of St. Paul
133 West 6th Street

The Cathedral of St. Paul was built in 1866, and stands as a monument of Victorian Gothic architecture. It replaced the congregation's first church building, a modest brick structure constructed by Erie masons William and James Hoskinson at a cost of $3,500. Details characteristic of the style, derivative of classic Gothic Revival, include contrasting colors and textures, pointed arches, steep roofs and exceptionally tall spires.

15. Taylor Mansion
150 West 6th Street

West 6th Street historically has been known as "Millionaire's Row" and the grand residences really get rolling with this 1890 offering in the Richardsonian Romanesque style by E. B. Green of Buffalo. An eclectic who designed over 100 Buffalo landmarks including the Albright-Knox Art Gallery, Green and his associates are responsible for several mansions on the street. Many in the first several blocks have been incorporated into Gannon University.

16. Gitnik Manse
162 West 6th Street

Gitnik Manse—a three-story, eighteen-room house that was built in 1885 by Erie lawyer Francis F. Marshall—now serves as Gannon University's office of admissions.

17. John Hill House
230 West 6th Street

The John Hill House, originally built around 1836 by William Johns, a former Burgess and prominent physician of the time, is a transitional building incorporating elements of both Greek Revival and Italian Villa architectural styles. In 1840, ownership passed into the hands of Pierre Simon Vincent Hamot, an Erie pioneer who had become a wealthy and successful merchant-banker. Hamot bought the Johns property for his daughter; his own imposing mansion overlooking the harbor was later donated for the purpose of establishing a hospital.

In 1854, the house was acquired by John Hill. Although a carpenter by tradewho soon developed into an accomplished builder and architect. He assisted on the new Court House and built a series of Romanesque Revival commercial structures along North Park Row and the west side of State Street. However, it was the "picturesque" additions which Hill made to his own residence which give it the distinct quality deserving of association with his name.

George Selden, who made a considerable fortune in the Erie City Iron Works manufacturing boilers, bought the house in 1888 for two nieces and never lived there, but it was the most opulent of the several Selden residences in the immediate neighborhood.

18. **First Presbyterian Church of the Covenant**
   southeast corner of Myrtle Street and West 6th Street

With its great height, steeply pitched roofs, and irregular, complex massing this 1929 church by Corbesier & W. E. Foster is an imposing edifice of English perpendicular Gothic design. The First Presbyterian Church organized on February 14, 1815. Over the years, several churches sprung forth from the Presbyterians, including Belle Valley in 1841, Park Church in 1855, and Central Church in 1871. In the summer of 1926, three independent downtown Presbyterian churches welded into the "Church of the Covenant." The congregation celebrated the dedication of the new church building on December 14, 1930.

19. **Woman's Club of Erie**
   259 West 6th Street

Another E.B. Green design in the Richardsonian Romanesque style, this 1892 house built for the Galbraith family now serves as the Woman's Club of Erie.

20. **The Boothby Inn**
   311 West 6th Street

Now a bed and breakfast inn, this red brick Victorian dates to 1888.

21. **Watson-Curtze Mansion**
   356 West Sixth Street

The firm of Green and Wicks of Buffalo delivered another Richardsonian Romanesque creation to the Erie streetscape in 1889, this one for Harrison Watson, president of the H.F. Watson Paper Company, manufacturers of roofing and lining papers and steam pipe and boiler packaging and coverings. The mansion has 24 rooms, 17 closets, 5 bathrooms and 12 fireplaces.

It was purchased in 1923 by Frederick Felix Curtze, president of the Erie Trust Company, Heisler Locomotive Works, Union Iron Works and the Keystone Fish Company. After his death in 1941 the house was offered to the School District of the City of Erie to be used as a museum.

22. **Erie Community Foundation**
   459 West 6th Street

Erie Community Foundation traces its history back to 1935 when Elisha H. Mack, co-founder of the Boston Store, created a charitable endowment fund. The Mack mansion features Neoclassical touches such as a Corinthian portico, corner quoins and dentilled cornice.

23. **Spencer House**
   519 West 6th Street

Built by prominent Erie banker Judah Colt Spencer for his son William in 1876, this building is a transitional dwelling incorporating elements of both Stick and Queen Anne styles. The visible stick-work in the apex of the truss of the central dormer is merely applied decoration with no structural relation to the underlying construction.

In 1852, J.C. Spencer founded the First National Bank of Erie, only the twelfth bank in the nation of its kind. When he died, William Spencer became chief executive officer of the institution. He held the influential position until 1920.

TURN RIGHT ON CHERRY STREET.
TURN RIGHT ON WEST 5TH STREET.

24. **Firefighters Historical Museum**
   428 Chestnut Street

The first station built on this site was in 1873 when equipment was hand-pulled. It was then known as the Eagle Hose Company. When the Erie Fire Department started to use horses in the late 1800s a barn was added to the west side of the structure, this was the stable area. The original two-story station was replaced with this building in 1904. The name was changed to Engine Company #4 because it is located in the 4th ward. All the stables were removed when the Erie Fire Department became motorized starting in 1912. The last horses were used up until 1921. This station closed in 1974 and opened as a museum two years later.

TURN LEFT ON PEACH STREET.
TURN RIGHT ON WEST 4TH
STREET.

25. McCrory's
24 North Washington Street

The Queen Anne style house was built in 1872 for George Carroll, an early settler and lumber dealer.

26. Modern Tool Square
northeast corner of State Street and 4th Street

Modern Tool was an 1850s era tool and die shop and later an automobile factory (the Payne Modern) that was slated for demolition until a redevelopment project of the mid 1980s converted it into an indoor markethouse and loft-style apartments. The indoor market failed, but the apartments remain.

TURN RIGHT ON STATE STREET.

27. Erie Art Museum
411 State Street

The Art Club of Erie was established in 1898 and met in the then-new Erie Library on Perry Square. It moved to the Watson-Curtze Mansion in the 1940s and in the 1950s found a home of its own next door in the Wood-Morrison House. In 1980 it moved here, in the Old Customs House.

Completed in 1839 as the Erie branch of the U.S. Bank of Pennsylvania, the Old Customs House was designed by architect William Kelly; the building is an elegant example of the Greek Revival style crafted in Vermont marble, brought from the quarry to the Erie Canal by oxcart, then to Buffalo, and across Lake Erie. The architect's name is carved into the portico, and can be easily seen from the doorway.

By 1843, the bank had gone out of business, and in 1849 the building was sold to the federal government for use as a customs house. Customs occupied the building until 1888. Today, the building houses the Erie Art Museum's galleries, offices, classrooms, and collection of over 5,000 objects.

28. Cashier's House
413 State Street

While William Kelly was working on the bank next door he also had the commission for this Cashier's House, a three-story, plastered brick, Greek Revival building The Coach House was also part of the 1839 complex. It was built primarily as the residence for the chief executive officer of the Erie Branch of the Bank of the United States. The bank closed in 1841, but the cashier continued to live in the house until his death in 1843. In 1850, the house was sold for $4,000 at half of its original cost. The interior of the Cashier's House is a rare example of Egyptian Revival architecture in Pennsylvania.

TURN LEFT ON DOVER STREET.

29. Erie County History Center
419 State Street

The Erie County History Center was once the Bonnell Block building. In 1839, Joseph and James Bonnell, new arrivals to Erie, purchased this parcel of land for the sum of $5,200 and engaged James and William Hoskinson to construct a three-story commercial building along the State Street frontage. Upon completion, the building was leased to the firm of Kellog and Clark, dealers in groceries, dry goods, hardware and sundries.

The real estate boom in Erie was short lived, however. The Bonnell brothers were forced into bankruptcy and disappeared from the Erie area in 1842. Later that same year, the Sheriff deeded the northern two-thirds of the building, adjacent to the Cashier's House, to Carson Graham. Numerous changes in ownership occurred for both sections of the building until the late 1900's.

Prior to hosting the administrative headquarters of the Erie County Historical Society, the complex was utilized by the Heyl Drug Company. The administrative offices of the Society moved into the renovated building in 1992 and it has been the headquarters of the Society since.

WALK ONE MORE BLOCK ON STATE STREET TO THE TOUR STARTING POINT IN PERRY SQUARE.

Look Up,

Germantown

(Philadelphia)

A Walking Tour of Germantown...

Germantown was founded in 1683 by a group of Netherlanders fleeing religious persecution. Francis Daniel Pastorius, rose to leadership, contacted William Penn, obtained land, and directly stimulated migration. Pastorius arrived on August 20 of that year, the other settlers reached Philadelphia on October 6. Germantown remained predominantly Dutch until 1709, when large numbers. of Germans began to settle here. Those immigrants overwhelmed the settlement and gave it a decidedly Germanic character for most of the 18th century.

The town grew rapidly. William Rittenhouse founded America's first paper mill on the Wissahickon Creek in 1690 and it was followed by textile mills and tanning yards. By 1758 some 350 houses stood in town, most of them occupied by Germans. The community was important enough to attract the attention of British General Sir William Howe who, after embarrassing the Americans at the Battle of Brandywine in the American Revolution in 1777, took a circuitous westerly route to occupy Germantown before marching on Philadelphia. General George Washington staged a bold counterattack on the British along today's Germantown Avenue and, although denied a great victory, infused his battered troops with critical confidence.

George Washington would return to Germantown after the war, this time as President of the United States. In 1793, when Philadelphia was the nation's capital, a Yellow Fever epidemic drove the government away from the foul air of the city and set up shop in Germantown. President Washington would come back the following summer to escape the heat of the city and establish America's first "summer White House."

Germantown remained independent until 1854 when it was absorbed by the city of Philadelphia. Five years later the street car ran from downtown up Germantown Avenue, providing an immediate and lasting effect upon the commercial nature of "Main Street." Despite the influx of shops and services, Germantown Avenue retained much of its mixed usage of churches, residences and schools. In 1965 the Colonial Germantown Historic District was designated a National Historic Landmark and many of its historical sites have been well preserved.

Our walking tour will take place entirely on Germantown Avenue that started as an Indian path and was enlarged into a road into the interior of young Pennsylvania. The thoroughfare boasts an unbroken heritage of residential and commercial use of over three centuries. We will begin in Market Square that was the center of the British line during the Battle of Germantown...

1. **Market Square**
   Germantown Avenue between Church
   and School House lanes

This half-acre was carved out for a market place as early as 1703. Crammed into this small space, in addition to the whirl of commerce was the engine house of the Fellowship Fire Engine Company, one of three Germantown volunteer groups, and the prison with its public stocks.

Today the public space has evolved into a passive park dominated by a Civil War *Soldiers' and Sailors' Monument*. This 1883 mustachioed soldier with gun in hand crafted by John Lachmier stands on a piece of granite brought from the Devil's Den, scene of fierce fighting at Gettysburg. The cannon on the north side was from the British frigate *Augusta*, sunk by the Americans during the Revolution.

2. **Impacting Your World Christian Center**
   5515 Germantown Avenue

This is the third church built here, the first having been erected in 1733 for the Church of the German Reformed Congregation of Germantown. Nikolaus Ludwig von Zinzendorf, German religious and social reformer and bishop of the Moravian Church, preached his first sermon in America here in 1741. During the Battle of Germantown the British captured a battalion of Virginians in the Ninth Regiment and locked them in the church until they were marched into Philadelphia after the battle was over. George Washington worshiped here when President of the United States and while a resident of Germantown. The old building was replaced in 1839 by one which made way for the present structure in 1888.

WALK SOUTH ON GERMANTOWN AVENUE.

3. **The Germantown Historical Society**
   5501 Germantown Avenue

Housed in a Colonial Revival brick building the Historical Society offers to the public a library and archives dating back to the 17th century. The museum on the ground floor has a changing exhibit from the Society's collection of over 20,000 artifacts. The organization was founded in 1900 as the Site and Relic Society of Germantown.

4. **Deshler-Morris House**
   5442 Germantown Avenue

This fine Georgian house was built in 1772 by merchant David Deshler; British General Sir William Howe occupied the house after the Battle of Germantown. In 1793 with Yellow Fever gripping the nation's capital of Philadelphia President George Washington and his cabinet sought relief in Germantown. Washington lived and conducted business in this house, then owned by Colonel Isaac Franks.

Colonel Franks and the President had some disagreements about the rent and costs along the way. Franks charged Washington $131.56, which included Franks' traveling costs to and from Bethlehem, the cost of furniture and bedding for his own family, the loss of a flatiron, one fork, four plates, three ducks, four fowl, a bushel of potatoes, and one hundred bushels of hay. Despite these extra costs, Washington returned to the house the next summer with his family.

Later the house was sold to Elliston and John Perot, and in 1834 to Elliston's son-in-law, Samuel B. Morris. Inside the house there is a portrait of the earlier Samuel Morris, signed by Washington. The Morris family lived in the house for over one hundred years before donating it to the National Park Service in 1948.

5. **Pine Place**
   5425 Germantown Avenue

Louisa May Alcott was born here on November 29, 1832. Her father, Amos Bronson Alcott, came from Boston to teach in Germantown. Alcott started out writing sensational stories about duels and suicides, opium addiction, bigamy, and murder. She called it "blood and thunder" literature, and said, "I seem to have a natural ambition for the lurid style." She published under male pseudonyms to keep from embarrassing her family. But in 1867, an editor suggested that she try writing what he called "a girl's book." The result was the now iconic *Little Women*, based on her own family. Alcott was disappointed at how popular *Little Women* became since it obligated her to keep writing more books in the same vein.

6. Trinity Lutheran Church
19 West Queen Lane at Germantown Avenue

Trinity Church dates to 1836; the church house was constructed in 1860, replacing the printing shop of Christopher Sower who manufactured America's first German Bible in 1743. The first Bible printed in America was in an Indian language. The first English-language Bible followed 40 years later.

7. Grumblethorpe
5267 Germantown Avenue

John Wister, a German immigrant, worked in his brother's button factory before building his own fortune in Philadelphia as a merchant and wine importer. Grumblethorpe was crafted in 1744 as a summer home. Stones for the house were quarried on the property and the timbers were hewn from oaks around the house.

The Wisters were staying in another home during the Battle of Germantown. General James Agnew occupied the house during the battle. He was wounded and died in the front parlor. His blood stains can still be seen on the floor. During the Yellow Fever epidemic the Wister family left Philadelphia and moved here full-time; family members lived here for over 160 years. Everything in Grumblethorpe, now open to the public, belonged to the Wister family. The equipment that Charles Jones Wister used for his endeavors as an astronomer, botanist and chemist is in pristine condition, so is the desk where Owen Wister wrote *The Virginian*.

8. Barron House
5106 Germantown Avenue

This house was owned by Commodore James Barron in the 1840s when he was commandant of the Philadelphia naval yard. Barron rose to prominence as commander of the frigate *USS Chesapeake* that confronted its British counterpart Leopard in 1807, one of the precipitating events of the War of 1812. Barron did not prepare the ship properly and quickly surrendered.

The *Chesapeake* affair was considered a disgrace to the United States Navy. Barron was convicted at a court martial and suspended from ser-

vice for five years. He sailed on merchant ships, and wound up spending the years of the War of 1812 in Denmark. When he finally returned to the United States in 1818, he tried to rejoin the Navy. Stephen Decatur, the nation's reigning naval hero, opposed the reappointment.

Barron felt that Decatur was treating him unfairly, and began writing letters insulting him and accusing him of treachery. Matters escalated, and Barron challenged Decatur to a duel. The two men met at a dueling ground in Bladensburg, Maryland, just outside the Washington, D.C. city limits, on March 22, 1820. The men fired at each other from a distance of about 24 feet. It has been said that each fired at the other's hip, so as to lessen the chance of a fatal injury. Decatur's shot struck Barron in the thigh; Barron's shot struck Decatur in the abdomen. Decatur died the next day. He was only 41 years old. Barron survived the duel and was reinstated in the Navy, though he never again commanded a ship. He died in 1851, at the age of 83.

9. Thones Kunders House Site
5109 Germantown Avenue

The Thones Kunders House was the site of the first meetings of the Society of Friends in Germantown. And it is where the first protest against slavery in the New World was signed in 1688.

10. Lower Burial Ground
corner of Logan Street and Germantown Avenue

In 1692 Leonard Arets set aside by deed a half-acre of ground for burial purposes for Lower Germantown. By 1750 this cemetery was becoming crowded so the trustees limited burials to citizens of Lower Germantown, and, as in so many cemeteries of the time, a space was designated as "Strangers' Ground."

Here among the old trees, rose bushes, and weathered stones lie 41 soldiers who fought in the Revolution and soldiers from War of 1812, the Seminole War, Mexican War, and Civil War. One of the graves of interest is that of Sergeant Charles S. Bringhurst, who three times climbed to the rampart atop Fort Sumter to replace the flag when it was shot down by Confederates during the opening engagement of the Civil War.

The earliest tombstone is of Samuel Coulson who died at the age of nine weeks on October 18, 1707.

William Hood, a Germantown resident, gave money for the front wall and gate in exchange for being allowed to select his own burial spot near the entrance. Hood died in Paris in 1850 and was buried in his chosen grave the very day the work was completed on the entrance gate and wall.

11. Loudoun
4650 Germantown Avenue

This imposing home has stood on a perch at the gateway to Germantown since 1801. The east end was built first and the opposite end followed in 1810. The stately Greek portico came along in 1830. It is named for Loudoun County in Virginia from where builder Thomas Armat hailed. There is some evidence that this site could have been more prominent still - had Philadelphia remained the nation's capital, the capitol itself would have been built where Loudoun now stands.

TURN AROUND AND WALK BACK UP GERMANTOWN AVENUE TO MARKET SQUARE AND BEGIN AN EXPLORATION OF UPPER GERMANTOWN.

12. Wister Mansion
northwest corner of Chelten Avenue and Germantown Avenue

The Wister Mansion in the park was built in 1803 by James Mathews and sold to A. John Wister in 1812. At one time part of the park was owned by Melchior Meng, a founder of Germantown Academy and a horticulturalist whose gardens were noted for their rare trees and shrubs. John Wister preserved and added to the collection while he lived here. The statue by the entrance is Wister, erected by his great grandson.

13. Green Tree Tavern
6023 Germantown Avenue

The Green Tree was built as a tavern by Daniel Pastorius, grandson of Francis Pastorius, the founder of Germantown. High in the side wall near the roof is a stone lettered "DPS 1748." The initials identify Daniel and his wife Sarah as the owners and builders. It operated under a variety of names including The Hornet's Nest, after a large one that was kept there as a curiosity.

Secretary of State Thomas Jefferson wrote to his friend James Madison in 1793 after the government had relocated in Germantown during the Yellow Fever epidemic that he had found a lodging for the both of them in a private home, "They will breakfast you," he wrote, "but you must mess in a tavern; there is a good one across the street."

That tavern is now owned by the First United Methodist Church and is used for church offices. The church moved the Tavern 100 feet up the Avenue in 1930, so that the Memorial Chapel could be added to the church.

14. Wyck
6026 Germantown Avenue

Wyck was home to nine generations of the same Quaker family; the middle portion of the house dates to around 1700. Famous architect William Strickland did the alterations on the farm in 1824. Wyck's grounds include a nationally known garden of old roses which grow in their original plan from the 1820s and early outbuildings that were part of Wyck's farm.

15. Germantown Mennonite Meetinghouse
6119 Germantown Avenue

This fieldstone meetinghouse was erected in 1770, replacing the "little log church" that was the first Mennonite meetinghouse in America, standing since 1708. In 1683 thirteen Mennonite and Quaker families sailed from Krefeld, Germany led by Francis Daniel Pastorius, and landed in Pennsylvania. The first permanent settlement of Mennonites in the new world was in Germantown. By 1690, however, the two groups split due to a conflict of interests. The Mennonites wanted a minister and the Quakers did not. William Rittenhouse, known as the first paper maker in the colonies, was the first Mennonite minister here.

16. Johnson House
6306 Germantown Avenue

This house was built in 1768 for John Johnson. During the Battle of Germantown the Johnson family hid in the cellar as musket shot and cannonballs struck the house. Three generations of the Quaker family worked to abolish slavery and improve living conditions for freed African Americans. In the 1850s this house was a station on the Underground Railroad.

TURN RIGHT ON PHILADELPHIA STREET.

17. Concord School
6309 Germantown Avenue at Washington Lane

The Concord School House, the first English-language school in Germantown, built on the corner of the Upper Burying Ground at Washington Lane and Germantown Avenue, was opened to students in October 1775. The burying ground was created in 1692 and the high front wall was completed in 1724. Here are buried fifty-two known and five unknown soldiers of the Revolution, as well as eleven from the War of 1812 and one from the Mexican War.

The school was supported by subscription and neighbors contributed to the fund, allowing any family that could afford the fee to enroll its children (around $2 per quarter, plus .25 for spelling books), including families of African descent who rented the school house in the 1850s. It served as a school room until 1892.

18. Upsala
6430 Germantown Avenue

Upsala is one of the finest examples of Federal architecture in Germantown. Dirck Jansen owned the land before 1775. The older, back part of the house was built around 1740. John Johnson Sr. is said to have bought the land in 1766. There is speculation over whether father or son owned the house first. John Johnson III, inherited the property in 1797 and built the much-admired front section of the house.

19. Cliveden
6401 Germantown Avenue

Cliveden, built from 1763-64 as the country estate of Benjamin Chew, stands as both one of America's finest examples of Late Georgian architecture, and as one of the nation's most important surviving battlefield landmarks from the American Revolution.

In dense morning fog of October 4, 1777 George Washington, desperate for some sort of victory for his ragtag army, launched a counterattack against the British, who were occupying Germantown on their march into Philadelphia. General John Sullivan smashed into an outpost led by Lt. Col. Thomas Musgrave and forced the outnumbered British into a rare retreat. Musgrave and about 120 men holed up in Cliveden.

The main American force approaching down the Germantown Road encountered the British-fortified Cliveden and General Henry Knox demanded Musgrave's surrender. Despite standing impotently isolated behind American lines, Musgrave refused, Knox began pounding the thick stone walls with six-pound cannon shells that produced no effect. A frontal charge achieved only American dead. The rebels attempted to burn the British out, but there was little that was flammable in Cliveden.

The fruitless half-hour assault bought the British valuable time and the American attack disintegrated into chaos in the still foggy morning. Although sent in disorganized retreat the Battle of Germantown buoyed the spirits of the Americans. Washington's audacious strike convinced European observers of American commitment to freedom and French military assistance would be shortly forthcoming.

Chew, a Colonial chief justice of Pennsylvania, refused to endorse either side in the conflict and was jailed for a time in 1777. He once again became a justice in pennsylvania after the war, serving until 1808, two years before his death. The main house, with its battle-scarred walls, is fronted by garden statuary, including two stone lions on the doorstep, which observed the events of the morning of October 4, 1777.

TURN AND WALK BACK DOWN GERMANTOWN AVENUE TO THE TOUR STARTING POINT.

Look Up,

Gettysburg

A Walking Tour of Gettysburg...

Gettysburg grew on the site of a farm belonging to Samuel Gettys which was part of the Marsh Creek Settlement, an area first purchased from the Iroquois Indians by the family of William Penn. It was Samuel's middle son, James, who purchased a 116-acre slice of the 381-acre farmstead and by 1786 he had laid out 210 lots around his home. Gettys was not merely a land speculator. He had an active interest in community affairs and served as burgess, town clerk, sheriff, treasurer and a state legislator. During the War of 1812 he was a brigadier general in the local militia. On March 18, 1815, James Gettys died at the age of 56, within a week of the deaths of his mother and his wife. By this time the town he founded was a thriving community; it became a crossroads town for the developing farms carved out by Scots-Irish and German settlers. The bustling new town was selected as the Adams County seat in 1800 and by 1806, when Gettysburg incorporated as a borough, over 80 houses appeared on the tax rolls.

Gettysburg's trajectory as a typical county seat and market town took a dramatic detour on July 1, 1863 when the Union Army of the Potomac, 92,000 men under General George Meade, clashed by chance with the invading Confederate Army of Northern Virginia, 70,000 troops led by General Robert E. Lee. Fighting raged for three days over 25 square miles around Gettysburg, culminating in a desperate Confederate charge across an open field into the center of the Union line under deadly fire. When the disastrous charge ended, the South's ranks were shattered and the ultimate outcome of the Civil War was never in doubt again. Lee had pressed the attack onto Northern soil and had been repulsed. It was his last major offensive of the Civil War. More men fought and more men died at Gettysburg than in any battle before or since on North American soil.

The town survived the battle mostly intact. It wasn't long before the agricultural economy sprinkled with light industry such as carriage- and wagon-making was humming again. But as important anniversaries of the battle ticked off over the years, veterans began returning and America's most famous battlefield became speckled with 1,400 monuments, statues and markers. The Gettysburg economy shifted to tourism. A century later, when departing President Dwight Eisenhower decided to settle in Gettysburg - in the first house he had ever owned - people had another reason to come visit.

Our walking tour of what bills itself as "The Most Famous Small Town In America" will begin where Abraham Lincoln stepped off a train on November 18, 1863, arriving in Gettysburg to dedicate a national cemetery and say a few, a very few, words - only 256 in fact...

1. Gettysburg Railroad Station
35 Carlisle Street

In the summer of 1858, The Gettysburg Railroad Company acquired a one-half acre lot from John H. McClellan, who owned what is now the Gettysburg Hotel. Three buildings were to be built on the property: a passenger station, engine house and freight station. Initial plans noted that the passenger station would cost $2,070. The station, built in the Italianate style with arched windows and low-pitched roof with eaves and decorative brackets began issuing tickets in May 1859. The building was technically a headhouse, as it was the western terminus of the railroad line. It was here that President Abraham Lincoln arrived on November 18, 1863 for the dedication of the Soldiers' National Cemetery.

WALK SOUTH ON CARLISLE STREET TOWARDS THE CENTER OF TOWN.

2. Majestic Theater
25 Carlisle Street

The Majestic Theater opened in 1925 as the largest vaudeville and silent movie theater in south-central Pennsylvania. In the 1950s, the theater gained worldwide attention when President Dwight D. Eisenhower and First Lady Mamie Eisenhower regularly attended performances. But time passed, the building changed hands and its original brilliance faded.

In 1992 Gettysburg College purchased the theater and partnered with the state and the Greater Adams County community to rehabilitate the space. $16 million later the renovated 60,000-square-foot Majestic Performing Arts and Cinema Center became a reminder of the days when a town's movie palace was the jewel of its Main Street.

Black-and-white photos of the original 1925 theater were used to recreate details including the chandeliers and carpet. The ceiling of the main theater, which seats more than 800 people, includes 1,500 pieces of pressed tin that were removed by hand, numbered and sent to a restoration company in New York. One-of-a-kind grand curtains of red and gold flank the stage. The main theater also features massive columns,

original stained-glass exit signs atop doorways, an art gallery, a patron's lounge, a balcony lobby and a grand staircase. Two smaller movie theaters are decorated in 1950s-era style and include cuddle seats. The building also houses a rehearsal hall, a dance studio, flexible space and large dressing rooms.

3. Hotel Gettysburg
1 Lincoln Square

In 1797, James Scott built Scott's Tavern on what is now Lincoln Square, Gettysburg's historic town center. A former York County sheriff, William McClellan, acquired the tavern in 1809 and renamed it the Indian Queen. After 1846 it was called the McClellan House for the brothers who owned it.

In the 1890s the old structure was replaced with an imposing building christened the Hotel Gettysburg, and so it remained through most of the 20th century. By the early 1900s, the hotel boasted electric lights, steam heat, hot and cold baths and a fine restaurant.

The hotel became part of a temporary White House in 1955 while President Eisenhower recovered from a heart attack at Gettysburg. In 1964, Eisenhower and his wife, Mamie, were Hotel Gettysburg's last guests before the owner closed its doors. The building, a victim of changes in postwar America's traveling habits, stood empty until a fire ravaged it in 1983. Through the initiative of Gettysburg College, the hotel was carefully restored in cooperation with the Historic Architectural Review Board.

4. Wills House
8 Lincoln Square, at southeast corner of York Street

The home of Gettysburg attorney David Wills, built in 1814, is the most famous building in Gettysburg. Wills is often given credit for hatching the idea of the Soldier's National Cemetery, for proposing that Pennsylvania provide, "...a common burial ground for the Union dead." President Abraham Lincoln was the overnight guest of David Wills on the eve of the dedication of the cemetery and it is assumed he polished and rehearsed the brief text of his Gettysburg Address during his stay in the house. " In honor of

Abraham Lincoln's 200th birthday on February 12, 2009, the David Wills House opened to the public as a museum.

TURN LEFT ON YORK STREET.

5. Wills-Tyson Building
11 York Street

Look up to see an artillery projectile protruding from the bricks just above the beltcourse. The Tyson brothers operated a photographic studio here during the war.

6. Nicholas Codori House
44 York Street

The Nicholas Codori House, crafted of brown fieldstone, is the oldest occupied house in Gettysburg. It was built in 1786 by Michael Hoke; Codori purchased it from the Hoke family for $1600. Nicholas Codori had 11 children and a thriving business so he purchased the property on either side of the house, building a large carriage house at the back of the east side and adding his meat market on the west side.

The Codoris hid in the basement of the house during the Battle of Gettysburg; when the street fighting occurred in the town on July 1, 1863, bullets entered their home above them. For months after the battle the house served as the Catholic chapel since St. Francis Xavier, the Codoris Catholic church, was full of wounded soldiers. The Codori family continued to live in the house until 1967.

7. Plank's Garage
northeast corner of York and Stratton streets

Baseball Hall of Fame pitcher Eddie Plank was born 10 years following the Civil War on his family's farm north of Gettysburg. Pitching mostly for the Philadelphia Athletics, Plank would become the first major league southpaw to win 300 games. After retiring, he opened an automobile garage on this corner in 1923. Three years later, he died from a stroke at the young age of fifty.

TURN RIGHT ON STRATTON STREET.

8. Gettysburg United Church of Christ
60 East High Street, at northwest corner of Stratton Street

The original German Reformed Church located here in 1814 served as a "Union brick church" with the town's Lutheran congregation until 1848. The current building, erected in 1851, was newly refurbished at the time of the battle. It became a hospital under fire, opened by Dr. Abraham Stout at the urging of his Confederate captors. For several days surgeons worked at operating tables in the "lecture room." Jennie Wade, the only civilian killed in the fighting, is buried in the churchyard.

TURN RIGHT ON HIGH STREET.

9. Common School
north side of High Street

The High Street, or "Common," School was Gettysburg's first consolidated public school building. Prior to its erection in 1857 classes were held in different buildings around town, often the home of the teacher. Samuel Sloan provided the town with an early example of the Italianate style, which was to become the most popular style in Gettysburg, with his design of this building. Like most of the town's public facilities it was pressed into use as a hospital during the Battle of Gettysburg. It would soon house Union and Confederate casualties on separate floors.

10. Adams County Prison
59 East High Street

As part of the deal to establish Gettysburg as the county seat the Getty family donated this land for a county prison. A two-story bastille-like building was erected in 1851 to replace the original detention center.

On July 2, 1863. Confederate General Robert E. Lee held a war council in the building. Following the battle, the prison was utilized by the Union Army provost marshal to retain soldiers and civilians charged with violating martial law.

In 1889 the County enlarged the building to three stories and continued its use until 1948. The library moved in for the next 40 years and most recently it has served as municipal offices.

TURN LEFT ON BALTIMORE STREET AND WALK UP THE EAST SIDE OF THE ROAD.

11. Gettysburg Presbyterian Church
208 Baltimore Street

The first Presbyterian church in the borough of Gettysburg was erected in 1813 at the corner of North Washington and Railroad Streets. The congregation moved to the present location in 1842. At five o'clock in the afternoon, following the morning ceremonies where he delivered his famous Gettysburg Address, President Lincoln attended a patriotic meeting in this church. The seat of President Lincoln is marked with a bronze plaque. All of the pews except the Lincoln pew have since been replaced. The present church building was erected in 1963 and contains the original rafters and dimensions, and simple decor of the building that was replaced.

On February 1, 1963, President and Mrs. Dwight D. Eisenhower became members of the church. The pew President Eisenhower occupied was so marked with a plaque.

12. Jennie Wade Birthplace
242 Baltimore Street

This small frame house, birthplace of the only civilian to die in three day of horrific fighting in Gettysburg, is typical of the working class housing found in the town during the mid-19th century.

13. Georgia Wade McClellan House
548 Baltimore Street

The story of Jennie Wade, Gettysburg's only civilian killed in the battle, is recounted in this restored house, riddled with more than 200 bullet holes. During the battle Jennie and her mother were visiting the home of sister Georgia Wade McClellan. On the morning of July 3, a stray bullet passed through two doors and struck the young woman while she was baking bread for convalescing troops. 20-year old Jennie Wade was the fiancée of Corporal Johnston H. "Jack" Skelly. Skelly was wounded in the Battle of Carter's Woods near Winchester, Virginia. He died July 12, 1863, without ever knowing of Jennie's fate.

CROSS THE STREET AND WALK BACK TOWARDS LINCOLN SQUARE ON THE WEST SIDE OF BALTIMORE STREET.

14. Farnsworth House
401 Baltimore Street

Now a bed-and-breakfast and tavern, this house was one of many used by Confederate sharpshooters during the Battle of Gettysburg. Over 100 bullet-scarred bricks attest to the desperate attempts to dislodge these deadly snipers.

15. Shriver House
309 Baltimore Street

George Washington Shriver was 23 when he paid $290 for a lot of ground on south Baltimore Hill. In addition to building his new home, George would also establish his new business - Shriver's Saloon & Ten-Pin Alley. The saloon would be located in the cellar while the two lane ten-pin bowling alley would be built in an enclosed building just behind the house.

The Shrivers were settling into their new home when the Civil War broke out in April 1861. In September, 1861, George mustered into Co. C of Cole's Cavalry. When cannon fire erupted in town in July 1863 Hettie shriver took her family to her parent's farm for safety. When she returned she discovered her house had been occupied by Confederate soldiers; two sharpshooters had been killed in an upstairs garret. Today the house operates as a museum dedicated to the civilian experience during the Civil War.

16. Prince of Peace Episcopal Church
20 West High Street, at southwest corner of Baltimore Street

The cornerstone of the Prince of Peace Episcopal Church was laid out on July 2, 1888, for the 25th anniversary of the Battle of Gettysburg. The church is a battlefield memorial - inside the large tower survivors from both armies placed more than 130 plaques in memory of their fallen comrades.

17. Adams County Library
140 Baltimore Street

The impressive Neoclassical building that houses the library was originally built as the Gettysburg Post Office.

18. "Penelope" Site
126 Baltimore Street

This is the 1863 site of the *Compiler* newspaper office, Gettysburg's weekly "voice" of the Democratic party, and the home of its outspoken publisher Henry Stahle.

During the Battle of Gettysburg Stahle took into his home a badly wounded Union officer and persuaded a Confederate surgeon to come and perform a life-saving leg amputation. This humanitarian act led to Stahle's temporary incarceration at Ft. McHenry in Baltimore for aiding the enemy to capture a Union officer, a baseless charge of disloyalty concocted by a local Republican for political revenge.

The breech of the cannon "Penelope," is seen protruding from the pavement nearby. Traditionally, "Penelope" was fired in Gettysburg's streets to celebrate Democratic election victories but was abruptly silenced in 1855 when an over-charge of powder ruptured her barrel. Fittingly the old political cannon was memorialized in front of the "voice" of the Democratic party, buried muzzle up in the pavement.

19. Adams County Court House
117 Baltimore Street, at southwest corner of Middle Street

Adams County chose Gettysburg as county seat in 1800; the first court met in the home of James Gettys' mother, Isabella. In 1859, this building was erected to replace a courthouse on the square The Court House was originally painted gray; the paint has since been removed; it continues to serve as a courthouse.

20. Adams County National Bank
16 Lincoln Square

The Adams County National Bank was organized in 1857; this Beaux Arts anchor on Lincoln Square was built in 1919.

TURN LEFT ON CHAMBERSBURG STREET.

21. 20 Chambersburg Street

The new Italianate style was popular in Gettysburg just prior to the Civil War; this well-preserved example of the art features the finest Italianate style doorway in town.

22. James Getty Hotel
27 Chambersburg Street

James Gettys, the founder of Gettysburg, sold his first plot of land in 1787 to John Troxell, Sr. In 1804, Troxell opened the Sign of the Buck tavern and roadhouse here to accommodate those traveling to the western frontier of Pennsylvania and beyond. The James Gettys Hotel closed in the 1960s and was used as an apartment building and then an American Youth Hostel. In March of 1995, the building was turned back into the James Gettys Hotel.

23. Christ Evangelical Lutheran Church
30 Chambersburg Street

Christ Evangelical Lutheran Church is the oldest structure in Gettysburg continuously used as a Church. It was founded in 1835 to be the English-speaking Lutheran Church in Gettysburg (St. James Lutheran Church, in existence since 1789, conducted its services in German). The structure was one of the first hospitals established during the Battle of Gettysburg, and at its peak accommodated approximately 150 wounded soldiers.

24. Epley Building
100 Chambersburg Street

This imposing example of Beaux Arts architecture dates to 1916.

RETRACE YOUR STEPS TO LINCOLN SQUARE AND TURN LEFT TO RETURN TO THE TOUR STARTING POINT, ONE BLOCK TO THE NORTH.

Look Up,

Greensburg

A Walking Tour of Greensburg...

Following the Revolutionary War, an inn was built along a wagon trail (today's East Pittsburgh Street) that stretched from Philadelphia west over the Appalachian Mountains to Fort Pitt, now Pittsburgh. A tiny settlement known as Newtown grew around the inn, today the intersection of Pittsburgh and Main streets.

After a raid in 1782 by Guyasuta-led Seneca Indians and British Canadian rangers burned Hannastown, the original Westmoreland County seat, Newtown was tabbed as the new county seat. In 1799 when the settlement was formally incorporated it adopted the name of Greensburg, after Revolutionary War General Nathaniel Greene.

Even though Greensburg was one of the few settlements in a vast agricultural region and even though it had the second post office in southwestern Pennsylvania (after Pittsburgh), there was very little growth here in the first half of the 19th century. By 1850 the population tally stood at 1,051. But Greensburg won a station on the Pennsylvania Railroad main line in 1852 and that made all the difference.

When coal and coke exploded in the region it was shipped from Greensburg. In the early 1900s the City could count more than 25 coal operators and shippers with offices in downtown. Many of the workers who came to mine the coal lived in "patch towns" near the mines with limited facilities. When it came time to go to town for supplies, Greensburg is where they went. This wealth helped the town outstrip its neighbors in growth and sophistication. The difference is apparent when walking the streets of Greensburg, not only in the substance of the buildings but in the quality of materials.

Our walking tour of historic Greensburg will visit the marble and granite and cast iron on display along Main Street but first we'll start in a piece of greenspace that was a cemetery at one time but no longer, save for one memorial that reads poignantly for an inscription that never came to pass: "The earthly remains of Arthur St. Clair are deposited beneath this humble monument which is erected to supply the place of a nobler one due from his country"...

1. St. Clair Park
    **northeast corner of North Maple Avenue
    and East Otterman Street**

The fingerprints of Arthur St. Clair, a Scot born in 1736, are all over the early history of North America, but, like fingerprints, without proper investigation they remain obscure. He first gained notice in Canada on the Plains of Abraham where his valor helped secure Quebec City for the British against the French in 1759. Later he was sent as the King's Magistrate by the Penn family to western Pennsylvania where he was awarded thousands of acres of land for his war service, including most of what is now Westmoreland County. In that capacity, Penn marched into Fort Pitt, newly claimed by the British through representatives of the Virginia colony and, without arms, took the settlement for Pennsylvania.

Fighting against the British in the American revolution, St. Clair was commissioned a brigadier general and rapidly made a major general. He crossed the Delaware with Washington and was with him at Trenton and Princeton and Morristown and, in the end, at Yorktown. After the war, St. Clair became president of the Congress of the United States Assembled. Under the Articles of Confederation, this was the highest office in the land. In this capacity he pushed forth the Northwest Ordinance from which would sprout six states.

Arthur St. Clair, an American patriot of the first rank, seemed destined to be immortalized on a coin. It was not to be. He pushed for the new Constitution that made his job obsolete in 1789 and he left for the frontier as governor general of the Northwest Territories. In 1791 he led new American troops against an uprising of Miami Indians in present-day Ohio. It became the worst rout by Native Americans in American military history, surpassing even Little Bighorn. More than 600 men died. St. Clair financed much of the expedition himself, expecting to be reimbursed by the Federal government. It did not happen. His military and political career were in tatters, his fortune gone, his estate, the Hermitage, sold off to pay creditors.

St. Clair returned to Westmoreland County where the shunned former president opened a tavern on the Forbes Road. In 1818, then in his eighties, he tumbled from the back of a wagon and died. Fellow members of the local Masons Lodge paid to bury him on the grounds of this park, one of the few places in America named in honor of Arthur St. Clair.

In addition to the hillside monument the park features a building from the early 1780s that was used for a school and place of worship by people of German Lutheran and Reformed churches. It was reconstructed and dedicated here in 1976.

EXIT THE PARK ON THE WEST SIDE THROUGH THE NORTH MAPLE STREET ENTRANCE. TURN LEFT ON NORTH MAPLE STREET AND RIGHT ON EAST OTTERMAN STREET. WALK ONE BLOCK TO MAIN STREET AND TURN LEFT.

2. **Westmoreland County Courthouse
    2 North Main Street**

This Beaux Arts tour-de-force is the fourth courthouse for Westmoreland County; fifth if you count the sessions held in Robert Hanna's tavern when the county was formed by an Act of Assembly on February 26, 1773. Newtown, now Greensburg, was selected as the permanent county seat in 1785 and this spot has always been reserved for the halls of justice.

The imposing four-story structure of light grey Maine granite was erected in 1906. The central dome, 175 feet above the ground, is of Italian Renaissance style, one of only two in the world designed by the courthouse's original architect, William Kauffman. The massive central dome is flanked on either side by two smaller ones above the main entrance, originally covered with ornamental gold and ivory terra-cotta. Roof edges and pediments are decorated with stone banisters and ornamental carving and figures.

Inside, beneath the 85-foot domed ceiling, is a vision of quality stonework. English-veined Italian marble decorates the public hall walls as well as the rotunda. Corridor floors and ceilings are laid with varicolored mosaics. Panels are set with marble mosaics in Renaissance patterns. A grand staircase of marble from the first floor opens upward to twin spirals to the second floor. Circular mezzanines on each floor of the rotunda are balustraded in white marble.

3. **Barclay-Westmoreland Trust**
   1 North Main Street

This limestone-and-granite building, richly decorated with Ionic pilasters, shields and garlands, was built for Barclay-Westmoreland Trust, founded in 1854, in 1928. An American coin-themed frieze features carved limestone ornamentation of sheaves of wheat from the back of pennies, Mercury dimes and Indian head nickels.

4. **Bank and Trust**
   41 North Main Street

This highly decorated Romanesque building from 1896 was originally the Bank and Trust building and has received few modifications decades after the last deposit was taken. The symmetrical heavy piered-stone arched windows of the ground floor give way to two-story and single-story arched brick windows, All the arches on every floor are supported by classical pilasters.

5. **First National Bank of Greensburg**
   111 South Main Street

The First National Bank of Greensburg is a Classical Revival stone-and-brick building that has been a mainstay of downtown since 1924. Paul Bartholomew, a busy city architect, did the seven-story design.

6. **McCrory's**
   126 South Main Street

McCrory's was one of Greensburg's five-and-dime stores in the early 1900s. This building has changed little from its opening in the 1920s except that the the historic variety store chains have disappeared from downtown landscapes and the basement level has been closed to the public.

7. **Masonic Temple**
   132 South Main Street

The Masonic temple dates to 1872 and is the oldest building in the Greensburg Downtown Historic District. Originally three floors, a fourth floor was added in 1876. The Italianate cast iron facade was popular in large cities and a testament to Greensburg's prosperity at the time.

8. **Troutman's Department Store**
   202-226 South Main Street

Troutman's was once the city's largest department store, now used for offices and seniors' housing. It has six stories with a limestone and terra-cotta facade in an Italianate style. The main portion was designed by Paul Bartholomew and built in 1923, with a more recent addition extending through to South Pennsylvania Avenue.

9. **First Evangelical Lutheran Church**
   246 East Main Street

The First Evangelical Lutheran Church was founded in 1784 in the log school near the public spring in St. Clair Park. The cornerstone for the present Gothic Revival building was laid on August 11, 1883.

10. **First Presbyterian Church**
    300 South Main Street

This English Gothic style church was built in 1917, of water-washed Massachusetts seamed-faced granite with sandstone trim. It was designed by the Boston architect Ralph Adams Cram, who also designed the Cathedral of Saint John the Divine, New York, and many of the buildings of Princeton University. Hexagonal towers flank the entrance with gabled buttresses and bracketed cornices along both sides with lancet stained glass windows. The congregation can trace its origins to 1788.

TURN AND WALK BACK NORTH ON MAIN STREET, RETRACING YOUR STEPS TO OTTERMAN STREET AND CONTINUE UP THE HILL.

11. **Union Trust Building**
    101 North Main Street at northwest corner of Otterman Street

The former Union Trust Building is a good example of the Classical Revival style with concrete pilasters and window hoods. Built in 1921, it once served as bank and office facilities, including the headquarters of the Westmoreland-Fayette Coal and Coke Company.

12. Belden Law Building
117 North Main Street

This commercial survivor from the 19th century was built of brick in the Queen Anne style in 1886.

13. Park Building
121 North Main Street

This Federal Revival building was first constructed as a residence and then did duty as the office for the Irwin Gas & Coal Company.

14. Greensburg Volunteer Fire Department
137 North Main Street

The Greensburg Volunteer Fire Department was organized on January 12, 1891 and included Hose Company #1 and Hose Company #2. The City's original firefighting equipment consisted of two hose carts and leather fire buckets. Greensburg Truck Company #2's first ladder truck arrived in Greensburg in 1891, along with two hose carts. This ladder truck could be hand drawn or horse drawn. This is the Social Hall entrance at the rear of the Central Fire Station on Pennsylvania Avenue. This downtown house contains most of the department's special equipment.

15. Trinity United Church
139 North Main Street

This Gothic Revival brick church with stone trim dates to the early 1880s; the congregation formed in 1849.

16. Christ Episcopal Church
145 North Main Street

This sandstone church, crafted in the Gothic Revival style, is the second on this site. It was built in 1889.

17. Westmoreland Museum of American Art
221 North Main Street

The Westmoreland Museum of American Art was established as the Woods Marchand Foundation in 1949 at the bequest of Mary Marchand Woods, a resident of Greensburg interested in the arts but without a personal collection. This visionary founder bequeathed her entire estate for the Museum facility to be built in Greensburg, where it was positioned to serve the people of rural Westmoreland County as well as the city of Pittsburgh. In 1959, the Museum opened its doors to the public and its focus became the collection and exhibition of American and southwestern Pennsylvania art.

18. Greensburg Academy site
301 North Main Street

On this site in 1811 the original Greensburg Academy was erected. This private school for boys and girls, with its commanding view of downtown Greensburg, inspired the name of the surrounding hilltop community, Academy Hill. In 1850, a fire of unknown origin destroyed the Greensburg Academy. Thereafter, the first public school to occupy Academy Hill was erected in 1862-63, with a subsequent school building erected in 1897. The existing school was erected in 1924. Thus, since 1862, this site has continuously provided facilities for public education in the City of Greensburg.

19. Blessed Sacrament Cathedral
300 North Main Street

The parish dates from March 10, 1789, when a group of laymen representing about 25 area families paid five shillings, the equivalent of less than $1 today, for the 1.5 acres that comprise the current site. Their intent was to build a Roman Catholic Church and public burial ground. Construction of a log church was started, then called to a halt because of a lack of funding. The space was never completed, never used, and the townspeople worshipped for the next 50 years at sites in Latrobe and Crabtree.

The second church of the parish was built in 1846; the present building came along in 1923. Built of sandstone with Indiana limestone trim, the English Gothic building was designed by Comes, Perry and McMullen in Pittsburgh.

20. Aquinas Academy
340 North Main Street

This is the parish elementary school of the next-door Blessed Sacrament Cathedral. It had originally been known as Saint Benedict School, then as Blessed Sacrament School until 1995 when its name was changed to Aquinas Academy due to a reorganization of the diocesan elementary schools. The oldest portion of the building, fronting Main Street, is a two-story red brick structure from 1904. There are also a 1954 addition and a 1961 addition, both fronting on Pennsylvania Avenue. A 1962 addition, set back from Main Street, was intended to serve as a convent.

21. Huff Mansion
424 North Main Street

The Academy Hill Historic District lies immediately north of the Greensburg business district; it was developed between 1880 and 1940 after an iron bridge spanned the railroad tracks that divided the two. The architecture of Academy Hill reflects the social differences prevalent in turn-of-the-century Greensburg - the high-style houses were built for the civic and industrial leaders and were sited near the top of the hill; the remainder of the neighborhood was developed for middle managers and the working class and exhibits less architectural detail.

Prominent among the architecturally impressive houses is the former home, now the YWCA, of William A. Huff, a founder and director of the First National Bank. Architect Ralph Adams Cram, who also designed the bank, drew up the plans for this Neo-Georgian mansion speckled with Ionic columns. Cram, a Boston architect, rarely took residential work and designed this as a favor for his friend Huff.

22. Jamison House
524 North Main Street

William Jamison was part of the family that established the Jamison Coal and Coke Company in 1892 that soon became industry leaders with control of over 20,000 acres of coal rights in southwestern Pennsylvania. His large 2 1/2-story Neo-Colonial Revival style home was built in 1903. It is a funeral home today.

TURN RIGHT ON KENNETH STREET. TURN RIGHT ON NORTH MAPLE STREET.

23. 416 North Maple Street

This block is chock full of handsome Colonial Revival houses from the first part of the 1900s.

TURN LEFT ON GRANT STREET. TURN RIGHT ON WALNUT STREET.

24. 334 Walnut Avenue

Paul Batholomew, who designed many buildings in the downtown historic district was also awash in commissions in Academy Hill. Seven of the homes in the neighborhood were created by the Cleveland-born architect; here he created a Tudor Revival style residence.

TURN RIGHT ON PARK STREET. TURN LEFT ON NORTH MAPLE STREET AND CROSS THE RAILROAD TRACKS TO RETURN TO THE TOUR STARTING POINT IN ST. CLAIR PARK.

Look Up,

Hamburg

A Walking Tour of Hamburg...

Settlement in the area dates to 1732. In 1779 when Martin Kaercher, Jr. received 250 acres of fertile land from his father instead of tilling the ground by the banks of the Schuylkill River he laid out building lots. In 1787 the little settlement was known as Kaercher Stadt or Kaerchertown. In 1792 the northernmost town in Berks County became its second postal designation, following Reading a few months earlier.

The name "Hamburgh" was adopted from the town of Hamburg, Germany since many of the first inhabitants were Germanic, a dialect that still lingers here today. The town began to blossom following the construction of the Centre Turnpike in 1812 from Reading to Pottsville. (both towns approximately 15 miles from Hamburg). And with the opening of the Schuylkill Canal in 1820 and the railroad which came soon after, Hamburg boomed.

Hamburg Borough, was organized in 1837, and has been called, "without a doubt one of the finest towns - architecturally - to be found anywhere in the state. Hamburg experienced its growth spurt during a period in architecture when ornamentation was popular. Victorian style in the homes and businesses in the town of Hamburg reflected the pride and attention to detail of its inhabitants no matter what the cost. Look down North 4th Street, South 3rd Street or North 5th Street and you'll find an abundance of ornate, Victorian cornices, gingerbread moldings, and brickwork - a tangible history of days gone by.

Our walking tour will begin at the Hamburg Public Library, one of the town buildings representative of the high style buildings that appeared during the Victorian Period...

1. Hamburg Public Library
35 N 3rd Street

The Hamburg Public Library borrowed freely from a variety of turn of the century styles and incorporated a few inventions of its own. The roof lines are more reminiscent of the Gothic Revival style, the arched windows and doorways are Romanesque Revival, rusticated lintel and arch stones borrow from Richardsonian Romanesque Revival, yet the eave crown moldings are of Classical Greek Revival profile and the dormer window is decorated with filigree reminiscent of the Stick Style. The interior details and moldings echo a modified expression of Roman architecture.

The library opened on November 5, 1904 and is the oldest library building still operating in Berks County. Funds for the building were donated by steel magnate Andrew Carnegie who supplied money for free libraries across the country. On the first day an estimated 500 people visited, and seventy-seven library cards were issued. The copper cupola roof was renovated in 2002. The rotunda in the inside is impressive, and much of the interior (wooden bookshelves, circulation desk, round bench in the entry) are original. Note the tin ceiling.

WALK NORTH ON 3RD STREET
(if facing the library, turn left).

2. Hamburg Municipal Center
61 N 3rd Street, southeast corner of Island Street

The Third Street School, erected in 1889, housed all elementary grades and after 1913, four years of high school. On February 25, 1924, at 4:30 p.m., fire was discovered in a hot air flue in the south wing. Though firemen fought the blaze for 12 hours, little was saved. The structure was rebuilt on the site and used as an elementary school until 1982. In 1987 the Borough of Hamburg purchased the property and relocated the Borough offices into the facility. It remains today as the Hamburg Municipal Center. The graceful iron fountain at the front corner (which predates the school) and the iron fence were most likely made by local iron works.

TURN RIGHT ON ISLAND STREET.

3. Bethany Methodist Church
321 Island Street, northeast corner of 3rd Street

This two-story church was built in 1913 of rubblestone in a rambling "Country" Gothic style with some Romanesque forms and Gothic details. It replaced the former Emanuel Union Church at this location that was heavily damaged by a rogue tornado on July 5, 1887. The weathervane is from the earlier church. Stained glass windows depict the life of Christ. The parsonage behind it along Island Street - so named because it leads to an island in the Schuylkill River - was built around 1904.

TURN RIGHT ON 4TH STREET.

4. Scott House
71 N 4th Street

This Federal style Victorian home was built in the 1870s for William Scott, a Hamburg carriage builder. The decorative window surrounds, arched doorway and footed windowsills give the home a formal look. The iron gate off to the side dates back to when the home was built.

5. 64 N 4th Street

This Federal style home intrigues with its gabled dormer and first-rate craftsmanship on the lentil brick work above the windows.

6. Schmick House
63 N 4th Street

Wilson Schmick was an early 20th century industrialist who tried to lure his wife away from Philadelphia by building this elegant mansion, complete with stained glass and art glass windows throughout the house. An exceptionally large one can be seen on the north wall. The twin wide gables are framed with corbelled layered diagonal brick peaks and elaborate chimneys. The ornate woodwork above is still topped with newel posts. Still, she refused to take the bait, stayed put in the big city and the house was sold.

7. 54 N 4th Street

This picturesque blend of Victorian styles was built for another town industrialist. Tudor-influenced details are placed over a heavy Queen Anne porch. An art glass window graces the exposed north wall. Corner quoins call to mind mid-19th century Italianate buildings.

8. 51-53 N 4th Street

These two Gothic Revival homes are joined together in the middle. Elaborate decorative wood trim is evident and trusses on either side of the center bay area is extensive. The chimneys on both homes are corbelled and have slate covers.

9. Miller House
45 N 4th Street

This Queen Anne from the late 1800s was the family home of the Millers, owners of the Robert P. Miller Underwear Mill in Shoemakersville. This home is a fine example of Queen Anne style architecture. It has a steeply pitched roof with a double row of snowbirds over a fine brick cladding. Arched soldier lentils above the windows are finely done and stone sills give the house a strong feeling. The brick work is precise. The front gable has accented symmetrical wooden detailed corner brackets. The house is situated above a terrace reached by a stone staircase and the wall in the front adds to the splendor.

10. 27-29 N 4th Street

A touch of the Gothic distinguishes this terrace-top double house. Note the finely crafted woodwork under the peaked gables.

11. Bailey House
21 N 4th Street

This is considered the oldest stone house still standing in Hamburg - the year 1811 is incised in a stone up near the peak. The elegance of this home lies in its hand-hewn stone that was hauled from the Blue Mountains by Abraham Bailey. It was built with fireplaces in nearly every room. Note the carefully fitted stone keystones in the arches above the windows.

12. 5-7 N 4th Street

These three-story buildings express a beautiful collection of Italianate woodwork, and have housed small shops and residences above them for many years. The tin ceiling has been beautifully restored in No. 7.

13. The American House
2 N 4th Street, northwest corner of State Street

This corner site has been a tavern/hotel for many years; however, its inception is unclear. The earliest record of real estate transaction is February 7, 1813. It changed hands many times until 1853 when it became a licensed hotel under Peter Fink and housed a tavern, eating house and oyster cellar. After being closed for many years, it is once again entertaining diners.

14. Confer
1 N 4th Street, northeast corner of State Street

Built in 1880 this Italianate style four-story building featured a large ballroom on the top floor for operas, dancing, and other affairs. The ground floor has housed many businesses over the years, including a liquor store (the reason for the bars on the side windows). An impressive portico once covered the sidewalk on both 4th and State Streets. The top windows inspired the town's Historic Hamburg logo.

15. Veterans of Foreign Wars Lodge
1 S 4th Street, southeast corner of State Street

This rambling, brick, Queen Anne style building with peaks, dormers and turrets was the machine shop of Snell and Meharg relocated from Reading to Hamburg. One of the partners, George Meharg, built this home that stayed in the possession of the Meharg family until the early 1950's when it became the social quarters for the Veterans of Foreign Wars.

16. 5-7 S 4th Street

At one time almost every building on this block featured a portico. Now this is one of the only ones left.

17. Hamburg Strand Theater
6 S 4th Street

Formerly a restaurant, this site was changed into a movie theater and opened on Christmas Day in 1920 with a showing of *The Whistling Devil*. Tickets for silent films cost 11 or 17 cents. The first "talkie" shown here was *Untamed* in March of 1930. This nostalgic one-screen theater remains family owned.

18. 13-15 S 4th Street

In 1908 this old former post office building was extensively remodeled into the National Bank establishment. Various businesses since then have kept the marble decor out front. The first mill burned down in 1875 and it was replaced by the present structure.

19. 16 S 4th Street

This property showcases the original stained leaded glass above the twin show windows which extends six feet inside the building. Also original is the tin ceiling and the brass and milk white light fixtures.

20. 17 S 4th Street

Dating to 1779, this is one of the oldest houses in Hamburg. It is reputed to have been one of the stop-over places for Negro slaves leaving the South for Canada on the "Underground Railroad."

21. First National Bank and Trust Company
26 S 4th Street

This two-story marble building, with a columned entrance brings a Classical Revival style with Greek detailing to downtown Hamburg. Built in 1927, it has 20-foot columns of white Vermont marble fluted in Corinthian capitals. It is the only marble-granite building in town.

22. Burkey & Driscoll's
38 S 4th Street

Established in 1852, Peter Burkey's cabinet making business shortly evolved into a furniture and undertaking enterprise. This is Hamburg's oldest business to be continually operated by the same family from 1852 to present. It is also the last of the once common funeral home/furniture store combinations left in Pennsylvania.

23. Miller's 5 & 10
43 S 4th Street

Miller's 5 & 10 was established in 1922 in the Miller family residence, built in 1819. For many years they sold homemade candy and ice cream. The store is little changed from those days.

24. Hamburg Savings and Trust Company
52-56 S 4th Street

The Hamburg Savings and Trust Company was founded in 1872 in a small single room across the street. The current building dates to 1923; the basement was leased to the Keystone Social Club for a bowling alley and club quarters which they still occupy.

25. Mill Creek

Mill Creek flows under under the street finally exposing itself here. The Flood of 1906 raged through this part of town, taking away Allen Romich's tinsmiths shop and Mr. Romich himself. The contents and that of Mr. Romich's, including stoves, tinware, and his cobbler's bench, and lumber was strewn along the creek banks and at the bridges. Romich's widow auctioned off the salvaged stoves and tinware. Lime was used to purify the water, but in spite of that, a typhoid epidemic broke out. Mr. Appel, assistant editor of the Hamburg *Item*, who worked so hard on the flood issue of the paper, was its first victim.

26. Leibensperger Funeral Home
143 S 3rd Street, northeast corner of Walnut Street

Built in 1829, it was formerly Loy's furniture and undertaking establishment. In 1935 Stephen T. Leibensperger purchased the property and converted the furniture store into a funeral parlor which still is owned by the Leibensperger family. The property still retains its original street portico.

27. 68-70 S 4th Street

This Federal-style house once featured lip-smacking treats from Gittle's Candy shop. It was also home to a tobacco shop, and later an insurance agency. It currently serves as a residence only. The show windows and portico are original.

28. Carpenters' Hall
320 Chestnut Street

Hamburg's first grist mill, powered by a millrace constructed along Church Street from Shomo's Dam between Franklin and Island Streets, was established on this site by town founder Martin Kaercher, Jr. The mill burned down in 1875 and was replaced by the present structure.

29. southwest corner of 4th and Pine streets

The Rotary Club donated this old-fashioned town clock in 2002.

30. 101 S 4th Street

This 19th century Victorian house got a French-inspired Second Empire mansard roof and Italianate door surround detailing. Originally owned by a succession of doctors it housed the Draft Board during World War II and today is divided into apartments.

31. Hamburg Union Fire Company #1
125 S 4th Street

Built in 1886, this building served to house fire equipment and also the borough office. Later acquisition of adjoining property allowed the addition of social quarters and a larger truck garage.

TURN RIGHT ON WALNUT STREET. TURN RIGHT ON 3RD STREET.

32. 124 S 3rd Street

Now an insurance office, this building with its portico and show windows has housed various shops over the years, including a stint as an oyster house,

33. First United Church of Christ
86 S 3rd Street

Built in 1898-99, this 2-1/2 story brownstone church done in the Gothic Revival style combining elements of Norman Gothic and English Perpendicular styles. The Tiffany stained glass windows are framed in heavy arched window heads of red stone. The church's pipe organ was purchased with $1,000 contributed by Andrew Carnegie. A 50-bell carillon was installed in 1971.

34. 73 S 3rd Street

This Federal-style house has original wooden shutters and door surround. Note the stone foundation and steps, the grates, and probably the only slate sidewalk left in town out front.

35. Burkey House
59 S 3rd Street

This house was built for Daniel Burkey, who owned the Burkey Furniture Business and Funeral Home and his sons assisted him in all his business efforts. Daniel Burkey was so appreciative that he built a home alongside of his for each of them.

36. Burkey Row
47-49-51-57 S 3rd Street

These are the houses the Burkey family patriarch built for his sons.

37. 41 S 3rd Street

This handsome brick home was built in 1918 and the young couple who moved into it lived there for more than 70 years. Notice the lead trim on the door and picture window.

38. 11 S 3rd Street

This frame building has seen many occupants, but from 1891 to 1930 it housed the newspaper plant and office of the *Hamburg Item*. After a fire in 1903, the paper was re-equipped and up and running in just a few weeks.

39. The Balthauser Building
2-10 S 3rd Street

Built in 1885 as Confer's Varieties, the style of this impressive market place has changed very little since then. For many years it was a department store and there was a farmer's market in the basement each Saturday.

40. Hamburg *Item* House
3rd and State streets

The Hamburg *Item* has been published since 1875. The "cast stone" facing blocks of this 1930 building were developed and manufactured by a local firm. The press room was at the rear, offices in the center, job printing upstairs, and until 1956 a store occupied the front of the building.

TURN RIGHT ON STATE STREET.

41. Adams & Bright Drug Store
306 State Street

A drug store opened in this building with a modified marble storefront and beautiful stained glass above the entry in 1906. Adams & Bright bought it in 1929 and installed a black marble soda fountain and some marble booths. The original counter is still there. An early telephone exchange was located on the second floor until 1914.

42. 308 State Street

This building was home to Wisser's bar and restaurant for many years, until 1994. The old bar and back-bar are still in place, as is the tin ceiling.

43. Dietrich's
320 State Street

From 1909 to 1920 this was the National movie theater. It was the American Legion during WWII, and then was remodeled to become a men's and boys' clothing store.

44. Hecky's Sandwich Shop
313-317 State Street

This imposing building dates to 1928 to house the business of Rau Bros., on the site of a former movie theater and an earlier blacksmith shop and carriage works. The Raus were tinsmiths, and were largely responsible for this being a "town of red tin roofs." Many of the ornate tin ceilings have been carefully preserved in businesses around town, including this one.

RETURN TO 3RD STREET AND TURN RIGHT.

45. 6 N 3rd Street

This site has at one time or another been a furniture store, bowling alley, grocery store and most recently a printing establishment.

46. 26-28 N 3rd Street

Two generations of the Seaman family made a wide variety of baked goods here beginning in 1887, delivering them first by horse and wagon, and later with a fleet of trucks. In 1941 it was sold to Maier's bakery, and they baked pies in the large building at the rear until 1957.

47. 308 State Street

This large building was the headquarters of the National Guard for many years. It was built in 1889 by the Blue Mountain Legion, a military company. Movies were shown here in the silent picture era. There were basketball games, roller skating, banquets, dances, and a cooking school.

YOU HAVE NOW RETURNED TO THE TOUR STARTING POINT.

Look Up,

Harrisburg

A Walking Tour of Harrisburg...

Harrisburg has been an important transportation center since the days of riverboat traffic; in colonial days, John Harris operated a ferry here. Its western boundary is formed by the Susquehanna River. This location played an important part in its selection as the capital of Pennsylvania in 1812 and Harrisburg played a large part in the early development of the Pennsylvania canal system and the subsequent development of the railroads, highways and airlines. Today, Harrisburg is one of the most important commercial centers and distribution points in the East.

At the dawn of the 20th Century, spurred by the design of New York's Central Park by Frederick Olmsted, a nationwide conservancy effort began. In Harrisburg that movement was spearheaded by J. Horace McFarland and Mira Lloyd Dock, who established Harrisburg's League of Municipal Improvements. In 1901, their visionary efforts, collectively known and "The City Beautiful Movement," created Harrisburg's first official park system and saw to its expansion over the next decade to include Riverfront Park, Reservoir Park, City Island and what is today known as the Capital Area Greenbelt.

Since that time Harrisburg has gone through many transformations. By the early 1980s, the once grand park system had become symbolic of the blighted city around it. Harrisburg was near bankruptcy and been declared the second most distressed city in the nation. The 1982 election of reformist Mayor Stephen R. Reed brought an investment of more than $29 million and a proverbial phoenix of greenery rising from the ashes of decades of neglect. New developers and preservationists have adhered to the program in the years since.

Our walking tour will start at the symbol of the Commonwealth, the State Capitol, a building President Theodore Roosevelt proclaimed as "the most beautiful building he had ever seen" when he attended its dedication in 1906...

1. Pennsylvania State Capitol
head of State Street at N 3rd Street

When John Harris Jr. laid out the town of Harrisburg in 1785 he gave land to the Commonwealth of Pennsylvania that was later used for the Capitol grounds after the government migrated from Philadelphia and Lancaster. The Italian Renaissance-style statehouse is the third state capitol to be in Harrisburg. The first capitol burned down in 1897 and the second was left unfinished when funding ran out.

The monumental design is by Joseph Miller Huston and was dedicated in 1906. After its completion, the Capitol was the site of a graft scandal when it was discovered that the construction and subsequent furnishing cost three times as much as what the General Assembly had appropriated.

The exterior is made from granite from Hardwick, Vermont. The Capitol Dome, rising 272 feet and weighing 52 million pounds, is topped by the gilded, brass statue of *Commonwealth* by Roland Hinton Perry. On the floor of the main hallway, tiles show Pennsylvania's history, symbols, insects and animals.

The large, bronze doors at the Capitol's main entrance were designed by Huston, were modeled by sculptor Otto Jahnsen and were both cast in one piece using the lost wax method of casting by the Henry Bonnard Bronze Company. The doors are decorated with scenes from the history of Pennsylvania, with busts of people who were important in the construction of the capitol. The entrance is flanked by two sculptures, *Love and Labor: The Unbroken Law* and *The Burden of Life: The Broken Law.*

TURN AROUND AND WALK DOWN STATE STREET TOWARDS THE SUSQUEHANNA RIVER.

2. Grace United Methodist Church
216 State Street

This church, built between 1873 and 1878, can be said to have saved Harrisburg from losing its status as the Capital of Pennsylvania. For most of the 19th century Philadelphia loyalists tried to bring the capital back east. When the Capitol Building burned in 1897 it was argued that Harrisburg had no facilities large enough to accommodate the Legislature and Administration. The Church opened it doors to the State Legislature, which occupied the sanctuary and Sunday School rooms until the interim Capitol was readied in 1899. During that time, the church's congregation worshiped at the Grand Opera House at Third and Walnut Streets. Grace Methodist was erected of limestone in the Gothic Revival style with one of the tallest and most distinctive spires in the City.

3. Saint Patrick's Cathedral
208 State Street

The magnificent Renaissance Revival-styled Seat of the Roman Catholic Diocese of Harrisburg is the second to rise from this prominent State Street property. Completed in 1907, Saint Patrick's Cathedral replaced its more modest predecessor, which was erected in 1827 and enlarged and remodeled over the years. In step with the construction of the new Capitol Building, old Saint Patrick's was replaced by this impressive and largest church building in Harrisburg, emulating in style the Basilica of Saint Peter in Rome.

RETURN TO THE STATE CAPITOL AND TURN LEFT ON N 3RD STREET.

4. State Museum of Pennsylvania
N 3rd Street and North Street

In 1903, Samuel W. Pennypacker, a member of the Historical Society of Pennsylvania became the Commonwealth's twenty-fourth governor. After Pennypacker took office, lawmakers drafted a bill for an appropriation of $50,000 for a new building for the state museum and archives. In 1964 a new depository for Pennsylvania's heritage was opened here. From an architectural history perspective, the William Penn Memorial Building reflects the style of Modern design for public buildings of the late 1950s and early 1960s that swept Harrisburg.

TURN LEFT ON NORTH STREET. TURN LEFT ON 2ND STREET.

5. **Hope Fire Station**
   606 N 2nd Street

The City's oldest surviving fire station was built in 1871. Rehabilitated and converted, the tin ceiling and spiral staircase are part of the building's original features.

RETURN TO NORTH STREET AND TURN LEFT.

6. **Harrisburg Central YMCA**
   701 N Front Street, northeast corner of North Street

Founded in 1844 in London, England, by George Williams, the Young Men's Christian Association quickly grew in the United States with Harrisburg, in 1854, being one of the first eight cities in the nation to establish a chapter. Located at various sites in the downtown during the last half of the 19th Century, the YMCA erected its first headquarters building in 1902 at the southwest corner of Second and Locust Streets. In 1931, the "Y" moved into the current impressive edifice of the Italian Romanesque style, incorporating elements from various baptisteries, cathedrals and churches in northern Italy.

7. **Old Waterworks**
   the foot of North Street at N Front Street

The stone portion dates to 1841. At one time, the City's principal facility pumped water from the old City Island filtration plant to the original reservoir on North Street and later to Reservoir Park. It was expanded in 1904. A recent renovation to adaptive use has created prestigious office space.

TURN LEFT ON N FRONT STREET.

8. **Civic Club of Harrisburg**
   612 N Front Street

This building, one of only two to survive on the west side of Front Street and ensconced within the idyllic setting of Riverfront Park, was erected between 1901 and 1903 by William Reynolds Fleming as a single family home which he named "Overlook." Fleming was one of the founders of the internationally known and Harrisburg area-headquartered engineering firm of Gannett Fleming, Inc. Designed in the half-timbered, English Tudor style, the house was willed to the Civic Club of Harrisburg upon the death of Fleming's widow, Virginia, in 1914.

9. **James Donald Cameron Mansion**
   404 N Front Street

Built in 1863, this Second Empire mansion was purchased in 1870 by J. Donald Cameron, son of Simon Cameron. The elder Cameron had served as Abraham Lincoln's first Secretary of War and was the organizer of one of the most powerful and lasting state political machines in U.S. history. J. Donald continued the Cameron legacy as Secretary of War to President Ulysses Grant and later as Pennsylvania U.S. Senator from 1877 to 1897. Grant visited this home while President and was reportedly seen smoking cigars while relaxing on the side veranda facing State Street. The house remained in the family until Mary Cameron died in 1959.

10. **William Maclay Mansion**
    401 N Front Street

This was the home of William Maclay; statesman, surveyor, lawyer America's first U.S. Senator and son-in-law of John Harris Jr., the founder of Harrisburg. Maclay's distinction of being the first U.S. Senator came after the Articles of Confederation provided for the organization of the new Federal government when the ninth state ratified the U.S. Constitution in 1788. Pennsylvania became the first state to elect its Senators through the State Legislature with Maclay being the first and Robert Morris, the second.

Erected in 1792, Maclay's dwelling originally had the appearance of a simple stone farmhouse with high foundation and elevated first floor. In 1908, the home was purchased by William E. Bailey, a descendant of an early Harrisburg iron and steel industrialist family, who enlisted the expertise of City architect Miller Kast to transform the house into a Georgian Revival masterpiece.

11. Flynn Building
305 N Front Street

In 1864 the state purchased a new Governor's residence at 313 N. Front Street in exchange for the previous Second Street home plus $20,000. The size of this house became inadequate as well. The adjoining lot was purchased, and an identical house was built during the administration of John W. Geary (1867-1873). A brownstone facade was later constructed to unify the two structures, and the expanded residence became known as "Keystone Hall."

Due to the poor condition of Keystone Hall by the 1940s some governors opted to reside in a fieldstone house at Fort Indiantown Gap Military Reservation, located 22 miles east of Harrisburg. In the early 1960s the residence, which had housed 17 governors and their families, was sold for $85,000 and razed. It was replaced with a parking lot. In 1990 the City's first condominium project opened on the site, with the building designed to complement the scale and character of historic Front Street.

12. Chapter House
221 N Front Street

This Second Empire-styled residence dates to 1870 and begins a trio of Cathedral buildings that exhibits a well-preserved cluster of distinctive architectural periods of old Front Street.

13. Episcopal Cathedral Church of St. Stephen
219 N Front Street

Although Harrisburg founder John Harris, Jr., was a member of the Church of England, it was not until 1826 that a permanent Episcopal church building was erected here. Territorial restructuring over the ensuing decades led to the creation of the Diocese of Harrisburg in 1904 (now the Diocese of Central Pennsylvania). Official designation of St. Stephens as a "Cathedral" Church would occur in 1932. St. Stephen's retains its Gothic Revival exterior from its original church.

14. Cathedral House
215 N Front Street

Now known as the Cathedral House, this classic Greek Revival-styled residential structure was acquired by St. Stephen's in 1918 for use as the home of the Church's Dean. Erected around 1840, it is one of the finest examples of this form of architecture in the Harrisburg area.

15. The Calder/Olmsted/McCormick Mansion
105 N Front Street

William Calder, Jr. was co-founder and president of the Harrisburg Car Works, president of the First National Bank of Harrisburg and was president and director of the Harrisburg Cotton Factory that stood at the current site of the Harrisburg Central YMCA. His father had been a pre-eminent Harrisburg stage coach operator and helped to establish the town's importance as a transportation center as the nucleus of early route development throughout the northeast. Calder Jr.'s original house was a fancy three story stone mansion in the Second Empire style with mansard roof. that was sold in 1901 to Marlin E. Olmsted, who served in the United States congress for eight terms. Olmsted converted the house to a palatial Italian Renaissance styled showpiece commensurate with the growth of Harrisburg's stature as State Capital. After Olmsted's death, his widow, Gertrude Howard Olmsted, who was known for serving many cultural and humanitarian causes in Harrisburg, in 1925 married former Harrisburg mayor, business leader, U.S. Ambassador and *Patriot-News* editor Vance McCormick of the Harrisburg McCormick Dynasty. They lived at the home until McCormick died in 1946 and she in 1953.

16. James McCormick Mansion
101 N Front Street

This house was built in 1869 by James McCormick, Jr. , a noted banker, industrialist, community leader and member of one of Harrisburg's oldest families. The house is one of the best surviving examples of the stylish mansions which would rise on Front Street after the Civil War. Second Empire in architectural style, the edifice is beautifully executed in design and detail. The house stayed in the McCormick family until the family willed it to the Harrisburg Public Library who sold it in 1976 for professional offices.

17. Harrisburg Public Library
southeast corner of N Front Street and Walnut Street

The Harrisburg Public Library was founded in 1899 at 125 Locust Street in a building erected by James McCormick, Jr., which still stands. McCormick lived around the corner at 101 N Front Street, just across Walnut Street from the side yard garden of the Haldeman Mansion at 27 N Front Street. The present library, of Georgian Revival style rendered in limestone, was constructed in 1914.

18. Art Association of Harrisburg
21 N Front Street

The former home of Governor William Findlay (1817-1821) is now the home of the Art Association, founded in 1926 with working artist studios and a school. The original 1815 brick building was surfaced with brownstone around 1850.

19. Governor's Row
N Front Street between Strawberry and Walnut streets

This outstanding row of townhouses built between 1812 and 1840 served as homes to several early Pennsylvania governors. They represent a variety of well-executed and painstakingly preserved architectural styles of the early to mid-19th century.

20. Market Street Bridge
N Front Street at Market Street

The Market Street Bridge, also known as the old Camelback Bridge, is a stone arch bridge that spans the Susquehanna River between Harrisburg and Wormleysburg. The current structure is the third bridge built at its current location and is the second oldest remaining bridge connecting Harrisburg's downtown and Riverfront Park with the West Shore.

Construction for the Camelback Bridge headed by Jacob Nailor began in 1814 and it was finally opened as a toll bridge in 1820. It was the first structure built anywhere to cross the Susquehanna River. The Camelback enjoyed a monopoly until the completion of the neighboring Walnut Street Bridge in 1890. In 1902 the Camelback Bridge was destroyed by a flood and in 1905 a two-lane replacement bridge was erected at the same location. The present structure, with its graceful stone-glad arches, is the result of the 1926 widening of the replacement bridge. Columns at the Harrisburg entrance to the bridge were salvaged from the old State Capitol which burned in 1897.

CROSS THE BRIDGE TO CITY ISLAND.

21. City Island
Susquehanna River at Market Street

Known in its early years as Turkey Island, Maclay's Island, Forster's Island and Hargast Island, this land was originally used for truck farming. It would not be until the municipal improvements of the early 20th century that the Island would begin to develop into the park that it is today. While amateur baseball teams played here as early as the 1880s, professional baseball arrived in 1903, hosting both the Harrisburg Athletics and Negro League Harrisburg Giants baseball clubs. Such notables as Satchel Paige and Babe Ruth played ball here. In 1908, Jim Thorpe won the high jump here for the Carlisle Indians in statewide competition.

The public works improvements of the early 20th century led to the construction of the City Island Filtration Plant, which extracted water from the river, filtered it in reservoirs which now define the edge of the Skyline Sports Complex, and pumped it by way of an under-the-riverbed tunnel to the Old Waterworks at Front and North Streets, which in turn pumped the water to the reservoirs in Reservoir Park. The bathhouse and concrete beach emerged by 1922 as the Island's popularity grew. In the mid-1980s minor league baseball returned to Harrisburg with the construction of Riverside Stadium.

RETURN TO HARRISBURG, USING EITHER THE MARKET STREET BRIDGE OR THE WALNUT STREET BRIDGE, THE PEDESTRIAN TRAVERSE ONE BLOCK TO THE NORTH.

22. Dauphin County Courthouse
southeast corner of Front Street and Market Street

Dauphin County's third and present courthouse since the 1785 creation of the County was completed in 1943 at this, the traditional and most prominent entrance to the City of Harrisburg. It replaced the second Courthouse, erected in 1860, which stood on the northeast corner of Market and Court Streets. The present building, designed by the noted Harrisburg architectural firm of Lawrie and Green in the Neoclassical revival interpretation of the Art Deco style, is a monumental edifice representing a temple of justice as the seat of the County Court system. The building's exterior is clad with white Georgia marble while its interior is laden with inscriptions, figurines, icons and carvings in wood, marble and glass tracing important elements to the founding and growth of Dauphin County as well as with symbols of law, justice and wisdom among many others. The main first floor lobby features an enlarged map of Dauphin County, depicting roads, towns and topographic features, which is inlayed in the terrazzo floor. The building is a treasure-trove of rich and unusual woods, a variety of marble and other quality building materials employed in a stylistic fashion making this a highly developed and beautifully executed example of the monolithic public building of its time. Note the stately front fountain and pool above where stands the statute of *Youth Crushing Evil*.

TURN RIGHT ON FRONT STREET AND TURN LEFT ON CHESTNUT STREET.

23. Crowne Plaza
northwest corner of 2nd Street and Chestnut Street

The current era of hostelries in Harrisburg can be defined as having begun in 1965 with the construction of the Holiday Inn Town, now The Crowne Plaza. Prior to that time, the Harrisburger and Penn-Harris Hotels, at Third and Locust and Third and Walnut Streets respectively, were the city's two principal hotels, both facing Capitol Park. The Harrisburger would close by 1968 and the Penn-Harris demolished in 1973. The Holiday Inn Town prevailed as the first newly constructed lodging facility since 1930. The 261-room rejuvenated hostelry was designated best Crowne Plaza in the western hemisphere upon opening in 2000.

24. Salem United Church of Christ
231 Chestnut Street

This is the oldest church building in the City, having been erected in 1822 by the German Reformed congregation on land designated for a church building by the original 1785 plan of Harrisburg.

TURN LEFT ON 3RD STREET.

25. Keystone Building
22 S Third Street

This Italianate commercial building reigned as the tallest building in Harrisburg from the time it was built in 1874 until 1906. It was the former printing house for pre-World War I daily and weekly newspapers.

RETURN TO CHESTNUT STREET AND TURN LEFT TO CONTINUE WALKING AWAY FROM THE RIVER.

26. Harrisburg Transportation Center
4th and Chestnut streets

The development of rail lines along the same routes as the earlier canal systems converged in downtown Harrisburg. The original portion of the present station was opened November 23, 1887 at 8:00 p.m. Constructed of pressed laid brick in red mortar, Hummelstown Brownstone and terra-cotta trim, the building cost $206,261. This complex was expanded in 1902 and 1910. Built by the mighty Pennsylvania Railroad, which established major operations in Harrisburg, it was the fourth train station on this site. By the 1920s more than 100 trains arrived and departed in th eQueen Anne style station. Now the Harrisburg Transportation Center, it is particularly distinguished by its lofty train sheds, a rarity in the United States.

TURN LEFT ON 4TH STREET.

27. Zion Lutheran Church
15 S 4th Street

"Tippecanoe and Tyler Too" was the familiar political slogan of the 1839 Presidential Campaign. That campaign began when William Henry Harrison and John Tyler were nominated as the Whig candidates for U.S. President and Vice President in this church, now altered from its original appearance. The Whig Convention here made Harrisburg the smallest city to ever host a U.S. presidential convention. Both men won and both eventually became President. The congregation of Zion Lutheran Church has been rooted to this property since the erection of its predecessor church on the same site in 1814, which burned in 1838.

CROSS MARKET STREET.

28. Harrisburg First Church of God
15 North 4th Street

Considered the mother church of the Church of God denomination, which was founded in Harrisburg in 1827 by Reverend John Winebrenner. This building dates to 1854.

RETURN TO MARKET STREET AND TURN RIGHT, TOWARDS THE RIVER.

29. 333 Market Street

At 341 feet in height, 333 Market Street represents the pinnacle of Harrisburg's robust skyline

and is not only the City's tallest building, but also the tallest of any building located between Philadelphia and Pittsburgh. Built in 1977, it replaced the popular 150-room William Penn Hotel, built in 1922, and the original Davenport Restaurant that grew into a national food service chain operating under several familiar trade names.

30. Kunkel Building
301 Market Street

This building was erected in 1914 as the home of the Mechanics Trust Company, a Harrisburg bank that later went bust during the Depression. It also served as one of Harrisburg's first high-rise office buildings, contributing to the early 20th Century urbanization of City Center. Listed in the *National Register of Historic Places*, the building is architecturally unique through its white, glazed terra-cotta, tiled exterior. In 1925, the structure was expanded from six bays to ten bays in depth through the application of the identical architectural style and height to that of the original structure. Originally known as the Kunkel Building in honor of Charles Kunkel, Chairman of the Mechanics Trust Company, the structure now serves as a tower for arts organizations, including the Susquehanna Art Museum.

31. Lochiel Hotel/Colonial Building
227 Market Steet; corner of E Market Street

This building was erected in 1835 in the Greek Revival style and was originally known as the Wilson Hotel. Such notables as Daniel Webster and singer Jenny Lind stayed here. In the late 1800s, the building was "Victorianized" through the creation of the mansard roof and window trim embellishments and was renamed the Lochiel Hotel. The hotel continued as a popular lodging destination until 1912 when it was transformed into the Colonial Theater, a lavishly decorated vaudeville theater house, which later doubled as a movie theater, and where many of the Nation's noteworthy actors took stage. Although efforts were launched to preserve the theater in the early 1980's, long-term neglect resulted in its physical collapse onto S Third Street in September, 1983, with no injuries. Because the building had been listed in the *National Register of Historic Places* several years earlier, extraordinary efforts were made to save the front portion of the structure.

32. Dauphin Deposit Trust Company
213 Market Street

Dauphin traces its history to the opening of the Harrisburg Savings Institution in Harrisburg, Pennsylvania, on September 28, 1835. Built the same year, this is the oldest bank building in metropolitan Harrisburg and still used for banking. The original Greek Revival design remains intact, inside and out with a dazzling interior with vaulted ceiling and Neoclassical cornicing and detailing. Note the granite hitching post on the front sidewalk that has been painstakingly preserved over the decades and may very well be as old as the bank building itself.

ARRIVE IN MARKET SQUARE AND TURN LEFT ON 2ND STREET.

33. M&T Tower
southeast corner of Market Street and 2nd Street

Crisply designed, this landmark Market Square office tower was completed in 1990 and serves as the home of several major law firms and to Harrisburg's main presence of M&T Bank. The building stands as a major contributor to the revitalization of the Market Square area.

34. Johnston Building
17-19 S Second Street

Originally only four stories in height, the Johnston Building was built in 1906 for the Johnston Paper Company, Harrisburg's first paper bag business founded by Robert A. Johnston in the 1880s. In 1912, two floors were added to the Italianate-styled building giving it a more urban presence. By the late 1970s, the building was a candidate for one of Harrisburg's earlier revitalization projects. It was thoroughly restored and became a fitting anchor to the south side of Market Square.

35. Market Square Presbyterian Church
20 S 2nd Street

The church was established on February 16, 1794 when a session was formed and the congregation gained its independence from its parent congregation, Paxton Presbyterian Church. Harrisburg's oldest Presbyterian congregation is also the oldest surviving building on Market Square, having been built in 1860. Its prominent Romanesque-styled church spire is the City's tallest at 193 feet.

36. Dauphin County Administrative Office Buildings
southwest corner of Second Street and Market Street

This renovated former bank now does duty as the newest addition to the Dauphin County Government Complex. It houses additional courtroom space, offices of the Dauphin County Commissioners and other operations of the County Administration.

TURN LEFT ON MARKET STREET.

37. Claster Building
112 Market Street

This building was erected in 1920 for the offices of the Pennsylvania Public Services Commission and was one of the first buildings in downtown Harrisburg intended to be leased for state offices. Originally known as the Claster Building, having been built by local merchant Henry C. Claster, it was acquired by Dauphin County as an expansion of the County Government Complex in the early 1980's. With many interior and exterior alterations made over the years, the County thoroughly overhauled the building including the reconstruction of previously altered curtain walls and windows to emulate its original 1920 Art Deco-styled appearance.

RETURN TO 2ND STREET AND TURN LEFT.

38. Penn National Tower
northwest corner of Second Street and Market Street

The world headquarters of Penn National Insurance was erected in 1996. The cross-vaulted roof design and distinctive Keystone icons enhance Harrisburg's skyline.

39. Martin Luther King Municipal Center
10 N 2nd Street

Built in 1982 to serve as Harrisburg's City Hall, this is the only municipal building in the world to be named after Dr. King. The interior features a stunning interior and sky lit atrium.

40. Hilton Harrisburg and Towers
northeast corner of Market Street and 2nd Street

When it opened amidst regalia and fanfare in the fall of 1990, the Hilton Harrisburg and Towers reclaimed Harrisburg's traditional role as Central Pennsylvania's primary destination for the lodging and conference industry. With 341 rooms, one of the largest ballrooms in Central Pennsylvania, fine restaurants, and enclosed walkway linkage to other downtown attractions, the Hilton Harrisburg and Towers has also been a catalyst to Harrisburg's growing after hours entertainment industry.

TURN RIGHT ON WALNUT STREET.

41. Old City Hall
423 Walnut Street

In the early 1900s, as the downtown area grew, many grand buildings were constructed to serve the growing needs of the community, as well as local and state governments. One of those impressive new structures, a cut-stone building, was designed in 1910 by prominent architect, Charles Lloyd, to serve as Tech High School. In 1928, Harrisburg's city government moved in and many dramatic changes were made to make the interior as imposing as the facade. A grand staircase in the lobby, offset by oak paneling, marble and brass accents and a cast plaster ceiling were a few of the unique architectural details added.

CROSS OVER THE STREET ONTO THE CAPITOL GROUNDS.

42. South Office Building
Capitol Grounds, southeast of the Capitol Building

This was the first separate building to be erected in the original Capitol Complex of the 20th century which would ultimately evolve into a grand Neoclassical and symmetrically organized collection of stately buildings. It was completed in 1921.

TURN LEFT AND WALK THROUGH THE CAPITOL COMPLEX HEADING TOWARDS THE RIVER.

43. Matthew Ryan Legislative Office Building
Capitol Grounds, south of the Capitol Building

By the late 1880s, the Old Capitol Building erected in 1822 was becoming limited in space due to the inevitable expansion of state government. What was originally known as the Executive, Library and Museum Building was designed by Philadelphia architect John T. Windrim in 1894 and is the oldest surviving structure in the Capitol Complex. Not only did the new structure house the library and museum rooms for Pennsylvania's growing collection of artifacts and artworks, but also the offices of three Governors who served between 1894 and 1906. Restored in the mid 1990s, the Old Museum Building, also known as the Capitol Annex, was renamed the Matthew J. Ryan Legislative Office Building, in honor of the legislator who was the longest serving Speaker of the House in Pennsylvania history.

WALK DOWN THE HILL ONTO 3RD STREET AND TURN RIGHT, HEADING BACK TOWARDS THE FRONT OF THE CAPITOL BUILDING AND THE TOUR STARTING POINT.

Look Up,

Honesdale

A Walking Tour of Honesdale...

Only in the latter half of the eighteenth century did settlers from Connecticut get around to clearing the land in the wooded northern hills of Wayne County. Dyberry Forks, which was to become the county seat, was then just a swampy wilderness at the point where the Dyberry River joins the Lackawaxen on its way to the Delaware River.

The town got started in the 1820s because of Maurice and William Wurts's coal business. To get their anthracite coal from the mines in Carbondale to seaboard cities, they decided to build a canal from Dyberry Forks to Rondout (now Kingston), New York, on the Hudson River. That was only the second of their two problems - the coal wasn't in Dyberry Forks - it was in Carbondale across 1,942-foot-high Farview Mountain. In 1825, backed by Philip Hone, a successful businessman turned mayor of New York City, the Wurtses succeeded in raising over $1 million for their Delaware and Hudson Canal Company, and they were off.

By October 1828, Philip Hone, inspecting the newly completed D&H Canal, marveled at the "stupendous stone work" and the impressive rock cuts - entirely achieved by men, mostly "wild Irish" immigrants, wielding pick and shovel and the unpredictable black blasting powder of the day. The canal negotiated a drop of 1,030 feet by means of a series of more than 100 locks, in the 108-mile journey to Kingston.

Honesdale was incorporated in 1831. Its sole purpose was to serve as the jumping off point for canal barges loaded with coal headed for New York City markets. That coal came over the mountain from Carbondale on a "gravity railroad" as loaded cars were hauled up on tracks on a series of planes, or inclines, to the top of Farview by stationary steam engines, then lowered by gravity down planes on the other side to the town of Waymart, finally coasting on a steady downgrade into Honesdale. Empty cars were brought back to Waymart by horse or mule.
At one time Honesdale had the largest stockpile of coal in the world.

By the mid-19th century Honesdale was a bustling waterfront town; it became the county seat in 1841. Our walking tour will begin in the parking lot in the center of town in front of the Visitor Center, that was actually a boat basin once at the start of the historical canal...

1. **Delaware and Hudson Canal**
   behind Main Street parking lot

The Delaware and Hudson Canal was a 108-mile, man-made waterway, an engineering feat of pre-industrial America that brought coal from the hills of Pennsylvania out to the Hudson River. From 1828 to 1898, mules pulled barges laden with anthracite coal along river valleys from Honesdale to Eddyville on the Rondout Creek near the villages of Kingston and Rondout. From here, it was shipped on barges down the Hudson to New York City and up the river to Canada.

At its peak over 5,000 boats were traveling the canal at one time, each loaded with as much as 160 tons of coal. The Canal operated successfully until the Delaware & Hudson Canal Company made a unique transition in 1898 into a railroad company, becoming America's oldest continuously operating transportation company.

WALK THROUGH THE PARKING LOT OUT TO MAIN STREET AND TURN RIGHT, WALKING EAST.

2. **Centennial Block**
   east side of Main Street, between 6th and 7th streets

In March 1871 W. Jonas Katz opened the doors of his little store for the first time. The full extent of his inventory was $41 worth of merchandise he had bought from a salesman. When he closed the till, first day's receipts were $31.14, an encouraging start. Katz Bros. Department Store would remain a fixture in town for the next 116 years.

The brothers were Samuel and Jacob who joined the business early on, before their store was destroyed by fire in 1875. the Katz brothers joined other entrepreneurs in constructing new buildings on Main Street between 6th and 7th Streets. J.A. Wood, a New York architect, was hired to design the new commercial block in Honesdale (he was also the architect for the Wayne County Court House). The block was completed in 1875, and became known as the "Centennial Block" in honor of our nation's one hundredth birthday.

The Centennial Block consists of multiple Italianate three-story brick buildings sharing a mix of architectural details, including segmental windows with decorative hoods and sills, and cornices with panels and brackets. Each building bears minor, but distinctive decorative differences. Three original bracketed Italianate storefronts are still visible at street level.

3. **Murray Co. Store**
   626 Main Street

The foundation for Murray Co. began in 1829 when Captain Ed Murray began selling goods on the newly constructed canal. In 1833 he opened the first Murray Store, which was destroyed by fire. The present building opened in 1907. It is the only four-story building on Main Street - known for years for its elevator and was fashioned from concrete blocks made locally by hand.

The store had hardware and appliance departments and expanded to the manufacturing of silos and cattle stalls under the Maple City name. In the early 1980s Fred Murray took over the family business and moved to Commercial Street. In 1987 he sold the business out of the family. In 1996 it closed, leaving Honesdale without a Murray store for the first time in 167 years.

TURN LEFT ON SIXTH STREET.

4. **The National Hotel/ VanGorder's Furniture**
   southwest corner of Sixth and Church streets

This corner was where the first house in Honesdale was built, a small plank cabin built by pioneer settler Samuel Kimble. He had bought 152 acres of the Indian Orchard Tract from Mordecai Roberts, Jr. in 1823. Kimble's northern boundary was an east-west line through what is now Central Park. In 1827, having been told that the proposed canal basin would be built south of his land and that the canal would ruin his planned farm, Kimble sold 100 acres to Maurice Wurts, Delaware & Hudson Canal entrepreneur. That land became the southern half of Honesdale.

In 1868 William Weaver built the National Hotel on the site. The large brick structure had 27 rooms and an opera house on the second floor. Each room had its own fireplace and those overlooking the street sported balconies. A stable for 110 horses was built next to it with a second story

137

access from the livery to the hotel. In 1929 the Athens Silk Company bought the hotel and it was for some years a silk mill. Ralph Van Gorder purchased the building in 1938 to house his growing used furniture business.

TURN LEFT ON CHURCH STREET.

5. **St. John's Evangelical Lutheran Church southwest corner of Church Street and 7th Street**

This Gothic church building was dedicated in October of 1904 to replace a wooden 1848 structure that was the congregation's home a block to the north. The early Honesdale Lutherans began organizing a congregation during the 1840s. At first they met in private homes and later rented a dwelling on Court Street opposite Beth Israel. This group of worshippers was known by the name "Die Deutsche Kirche" (The German Church). The land was given by the Delaware and Hudson Canal Co.

6. **Zenas Russell House 803 Church Street**

Zenas Russell was born in Madison County, New York in 1806 and came to the nascent Honesdale as a merchant at the age of 22. He was a member of Honesdale's first town council and in 1830 a director of the newly formed Honesdale Bank. By 1863 he was president of the bank, an organizer the Honesdale Gas Company. and was a charter member of Grace Episcopal Church. The triple brick-walled house was constructed in 1861, blending an Italianate core with Greek Revival porches.

Highlights for Children, a staple in elementary school classrooms since 1946, was the dream of Dr. Garry Cleveland Myers and his wife Caroline Clark Myers. They ground out that first issue in a two-room office over a car dealership in town. Mrs. Myers then drove to Columbus, Ohio, to deliver the artwork to a printer with a first issue print order of twenty thousand copies. The magazine purchased the house in 1963 and has run its editorial offices here ever since.

7. **Whitney House 823 Church Street**

Allis Whitney, who owned the Whitney Livery and Exchange Stables located in the large stone building across the street, bought this house in 1865. He advertised "both open and closed carriages for weddings, funerals, and extra occasions, with twenty head of well-groomed horses." His son, Major George H. Whitney was active in the organization of Company E, 13th Regiment of the PA National Guard, where he held every position from private to major. He was in the front lines during the Spanish American War. Whitney was best remembered as leading every Honesdale parade on his handsome snow-white charger. The horse was also trained to answer the fire bells, and would race to the firehouse upon hearing them. The house is a fine example of Folk Victorian architecture and was carefully restored by *Highlights for Children* after the magazine purchased the house for offices in 1978. All the paint was removed from the exterior bricks and the woodwork rehabilitated.

8. **Grace Episcopal Church southeast corner of Church Street and 9th Street**

The Protestant Episcopal Church of Honesdale originated February 13, 1832 at the Charles Forbes Inn, now the site of the Wayne Hotel. The present building site was deeded to the Episcopal congregation by the Delaware & Hudson Canal Co., and a wooden structure was erected in September 1834. This building was later moved to a vacant lot to allow for the construction of a new church. The old Grace Church was eventually sold to the German Catholic Church in 1852 and was destroyed by fire in 1859. In 1854 the Episcopal Parish erected the present angular church in the Gothic Revival style from locally quarried stone. The adjoining stone rectory was completed in 1876, and in 1879 the spire was erected in memory of one of the founders, Zenas H. Russell, by his family.

CROSS OVER INTO CENTRAL PARK.

9. Central Park
between 9th and 10th streets and Court and Church streets

The land for the park was donated by Jason Torrey and by the Delaware and Hudson Canal Company in 1834. A wooden fence enclosed the square for many years. The *Wayne County Herald* of October 4, 1848 noted that "the crowd gathered for the hanging of Harris Bell, clambered on and collapsed the wooded park fence." In the 1850s the local militia held occasional military reviews in the park. The name change from public square to Central Park seems to have occurred during this period.

The statue of a Union soldier in the position of old-time parade rest was chiseled of Quincy marble and bears the names of the 353 Wayne County men who died of wounds or disease during the Civil War. The monument was one of the first erected in the state and was dedicated with appropriate ceremony in 1869 by Pennsylvania Governor John W. Geary. The fountain in Central Park was built seven years later in commemoration of America's centennial.

LEAVE THE PARK ON THE SOUTHEAST CORNER, AT COURT STREET AND 9TH STREET.

10. Dimmick Mansion
northeast corner of 9th Street and Court Street

The first house on this corner of Court and Ninth Streets was a clapboard building belonging to Honesdale merchant Charles C. Graves and his wife Julia. He sold in 1859 to Samuel Dimmick and four years later it burned to the ground. Dimmick, a lawyer active in Republican politics, erected this Italianate brick building with Second Empire mansard roof at a cost of $40,000. It had twenty-two rooms, rare chestnut woodwork, and ten-foot high front doors. Samuel Dimmick was Attorney General of Pennsylvania when he died in office in 1875 at the age 52.

In 1919 the house was bought by The Wayne County Memorial Hospital Association and after renovations was opened as the first hospital in Wayne County. When a new hospital was built on Park Street the building was acquired by the Honesdale Gospel Tabernacle and was a church for the next forty years. In 1992 the County of Wayne purchased the property for much needed office space.

11. Wayne County Courthouse
923 Court Street

The first county courthouse was in Bethany, the county seat from 1800 to 1841. During the legislative sessions of 1840-41, Senator Ebenezer Kingsbury quietly secured the passage of an act for removal and on May 4, 1841 the county commissioners accepted a plot of land opposite the public square for new government buildings. The land was a joint gift of the Jason Torrey estate and the Delaware and Hudson Canal Company.

After many years of discussion of the need for a new building, the commissioners adopted a resolution to begin construction in 1876. J.A. Wood of New York was selected as architect and the massive stone walls of the foundation were begun. During the next two years, little progress was made on the structure as "The Courthouse Wars" raged. Taxpayers were angry, legal disputes abounded and political disputes flared. Finally the commissioners resolved to complete the building and $130,000 later, the new Italianate courthouse was ready in 1880.

WALK NORTH ON COURT STREET TO 10TH STREET AND TURN RIGHT. GO TO THE END OF THE ROAD AT THE BANKS OF THE LACKAWAXEN RIVER.

12. Old Stone Jail
south side of 10th Street at Lackawaxen River

This imposing rough stone jail was built in 1859 to replace a wooden jail on this site. The rough stone of the exterior continues on the inside walls and floor as well. Passing through the heavy iron front door, the prisoner was led to one of five cells, each measuring about twelve feet by nine feet with arched ceilings. The opening to each cell was considerably lower than a normal doorway, making it necessary for even a man of medium stature to stoop to gain entry. The only light slipped through a long narrow vertical slit for a window.

The dreariness of this dungeon was the fate for Wayne County ne'er-do-wells until 1936. More than one prisoner committed suicide and there were several escapes, including through the cupola on the roof that was accessed via a trap door.

TURN AND WALK BACK ON 10TH STREET PAST CENTRAL PARK TO CHURCH STREET.

13. First Presbyterian Church
201 10th Street

The Presbyterians were the pioneer church organizers in Honesdale, beginning in the "Old Tabernacle," a log cabin structure located at the confluence of the Dyberry and Lackawaxen rivers. One of the first members was Maurice Wurtz, the originator of the D & H Canal. The original Presbyterian Church was a wooden structure erected in 1837 at this site; the current building was dedicated on June 25, 1868.

TURN RIGHT ON CHURCH STREET.

14. Central United Methodist Church
205 11th Street

Methodism in Honesdale dates back to 1825, when the Reverend Sophoronius Stocking, a circuit preacher, came to the Borough and organized a church. In 1834, Jason Torrey presented the Methodist society with a lot on lower Ridge Street, and a wooden structure (later converted into apartments) was erected that same year. The site for the present structure was purchased in 1872, and was dedicated on July 1, 1874.

15. Baptist Church
southeast corner of Church Street an 12th Street

The Baptist denomination has the honor of establishing the first church in Wayne County, dating back to June of 1796. However, the Honesdale church was first organized in 1833 by Reverend Henry Curtis, and services were first held in the "Old Tabernacle," the same building used by the Methodists and Presbyterians in their formative stages.

In 1843 the site of the present building on Church and Twelfth Streets was purchased and construction of a wooden edifice begun. The church was dedicated on July 30, 1845, and remains the oldest house of worship in the Borough of Honesdale.

TURN LEFT ON 12TH STREET AND TURN RIGHT ON MAIN STREET. WALK TO THE BRIDGE OVER THE LACKAWAXEN RIVER.

16. The Wayne Hotel
1202 Main Street

Charles Forbes built Honesdale's first lodging house in 1827, the same year as the D&H canal was being constructed. The Forbes House was a large wooden structure with long two-story porches and was the town place to hobnob for more than six decades. John Weaver bought the Wayne County House, as it came to be known, in 1891 and had the present large brick building constructed around the old wood hotel. When the new structure was completed, the old one within it was razed. Today the brick exterior is just as it was when built, with HOTEL WAYNE in dark brick high on the street-facing facades. The beautiful iron posts and balustrade of the porch were recently restored. Just west of the porch was once the entrance to the livery stable, and is now a commercial space.

TURN AND WALK SOUTH ON MAIN STREET.

17. Honesdale City Hall
958 Main Street

Built in 1893, this Romanesque Revival brick-and-stone building once sported cupolas atop the building's two towers but they were removed because of maintenance issues. Above the main entrance are a large arch and a balcony that runs between the two towers. Years ago local dignitaries used the balcony to make their public speeches. For many years the building was also the home to the Protection Engine No. 3 Fire Company.

18. Lincoln Nomination Site
115 9th Street

Horace Greeley, a prominent newspaper editor from New York, came frequently to the northeast corner of Pennsylvania, visiting both Pike and Wayne counties. The area was a familiar vacation spot for middle class families from New York or New Jersey. According to local tradition, the meeting to plan Lincoln's future took place in Honesdale in 1859 at the law office of Samuel Dimmick.

But local tradition and historical reality are at odds in the case of this marker. There may have been a political meeting in northeastern Pennsylvania to plot strategy for the 1860 Republican convention, and Horace Greeley may have attended it, but it was definitely not his intention to "boom" Lincoln for president. The editor recalled that he had "endeavored to fix on the proper candidate for President," for months before the convention, but remembered clearly that Lincoln was not his preference. "My choice was Edward Bates, of St. Louis," he noted in his memoir.

RETRACE YOUR STEPS TO MAIN STREET AND TURN LEFT.

19. Jason Torrey Land Office
810 Main Street

Built in 1830 and one of the oldest brick buildings in Wayne County, this was the land office of Jason Torrey. Torrey came to Mt. Pleasant in 1793 and moved to Bethany in 1801. He was a land surveyor and wound up buying much of what he surveyed. His family owned most of the land in and around Honesdale. He was one of the largest land holders in Wayne County and owned considerable territory in neighboring counties as well.

In 1981 the Wayne County Historical Society moved the office from its original location at the terminus of the canal and it's gravity railroad, saving it from demolition. A restoration of the exterior took $85,000 and 18 years to finish.

20. Delaware & Hudson Canal Office/ Honesdale Museum
810 Main Street

The canal company built this brick building in 1860 after losing at least one prior office in Honesdale to fire. Strategically locating it near where the company's gravity railroad and canal met, the employees inside could keep a close eye on the activities outside their back door.

In 1923, with the canal era over, the Wayne County Historical Society, was granted a lease to use the north half of the building for storage while the Hudson Coal Co. used the south half. The Society opened the museum to the public in 1939. Its centerpiece exhibit is a full-size replica of the *Stourbridge Lion*. On August 8, 1829, its namesake, the first locomotive to turn wheel on commercial track in the United States, made its first run here in Honesdale.

With the hope of finding a better way for hauling coal from Carbondale to Honesdale other than the gravity railroad that ran with the help of cables to the head of the canal, the D&H Canal Company ordered a steam locomotive from Stourbridge, England. The engine was called the *Stourbridge Lion* because a huge lion's head was painted on the front of the boiler. Unfortunately the engine proved too heavy for the wooden tracks and was never used again. At the end of the 19th century, the remaining scattered pieces were reassembled and put on permanent exhibition at the Smithsonian Institute in Washington, D.C.

21. Honesdale National Bank
724 Main Street

During the canal era, this was a huge basin of water used for the storage and repair of canal boats; a bridge carried Main Street across the water. Established in 1836, The Honesdale National Bank is "the oldest Independently owned Community Bank headquartered in Northeastern Pennsylvania." It occupied various buildings before moving here after the basin was filled in and the present building of local Forest City stone and Indiana limestone trim was erected in 1896.

22. Wayne County National Bank
   717 Main Street

Wayne Bank was founded on November 4, 1871, and was known as the Wayne County Savings Bank. Early financing included everything from boat building and harness manufacturing to tanneries and farming. The shutdown of the Canal at the end of the 19th century forced the Bank to change with the times by financing the expansion of the county into other industries such as glassworks, textile factories and logging.

In 1924, the Bank' moved to the present headquarters between 7th and 8th Streets on Main Street. The majesty of the building's limestone and marble facade continues to represent the image of stateliness and security favored by banks in those days. The Bank's heart remains the massive 12-foot high, polished steel vault, which when opened looks like a giant complex time-piece, a must see on any visitor's itinerary.

YOU HAVE NOW REACHED THE TOUR STARTING POINT.

Look Up,

Indiana

A Walking Tour of Indiana...

One of the few founding fathers to sign the Declaration of Independence, the Articles of Confederation, and the Federal Constitution, George Clymer was orphaned in 1740, only a year after his birth in Philadelphia. Apprenticed to the mercantile business by a wealthy uncle, he became a leading Colonial merchant after marrying his senior partner's daughter, Elizabeth, in 1765. Like many other contemporaries, Clymer also speculated in western lands, and donated the land upon which the town of Indiana was laid out in the early 1800s after the county was formed on March 30, 1803 from Westmoreland and Lycoming counties. Its name memorializes the first inhabitants.

The county's first major industry was the manufacture of salt, made from evaporating salt water pumped from wells. The salt boom in the southwestern part of the county accounted for the name of the town of Saltsburg. Coal mining soon rivaled farming as the backbone of the region's economy.

Today, Indiana is known for two things that are indispensable at Christmas time: the Christmas tree and Jimmy Stewart. It seems growing pine and spruce as a farm crop started in Indiana County in 1918. In 1944 a group of growers organized the Pennsylvania Christmas Tree Growers Association and by the 1950s an estimated 700,000 trees were being cut each year around Indiana. An Associated Press news story tagged Indiana County as the "Christmas Tree Capital of the World," a title it guards ferociously. Shortly after Indiana began receiving nationwide publicity the state of Washington tried to appropriate the title and an Indiana nurseryman produced an order he had for 15,000 trees to be shipped to Tacoma, Washington.

James Maitland Stewart was born in his parent's home at 975 Philadelphia Street in Indiana on May 20, 1908. The Stewarts trace their roots in Indiana County back to 1772 when Jimmy's third great-grandfather Fergus Moorhead first arrived and was captured by Indians. The Stewart family hardware store, known locally as the "big warehouse," was a fixture in Indiana since 1848. After experiencing an All-American childhood in Indiana (he was an enthusiastic Boy Scout) that imbued him with the values that would later show up on the silver screen, Jimmy Stewart left for his father's alma mater, Princeton University, in 1928. His on-stage performances attracted enough attention that he would not return after school to take up business in the family store.

Jimmy Stewart never forgot his roots in Indiana and our walking tour will begin at a life-size statue that the actor himself dedicated on the occasion of his 75th birthday...

1. *Hometown Hero - Jimmy Stewart*
   825 Philadelphia Street

Jimmy Stewart was born and raised in this timber-and-coal town, enjoying a boyhood that was, by all accounts, the typical small-town American experience similar to that often portrayed in his films. His hometown honored Stewart with this bronze statue on the occasion of his 75th birthday in 1983. Well, not exactly this statue. The $100,000 tribute wasn't ready in time for its dedication so a look-alike fiberglass statue was substituted. No one noticed the difference -- not even Jimmy, who flew in from California for the dedication. The festive 75th birthday blast included a fly-over of Air Force jets and a telephone call from President Ronald Reagan.

The real statue was eventually completed, and the fiberglass statue was moved next door as a display inside the Jimmy Stewart Museum, which opened in 1996. Directly across Philadelphia Street from the statue is the former location of J.M. Stewart & Sons Hardware, where young Jimmy worked and proud father Alex later displayed Jimmy's Academy Award Oscar statue. One block west on Philadelphia Street, a bronze plaque marks the doorstep which led to the house where Stewart was born. His boyhood home is three blocks to the north, on Jimmy Stewart Boulevard at the base of a long set of concrete steps that lead up Vinegar Hill.

2. **Indiana County Courthouse**
   825 Philadelphia Street

This Colonial Revival courthouse with hipped roof replaced its showier predecessor down the street in the 1970s, ending its more than a century of service. In addition to the Jimmy Stewart statue out front the grounds also feature the Indiana County War Memorial.

WALK WEST ON
PHILADELPHIA STREET.

3. **Indiana County Library**
   845 Philadelphia Street

Indiana Free Library started in a reading room starting in 1907 in a building not that far from where it is now. This building was constructed in 1912 as the YMCA. It would be several decades before the library moved in. The library is also home to the Jimmy Stewart Museum that displays memorabilia from the actor's time in Indiana and his Hollywood career.

TURN LEFT ON
SOUTH 9TH STREET.

4. **Christ Church**
   902 Philadelphia Street

After first assembling in 1831, the small Episcopal congregation met for 25 years in the homes of members, schoolhouses, and the Court House before a church was built on this site. It was destroyed by fire in December 1899 and the current church dates to 1901.

TURN LEFT ON CHURCH STREET.

5. **Grace United Methodist Church**
   northwest corner of Church and 7th streets

In his original 1803 plat of the town George Clymer designated the block between 6th & 7th streets to be reserved for churches. This Georgian Revival building with triangular pediments and soaring steeple is the third church built by Indiana's Methodists, completed in 1932 succeeding previous sanctuaries from 1876 and 1841.

6. **Cavalry Presbyterian Church**
   southeast corner of 7th Street and Church Street

This congregation was organized in 1807 as the First Presbyterian Church in Indiana. Meeting first in homes and, after 1809, in the County Courthouse, the congregation erected its first building in 1827 on this site - ground donated by town founder George Clymer. In 1858 a second church replaced the initial building.

In 1904 work began on the third and present building, a Victorian eclectic structure designed by J.C. Fulton of Uniontown. Built of Hummelstown brownstone by Indiana contractor John S. Hastings, the new edifice was completed in 1906. Its octagonal sanctuary, dominated by an art glass dome 28 feet in diameter, incorporates the central pulpit and semi-circular pew arrangement of the "Akron Plan," allowing worshipers to hear and see easily from any seat.

TURN RIGHT ON SOUTH 7TH STREET. TURN LEFT ON SCHOOL STREET.

7. **Silas M. Clark House**
   200 South 6th Street, at Wayne Avenue and School Street

This Italian villa-style brick dwelling was built in 1870 for Silas M. Clark, a judge on the Pennsylvania Supreme Court. He would later help start the Indiana Normal School. Dominated by a tall, square central tower, the distinguished house features decorative S-brackets, a low pitched gable roof, a bay window, round-headed windows, and brick corner quoins. Today it is the home of the Historical and Genealogical Society of Indiana County.

TURN RIGHT ON WAYNE AVENUE IN FRONT OF THE CLARK HOUSE.

8. **National Guard Armory**
   121 Wayne Avenue

Built in 1922, this Art Deco structure is now home to the library and research center of the Historical and Genealogical Society. It housed a drill hall on the first floor.

TURN LEFT ON WASHINGTON STREET.

9. *The Doughboy*
   Indiana Memorial Park

The Doughboy was dedicated May 30, 1925 to the Indiana men and women who served during World War I; veterans of subsequent wars were honored with plaques. *The Doughboy* is located on land what was once part of an old cemetery that had burials dating from as early as 1803 to 1875 - and this perhaps accounts for its tumultuous history.

A religious group had acquired the area as a gift and began constructing a church but ran short of funds. It planned to sell the trees and part of the land to finance the building on another part. The local veterans opposed the idea of selling the land and, led by Alex Stewart, local hardware merchant and the father of screen legend Jimmy Stewart, mounted a campaign to erect a memorial on the property. A local bank made a gift of the tall impressive pedestal to the Mothers of Democracy in 1922 and a local individual made a gift of The Doughboy sculpture.

After discovering a hole dug for *The Doughboy's* foundation, the church group filled it in. Stewart, Jimmy and others dug the hole again and the church group filled it again - this time, erecting a fence and posting a "No Trespassing" sign. Undaunted, Stewart invited his associates and members of the church group to meet him at the site and when the group was assembled, he cut the fence, crossed into the area and defied anyone to do anything about it. Stories in Indiana differ as to whether he spent time in jail, and if so, how much. In the end, the city bought the land and *The Doughboy* was erected where Stewart and his associates had wanted it to be placed.

TURN LEFT ON 6TH STREET.

10. **J. P. Carter House**
    209 South 6th Street

This seems like a particularly contentious corner of town. The builder, J.P. Carter, deliberately constructed a larger house than that of his neighbor across the street, Silas M. Clark, in retaliation for Clark's having secured the service of the architect whom Carter wanted. It cost $30,000 to build in 1870.

11. **Bennett House**
    145 South 6th Street

This Victorian Romanesque house was built in contrasting colors of golden tan and dusty rose under a green tile roof for Michael Bennett in 1915. The walls and floors are cast concrete. At one time, there were two elevators and a swimming pool in the basement.

12. John W. Sutton House
134 South 6th Street

This Second Empire-influenced house was constructed in 1882-1883 for John W. Sutton, son of the purchaser of the land for the Normal School (now Indiana University) to train women to become teachers. It features a mansard roof, dormers, and brick quoins. The house was used as the manse for the Calvary United Presbyterian Church from 1920 until 1963, when it was sold at auction for $17,050.

13. Zion Lutheran Manse
114 South Sixth Street

An asymmetrical Queen Anne style residence featuring wrap-around porch and gingerbread tower, the manse was built in 1899. This style displays a variety of interior and exterior materials, forms, colors, and textures. Projecting turrets and brick chimneys give the house a top-heavy appearance.

14. Zion Lutheran Church
6th Street and Church Street

George Baum of Philadelphia designed this church in 1923 for the congregation, which can trace its roots back to 1813. Built of steel-framed veneered stone, the Gothic Revival church features weathering, buttresses, and large pointed stained glass windows with tracery. Constructed at a cost of $225,000, it replaced a Neo-Gothic church built in 1880.

15. James Mitchell House
57 South Sixth Street

Built in 1849 by local merchant James Mitchell, this Federal style brick structure has an unusual second front doorway since the house originally served as both a residence and a general merchandising store.

16. David Ralston House
33-41 South Sixth Street

A double brick Federal House with a later single addition built in 1843, it is presently three separate units used as offices and dwellings. Para-pet chimneys are still evident on the south gable end. Ralston, a local merchant, built the house when he moved to Indiana from the Shelocta area to become sheriff. Bennett Whissel used it as a hotel. James Mitchell also owned this structure and ran an inn called the "Mansion House."

TURN RIGHT ON PHILADELPHIA STREET.

17. Alexander W. Taylor House
532 Philadelphia Street

This is believed to be the oldest structure in Indiana, built of stone by John Lucas, sometime around 1817. Also born in town around that time was Alexander Wilson Taylor. Taylor graduated from the Dickinson School of Law at Carlisle and commenced practice in Indiana. A member of the new Republican party, he was elected to the 43rd Congress. The house stayed in the Taylor family until 1950 when it began a long tenure as a television shop.

18. Griffith Building
555 Philadelphia Street

This two-story Queen Anne brick building dates to 1892 and features elaborate woodwork that betray the opulence of the age. H.P. Griffith was a town dentist who ran his practice here until his death in 1956.

19. William Houston House
581 Philadelphia Street

Constructed in 1823 by Houston, a merchant and member of the Pennsylvania House of Representatives, this is the second oldest of Indiana's buildings and longest continually used commercial building. The massive H-parapet chimney is a trademark of the Federal style. Note the west wall and the iron brackets that tie the brick wall into the structure. The house was used as the town's first bank by Hogue and Company in 1858.

TURN AND RETRACE YOUR STEPS TO 6TH STREET AND TURN RIGHT, WALKING UP THE EAST SIDE OF THE STREET.

20. Coventry Inn
11 North 6th Street

Charles Runyon owned the Roadster Factory, a company that provided parts and equipment for British sports cars in Indiana County. That's unlikely enough, so why not create an authentic English pub on the downtown streets? To ramp up the audacity another notch, Runyon created a mythical prototype, the Coventry Inn, that first operated in Bidford-on-Avon in 1497. So he was going to replicate the Coventry for its 500th anniversary. And, of course, he would start with some oak beams that had survived when the "original" was bombed out of existence in a German air raid in World War II.

The timbers, regardless of origin, were imported from England and pinned together with oak pegs. His English pub features the half-timbering of a 15th century Tudor building and also sports a heavy iron-strap door and a massive chimney topped with decorative clay pots. Begun in 1990, it opened in time to celebrate the great anniversary in 1997.

21. *Messenger* Building
15 North Sixth Street

This building dates to the 1840s and housed the Indiana *Messenger*, a local independent journal established around 1850. It's Italianate commercial style displays highly embellished cast iron window heads and a decorative, bracketed cornice.

22. Brown Hotel
northeast corner of 6th Street and Water Street

This is the last remaining 19th century hotel in Indiana, but it didn't make it to the 21st century without a struggle. A roof fire caused $70,000 in damage in 1933 but was restored to its original Italianate design with unusual jerkin-head cross gables incorporated into the hipped roof construction. Built in the 1870s on the site of the earlier Hines House, the hostelry operated under a string of names: Reiders' Hotel in the 1880s, Gompers' House in 1887, Clawson Hotel from 1890-1915, and finally the Brown Hotel in the 1930s.

CROSS 6TH STREET AND TURN LEFT, WALKING BACK TOWARDS PHILADELPHIA STREET AND THE TOWN CENTER.

23. Indiana County Sheriff's House and Jail
29 North Sixth Street

This exuberant Victorian, built in 1887, was the fourth county jail. It features cut stone quoins, decorative window heads, and ornately turned woodwork on the portico. A "Bridge of Sighs" connected the jail with the courthouse next door on the corner. Executions were carried out in the courtyard between the house and the old courthouse. The last hanging was on November 23, 1913. The house and jail have been restored by the NBOC Bank and are used for offices.

TURN RIGHT ON PHILADELPHIA STREET.

24. Old Courthouse Building
601 Philadelphia Street

A courthouse appeared on this corner in the center of town shortly after the county was formed in 1803. J.W. Drum designed this replacement in 1870 at the cost of $186,000. He blended classical elements, such as the grand colonnade of fluted iron columns topped with Corinthian capitals with the then-modern Second Empire style mansard roof. The golden clock tower consists of a podium, belfry, and cupola. When the county moved down the street in the 1970s, the courthouse was saved from destruction by NBOC, which took out a 99-year lease and poured an estimated half-million dollars into restoration.

25. NBOC Bank
600 Philadelphia Street

The First National Bank was organized in 1864 from the cinders of Hogue and Company that had started in 1858. This Neoclassical vault lined with Doric columns and pilasters was built in 1929 on the cusp of the Depression and no matter how much strength and security its appearance radiated, it couldn't keep the bank from going under in 1934.

26. Indiana Theater
637 Philadelphia Street

The theater started as a dream of Judge John Elkin, a prominent citizen of Indiana in the early 1900s. The judge died in 1915 before his performance hall could become a reality but his wife, Adda, continued with the project and the Indiana Theater opened July 24, 1924. It was constructed as a 1,500-seat Vaudeville & Movie Theater but was converted in 1928 to a much smaller theater, rendering it primarily a movie venue. After being dark for two decades the movie house re-opened in 2001.

27. The Coney
642 Philadelphia Street

The original Coney Island was opened in 1933 by Jimmy George two doors down from Stewart's hardware on the 800 block of Philadelphia Street. In 1965 Coney Island moved to 11 Carpenter Avenue which still holds the back bar and the rear seating area. Thirty years later in 1995 the business stretched out to meet Philadelphia Street and eventually devoured four storefronts.

The Suttons and Wilsons, founding fathers of Indiana University and the Kiski School, erected the corner building that houses the "Old Coney" in 1853 as Indiana's first dry goods store. The Coney's main entrance is through the old Wilson, Sutton & Company Store, constructed in 1880 with a rounded, decorative cornice. The Rend Brothers Building dates to 1895 and the adjacent building was constructed as the First National Bank around the same time.

28. Mrs. C.B.M. White Building
655 Philadelphia Street

The Mrs. C.B.M. White building was one of two commercial buildings constructed in 1915 for Harry White, noted Indiana judge, politician, and businessman. Prior to the establishment of the current H.B. Culpeppers this three story brick structure was home of the following businesses: Dairy Dell, Family Host Cafeteria, Landmark, and Michael's.

29. Luxenberg's
717 Philadelphia Street

Founded in 1916, Luxenberg's Jewelers is approaching 100 years in business at this location. The building was constructed in 1907 as an Elks Lodge.

30. Rose Building
740 Philadelphia Street

The Rose Building, constructed for S.W. Rose, proprietor of the Bon Ton Department Store, represents the apogee in high-style retailing in Indiana. Rose occupied the white, glazed brick building in 1918. Its multistory arches recall Italian Renaissance loggias while the building's clean lines and lack of ornamentation anticipate the Modern architectural styles a decade away.

YOU HAVE NOW RETURNED TO THE TOUR STARTING POINT.

Look Up,

Jim Thorpe

A Walking Tour of Jim Thorpe...

In 1791 Philip Ginder went digging at Summit Hill to cut a millstone and found himself picking through underlying black rock. It was anthracite and lured Colonel Jacob Weiss of Philadelphia to purchase some 10,000 acres of land around Summit Hill. It's one thing to own a mountain of coal, it is, however, quite another to do anything with it. At the time it was difficult to find a good road from city to city, let alone out of the mountains of northeast Pennsylvania. And even if there was easy transportation, people were only using soft coal - there was no market for hard coal.

The market developed after the War of 1812 and when Josiah White devised a canal system that released needed freshets of water to float barges on the shallow parts of the Lehigh River the game was on. Mauch Chunk, an Indian word roughly translating to "Bear Mountain," was founded in 1820 and in 1827 coal excavated from the mines on Summit Hill began rolling into town on America's first gravity railroad. Gravity took unpowered wooden coal cars down a switchbacking rail into the town to meet the barges on the Lehigh. Meanwhile, mules hauled the empty cars back up the mountain on a parallel track for the next load. Steam power eventually replaced the mules but the gravity railroad lasted until 1933 - its final years spent as one of America's first rollercoasters and a popular tourist destination for thrill seekers. Today it is a recreational hiker-biker trail.

Even though it was a coal town, local entrepreneurs saw the value of their breathtaking mountain setting early on. In 1824, when there were only 19 log buildings in town, the Mansion House was begun on Susquehanna Street, touted as America's largest hotel. Within a decade the Broadway House and White Swan hotels would open and soon Mauch Chunk was billing itself as "America's Switzerland."

A fire swept through town in 1849, destroying most of the vernacular building stock. Mauch Chunk, by now flush with coal cash, went on a rebuilding spree that would last through the rest of the century. And that would be it for building in Mauch Chunk. The coal industry collapsed in the early 1900s and the coming of the automobile brought other, more fashionable, mountain resorts into easy reach. The town's fortunes spiraled downhill - fast. An odd bargain to house the remains of Jim Thorpe, the greatest athlete of the first half of the 20th century, in exchange for renaming the town united Mauch Chunk with East Mauch Chunk in 1954 but never attracted the anticipated tribute-paying tourists.

It would be another generation before those tourists rediscovered the charms of Mauch Chunk and our walking tour will follow the narrow streets that have seen scarcely a modern intrusion since the coal boom days ended so many years ago...

FROM THE PARKING LOT ALONG THE RIVER, WALK TO THE STOP LIGHT AT BROADWAY AND SUSQUEHANNA STREET. TURN RIGHT AND WALK UP THE STEPS TO THE LEFT OF THE STATUE.

1. Asa Packer Mansion
Packer Hill Road

The mansion of Asa Packer, built in 1860, sits high above the town of Jim Thorpe. Packer came to town in 1822 as a 17-year old apprentice boatbuilder. He died 57 years later as a millionaire, after founding boatyards, construction and mining companies, the Lehigh Valley Railroad, and Lehigh University. His three-story Victorian Italianate building has a center hall plan, though at each end of the house is a one-room extension with a bowed end. Designed in 1861 by architect Samuel Sloan of Philadelphia, the home was built over a cast iron frame at the cost of $14,000 and renovated twenty years later with another $85,000.

Several stylistic details mark the exterior, including an Italianate roof and elaborate wooden brackets, Gothic window arches, and Gothic gingerbread trefoil motifs trimming the verandah. Inside, the Main Hallway features fine woodcarvings by European artisans, again using the Gothic motif throughout. The chandelier is said to have been the model for the one that appears in *Gone With The Wind*. The most amazing story about this National Historic Landmark, now open for tours, is that the mansion was boarded up from 1912 until 1956 and it was never vandalized and nothing was ever stolen from the house.

2. Harry Packer Mansion
Packer Hill Road

Asa Packer built another Victorian mansion next to his own home as a Lehigh Valley Railroad company owned home. This home was later lived in by his railroad engineer son, Harry Packer, and the Harry Packer Mansion is now used as an inn.

FOLLOW PACKER HILL ROAD BACK DOWN THE HILL TO ROUTE 209 AT THE BOTTOM.

3. Kemmerer Park
beneath the Packer Mansions on Packer Hill Road

These grounds were once the site of the grand 19-room mansion of coal baron Mahlon Kemmerer. When Kemmerer died in 1925 none of his children took interest in his luxurious home which was demolished in 1927 to make way for a public park and playground. Standing at the far end of the park is the Carriage House, larger and more substantial than most houses of the era. Featuring Victorian-era details, the multi-gabled building accented by a commanding cupola is in deteriorating condition and awaiting restoration.

TURN RIGHT AND WALK TOWARDS TOWN (THE LEHIGH RIVER IS ON YOUR LEFT).

4. Central Railroad of New Jersey Station
foot of Broadway at Lehigh Avenue

Constructed in 1868, the Central Railroad of New Jersey Station was designed by the Wilson Brothers of Philadelphia. Once considered one of the finest passenger stations on the Jersey central line, the main mass of the station is covered by a gable roof and supported by brackets with a prominent cylindrical tower at the end. With the discontinuance of passenger service in 1963, the station began to deteriorate, and on March 31, 1972, 106 years to the day the Jersey Central had begun its operation of the Lehigh and Susquehanna Division, the station was officially closed. Listed in the National Register in 1976 the station now houses the Tourist Welcoming Center.

WALK THROUGH THE PARK IN FRONT OF THE TRAIN STATION TO THE INTERSECTION OF SUSQUEHANNA STREET AND RACE STREET.

5. Hooven Mercantile Co.
41 Susquehanna Street

The Hooven Mercantile Co. was established in 1882 as a distributor of coffee, tea and spices. It was renovated in 1984 as a combination of museums and specialty shops. On the second floor, the Old Mauch Chunk Model Train Display and Hobby & Gift Shop offers a brief history on the world of model trains. This display features 13 separate mainlines, realistic landscaping, more than 100 bridges and trestles, over 200 structures, including a burning building.

WALK UP RACE STREET.

6. St. Mark's Church
21 Race Street

The first Episcopal services were held in Mauch Chunk in 1829 but it wasn't until 1848 that the first church was ready for occupancy. On June 16, 1867 it was demolished to make way for the present church, designed by Richard Upjohn and now a National Historic Landmark. In 1876 the original bell was replaced by a chime of nine bells cast by the Jones foundry of Troy, New York. Each bell was given by or in memory of a prominent member of the parish. As the wealth of the citizens of old Mauch Chunk grew, so did the richness of the memorials they lavished on their church. This church contains Tiffany Glass Windows, Minton Tile Floors, and an incredible stone labyrinth.

Through the generosity of Mary Packer Cummings, the entire church was renovated and redecorated, including the installation of an Otis elevator. The story goes that just before the elevator was completed, Mrs. Cummings fell ill and died. The first official use of the elevator was to carry her casket up to the main church for her funeral service on November 1, 1912.

7. Stone Row
25 Race Street

Asa Packer erected these 16 row house for engineers and foremen of the Lehigh Valley Railroad in 1848. Built of stone, the houses may have been a copy of Elfreth's Alley in Philadelphia. All houses are sturdily constructed and well designed. A stone wall divides every other dwelling to help cut down on noise. The three-story row houses were individualized by variations in dormer, bay window and door and window trim.

AT THE END OF RACE STREET TURN LEFT ON WEST BROADWAY.

8. Mauch Chunk Opera House
14 West Broadway

The Mauch Chunk Opera House was designed by Philadelphia architect Addison Hutton in 1882 to function as an open-air farmer's market on the first floor and a second story concert hall. It was said to be "of ample size, appropriately and elegantly finished and furnished, and possessed the important requisite of excellent acoustic properties." The Opera House would become a regular stop on the old Vaudeville Circuit. Al Jolsen performed here regularly as well as John Phillips Sousa who delighted audiences with an annual show.

In 1927, the building was purchased by the Comerford amusement chain, who renovated extensively, eliminating its Italianate tower. During the next three decades the Opera House became known as the Capitol Theater, a movie house. It officially closed on April 27, 1959. The building was then purchased by Berkeley Bags Company, a pocketbook manufacturer, and used for many years as a warehouse before being reborn as a venue for live performance and cultural events.

9. Marion Hose Company #1
16 West Broadway

The Marion Hose Company #1 was the first fire company in Carbon County, erected in 1885. Aside from the function of protecting Mauch Chunk from the ravages of fire, the Marion Hose was a community center. It was the location of numerous social and cultural events and the site of the first art exhibition held in Mauch Chunk.

10. Anita Shapolsky Art Foundation's
Exhibition Center
20 West Broadway

This one-time Presbyterian Church from the late 1800s provides an unusual and dramatic building to showcase the Foundation's collection of American Abstract Expressionist art. The church has a most unusual layout with two stories, a stage, and full living quarters in the rear. The second floor has a stunning collection of beautiful stained glass windows by Tiffany, La-Farge, and others.

11. Mauch Chunk Museum and Cultural Center
41 West Broadway

The Museum is housed in the former St. Paul's Methodist Church building in the Jim Thorpe Historic District. Constructed in 1843 of red brick with high ornate ceiling, the church is a magnificent example of Victorian ecclesiastical architecture. The museum contains Switchback Railroad and canal lock models and displays of Jim Thorpe - the athlete and the town.

12. 1855 School
43 West Broadway

This fortress-like Italianate building was actually constructed in 1855 as the town school. In the 1930s it was converted into a factory and is now adapted for residential use.

13. Old Carbon County Jail Museum
128 West Broadway

The Carbon County Jail is an excellent example of 19th-century prison construction, designed and built from 1869 to 1870. The jail is a two-story rusticated stone building with thick, massive walls and a tower. The jail could hold 29 prisoners. It was an active prison until 1995.

In 1875, the jail was crowded with miners accused of a series of murders on behalf of what the mine owners, railroad men, the prosecutors, anti-labor and anti-Catholic nativists, and the press described as an ominous terrorist conspiracy— the Molly Maguires, taking their name from the legendary widow Molly Maguire, said to have led anti-landlord resistance in the 1840s.

The trials of the Molly Maguires, which received incendiary and biased press coverage, were patently unfair: prosecuting attorneys worked for the railroad or mining companies (not the state); Irish Catholics were not allowed to serve on the juries; some juries consisted primarily of German-speakers who knew little or no English; and in a number of trials, the sole prosecuting evidence came either from James McParlan, who admitted to attending meetings where assassinations were planned, but did not warn the intended victims, or from men who after being convicted of murder, became prosecution witnesses in order to lessen their sentences. The convictions and death sentences crushed the Molly Maguires and the cause of organized labor suffered as a result of the trials and the identification of the Molly Maguires with the mine union movement. Of the twenty convicted Molly Maguires, seven men were hanged here at the Carbon County Jail while the other men were hanged in Pottsville.

14. Immaculate Conception Church
180 West Broadway

There is record of a circuit-riding priest coming to the area to serve the scattered Catholic population as early as 1797 but it wasn't until 1852 that the congregation, mostly Irish refugees, had a permanent home. The original brick-and-frame church was replaced in 1906 with this handsome Romanesque sanctuary built of North Carolina granite trimmed with Indiana limestone.

TURN AND WALK BACK DOWN THE HILL ON WEST BROADWAY.

15. Millionaires Row
Broadway, beneath Hill Road

Instead of mansions, some of Mauch Chunk's wealthiest denizens built stately townhouses in the fashion of Philadelphia and New York. As many as 13 millionaires were thought to reside along Broadway in the late 1800s. This four-story brick house at 72 Broadway sports a Second Empire mansard roof and, like many of its neighbors, a terraced garden in the back.

16. YMCA
69 Broadway

The YMCA, now a human services center, was built in 1893; the four Ionic columns on the upper facade may have been salvaged from the town's second courthouse that was razed for the current courthouse that was also built that year.

17. Dimmick Memorial Library
54 Broadway

Milton Dimmick, son of Milo Dimmick a local lawyer and congressman, died in 1884 at the age of 36 and left money to establish a library in the name of his family. The original Dimmick House is located one block up Broadway from the library. The cottage style, cross-gabled library designed by T. Roney Williamson opened its doors on October 1, 1890.

18. IOOF Building
39 Broadway

Originally a two-story structure built in 1844, the Odd Fellows Hall was substantially enlarged and altered in the Italianate style sometime after the Great Fire of 1849. The first floor commercial front with lead glass windows dates to the turn of the century.

19. Stroh Building
30-32 Broadway

In the late 19th century the building trades made a distinction between clay-based terra-cotta and artificial stone. Artificial stone was manufactured from a mixture of cement, sand, water, and stone aggregate that was poured into molds. Like cast iron, its popularity lay largely in its cheapness. Well-done cast stone is detectable only to an experienced eye and one of the best of its form in Pennsylvania is the 1898 Stroh Building. It is fully constructed of artificial materials: Pompeian brick front is trimmed with what appears to be cast-brownstone sills and lintels, ground story iron piers with an in-fill of mid-twentieth century artificial stone, and a sheet-metal cornice and parapet with a terra-cotta gable.

20. The Inn at Jim Thorpe
24 Broadway

Cornelius Connor built the White Swan Hotel here in 1833, one of several large, rambling, grand hotels in the town. After the inn was destroyed in the Great Fire of 1849 Connor rebuilt as the New American Hotel that stood as the jewel of Mauch Chunk accommodations until the Great Depression. Among the dignitaries staying here were General Ulysses S. Grant, President William H. Taft, Buffalo Bill Cody, Thomas Edison and John D. Rockefeller. The inn fell into disrepair in the 1930s until it was restored in the 1980s, becoming a catalyst for the rebirth of the town's tourist trade.

21. Jim Thorpe National Bank
12 Broadway

In 1852, Rockwood, Hazard & Company purchased, from the Lehigh Coal and Navigation Company, a stone building erected in 1829 on this site. This was the beginning of a private bank known as the "Savings Shoppe" that would be the Mauch Chunk Bank when it became the first chartered bank in Carbon County in 1855. In 1863 a new building on the site was created as the First National Bank of Mauch Chunk. The brick building, recently stripped of its white paint, features cast iron detail and marble veneer in the Baroque style. The First National Bank of Mauch Chunk consolidated with the Linderman National Bank in 1902 and was chartered by the United States Treasury Department as The Mauch Chunk National Bank (Jim Thorpe National Bank).

21. Lehigh Coal and Navigation Building
1 Susquehanna Street at southwest corner of Broadway

Josiah White was born in 1781, about ten years before the discovery of anthracite coal in the wilderness that was Carbon County. When he arrived in the Lehigh Valley he envisioned the shallow river carrying the "black diamonds" out to America's biggest cities. White invented an ingenious method that allowed canal locks to be closed quickly by only a single man to rapidly create navigable water. His unique "bear trap lock" system tamed the Lehigh River and created the inland highway through the gorge he sought. On August 8, 1818, The Lehigh Navigation system was created. A second company, the Lehigh Coal Company was formed to mine the coal. Between 1820 and 1883 some 21 million tons of coal were shipped down the Lehigh River.

At that time the firm was ready for a new headquarters. Addison Hutton, the town's go-to-architect for statement buildings, created the Lehigh Coal and Navigation Building with red brick, terra-cotta and carved sandstone trim. He designed the building to be fire proof using cast and wrought iron structural units. The building never burned but the company flamed out when petroleum replaced coal and the offices were abandoned. The town's most spectacular building, sited at its most prominent location, eroded in disrepair until it was resuscitated for residential use in the 1970s.

22. **Carbon County Courthouse**
    4 Broadway

This is the third courthouse located on this site. The first, built sometime after 1843, was destroyed in the 1849 fire. The second was an imposing Greek Revival structure demolished to make way for the current sandstone structure, designed by L. S. Jacoby of Allentown. On the building's centennial in 1983, it was refurbished, leaving original Victorian courtroom preserved.

TURN LEFT ON HAZARD SQUARE.

23. **Hotel Switzerland**
    5 Hazard Square

The Hotel Switzerland has been entertaining guests since 1830; this block was once known as Hotel Row in Mauch Chunk with the Central, Switzerland and Armbruster houses. Only the Switzerland remains.

24. **Civil War Monument**
    north end of Carbon County Courthouse

The dedication of the town's Civil War Monument took place on Memorial Day, 1922.

TURN RIGHT TO RETURN TO THE PARKING LOT.

Look Up,

Johnstown

A Walking Tour of Johnstown...

Johnstown is best known for the flood that decimated the town on May 31, 1889 killing 2,209 people in one of the country's greatest calamities. What is lesser known is that Johnstown has been visited twice more by great, rampaging waters - a flood in 1936 that caused significantly more property damage than 1889 and in 1977 when relentless rains brought five times as much - 128 million gallons - water into the city.

Around the floods Johnstown was a prosperous and hard-working mill town. The Pennsylvania Canal reached Johnstown in 1830 and the Pennsylvania Railroad arrived in 1854, two years after the Cambria Iron Company was founded in the Conemaugh Valley. The Cambria Iron Company of Johnstown was the greatest of the early modern iron and steel works, a forerunner of Bethlehem Steel Company and the United States Steel Corporation. It was the site of several major technological innovations that were copied throughout the world, including early use of the Bessemer process for refining steel and many new methods of heating, handling and rolling steel.

As Cambria became one of the nation's largest iron and steel producers it employed as many as 7,000 workers. The wealth spilled into Johnstown - by 1901 there were enough shoppers to support 11 department stores in the downtown area. The most modern buildings of the day, many that still line the Johnstown streets, were erected to replace ones destroyed in the Great Flood of 1889.

Those streets look remarkably what founder Joseph Schantz (Johns), envisioned when he plotted and planned the first permanent settlement in 1800. An Amish farmer, Schantz arrived in Philadelphia from Switzerland in 1769 and set his sights westward. During his life-time he used the name "Schantz" (Johns) on most of his land deeds and "Jantzin" (Johnson) in his family Bible records. In 1793 Johns bought a tract of land between the Conemaugh and Stonycreek rivers, built a cabin, cleared some land and began to farm.

Anticipating the creation of a new county (Cambria County in 1804), Joseph Johns hoped that his land would be chosen as the county seat. With this in mind, he laid out the first village lots and streets in 1800. He called his settlement "Conemaugh Old Town."

Our walking tour historic downtown Johnstown will begin in Central Park, a greenspace that remains the same public space as it was in 1800 when it was so designated by town founder Joseph Johns...

1. **Central Park**
   bounded by Main Street, Franklin Street, Locust Street and Gazebo Park

The city's basic street and alley plan, and several public spaces set aside by Johns, have remained intact for nearly 200 years. By the mid-19th century, a firehouse, butcher shop, jailhouse, and a large market stood here on the public square. During the Civil War, soldiers used Central Park as a drill field. Children came with their parents to see circuses or watch the town's two baseball teams, the "Kickenapawlings" and "Iron Club," practice. In 1872, the grounds were cleared of all buildings and laid out as a formal park. There was an ornate water fountain in the center. Nearly 100 planted trees offered shade in the summer.

The years of landscaping were wiped out in seconds by the flood wave. When the waters receded, debris 10 to 15 feet high filled the park. Within four days the wreckage was cleared to make room for tents that would house the 14th Regiment from Pittsburgh. After the troops departed, the park was lined with temporary wooden stores for a year before the square was restored as a park and new trees were planted. The original dimensions of the Johns Plan were re-instituted following the 1889 flood. This statute of Joseph Johns was erected by residents of German descent in 1937.

WALK TO THE SOUTHWEST CORNER OF CENTRAL PARK AT THE CORNER OF MAIN STREET AND GAZEBO PARK.

2. **Park Building**
   423 Main Street

This four-story building was designed by popular local architect George Wild for the Knights of Pythias, and completed in 1914. The Garden Theater (later Park) occupied the first floor and upper floors were used for offices. The Park Building features a patterned facade in light mortar, dark brick and light stone. The building features tile mosaics, Doric pilasters and a circular terra-cotta tile medallion at the upper center.

WALK EAST ON MAIN STREET ACROSS CENTRAL PARK.

3. **Nathan's Department Store**
   430 Main Street

Now known as Central Park Commons, this four-story store was built as Nathan's Department Store in 1917. Family-owned and operated, Nathan's had been operating in Johnstown since the late 1880s. The Early Modern design features brick exterior walls, Chicago-style windows, a classically styled cornice and one of the few remaining examples of glazed architectural terra-cotta work on a large scale in the Johnstown area.

Nathan's Department Store went out of business in the 1929 and the building was leased to the S. S. Kresge Company for decades. The Central Park Commons building is listed on the *National Register of Historic Places*.

4. **Alma Hall**
   442 Main Street

The International Order of Odd Fellows built Johnstown's tallest building in 1884. This four-story Queen Anne-style brick building features incised artwork on inset stone blocks, elliptical brick arches, and corbelled brickwork. Office space was rented out on the first and second floors. The third and fourth floors contained meeting halls. It remains the headquarters for Alma Lodge 523 today.

Shielded by the Methodist Episcopal Church, it survived the flood wave in 1889 and gave refuge to 264 people during the night of May 31. Two babies were born on the upper floors of Alma Hall that night with 18 feet of water crushing the walls of the building.

5. **AmeriServ Bank Building**
   southwest corner of Main and Franklin streets

The older 10-story United States Bank Building to the rear was constructed in 1910; the modern addition in the Brutalist style sits heavily on the corner.

TURN RIGHT ON FRANKLIN STREET.

6. Original *Johnstown Tribune* Building
209 Franklin Street

This commercial building was built in 1883 as the home of the *Johnstown Tribune*, a newspaper that had begun in 1853 as the weekly *Cambria Tribune*. It went daily in 1873. The rear wall of the print shop collapsed during the flood but the building survived. And so did the paper. In 1952 it merged with a competing daily, the *Johnstown Democrat*, a paper that traced its roots back to 1863, to form today's *Tribune-Democrat*.

7. 211 Franklin Street

Next door is another survivor of the Johnstown Flood of 1889. The Gothic Revival building was originally the Moses Tailor Shop when it was built in 1884. It has a fleur de lis incised in stone and an elliptical arch.

TURN LEFT ON VINE STREET.

8. Schrader's Florist Shop
510 Vine Street

This is Johnstown's most decorative Second Empire style building, built in 1890. It features a slate mansard roof, stained glass windows and two small second-story corner porches.

TURN AND WALK WEST ON VINE STREET.

9. Conrad Building
301 Franklin Street at Vine Street

Built around 1900, the Conrad Building is a triangular-shaped office building in the Romanesque style. Its features include a massive cornice, open round arches framing the doorways and windows, brick arcading over the upper floor windows and decoratively patterned brickwork.

10. Franklin Street Bridge
Franklin Street, at Vine Street

This 230-foot metal truss bridge, one of many in Johnstown, was built in 1937 to replace an earlier bridge swept away by the 1936 flood.

11. Crown American Building
417 Vine Street

Architect Michael Graves designed the Crown American Building, constructed in 1989. Its classically inspired style draws inspiration from its surrounding brethren.

12. First Methodist Church
436 Spruce Street, at southwest corner of Washington Avenue

Erected in 1911, this rusticated brownstone landmark has a massive 90-foot center tower surrounded by gable and hipped roof pavilions. It sports an Akron style interior, with the entrance in one corner and the pulpit in the opposite. The stained glass windows were produced locally by William Heslop.

13. First Lutheran Church
415 Vine Street

Constructed in 1920 in the Gothic Revival style, the First Lutheran Church presents a skyline of pointed arch windows, a massive corner tower, stained glass windows and stone facing. An earlier Lutheran church around the corner on Franklin Street burned in 1918.

TURN RIGHT ON MARKET STREET.

14. 227 Market Street

Built around 1890, this Second Empire style building retains decorative molded lintels, metal "shingle pattern" roofing and bracketed cornice. It also retains its original use pattern, with retail shops n the ground floor and apartments above.

TURN RIGHT ON MAIN STREET AND WALK DOWN THE SOUTH SIDE OF THE STREET.

15. Lincoln Center
416 Main Street

Inside this modern building is the facade of a Presbyterian church that was dedicated in 1866. The church survived the flood and served afterwards as one of six temporary morgues set up in the valley. Volunteer undertakers from Pittsburgh and other parts of the state embalmed bodies that were brought to the church. Of the 2,209 total dead, 755 were never identified.

In the 1900s the church was converted into a performing center, first the Nemo and later the Embassy. The facade of the old church, including a stained glass window, has been incorporated into the Lincoln Center complex.

CROSS THE STREET AND WALK BACK TOWARDS MARKET STREET.

16. 407 Main Street

Completed in 1920, this Beaux Arts style three-story building was constructed for the Farmers Trust and Mortgage. later, it was used by the Johnstown Savings Bank and the Moxham National Bank.

17. City Hall
northeast corner of Main Street and Market Street

Joseph Johns set aside space on all four corners of this intersection for "parklets." Three remain and only the corner containing City Hall is occupied. Constructed in 1900 to replace an earlier building on this site, the new City Hall held special significance for the community. Here one of the flood's most beneficial changes to the town took place - the consolidation of many of the valley's small boroughs into the City of Johnstown. Before the flood, each borough guarded its governing rights but rebuilding together made more sense and so consolidation was voted in on November 6, 1889.

The city fathers wanted to be sure that the new City Hall, constructed in 1900 to replace an earlier municipal building on the site, symbolized what they believed was the modern, progressive nature of Johnstown. To that end, Charles Robinson of Altoona designed a Richardsonian Romanesque structure, which at the time was the style of choice in America for monumental civic buildings. Walter Myton served as project architect; he designed at least forty residences in the area, along with as many churches, schools, and stores.

A square wooden cupola, rising out of the western end of the roof, contains miniature features found in the larger building, such as false arches with voussoirs and small arched balconies. It also has clock faces on all four sides. Note also the markers on the wall of City Hall, showing high water lines during Johnstown's three worst floods. Flood control measures were taken after the 1936 disaster, yet in 1977, a "once in 500 years" storm caused a flood resulting in 85 deaths and $200 million in damage.

For decades, one of the residents of the parklets around Market and Main streets was Morley's dog, a statue made in the late 1800s by J.W. Fiske Iron Works, a New York City-based maker and retailer of ornamental iron and zinc products. Cambria Iron executive James Morley bought the statue and placed it in his lawn at Main and Walnut, where it stood until being washed away by the floodwaters of May 31, 1889. Recovered in the debris pile, it was returned to Morley. In the 1940s, the statue was donated to the city, and became a beloved icon. It has since been removed in anticipation of needed restoration.

Over time people came to believe that Morley was a dog that saved a child during the great flood. There was such a dog, a Newfoundland named Romey who saved three people, but Morley's Dog has nothing to do with that incident. This misconception was spread further by a reference in the 1977 Paul Newman movie *Slap Shot*, filmed in Johnstown.

18. State Theater
336 Main Street

The State was one of the last theaters built in Johnstown, opening on July 4, 1926. It rapidly became known as the "Million Dollar State. Patrons were greeted in the lobby by an elaborate crystal chandelier made up of 62,000 separate pieces of glass and 164 lights. Three kinds of marble were used for the lobby and the sweeping stairway up to the balcony — cream-colored travertine for the columns, black onyx for the stairway base, and tan tavernelle for the steps. The Wurlitzer theater organ was rumored to have cost $35,000 by itself.

The symmetrical, five-bay, Neoclassical design features a façade constructed entirely of glazed terra-cotta. Six multi-story Corinthian pilasters grace that facade. The top level of windows features projecting moldings, visually supported by brackets and medallions. Above the top level of windows there is a projecting classical cornice supported by dentils and medallions. The façade is topped by a full, classical, five-bay entablature. The panels are separated by engaged pilasters decorated with a medallion.

19. William Horace Rose House
229 Main Street

William Horace Rose, a prominent Johnstown attorney, was seriously injured in the Johnstown Flood and two of his sons were feared lost - all clinging to wreckage as they floated away. The following day the family was reunited and the only Rose casualty was the loss of their home. This ornate Queen Anne style residence was built to replace it. When all the boroughs consolidated into the new City of Johnstown in 1900, Rose was elected the first Mayor.

20. Inclined Plane
Main Street and St. Johns Street

Built after the Johnstown flood of 1889, the Inclined Plane's original purpose was to connect the Westmont Borough area to the downtown to develop that area residentially. During Johnstown's two other floods in 1936 and and 1977, the Incline became a lifesaver for people, helping people to escape downtown as well as to ship supplies in the valley.

In its heyday, the Incline carried approximately 1,000,000 passengers a year to and from the downtown area. This was largely due to the steel mills that were in operation. As better roads were built in the vicinity of the Incline following World War II, use of the railway declined, and it was closed in 1962. In 1984, the Johnstown Inclined Plane was completely rebuilt at a cost of $3.5 million. Today the Incline welcomes visitors and locals alike, carrying approximately 100,000 passengers a year.

The Johnstown Inclined Plane is the steepest vehicular incline in the world, meaning its 30' cars, which are large enough to hold 65 people, 6 motorcycles, or a vehicle, travel at the steepest grade for cars their size.

TURN RIGHT ON JOHNS STREET.

21. The Point

This wedge-shaped tract of land at the junction of the Stoneycreek and Little Conemaugh Rivers was set aside in 1800 by Johnstown's founder, Joseph Johns, for the town's "common and public amusements." Except for occasional baseball games, the Point was used very little before the 1889 flood. Instead, trash was dumped at the Point, narrowing the river channels and increasing the possibility of flooding. Sections of the river also were filled in by the Cambria Iron Company and the Pennsylvania Railroad to gain more ground for tracks and structures. These encroachments led to frequent minor flooding during Johnstown's first century.

Dumping debris into the river was outlawed in 1883, but the law was not enforced. Even if it had been, many other factors contributed to the threatening flood situation which was becoming more and more severe. The rapid growth of population and industry in the valley led to the deforestation of surrounding mountainsides. Without trees, water released by thaws and storms rushed down the slopes, eroding soil which was carried into the rivers and deposited near the Point. Here, the flow of water through the valley was obstructed.

Johnstown suffered seven floods between 1881 and 1889. On May 31, 1889, the Point and the lower end of town already stood in water up to seven feet deep by 1:30 p.m. The main flood wave hit about 4:10 p.m. and wreckage piled up behind the stone railroad bridge, completely covering four acres. It would be the only bridge to survive the flood.

Weeks after the flood, when all debris was cleared, earth dug from the cellars and streets of Johnstown was dumped at the Point, thus raising its height five feet. The concrete walls that now line the rivers were the result of a five year flood control program (1938-1943) which cost more than $8 million. Except for the extraordinary flood of 1977, the widened channels and paved river banks have enabled flood waters to move rapidly through the valley without damaging Johnstown, which understandably has been nicknamed "Flood City."

The current Point Stadium baseball field was

built in 2005 to replace the original Point Stadium, home of the Johnstown Johnnies, that had hosted minor league baseball here since 1926.

TURN RIGHT ON LOCUST STREET. TURN LEFT ON WALNUT STREET.

22. Bethlehem Steel Corporate Office
119 Walnut Street, at northeast corner of Locust Street

Built in the 1950s, this modern office building was one of the last projects undertaken by New York City' most celebrated 19th century architectural firm, McKim, Mead & White. The steel company's original 1911 office building is behind it at 333 Locust Street.

23. Johnstown Flood Museum/Cambria Free Library
304 Washington Street, at southeast corner of Walnut Street

Four months after the devastating 1889 flood, Andrew Carnegie journeyed from Pittsburgh to visit the local steelworks and see the ruins of Johnstown. One of the nation's richest men, he was better known in Johnstown as a member of the South Fork Fishing and Hunting Club. The club was responsible for the South Fork Dam which gave way and sent 20 million tons of water rushing onto the city of Johnstown. This is the site of the former Cambria Library which, along with its librarian, disappeared in the flood waters. Carnegie donated the money to erect a new library on the same site.

The French Gothic style library was designed by Philadelphia architect Addison Hutton; it is the oldest public building in downtown Johnstown. It was similar to Johnstown's first library, which had been financed by the Cambria Iron Company. Like its predecessor, the new Library contained 8,000 standard works and had spacious, comfortable reading rooms. On the third floor there was a gymnasium which included a large exercise track made of padded leather. The library proper was on the second floor. In 1973,the public library moved to a new building and this structure became the Johnstown Flood Museum.

TURN RIGHT ON WASHINGTON STREET.

24. Cambria Iron Company General Office
317 Washington Street

Johnstown, in 1889, was a company town. Some 7,000 men and women worked for Cambria Iron Company and many of them rented one of the 700 company houses throughout the Conemaugh Valley. Groceries and supplies were purchased at the company store and medical attention could be obtained at the company-financed hospital.

In addition to being one of the world's leading steel producers, the company owned thousands of acres of mineral lands, 35 miles of railroad track and some 1,500 railroad cars. The company also held extensive real estate, such as a theater, a company executives' club, shoe and furniture stores, wire, flour, and woolen mills, and several farms located on surrounding hillsides.

This two-building office complex was the business center for the Cambria empire and one of the few structures on this street that survived the 1889 flood. Its two sections, built in 1881 and 1885, reflect the changing popularity in architectural styles. The western section was built first in orderly Palladian symmetry with a hipped roof, stone belt course and stone window surrounds. The eastern section features an asymmetrical massing with large dormers and brownstone detailing designed by prominent Philadelphia architect Addison Hutton.

25. Penn Traffic Building
319 Washington Street

What began as a modest two-story store operating as Stiles, Allen & Company evolved into Johnstown's greatest emporium. During the year of 1865 the store was replaced by a three-story brick structure which was considered the most extensive and best equipped general merchandise establishment within 100 miles. Operating as Wood, Morrell & Co., it was considered Cambria Iron's company store. The largest part of the building was destroyed the Great Flood of 1889.

A larger, grander building under the auspices of Penn Traffic Company was built but on the night of Aug. 28, 1905, it was completely wiped

165

out by a fire which raged from 11 o'clock until the following morning. The current five-story French Renaissance-styled building is attributed to the Buzer Bros. construction firm of Pittsburgh. It features pressed brick walls and semi-glazed white tile details. When it opened it was unsurpassed in beauty and customer comforts by any retail establishment between Philadelphia and Pittsburgh. By a unique architectural device, each floor was separated as to prevent the spread of fire beyond the confines of a single floor.

Additions were made in 1924 and 1949 and the Penn Traffic Building became the largest building in downtown Johnstown, swallowing up an entire block. The Penn Traffic Store closed in 1977 and is now used as an office building and federal court.

26. Public Safety Building
   401 Washington Street

Dating from 1925, the Public Safety Building presents a transition to modern office construction with clean lines and minimal architectural detailing. The ornamentation is limited to bas relief eagles and hard pressed brick walls.

TURN RIGHT ON MARKET STREET.

27. St. Mark's Episcopal Church
   325 Locust Street, at northwest corner of
   Market Street

Responding to her first major disaster since the founding of the American Red Cross in 1881, Clara Barton arrived in Johnstown on June 5, 1889, accompanied by fifty doctors and nurses. At age 67, Miss Barton worked tirelessly for the relief of the valley's survivors. The Red Cross directly served over 25,000 victims of the Johnstown Flood in its first real test for disaster relief. Here, where St. Mark's Episcopal Church now stands, the Red Cross built a hotel for "the wealthy, the elegant, the cultured leaders of society, and the fathers of the town." After finding many of these men homeless and working long hours in the mud and rain to help in the grueling clean-up, Miss Barton reasoned: "As the salvation of the town depended in great measure upon the efforts of these men, it was vitally necessary that their lives should be preserved . . ."

A previous St. Mark's Episcopal Church had stood here until it and its pastor were swept away by the flood. The "Locust Street Red Cross Hotel" was constructed in fast order. On the outside, the hotel looked much like the large Red Cross warehouse only fifty yards away, but on the inside it was homelike and comfortable. It had hot and cold running water, gas heat, and furnishings donated by companies from far and near. The Red Cross relief effort continued in the valley another two months. Clothing, medicine, furniture, and domestic supplies were freely distributed to all flood refugees.

The stone Gothic Revival St. Mark's Church was erected in 1891 and features a corner steeple, pointed arch openings throughout and battlement-type windows. The bell is among several relics salvaged from the original church.

28. Old Johnstown Post Office
   131 Market Street, at southeast corner of
   Locust Street

Designed by James Knox Taylor, the 1912 building incorporates a Classical Revival design. The terra-cotta temple is lined by simple Doric columns, full Classical entablature and four brass plaques representing the seal of the President, the Commonwealth of Pennsylvania, the Department of Justice and the Postal Department.

TURN LEFT ON LOCUST STREET.

29. Mayer Building
   414 Locust Street

This eight-story apartment building with terra-cotta classical details such as keystones, cornice and storefront pilasters was designed by Johnstown architect Walter Myton in 1913.

30. G.A.R. Building
   132 Gazebo Place, at southwest corner of
   Locust Street

The Grand Army of the Republic chapter, which once had more than 300 members, constructed this building in 1893. It features Romanesque details including heavy stone arches and carved stone sculptures of military icons: cannon, artillery and swords.

31. *Tribune-Democrat* Building
425 Locust Street

The *Tribune-Democrat* moved here from Franklin Street in 1919. An annex to the classically-inspired building was constructed around 1940.

32. Ellis Building
435-449 Locust Street, at northwest corner of Franklin Street

The oldest department store building remaining in Johnstown, the Ellis Building was constructed in 1905 in the Romanesque style. It is distinguished by a brick colonnade at the roofline, rounded windows, decorative arches, decorative brickwork, pilasters and projecting bay windows. The 1931 Art Deco addition features vertically aligned window bays and glazed terra-cotta incorporating shell and plant motifs.

33. First Methodist Episcopal Church
131 Franklin Street, at southeast corner of Locust Street

This is the only surviving downtown church that predates the Johnstown Flood. It is famous for having split the flood wave, allowing several buildings on Main Street to avoid a direct smash. The Reverend Henry L. Chapman, pastor of the First Methodist Episcopal Church in 1889, was preparing his Sunday sermon when a B &O Railroad car floated by in front of the parsonage. He rushed his family to the attic. From the attic windows they watched as the row of frame houses down the street was whisked away by the flood waters. "Pale, frightened, and awestricken," they waited through the long night, "expecting each moment to be swept away. "The Chapman family survived mainly because their house stood close to the massive sandstone church, which took the brunt of the flood without a crack in its walls although water broke through the windows and poured into the sanctuary some 18 feet deep, causing the floor to cave in, ruining the plaster, and destroying the choir gallery and numerous pews.

Built in the Gothic Revival style, its design is credited to mill designer and inventor George Fritz. Constructed in 1869, the stone church has a steeply pitched roof, an 80-foot tall corner spire, pointed arch window and door openings, buttresses, and rose windows.

34. Johnstown Post Office
111 Franklin Street, at northeast corner of Locust Street

This is a notable 1938 Art Moderne design by Lorimer Rich and still serves as the town post office. It features a smooth black stone facade, vertical window bays, and iron window frames. The stylized eagle sculpture was a New Deal art project of the Franklin Roosevelt administration.

35. St. John Gualbert Cathedral
117 Clinton Street, at northeast corner of Locust Street

Johnstown's most ornate church appeared on the streetscape in 1896. It combines pressed brick, brownstone and rough-faced terra-cotta. Distinctive ornamentation includes a wheel window, stained glass windows and a huge corner bell tower. Patterned after St. Mark's in Venice, Italy, the church is one of the first examples of the use of structural steel in an ecclesiastical building.

The original St. John's burned during the 1889 Flood. The roiling waters overturned houses that had coal stoves in their kitchens and one crashed into the church with enough smoldering embers to ignite the structure above the waterline.

TURN RIGHT ON CLINTON STREET.

36. Coney Island Lunch
127 Clinton Street

Coney Island was founded in 1916 and has been operated by four generations of the Contacos family.

37. Widmann Building
139 Clinton Street

Built in 1892 by John Widmann, it was originally a grocery. The handsome Romanesque style building includes a rough sandstone exterior, buff and pink sandstone pillars, keystones and stone belt courses.

38. Carnegie Building
605 Main Street, at northeast corner of Clinton Street

The seven-story Carnegie Building was originally the Title Trust and Guarantee Building. This prominent downtown office building has a stone veneer on the first floor and a huge metal bracketed cornice.

TURN RIGHT ON MAIN STREET.

39. Fend Building
542-544 Main Street

This three-story Romanesque-style building, constructed in 1893, is distinguished by its highly detailed brickwork, round arches, decorative tiles, and the blind arcade at the cornice level.

40. Bantley Building
538 Main Street

This building, constructed by Gottlieb Bantley, wasn't even a year old when it was battered by flood water. Some of the tightly-packed commercial buildings on Main Street were able to withstand the force of the water thanks to their accumulated bulk. Here it appears two-thirds of the building survived. The Bantley Building features decorative brickwork and stone lintels and sills.

41. Johnstown Bank & Trust Company
534 Main Street

This ten-story bank and office building, designed in the Classical Revival style with pilasters and cartouches decorating the top floor was built in 1915; the first floor Colonial Revival details were later additions.

42. Woolf & Reynolds Building
526 Main Street

The "Home of Good Clothes," Woolf & Reynolds, opened here in 1908. The popular men's clothing store has a molded metal facade with Classical Revival decorative features and large Chicago style windows.

43. Miller-Zimmerman Block
525 Main Street

The Miller-Zimmerman Block was built in 1890 to house a tailor and menswear shop for Miller and studio space for Zimmerman, a photographer. Note the original, ornate metal cornice.

44. Stenger Store
523 Main Street

Built in 1883, the former Stenger Dry Goods Store features brick corbelling, pilasters and an elaborate metal cornice.

45. J.T. Kelly Building
502 Main Street

Built in 1913, this narrow, three-story building was originally a small restaurant. Built in the Romanesque style, it features rusticate stonework, small marble columns and stained glass windows.

46. Dibert Building
500 Main Street

This Italianate style commercial building was constructed in 1889. It was started by David Dibert, who perished in the Johnstown Flood, and completed by his son, Scott. It features arches at the third and fourth floors, arched windows, incised brickwork, tapestry brickwork, a corner turret, and an intact cast-iron cornice.

YOU HAVE NOW RETURNED TO THE TOUR STARTING POINT AT CENTRAL PARK.

Look Up,

Kennett Square

A Walking Tour of Kennett Square...

The name Kennett originates with Francis Smith who came to this region in 1686. He was a native of Devizes, in Wiltshire, England, in which there is a village called "Kennet." The name is first mentioned in court records in 1705. In the seventeenth and eighteenth centuries Kennett was a small village located where the road from Chester to Baltimore intersected with the road from Lancaster to Wilmington. It was at this intersection that the Unicorn Tavern was built in 1735 by Joseph Musgrave, the largest landowner in what is now Kennett Square. In 1776 Musgrave sold his property to Colonel Joseph Shippen, the uncle of Peggy Shippen, who became the wife of Benedict Arnold. His later treachery was said to be inspired by a need to keep her in the style she was born to.

Travelers found the village a good place to stop, including Baron Wilhelm van Knyphausen and General Sir William Howe, who stayed for one night before marching to the Battle of the Brandywine against George Washington at Chadds Ford in 1777. By 1810 there was a village of about eight dwellings, five of which were log, but it was not until 1853 that a group of citizens petitioned the Court of Quarter Sessions of Chester to form a borough. Antebellum Kennett was an important region in the Underground Railroad, and many prominent citizens of Kennett Square and the surrounding region played an important role in securing freedom for runaway slaves.

It was in Kennett Square that the grain drill was invented by Samuel and Moses Pennock (patented on March 12, 1841), and improvements for the corn sheller and harvester (1857), and the first four-wheel road machine (1877). Other local inventors included James Green (a hayknife), Bernard Wiley (the famous Wiley Plow), John Chambers (an asbestos stove plate), and Cyrus Chambers (a machine for folding papers and a brickmaking machin)e. It was on the Chamber's property that the first circular saw was built in 1835. Another large business was the Fibre Specialty Manufacturing Company, later known as NVF, which built its first plant in Kennett Square in 1898 and is now closed.

Kennett Square's most famous citizen was Bayard Taylor. a nineteenth-century author, diplomat, poet, and journalist who published over forty books, including *Views A-foot*, *Eldorado*, a translation of Faust (which Mark Twain called the best of all English translations), and a local favorite, *The Story of Kennett*. Bayard Taylor died in Berlin while serving as Minister to Germany.

Our walking tour will start one block north of the Town center at State Street and Union Street where there is a municipal parking garage...

1. **The Brosius House**
    119 East Linden Street

Edwin Brosius built a pottery at the corner of Broad and Linden streets around 1844. The Brosius home serves as a fine example of the Federal style, having been updated later in the century. The more modern Italianate details of the structure are seen in the ornate bracketed cornice and the iron porch with the balcony above. An added wooden porch protects the center doorway with its sidelights and transom on the south elevation.

2. **District Court and Old Ben Butler**
    southwest corner of East Linden and
    North Broad streets

The official opening of the former municipal building was April 17, 1939. The building was completed by WPA labor. In 1861 Bayard Taylor presented the home guard of Kennett Square with a cannon cast at the Pennock Foundry at State & Willow Streets. It became known as "Old Ben Butler," fired to hail Union victories in the Civil War.

3. **The Walls House**
    219 East Linden Street

At the turn of the 20th century the house served as parsonage for a church next door. Later it was the home of Dr. Orville R. Walls, a graduate of the Meharry Medical School in Nashville, Tennessee in 1936.

4. **Bethel A.M.E. Church**
    301 East Linden Street

Early records show that a number of free blacks had owned land in the town of Kennett Square from as early as the 1850s. The African Methodist Episcopalian Church was officially founded in 1894. A lot was purchased on East Linden Street and a building was erected and dedicated in July, 1895. The structure underwent extensive renovations in 1973, although the fine example of a federal steeple is still evident at the south end.

5. **New Garden Church**
    309 East Linden Street

On September 4, 1824, the Union African Methodist Episcopalian Church purchased one acre of land from Joseph Broman for $50 at Buck Toe Hill in New Garden Township. A log building constructed on the site was later destroyed by fire, and was replaced by a stone building. In 1904, property was purchased on East Linden Street and a new building erected with the stone from the original church. The new church was dedicated on February 18, 1911.

6. **The Vincent Barnard House**
    315 East Linden Street

Vincent Barnard, 1825-1871, was a local naturalist who came to Kennett Square to work for Samuel Pennock, and whose daughter Joanna, he married. At the time of his death he had a two-acre botanical garden containing numerous rare and indigenous specimens of trees and flowers.

TURN RIGHT ON WILLOW STREET.
TURN RIGHT ON STATE STREET.

7. **The Kennett Square Inn**
    201 East State Street

Built between 1820 and 1839, this structure is a combination of a two-bay Penn plan on the west side and a four-bay Federal plan on the east side.

TURN LEFT ON BROAD STREET.
TURN LEFT ON APPLE ALLEY.

8. **Hicks-Schmaltz House**
    120 South Marshall Street

Built before 1908 in the Queen Anne style by Harry K. Hicks, this home is characterized by its eclectic mix of contrasting materials and patterns: the use of stucco, clapboard, decorative shingles, and half-timbering. Hermann Schmaltz, a native of Germany, came to America in 1884. In 1903, he settled in Kennett Square, where he owned and operated a hardware, plumbing and heating business, and later moved into the Hicks house. Today it is home to Borough offices.

TURN RIGHT ON MARSHALL STREET.

9. Sharpless Lewis House
211 Marshall Street

Most of the original features of this Stick style house are intact, although the stucco on the second floor was originally wood. Automation of wood working allowed for mass production of decorative elements.

10. Eli & Lewis Thompson House
221 Marshall Street

This 1882 Gothic house has wooden posts and scrolled brackets trimming the first floor porch. A barn which is approximately the same age as the house occupies the property as well. Eli Thompson was the father-in-law of William Swayne who built his greenhouses across the street. Swayne was not only a successful florist, but along with Harry Hicks, built the first mushroom house in Kennett Square in 1885, laying the skids for Kennett Square to become "Mushroom Capital of the World."

11. Roberts House
222 Marshall Street

This home is Queen Anne/Gothic stick style built about 1880. A gambrel-roofed cross gable has a decorative pendant and a window with a Gothic arch. A one-story shed roofed porch has chamfered posts and open brackets.

TURN RIGHT ON SOUTH BROAD STREET. WALK OF THE EAST SIDE OF THE STREET.

12. Chandler House
219 South Broad Street; northeast corner of Juniper Street

This house was built by Samuel D. Chandler, a local pharmacist, in the Second Empire style. Note the three distinct slate patterns in the mansard roof - diamond, brick, and fish-scale. The detailed and carved cornices are similar to the closely related Italianate style.

13. Presbyterian Parsonage (Manse)
213 South Broad Street

Built in about 1884 in the Stick Style, this brick house is an excellent example of its type and appears to retain nearly all its original exterior features including roof and porch trim. Note the drop-finial at the apex and bargeboards with unique bulls-eye detail at the porch eaves, the Gothic window beneath the apex detail, and the type of bonding used between brick courses. It was used as a parsonage for the church next door until the 1960s.

14. The Presbyterian Church of Kennett Square
211 South Broad Street

In the early 1860s when Kennett Square numbered between 500 and 600 people, the Lower Brandywine Presbyterian Church organized when there was but one Presbyterian living in the town. In 1865 a brick building was erected at a cost of $6,200. The major portion of the present stone church was built between 1909-1916. The building was further remodeled in 1928, after a damaging fire.

CROSS THE STREET AND WALK BACK DOWN THE WEST SIDE OF SOUTH BROAD STREET TOWARDS JUNIPER STREET.

15. United Methodist Church of the Open Door
210 South Broad Street

This church is now home to Methodists but in the past has been a Lutheran Church and before that, an Episcopal Church. Note the variety of patterns and character of the slate roof, modified buttresses, and Gothic windows.

16. McMullen-Walton House
216 South Broad Street

The house was built in 1869 by Joseph McMullen, a Burgess of Kennett Square. The decorative trusses in the gables are a common architectural detail in town. This one is in the form of a rising sun, a popular symbol for a rising country.

17. Gregg House
307 South Broad Street

This two-and-a-half story brick house house dates to the early 1900s when A.W. Gregg, a physician, lived at this address. This is in the Queen Anne style, notable for its large and irregular shape. Note the upper balcony and lamp black used in the mortar. The gable also uses the sun motif.

18. Isaac Pyle House
312 South Broad Street

This 1870 house has beautiful filigree ironwork and a striped "circus tent" tin porch roof, a popular decorative effect.

19. Kennett Square Academy
313 South Broad Street

This large building is three stories high above a raised basement, and has a flat roof with projecting cornice. Stucco now covers the exterior brick walls. It was built in 1870 as Swithin C. Shortlidge's Kennett Square Academy for Young Men and Boys and Kennett Seminary for Young Ladies and Girls.

20. Mary Phillips House
318 South Broad Street

Now apartments, this 1871 Gothic-inspired house was the boyhood home of Hall-of-Fame baseball pitcher Herb Pennock. Pennock was born in Kennett Square on February 10, 1894 and began his 22-year big league career at the age of 18, winning 241 games, most with the powerhouse New York Yankee teams of the 1920s.

21. Woodward House
332 South Broad Street

This house was built in 1858 by Thomas Pyle for the Woodward family, resembling Colonial houses across the street at 323 and 325 South Broad Street. In about 1888, the exterior got a drastic facelift under the guidance of a Dutch architect who had recently come to town. At this time, the tower, circular porch, and Victorian gingerbread were added.

22. Gawthrop House
402 South Broad Street

This house was built in 1879 by James Gawthrop, founder a coal and lumber business. An eclectic combination of Queen Anne and Stick styles, it is one of the more unusual houses in the Historic District. Particularly interesting is the six-sided turret with the original cap. Note the Gothic window in the gable peak on the facade, and the cross gable filled with lattice work above the entrance. Heavy turned posts connected by a wooden balustrade, support the roof of the wrap-around porch.

TURN RIGHT ON MULBERRY STREET. TURN RIGHT ON SOUTH UNION STREET.

23. Catherine Reed House
401 South Union Street

Once the home of Catherine Reed, a seamstress, the entrances in the central bays are topped by transoms. A wooden balustrade connects the heavy turned posts with solid brackets which support the flat roof and its wraparound porch.

24. Lamborn House
341 South Union Street

This stucco house was originally brick and had an iron gate around the property. This house was built by Emma Taylor Lamborn, a sister of Bayard Taylor. It was here that their mother died in 1890. Note the ocular window. The original brick sidewalks still remain.

25. Kirk House
316 South Union Street

This is a brick house with wrap-around porch. Note the bonding mid-way between the second story and the barn in the rear of the property.

26. Philips-Grason House
306 South Union Street

This is a large Victorian house built in the Queen Anne style. Of special note are the beautiful tulip-shaped porch railing, stain glass windows, and three-story tower with conical slate roof. There is a large carriage house in the rear alley.

27. Lydia Walton House
231 South Union Street

This 1860s house was the home of Lydia Walton, elected in 1869 to the post of school director. Since 1908, as stipulated in her will, $40 annually has been distributed to buy shoes and mittens for needy children in the borough. Next door, at 233 South Union Street, is the former site of The Walker House, home of James Walker, who played a role in the Underground Railroad in antebellum Kennett Square.

28. Samuel Pennock House
222 South Union Street

Cypress Lawn was built in 1864 by Samuel Pennock, founder of the American Road Machine Company and inventor of the snow plow and various road grading machines. The house has a Queen Anne porch which was added later.

29. Dr. Sumner Stebbins House
221 South Union Street

Dr. Sumner Stebbins was a noted doctor, temperance orator, and abolitionist. His wife, Mary Ann Peirce, was the daughter of Joshua Peirce, who, along with his twin brother, began the planting of the arboretum known as Peirce's Park, which later became part of Longwood Gardens. Another noted resident of this house was William Marshall Swayne, an artist and sculptor. In 1878, he completed a plaster bust of local author Bayard Taylor, which is now prominently displayed in the Bayard Taylor Memorial Library. Another of Swayne's outstanding works was a bust of Abraham Lincoln. This Victorian home was built in 1845.

30. Samuel Martin House
209-211 South Union Street

Samuel Martin started his career in Kennett as a school teacher and went on to build many of its houses and a school.

31. Pyle House
208 South Union Street

This Queen Anne style house dates from about 1907, and has one of the most outstanding porches in town. Also of note is the octagonal tower and gable-roofed dormers with multi-pane windows.

32. Entrikin House,
204 South Union Street

This house dates from about 1907 and is in the Queen Anne style. Note the hexagonal dormer with peaked roof which faces the street.

33. Garage Community & Youth Center
115 South Union Street

This car garage, built in 1923, was vacant when a local business leader and youth pastor set about renovating the building to provide services for young people. The Garage Community & Youth Center is the only place in Kennett Square that is open just for middle and high school students.

34. Genesis HealthCare
northeast corner of State Street and Union Street

Here, on September 11, 1777, 12,000 British and 5,000 Hessian troops gathered prior to marching east for what later became known as the Battle of the Brandywine. On the northwest corner was the site of the oldest building in Kennett Square, the Unicorn Tavern, and on the southeast corner was the site of Bayard Taylor's birthplace. On the northeast corner was the original site of Evan P. Green's mercantile store, and later the Chalfant Block. The structure was razed in 1996, and the present building constructed as the national headquarters of Genesis HealthCare. In the tower of the office building are three faces of the original workings of the Kennett Town Clock.

35. Miller-Hannum House
200 North Union Street

This Federal-style house dates from 1820. It has a dormer with a segmentally-arched roof and brick dentillated trim the cornice. The windows can be opened from the bottom and act as a walk through.

36. Chalfant Mansion
   220 North Union Street

A fine example of Queen Anne architecture attributed to the firm of Frank Furness, the ornate north aspect date stone is inscribed "WSC 1884." Note the elaborate corbeled brickwork on the three chimneys, restored in 1987.

37. M. Ellen Taylor House
   233 North Union Street

This Queen Anne/Stick style house, built in 1876 on land deeded to her by her father Joshua, has a gable roof with large cross gable on the facade tops. Fish-scale wood shingles cover a two-story bay window at the side and the cross gable. Ellen was Bayard Taylor's first cousin.

38. Gilmore-Marshall-Pennock House
   234 North Union Street

"Robinhurst" was built in 1859 in the Federal style, and was once the home of Charles Pennock, local banker and well-known ornithologist. He was an eccentric who suffered amnesia, disappeared, and resurfaced in Florida under an assumed name. He eventually returned to Kennett. Behind the house is a large wooden carriage house with lacy barge boards and a steep gable roof.

39. Joshua Taylor House
   315 North Union Street

Fairthorn is the oldest house in the historic district, and was the home of Bayard Taylor's grandparents. The house served as the setting for his novel *The Story of Kennett*, written in 1866.

TURN AROUND AND WALK BACK DOWN NORTH UNION STREET TO THE TOUR STARTING POINT AT THE PARKING GARAGE ON LINDEN STREET.

Look Up,

Lancaster

A Walking Tour of Lancaster...

Most of the land that would become the City of Lancaster was owned by Andrew Hamilton. The settlement here was known as "Hickory Town" and dated to 1709. Andrew's son James was deeded 500 acres of this land in 1733, and designed the layout of the city in a plan of straight streets and rectangular property lots. Still very much linking to England, the new town adopted the symbol of the red rose from the mother country. The town became a borough in 1742 and a chartered city in 1818.

During the Revolutionary War, Lancaster was an important munitions center, and when the British captured Philadelphia the Continental Congress headed here, the largest inland city in America at the time. The Congress only stayed a day, however, September 27, 1777, before moving on to York where they could put the Susquehanna River between themselves and the British.

The colonial city owed its early prosperity to its strategic position at a transportation crossroads. After the American Revolution, the city of Lancaster became an iron-foundry center. Two of the most common products needed by pioneers to settle the frontier were manufactured in Lancaster: the Conestoga wagon, named after the Conestoga River that flows through the city, and the Pennsylvania long rifle.

In 1795 the Philadelphia and Lancaster Turnpike opened, linking the two cities. It was considered the first engineered long-distance road in the United States, designed by Scottish engineer John Loudon MacAdam. It became the first paved road in the country and later a link in the Lincoln Highway, the nation's first transcontinental road.

Our walking tour will head right down that historic road in the center of Lancaster, starting in a town square that existed in the original platting of the town as "Centre Square" but is known today as Penn Square...

1. *Soldiers and Sailors Monument*
    northeast corner of Penn Square at King Street and Queen Street

The Soldier and Sailor Monument has stood as the symbolic centerpiece of Lancaster since July 4, 1874. The monument's original intention was to pay tribute to Lancastrian Union soldiers killed during the Civil War but has since come to represent those killed in all American conflicts. The monument stands on the exact spot where the Second Continental Congress met during the Revolutionary War on September 27, 1777, in the old Lancaster Courthouse. The courthouse burned down in 1784. Lewis Haldy designed the 43-foot tall Gothic Revival monument of Rhode Island granite.

CROSS THE STREET TO THE LANCASTER VISITORS CENTER AND BEGIN YOUR TOUR OF PENN SQUARE, WALKING CLOCKWISE.

2. **The Lancaster Cultural History Museum**
    13 West King Street

Originally commissioned as "a public office house" in 1795, this three-and-one-half-story brick building laid in Flemish bond, is one of Lancaster's most important Georgian structures. The building features decorative accents cut in stone, including arches, keystones and belt courses. The business of the Commonwealth was conducted here when Lancaster was the capital of the state from 1799 to 1812 and later served as Lancaster's City Hall from 1854 until 1930. Now a museum and visitor center, it has also been used as a Masonic lodge meeting hall, a post office and a library. It is the oldest building on Penn Square.

3. **Central Market**
    northwest corner of Penn Square

A market has operated in this vicinity since Lancaster's founding in 1730, making Central Market the oldest continuously operating farmer's market in the United States. The current building dates to 1889 and was constructed of locally produced brick with twin towers and a centered

gable. One of the best examples of Romanesque Revival architecture in Lancaster County, it sits on a a base of rock-faced brownstone with similar decoration given to window heads and sills. It was designed by Philadelphia architect James H. Warner.

4. **Griest Building**
    8 North Queen Street

At 14 stories and 187 feet, the Griest Building is Lancaster's only classical skyscraper. Faced in Indiana limestone and terra-cotta on the top two floors, it was designed in the Beaux Arts style in 1925 by Lancaster's most prominent architect C. Emlen Urban. There are Corinthian pilasters at the ground level and at the twelfth floor. When constructed the Griest Building was a showcase of local craftsmanship; the interior featured a large two-story lobby with Tennessee marble floors and Italian marble railings and wall bases. The walls and ceilings were decorated with fresco-covered plaster. The original interior design has been significantly altered.

William Walton Griest was an influential Republican Congressman and president of the Lancaster Public Utilities. The Hirsch Building was demolished to make way for this building at the town's most important intersection in 1924. It was constructed to house the offices of The Conestoga Traction Company, The Edison Electric Company, and The Lancaster Gas Light and Fuel Company.

CROSS OVER QUEEN STREET AND KING STREET TO CONTINUE AROUND PENN SQUARE.

5. **Lancaster County Convention Center**
    southeast corner of Penn Square

Anchoring Downtown Lancaster and boldly incorporating the 110-year-old Beaux Arts facade of the historic former Watt & Shand department store, the integrated convention center / hotel facility offers a combined 90,000 square feet of meeting space and the latest technology for conventions, events, and trade shows. Designed by C. Emlen Urban with four imposing stories of buff brick with elaborate terra-cotta and marble ornamentation, this Watt & Shand icon anchored the downtown retail area from 1898 until 1995. The original Watt & Shand store opened on this site in 1878. Its towering columns and ornate facade are a distinguished example of the Beaux-Arts style often used by Urban. Major additions extending west toward South Queen Street were built between 1916 and 1925.

EXIT PENN SQUARE BY WALKING SOUTH ON QUEEN STREET.

6. Jasper Yeates House
24-26 South Queen Street

Built by John Miller, a blacksmith, hardware merchant, land speculator, and founder of the nearby town of Millersville, this Georgian house was built from 1765-1766 and considered the finest in town in its day. The exterior design illustrates the close relation of high-style Lancaster architecture to its Philadelphia relatives.

Two hundred years later the building was no longer recognizable as the one that graced pre-Revolutionary Lancaster streets. A fourth story was added in 1882 and a modern storefront was installed in the 1950s. A major restoration in the 1970s restored the building to its original appearance. It carries the name of Jasper Yeates, attorney and judge, and a delegate to the Pennsylvania Convention for ratification of the United States Constitution in 1787. Yeates lived here from 1775 to 1817.

7. William Montgomery House
19-21 South Queen Street

This townhouse, thoroughly restored, is one of Lancaster's finest Federal period mansions. Built circa 1804 for William Montgomery, it is the only documented local work by architect Stephen Hills, designer of the first Capitol building in Harrisburg. William Montgomery was a prominent Lancaster attorney with numerous real estate investments. In 1820, he purchased Rock Ford, the former home of General Edward Hand located in Lancaster's Central Park, for use as a tenant farm. The parapeted chimney and fanlight window on the south gable wall are original.

8. Home and Office of Thaddeus Stevens
45-47 South Queen Street

Another complete restoration has brought this building back to the days when it was the home and law office of Lancaster attorney, U.S. Congressman, and abolitionist Thaddeus Stevens from 1843 until his death in 1868. During the presidency of Abraham Lincoln, Stevens served as chairman of the powerful House Ways and Means Committee. After the Civil War, he led the Radical Republicans and pushed for strict enforcement of civil rights for freed African Americans, guiding the passage of the Thirteenth and Fourteenth Amendments.

9. Southern Market
100 South Queen Street at southwest corner of Vine Street

The Farmers' Southern Market is the only one of the four major private markets constructed during the 19th century that has remained largely intact. Built in the Queen Anne style in 1888, this large, richly detailed markethouse was the first major work by architect C. Emlen Urban, designed when he was only 25 years old. With a width of 90 feet and a length of 250 feet, this large building is spanned by an arched roof. The corner towers have pyramidal roofs with dormer windows. The date "1888" appears in terra-cotta within the center pediment, flanked by round medallions containing the heads of a bull and ram -- appropriate ornamentation for a former farmers' market.

RETRACE YOUR STEPS ONE BLOCK TO KING STREET AND TURN RIGHT.

10. 18 East King Street

Throughout the nineteenth century and for much of the first half of the twentieth, this first block of East King boasted numerous businesses selling varied merchandise, including shoes, hardware, fruit, groceries, china, furniture, wine, carpets, jewelry and dry goods. This building dates to about 1910 and housed the Stauffer & Breneman clothing store in the 1920s, followed in the 1930s by a men's clothing store owned by Edwin

Piersol. The letter "E" that appears in the carved cartouche on the parapet may stand for Piersol, or his wife Elizabeth. The brick storefront façade is an alteration but the second and third floors are likely original.

11. Lancaster County Courthouse
43 East King Street

This is the third county courthouse; the first two brick buildings stood a block away on Penn Square. The oldest section of this monumental cut-stone building was designed by Samuel Sloan, a nationally respected Philadelphia architect, in the Roman Revival temple form in the 1850s. The T-shaped rear wing was added in 1896 from the pen of local architect James H. Warner. Warner, who designed the Central Market, matched the materials and details of Sloans' original building. In 1927, two wings flanking the exterior staircase were built from designs by C. Emlen Urban to blend with the previous construction. The cupola contains a clock with four dials and a statue of *Justice* holding scales sits atop the central dome.

12. Farmer's Trust Company
46-52 East King Street

Built for the Farmer's Trust Company in 1929 and designed by Lancaster architect Melvern R. Evans, this bank building reflects the Georgian Revival style of the early twentieth century. The façade of this brick building features three dormers on the mansard roof, set behind a cement balustrade. Two large windows flank the center entry door, which is topped by a decorative cement swag.

TURN RIGHT ON DUKE STREET.

13. Trinity Lutheran Church
31 South Duke Street

Formally organized in 1730, Trinity is the oldest church in Lancaster and one of the oldest in Pennsylvania. The congregation worshiped in a small stone church on Duke of Cumberland Street for thirty years. Construction of the present brick building began in 1761. In 1766 the new church was dedicated with Henry Melchior Muhlenberg, the patriarch of the Lutheran Church in America,

officiating. The 195-foot tower was added to the Georgian rectangular building in 1794, and the two vestibules were added in 1853.

RETURN TO EAST KING STREET AND TURN RIGHT.

14. Hotel Weber
105 East King Street

The Buck Tavern operated on this site as early as 1765, and later served as the Leopard Hotel until the property was purchased by Samuel R. Weber in 1903. He built the Hotel Weber which later became the King Douglas. The building continued to function as a hotel through the 1980s.

15. 110-112 East King Street

The oldest sections of this building pre-date the American Revolution. The arched dormer windows with applied keystones reflect high-style from the 1700s, while the bracketed cornice beneath the roof reflects a remodeling in the 1800s. The row of shopfront-residences at 106 through 124 East King all pre-date 1810, representing the largest group of buildings from this period still surviving within the city.

16. Demuth Tobacco Shop
114-116 East King Street

This is believed to be the oldest tobacco shop in the country owned continuously by the same family. Established by Christopher Demuth in 1770, it was first remodeled about 1840, and a Victorian store-front was added about 1875. It was remodeled again in 1917 in the Colonial Revival style, designed by C. Emlen Urban.

17. Demuth Foundation
118-120 East King Street

John Messencope, a blacksmith, built this house around 1760. He operated the William Pitt, Earl of Chatham tavern here. By the late 1800s, the building was owned by H.C. Demuth, proprietor of the tobacco store next door. The renowned modernist artist Charles Demuth moved with his family from 109 North Lime Street to this house in 1889, at the age of six, and died here in 1935. The building now houses the Demuth Museum, accessed through a side alleyway leading to the rear courtyard and gardens.

18. Bausman House
121 East King Street

William Bausman, a German settler, created this cut-sandstone five-bay façade house with Georgian features in 1762; it is unique in an area dominated by brick buildings. Bausman became prominent in Lancaster's Colonial-era government and served as Chief Burgess (a position comparable to the modern office of mayor) and also ran a tavern next door. A datestone lies between two second-floor windows and, at the corner of the cornice, the sculpted head of an "eavesdropper" peers down at pedestrians.

19. Messencope House
124 East King Street

Built as a residence in 1802, this structure is one of the latest pure Georgian house styles in Lancaster City. Although the first-floor façade was altered in the 1870s, its Georgian features were restored in 1978. Showing how new and old architecture can sympathetically co-exist in Lancaster, the adjoining brick building at 126 East King, housing law offices, was constructed in 1983-1984.

20. Excelsior Hall
125 East King Street

John Sprenger established a brewery on this site in the 1850s. In 1873, he built Excelsior Hall next door, which functioned as a beer hall, public hall, meeting hall, and occasional hotel. The family lost the properties, some of the most valuable private holdings in the town at a sheriff's sale in 1880, and the Sprenger Brewery moved to a new site at South Lime and Locust Streets. Meanwhile this became home to the Westenberger, Maley, and Myers furniture store. Excelsior Hall's ornate Victorian façade and mansard roof were restored by the City of Lancaster in the 1990s.

21. Sign of the Ship
171 East King Street

This Colonial tavern, built in 1761, picked up a Victorian storefront and third-story mansard roof a century later. In the 1880s, the property housed George Brady's bread and cake bakery; the baking was done in the rear wing along North Lime Street. Fisher & Brothers grocery store became the occupant in the 1890s. The building was severely damaged by fire in 2002 but was quickly restored.

22. 204 East King Street

This is the oldest building on the block, erected in the 1780s. It was a fashionable home as evidenced by the dormer windows with rounded tops, keystones over the windows, the belt course between the first and second floors, and a brick watertable. The house seen today is the result of an enlargement in 1815.

23. 208 East King Street

This little building only dates to the 1920s and is a whimsical example of the Colonial Revival style that gripped America in the beginning of the last century. There is a broken pediment over the entry door, topped with an urn. Just above is a miniature three-part Palladian window. The windows, including the modern glass storefronts on the ground floor are decorated with stone keystones and angled bricks.

24. 212-212A East King Street

This building was constructed in 1860, but picked up its current Romanesque form in the 1890s when architect C. Emlen Urban moved here. Urban lived in this building until 1914.

25. Moose Home
224 East King Street

This two-story, multi-hued brick meeting hall was built in 1931. Its Colonial Revival façade is characterized by the twin arched entries and concrete ornamentation above the windows and doors.

26. William Peiper Mansion
235 East King Street

This was the home of Colonel William Peiper, cashier of the Lancaster County National Bank. He started the house, constructed of red pressed brick, in 1879 but died suddenly in 1881 before it could be finished. His widow took on the task of putting the finishing touches of a rare Eastlake house in Lancaster. The façade presents elaborate brownstone carvings, incised trim around the windows, and use of ornamental iron. After Mrs. Peiper's death in 1914 the building was sold to a local fraternal organization.

27. Eastern Market
308 East King Street

Built on the site of the Colonial-era Indian Queen tavern, this is one of five Victorian-era markethouses that once served Lancaster. Constructed in 1883 in the Second Empire style with a three-story corner tower and bell-curved roof, it was designed by builder-architect John Evans. When first opened, Eastern Market contained 168 farmers' stalls and 23 butchers' stalls. When Eastern Market closed in 1927, large plate-glass display windows were added and it was used as an automobile salesroom. An outdoor summer farmer's market was reintroduced at the site in 2006.

28. Fairmount Hotel
402 East King Street

Edward Stewart built this brick inn in 1807; the oldest structure along the 400 block. The dormer windows and brick watertable are original. It continued to operate almost 200 years - until 2002 - and is one of Lancaster's few early tavern buildings that still survives.

29. 409 East King Street

This excellent Colonial Revival example from the early 1900s has an elliptical fanlight and leaded-glass sidelights surrounding the entry door, an address stone to the left of the doorway, and an oval 1915 datestone on the gable-end wall above the side porch.

30. 419 East King Street

Dating from 1895, this brick building is an excellent example of the Chateauesque style, resembling a castle or French chateau, with a steep pyramidal roof and a railing along the ridge, and beige cut-stone frames surrounding the windows and door. Part of the eastern section of the original building was demolished to make way for construction of the adjacent movie theatre.

31. King Theater
423 East King Street

Built between 1948 and 1950 as the King Theatre, this Art Deco entertainment center featured marble decoration at the lobby entry. The tall front wall makes this one-story building appear to have a second floor, while the brickwork in the central section gives the wall an accordion-like appearance. The theater was converted into 43 senior citizen apartments about 1990.

TURN AND WALK ONE-HALF BLOCK BACK TO PLUM STREET AND TURN RIGHT. TURN LEFT ON ORANGE STREET.

32. Colonial Mansion
northwest corner of Orange Street and Shippen Street

This house, of true Georgian style, was built about 1750. John Passmore, first mayor of Lancaster, occupied the house at one time.

TURN RIGHT ON SHIPPEN STREET. TURN LEFT ON MARION STREET. TURN RIGHT ON LIME STREET.

33. Lancaster Mansion of Art
135 North Lime Street

Currently the home of the Lancaster Museum of Art, the Grubb Mansion is one of Lancaster County's best examples of the Greek Revival style. It was built in 1845 by ironmaster Clement Bates Grubb. The house still sits on its own city block, now known as Musser Park. The museum was founded in 1965 in the building.

WALK SOUTH ON LIME STREET
BACK TO ORANGE STREET AND
CROSS IT.

34. John Black Mansion
47 North Lime Street

This is one of the few examples of the Greek Revival style in Lancaster. Built in 1852, classical details include the entry porch supported by thick Tuscan columns and the sidelights flanking the front door. The house was remodeled in the 1880s to add elements of the newly fashionable Queen Anne style, including the multi-paned window sash and ornamental chimneys.

35. Frank Furness House
24 North Lime Street

This is Lancaster's only known work by the celebrated Philadelphia Victorian architect Frank Furness. Furness was famous for his picturesque train stations, banks, churches and ornate homes. This L-shaped brick house from 1886-1888 features a combination of gabled and hipped roofs, a side porch with bracketed posts, and a sandstone water table.

WALK NORTH ON LIME STREET
BACK TO ORANGE STREET AND
TURN LEFT.

36. Shippen House
northwest corner of Orange Street and Lime Street

This is the site of a house occupied from 1751-1781 by Edward Shippen; lawyer, judge, Chairman Committee of Observation, and grand-father of Peggy Shippen, who would marry Benedict Arnold. An earlier occupant was Thomas Cookson, first Burgess of Lancaster Borough.

37. Reuben Baer Mansion
141 East Orange Street

This residence was built in 1874 for Reuben Baer, a partner in the firm that published the popular *Baer's Almanac*. It is Lancaster's best example of an asymmetrical Italianate villa.

38. First Presbyterian Church
140 East Orange Street

The earliest mention of a Presbyterian ministry in Lancaster dates from 1742. For many years, services were held in the first Lancaster County Courthouse in Penn Square. The church acquired part of its present lot in 1763, and the first building on the site was built in 1770. The current Greek Revival building was built in 1851. President James Buchanan and Congressman Thaddeus Stevens were both members here.

39. Hamilton Club
106 East Orange Street

Named in honor of James Hamilton, a prominent political figure in Colonial America and planner of the City of Lancaster, the Hamilton Club was founded in 1889 with an original membership of 31. This is the club's third home, purchased in 1912. It was constructed in 1890 as a private residence for Catherine Haldeman Long and is considered the earliest domestic example of the Chateauesque style in Lancaster County.

40. St. James Episcopal Church
119 North Duke Street, at northeast corner of East Orange Street

The congregation was founded in 1744 and the original structure was built between 1746 and 1753; this building was begun in 1820 in the Federal style but was covered in the 1880s with dark pressed brick to give it a Romanesque look. George Ross, signer of the Declaration of Independence, was vestryman. Buried in the walled cemetery, just west of Cherry Street, are the patriots Edward Shippen, William Atlee, Edward Hand, and Jasper Yeates. It is the most intact eighteenth-century cemetery within city limits.

41. Reformed Church
40 East Orange Street

A congregation of German, Swiss, and French settlers formed about 1729 and the log church they built here in 1736 was Lancaster's first. It was followed by a stone building in 1753 and this brick church in 1854. Philip Otterbein, William Hendel, and Henry Harbaugh were pastors.

TURN RIGHT ON QUEEN STREET.
TURN LEFT ON CHESTNUT
STREET.

42. Davidson Building
11-17 West Chestnut Street

This golden brick store and apartment building was designed by C. Emlen Urban and constructed in 1898 for Long and Davidson, wholesale shoe dealers, It features terra-cotta decorations and a metal cornice.

43. Miller & Hartman Building
21-23 West Chestnut Street

Built in 1873 as Miller & Hartman, wholesale grocery store and warehouse, this building has Lancaster's only intact cast iron storefront.

44. Lancaster Post Office
50 West Chestnut Street

A monumental Beaux Arts building constructed in 1929, this building displays classical motifs of pilasters, dentiled cornice and stylized eagle on its limestone façade.

Detour: To see some of Lancaster's most beautiful Victorian residences, continue on Chestnut Street; otherwise turn left on Prince Street and pick up the tour at Stop 54.

45. St. John's Episcopal Church
321 West Chestnut Street, at northwest corner of Mulberry Street

St. John's was founded in 1853 at its present location on Chestnut and Mulberry Streets. It was the first Episcopal congregation in Pennsylvania to be established without a pew rental system, and so was called St. John's Free Church. Wealthy and poor parishioners were able to come together as equals in their worship of God, an unusual practice at that time for Episcopal congregations. The original brick Gothic church building was constructed in 1853 and rebuilt in 1938, after a fire. The Parish House, located just to the west, is an excellent example of Gothic residential architecture.

46. Thaddeus Stevens Girls High School
northeast corner of Chestnut and Charlotte streets

This beautiful three-story building was designed in the Beaux Arts style by C. Emlen Urban. Now an apartment building, this former public school features a third floor auditorium with French Renaissance style plasterwork.

TURN RIGHT ON NORTH CHARLOTTE STREET.

47. 233 North Charlotte Street

Designed by Philadelphia architects Hazelhurst and Huckels, this elaborate Queen Anne style house was constructed in 1883-1885 for William Zahm Sener, a wealthy businessman.

48. Charles Steinman Foltz House
249 North Charlotte Street

The three-story brick-and-stucco house displays the projecting eaves and simple finishes characteristic of the popular Arts and Crafts movement. The house was constructed in 1897-1899, from designs by William Pritchett, Jr.

TURN LEFT ON WALNUT STREET.

49. 412-422 West Walnut Street

These six dwellings were built by Barton B. Martin in 1883, for speculative rental and resale purposes. This is one of the best preserved Victorian rows of houses in Lancaster. Fine Italianate style details include the bracketed cornices, arched and ornamented hood molds over the windows, and bracketed entry hoods.

TURN LEFT ON LANCASTER AVENUE.

50. 238 Lancaster Avenue

Constructed in 1893 as the Western Methodist Episcopal Church, this Gothic Revival style building combines the massing of the Perpendicular Gothic style and wooden ornamental details in the simpler Carpenter Gothic style. Highlights include the two towers and a large Gothic multi-arched window.

TURN LEFT ON CHESTNUT STREET.

51. Jonas B. Martin Mansion
423 West Chestnut Street

Queen Anne style details are evident in this house constructed in the 1880s. The multi-intersecting gables, projecting dormers, and ornate chimney stacks are just some the lavish ornamental features of this building. It was built for the brother of lumber baron Barton B. Martin whose house was...

52. West Lawn
403 West Chestnut Street

This three-story mansion is one of Lancaster County's finest examples of the Second Empire style, and one of the outstanding villas in Pennsylvania. It was constructed in 1873-1874 for Barton B. Martin, a wealthy lumber and coal merchant, and real estate developer. Notable features include the mansard roof with dormer windows, window caps with console brackets, and reconstructed porch with Corinthian columns.

53. McComony Mansion
402 West Chestnut Street

This Queen Anne style house was built in 1883. The mansion displays half-timbered gables, clustered chimney stacks, stained glass window, and an original entry porch.

WALK EAST ON CHESTNUT STREET TO REJOIN THE TOUR AT PRINCE STREET AND TURN RIGHT.

54. Sehner-Ellicott-von Hess House
123 North Prince Street

This building has been the home of the Historic Preservation Trust of Lancaster County since 1966, when a group of preservation advocates saved it from being demolished as part of an ur-ban renewal project. Soon afterward, the house was extensively renovated to reflect its appearance in the 18th century.

The house was once the home of Andrew Ellicott, a surveyor who completed Pierre L'Enfant's plan for Washington, D.C. In 1803, Meriwether Lewis visited Ellicott to learn the latest surveying techniques in preparation for his 1804 expedition with William Clark. An exhibition in the house recounts key moments in Ellicott's career.

55. Fulton Opera House
12 North Prince Street

Christopher Hager, a Lancaster merchant and civic leader, had a dream - to create a building that would serve as a community center for meetings, lectures, concerts, and theatrical performances. He commissioned the renowned Philadelphia architect Samuel Sloan to create this building, which was erected in 1852. Named Fulton Hall, after the county's steam engine pioneer, Robert Fulton, it was built on the foundation of Lancaster's pre-Revolutionary jail, where in 1763, a vigilante gang known as the "Paxtang Boys" massacred the last of the Conestoga Indians being held there for their protection. This was a monumental event throughout the colonies and became the subject matter for the first plays ever written on American soil - *A Dialogue Between Andrew Trueman and Thomas Zealot About the Killing the Indians at Cannestogoe and Lancaster* and *The Paxton Boys, a Farce*. The exterior wall of the jail courtyard is now the back wall of the theatre.

From a meeting hall, to the "Queen of the Roadhouses" through vaudeville, the movies, near destruction, salvation and on to the cutting edge of contemporary theatre, the history of the Fulton Opera House, considered to be the nation's oldest continuously operating theatre, is one of only eight theaters to be named a National Historic Landmark. Many of the "greats" of the American and International stage have performed on her boards. The list is extensive and includes most of the Barrymore family, Sarah Bernhardt, W. C. Fields, Alfred Lunt, Al Jolson, and Irene Dunne, Mark Twain, a young actress named Helen Brown (later known as Helen Hayes), Marcel Marceau and hundreds more.

TURN AND WALK BACK TO
ORANGE STREET. TURN RIGHT.
TURN RIGHT ON QUEEN STREET.

56. Eichholtz Building
43-45 North Queen Street

This 1925 building was constructed of "Straub blocks," a type of cement building material developed in Lancaster. The façade has a streamlined look that reflects tastes of the day. The first tenant in this building was the Ross Store, Lancaster's first chain department store.

57. Reilly Brothers & Raub Building
44 North Queen Street

This building has one of the most intact original storefronts along this stretch of North Queen, the oldest retail block in the city. Built in 1911 as a hardware store, it was designed by C. Emlen Urban in a French Renaissance style. While the city's other commercial buildings typically used brick, tile and terra-cotta, this refined façade employs granite, Indiana limestone and copper. The original metal signage appears just above the storefront opening, while the tall paired windows on the upper floors are separated by copper friezes.

58. New Era Building
39-41 North Queen Street

This circa 1890 Queen Anne style brick building is crowned by a cornice of corbelled brick, wood and pressed metal with a center pediment framing a sunburst motif, beneath which is the original "New Era" signage. Designed initially to be a tavern, the building was sold before construction was completed to the New Era printing company.

59. Shaub's Shoe Store
20 North Queen Street

Built in 1929, this store represents one of the most intact Art Deco style buildings in Lancaster. It is also among the oldest businesses in the city to be owned by the same family and operated continuously at the original site. Art Deco ornamentation includes the decorative geometric band along the roof cornice, the cast metal framing the second floor, the lamp hanging above the arched doorway to the right, and the rich inlaid wood panels inside the display windows.

YOU HAVE NOW RETURNED TO
THE TOUR STARTING POINT IN
PENN SQUARE.

Look Up,

Lebanon

A Walking Tour of Lebanon...

Originally occupied by Algonquin Indian Tribes, the Lebanon Valley was part of a 1681 land-grant by King Charles II of England to William Penn. Pennsylvania was described as a place to go for religious sovereignty and inexpensive land. First settled in 1723, Lebanon County's initial colonists, prior to 1720, were Scotch-Irish. By 1729, the predominant settlers were German. Some worked as missionaries and others seeking religious freedom came for the land.

The Lebanon Valley went through a terrible period during the French-Indian War. Forts were constructed in an attempt to stop attacks, but Indian attacks continued until 1763. The Revolutionary War was significant in Lebanon history as well. British and Hessian prisoners were held captive in the region and worked for the Cornwall Furnace, making cannons and munitions.

By 1790, most of the German settlers who had immigrated to Lebanon County for religious freedom, were of the middle class. These Germans became known as the Pennsylvania Dutch, and they included such groups as the Mennonites, the Dunkers, the German Reformed, the Lutherans and Moravians. The Pennsylvania Dutch built farming communities and churches, bringing ministers and educators to the community. These people and their way of life had a great influence on the industry, farming, religion and other qualities of life that Lebanon knows today.

George Steitz is given credit for laying out the present city of Lebanon in the 1740s. The town was located in what was then Lebanon Township in Lancaster County and was commonly called Steitz Town or Steiza, after its proprietor. The village was renamed Lebanon in 1758 and became the county seat when Lebanon County was created by an Act of Assembly in 1813 from portions of Dauphin and Lancaster Counties. Lebanon received its charter as a borough in 1821 and as a city in 1885.

Our walking tour will begin at the former Market Square at Cumberland Street and Ninth Street where you find free parking in the municipal lot...

1. **Municipal Parking Lot**
   southeast corner of 9th Street and
   Cumberland Street

This was Market Square in Lebanon, which was lined with wooden sheds into the late 19th century. The market stood on either side of Cumberland Street, making available the finest of Lebanon County produce. The parking lot is the site of the annual Bologna Drop every New Year's Eve.

BEGIN ON S 9TH STREET, ACROSS FROM THE PARKING LOT AND APPROACH CUMBERLAND STREET FROM THE SOUTH.

2. **American House**
   25 S 9th Street

Now an assisted living facility, the American House was long a public hostelry. Its fine stone front elevation still bears two stones which tell much of the story of its erection before the American Revolution in 1771, inscribed in German. The third story was added in 1855 when it was owned by John Gloninger.

3. **Lincoln Republican Club**
   17 S 9th Street

The Lincoln Republican Club was established in 1935; the brick Federal-style building dates to 1941.

4. **Standard Motor Car Company building**
   15 S 9th Street

This building was once the dealership of the Standard Motor Car Co. that was organized in 1922 from the old Standard Steel Car Company that was in existence from 1913.

5. **Cavalry Chapel**
   9 S 9th Street

Founded by actors just after the Civil War, the Benevolent and Protective Order of Elks was originally known as the Jolly Corks. This building once served as the lodge for the BPOE.

6. **Filbert's Store**
   southwest corner of Cumberland Street
   and S 9th Street

This corner was the site of Philip Greenawalt's home. A native of Germany, Greenawalt came to America in 1749 and settled first in Lancaster County. At the outbreak of the Revolution he was commissioned Colonel of the first battalion of Lancaster County and fought alongside George Washington at Trenton and Princeton and Brandywine and Valley Forge. Greenawalt died in 1802 and afterwards the double-story frame building was converted into a string of stores and businesses. Its current appearance dates to extensive improvements made in the 1890s for Filbert's wholesale liquor house, absent a corner turret.

TURN LEFT ON CUMBERLAND STREET.

7. **Stoy Museum/Cumberland County**
   Historical Society
   924 Cumberland Street

The original front portion of the Stoy Museum was built in 1773 as a home for Dr. William Henry Stoy, a local minister and prominent Revolutionary War doctor. The upstairs rooms were used as Lebanon County's first courthouse when the county was established in 1813. James Buchanan, fifteenth President of the United States, practiced law there as a young attorney. John Andrew Shulze was the new county's first prothonotary and later became the sixth Governor of Pennsylvania.

8. **Swan Tavern**
   1002 Cumberland Street

This Revolutionary-era hostelry was the Swan Tavern when George Washington slept here during the summer of 1792. For much of the next two hundred years, it took on the name of its famous patron - the George Washington Tavern.

TURN RIGHT ON S 10TH STREET.

9. **Moravian Church**
   29 N 10th Street

The Moravian Church in Lebanon County dates to 1747. On December 19, 1848, just 100 years after its formal organization, the congregation moved to the center of Lebanon. Within its first year a sanctuary at 10th & Spring streets was consecrated.

On June 2, 1853, the parsonage built on the north side of the building was completed. The church was completely destroyed by fire on June 29, 1858 but within a year a second building was completed and consecrated on June 5, 1859. The congregation moved to South Lebanon Township in 2005.

10. **Stevens Towers**
    930 Willow Street; southeast corner of S 10th Street

Stevens Towers, a state-of-the-art place for Lebanon County seniors to live incorporates the old bell tower from the Stevens School.

TURN RIGHT ON WILLOW STREET.

11. **Nevin Hall**
    931 Willow Street

Nevin Hall, with a Second Empire mansard roof, dates to 1886.

12. **St. John's Reformed Church**
    925 Willow Street

This handsome brownstone church was built in 1859.

13. **YMCA**
    901 Willow Street

Now an assisted living facility, the ornate Neo-classical brick building was the YMCA when it opened in 1906.

14. **New Life Chapel**
    100 N 9th Street

The main section of this church building dates to 1867.

TURN RIGHT ON N 9TH STREET.

15. **Zion Lutheran Church**
    28 N 9th Street

This lovely brick church on a rough-faced stone base dates to 1874.

RETURN TO WILLOW STREET AND TURN RIGHT.

16. **Salem Evangelical Lutheran Church northwest corner to Willow Street and N 8th Street**

On this site in 1766 was erected the first church and school house in the City of Lebanon. On the tower of this building hangs a bell cast in 1773 which proclaimed in Lebanon County the signing of the Declaration of Independence. The first regular pastor of this church, Frederick Augustus Conrad Muhlenberg, was president of the convention that adopted the constitution of the United States and Speaker of the first House of Representatives. The cornerstone of this building was laid in 1796 and consecrated two years later. It was renovated to a two-story structure in 1848.

TURN LEFT ON N 8TH STREET.

17. **Salem Lutheran Church/Schmauck Memorial Chapel**
    119 N 8th Street

The cornerstone for this Tudor-Gothic structure was laid in 1898 and it was built entirely of stone, steel, copper, and slate. It provides lofty arches and a vaulted roof. The altar, stair and balcony rails, pulpit, baptismal font, and lectern were all hand carved. In 1928, the chapel was renovated and the Skinner organ installed. The organ was modernized in 1995.

18. **Cornwall and Lebanon Railroad Station**
    161 N. 8th Street

The operation of the Cornwall iron ore mines - one of the world's great iron mines and oldest continuously operated mine in the New World - and furnaces were acquired by Robert Coleman, who later passed controlling interest to his great grandson, Robert Habersham Coleman. As production increased and the markets expanded, the Coleman family acknowledged the need for rail service. In 1853, R.W. Coleman, William Coleman, and G. Dawson Coleman formed the North Lebanon Railroad, later renamed the Cornwall Railroad Company, to connect the ore hills to the Union Canal landings in Lebanon. In 1883, as even wider markets were sought, R.H. Coleman built the Cornwall and Lebanon Railroad which ran from Lebanon to Cornwall and through the Conewago Hills to Elizabethtown. The railroad was built to connect holdings to the Pennsylvania Railroad at Conewago, thereby opening Cornwall and Lebanon to markets in Philadelphia, Pittsburgh, and west. Both of these lines provided passenger service throughout the county and to two favorite local picnic and recreation areas, the Mount Gretna Park and Penryn Park.

The 1883 station was designed by architect George Watson Hewitt, in partnership with his brother William. William created many Philadelphia landmarks including the Bellevue-Stratford Hotel, Academy of Fine Arts, and Hahnemann Hospital.

The wealth of the builder, Robert Coleman allowed an architectural quality unique among small town railroad stations. It is also unusual that a grand structure such as the Cornwall and Lebanon Station was built for a railroad with only 22 miles of track.

TURN AND WALK BACK SOUTH ALONG 8TH STREET TO CUMBERLAND STREET AND TURN LEFT.

19. First National Bank
760 Cumberland Street

This Neoclassical bank with engaged fluted columns was built in 1914.

20. Wertz Candies
718 Cumberland Street

The Wertz family has been churning out handmade candies since 1931 when William Wertz made his first chocolates. Wertz is famous for its Opera Fudge, a Lebanon tradition that dates to the days when the City had an Opera House and patrons would routinely stop in for candy while walking down Cumberland Street. Opera fudge is not a fudge at all. It is a deliciously rich, creamy fondant made with heavy cream from local dairies, delicately flavored with vanilla and coated in pure chocolate liquor. Wertz Candies was featured on the popular television series, *Dirty Jobs*.

TURN AROUND AND RETURN TO 8TH STREET. TURN LEFT.

21. Samler Building
northwest corner of Cumberland Street and 8th Street

This trademark building of downtown Lebanon featured the City's first elevator when it opened.

22. Sirro's Italian Ice
7 S 8th Street

This brick building dating to 1876 is typical of the Italianate commercial structures that sprouted in downtown Lebanon in the years following the Civil War. Note the fanciful cornice.

23. Lebanon Farmers Market
35 S 8th Street

This was the site of the Lebanon County courthouse and jail that gained national notoriety in 1879 during the trial of the Blue Eyed Six, a band of business associates who conspired to murder an indigent neighbor for $8,000 in insurance money. At the time it was common to purchase assessment life insurance on people in whom one had no legal interest, a practice which was ended by law after this case. The six conspirators, who coincidentally all had blue eyes leading to the catchy moniker in the press, were all convicted after a six-month trial. Five were hanged in the courtyard here. Fire destroyed the structure just a few years later.

After the fiery destruction of the Lebanon County Jail, construction began on the Market House. In 1892 after nearly a two-year construction process the Lebanon Farmers Market was dedicated. Chickens, fresh produce, eggs, beef and milk were easily available and farm fresh at the Lebanon Market since it was one of the first places in Lebanon County to offer cold storage and refrigeration.

From the Lebanon Family Theatre featuring almost daily Vaudeville performances in the early days to being the home of the Crestview Secretarial School in the 1950s, the Market House has been home to many. But its longest tenant was the S. Kantor Sewing Company that operated in the building from the 1930s until just a few years ago. Lebanon had over 60 sewing factories at one time, but the S. Kantor is one of only a handful of survivors. In 2007 the 30,000-square foot historic facility. occupying nearly one-half the block, was restored to its original 1892 Farm Market Building appearance.

24. **Edible Arrangements**
    37 S 8th Street

An attractive terra-cotta facade marks this 1888 commercial building.

RETURN TO CUMBERLAND STREET AND TURN LEFT.

25. **Mann Building**
    815-817 Cumberland Street

This ornate commercial building was constructed in 1900 and housed the Farmers Trust Bank for many decades.

26. **Lebanon National Bank**
    northeast corner of Cumberland Street and 9th Street

On this corner William Moore lived in a stone house in the early 1800s. Moore was instrumental in establishing the first bank in Lebanon, and became its first president. A substantial brick bank was erected here in the 1880s, eventually replaced with the present Neoclassical building.

YOU HAVE NOW RETURNED TO THE TOUR STARTING POINT.

Look Up,

Lewisburg

A Walking Tour of Lewisburg...

Lewisburg was founded in 1784 by Ludwig Derr, a settler in the area since the 1760s. Derr had purchased several tracts of land from the family of William Penn and other neighboring land owners; the largest of which was known as "The Prescott." In 1783, he worked with Samuel Weiser (son of Conrad Weiser, the famous Indian liaison who died in 1760, and with whose family Derr's own paternal family had been friends) to layout his combined land tracts, and create Derrstown.

The name was later, after Derr's death, changed to Lewisburg. Much has been considered regarding 'how' the name changed from Derrstown to Lewisburg. The most likely truth is that Derr's first name "Ludwig" translated into English as "Louis" but, being of German decent, it was spelled "Lewis." Later, after Derr's death, the traditional Germanic "burg" was appended to his first name to create Lewisburg.

The street names that run east and west are a local urban mystery. St. George, St. Catherine, and St. Louis etc...they appear to be named for Saints. However, since Derr was a Lutheran and did not pay homage to Catholic saints, this is unlikely. Rather, the street names are more likely named for Derr's family members, as those streets are consecutively parallel, and emanate from what was then Derr's home.

Another mystery surrounding Lewisburg, is the disappearance of its founder, Ludwig Derr. After selling many lots of land, Derr set off for Philadelphia to sell additional lots. Shortly after arriving, records indicate some of his lots had sold. However, Ludwig Derr simply disappears from history in that city. Derr's son George went to Philadelphia to search for his father, but returned a short time later knowing nothing more than when he set out.

Over the centuries, Lewisburg has been a center of commerce in Union County. Its tributary off of the Susquehanna River was used for logging and shipping, and remains of old factories and other ancient stone structures exist along the river banks. The town's most famous landmark are its three-globe streetlights. Installation of the cast iron standards began in 1912 when Market Street was being paved with brick. Today approximately 1,500 of these lights line Lewisburg's streets. The standards are made by the nearby Watsontown Foundry and wired by Citizen Electric.

Our walking tour will begin five blocks away from the Susquehanna River in Hufnagel Park and head down Market Street towards the water...

1. **Reading Depot**
   South Fifth Street

This is the only reminder of the once important railroad system that helped bring prosperity to Lewisburg in the 19th century.

2. **The Chamberlin Building**
   434 Market Street

Elements of the original Federal style of this building can be seen along N 5th Street. The addition of the cast iron front was part of the 1870s renovation. A building technology rather than an architectural style, this technique employed iron in a new structural form which allowed large openings, principally along a street front. These structures were often loft buildings with ground-floor commercial establishments and some type of light manufacturing on the upper floors. Beaux Arts style elements can be seen in the decoration and the rounded arches and columns.

TURN RIGHT ON MARKET STREET AND WALK EAST.

3. **Campus Theatre**
   413 Market Street

Dating to 1940 and featuring Bucknell's school colors, blue and orange, and mascot bison, this is Lewisburg's only Art Deco building. Glazed tiles, glass block, steel windows, aluminum and neon lights combine to produce forms which often reflected the ideals of the building's inhabitants. In 2004, the theater underwent a major restoration to the marquee to bring back the Art Deco glory.

4. **Sun Bank**
   311 Market Street

This 1899 bank sprung to life in the Beaux Arts style, evidenced by the elaborate stone frieze and brackets, and the Ionic columns; with their elegant fluted shafts, detailed bases and scroll-like volutes at their capitals. Note the rounded windows, round arches connecting the columns, and the metal cross-hatched grilles on the windows.

5. **Post Office/Courthouse**
   southwest corner of South 3rd Street and Market Street

It was common practice for the federal government to construct massive combination post office/courthouses in big cities like Philadelphia and Pittsburgh, but not so common in smaller towns like Lewisburg. In this case, the building must express the dignity and solemnity of the judicial system. The four-story Neoclassical building, the tallest on Market Street, distinguishes itself from its commercial neighbors by the 10-step elevated entrance, massive Doric columns, and brass doors. It opened in 1932.

6. **Sovereign Bank**
   239 Market Street

Continuing the Greek Revival motif on this corner, a set of sturdy Doric columns greets depositors here.

7. **Cameron House**
   201 Market Street

In 1830 William Cameron built a Federal style residence that 20 years later was remodeled into the headquarters for the Lewisburg National Bank. In the 1880s Jane Cameron renovated it back into a Queen Anne-style family home. She added porches, stained glass, towers and gables, and terra-cotta decorations. The original vault and stone interior walls of the bank remain in the house. She also added a matching carriage house that is one of only a few such structures in the United States not converted to a residence.

8. **Bradley Shoemaker Gallery**
   200 Market Street

This Shingle Style home migrated from the New England seashore and uses wood shingles on vertical wall surfaces, often with decorative overlays. This is an 1890 renovation of an original structure was of logs slabs, chinked with mortar and horsehair. glass panes and a conical roof with fancy shingles. Blue colored glass in diamond shaped windows decorate the east side. A pharmacy was in continuous operation here from 1845 to 1990 — a record in the United States.

9. **Lewisburg Hotel**
   136 Market Street

Originally two stories when it opened as Kline's Hotel in 1834, a third and fourth story were added in subsequent renovations (the fourth story was added to accommodate the addition of an elevator). A Mt. Vernon style portico was added in 1938 by local architect Malcolm Clinger. The 1997 renovation successfully united the hotel with the smaller motel behind it, including replacing a flat roof with the gabled roof with dormers. Between 1834 and 1900 every Pennsylvania governor slept here.

10. **133-139 Market Street**

The stone foundation and belt course, Queen Anne shingles in the gable and side entry add interest to this brick commercial building.

11. **Lewisburg Club**
    131 Market Street

In 1906 the Lewisburg Club was organized as the focal point for the three service clubs - Kiwanis, Lions and Rotary. In 1911 this building was purchased for $6,000 to be the home for the service clubs and community activities. It was originally a simple brick structure built sometime between 1800 and 1814 on land conveyed by Ludwig Derr to Carl Ellenkhuysen. In 1906 the brick was overlaid with rustic yellow sandstone and accented with brownstone, a hard dark sandstone. It is the only brownstone building in Lewisburg. Notice the striking overhanging bay window at the second floor level and the lovely stained glass as well.

12. **Christy Mathewson House**
    129 Market Street

Legendary baseball pitcher and winner of 373 major league games with the New York Giants, Christy Mathewson was born in Factoryville and went to school at Bucknell. The most famous of all Bison athletes, Mathewson was better known on campus as a hard hitting fullback and outstanding kicker on the gridiron although he also played baseball and basketball. "Matty," was also well-known as a gentleman and a true scholar-athlete. He was president of his class and a member of the glee club. Mathewson, who was one of the five original members of the Baseball Hall of Fame, and his wife, Jane Stoughton, lived here. He is buried at Lewisburg Cemetery on South 7th Street. The early brick building was later stuccoed and the corner quoins and ornate portico and cornice added.

13. **124 Market Street**

This brick townhouse was built in 1830; the ornamental Italianate details were later additions.

14. **110 and 112 Market Street**

These twin Federal-style brick homes feature protruding fronts and off-center entrance.

15. **Lewisburg Inn**
    101 Market Street

This building was formerly the Lewisburg Inn. Built in 1825, it is thought to have contained only the portion from the corner to the bay window. It was the home of James Fleming Linn whose two sons were John Blair Linn, author of *Annals of Buffalo Valley* (1857) and James Merrill Linn, author of chapters in *History of Juniata and Susquehanna Valleys*. The house had a water tank in the attic which supplied the first running water in Lewisburg.

16. **Halfpenny Mansion**
    100 Market Street

Built in 1819 by merchant William Hayes, the stone Halfpenny mansion symbolized Lewisburg during the days of the woolen mill boom. The third story, front porch and balcony are not original.

17. **Abbot Green House**
    43 Market Street

The original owner of this house, General Abbot Green, directed the work on the West Branch Canal in 1827. The fancy wooden trim, the peak in the roof, and the porch were all later additions.

18. Wm. D. Himmelreich Memorial Library
   18 Market Street

Completed in 1902, the town library was designed to conform with the Greek Revival architecture of the church next door.

19. First Presbyterian Church
   14 Market Street

Built in 1856 by Jonathan Nesbit, this is Lewisburg's finest example of Greek Revival architecture. Details include a beautiful spire and belfry with curved supporting brackets, tall entablature with fluted columns and Ionic capitals, a fanlighted door, and a Classical pediment. The 1869 residence with its ornate trim was the boyhood home of Norman Thomas, many times the Socialist candidate for President.

20. Packwood House
   10-12 Market Street

Packwood House is among the oldest log-built structures of its kind in Pennsylvania, originally constructed as a two-story log cabin between 1796 and 1799. It initially served as a tavern and inn for river travelers along the Susquehanna. In the early 19th century, with the construction of the Pennsylvania Canal's crosscut at Lewisburg, the tavern evolved into a hotel known as the American House. The hotel eventually expanded into an impressive three-story 27-room structure in the mid-19th century.

In the 1860s, with the arrival of the Pennsylvania Railroad, interest in river travel faded and the hotel soon lost much of its business. The American House closed in the late 1880s, and the structure was converted into three townhouses.

TURN RIGHT ON WATER STREET.

21. 37 South Water Street

The earliest homes in the county which remain largely unaltered are the stone houses. This is the oldest stone house, from 1786, still standing in Lewisburg. A log annex (now covered with shingles) attached to the house on the south side was originally a store, and later served as the first school in Lewisburg.

TURN RIGHT ON ST. LOUIS STREET. TURN RIGHT ON SOUTH 2ND STREET AND WALK DOWN THE EAST SIDE OF THE STREET.

22. Tuscan Villa
   60 South 2nd Street

Built in 1869 for James Marsh, it became the home of Congressman Benjamin Focht in 1915. The Italianate villa was one of the many romantic styles popular in the latter part of the nineteenth century, characterized here by the deep roof overhang with carved brackets, corner quoins, tall and narrow windows with interesting mullions, shaped window hoods ending in a drop at the sides, decoratively carved fascia boards beneath the roof with oval lie-on-your-stomach windows, and an arched double-door entrance.

23. George B. Miller House
   54 South 2nd Street

George Barron Miller, son of George F. Miller, built this home in 1884. Notice the deep frieze under the roof and the jig-saw cut-outs on the porch.

24. George F. Miller House
   43 South 2nd Street

Built in 1856 by George F. Miller, Congressman during the Civil War, this is a late example of brick Federal architecture. This building also has many unusual features not typical of the Federal style: three story construction, hard-fired brick facing with tight joints and slender rows of mortar, (but with sides of soft-fired common brick), window ledges of marble, (unlike the more economical stone or wood) and larger windows than in earlier Federal houses.

25. 37-39 South Second Street

This Early Federal structure is typical of Lewisburg, before the building boom of 1842-1860. Note the wooden clapboard, overall simplicity and doorways that open directly onto the street.

TURN AROUND AND RETURN TO ST. LOUIS STREET.

26. Cronrath Funeral Home
106 South 2nd Street; southeast corner of South 2nd Street and St. Louis Street

This house offers many of the hallmarks of the Queen Anne style: decorative wooden shingles beneath gables, a terra-cotta roof crest shaped in metal like scales on a dragon's back, a multi-colored slate roof, fish-scale shingles under the gable facing South 2nd Street, a peculiar isolated gable arising from the roof on the North side and leaded and stained glass windows. This one was built in 1888 by the Matlack family.

27. Union County Court House
southwest corner of South 2nd Street and St. Louis Street

The original wing of the Greek Revival courthouse was built in 1856-57 with private funds pledged during the movement to encourage the division of Union County. Lewis Palmer was the designer and Henry Noll was the head carpenter. Note the corner pilasters (flattened columns that stand out in relief from the wall); imposing columns with Ionic capitals; and the classical triangular pediment with Greek dentils above the capitals. A fine example of a cupola, with recently restored copper roof, houses the bell donated by Simon Cameron, Secretary of War in President Lincoln's cabinet. The new complementary addition was completed in 1973.

TURN RIGHT ON SOUTH THIRD STREET.

28. 60 South Third Street

This house was typical of the frame houses built in Lewisburg in the 1850s. The rear wing was added in 1880 by Robert Lawshe.

29. Beaver Memorial United Methodist Church
40 South Third Street

This church and parsonage (the fourth in a series of buildings for the Methodists) was erected during 1889-1890 in the Ruskinian Gothic style, named for John Ruskin, an English architectural critic and social reformer who disdained what he perceived to be the increasing emphasis on function over form in the architecture and engineering of his day. Notice the asymmetrical design of this buff sandstone church and ornamental finial at the top of the church's spire and roof peak.

TURN AROUND AND WALK BACK TOWARDS ST. LOUIS STREET.

30. First Baptist Church
51 Third Street

The First Baptist Church was dedicated in 1870. The original spire, which was 175 feet high, was shingled by a president of Bucknell University, Justin R. Loomis, who designed the building. This church exemplifies the Gothic Revival style, one of the most popular architectural styles of the mid-19th century. This church's steeply pitched roof, simple facade, pointed-arch stained glass windows, buttressed walls, and tall, thin spire are all characteristic of this style. The dark exterior stones are hornfels; a hard, very fine-grained rock that has cooled and solidified from liquid magma after intruding into, and forming a vein within, surrounding rock.

31. Christ's Evangelical Lutheran Church
southeast corner of South 3rd Street and St. Louis Street

Notice the rough appearance of the red sandstone facade, the broad round arches; the squat, square, medieval looking tower, the smaller windows, deeper door openings and the general absence of carved or applied ornament. This heavy Romanesque style was popularized by Henry Hobson Richardson in the 1880s and 1890s and especially popular in civic and ecclesiastic buildings.

TURN RIGHT ON ST. LOUIS STREET AND RETURN TO HUFNAGEL PARK.

Look Up, Ligonier

A Walking Tour of Ligonier...

During the French and Indian War, British General John Forbes was assigned the daunting task of seizing Fort Duquesne, the French citadel at the forks of the Allegheny and Monongahela rivers. He ordered construction of a new road across Pennsylvania, guarded by a chain of fortifications, the final link being the "Post at Loyalhanna," fifty miles from his objective, to serve as a supply depot and staging area for a British-American army of 5000 troops. The fort was constructed in September 1758 and named "Fort Ligonier" after Forbes' superior, Sir John Ligonier, commander-in-chief in Great Britain. There are two other sites in America that honor the grizzled warrior who was made the Earl of Ligonier in 1766 at the age of 87, four years before his death. One is a small bay on Lake Champlain and the other a town in Indiana that was founded by a pioneer from the Ligonier Valley.

The town was laid out by John Ramsey in 1817. He rode out from Chambersburg to build a mill on his newly acquired 672 acres of land on the north bank of the Loyalhanna Creek. When the borough was incorporated in 1834, a Ramsey descendent changed the name of Ramseytown to the more exotic "Ligonier." Perhaps he was anticipating attracting vacationing tourists in the future. He certainly anticipated the town becoming the most important in the area, designing it round a central diamond awaiting a county courthouse. The designation as a county seat never came but the tourists did and Ligonier has been a resort destination for Pittsburghers since the 1800s.

But growth came slowly; it was non-existent for a time, in fact. In its early days Ligonier was a welcome stop for stagecoach and commercial wagon traffic between Philadelphia and Pittsburgh. But in 1952 the Pennsylvania Railroad was completed across the state and it ran not through Ligonier but Latrobe ten miles away. The population of actually declined from 350 people in 1860 to 317 in 1870.

It would not be until 1878 that udge Thomas Mellon, scion of what was to become one of the 20th century's greatest family fortunes, completed a 10-mile feeder line with the Ligonier Valley Railroad that fortunes reversed. Ligonier's character, however, continued to remain less commercial than some of its more advanced neighbors. Its reputation as a summer excursion destination was assured in the 1890s when the Mellons developed Idlewild, a picnicking park that is considered the nation's third oldest amusement park still in operation today.

When the Lincoln Highway, America's first paved transcontinental road, rolled through Ligonier in 1919 it brought more tourists, not industry. Our walking tour will explore the remnants of that historic road that is now the town's Main Street...

1. **The Diamond**
   Market Street and Main Street

Before Ligonier's Diamond was landscaped as a park in 1894, it served much of the 19th century as a corral and parking area for wagon horses and cattle. Its present design, including the bandstand, was created in 1971. A cast iron water fountain installed in 1894 with separate drinking positions for man, dog and horse, retains its historic position on the square's north side.

EXIT THE DIAMOND ONTO WEST MAIN STREET (THE METHODIST CHURCH WILL BE ON YOUR LEFT).

2. **Heritage United Methodist Church**
   southwest corner of the Diamond

The Redstone Circuit of the Methodists was formed in 1784. It comprised all the territory west of the Allegheny Mountains. In 1788, the Ligonier Methodist Episcopal Church was established in "name, style and title" authorized by a letter from John Wesley which was dated September 19, 1788 and postmarked Bristol, England. Jacob Shaw held the first services in his home. The congregation consisted of five of his family and one other.

For a time, services were held in an old pottery on Main Street. A lot on the corner of St. Clair and Church Streets was purchased for twenty dollars and a small wooden church was erected. The congregation outgrew the little church by 1857 and land was bought at the present site on which a brick church was constructed. It served the congregation until 1902 when it was torn down to make room for the larger present church. The bluestone for the building was quarried from Laurel Mountain. The new $25,000 church was dedicated debt-free in 1903.

3. **131 West Main Street**

This house survives from the turnpike era of 1830-1850. Although altered for retail use, its original five-bay, center door Federal facade and Flemish bond (alternating headers and stretchers) brickwork is still in evidence.

4. **Weaver Building**
   137 West Main Street

This three-story commercial/apartment brick building was constructed in 1924 during the Lincoln Highway era.

5. **Ligonier Theater Building**
   208 West Main Street

In 1920 A.J. McColley constructed this building for his Ford dealership and automobile repair garage. After financial reversals in the 1930s he sold the building which was eventually converted into a movie theater by Vilie Alexas of Johnstown. The Mellon family acquired the building in 1966 and remodeled it in an attempt to make it smaller and profitable in an age of the emerging movie multiplex. The losing battle was abandoned and the family sold the property in 1993. New ownership struggled on until 1997 before the theater closed. In 2003 the Valley Players of Ligonier purchased the building and have breathed life back into the performing arts center.

6. **Pioneer Presbyterian Church**
   240 West Main Street

In 1866 the Presbyterians in Ligonier were organized. This sanctuary, the oldest church in town, dates to 1878.

7. **Ligonier Armory**
   358 West Main Street at Walnut Street

The Ligonier Armory for Company D, 103rd Medical Regiment of the Pennsylvania National Guard was built in 1938 as a Depression-relief project on property belonging to the Ligonier Valley Railroad. The utilitarian building is constructed of brick, originally laid out on a T plan. Architect Robert T. Brocker added a simple yet refined Art Moderne finish. The armory contains a drill hall, kitchen, locker room, offices and storage rooms.

TURN AND RETRACE YOUR STEPS BACK TO THE DIAMOND. TURN LEFT ON NORTH MARKET STREET.

8. Mellon Bank
112 North Market Street

Thomas Mellon was a lawyer, judge and banker, founding Mellon Bank precursor T. Mellon & Sons in 1869. In 1877, Mellon was approached to finance the Ligonier Valley Railroad. In 1878 he acquired land around the railroad just west of Ligonier where he began a picnic park, Idlewild. Additional land in the Ligonier Valley which he once owned is now the Rolling Rock Club. By the end of the 20th century Mellon Bank would be the largest financial institution in America outside of New York City. This is the first bank Mellon built in Ligonier.

9. Covenant Presbyterian Church
200 North Street at Church Street

The beautiful stone Covenant Church was completed in 1902: the Presbyterian burying ground dating back adjacent dates to 1798. Many of the town's founding families are buried here.

TURN AND RETRACE YOUR STEPS BACK TO THE DIAMOND. TURN LEFT ON EAST MAIN STREET AND STAY ON THE NORTH (LEFT) SIDE OF THE STREET.

10. Town Hall
northeast corner of Diamond

This Colonial Revival government building replaced the historic Ligonier House on the Diamond in 1967.

11. Odd Fellows Hall
136-138 East Main Street

This property was purchased by trustees of Ligonier Lodge #964 IOOF in 1920. The original structure, was torn down and replaced by a brick building with two double front store rooms and a meeting room on the second floor.

12. Ambrose House
144 East Main Street

This two-story building features Victorian elements such as corner tower, fish-scale shingles and Stick Style woodwork in the gable. It became the home of Dr. Jacob T. Ambrose, a veteran of the Civil War, in 1883. A smaller building, located at 140 East Main, later was used for his physician's office. For the first 26 years of his 50-year practice, Ambrose traveled on horseback to his patients. Roy Sibel next opened his funeral home here.

13. McColly House
204 East Main Street

It is believed that bricks for both buildings at this location came from the Robb brick works, which was located near the present entrance to Ligonier Valley Cemetery on Route 711 South. In 1870 Bales McColly, a former Westmoreland County Prothonotary, purchased the property for his residence and used the smaller building for his saddle and harness shop.

14. 224 East Main Street

This unornamented Victorian from the late 1800s stands out on Main Street with its Queen Anne asymmetrical massing, corner turret and wraparound porch. It features a small Colonial Revival three-part Palladian window in the gable. The iron fence was a late 20th century addition.

15. Ramsey House
228 East Main Street

This was the residence of Colonel John Ramsey, who laid out the town lots in 1817. The Federal-style brick residence features a symmetrical design around a center entry hall and a two-sided stepped entrance. Eventually, more rooms were added to the rear, a side porch tacked on and a garage placed in the back of the lot.

16. Ashcom House
230 East Main Street

This plank house was built by William Ashcom in 1780; a room for a cobbler's shop, with its own entrance, was added around 1799 at the east side of the building. This is believed to be the oldest home in Ligonier Borough.

17. Lowry Shop
304-306 East Main Street

C.A. Lowry operated an undertaking and furniture making business in the smaller building and resided in the adjacent building in 1871. In 1936, Ford F. Kinsey purchased the property, operating a service station in the smaller building. The stone wall was built after the street surface was lowered. In the 1940s two millstones were placed at each side of the stone wall and the cement pineapple added.

18. Albright Evangelical Church
324 East Main Street

If you peek in the alley on the west side of this square brick building you can see the outline of when it was a Gothic style church built in 1882. The concrete block section on the east side of the building was added when the facility became a school bus garage.

CROSS THE STREET AND FIND THE HISTORICAL MARKER.

19. Fort Ligonier Historical Marker
301 East Main Street

Fort Ligonier, built by order of General Forbes, was located 200 yards west of this marker.

20. 237 East Main Street

This is the middle of three adjoining lots purchased by the Weimer family from Somerset County. Items were made in the carpentry shop at 235 East Main and brought here for painting, varnishing and storing. The building originally faced on to East Main, but was turned 90 degrees enlarging the adjoining lot on the east and facing a wide door on the second floor to the street. This allowed for caskets stored there to be slid down onto wagons. The brick addition to the rear was built in the 1990s.

21. 235 East Main Street

This two-story structure was built, around 1813, using plank and clapboard. It was framed with seven-inch square white oak hand-hewn timbers held in place with wooden pins. The second floor did not have any flooring, only hand hewn joists for the overhead storing of lumber to be used in the making of cabinets and caskets. In the mid-1950s it became Don Robb's workshop for the custom manufacturing of specialty rods and other tackles for fishermen from all over the country.

22. Crawford Metal Shop
233 East Main Street

Built in 1888, this building was constructed of wood siding and tin ceilings by John W. Crawford, who operated it as the Crawford Sheet Metal Shop. John's son, Frank W., purchased the building in 1918 and it became the Crawford Sheet Metal and Roofing Shop. The original windows and the tin ceilings remain there today, however, the ceilings were covered over during remodeling.

23. Barnes Mansion
223 East Main Street

Built in 1921 by Earl McCune of McKeesport, this two-and-a-half story, buff brick structure was constructed from tile-backed brick. It housed the McCune family and the Jackson Barber Shop. In 1950, the building was sold to the Ligonier Valley Library Association. It remained a library until 1968. The building then became the Fern Museum of Clocks for a time.

24. 219 East Main Street

This 1880s structure was originally a six-room residence. Indented in the newel post at the foot of the original stairway is a glass ball, which according to Victorian lore, was placed there when the mortgage was paid. In the 1930s and 1940s, Marion Horner operated Horner's Tourist Rooms, popular with Pittsburghers spending their summers in Ligonier.

25. 209 East Main Street

Built around 1820 or 1830 as a large residence, the unusual feature of this building is the facade. It appears to be painted stone or brick, but it is wood. The smaller attached building, at 211 East Main, was added, along with a third floor, in the early 1900s.

26. Marker House
201 East Main Street

This three-bay, Federal period brick house, that retains much of its original woodwork, was built about 1840 for Noah M. Marker, a prominent merchant and state legislator. This house later became the home and office of one of the town's early physicians, E. E. McAdoo. In later life a large dining room was added and it became a restaurant.

27. National Hotel
149 East Main Street

The National Hotel was built on this site in the mid 1800s. Hotel rates were $1.50 per day, with free transportation to and from the train station located on the west side of town. In 1918, Roy Sibel purchased the property and used it for his furniture store, undertaking business and residence. When he went out of the furniture business in the 1930s, Sibel rented out the space for Pon's Family Restaurant. In 1955, Sibel sold the property to the VFW Home Association.

WALK ONE MORE BLOCK TO REACH THE TOUR STARTING POINT ON THE DIAMOND.

Look Up,

Meadville

A Walking Tour of Meadville...

David Mead, Connecticut-born in 1752, was the pioneer to the waters of the French Creek, following land claims from his native colony through the Wyoming lands of northeast Pennsylvania to these lands of the Iroquois Indians where Chief Custaloga had built a village known as Cussewago. Mead led a small band of settlers that included his brothers, their wives and families and optimistically laid out the original town plat in 1792 in the face of looming Indian hostilities. But by the next year he had sold a few lots and Meadville was off and running.

In 1800, the Pennsylvania counties of Armstrong, Beaver, Butler, Crawford, Erie, Mercer, Warren and Venango were cleaved from a part of Allegheny County. The population of Crawford County was then 2,346. Owing to the sparse population of the new counties, Erie, Mercer, Warren and Venango were included in the Crawford County District with the courts of justice located in Meadville. By the mid nineteenth century, Meadville was the most prominent and elegant community in this part of Pennsylvania. It had a reputation for education (Allegheny College was the second school west of the Allegheny Mountains when it was established in 1815), religion (the Meadville Theological School was a minister-generator for the Unitarian church), and law (the town was the birthplace of the direct primary system of elections in the United States).

The big boost for commerce arrived with the Atlantic and Great Western Railway of Pennsylvania (now the Erie Railroad) in October 1862. With Meadville practically half way between New York and Chicago, the railroad opened a wide area of markets to the farms and industries of Crawford County. Meadville was also well-positioned as the gateway town to the new oil boom that came with Edwin Drake's new oil wells in the region in 1859. With its already well-established base, Meadville enjoyed the boom without crashing in the bust of the oil days.

Meadville's 20th century notoriety began in Chicago in 1893 when Whitcomb L. Judson invented the hookless fastener. Meadville's Lewis Walker moved the enterprise back to Pennsylvania where Gideon Sundback invented the fastener used everywhere today. It was not a money-maker, however, until 1923 when the B.F. Goodrich Company used it on a new line of rubber galoshes. The new shoes were called Zippers - the galoshes forgotten today but not so their little metal fastener. Meadville became known as the "Zipper Capital of the World."

Our walking tour will visit commercial, residential, ecclesiastical and governmental sites all fastened together by Diamond Park, still a public use green area as planned more than 200 years ago, and where our explorations will commence...

1. **Diamond Park**
   Main Street between Chestnut Street and Walnut Street

When Evans W. Shippen, a Philadelphia foundry owner who was the son of Sixth Judicial District Judge Henry Shippen, gave a multi-tiered structure overflowing with lion heads, fish and seahorses to the town as a gift Meadville was perplexed as to what to do with it. So the powers that be took the fountain and placed it in a fenced field where cows grazed as they were driven to markets in Pittsburgh and Diamond Park was born. Originally the cast iron fountain was painted in multicolored hues, but has since been painted green. The fountain, currently facing $100,000 in repairs, is listed as a significant sculpture on the Smithsonian American Art Museum's Art Inventories Catalog.

Diamond Park is now dotted with public monuments. The first to be erected was the *Pioneer Statue*, dedicated on May 12, 1888 to "mark the hundredth anniversary of the settlement of Crawford County." In 1891 came a Civil War monument and in 1916 a **Firemen's Memorial Statue.**

STAND IN THE CENTER OF DIAMOND PARK AND FACE WEST (THE MOST IMPOSING BUILDING, THE COURTHOUSE, WILL BE AT YOUR BACK) AND TRAVEL CLOCKWISE AROUND THE PUBLIC GREEN.

2. **Judge Derickson House and Office**
   902/918 Diamond Park

David Derickson, a prominent Meadville citizen and attorney, built a Jefferson Classical one-story Revival structure at 918 Diamond for use as a law office. Derickson built the neighboring single classical brick structure around 1830. In addition, Derickson later built a Second Empire structure on the same block. All three of these buildings remain today, facing the Diamond. Derickson, in addition to being a counselor-of-law, also served as Deputy Attorney General and District Judge in Pennsylvania.

3. **Founder's House**
   908 Diamond Park

The Founders House stands on the property where once stood the log courthouse where Allegheny College was founded. The site was also the founding location of Meadville's Chamber of Commerce, the third oldest in the country. Allegheny College purchased the property in 2008 and completely refurbished it.

4. **Meadville Armory**
   894 Diamond Park

This brick armory with parapet walls and crenellation served the National Guard for over 100 years before a recent move into a $20 million training and preparedness facility.

5. **Christ Episcopal Church**
   870 Diamond Park

The Episcopalian congregation in Crawford County traces its beginnings back to 1825 and two years later an English Village Gothic church was begun. The current sanctuary dates to the 1880s and blends Romanesque elements onto the basic Gothic visage. An elaborate rose window dominates the gable. The bell tower soars into a pointed steeple. The sandstone tracery is especially fine.

6. **Meadville Public Library**
   848 North Main Street

The first library was established in 1812 with 150 volumes. The library contained the standard works of the time in history, biography and travel, but by policy, no fiction. A citizen could use the library if he donated a dollar and a volume annually.

In 1868, the City Library of Meadville was formed. Anyone could become a member by paying a dollar. In 1879 the Meadville Library Art and Historical Association was organized by joining the library with the Art and Historical Societies. In order to buy a building, shares of stock were sold for $25.00. One can still buy a share of stock for $25.00. The Library was supported by rentals, gifts and annual association dues of five dollars. In 1895 the library was opened to citizenry free of charge.

In 1924 a fund drive for $100,000 to finance a new library building was begun. Within a week the total was raised , all from local sources. The new building opened its doors in 1926, and the same building continues to be the home of the library. The building was designed by Edward L. Tilton, a leading architect of the day and an expert on libraries. It used the same red brick and sandstone as the high school across the street and on all four sides huge arched windows extended from floor to ceiling "leaving no shadow to distract the reader."

7. Meadville Junior High School/Parkville Commons
North Main Street

This collegiate style school replaced the 1888 Centennial High School on Market Street in 1923. It was constructed around a courtyard and featured gymnasiums for boys and gils and an acoustically perfect auditorium. It was reconstituted as a junior high school and then abandoned altogether. It is currently awaiting private development.

8. Tarr Mansion
871-873 Diamond Park

100 years before Jed Clampett discovered some bubblin' crude and "loaded up the truck and moved to Beverly" there were the Tarrs of Oil Creek. In 1861 oil was discovered on his farm that is now Oil Creek State Park. It was the largest oil strike ever found up to that time. After receiving well over $1,000,000 in royalties, James Tarr in 1865 sold his interest in the farm for $2,000,000 in gold. And the family moved to Meadville. The Tarrs built this exquisite High Victorian Italianate mansion that exhibits all the requisites of the form including tall, slender windows, molded window hoods and an elaborate bracketed cornice. The building has been subdivided into offices.

9. Crawford County Courthouse
903 Diamond Park

A courthouse and jail were built here in 1820; still the site of the County Courthouse. A Second Empire Style Courthouse was built late in the 1800s only to be expanded and encased in a Georgian Revival Style building in the 1950s.

10. First Baptist Church
353 Chestnut Street

The cornerstone for this stone church building was laid in 1904. Access on the Diamond is accomplished through an arcade-style entry that blends the wide, muscular arches of the Richardsonian Romanesque style and the pointed remnants of the Gothic style. The gabled entrance is dominated by a rose window. The corner bell tower is topped by a crenellated parapet.

11. Unitarian Universalist Church of Meadville
346 Chestnut Street

The name of Meadville rang familiar in liberal religious circles through the existence here of an important religious institution, the Meadville Theological School, founded in 1844 in great part through the efforts of Harm Jan Huidekoper and his sons. Meadville thus was the temporary home of hundreds of young men who became Unitarian ministers and supplied pulpits all across the nation. The school remained here for 82 years, but in 1926 was moved to Chicago as an entity of the Federated Theological Faculty of the University of Chicago, where it preserves the town's memory in its name: the Meadville Lombard Theological School.

The Unitarian Church in town was established ii 1825 when a group of 32 worshipers broke away from the local Presbyterian church. It was formally organized in 1829 as the independent Congregational Church. Three families had important roles in the church's early history: Harm Jan Huidekoper established the church; Margaret Shippen and Harm Jan Huidekoper provided the congregation with land; and George W. Cullum, who would later play a part in rebuilding South Carolina's Fort Sumter, ground zero for the Civil War, designed the imposing Greek Revival church. Looking out on Diamond Park behind a portico of stout, fluted Doric columns, buildings, the church is remarkably true to its original aspect of 1836.

12. John McCloskey House
363 Chestnut Street

These blocks of Chestnut Street developed into the town's most prestigious address. John Newton McCloskey was born at Saegerstown on St. Patrick's Day, 1839. He attended the State Normal School at Edinboro, read law, and was admitted to practice in the courts of Crawford County, where he acquired wealth and distinction. His house blends the asymmetrical massing of the Victorian age with the Colonial Revival detailing popularized in the early 1900s.

13. Judge Shippen House
403 Chestnut Street

Henry Shippen arrived in the village of Meadville in 1825 after being appointed Judge of the Sixth Judicial District. The grandson of Philadelphia's first mayor, Shippen built this sophisticated Federal-style brick house in 1838 to accommodate his growing family. Unfortunately Shippen died a year later leaving his widow, Margaret, to rear their ten children. The oldest son, Evan, an iron furnace manager in Lancaster, York and Philadelphia during the 1850s and 60s (he is the one who donated the fountain where the tour began), converted the house to the Second Empire style. On the interior the house was partitioned into two apartments, but all the original woodwork was retained.

14. Huidekoper Land Office
423 Chestnut Street

Harm Jan Huidekoper was a native of Holland, born in Hoogeveen, in the district of Drenthe, April 3, 1776. He sailed for New York in 1796, spending the 63 days at sea in the study of the English language and so great was his advancement that when the voyage had ended he was able to find employment as bookkeeper for the Holland Land Company.

The firm's agent in Western Pennsylvania, Major Roger Alden, was incompetent as a bookkeeper, and as a result great confusion was produced in the agency's accounts. To adjust these, Huideko-

per was sent to Meadville, making the journey on horseback. When Alden resigned two years later, Huidekoper replaced him. Following legal difficulties in 1836 the company decided to close out its interests in New York and Pennsylvania and Huidekoper purchased all its lands in Erie, Crawford, Warren and Venango counties, paying for them the sum of $187,000. This was added to prior purchases of considerable magnitude from the Pennsylvania Population Company. Subsequent generations of Huidekopers managed their land business from this office; the family built several substantial homes around town, including a hilltop landmark on Terrace Street.

Today the 1850s building houses the Johnson-Shaw Stereoscopic Museum, an expansive collection of stereoviews, lantern slides, historic documents, books and equipment manufactured by Keystone View Company, the largest maker of stereoscopic views in the United States.

15. McClintock-Fuller House
485 Chestnut Street

This excellent brick Victorian structure has two trefoil windows and fleur-de-lis decorated gable vergeboards, Gothic elements, interestingly imposed on an Italianate mass.

TURN AND WALK BACK DOWN CHESTNUT STREET TO THE TOWN CENTER.

16. Stone United Methodist Church
956 South Main Street

Circuit riding preachers established the Stone United Methodist congregation in 1806. When this church was built in 1825 it became the hub of the enthusiastic French Creek circuit. After a fire in 1927 all the church's English Gothic origins were replicated - lancet windows, small buttresses and stained glass windows.

17. Masonic Building
310 Chestnut Street

This early 20th century brick building was constructed for Crawford Lodge No. 234 when they moved up from Water Street. The five-story hall is in the Second Renaissance Revival style.

18. Federal Building
296 Chestnut Street

This beautifully constructed Georgian Revival federal building, teeming with high-quality building materials, dates to World War I. A white marble balustrade emphasizes the roofline and white granite quoins embrace the corners. The Chestnut Street facade is graced by a trio of Palladian windows. Inside, the lobby features black walnut carved woodwork, terrazzo floors and brass grillwork.

19. Academy of Music
275 Chestnut Street

The theater was built in 1886 and operated as an opera house under the name of the Academy of Music. It was was built by Ernest Hempstead. It hosted live stage shows up into the 1920's when it began to share the stage with silent films and eventually was converted to a movie theater. The building was damaged by fire and closed in the 1980s but a restoration has brought the building, listed on the *National Register of Historic Places*, back to its original appearance.

20. Eldred Building
245 Chestnut Street

Albert I. Eldred was born in Spartansburg in 1885 and after attending the Meadville Commercial College and Allegheny College he entered the leather goods business with the firm of Grove & Eldred for six years. He later added various novelty lines and china when he constructed this building for his own firm.

21. Crawford County Trust Building
231 Chestnut Street

Crawford County Trust organized in 1900 under the direction of Albert Milton Fuller and quickly established itself in the community, paying "four per cent on all Savings Accounts." There were enough depositors by 1920 to build Meadville's only "skyscraper." It is a classically-influenced truncated six-story version of early high-rises in America with a base-shaft-capital design that mimics ancient columns.

TURN RIGHT ON MARKET STREET.

22. Meadville Market House
205 East Harford Street

As the county seat and market center for the region, it seemed long overdue when the town cleared a square in the downtown business district and put up a one-floor brick market house in 1870. No longer did farmers need to peddle their fruits and vegetables from curbside wagons on the street or go door-to-door. From the get-go it was a success and in 1917 a second floor and additional bays were added. After a centennial restoration in 1970, the Market House carries on as the oldest continuous market use structure in Pennsylvania.

TURN RIGHT ON CENTER STREET.

23. Central Station
875 Park Avenue at Center Street

Prior to 1915 the community was served by volunteer hose, pumper and ladder departments around town. Fire horses had stables in City Hall. With the coming of this building, Meadville switched to a new motorized engine fleet and a full-time, paid fire-fighting force. Today, the handsome orange brick building serves as a fire station-themed eatery.

CONTINUE WALKING TWO BLOCKS TO THE TOUR STARTING POINT IN DIAMOND PARK.

Look Up,

Media

A Walking Tour of Media...

After receiving the colony of Pennsylvania from England's King Charles II in 1681, William Penn sold a parcel of land to Thomas Minshall, who emigrated from England in 1702. Minshall's farming land was set up outside the town limits of the Village of Providence, which contained a blacksmith, wheelwright, stables, outbuildings, and a few small houses and farmland areas.

The community name derives from Latin for "middle," because of its location in the center of Delaware County. It is also situated at the highest point in Delaware County and approximately 12 miles from Philadelphia. Over time, there was a growing public demand for the county seat to be relocated from its southern location in Chester to a more central site. In response, the Borough of Media was incorporated by a special Act of Assembly in 1850, and the Greek Revival courthouse was completed the next year.

The beauty and healthfulness of Media, the picturesque surrounding hills and valleys, the fact that the sale of liquor was prohibited in the borough from the start, and its easy accessibility from Philadelphia caused many people to seek summer homes in the town. For those just looking for a respite from the city there were spacious "country houses" that took on guests.

In this tradition of recreation and leisure our walking tour will begin at the Media Theatre on State Street in the eastern end of town...

1. **Media Theatre**
   104 East State Street

Built in 1927 by Samuel Dembow as Media's third and largest movie theatre, it was designed by Louis Magziner as a Beaux Arts structure with Art Deco design elements. The interior was decorated in the English Renaissance style by Harris Brodsky. The theatre opened in August 1927 with a screening of *The Jazz Singer* starring Al Jolson, the first motion picture with sound. Admission was 25 cents. The theatre served for nearly 75 years as a movie palace displaying the magic of motion picture to generations of Media residents before Walter M. Strine converted it into the Media Theatre for the Performing Arts in 1994.

2. **Media High School**
   northeast corner of East State Street and Monroe Street

Constructed in 1914 of local granite schist stone in Tudor Revival with strong medieval details, this was the Media High School through 1966. It was formerly the site of the county poor farm and the famous Shortlidge Academy for Boys.

3. **Media Armory**
   12 East State Street

Built in 1908, the raised two-story Tudor Revival with flying Buttresses was headquarters for the Cooper Rifles, a military unit which was organized in 1877. It later housed Company M, 111th Infantry, Pennsylvania National Guard which left Media as a body in 1917 to serve in the First World War. It was designed by renowned architect William S. Price and M H. McClanahan. Price is recognized as one of the fathers of the "Modern School" of American architecture.

4. *Ledger* **Building**
   southwest corner of State Street and Jackson Street

John B. Robinson, a Congressman and local political figure, who was editor of the *Media Ledger*, a well known weekly newspaper at the turn of the century built this in 1895.

5. **Old Media Borough Hall**
   1 West State Street, northwest corner of State Street and Jackson Street

In the days before the creation of the town, today's central location was the site of the Way Homestead, one of Media's original farms in 1850. Isaac Chalfont later built a livery stable here with stagecoach service to Chester. The fare was 25 cents one way. The present Neoclassical building was constructed as a post office in 1918. In 1969 it was converted into municipal offices and police station. Today it functions as a restaurant.

TURN RIGHT (NORTH) ON JACKSON STREET. TURN LEFT ON FRONT STREET.

6. **south side of Front Street between Jackson and Olive streets**

This typical block of Media row homes dates from 1880. They retain original brick walks and facades.

TURN RIGHT ON OLIVE STREET.

7. *Soldiers' Monument*
   east lawn of the Delaware County Court House

This granite infantryman stands as a memorial to the Delaware County artillery, navy and cavalry - and the "patriotic women who aided the defenders of our country" - during the Civil War. The monument was dedicated in 1885.

RETURN TO FRONT STREET AND TURN RIGHT (WEST).

8. *Delaware County Record* **Building**
   112 Front Street

The row of brick buildings between South Avenue and Olive Street and South Avenue was Media's first office district and dates from the 1850s. Number 112 in 1878 was the home of the *Delaware County Record*, a widely known and respected weekly newspaper of the period.

The *Delaware County Record* was established by J. W. Batting & Co., the company being C. D. Williamson and Joseph Chadwick, on March 23, 1878, as an independent local newspaper. Originally an eight-column paper, twenty by twenty-seven inches, page measure, it was so successful that the proprietors enlarged it to nine columns in less than a year from the time it was started. This block is now a borough historic district and retains the atmosphere of Media's early days.

RETURN TO OLIVE STREET AND TURN RIGHT (SOUTH). TURN RIGHT (WEST) ON STATE STREET.

9. Haldeman's Store
101 West State Street

Isaac Haldeman, first president of Media Borough Council, built this grocery and dry goods store in 1854. Haldeman was one of the original movers in the establishment of the First National Bank of Media, was a member of its board of directors, and its president from the day of organization until his death. The bank was organized February 22, 1864, chartered March 12th, and opened for business on March 21st in the second story of Haldeman's store building.

10. Burdsall & Adams Cigar Factory
106 West State Street

In 1900 this was Media's leading industry, employing fifty people. The famous Burdsall & Adams cigar cost 5 cents. The building dates to 1879.

11. First National Bank of Media (Provident National Bank)
114 West State Street

Designed by Albert Dilks and constructed in 1900, the first permanent home of the First National Bank of Media is a landmark example of the rare Chateauesque style, with numerous stylistic references to French Renaissance and Richardson Romanesque detail and form. The great bronze doors at the front are original.

12. Phoenix Building
115-117 West State Street

This commercial building dates to 1895 and the facade features tiers of Romanesque arches and broad corner quoins.

13. Beatty Building
northwest corner of State Street and South Avenue

Dating from 1849, this was the first commercial structure erected in Media and continues in business use today. The lot on which it is located was purchased for $367.50 during the original sale of ground in Media by the County Commissioners.

TURN RIGHT (NORTH) ON SOUTH AVENUE. WALK UP THE EAST (RIGHT SIDE OF THE STREET).

14. Delaware County Institute of Science
northwest corner of South Avenue and Jasper Street (Veterans Square)

The first meeting of the Institute was held in Upper Providence on the 21st of September, 1833, by five persons - George Miller, Minshall Painter, John Miller, George Smith, and John Cassin. An acre of land was purchased near Rose Tree, and in 1837 a two-story brick building was erected, which was formally opened in September of that year, upon which occasion an address was delivered by Dr. Robert M. Patterson, then director of the United States Mint. The present three-story temple-like Greek Revival brick structure was built in 1867. Dr. George Smith was president from the first till his death, February, 1882.

15. Delaware County Court House
Front Street at the head of South Street

The original section was completed in 1851 with one courtroom. The structure was later expanded and altered in 1871, 1913 and 1929. It is generally regarded as one of the handsomest court houses in the eastern United States. William Jennings Bryan once orated from the front steps and Ronald Reagan also spoke here.

TURN AROUND AND WALK DOWN THE EAST SIDE OF SOUTH AVENUE.

16. Legal Row
South Street between Jasper and Front streets

This was the first business district of Media, occupied by lawyers and early merchants in 1850. An early photographic studio, Thompson's Daguerreotypes, as well as a druggist and chemist were located here.

17. Plymouth Hall (Charter House)
northeast corner of State Street and South Street

This house, one of the notable institutions of Media as a place of happy entertainment for "the wayfarer and the stranger," was a monument to those zealous friends of temperance who triumphed after a hard fight and made the prohibition of the liquor traffic one of the provisions of the town charter.

TURN RIGHT ON STATE STREET.

18. Delaware County American Building
212 West State Street

The first newspaper in Media was *The Union and Delaware County Democrat*, a small sheet started prior to June, 1852, by Charles B. Stowe. The town was then quite small, and it is not strange that the obituary of the little sheet should have appeared in the *Republican* as early as Dec. 29, 1854. It read as follows: "DEAD. - *The Union and Delaware County Democrat*, published at Media in this county, has adjourned sine die, its editor having removed to West Chester. A good opportunity is now presented to an enterprising man with a few thousand dollars, who desires to embark in the printing and publishing business."

The next newspaper venture in the new county-seat was destined to be a more successful one, and to result in the permanent establishment of the *Delaware County American*. The paper was started as the *Media Advertiser* by Thomas V. Cooper and D. A. Vernon on March 1, 1855. Its politics were Republican. The publication office was here on State Street.

19. Engle Bakery
216 West State Street

This was originally the German bakery of Christian Schur in 1892 and later purchased by Harry Engle who baked bread, cakes and confectionary here. Homemade ice cream was 5 cents a plate.

TURN RIGHT ON ORANGE STREET.

20. Williamson House
southwest corner of Orange Street and Front Street

Built in 1850 by Charles R. Williamson, a borough councilman and businessman. The Federal-style house has been used as a residence, post office, grocery store and shoe factory during its history. The structure was restored as law offices in 1976.

RETURN TO STATE STREET AND TURN RIGHT.

21. Cooper House
330 West State Street

This was the first home in Media of Thomas V. Cooper, state legislator and president of the Pennsylvania State Senate in 1878. This house was built prior to 1870. Number 330A was later used as an office by Dr. Philip Jaisohn, a famous Korean patriot and founding father of Korean independence from Japan. He settled in Media after service as a medical officer in three wars for which he was commended by Congress in 1946.

22. 331-341 West State Street

One of the last undisturbed blocks of old Media, Nos. 331-341 were built between 1855 and 1873.

TURN RIGHT ON LEMON STREET.

23. First School House
8 Lemon Street

In 1853 a small brick school-house was erected here, which was the first in the new town. Media became a separate school district early in 1856 and a new school was ready in 1860. The lot and building were sold to Charles R. Williamson for five hundred and fifty dollars.

TURN LEFT ON FRONT STREET.

24. Broomall House
West Street at the head of Front Street

Built in 1873 it was the home of John M. Broomall, a county judge, Civil War Congressman, and friend of Abraham Lincoln. It is a typical Victorian estate house of the latter half of the nineteenth century.

TURN LEFT ON WEST STREET. TURN LEFT ON BALTIMORE AVENUE. TURN RIGHT ON ORANGE STREET.

25. Hillhurst
216 South Orange Street

Built in 1890 by John Biddle as a Queen Anne summer cottage, it was designed by Addison Hutton, a famous Quaker architect of the Victorian period. This site was once part of the John Hill farm, one of the original properties composing what is now Media. H. Jones Brooke purchased the ground and erected the Brooke Hall Female Seminary in 1856, one block to the west. It's most famous graduate was Ida Saxton, wife of President William McKinley.

26. Christ Church
311 South Orange Street

During the summer of 1853 the first Episcopalian religious services in Media were held in the court-house, then recently built. From that time until the present church edifice was constructed services were held in the courthouse and in the Methodist Church. The corner-stone of the present church edifice was laid July 5, 1858.

RETURN TO BALTIMORE AVENUE AND TURN RIGHT.

27. Towne House
117 Veterans Square

The Towne House was founded in 1951 by Silvio "Babe" D'Ignazio. He acquired the nickname as either the youngest child in an Italian family or for his exploits on the football field as a center for the Pennsylvania Military College (now Widener University) where he was as strong as Paul Bunyan's blue ox, Babe. It was only one small row house at the time, but new rooms were added over the years. After D"Ignazio passed away in 2008 at the age of 90 the road in front of the Towne House was re-christened "Babe's Way."

28. Media Presbyterian Church
30 East Baltimore Avenue

The church - Media's first - was built on one of two lots donated to the church by Mr. John Beatty from 40 acres he had purchased in 1853. On October 11, 1855, the Media Presbyterian Church, designed by Philadelphia architect John McArthur, was dedicated. The church operated in the beginning as a mission of the Middletown Presbyterian Church. The total cost for construction was $10,500, financed partly through contributions with the balance of $3,500 paid for by the Presbytery of Philadelphia. The money promised by the Presbytery of Philadelphia was eventually paid but only after a long delay. Reverend Dale mortgaged his home and personally carried the debt for a long time. This was done so that the contractor could be paid and the construction of the church proceed without interruption.

TURN LEFT ON CHURCH STREET. TURN RIGHT ON STATE STREET.

29. SEPTA Trolley Line

Media is the last suburban town in America with a trolley running down its main street.

RETURN TO THE TOUR STARTING POINT AT THE MEDIA THEATRE.

Look Up,

Milford

A Walking Tour of Milford...

In 1793 when a deadly wave of yellow fever swept through Philadelphia, those who could afford to leave, did. One who left was President George Washington, who moved to Germantown, about ten miles away. Another who could afford to leave was John Biddis. Biddis began his career as a tavern owner who later invented a new white lead paint in 1783. He opened a paint factory and soon was making the city's first wallpaper. Another invention tanned hides with gums from the barks of various trees. Biddis was 44 years of age when he removed his family from Philadelphia to the healthy air along the Delaware River in what was then known as Wells Ferry.

Thomas Quick had settled the area in 1733 where various ferries operated, most enduringly, one by Andrew Dingman. Biddis bought a huge swath of land, large enough to lay out 530 lots in 1796 and he had enough land left over to offer buyers two acres outside of town for every acre purchased in town. Biddis began paper construction in a mill to be built on the Sawkill Creek, the first in the United States to use wood pulp rather than rags (another invention of his) and so named his new village "Milford." Soon a second mill was operating, this one reusing wool. In 1806 he was charged by the governor with building the first bridge across the Delaware River when he died. His children took up residence here rather than Philadelphia and many streets you will be walking on carry their names - Ann, Catharine, and so on.

Pike County was birthed from Wayne County in 1814, named, like several around the United States, for explorer Zebulon Pike. Milford, the county seat, was incorporated in 1874. The first family of Milford was the Pinchots, who arrived in 1816 and opened a mercantile operation, The French Store. In 1850, by the time 19-year old James was ready to enter the family business there was no room so he trundled off to New York City and made a fortune in the wallpaper trade. He retired after 25 years and by 1886 had built the French-influenced Grey Towers in his hometown.

At the time his son Gifford was 21 and instilled with a love of nature. When his friend Theodore Roosevelt became President in 1900, Gifford Pinchot was named the first Chief Forester of the United States Forest Service. During his tenure, national forests tripled in size to 193 million acres. Later, Pinchot became one of Pennsylvania's most popular and progressive governors, wiping out a $30 million budget deficit and paving rural roads to "get the farmer out of the mud."
The Pinchots donated Grey Towers to the American public in 1963.

Our walking tour will begin at an historic building constructed by the Pinchots in 1907 that was intended for use by commercial shops on the first floor and for classrooms for Yale University's Forest School on the upper floors...

1. **Forest Hall**
   200 Broad Street at northeast corner of
   East Harford Street

Calvert Vaux, designer of the Metropolitan Museum of Art, used native bluestone to craft the old Milford Post Office on the corner in 1863. Studio space upstairs was utilized by such artists as John Ferguson Weir and others of the Hudson River School. The Second Empire building is topped by a steep hipped roof with segmented dormers and classical details. Side mansard roofs flank the center with an eyebrow dormer looking out over Broad Street.

The monumental building that dominates the block lays claim to the birthplace of the American Conservation movement. It was built for James Pinchot in 1904, father of Gifford. Gifford Pinchot studied in France and became the first American trained in forestry. He was named Chief Forester of the U. S. Division of Forestry and served under his good friend Theodore Roosevelt from 1898 to 1910. Together the two placed over 200 million acres of national forest under scientific land management. At one time this building was the summer school for Yale University School of Forestry. The first five chiefs of the United States Forest Service were all either instructors or students at Forest Hall.

The massive masonry building was designed by Hunt & Hunt, successor to famed New York architect Richard Morris Hunt and leading proponent of French Chateauesque architecture in America. Four hipped dormers with French windows face the front and back of the building. On the corner of the facade is a two-story, round oriel window complete with pendant and finial.

WALK EAST ON BROAD STREET.

2. **Normandy Cottage**
   219 Broad Street

This Tudor Revival cottage was built in 1903 in the original Pinchot family garden by James Pinchot for his son Amos. The playful exterior is splashed with a variety of textures: steep roof with fish-scale slate shingles, bluestone used with the chimney and corner quoins, rubble stone with half-timbering and stucco, and round glass decorations that may be the bottom of glass bottles.

3. **First Presbyterian Church**
   300 Broad Street

The church began as a Sunday School in "The Old Jail House" in 1824. Architect George Barton produced this Romanesque-influenced church of locally produced bricks fifty years later. The triple windows are banded with sandstone to give the facade a polychrome surface decoration. The bell tower and clock were donated in 1887 by William Bross, Lt. Governor of Illinois and president of the Chicago-based *Tribune* company. Bross, the first signer of the constitutional amendment abolishing slavery, grew up in Milford and attended the Milford Academy.

TURN LEFT ON WEST ANN STREET.

4. **Hissam House**
   108 West Ann Street

This traditional British folk house dates to before the American Revolution. The stylish Georgian door surround was added at a later date to give the house a little pizzazz.

5. **Quick House**
   110 West Ann Street

Another vernacular home from around 1800, the gable-fronted house has been updated with a splashy front porch, spandrels and one-story bay window.

6. **Armstrong House**
   206 West Anne Street

Tucked behind a white picket fence, this Queen Anne house from 1901 features a steep hipped roof and a battery of picturesque oriel windows.

7. **208 West Anne Street**

This attractive Queen Anne style house dates to the 1870s. Signature touches include fine spindle work on the porch banisters and fish-scale shingling. Through the adjoining alley is a carriage house that once served as a viewing parlor for an undertaker. Lenni Lenape Chief Indian Cloud was laid out to rest here.

8. Armstrong House
209 West Ann Street

This brick Italianate residence from 1875 may take its veranda, bay window and tower design from Calvert Vaux's influential architecture pattern book, *Villas and Cottages*. The decorative details such as double-hooded window crown groupings with keystones, bracketed cornices, porch details and cupola are all hallmarks of this popular style.

WALK PAST THE PARK ALONG THE ALLEYWAY IN FRONT OF THE ARMSTRONG HOUSE TO WEST CATHARINE STRET AND TURN RIGHT.

9. 205 West Catharine Street

This Second Empire house with single bracketed mansard roof, wide cut-out spandrels on the front veranda, round window and door surrounds, dates to the early 1870s.

10. Episcopal Church
321 5th Street at southeast corner of Catharine Street

The Church of the Good Shepherd was organized on April 3, 1871. The cornerstone of the first church building at Fifth and Catharine Streets was laid in June 1871 and on September 14, 1877 the church was consecrated. The rectory was started in the spring of 1891. Around the same time, the parish hall was added for Sunday School, dinner, dances and other functions.

11. Milford Borough Building
109 West Catharine Street

E.S. Wolfe designed this building for the town government offices to greet a new century in a new building. He used indigenous bluestone, often seen around town not only in buildings but sidewalks as well. When built in 1899 the tower was capped with an open metal form to support the fire alarm bell.

12. Bloomgarden Building
320-322 Broad Street, northeast corner of Church Street

Over the years this building has housed a bank and a succession of retail stores. The third floor was known as Brown's Hall and hosted civic events. The Italianate style reveals itself here in the recessed window openings, stone quoining at the corners and the decorative cornice. Look up and notice the small pediment brackets which start above the roof-line and extend through the cornice and wide frieze band.

TURN LEFT ON BROAD STREET.

13. Hotel Fauchère
401 Broad Street, southwest corner of Catharine Street

Louis Fauchère, former chef at Delmonico's Restaurant in New York City, opened this hotel in 1852 as a summer business. Fauchère would work during the winter months at restaurants in New York City. The present Italianate style building opened in 1880, with twenty–four sleeping rooms and other apartments, including a beautiful dining room at the rear of the house enclosed with glass. Having worked at America's most famous restaurant, and staying friends with his fellow French-speaking Swiss, the Delmonico brothers, helped lure prominent politicians, artists and others to the hotel. In the guest register have been Andrew Carnegie, Robert Frost, Mae West, Babe Ruth, Henry Ford and three United States presidents.

14. Tom Quick Inn
441 Broad Street

The Tom Quick Inn was originally two different hotels, the Terwilliger House and the Centre Square House. Amanda Beck Terwilliger built her three-story hostelry in 1880 and George A. Frieh opened The Centre Square House two years later. In 1950 Robert Phillips joined the nearly identical Second Empire hotels to form the Tom Quick Inn.

15. Pike County Court House
412-414 Broad Street

Architect George Barton blended the popular Second Empire style with classical elements in 1874 to provide Pike County with a suitably impressive courthouse. The mansard roof with cornice brackets and round, arched windows are standard-bearers for this French style. The roofline is rich with Palladian dormers, a classical pediment and domed cupola with paired pilasters. The tall 75-foot shaft, erected in 1899 and dedicated a year later on the site of Northampton County's first courthouse, was dedicated to the area's Civil War dead.

16. "Old Jail House"
500 Broad Street

This vernacular structure is side-gabled with masonry of rubble stone. It is the second oldest court house in Pennsylvania, constructed in 1814, and served in that capacity until the completion of the new court house across the street. For decades it did time as the county jail - look for five windows that were filled in with stone to keep prisoners from escaping. Atop the hexagonal cupola is a weather vane with the state fish, a wiggling brook trout.

17. Wallace House
501 Broad Street

This was a simple three-room house when it was built in 1835 before it received a complete transformation in the popular Greek Revival style of the day. Side wings were added and a dominant Doric portico applied to the front center.

TURN RIGHT ON EAST HIGH STREET.

18. The Judge School
111 East High Street

In the 1920s this was a fashionable hotel called The Windsor before Margaret Duer Judge converted it into a school for exceptional children. The imposing eclectic house sits back in its lot and has been called the most important wood-frame structure in the Milford Historical District. Starting at the roof the original finial sits atop the bell cupola and shares the skyline with chimney pots, tile cresting, patterned fish-scale slate shingles, gables, dormers, and stick spandrels with pendants. Circular porches wrap around the facade. If that wasn't enough going on architecturally, partial wagon wheels decorate the front and side entrance stairs.

TURN RIGHT ON FOURTH STREET. TURN LEFT ON EAST CATHARINE STREET.

19. 207 East Catharine Street

This gable-front-and-wing house folk Victorian dates to the 1880s. The cornice features brackets that were common at that time and the gracefully curving porch stands out.

TURN RIGHT ON THIRD STREET AND TURN LEFT ON EAST ANN STREET.

20. 306 East Ann Street

Architect A.S. Brown crafted this Queen Anne house in 1898 as an early experiment in passive solar energy. Windows were placed to take advantage of the prevailing sun. White fir trees were strategically planted on the corners of the property to moderate the effects of temperature. The roof forms include gambrel, gable and hip. Subsequent owners have redesigned the plain, cedar shake wall pattern in the front with a dramatic hexagon and diamond design. Other changes include the eye-catching sunburst in the porch gable.

TURN AND WALK UP EAST ANN STREET, TOWARDS THE CENTER OF TOWN.

21. Forsythe Hall
212 3rd Street at the norhteast corner of East Ann Street

This 1898 Queen Anne house was restored to its century-old appearance after recent owners uncovered an old photograph of the house.

22. Methodist Church
206 East Ann Street

This is a Gothic church from 1864, highlighted by beautiful stained-glass lancet windows. The first Methodist-Episcopal church was built in 1826 just north of the "Jersey Bridge" on the banks of the Delaware. After recurrent flooding a new church was erected in the current parking lot. The belltower is considered a local adaptation of the Italianate style.

23. Milford Academy
200 East Ann Street

The unusual size and number of the windows betray this house's beginnings in the 1850s as the Milford Academy; the windows provided light for teaching in the classroom and studying in the dormitory above. At the turn of the 19th century new owners lifted and turned the entire building so the gable-end faced East Ann Street and added a front porch to make the structure look more like a house. It was common practice to move buildings as a way to preserve resources and, more importantly, money.

TURN LEFT ON FOURTH STREET.

24. Milford Masonic Lodge `
204 Fourth Street

This three-story, red-brick building was built in 1875 as a general store. For a time it housed a pill manufacturer. In 1901 it became home of the Milford Masonic Lodge. With the exception of the modern front door, the Italianate facade is intact with a heavy cornice over the first floor and a large glass store front.

TURN LEFT ON EAST HARFORD STREET.

25. Mansard Building
205 East Harford Street

This Second Empire house retains much of its detail from the early 1870s - straight mansard roof with fish-scale shingles, molded cornices, decorative brackets supporting a wide overhanging eave. Simple round window surrounds with original fitting windows and shutters plus chamfered porch supports complete the effect.

TURN AND RETRACE YOUR STEPS ON EAST HARFORD STREET, WALKING TOWARDS THE CENTER OF TOWN.

26. Harford House
201 East Harford Street

This is the oldest house in Milford. Although it has undergone alterations it is essentially the same building that stood in the 1700s. The house is oriented with its gable-end to the street and the main entrance set off to the south, perhaps to have once faced Sawkill Creek. Nineteenth-century changes can be found in the tiny Gothic window in the gable and scalloped Doric capitals on the front porch posts. The rear barn dating to 1800 has one remaining "Indian shutter" that could be closed against attack. The house was built by Robert Harford and sufficiently grand to host the Marquis de Lafayette on a tour of America in 1824.

27. The Egg House
110 East Harford Street

This picturesque Italianate villa, built in 1862 by Cyril C.D. Pinchot, grandfather of Governor Gifford Pinchot, also blends Greek Revival details such as the dentils between elaborate double brackets and classical pediments as window caps. Egg-shape decorations grace the pillars of the veranda. The roofline is distinguished by a cupola decorated with drop pendants and a finial. All is beautifully preserved behind a cast-iron harp fence.

28. Gulick House
106 East Harford Street

This house from the 1870s show elements of the Stick Style with its simple porch spandrels, a cut-away bay window with curved flat braces, and truss work in the gables.

29. Dimmick Inn
101 East Harford Street

Samuel Dimmick built this inn in 1856 to replace an earlier structure that had stood since 1828 before falling in a fire. Dimmick was County Treasurer, Commissioner and Justice of the Peace and the day to day operations were handled by his daughter Frances, familiarly known as "Miss Fan." Miss Fan played the fiddle, fished, rode horses and favored wearing men's clothing. Under her guidance the Dimmick Inn became as much an area tourist attraction as the mountains and waterfalls. She may never have left Dimmick Inn - her ghost is said to haunt the building to this day.

30. Community House & Pike County Library
201 Broad Street at southeast corner of East Harford Street

Cyrille Pinchot built this early Greek Revival house in the 1820s. It demonstrates such classical elements as a dentiled cornice, pilasters, and door surrounds with rectangular transom and sidelights. The second story round-hooded window is topped with a keystone in the molding. The imposing front portico with two sets of Ionic columns was matched by a side portico during an early 1900s alteration. The building serves today as library and meeting center for Pike County.

YOU HAVE NOW RETURNED TO THE TOUR STARTING POINT.

Look Up,

New Castle

A Walking Tour of New Castle...

In 1798, John Carlysle Stewart, a civil engineer, traveled to western Pennsylvania to resurvey the "donation lands" granted by the government to Revolutionary War veterans. In the course of performing his task, he discovered that the original survey forgot to stake out 50 acres at the confluence of the Shenango River and Neshannock Creek. Stewart claimed it for himself.

Stewart laid out the town of New Castle, named for his hometown in Delaware, in April of 1798; the town became a borough in 1825, having a population of about 300. Business began to flourish with the construction of the canal system which made its way through the city. Numerous manufacturing plants located in New Castle because of the availability of transportation facilities and ready access to raw material markets. The canal system was later supplemented and then replaced by the railroad system which offered greater speed and capacity for freight as well as year round service.

In the 1870s, the city became a major hub of the Pittsburgh and Lake Erie Railroad and by 1900 was one of the fastest growing cities in the country, heralded as the tin plate capital of the world. The population swelled from 11,600 in 1890 to 28,339 in 1900, and to 38,280 in 1910, as immigrants flocked to the city to work in the mills. Steel and paper mills, foundries, a bronze bushing factory, and car-construction plants contributed to the economy. In addition, the Shenango China produced here would find its way onto the White House dinner tables of Presidents Dwight D. Eisenhower and Lyndon B. Johnson.

New Castle has been known for decades as the Fireworks Capital of America; it is home to Zambelli Fireworks, the largest manufacturer and exhibitor of fireworks today. Our walking tour will begin at Zambelli Plaza that has been designed to be a focal point of downtown New Castle where the two major roads of East Washington and Mill streets join and a fireworks sculpture illuminates the night...

WALK SOUTH ON MILL STREET, TOWARDS THE SHENANGO RIVER.

1. Cascade Center
11 South Mill Street at southeast corner of East Washington Street

This site is the birthplace of the legendary Warner Brothers movie studio of Hollywood fame. The four founding Warner brothers (born Wonskolaser in their native Poland) emigrated to Ontario, Canada and later moved to nearby Youngstown, Ohio. In 1903, Harry, Sam and Jack showing a used copy of *The Great Train Robbery* at Idora Park in Youngstown, and then traveled to New Castle to screen the movie in a vacant store on the site of what would become the Cascade Center. This makeshift theatre, called the Bijou, was furnished with chairs borrowed from a local funeral home. In 1906, the brothers purchased a small theater on this site, which they called the Cascade Movie Palace, taking its name from nearby Cascade Park. The Warners maintained the theater until moving into film distribution in 1907. Within a decade they were in Hollywood producing movies.

The buildings eventually fell into disrepair and the Cascade was demolished to make way for a parking lot. In 1996, parts of the wall of the building that housed the Bijou collapsed onto East Washington Street. The city of New Castle was very close to issuing a condemnation notice to the building, but its historical significance led to redevelopment plans.

TURN RIGHT ON EAST WASHINGTON STREET.

2. Stritmater's Brothers
126 East Washington Street

Brothers W.A. and J.R. Stritmater, dealers in dry goods, millinery, carpets, merchant tailoring, boots and shoes, began business on East Washington Street in 1876. The original ground floor has been compromised but the bothers would recognize the upper facade if they walked down the street today.

3. Huntington National Bank
101 East Washington Street

Some of the finest buildings in northwestern Pennsylvania were built for banking institutions along East Washington Street, New Castle's main thoroughfare.

4. First Commonwealth Bank
27 East Washington Street

This sturdy vault combines elements of Art Deco (small, square glass panes), Classical (Ionic columns) and Beaux-Arts (sculptured facade at the cornice).

5. Kennedy Square
East Washington and Jefferson streets

When John Carlysle Stewart platted the town he set aside this piece of land as the town square. In one form or another, it has remained the town square ever since. The square has been reconfigured several times. Like most town squares in Western Pennsylvania, it is known as "The Diamond." In 1846 a brick market house was built here. In 1886, the Ladies Park Association was organized for the purpose of beautifying the public square, which as one member put it was "as desolate as the Sahara."

By 1891, the Association had begun raising money for a monument to commemorate the soldiers who had died during the Civil War. In 1893, the granite for the monument was shipped from Quincy, Illinois, and work was begun. The monument was finished in 1896, and on December 15, 1897, the statue was placed on the top. The cannon was placed in the park and later a plaque with the Gettysburg address was placed by the monument. There are now stone monuments to the men who served in the Spanish-American War and World War I.

In the 1960s the square was officially dedicated to John F. Kennedy when a memorial fountain was erected. The western portion of the diamond was wiped out by a runaway truck coming down the North Hill on Jefferson Street in May of 2006.

6. Coney Island
9 East Washington Street

New Castle fancies itself as the "hot dog capital of the world" - its chili dogs are the product of Greek immigrants who came to town in the early 1900s and established restaurants along with their homes. Since 1923, Coney Island has been serving its famous hot dogs when cooks would stack up to 20 hot dogs on their forearms in order to speed up the addition of condiments. Over the years Coney Island has grown into multiple locations and continues to be one of the most popular hot dog destinations in America.

7. United States Post Office
south side of Kennedy Square

The old Post Office was designed by the W. G. Eckles Company in the 1930s with a massive front of fluted Doric columns. Now it is used as an office building.

8. First Christian Church
23 West Washington Street

The First Christian Church in New Castle was formally organized in March of 1856. At that time, the congregation met at the old Covenant Church. They moved into their own church on North Street in April 1858. In February 1868, the congregation moved into their present building on West Washington Street, a building with only a sanctuary and steeple.

TURN RIGHT ON BEAVER STREET.

9. St. Mary's Catholic Church
124 North Beaver Street

In 1866 the cornerstone for this Gothic-inspired church was laid on a large lot purchased for $4,000 on the corner of Beaver and North Streets. Five years and $15,000 later the sanctuary was ready for services.

TURN RIGHT ON NORTH STREET.
TURN LEFT ON JEFFERSON STREET.

10. First Presbyterian Church
125 North Jefferson Street

The first Presbyterian services in town were held under a tent set up over an outdoor pulpit roofed over and partly enclosed on three sides. Worshipers sat on logs and stumps in the open air.

In 1804 the first house of worship was built of round logs in a dense thicket near a tannery a little east of the present intersection of West Falls and Shenango streets. This was the first church building in New Castle. At that time there were only two log cabins in downtown New Castle. The congregation's first brick building was constructed here in 1825.

The fourth church for the Presbyterians was located here in 1845 and served almost 50 years until it was replaced with the current Richardsonian Romanesque styled brick-and-stone church in 1896. It was designed by S.W. Foulke, a leading practitioner of the Romanesque style throughout the Ohio Valley and Appalachia; he had planned that the main tower should be about ten feet higher than it is, but the financial panic of 1893 drained enough funds that the church was completed with the tower at its present height.

11. Municipal Building
230 North Jefferson Street

The Municipal Building features a stylish Art Deco facade that harkens back to New Castle's glory days of the 1920s.

12. Raney-Jameson Castle
330 North Jefferson Street

This Queen Anne mansion constructed of coursed, rock faced limestone was built in 1892 for Leander Raney, who owned the Raney & Burger Iron Works and Raney Milling Company. Also designed by S.W. Foulke, it features a round tower in the south bay with a conical roof, a square turret and a main gable with decorative patterns. The house was purchased in 1907 by David Jameson, one of the founders of Citizens Bank and through whose efforts the Jameson Memorial Hospital was established. The castle was badly damaged by fire in May 1998.

13. Greer House
408 North Jefferson Street

The residence was built in 1904-1905 for George Greer, Lawrence County's Tin King. Frank Foulke designed the three-story, rectangular plan Colonial Revival residence on a rock-faced coursed limestone foundation. It has a full front porch with clustered and fluted Ionic columns on limestone piers, with a short open balustrade. It was lived in by the Greer family until 1965 and was donated by the subsequent owners, the Clavellis, in 1982 to the Lawrence County Historical Society and is now a museum.

TURN RIGHT ON LINCOLN AVENUE.

14. The Scottish Rite Cathedral
110-120 East Lincoln Street

The Scottish Rite Cathedral was constructed in 1924-1925 for the FreeMasons Lodge #433 at the cost of $1,750,000. It is a Neoclassical design by R. G. Schmid Co. of Chicago. The foundations consist of 916 concrete piles, 20 to 28 feet long. The main facade on Lincoln Street is two stories and nine bays wide. It has two-light windows in frieze, the architrave with "Scottish Rite Cathedral" and monumental engaged stone Ionic columns. The Cathedral is perfectly placed on the crest of the hill.

The interior contains a ballroom, banquet room and theater, as well as Masons' lodge rooms and various smaller chambers. The theater seating capacity is 3,240, consisting of the main floor and two balconies.

15. Henderson House
northwest corner of Lincoln Street
and Highland Avenue

The two and one-half story Queen Anne residences with patterned masonry was built in 1895 for Mathias Holstein Henderson, vice-president of the Lawrence Savings and Trust Bank. The prominently situated, ivy-coated mansion is most notable for its distinctive red tile roofing.

16. Ohl House
208 East Lincoln Street

The house was built in 1899 for Edwin Newton Ohl, an executive with Republic Iron and Steel. He later became president of United Iron and Steel (1906), president of New Castle Portland Cement Company (1908) and was a director of the First National Bank. The Queen Anne mansion sports a high hip roof, a tower with conical roof located in west bay, and prominent gabled roof dormers.

RETURN TO HIGHLAND AVENUE AND TURN LEFT TO WALK DOWN THE HILL BACK TOWARD DOWNTOWN.

17. Johnson House
318 Highland Avenue

The home was built for George W. Johnson in 1901. Johnson was a leading local industrialist involved in limestone, iron and bronze production. He was principal owner of the American Car and Ship Hardware Company in 1901, which he later purchased and renamed Johnson Bronze. The home was designed by local architect Harry W. Wirsing who created an symmetrical Colonial Revival mansion of bowed bays with prominent, classically inspired roof dormers with open pediments, Ionic pilaster and decorative round top windows. There is a central stained glass window at the second floor with stained glass circular windows to each side.

18. Bower House
460 Northampton Street

John Bower was a local merchant and tailor and pioneer home builder in the historic North Hill district. This Second Empire mansion dates to 1889. Noteworthy are the mansard roof with slate shingles and paired brackets under the eaves and spindle woodworking on the porch.

19. Reis House
   312 Highland Avenue

This Queen Anne frame residence was built for industrialist William Reis. Many members of the Reis family lived in the house including politician William M. Brown, a Pennsylvania senator and, in 1902, the Lt. Governor of the Commonwealth. A turret is located in the south bay with a conical slate roof and a small elaborate spindle balcony in the North Bay. There is a veranda with spindle work, open balustrade and frieze.

20. Trinity Episcopal Church
   212 North Mill Street

The first Protestant Episcopal services were held in New Castle in 1843, at the home of Dr. A. Andrews, who had settled here in 1834; the parish was organized five years later. The present handsome church building was erected in 1902, and is the only stone church in the town.

21. New Castle Lodge, No. 69
   127 North Mill Street

This classically inspired lodge hall was built for the fraternal organization, the New Castle Lodge, No. 69, Benevolent Protective Order of Elks, founded in 1887. It features symmetrical proportions and Doric columns, both large and small.

CONTINUE DOWN MILL STREET
TO THE TOUR STARTING POINT.

Look Up, Norristown

A Walking Tour of Norristown...

There was nothing organic about the birth of Norristown. In 1784, Montgomery County was created out of Philadelphia County by an act of the Commonwealth. A 27-1/2 acre parcel in what is now Norristown Borough was stipulated to be purchased for the new county's seat of government, making it one of the earliest established in Pennsylvania. It took the name of an ancient landowner in the area, Isaac Norris. Norris had been mayor of Philadelphia 60 years earlier - Ben Franklin had just gotten to town and George Washington wasn't even born yet. Norris himself was born in England in 1671 - and thus may be the oldest person for whom a Pennsylvania town is named.

Norristown was not destined to be a sleepy government town. Water power draining into the Schuylkill River along the Stoney Creek and Saw Mill Run encouraged early industry and Norristown was superbly sited to take advantage of early American transportation. The Schuylkill Canal was completed in 1826 and the Reading Railroad arrived in 1834. Horse drawn trolley cars ran through town by the 1880s and Norristown had some of the earliest electrified trolley lines in America. When the Philadelphia and Western electrified high speed line was constructed in 1912, Norristown was in easy commuting distance of Philadelphia, 20 miles away. It was heady enough for borough boosters to proclaim in Centennial literature that year that, "Norristown is now the biggest, busiest, brightest Borough in the world."

Now on the eve of the centennial of that Centennial proclamation, our walking tour will investigate how that boast holds up, beginning at the county court house at the heart of the Norristown Central Historic District...

1. Montgomery County Court House
2 East Airy Street at southeast corner of Swede Street

The oldest part of the Court House, which faces Swede Street, is of the Greek Revival style. It was built as the result of a competition of 1849 between Thomas U. Walter (architect of Girard College and later of the U.S. Capitol dome) and Napoleon LeBrun, designer of Philadelphia's Academy of Music and Cathedral of Sts. Peter and Paul. LeBrun's successful design originally featured a steeple that was even higher than the Presbyterian church's to the east, and it was criticized as being out of keeping with the Greek Revival style. The steeple was replaced by the dome in a substantial renovation of 1904. The interior of the Court House dates largely from that time, when the stained glass ceilings in courtrooms A, B, and C were installed.

WALK SOUTH ON SWEDE STREET. (THE COURT HOUSE WILL BE ON YOUR LEFT).

2. Courthouse Plaza and Public Square
Main Street at Swede Street

Courthouse Plaza is home to several notable memorials, the first being erected in 1868 to "the brave soldiers and sailors who fell defending the Union during the Great Rebellion." Others include remembrances of David Rittenhouse, who calculated and observed the transit of Venus at his home in Norrtion in 1769, of Military Order of Purple Heart recipients, of Montgomery County sons and daughters lost in the Vietnam War, and to the victims of the World Trade Center attacks, sculpted with a twisted piece of I-beam from the North Tower. This square was owned by the University of Pennsylvania - rent was one acorn per year.

TURN RIGHT ON WEST MAIN STREET.

3. Penn Norristown Trust Building
1 West Main Street at northwest corner of Swede Street

In 1850, 24-year old Jacob Morton Albertson arrived in Norristown as a surveyor. By 1857 he was successful enough to establish his own private banking business. In 1889, with his sons aboard, the Albertson Trust and Safe Company was incorporated. In 1904 the bank was renamed the Penn Trust Company and when it merged with Norristown Trust twenty years later this handsome Renaissance Revival headquarters was constructed.

4. Cherry Court
104 West Main Street

Cherry Court, now a government office building, began life as a decorated Colonial Revival headquarters for the Town and Country Building and Loan Association that was founded in 1924.

5. Masonic Building
106 West Main Street

The Masons organized in Norristown in 1823; their Italianate-influenced temple with tall, slender windows, bracketed cornice and window hoods was constructed in 1854.

6. Montgomery National Bank
108 West Main Street

Norristown's first bank, the Montgomery National Bank, originally the Bank of Montgomery County when chartered in 1815, was built on Main Street in 1854. It was still the only bank in Montgomery County when it was built and would remain so another three years until the opening of the Bank of Pottstown. The Greek Revival building is brick with a marble front.

TURN AND WALK EAST ON MAIN STREET TO GREEN STREET.

7. Humane Fire Company
129 East Main Street at northwest corner of Green Street

Norristown's fourth fire department organized on July 27, 1852 and members officially adopted the name Humane Fire Engine Company No. 1 of Norristown, Pa. The name Humane was selected because the committee purchased their first piece of apparatus from the Humane Fire Company of Philadelphia No. 1. The company, still in operation moved into their current building in 1882.

RETURN TO DEKALB STREET AND TURN RIGHT.

8. Centre Theater
208 DeKalb Street

This Greek Revival building opened in 1851 as a lodge hall and public auditorium for the Odd Fellows; a mansard fourth story was applied in 1858. Many famous figures spoke here, including Abraham Lincoln, Mark Twain, Charles Dickens, and Daniel Webster. Until 1873, when the Music Hall was opened on Main Street, the Odd Fellows auditorium functioned as the entertainment center in town. In 1868, native son, General Winfield Scott Hancock accepted the nomination of the National Democratic Party to run for President in the hall and ran his campaign from the Lodge.

Early acts on the Vaudeville Circuit performed here and Phineas Taylor Barnum presented General Tom Thumb, world famous midget, and his wife, Lavinia Snow to a Norristown packed house. In 1910 the building was bought by the Gas Company of Montgomery County and began its longest run as office suites. In the 1990s it was acquired by the Greater Norristown Corporation who have returned it to is roots as the Centre Theater.

9. St. George Coptic Orthodox Church
411 DeKalb Street

This splendid Greek Revival church was built in 1863 as the Trinity Evangelical Lutheran church, replacing an 1849 church. This building was renovated at the turn of the century by Louis Comfort Tiffany and boasts Tiffany stained glass windows, a Tiffany glass mosaic, and an alabaster and gilt-bronze altar rail.

10. Jamison House
southeast corner of DeKalb and Airy Streets

Built in 1850 in the Greek Revival style for William Jamison, son of the founder of Jamison Mills, this property once included stables and outbuildings extending all the way to Green Street. The original small spindly balustrade near the center of the flat roof has been removed. There is a story that the house was originally to be only three stories, but when Jamison heard of the plans for the vast church tower to be erected across Airy Street, he feared his manse would be dwarfed so he had another story added in such haste that it was one big room. This was used as a ballroom for the rest of the century except when used by the children for rollerskating.

11. The First Presbyterian Church At Norristown
113 East Airy Street at northeast corner of DeKalb Street

Completed in 1854, the soaring spire remains as much a landmark above the town today as it was 150 years ago. The Italianate building presents a Greek Revival façade on Airy Street.

TURN LEFT ON AIRY STREET.

12. Montgomery County Jail
north side of East Airy Street between Church Street and DeKalb Street

The prison was constructed in 1853, as part of the same plan as the Court House. Also designed by Napoleon LeBrun, the original competition drawings show versions of the buildings in both Gothic and classical styles; Gothic was chosen here. The facade is of solid granite. There is an underground tunnel for conveying prisoners to and from the Court House.

13. Post Office
   28 East Airy Street

This Art Deco structure was completed as a Depression-era project by James Wetmore and Harry McMurtie. It has a lobby adorned with Works Project Association murals by Paul Mays and groundbreaking aluminum Deco/Classical metalwork. Note the decorative friezes at the top of the building.

14. St. John's Episcopal Church
   23 E Airy Street

St. John's Church stands as the oldest church building in continuous use by an Episcopal congregation in Montgomery County and as the first Episcopal parish organized after the Revolutionary War in the Diocese of Pennsylvania. Founded during the Summer of 1812 as "The Rector, Wardens, and Vestrymen of St. John's Church at Norristown in the County of Montgomery," the church building completed in 1815 is the oldest in Norristown. At his consecration Reverend William Allen White, noted that "the size and beauty of the building does great credit to the zeal of the few members of our communion resident in the small town and its vicinity."

15. Stinson House
   11 East Airy Street, northeast corner of Church Street

This Greek Revival townhouse was fashioned for Elijah Thomas in 1856. It was the former home of Mary Stinson, thought to be the first female professionally accredited psychiatrist in America. She left her fortune to found a home for elderly women.

WALK A FEW STEPS TO SWEDE STREET AND THE START OF THE TOUR.

Look Up,

☆Oakland

(Pittsburgh)

A Walking Tour of Oakland...

Oakland lays claim to being the third largest "downtown" in Pennsylvania after Center City Philadelphia and Downtown Pittsburgh. It is stuffed with museums, prestigious universities, fabled eateries, live entertainment venues, public art, spiritual centers and a huge quotient of "hipness."

In 1905, Franklin Nicola, who had purchased land from the estate of Mary Schenley two years earlier, put forth a development plan in the City Beautiful style, then sweeping across America, for Oakland. The City Beautiful movement favored boulevards, parks, and formal civic buildings in the Beaux-Arts style evoking ancient Greece and the Italian Renaissance. Although Nicola's plan was not fully implemented, including a never-constructed Oakland town hall, it produced several important landmarks. Oakland is, in fact, now home to three historic districts: The Schenley Farms National Historic District, the Oakland Civic Center Historic District and the Oakland Square Historic District.

Other major landmark buildings were added to Oakland after the pursuit of Nicola's designs had ended, including the Cathedral of Learning and Heinz Memorial Chapel of the University of Pittsburgh and Andrew Carnegie's contributions to the school he founded and the massive civic project that eventually became the Carnegie Museums and Library.

Our walking tour will travel down the two main thoroughfares that bustle with activity through Oakland, Forbes Avenue and Fifth Avenue, but first we'll begin in the bucolic open spaces of a great city park that was donated by a girl who ran away to elope when she was just a teenager...

1. Schenley Park
Boulevard of the Allies

Mary Elizabeth Croghan did not spend much of her 77 years in Pittsburgh, but few have matched her lasting influence on the city. Born near Louisville in 1826, Mary was the daughter of frontier businessman James O'Hara and stood to inherit large tracts of Pittsburgh land. That inheritance was jeopardized when, at the age of 15 in a Staten Island boarding school, she eloped with a 43-year old British sea captain named Edward Schenley. The incident became a highly publicized scandal on both sides of the Atlantic, not helped by the fact that Captain Schenley was AWOL from his post in British Guiana at the time and it was his third elopement. Mary's enraged father voided her inheritance by an act of the state legislature. Years later after he had calmed down, the two reconciled in England and in 1850 she received her full inheritance. Through the years she donated freely to Pittsburgh churches and public schools and in 1889 she gave the land that would become the 456-acre Schenley Park.

WALK TO SCHENLEY DRIVE IN THE NORTHWEST SECTION OF THE PARK.

2. Phipps Conservatory and Botanical Gardens
One Schenley Drive

Phipps Conservatory and Botanical Gardens in the park was a gift to Pittsburgh from steel and real estate baron Henry Phipps in 1893. Phipps directed the building of a splendid Victorian glasshouse designed by the renowned architectural firm of Lord and Burnham. Today Phipps Conservatory is one of the largest celebrations of botanical diversity in the country.

WALK OUT OF THE PARK PAST PHIPPS CONSERVATORY AND BEAR LEFT ON ROBERTO CLEMENTE DRIVE.

3. Frick Fine Arts Building
Schenley Drive

The Frick Fine Arts building houses famous reproductions of 15th-century Florentine Renaissance artworks by Russian artist Nicholas Lochoff. In 1911, Lochoff was commissioned by the Moscow Museum of Fine Arts to travel to Italy and make a series of copies of the finest examples of Renaissance Art. Those copies, considered by some to be the closest replicas to the original works, were acquired and placed in the Fine Arts building. The building's Italian Renaissance architecture, complete with a cloister-style inner courtyard, makes it truly unique in Pittsburgh. The fountain outside the Frick Fine Arts building was designed by Victor Brenner, the same man who sculpted the portrait of Abraham Lincoln on the U.S. penny.

4. Forbes Field Site
Bouquet Street at Roberto Clemente Drive and Sennott Street

This was the location of one of the most storied ballparks in baseball history - Forbes Field. Named for General John Forbes, the British general in the French and Indian War who captured Fort Duquesne and renamed it Fort Pitt in 1758, the home of the Pittsburgh Pirates opened on June 30, 1909. The stadium saw Pittsburgh World Championships in 1909, 1925 and 1960, all in seven games. The Pirates never lost a World Series in Forbes Field. It closed in 1970 and was demolished on July 28. 1971.

Babe Ruth hit the last three of his 714 regular season home runs in Forbes Field as a member of the Boston Braves on Saturday, May 25, 1935. That the final blow, which was the first ever to clear the right field roof, came to rest on the roof of 318 Boquet Street, a rowhouse which survives to this day. Today a plaque marks the spot where the most famous home run in World Series history, Bill Mazeroski's Game 7-winning homer left the park in 1960 and flew into the trees. The center-field and right-center brick walls still stand, along with the base of the flagpole. Home plate remains in almost its exact original location, and is now encased in glass on the first-floor walkway of the University of Pittsburgh's Wesley W. Posvar Hall across the street.

WALK OVER TO FORBES AVENUE AND TURN RIGHT, HEADING EAST.

5.   Stephen Foster Memorial
4301 Forbes Avenue

The Stephen Collins Foster Memorial is an academic facility of the University of Pittsburgh conceived in 1927 when the Tuesday Musical Club, founded in 1889 by affluent female musicians, and University of Pittsburgh Chancellor John Bowman agreed to collaborate on a performance hall dedicated to native son Stephen Foster that would house the club's recitals. The main structure houses the two theaters: the 478-seat Charity Randall Theatre and 151-seat Henry Heymann Theatre. The left wing of the building houses the Stephen Foster Memorial Museum and the Center for American Music which contains the University of Pittsburgh's Foster Hall Collection that includes manuscripts, copies of over 200 of his musical compositions, examples of recordings, songsters, broadside, programs, books, various memorabilia, and several musical instruments, including one of Foster's pianos.

6.   University of Pittsburgh Log Cabin
Forbes Avenue opposite Schenley Plaza

Tradition holds that the University of Pittsburgh, then the Pittsburgh Academy in the 1780s, began life in a log cabin. Not this one though. That long-ago classroom was replaced by a brick building in the 1790s downtown near the Point. That building, and most of Pittsburgh, was destroyed by fires in the 1840s, taking most of the school records with it. This particular cabin, from Yatesboro, Pennsylvania, was purchased at an auction for $1,000 by Charles Fagan III, who donated it to the university. It was placed here to commemorate the university's bicentennial in 1987.

7.   Cathedral of Learning
Forbes Avenue

The Cathedral of Learning is the second-tallest education building in the world—42 stories and 535 feet tall. It is also the geographic and traditional heart of the University of Pittsburgh campus. Begun by Chancellor John Bowman in

1926 and dedicated in 1937, the building was realized with the help of contributions from men, women, and children throughout the region and the world. During the peak of the Depression, when funding for the project became especially challenging, school children were encouraged to contribute a dime to "buy a brick." In addition to the magnificent three-story "Commons Room" at ground level, behind its 2,529 windows the Cathedral of Learning also contains classrooms (including the internationally renowned Nationality Classrooms), the University's administrative offices, libraries, a computer center, and a restaurant.

8.   Carnegie Museums and Library
4400 Forbes Avenue

The establishment of the Carnegie Library of Pittsburgh was forecast in a letter, November 25, 1881, from Andrew Carnegie to the Mayor of Pittsburgh in which Mr. Carnegie offered to donate $250,000 for a free library, provided the City would agree to provide the land and appropriate $15,000 annually for its maintenance. This offer could not be accepted, because at that time Pittsburgh was not authorized to expend funds to maintain a public library. Ten years later the City was legally allowed to accept the offer but Pittsburgh had grown so much since the original offer that Carnegie upped his commitment to a million dollars for a larger building combining reference and circulating libraries, art galleries, and meeting rooms for learned societies.

The original building was designed by Longfellow, Alden & Harlow in 1895 and, with millions more of Carnegie's dollars, a major addition came in 1907. Today the immense Institute building is actually a multi-purpose complex of library, lecture hall, music hall, natural science museum and art museum hosting more than one million visitors a year.

9.   St. Nicholas Greek Orthodox Church
419 South Dithridge Street at Forbes Avenue

St. Nicholas can trace its membership back to the turn of the century, when many of the first Greek immigrants made their way to Pittsburgh. Among them were men who were enlisted by the city's early industrialists to paint the buildings and smokestacks of the iron and steel mills. The present church with Greek portico was purchased in 1923. It was built in 1904 as the 1st Congregational Church.

WALK BACK A FEW STEPS AND TURN RIGHT ON BELLEFIELD AVENUE.

10. Heinz Chapel
115 Federal Street

The non-denominational Neo-Gothic Chapel's origins lie with Henry John Heinz, the founder of the H.J. Heinz Company. His will made arrangements to honor his mother, Anna Margaretta Heinz, with a building at the University. The building, designed by Charles Z. Klauder, was dedicated in 1938, featuring carved limestone walls, oak woodwork, and ironwork from craftsmen from throughout the northeastern United States. Its 23 exquisitely detailed stained glass windows depict 391 sacred and secular figures who are famous in religion, history, medicine, science, and the arts. The 73-foot transept windows by C. Connick Studios are among the tallest in the world and depict an equal number of women and men.

11. Bellefield Hall
315 South Bellefield Avenue

Bellefield Hall, constructed in 1924, was designed by architect Benno Janssen by combining the facades of the Italianate Palazzo Piccolomini delle Papesse in Siena with the the 18th-century Lee House at Stratford in Virginia for the Flemish-bond brick finish and the high basement. Bellefield Hall, a Pittsburgh History and Landmarks Foundation Historic Landmark, was originally home to the Young Men's and Women's Hebrew Association and is today home to a variety of University of Pittsburgh offices and services, most notably the old athletic association pool. The iron work for the lamps at the classical entranceway was done by Samuel Yellin.

12. Bellefield Towers
northeast corner of Bellefield Avenue and Fifth Avenue

The First United Presbyterian Church was displaced from downtown Pittsburgh in 1896 and built a new Gothic home on this corner. In the 1960s the church merged with the nearby Bellefield church which became an official Presbyterian church in 1866 on the former Bellefield Farm that once occupied most of what became eastern Oakland. The congregation traces its origins to a small prayer group in the 1830s. The new, united congregation moved away but left the building with the more historic Bellefield moniker. When the property was developed in the 1980s as a residential complex the church's distinctive bell tower was retained and the whole complex took the adopted Bellefield name.

TURN RIGHT ON FIFTH AVENUE.

13. Mellon Institute
southeast corner of Fifth Avenue and South Bellefield Avenue

Mellon Institute of Industrial Research, founded in 1913 by Andrew W. Mellon and Richard B. Mellon, merged with the Carnegie Institute of Technology in 1967 to form Carnegie Mellon University. While it ceased to exist as a distinct institution, the landmark building bearing its name remains. Designed by architect Benno Janssen, the building would seem low in height but three floors were built into rock below the street level, natural light being provided by interior courts. The entrance to the edifice, from the gradually-ascending steps, is at the fourth story. The monumental colonnade of 62 Ionic limestone columns is the largest in the world, completed and dedicated posthumously to the Mellon brothers in May 1937.

14. St. Paul's Cathedral
northwest corner of Fifth Avenue and Craig Street

The first Roman Catholic Cathedral was sited in downtown Pittsburgh on Grant Street, exactly where Henry Frick wanted to build his Union Trust building. Money trumped history and the church took Frick's dollars and commissioned Egan & Prindeville Architects in 1906, for this commanding house of worship with English and German Gothic features.

15. Fairfax Apartment Building
4614 Fifth Avenue

The Fairfax Apartment Building was designed by P.M. Julian in 1926. The Fairfax features coats of arms, Scottish strap work and the use of terra-cotta molded decorations.

16. Central Catholic High School
4720 Fifth Street

The castle-like Central Catholic High School, a designated historic landmark dating to 1927, is built in the Flemish Gothic style by E.J. Weber with soaring towers and stabilizing buttresses in patterns of light and dark-colored bricks.

TURN LEFT ON CLYDE STREET.

17. First Church of Christ, Scientist
635 Clyde Street at Fifth Avenue

This church was designed by S. S. Beman in 1904. Beman had made a reputation for Chicago skyscrapers but across the country he achieved acclaim for his Christian Science churches, including the Mother Church in Boston. Notice the porch on this building.

RETURN TO FIFTH AVENUE AND TURN LEFT.

18. Holy Spirit Byzantine Catholic Church
4815 Fifth Avenue

During the first decade of the twentieth century, immigrants from Carpatho-Ruthenia, a small portion of the vast Austro-Hungarian Empire, began to settle in the Oakland section of the City of Pittsburgh, lured by the promise of a better life in the City's steel mills. The congregation organized in 1907 and the present church, notable for its mosaic wall depicting the Old Testament prophets, was dedicated in 1962.

19. WQED-TV
4802 Fifth Avenue

These are the studios of WQED, the first educational television station in the country.

20. Rodef Shalom
4905 Fifth Avenue

Rodef Shalom, the oldest Jewish Congregation in Western Pennsylvania and the largest Reform congregation in the area, was chartered by the Commonwealth of Pennsylvania in 1856, though its origins go back to the late 1840s. Architect Henry Hornbostel used local cream-colored brick, handmade Guastavino tiles and terra-cotta to create this traditional synagogue in 1907.

On the grounds is the largest biblical botanical garden in North America (1/3 acre) and the only one with an ongoing program of research and publication. Visitors are able to experience the land of the Bible in a setting that includes a waterfall, a desert, a stream and the Jordan River, which meanders through the garden from Lake Galilee to the Dead Sea. All of the plants in the garden are labeled with biblical verses accompanying them. The garden features more than 100 temperate and tropical plants in addition to special new program plantings each year. See wheat, barley, millet and many herbs grown by the ancient Israelites along with olives, dates, pomegranates, figs, and cedars. The gardens are open during the summer.

TURN RIGHT ON MOREWOOD AVENUE.

21. Mudge House
5000 Forbes Avenue at southwest corner of Morewod Avenue

In 1958, industrialist Edmund W. Mudge, a pig iron and coke magnate, donated their bow-fronted Fifth Avenue mansion to Carnegie Mellon University. It has been used ever since as student housing.

TURN RIGHT ON FORBES AVENUE.

21. U.S. Bureau of Mines/Hamburg Hall
4800 Forbes Avenue

The northwestern part of the Carnegie-Mellon campus was acquired from the U.S. Bureau of Mines in the 1980s. This Beaux Arts building, designed by Henry Hornbostel, was dedicated in 1917 as the Pittsburgh Experiment Station. Here, at the largest of the Bureau's test stations, investigations were conducted on first-aid and rescue methods, fuel problems, petroleum uses and chemical research. Today it is a school administration building.

TURN LEFT ON BOUNDARY STREET.

22. Hammerschlag Hall
5000 Forbes Avenue

Andrew Carnegie and William H. Frew, chairman of the Board of Trustees of The Carnegie Institute and Carnegie's lawyer in Pittsburgh, hired New York electrical wizard Arthur Hamerschlag in 1903 as the first director of the fledgling Carnegie Technical Schools. Its aim was not to compete with the nearby University of Pittsburgh, but to provide practical vocational training in the industrial trades and to offer 3-year diplomas, not bachelor's degrees.

Hamerschlag built the campus in partnership with Carnegie himself and the architect Henry Hornbostel. But progress was slow. Industrial unions had their own apprenticeship programs, and it was challenging to attract and retain faculty, most of whom preferred to work for degree-granting institutions. So in 1912, the Carnegie Technical Schools were renamed Carnegie Institute of Technology. Hamerschlag then led the development of bachelor's and master's degree programs, and the college took off. Hammerschlag Hall, now the home of the Department of Electrical and Computer Engineering, was positioned to ride the crest of Junction Hollow and to be a towering, commanding focal point for the college campus.

CONTINUE ON BOUNDARY STREET INTO SCHENLEY PARK AND THE TOUR STARTING POINT.

Look Up,

Philadelphia

(Benjamin Franklin Parkway)

A Walking Tour of Benjamin Franklin Parkway...

The model for Benjamin Franklin Parkway is the Champs Elysees in Paris, France — a wide, pastoral avenue connecting City Hall to the world's largest municipal park, Fairmount Park. It did not come easy. When formal planning got underway prior to World War I there was a mass of buildings between there and there.

The designers of the Parkway were Paul Cret and Jacques Greber and the mass removal of those buildings - and the displacing of the people who lived in them - was a startlingly bold stroke for a conservative city often accused of preferring to live in the days of the Founding Fathers. By 1919 a stretch of Parkway could be seen and within a decade fountains, small parks, statues and monuments and formal public buildings began to take their place on the Parkway. By 1935 the Franklin Institute, the Free Library of Philadelphia, the Philadelphia Museum of Art at the head of the avenue, and the Rodin Museum could be seen along the mile-long parkway.

Our walking tour will begin in the heart of Center City and head out along the Benjamin Franklin Parkway...

1. **LOVE Park**
   John F. Kennedy and Benjamin Franklin parkways

LOVE Park was designed by Vincent Kling in 1965 as the anchor space for Benjamin Franklin Parkway. It covers an underground parking garage. The main features of the plaza are curved granite steps and a single spout fountain which was added in 1969. The now famous LOVE sculpture, designed by Robert Indiana, was first placed in the plaza in 1976 as part of the United States' Bicentennial celebration.

WALK WEST ON ARCH STREET, TOWARDS THE SCHUYLKILL RIVER.

2. **Insurance Company of North America**
   1600 Arch Street

Since 1925, this 16-story, steel frame, brick-and-stone structure has been the home of the oldest capital stock insurance company in America. Incorporated in 1794, INA pioneered many forms of insurance, in particular marine underwriting.

3. **Arch Street Presbyterian Church**
   1724 Arch Street, southeast corner of 18th Street

Regarded as a magnificent example of the classical revival in American architecture, Joseph C. Hoxie of Camden was built as the West Arch Street Presbyterian Church. The cornerstone was laid in May, 1853 and the church was dedicated in October, 1855. The large copper dome surmounts a Corinthian-porticoed corner building that is one of Philadelphia's most beautiful.

TURN RIGHT ON 18TH STREET.

4. **Cathedral of Saints Peter and Paul**
   18th and Race streets

Opposite the monument, across Race Street, was the residence of the cardinal of the Roman Catholic Archdiocese of Philadelphia. Behind the residence, The reddish brownstone Cathedral of Saints Peter and Paul was built between 1846 and 1864 under the direction of Napoleon Le Brun, who designed the Academy of Music, and John Notman, whose buildings include the Athenaeum and the Church of the Holy Trinity. Notman worked the exterior Palladian facade and copper dome in the Italian Renaissance manner and the interior is spacious with magnificent proportions reminiscent of Roman churches. It was largely decorated by Constantino Brumidi (1805-90), who painted the dome of the Capitol in Washington.

TURN LEFT ON RACE STREET.

5. **Academy of Natural Sciences**
   southwest corner of Race and 19th streets

America's first natural history museum was founded in 1812 in John Speakman's apothecary shop by a small group of local devotees to nature to advance scientific knowledge for people, encourage learning, and as a way to "occupy their time in the fashionable interest of Nature." The Philadelphia Academy of Natural Sciences was chartered by the Pennsylvania legislature four years later and opened its collections to the public in 1828. Three times it outgrew its buildings but in 1876 the Academy moved into this building that has managed to corral its 17 million specimens. The Academy of Natural Sciences was the first museum in the world to display a mounted dinosaur skeleton.

TURN LEFT ON 20TH STREET.

6. **St. Clements Episcopal Church**
   20th and Cherry streets

The Episcopalians have some of Philadelphia's most interesting and historic churches and by and large the ones with the greatest architectural beauty, such as this one by John Notman in 1859. It was actually built as golf courses are today - to attract new homebuyers.

TURN AROUND ON 20TH STREET AND WALK TOWARDS BENJAMIN FRANKLIN PARKWAY.

7. The Franklin Institute Science Museum
   222 N 20th Street

The Franklin Institute opened in 1824 in Independence Hall and is the oldest organization in the United States devoted to the study and promotion of mechanical arts and applied sciences. The current building, braced by Corinthian porticos dates to the early 1930s and was designed by John T. Windrim. In the museum's rotunda is the Benjamin Franklin National Memorial, with a 20-foot-tall marble statue of the scientist and Founding Father by James Earle Fraser.

8. Logan Square

Logan Circle is one of Penn's original five squares - the generically monikered Northwest Square. Liek the others, save today's Rittenhouse Square, it was once used as a burying ground and site of public hangings. On February 7, 1823, William Gross was hanged here — the last public execution held on the spot. In 1825 it was renamed for James Logan and 17 years later, after being an open pasture for 150 years, it was a punishable offense to take a cow, horse, cart wagon or carriage into the square. Eventually the graves, mounds and hillocks were removed or leveled.

The square became a circle and in 1924 the Swann Memorial Fountain by Alexander Stirling Calder was dedicated as its centerpiece. William Cary Swann was the founder of the Philadelphia Fountain Society whose mission was to install drinking fountains and horse troughs across the city. The three figures in the center represent the trio of waterways that define Philadelphia - the Delaware River, the Schuylkill River and the Wissahickon Creek.

9. Free Library of Philadelphia
   1901 Vine Street on Logan Circle

The Free Library of Philadelphia was founded in 1894, housed in City Hall. Horace Trumbauer, one of America's finest practitioners of France's Ecole des Beaux Arts, designed this building in 1917 and it opened in 1927. The Central Branch of the city's public library system soon became a popular repository for everything from Sumerian cuneiform tablets to the works of Beatrix Potter. With more than 100,000 books and manuscripts,

it is one of the country's great libraries. The Rare Book Department, which has holdings spanning 5000 years, is housed on the third floor in a handsome Georgian room that was removed from William McInitre Elkins' home in Whitemarsh, on the outskirts of Philadelphia, and installed in the library in 1949. Richly paneled, the room contains Mr. Elkins own fine library, a notable collection of Dickens' letters and editions, Dickens' desk and candleholder and even his pet raven which was stuffed in 1841.

TURN LEFT AND WALK UP BENJAMIN FRANKLIN PARKWAY.

10. Benjamin Franklin Parkway

More so than most, Philadelphia is a city of well-ordered right angles, much as William Penn envisioned it in 1682. But when the World's Columbian Exposition in Chicago in 1893 ushered in a "City Beautiful" movement in America some began to dream of a wide, park-like boulevard to connect City Hall with Fairmount Park. Paul Philippe Cret was hired in 1907 to make the dream a reality, laying a diagonal vector across the city's checkerboard.

Demolition cleared away scores of residences in a massive urban renewal effort. Several of the city's biggest institutions - the library, museums and some government buildings moved to the new Parkway but many are sited at an angle leaving gaps in the route that are poorly defined.

11. Rodin Museum
   22nd Street and Benjamin Franklin Parkway

This is the only building that Paul Philippe Cret designed along his parkway. It houses the largest collection of sculptures - more than 120 - by Auguste Rodin outside of France, brought together by Jules Mastbaum, an early film exhibitor in Philadelphia, who began assembling the works in 1913 with the idea of eventually donating them to the city. Mastbaum hired Jacques Greber, the French landscape architect responsible for the layout of the Benjamin Franklin Parkway to design the elegant gardens. He died before the project was completed in 1929.

12. Parkway House
22nd Street and Pennsylvania Avenue

Erected in 1953, this colossal apartment complex that blends elements of Art Deco and International styles, steps down to the Parkway. It is not without its detractors, one of whom observed that the city allowed its crown jewel, the Museum of Art to be "overshadowed by the most monstrous apartment building ever to disfigure the skyline and physiognomy of Philadelphia - or perhaps of any great city."

13. Eakins Oval
2600 Benjamin Franklin Parkway

The plaza is named for Thomas Eakins (1844-1916), the great Philadelphia painter who is best known for The Gross Clinic and The Agnew Clinic, leads to three fountains. The center fountain, dedicated to George Washington, was erected by the Society of the Cincinnati of Pennsylvania. Executed by Rudolf Siemering in 1897, it was originally placed in Fairmount Park before moving to this prominent spot on the Parkway in 1928. The four figures and the animals overlooking the pools at the base represent four great waterways of America — the Mississippi, the Potomac, the Delaware and the Hudson.

Flanking the Washington Monument are twin fountains designed by the architects of the Philadelphia Museum of Art, Horace Trumbauer, C. Clark Zantzinger and Charles L. Borie, Jr. One is dedicated to the inventor John Ericcson who designed the great Civil War ironclad Monitor; the other to Eli Kirk Price who spearheaded the movement to create the Parkway. Across the roadway, Auguste Kiss's Mounted Amazon Attacked by a Panther and Albert Wolff's The Lion Fighter flank the museum steps.

14. Philadelphia Museum of Art
2600 Benjamin Franklin Parkway

Founded during the nation's first centennial in 1876 as a museum of decorative arts, the Museum soon outgrew its quarters in Fairmount Park's Memorial Hall. Horace Trumbauer, C. Clark Zantzinger and Charles L. Borie, Jr. collaborated to create Philadelphia's Parthenon majestically atop a rise at the end of the Benjamin Franklin Parkway.

Trumbauer devised the scheme of three linked Greek temples facing in toward a common court. Begun in 1919 the first section of the Beaux Arts building finished in golden Minnesota dolomite with blue tile roofs opened in 1928.

The pediment or tympanum on the north wing was done by Carl Paul Jennewein and illustrates the theme of sacred and profane love. There are thirteen classical figures, the central one of Zeus signifying the creative force, with Demeter, the laurel tree, Theseus, Aphrodite and Eros to the sides. Unfortunately, funds were never available to complete it with similar groups on the central and south buildings.

Movie-lovers will remember the long set of steps in front of the museum as the spot where boxing underdog, Rocky Balboa, made his triumphant run — arriving at the top with hands raised aloft in triumph. There is a ground floor entrance on the river side of the museum for those not similarly inspired.

WALK AROUND THE MUSEUM OF ART TO THE SCHUYLKILL RIVER.

15. Fairmount Waterworks
east side of Schuylkill River below the Museum of Art

Perched on the banks of the Schuylkill River, the Water Works was not only a source of the City's water, its rambling Classic architecture and cutting-edge engineering made it an international 19th century tourist attraction. Built between 1812 and 1815 by Frederick Graff, the waterworks comprise a dam, pumphouse and reservoir. Water was pumped from the river into a reservoir (where the Art Museum now stands) and then distributed through the city via wooden water mains. Graff was a draftsman on the city's first waterworks built between 1799 and 1801 after which he became superintendent of the Philadelphia Waterworks. he remained at the post 42 years, becoming the young nation's foremost authority on supplying fresh water.

TURN LEFT ON KELLY DRIVE.

16. Boathouse Row
Kelly Drive on the Schuylkill River

Historically, the Schuylkill River became attractive to rowers after the construction of the Fairmount Water Works, where the dam slowed the water down to a calmer current and provided space for a wide, mile-and-a-quarter course that still exists today. Boathouse Row, home to Philadelphia's rowing community, is a leading epicenter of the nation's championship aspirations for the sport. It is a magnet for the grass roots development of national and world championship medalists and has been home to a long list of Olympic competitors and coaches. Philadelphia hosts nearly twice as many regattas as the closest competitor city, Boston.

The picturesque Victorian boathouses are simple, roomy and functional. The Undine Barge Club, erected 1882-83, was designed by Frank Furness, America's finest practitioner of the style. The clubs outline their boathouses with lights — always an enchanting sight for those driving the opposite side of the river by night.

WALK UP THE HILL ACROSS KELLY DRIVE INTO FAIRMOUNT PARK AND LEMON HILL DRIVE.

17. Lemon Hill
Lemon Hill Avenue above Boathouse Row

The estate was known in 1770 as The Hills, and from that year until 1799 it was the home of Robert Morris, Declaration of Independence signer, and a major financier of the Revolution. Morris built a greenhouse on the property, one of the first such in the country. He later went bankrupt due to his land speculations, and Henry Pratt, a Philadelphia merchant, purchased the main part of the property at a sheriff's sale in 1799. The present house was built in that year and the next. Pratt planted lemon trees here and hence the estate became known as Lemon Hill. Pratt died in 1838 and the city purchased the estate in 1844, the first of the Fairmount Park houses to be acquired.

The house is rectangular, with a central bay on the river side that rises three stories. Oval rooms give the home a unique flavor. The lightly concave doors have superb proportions and are strikingly beautiful. The exterior walls are stucco with granite trim.

RETURN TO KELLY DRIVE AND BACKTRACK TO FAIRMOUNT AVENUE. AND TURN LEFT.

18. Fidelity Mutual Life Insurance Company Building
Fairmount and Pennsylvania avenues

The same firm that designed the Philadelphia Museum of Art did this building for the Fidelity Mutual Life Insurance Company in 1926. Zantzinger, Borie, and Medary created monumental entrance arches that flank the Beaux-Arts Deco block-long structure. The naturalistic carvings adorning the building were sculpted by Lee Lawrie. Ironically, the Museum of Art came calling in 2007 and opened an expansion in the building.

19. Eastern State Penitentiary
North 22nd Street and Fairmount Avenue

Eastern State Penitentiary has been called the most influential building constructed in the United States. When Eastern State opened in 1829, visitors from around the world marveled at the medieval fortress created by John Havilland. But it was the Quaker-inspired belief that solitary confinement could reform criminals that made Cherry Hill Penitentiary, as it was then called, a model for prison design world wide. An estimated 300 prisons on four continents are based on Eastern's distinctive "wagon-wheel" floor plan. Once the most expensive building in the USA, Eastern State was finally abandoned in 1971 after 142 years in use. A National Historic Landmark, the prison is open for tours that include include a restored 19th-century cell, the warden's office, several cellblocks, exercise yards, death row and critically acclaimed art installations.

WALK SOUTH ON 22ND STREET. TURN RIGHT ON GREEN STREET.

20. Kemble-Bergdoll House
2201-5 Green Street

This Renaissance Revival mansion was built in 1889 for People's Bank president William Kemble and later bought by the Bergdolls whose brewery on Girard Avenue was one of Philadelphia's largest and best known. Prohibition in 1920 caused the brewery to go out of business. The brownstone house was designed by James A. Windrim.

21. 2223 Green Street

This Green Street rowhouse with the unusual brick and tile facade was designed by Willis Hale. It was one of several in the area owned by the Fleisher family, wealthy textile manufacturers and one of several on the block done by Hale.

22. St. Francis Xavier Church
northeast corner of 24th and Green streets

The grand Romanesque structure adorning the northeast corner of 24th and Green Streets is the oldest church in the neighborhood. Completed in 1898, this building replaced the old church that was located at 25th and Biddle (approximately where the Art Museum steps are today). The parish itself began in 1839. While the building has many striking features, the tower is the most prominent. The spire is one hundred, fifty-two feet tall. It is one of the most recognized landmarks in the neighborhood. The stained glass windows are beautiful, especially the circular one above the main entrance. It's 22 feet in diameter, and its fine stonework reminds one of lace.

TURN LEFT ON 24TH STREET AND TURN LEFT ON PENNSYLVANIA AVENUE.TURN LEFT ON HAMILTON STREET. TURN RIGHT ON 20TH STREET.

23. Reading Company Grain Elevator
411 North 20th Street

Philadelphia was once a distribution center for grain grown in the farmlands of Pennsylvania. For a long time grain elevators were a common sight in the city, but only this one remains. The Reading Company Grain Elevator was built in 1925 on the site of a grain elevator that had been there since the Civil War and which was destroyed in a grain explosion. The hulking grey structure was designed by staff architects of the Reading Railroad and was built using a continuous poured in place concrete process. Grain was delivered by wagon to the entrance then stored in the silos until it was loaded onto trains and taken to the Port Richmond on the Delaware River. Abandoned in the 1950s, the building was purchased in 1976 by an interior designer, who converted the lower floors into offices. The silos were left untouched, but the machinery towers were transformed into a penthouse apartment. The place was added to the National Register of Historic Places in 1982.

CONTINUE TO THE BENJAMIN FRANKLIN PARKWAY AND RETURN TO THE TOUR STARTING POINT.

Look Up,

Philadelphia

(Center City)

A Walking Tour of Center City...

When William Penn founded Philadelphia in 1682 he saw a city that would one day stretch from the Delaware River to the Schuylkill River. He had surveyor Thomas Holme lay out a plan for the city to match that far-reaching vision. For the next 100 years the city still clustered only six blocks from the Delaware River.

By the early nineteenth century, development had reached Center Square (now site of City Hall) and continued westward to the Schuylkill and beyond into West Philadelphia. Things were happening so rapidly that the Consolidation of 1854 recognized this fact by enlarging the city boundaries to match those of Philadelphia County.

The city's banks and businesses and small manufacturers marched westward as the city grew. By 1900 Center City claimed not only Philadelphia's government and moneyed interests but its railroads and great retail emporiums. Center City today continues to be the pulsing heart of the city with America's most formidable historical to the east and majestic residential neighborhoods to the west.

Our walking tour will begin at one of America's most magnificent buildings recently restored...

1. City Hall
Broad & Market streets

City Hall is built on the area designated by William Penn as Centre Square. It was a public square from the city's founding in 1682 until construction of City Hall began upon the site in 1871. Working on a French Second Empire design by Scottish architect John McArthur, Jr., it was intended to be the tallest building in the world but when it was finally finished 30 years - and eight mayors - later City Hall was surpassed by both the Eiffel Tower and Washington Monument. Instead, it hung its hat on the fact that at 547 feet it was the world's tallest habitable building, a title it held for less than a decade. Today it remains the tallest masonry building ever constructed.

The building is topped by an 11.3-m (37 ft), 27-ton bronze statue of city founder William Penn, one of 250 sculptures created by Alexander Milne Calder that adorn the building inside and out. The statue is the tallest atop any building in the world. Penn's statue is hollow, and a narrow access tunnel through it leads to a small (22-inch-diameter) hatch atop the hat.

LEAVE CITY HALL AND HEAD EAST ON MARKET STREET.

2. John Wanamaker's
1300 Market Street

John Wanamaker opened his first men's store in his hometown in 1861 at the age of 23. Called "Oak Hall," the new emporium stood at Sixth and Market Streets on the site of George Washington's Presidential home. Oak Hall grew substantially based on Wanamaker's then-revolutionary principle: "One price and goods returnable". In 1869, he opened his second store at 818 Chestnut Street under his own name. Wanamaker's genius for advertising soon created one of the world's great retailing empires.

This building, an unremarkable Renaissance palazzo of limestone and granite, opened in 1911. The splendor lies within, starting with a five-story central atrium. On the second level is the legendary pipe organ, 30,000 pipes strong. It is America's largest. How important was the opening of this new John Wanamaker's? President William

Howard Taft was on hand for the grand opening.

3. PSFS Building
12 S 12th Street, southwest corner of Market Street

This is the third headquarters for the Philadelphia Saving Fund Society. George Howe took the design for his tower in a completely new direction and built the first International style skyscraper in the country. The sleek 33-story tower rests atop a curving base of polished black granite and the guts of the building's operating system reside in an adjoining tower. The interior details, which included Cartier-designed clocks and custom designed furniture, fostered a new era of modernism when it was completed in 1932.

4. Reading Terminal
Market Street between 11th and 12th streets

The Reading Railroad is long gone, existing today only on Monopoly game boards. This is the line's only Center City facility, the arches and balustrades of the headhouse designed by Francis Hatch Kimball in 1891. Its outstanding architectural feature is a curved, arcaded bay looming over Market Street from its fourth floor perch where Kimball sliced away a corner.

5. Reading Terminal Market
12th and Market streets

When the Reading Railroad wanted to come into Philadelphia the only suitable location was already occupied by the venerable Franklin Market. To get the right to build its terminal the line had to incorporate the market into its design. The Reading Terminal Market, established in 1892 is the nation's oldest continuously operating farmers' market. Cuisine from across the globe is available from more than 80 unique merchants, three of which are descendants of original stand holders from when it opened more than 110 years ago. The northwestern corner of the market is devoted to Amish merchants from Lancaster County, who bring their farm-fresh products and distinctive prepared dishes to the Market Wednesday through Saturday.

6. **The Gallery**
   Market Street, between 11th
   and 9th streets

This pioneering downtown shopping mall was developed between 1974 and 1977.

7. **United States Post Office and**
   Court House
   9th and Market streets

The first buildings on this site were part of the University of Pennsylvania campus from 1800 to 1870. The current Depression-era classical monolith replaced a rambling Victorian post office from the 1870s. Along the 9th street side of the building are relief panels of energetic postal workers carved into limestone by Edmond Amateis.

8. **Strawbridge & Clothier**
   8th and Market streets

Quakers Justus Clayton Strawbridge and Isaac Hallowell Clothier opened a dry goods store in 1862. In 1868 Strawbridge & Clothier purchased a 3-story brick building on the northeast corner of Market and 8th Streets which had been Thomas Jefferson's office in 1790 while he served as Secretary of State. Soon the old building was replaced by a new 5-story department store offering a variety of fixed price merchandise under one roof. By 1896, when the present building was erected, Strawbridge & Clothier was a Philadelphia retailing institution on a par with Wanamaker's. In 1929, Strawbridge & Clothier opened one of the first suburban branch department stores in the nation, located in the Suburban Square shopping center in Ardmore. The historical flagship closed in 2006.

9. **Lit Brothers**
   Market Street between 8th and 7th streets

Samuel and Jacob Lit opened the first store at Eight and Market Streets in 1893. Over the next 15 years the brothers methodically bought up the surrounding stores until they had the entire block. The flagship store, with new structures on either end, opened in 1907. Like many department stores of its time, the store was an assemblage of several buildings built over time, which were joined so the interior appeared as one building. The unique façade of this building's front on Market Street caused it to become known as the "cast iron" building. After the store closed in 1977, it was in danger of demolition but was luckily redeveloped as office and commercial space in the late 1980s.

TURN RIGHT ON 7TH STREET.

10. **Atwater Kent Museum**
    15 S 7th Street

John Haviland, who was also the architect of Eastern State Penitentiary, designed the 1826 Greek Revival building that was the original home of the Franklin Institute. A. Atwater Kent, a wealthy inventor who manufactured early radios in Philadelphia, bought the building in 1938 and gave it to the city to establish a museum dedicated to Philadelphia's cultural and industrial history.

TURN RIGHT ON CHESTNUT STREET.

11. **Jeweler's Row**
    8th and Chestnut streets

The first person to build here, when it was still on the outskirts of the city was Robert Morris, the "Financier of the Revolution." Morris retained Pierre Charles L'Enfant, who would layout the new capital of Washington, to work on his estate. The mansion would bankrupt Morris and land him in debtor's prison. "Morris' Folly" would never be finished.

Developer William Sansom bought part of the property and hired builder and architect Thomas Carstairs to construct one of America's first speculative housing developments. Now the area on Sansom Street, between Seventh and Eighth streets, and on Eighth Street between Chestnut and Walnut street, is home to Jewelers' Row. It is the oldest diamond district in America, and second in size only to the one in New York City. Some of the businesses have been owned by the same family for five generations; the oldest dates to 1851.

12. Benjamin Franklin Hotel
834 Chestnut Street

Opened in 1925 as the Benjamin Franklin Hotel, Horace Trumbauer incorporated many Neoclassical elements in its limestone and brick design. In the mid-1980s the hotel was renovated and reopened as the Benjamin Franklin House. Affectionately referred to as "The Ben" by many Philadelphians, the building currently has 412 apartments and boasts one of city's largest ballrooms.

TURN LEFT ON 9TH STREET.

13. Walnut Street Theater
825 Walnut Street, northeast corner of 9th Street

What began as a circus in 1809 is today the oldest continuously used theater in the country. It was once owned by the great classical actor - and brother of the presidential assassin, Edwin Booth. The Walnut Street Theater can claim installing the nation's first gas footlights (1837) and air conditioning with Mr. Barry's Patent Cool Air Machine (1855).

TURN RIGHT ON WALNUT STREET.

14. Thomas Jefferson University
1020 Locust Street

The main building dates to 1907. In Alumni Hall are three life-size portraits by Thomas Eakins, one of America's greatest 19th-century realist painters. The gallery was inaugurated in 1982 to celebrate the portraits of three eminent university medical professors: Samuel Gross, Benjamin H. Rand and William S. Forbes. Two portraits hanging in the gallery offer sympathetic images of Jefferson professors whom Eakins knew — one, Dr. Rand, with his cat. The gallery also displays early stethoscopes, syringes and other medical instruments from the University's collection.

Eakins actually studied anatomy at Jefferson, seeing it as a crucial part of an artist's education. The compelling honesty of *The Gross Clinic* (recently sold to the Philadelphia Museum of Art and replaced with a copy) reflects Eakins's uncompromising approach to art and life; he lost his position teaching at the Pennsylvania Academy of Fine Arts in a dispute over the use of nudity in an art class, and not until late in life did he begin to receive the acclaim he deserved.

TURN RIGHT ON 10TH STREET.

15. Federal Reserve Bank
10th and Chestnut streets

This classical government building, with a facade of square Doric columns, was designed by Paul Phillippe Cret in the 1930s. The highly fenestrated upper floors contain offices; the Federal Reserve, one of the 12 branches of the nation's central bank, has since relocated on Independence Mall.

16. Victory Building
1001 Chestnut Street, northwest corner of 10th Street

This Second Empire granite office building by Henry Fernbach was half its current size when constructed in the 1870s. The balustrade marks the former roofline when this was a branch office of the New York Life Insurance Company capped by a mansard roof.

17. St. Stephen's Church
19 S 10th Street

This is the site where Benjamin Franklin flew his kite to conduct electricity experiments. Several of the 19th century's greatest architects and artists had a hand in St. Stephen's. William Strickland employed an early Gothic interpretation to build it in 1823. The church is the only surviving example of his Gothic style. In the late 1870s Frank Furness added the north transept and vestry and the marble Angel of Purity was sculpted by Augustus Saint-Gaudens.

RETURN TO CHESTNUT STREET AND TURN RIGHT.

259

18. Widener Building
Chestnut Street between Broad and Juniper streets

The Widener Building was designed in 1914 by Horace Trumbauer for Peter A. B. Widener, one of three men who built the trolley system in the late 19th century. The 18-story, 385,000-square-foot building was gutted in 1991 and $80 million spent to restore the tower. There are superb Corinthian pilasters and soaring vaulted entries on both the south and north ends of the building.

19. Girard Trust Company
34-36 South Broad Street

The influential New York architectural firm of McKim, Mead & White left little imprint on Philadelphia but the office executed this stately Ionic temple crowned with a beautifully proportioned dome. The exterior is finished in sparkling white Georgia marble.

TURN LEFT ON SOUTH BROAD STREET.

20. Union League Club
140 South Broad Street

John Fraser designed this Second Empire-influenced club building in the waning days of the Civil War when the union League split from the Union Club over war policy. This fine brownstone was given a Beaux Arts limestone addition a half-century later by Horace Trumbauer.

21. The Bellevue
southwest corner of Broad and Walnut streets

George Boldt, a Prussian immigrant and his Philadelphia-born wife, Louise Kehrer Boldt, opened an earlier facility, the Bellevue Hotel, in 1881. A small boutique inn, it quickly became nationally-known for its high standard of service, fine cuisine, and elite clientele. The Boldts expanded by acquiring the Stratford Hotel across the street. Both were supplanted by construction of the grand Bellevue-Stratford Hotel, designed in the French Renaissance style by Philadelphia architects, brothers George and William Dewitt.

The present building opened in 1904. Over two years in the making and costing over $8,000,000 (in 1904 dollars), the Bellevue-Stratford was described at the time as the most luxurious hotel in the nation and perhaps the most spectacular hotel building in the world. It initially had 1,090 guest rooms, the most magnificent ballroom in the United States, delicate lighting fixtures designed by Thomas Edition, Tiffany and Lilac glass embellishments, and the most celebrated marble and hand-worked iron elliptical staircase in the city. The rusticated building has gone through many owners in its 100+ years but is still one of America's most beautiful hotels.

22. Academy of Music
1420 Locust Street at the southwest corner of Broad Street

Napoleon LeBrun built the Academy of Music in 1857, modeling its lavish interior on La Scala Opera House in Milan. It is the oldest known opera house continuously in use in the United States and has often been praised as the finest. The Academy is home to the Opera Company of Philadelphia, the Pennsylvania Ballet and "Broadway at the Academy," a series of national productions. For more than a century, its most famous resident was the Philadelphia Orchestra, which returns every January to play the Academy Anniversary Concert and Ball.

23. The Kimball Center for the Performing Arts
Broad and Spruce streets

The brightest light on the Avenue of the Arts is the dazzling regional performing arts center, whose discreet brick exterior rises to a bold 150-foot glass vaulted rooftop for startling views of the city. The Philadelphia Orchestra's need for a modern concert hall coupled with the city's need for a venue to serve the community and visiting artists proved the catalyst for the Kimball, completed in December 2001 by architect Rafael Vinyl and the acoustic team Artec. The facility is named for sportswear manufacturer and Philadelphian Sidney Kimball, the largest private donor.

24. University of the Arts
320 South Broad Street, northwest corner of Pine Street

The serious Doric facade designed by John Haviland in 1826 was for the Pennsylvania Institution for the Deaf and Dumb which it remained until 1893 when the College of Art and design moved here. It was spruced up in 1983 when it became the Broad Street face of the complex known as the University of the Arts.

TURN AROUND AND WALK BACK UP BROAD STREET TOWARDS CITY HALL. TURN LEFT ON SPRUCE STREET.

25. Drake Tower
1512-14 Spruce Street

The Drake was designed as a hotel in 1929 by architects Ritter & Shay who delivered a 30-story slab skyscraper whose length is several times its width. The Drake is an Art Deco masterpiece with a Spanish Baroque red-tiled roof and turrets and sculptured terra-cotta ornaments. The warm orange brick has turned brown and drab as the building has made the transition to apartment house.

TURN RIGHT ON 15TH STREET.

26. Bookbinders Seafood House
215 South 15th Street

Philadelphia's most famous restaurant - name, at least - opened as an oyster saloon in 1893 on Fifth Street near South Street by Dutch immigrant Samuel Bookbinder. In 1898, Bookbinder moved down closer to the docks at Second and Walnut. The restaurant left the family in the 1930s when it was bequeathed to the Jewish Federated Charities.

In 1935 two of Samuel Bookbinder's sons opened Bookbinders Seafood House here. When new owners took over the Second and Walnut restaurant they added "Old Original" to differentiate it from the new family operation. The family business shuttered in 2004, the family's old restaurant, no longer in the family, closed in 2009.

27. Drexel Building
135-43 South 15th Street, southeast corner of Moravian Street

Some buildings are designed to appear taller than they actually are; this one strives to seem shorter. The bottom two stores are designed to look like one story. The entire Florentine palazzo-styled building, executed in the 1920s, is faced with rusticated granite.

28. Packard Building
southeast corner of 15th and Chestnut streets

Samuel Yellin, a Polish-born craftsman, contributed the pair of monumental 10-ten wrought iron gates at the entrance to the Packard Building, decorated with an overall design of squares within squares. At the center of each square is a flower surrounded by a ribbon and scroll work. Additional Samuel Yellin metalwork include two large sconces that flank the entrance. The Packard Building was designed by the busy firm of Ritter & Shay in 1924.

TURN RIGHT ON CHESTNUT STREET.

29. Jacob Reed's Sons Store
1424-26 Chestnut Street

The large, inviting Palladian entranceway leads to one of Philadelphia's finest retail facades and interiors, built in 1904. The handmade tiles on the front of the building came from Henry Chapman Mercer's Moravian Pottery and Tile Works in Doylestown. The Reeds were selling fashionable duds for men Of means.

TURN AROUND AND WALK THE OTHER WAY ON CHESTNUT STREET, TOWARDS THE SCHUYLKILL RIVER.

30. WCAU Building
1620 Chestnut Street

Built in 1928 by Harry Sternfield and Gabriel Roth, this is one of Philadelphia's most joyful Art Deco buildings. It is meant to resemble a radio and the glass tower was lit in blue at night when the statin was on the air. WCAU projected one of the most powerful signals in the country and could be heard clearly at night across the country. The building was renovated in the 1980s for the Art Institute of Philadelphia.

TURN RIGHT ON 17TH STREET.

31. Liberty Place
Market Street, between 16th and 17th streets

For generations a "gentleman's agreement" was strictly abided by developers in Philadelphia - no building would be higher that William Penn's statue of City Hall. While other cities engaged in battles to build soul-less skyscrapers ever higher, Philadelphia retained a charm unique among major cities with its tradition. It all ended in the 1980s when Willard Rouse built One Liberty Place and Two Liberty Place, reaching sixty and fifty-eight stories, respectively.

32. Suburban Station
16th Street and John F. Kennedy Boulevard

When Broad Street Station gave way to 30th Street Station the new depot across the Schuylkill River was just a tad far afield for the Center City commuter. So Suburban Station was created at the same time, 1924 to 1929. It is essentially a train statin stuck in the basement of an office building. Little is done to announce its presence but the commuters know where they are going.

TURN RIGHT ON JOHN F. KENNEDY BOULEVARD.

33. LOVE Park
John F. Kennedy and Benjamin Franklin parkways

LOVE Park was designed by Vincent Kling in 1965 as the anchor space for Benjamin Franklin Parkway. It covers an underground parking garage. The main features of the plaza are curved granite steps and a single spout fountain which was added in 1969. The now famous LOVE sculpture, designed by Robert Indiana, was first placed in the plaza in 1976 as part of the United States' Bicentennial celebration.

TURN LEFT ON NORTH BROAD STREET.

34. Masonic Temple
1 North Broad Street, northeast corner of Filbert Street

Designed by architect James Windrim, the Masonic Temple was constructed over a period of five years – completed in 1873 – at the astonishing sum of $1.6 million. The process of decorating the interior, performed mostly under the supervision of artist George Herzog, took nearly twenty years to complete. The Masonic Temple is the headquarters for the Grand Lodge of F. & A.M. of Pennsylvania, and also serves as the meeting place for twenty-eight Philadelphia lodges. Freemasonry is the oldest continuously existing fraternal organization in the world and Philadelphia's were the first in the colonies.

TURN RIGHT ON ARCH STREET.

35. A.J. Holman and Company
1222-26 Arch Street

This well-preserved factory facade dates to 1881. A.J. Holman, America's oldest bible publisher, manufactured books here.

RETURN TO NORTH BROAD STREET AND TURN RIGHT.

36. Pennsylvania Academy of the Fine Arts
southwest corner of Broad and Cherry streets

The Pennsylvania Academy of Fine Arts is the finest example of Frank Furness's work. The richly ornamented exterior — executed in juxtapositions of sandstone, pink granite, red brick and purplish terra-cotta — is somber by comparison with the interior where gold floral patterns are set on walls of Venetian red beneath a blue ceiling sprinkled with silver stars. The High Victorian Gothic building was completed in 1876; the Academy had its origins in Charles Wilson Peale's natural history museum that he opened in 1794.

TURN AROUND AND RETURN TO THE TOUR STARTING POINT AT CITY HALL OR CONTINUE UP BROAD STREET ANOTHER FOUR BLOCKS...

37. Packard Motor Car Building
317 North Broad Street

The early 20th century was an era of new prosperity for Philadelphia. The popular new automobile was becoming an affordable luxury and people flocked to the auto dealerships located along Broad Street to see the new models. The dealerships were lavish temples and the showroom of the Packard Motor Car Company was a prime example. Packard commissioned acclaimed midwestern architect, Albert Kahn, to create a building that would be unrivaled in Philadelphia. From the limestone and terra-cotta trim on the exterior to the majestic two-story lobby inside, the Packard was designed to be the model of excellence. The Packard automobile is long gone but the building has survived, still catering to those who long for luxury - this time as apartments.

38. *Philadelphia Inquirer/ Daily News* Building
401 North Broad Street

The *Philadelphia Inquirer* began on June 1, 1829 actually as the *Pennsylvania Inquirer*. the name became lost when, six months later, Jesper Harding purchased the paper as one of many he would acquire over the next 30 years. Harding built his own paper mill to supply his press and became successful enough to obtain the first American rights to publish several of Charles Dicken's novels in serial form in his paper, including Barnaby Rudge and Master Humphrey's Clock.

When his son, William W. Harding became the owner in 1859, the name of the paper was changed to the *Philadelphia Inquirer*. Circulation grew from 7,000 in 1859 to 70,000 by 1863, possibly based on its excellent reporting of the Civil War. Harding sold the paper to British-born James Elverson in 1889 who used the paper to initiate civic improvements, promoting the Reading Terminal and Benjamin Franklin Parkway.

Elverson's son became publisher after his father's death in 1911 and built the Elverson Building in 1924, applying an Italian Renaissance style to a large building. He and his wife used the 12th and 13th floors for living space. The imposing white building, with its lantern top, housed the newspaper office and printing plant.

TURN AROUND AND RETURN TO THE TOUR STARTING POINT AT CITY HALL.

Look Up,

Philadelphia

(Old City)

A Walking Tour of Old City...

William Penn envisaged a beautiful waterfront for his city — something similar to the embankment in London, but this was not to be. The area early became a scene of great commercial activity, and wharves, warehouses, and taverns sprang up, as they have for centuries, in waterfront cities throughout the world. The district is thus one of the oldest and most historic in the city, for it was from the banks of the Delaware that Philadelphia grew westward toward the Schuylkill River.

Construction was started on Independence Hall in 1732, only fifty years after the founding of the city by William Penn. At the time, the area between 5th and 6th Streets, where the most ambitious building ever planned in the American colonies was being built, was still on the edge of things. Forty years later, when events leading to a declaration of independence by a gathering of rebels made this the birthplace of America the city had grown as far as 8th Street. The port was thriving but the streets were still unpaved.

There were dwellings in Old City — Elfreth's Alley and Loxley Court attest to that — but they were modest homes in contrast to the larger ones to be seen in Society Hill. By the 1960s Old City had long ago ceased to be the city's pulsing financial center. Manufacturers had departed as well. Cheaper rents now again attracted artisans and craftspeople. The spacious 19th century buildings offered a perfect locale for contemporary art galleries and stores offering the fine crafts of this new population — particularly furniture. Today, Old City is home to more than 30 galleries interwoven in the historic district.

This walking tour will start at Philadelphia's number one tourist attraction - at the south end of Independence Mall where the Liberty Bell stands opposite Independence Hall...

1. **Liberty Bell Center**
   6th & Market streets

The Pennsylvania Assembly ordered the Bell in 1751 to commemorate the 50-year anniversary of William Penn's 1701 Charter of Privileges, Pennsylvania's original Constitution. Historians are skeptical that the Bell actually rang out the chimes of freedom as tradition holds. Abolitionists in the 1830s were the first to seize the bell as emblematic of their cause; after the divisive Civil War, Americans sought a symbol of unity. The flag became one such symbol, and the Liberty Bell another. To help heal the wounds of the war, the Liberty Bell would travel across the country. Back in Philadelphia, now a national icon, it has had several homes, this is the latest.

2. **Pennsylvania State House/**
   Independence Hall
   Chestnut Street between 5th and
   6th streets

Construction of the Pennsylvania State House, which came to be known as Independence Hall, began in 1732. At the time it was the most ambitious public building in the thirteen colonies and since the Provincial government paid for construction as they went along, it took 21 years to complete. The building has undergone many restorations, notably by Greek revival architect John Haviland in 1830, and served a number of purposes. The second floor was once home to Charles Willson Peale's museum of natural history and the basement was once the city's dog pound.

In 1950 the National Park Service returned it to its 1776 appearance finalizing its status as the birthplace of the United States. It was within its walls that the Declaration of Independence was adopted. It was here that the Constitution of the United States was debated, drafted and signed.

3. **Congress Hall**
   southeast corner of Chestnut and
   6th streets

Independence Hall is flanked on on its left by Congress Hall, occupied from 1790-1800 by the new United States Congress. The first floor was occupied by the House of Representatives. The upper floor was occupied appropriately, by the upper house, or the Senate. In 1793, President George Washington was inaugurated here for a second term. Four years later, in a scene unlike any the world had ever seen, George Washington ended his presidency and voluntarily passed the reins of power to his successor, John Adams. At the close of the ceremony, John Adams waited for Washington to lead the exit, as everyone had grown accustomed to, but Washington insisted on leaving the room after the new President. Finally, and perhaps most important of all, the Bill of Rights was ratified while Congress met in these rooms.

4. *Public Ledger* **Building**
   southwest corner of 6th and
   Chestnut streets

The *Public Ledger* was Philadelphia's most widely read daily paper as soon as it hit the streets in 1836 as the city's first penny paper. After the Civil War the paper settled on this corner and in 1913 it was purchased by Cyrus H.K. Curtis who ran a magazine empire next door. He commissioned Horace Trumbauer to do this Georgian Revival office building in 1924. The Ledger had only a decade to live at the time, in 1934 it merged into the *Philadelphia Inquirer*.

TURN AROUND AND WALK UP INDEPENDENCE MALL, AWAY FROM INDEPENDENCE HALL.

5. **Rohm and Haas Corporate Headquarters**
   100 Independence Mall West

The chemical company was the first private investor to build on Independence Mall, moving here in 1964 from Washington Square. The nine-story building with translucent, corrugated sunscreens (made of Rohm and Haas's principal product, Plexiglass) became a standard for redevelopment around the historic area. Designed by Pietr Belluschi, with more than 1,000 building designs to his credit, the Rohm and Haas Headquarters and is considered one of the best examples of the International style.

6. The Bourse
11 South 5th Street, east side of
Independence Mall

Designed by brothers G.W. and W.D Hewitt in 1893, the Philadelphia Bourse was the first in the world to house simultaneously a stock exchange, maritime exchange, and grain-trading center. Under the guidance of Philadelphia businessman George Bartol, the exchange thrived but the building was cast adrift when the business center of the city moved away from the river in the mid 20th century. Unlike many of its Victorian-age cousins the Bourse did not meet a grisly end in front of a wrecking ball but was renovated in 1982 into a combination shopping mall and office complex.

7. Christ Church Burial Ground
southeast corner of 5th Street and
Arch Street

In 1719 the Christ Church burial ground was full, and the neighboring lands proved too marshy to be useful for burials. So land was purchased on the outskirts of the city (three blocks away at the time.) The earliest tombstone dates to 1720. Eventually five signers of the Declaration of Independence are buried here. Hundreds of Colonial, Revolutionary and Post-Revolutionary notables are interred in Christ Church Burial Ground but the most famous of whom is Benjamin Franklin who is buried here with his wife Deborah. The grave can be seen through the fence on Arch Street if the burying ground is closed.

8. National Constitution Center
525 Arch Street

The first-ever national museum honoring the U.S. Constitution tells the story of the document that framed the American idea. The center opened in 2003.

9. The United States Mint
5th and Arch streets

The United States' first mint — indeed the first structure sanctioned by the United States government — was erected in 1792, just two blocks from the present site. Many citizens of the new nation were deeply suspicious of federal power. They were accustomed to using coins issued by their own state banks, along with various forms of foreign currency. The suggestion of a single federal mint producing a uniform coinage was disturbing. George and Martha Washington donated the silver for the first coins.

As a new capital city was being built along the banks of the Potomac, it was expected that the Mint would move there. Yet in 1800, when Washington, D.C., was ready, the government did not have the money to replace what was already an efficient operation. An Act of Congress in 1828 ensured that the Mint would remain permanently in Philadelphia.

This block-long monolithic structure is the fourth Philadelphia mint, completed in 1969. It is the largest mint in the world, capable of producing 30 million coins a day.

CONTINUE UP 5TH STREET PAST INDEPENDENCE MALL. TURN RIGHT ON NEW STREET.

10. St. Augustine Church
northwest corner of 4th and New streets

On the night of May 8, 1844 anti-Catholic, anti-immigrant rioters attacked and burned St. Augustine, at the time the largest church in the city. By dawn only a single wall of the church, whose cornerstone had been laid in 1796, was left standing. Amid the rubble, the historic Sister Bell, symbolic of Penn's dream of religious and personal freedom, lay burned and smashed, destroyed by the fire. Church records were spared however, by a quick-thinking pastor who hid them in a furnace to protect them.

Due to the burning of the church and other violence a state law requiring police forces was enacted in 1845. The violence also led to the consolidation of the city and county in 1854.

The architect chosen to rebuild was Napoleon LeBrun who also designed the Philadelphia Academy of Music. LeBrun gave the church a Palladian style. Inside are stunning ceiling frescoes by Filippo Costaggini who painted part of the frieze on the rotunda of the nation's Capitol.

The new church saw disaster of it own in 1992 when its steeple blew off during a brutal winter storm and fell onto the Benjamin Franklin

Bridge. the bridge was closed for three days and a fifty-foot hole opened in the church's ceiling but no one was hurt.

11. St. George's United Methodist Church
235 N 4th Street

Methodists scattered across Philadelphia met in private homes until this church, built in 1763 and belonging to a German Reformed Congregation, was purchased in 1769. Now known as "The Cradle of American Methodism," it is the world's oldest Methodist church in continuous use and the seat of the first three conferences of American methodism.

British forces occupying Philadelphia in 1777 noticed the church still had a dirt floor and a door that opened conveniently onto the street and set up a cavalry school inside. Engineers planning the Benjamin Franklin Bridge were ordered by the court to move the bridge 14 feet. The sidewalk was lowered in the process and that is why St. George's is entered via steps at its second level.

TURN RIGHT ON 4TH STREET.

12. Benjamin Franklin Bridge
Delaware River at Vine Street

For almost 250 years the only way to reach New Jersey was by ferry. It took the world's longest suspension bridge in 1926 to change all that (a title it held for only three years). Paul Phillippe Cret created one of the country's most beautiful bridges, far surpassing the quality of its original name - the Delaware River Port Authority Bridge. In 1956, befitting the grandeur and wonder of the span, it was renamed for Ben Franklin. As for cold hard facts, the length of the main span is 1,750 feet, the full length of the bridge is just short of two miles, the towers are 380 feet high and the drop to the water is 135 feet.

TURN LEFT ON ARCH STREET.

13. Arch Street Friends Meetinghouse
330 Arch Street

The religious Society of Friends was founded in 1600s England by George Fox. Originally the sect was derided for "quaking" before God but the insult was good-naturedly adopted by the Friends. Persecuted in England, the Quakers, under William Penn, created their own colony of Pennsylvania in 1682. Penn donated the land here to be used as a burial ground in 1701. The long, center-pedimented brick building was begun in 1803 with the wings added in 1811. The Arch Street Meeting House is the oldest still in use in Philadelphia and the largest in the world.

14. St. Charles Hotel
60 N 3rd Street, southwest corner of
Arch Street

The old hostelry with its bar on the ground floor and guest rooms above was typical of the accommodations travelers to America's largest city in the early 1800s could expect to find. It sports one of the city's earliest cast-iron facades, dating to 1851.

15. Betsy Ross House
239 Arch Street

Betsy Ross did not design the American flag; probably never sewed one in fact. She may never have even lived in this house, let alone be buried here. But the legend has helped make this modest dwelling one of the best preserved example of a working class abode in Colonial America. Today it is the third most visited historic site in Philadelphia.

TURN RIGHT ON 2ND STREET.

16. National Products Building
109 N 2nd Street

Harry Caplan opened National Products, a supplier of kitchen equipment to the restaurant trade, in 1929. Caplan acquired adjacent parcels to create what is now known as the National Products property. The orange tiled Art Deco facade was added in 1957. National Products stopped operating out of this facility in 1996. It sat empty and was in danger of demolition but a compromise was brokered to allow the facade to remain during its conversion into condominiums.

TURN AROUND AND CROSS ARCH STREET AND MAKE A RIGHT ON ELFRETH'S ALLEY.

17. Elfreth's Alley
between Front and 2nd streets, north of Arch Street

The cozy confines of Elfreth's Alley are often referred to as the oldest continuously inhabited street in America. It was opened shortly before 1702 by Arthur Wells, a blacksmith, and John Gilbert, a bolter, when the Delaware River flowed next to the alley. Shortly thereafter it took on the name of Jeremiah Elfreth, a blacksmith and land speculator, who built and rented out many of the alley's homes. Often the homes were rented to fellow artisans.

The oldest houses are thought to be 122 and 124, which were built between 1725 and 1727. The early 18th century houses stand two-and-a-half stories and later Federal-era townhouses are a bit more lavish with a full third story and often boasting a porch. Try not to miss walking the cobblestones into Bladen's Court located midway down the street, which is basically an alley within an alley that leads into a charming circular courtyard. Mirrors called busybodies project from the second floor windows of many of the houses. These allowed those on second floors the ability to see who was knocking on their front doors.

TURN RIGHT ON FRONT STREET.

18. Smythe Stores
100-111 Arch Street, northwest corner of Front Street

The warehouse district on Philadelphia's waterfront was peppered with commercial buildings gussied up with cast iron facades in the Victorian era of the mid-19th century. The finest of these facades belonged to the four-story Smythe Stores, an Italianate style built between 1855 and 1857. Look closely at the building and you will notice that the central section has been reproduced in fiberglass when the building was converted to apartments in the 1980s.

19. Girard Warehouses
18-30 Front Street

The rugged commercial buildings along Front Street were built to accommodate the busy waterfront when the Delaware River lapped up on its doorstep. The Girard Warehouses, faced in granite on the first floor storefronts with upper floors in brick, date to 1810. At 46 North Front Street, at the northwest corner of Cuthbert Street, is a 1785 home-store built for John Clifford. It became a store and warehouse from 1821.

TURN RIGHT ON CHURCH STREET.

20. Christ Church
2nd Street, northwest corner of Church Street

Organized in 1695 during the reign of William and Mary, it was built between 1727 and 1744 by Dr. John Kearsley in the style of the fabulous English churches done by Sir Christopher Wren. Palladian elements such as double rows of arched windows and balustraded parapets have led architectural historians to praise Christ church as "the most advanced and completely English church in Colonial America."

The church's 196-foot high steeple that was the most identifiable city landmark for ships sailing up the Delaware River for decades was added in 1754 by Scotsman Robert Smith. Benjamin Franklin organized three lotteries to finance the payment of the church's steeple and bells. Inside is the "600-year-old font" in which William Penn was baptized; sent to the colonies by All Hallow's Church, Barking by-the-Tower, England.

The Second Continental Congress worshipped here as a body in 1775-76. Pew 70 was Ben Franklin's; George Washington sat in Pew 56. The box pews were all rented, the balconies were rented with a few free pews there for servants and slaves of parishioners. There is ecclesiastical history as well - in 1789 the First Convention of the American Episcopal Church was held here.

TURN LEFT ON 2ND STREET.
TURN RIGHT ON MARKET STREET.

21. Franklin Court
316-322 Market Street

Benjamin Franklin moved from Boston to Philadelphia at the age of 17. He was a printer, diplomat, inventor, publisher, author, statesman, Postmaster, and more. He founded the Library Company, Pennsylvania Hospital, American Philosophical Society, and the University of Pennsylvania.

Franklin's house and print shop were in the courtyard in the interior of this block but were razed in 1812. What is known of the house is that it was 3 stories high, covered 33 feet square, and included 10 rooms. The house was razed in 1812. Because no historical records of the look of the exterior exist, the space once occupied by the house is marked by an oversized "Ghost Structure" designed by world-famous architect Robert Venturi. You can look through portals to see into Franklin's privy pits, wells, and foundation.

At 316 Market Street is the only active post office in the United States that does not fly a United States flag (because there wasn't yet one in 1775). The postmark "B. Free Franklin" is still used to cancel stamps. James Wilson, an editor of The Aurora, lived at 322 Market Street. His grandson, Woodrow, became the 28th President of the United States.

RETURN TO 3RD STREET AND TURN RIGHT.

22. Leland Building
37-39 S 3rd Street

Stephen Decatur Button designed this commercial building in 1855. The use of continuous vertical piers and lack of ornamentation are said to have influenced a young Louis Sullivan, the father of the modern skyscraper, when he lived in Philadelphia while working for Furness & Hewitt in 1873.

TURN LEFT ON CHESTNUT STREET.

23. Elliott and Leland Buildings
235-237 Chestnut Street

These handsome commercial buildings were designed by Joseph C. Hoxie in the Italianate style, executed in granite. They date to 1853-54.

24. Customs House
100 S 2nd Street, southwest corner of Chestnut Street

Built in 1933, this is the final major work by Ritter & Shay, Philadelphia's most prominent designers of Art Deco skyscrapers.

TURN RIGHT ON 2ND STREET.

25. City Tavern
northwest corner of 2nd and Walnut streets

City Tavern, also called the Merchants' Coffee House, was the political, social, and business center of the new United States. Jefferson, Adams, Franklin, and Paul Revere all ate here. When the British occupied Philadelphia, they and their Tory sympathizers partied here. In 1789, George Washington celebrated here with 250 Philadelphia bluebloods prior to his inaugural in New York City. The Tavern burned down in 1854; this building is a 1975 reconstruction.

TURN RIGHT ON WALNUT STREET.

26. Merchants' Exchange
143 S 3rd Street, northeast corner of Walnut Street

After Dock Creek was filled in Philadelphia suddenly had a curved street intruding on William Penn's carefully laid out street grid of 90-degree angles. When the city decided in 1832 to rescue traders from the cramped and noisy meetings in coffeehouses and taverns by building a grand "temple of commerce" architect William Strickland solved the conundrum of the odd-shaped lot with a semi-circular Corinthian portico.

The Philadelphia Stock Exchange followed most city businesses to Broad Street after the Civil War and the much-admired building began a steady decline. In 1922 it was sold to a firm that made it a Produce Exchange. An open-air market surrounded the Exchange. Vendors hawked vegetables from pushcarts. A gas station was built on the Dock Street side. Finally in 1952 the building was incorporated into Independence Park and today is the oldest standing stock-exchange building in America.

TURN RIGHT ON 3RD STREET.

27. First Bank of the United States
120 S 3rd Street

This building, considered the oldest in America with a classical facade, was built in 1797 to be most imposing building in the country - at a staggering cost of $110,168.05. Samuel Blodget delivered one of the best works of public architecture of the 18th century with his Corinthian portico and fully marble facade. The bank was championed by Alexander Hamilton and chartered in 1791 to mitigate the colossal war debt from the Revolutionary War. The central bank's charter was only in effect for 20 years; Congress voted to abandon the bank in 1811. Stephen Girard, one of the first financial moguls, purchased the building and operated it as a private bank for a time. America's first bank building was restored for the Bicentennial in 1976.

TURN LEFT ON
CHESTNUT STREET.

28. Carpenters' Hall
320 Chestnut Street

The Carpenters' Company was founded in 1724 and is the oldest trade guild in the country. This building was brand new in 1774 when it was let to the First Continental Congress who were planning a rebellion against England. Later it also served as the headquarters of the First Bank of the United States.

Carpenters' Hall is important architecturally as well as historically. Designed by master builder Robert Smith, a Carpenters' Company member, it is the first Philadelphia building to employ a Greek Cross plan behind a handsome pedimented doorway with Doric detailing. Three Palladian windows line the second floor under which are stone balustrades. The belt course (band separat-

ing the floors) is unusual in that it is outlined in wood instead of brick.

29. Second Bank of the United States
420 Chestnut Street

Just as war debt spawned the First Bank of the United States debt after the Revolution, so too did it cause the creation of the Second Bank of the United States. To help a cash-strapped nation after the War of 1812, Congress authorized and President James Madison signed a bill chartering the bank for 20 years.

William Strickland, a 27-year old painter, won a design competition to create the new bank in 1815. Strickland chose the Parthenon in Greece as his model for the exterior; inside he built a Roman rotunda. Strickland became America's foremost proponent of the Greek Revival style, launching the first truly American architectural movement. Today the building houses an extraordinary portrait gallery including, among other treasures, George Washington's death mask.

30. Bank of Pennsylvania
421 Walnut Street

Bank Row emerged across the street from the Second Bank of the United States. The ornate Italian Renaissance Bank of Pennsylvania building was designed in 1859 by John M. Gries.

31. Farmers' and Mechanics' Bank
427 Chestnut Street

In its systematic cleansing of all obsolete buildings erected after 1840 by Philadelphia's urban renewal plan, this sparkling Italianate marble bank was somehow spared and lovingly restored in the 1980s. It was also designed by John M. Gries with corner quoins, heavy modillions and relief panels.

CONTINUE WALKING ONE
BLOCK ON CHESTNUT STREET
TO THE TOUR STARTING POINT
AT THE LIBERTY BELL.

Look Up,

Philadelphia

(Rittenhouse Square)

A Walking Tour of Rittenhouse Square...

Rittenhouse Square, one of William Penn's original five, was known as the southwest square until 1825 when it was named for the astronomer-clockmaker, David Rittenhouse (1732-96). This amazing man of universal talents — one of many in 18th century Philadelphia — was a descendant of William Rittenhouse, who built the first paper mill in America in Germantown. He was at various times a member of the General Assembly and the State Constitutional Convention, and president of the Council of Safety. His survey of the Maryland-Pennsylvania boundary in 1763-64, to settle a dispute between the Penns and Lord Baltimore, was so accurate it was accepted and followed by Charles Mason and Jeremiah Dixon when they surveyed the "line" for which they are still remembered. Professor of Astronomy at the University of Pennsylvania and inventor of the collimating telescope, he was also president of the American Philosophical Society and the first director of the United States Mint.

Rittenhouse Square has always denoted quality. The first house facing the Square was erected in 1840. During its next century the Square kept its residential quality. In 1913, the architect Paul Cret, who was one of the men responsible for Benjamin Franklin Parkway and many of its buildings, designed the Square's entrances, central plaza with the stone railings, pool and fountain. To have lived near or on the Square was a mark of prestige. Today, private homes are gone, but it still counts for something to live on the Square. There are several houses still standing, but they have been converted into apartments. With cooperative apartments and condominiums displacing private dwellings in the last three decades, some of the Old Guard still live on here — in these homes in the sky rather than family mansions.

The immediate surrounding streets around Rittenhouse Square are a microcosm of all Philadelphia has to offer. Within easy walking distance are eclectic shopping boutiques, world-class restaurants, the skyscrapers of the city's business community, the cultural resonance of unique museums and galleries and, to the south and east, some of America's most charming big city residential streets.

Our walking tour will begin strolling the leafy walkways that crisscross the plaza of Philadelphia's most desirable address...

1. **Rittenhouse Square**
   bounded by 18th Street on the east,
   South Rittenhouse Square on the south,
   West Rittenhouse Square (an offset of
   19th Street) on the west and Walnut
   Street on the north

The Rittenhouse Square one sees today is mostly the work of Paul Phillipe Cret who laid out this urban oasis in 1913. The main walkways are diagonal, beginning at the corners and meeting at a central oval. Classical urns, many bearing relief figures of ancient Greeks, rest on pedestals at the entrances and elsewhere throughout the square. Ornamental lampposts contribute to an air of old-fashioned gentility. A low fence surrounds the square, and balustrades adorn the corner entrances.

Several of the city's best-loved outdoor sculptures reside in Rittenhouse Square. The dramatic *Lion Crushing a Serpent* by the French Romantic sculptor Antoine-Louis Barye, created in 1832, symbolizes the power of good (the lion) conquering evil (the serpent). This bronze cast was made about 1890.

At the other end of the central plaza, within the reflecting pool, is Paul Manship's *Duck Girl* of 1911, a lyrical bronze of a young girl carrying a duck under one arm. A favorite of the children is Albert Laessle's *Billy*, a two-foot-high bronze goat whose head, horns, and spine have been worn to a shiny gold color by countless small admirers. The central gatehouse once stood in Fairmount Park during the Centennial of 1876.

WALK TO THE SOUTHEAST CORNER OF THE SQUARE.

2. **Thomas A. Reilly House**
   1804 Rittenhouse Square

Frank Furness, America's finest Victorian architect, did much of his residential work on the streets around Rittenhouse Square. Here he is represented on the Square itself with this memorable stone townhouse from the 1890s, packing a great deal of decorative detail into an obviously limited space.

3. **Philadelphia Art Alliance**
   251 S 18th Street

This serious looking building was not a bank or arsenal but a house, the former Samuel Price Wetherill mansion. It was designed in 1909 by Philadelphian Frank Miles Day. Christine Wetherill Stevenson, who grew up here, founded the Philadelphia Art Alliance in the building in 1926. One of the most active organizations of its kind, the Art Alliance sponsors art exhibits, dramatic and poetry readings, dance and musical events, architectural displays and lectures of all kinds. Most are free to the public, as are the galleries.

4. **Barclay Hotel**
   237 S 18th Street

On the southeast corner of Rittenhouse Square is the site of what was once the most famous hotel in Philadelphia. It was owned by John McShain, the millionaire Philadelphia builder who also owned the Lakes of Killarney in Ireland. The scene of some of society's most glittering private parties, it has also housed almost every distinguished celebrity who has traveled to Philadelphia. It has since been converted to condominiums.

LEAVE RITTENHOUSE SQUARE BY WALKING EAST ON LOCUST STREET.

5. **Curtis Institute of Music**
   1726 Locust Street, southeast corner
   of 18th Street

Founded in 1924 by Mrs. Mary Louise Curtis Bok Zimbalist, The Curtis Institute is a unique conservatory of music for it is entirely a scholarship school. Some of the noted musicians who have attended Curtis are Samuel Barber, Leonard Bernstein, and Anna Moffo.

The Institute occupies three townhouses around Rittenhouse Square. The main building was the home of George Childs Drexel, a banker and son of the founder of Drexel Institute, Anthony Joseph Drexel, co-founder of the *Public Ledger*. Across Mozart Place is the school library housed in Knapp Hall. Originally it was the home of Theodore F. Cramp, a shipbuilding magnate, and later the salon of Elizabeth Arden, the cosmetician. A copy of a French townhouse, as is the one adjoining it, Knapp Hall strikes a note of elegance along the quiet street.

6. 1629 Locust Street

This white limestone Beaux Arts townhome was created by Horace Trumbauer in 1892.

7. St. Mark's Episcopal Church
1625 Locust Street

St. Mark's Episcopal Church was founded in 1848. The church building was begun that year on plans drawn up by John Notman, dedicated in 1850, and finished in 1851 when the tower was completed. An example of Gothic Revival, the parish buildings and the garden create an effect not unlike that of an English church.

8. 1622 Locust Street

This Italian Renaissance Revival in brownstone by John Notman dates to the 1850s. It is one of three he designed on the 1600 block of Locust Street, including 1620 next door and 1604.

9. 1606 Locust Street

George W. Childs (1829-94), the publisher of the Philadelphia Public Ledger and one of the most influential men in America made his home at 1606 Locust from 1855 to 1872.

TURN RIGHT ON 16TH STREET AND RIGHT ON LATIMER STREET.

10. Print Center
1614 Latimer Street

The Print Center has been a Philadelphia institution since 1915. This famous organization has more than a 1000 members from all over the world, composed of artists, collectors and others whose interest in prints has brought them together. There are shows continually throughout the year and it is extremely pleasant to stop by and browse. Next door, at 1616, is the Cosmopolitan Club, a women's club with a long history of interest in the arts, politics and the humanities, has its clubrooms.

RETURN TO 16TH STREET AND TURN LEFT. TURN RIGHT ON WALNUT STREET.

11. Le Bec-Fin
1523 Walnut Street

Owner and founder Georges Perrier trained at La Pyramide in France and started working in Philadelphia in the late 1960's. He started his own restaurant in 1970, naming it after the French colloquialism for "Fine Palate." By 1981, Le Bec-Fin was known as the leader of the "Philadelphia restaurant revolution" and began garnering numerous awards. It consistently rates five-stars and is widely regarded as the best restaurant in Philadelphia and the finest French restaurant in America.

TURN AROUND AND WALK WEST ON WALNUT STREET BACK TO RITTENHOUSE SQUARE.

12. Van Rensselaer House
northwest corner of 18th and
Walnut streets

Facing the Square on the northeast corner is the former home of Alexander Van Rensselaer, a financier and supporter of the Philadelphia Orchestra under Leopold Stokowski. One of the few splendid old mansions to survive, it once housed the Pennsylvania Athletic Club. The Alison Building next door contains the offices of the Presbyterian Ministers' Fund, the oldest life insurance company in the world (1717). Adjacent to it, at 1811 Walnut Street and also facing the Square, is the Rittenhouse Club, another of the city's old and exclusive clubs. The author Henry James used to sit at a window and view this Square, too, with his worldly eye.

13. Holy Trinity Church
Walnut Street, northwest corner of
West Rittenhouse Square

The Church of the Holy Trinity, designed by John Notman in 1859, provides an ecclesiastical presence on the square. It is one of the first accurate Romanesque buildings in the United States, replete with an asymmetric tower, rose window, and recessed geometric doorway. One of the city's most fashionable congregations,one of its rectors, Reverend Phillips Brooks (1835-93), penned the words to the Christmas standard "O Little Town of Bethlehem."

14. Rittenhouse Hotel
210 West Rittenhouse Square

The unusual white horizontal zig zags have drawn mixed reviews on this 33-story tower. The Belgian stone courtyard, fountain and manicured gardens featuring the beguiling statue Welcome by Evangelos Frudakis draw more universal praise.

LEAVE RITTENHOUSE SQUARE TO THE NORTH ON 19TH STREET. TURN LEFT ON CHESTNUT STREET.

15. Boyd Theater
1908 Chestnut Street

Opened on Christmas Day 1928, the Boyd is the last surviving major movie palace in Philadelphia - although it has had to weather some rough times. The 2,450-seat capacity, Art Deco first-run moving picture theatre was built for Alexander R. Boyd and designed by one of the great Philadelphia theater architects, Hoffman-Henon. Its carved limestone facade was etched with touches of color. A towering vertical sign with many angular surfaces towered over the handsome marquee, the underside of which was crafted into swirls of crystallized glass illuminated from within. On the inside, custom designed area and aisle rugs, ceiling height carved mirrors of many hues, modern statues in wall niches, and multitudinous crystal and glass lighting fixtures added to the rich ambiance. The Boyd had a fully equipped stage and an organ and orchestra pit, which could be raised and lowered electrically. The National Trust for Historic Preservation named the Boyd Theater on its 2008 List of America's 11 Most Endangered Historic Places.

16. First Unitarian Church
2125 Chestnut Street

Philadelphia's most famous Victorian architect Frank Furness designed this church for his father, the Reverend William Henry Furness. The First Unitarian Church of Philadelphia was founded in 1769. The Parish House was finished in 1884; the cornerstone for the church was laid in 1885 and it was dedicated in 1886.

17. The Coronado
northwest corner of 22nd and
Chestnut streets

When the Coronado, a 10-story building designed by Milligan and Webber in 1910, was sold in 2003 for $5.7 million, or $175,000 a unit it established a new threshold for the highest per-unit sale price for the region.

TURN RIGHT ON 22ND STREET.

18. Mutter Museum
19 S 22nd Street

The world-famous Mutter Museum is run by the College of Physicians, founded in 1787. It was named for Dr. Thomas Mutter and is a fantastic collection of medical curiosities — there is no other description for it. Some of it is not for the faint-hearted. Among the rarities exhibited are part of President Grover Cleveland's jawbone. There are bones shattered by bullets, others showing wounds, breaks, etc., and skulls bearing the personal data and medical history of their owners. Particularly fascinating is a cast of the original Siamese twins, Chang and Eng Bunker, who were sixty-three at the time of their death in 1874. The chair they used is here, a pathetic small wooden one, and their liver has been preserved in a jar. An entire drawer is devoted to buttons, coins, and other objects that have been retrieved from human stomachs.

TURN AROUND AND WALK SOUTH ON 22ND STREET. TURN LEFT ON WALNUT STREET. TURN RIGHT ON 21ST STREET.

19. Thomas Hockley House
235 S 21st Street

An unusual recessed corner entrance sets the stage for this picturesque house by Frank Furness from 1875. A rich diversity of materials, pointed dormers, steep mansard roof, pointed arches with polychrome voussoirs are all thrown into this Victorian home.

TURN RIGHT ON SPRUCE STREET.

20. 2132-34 Spruce Street

These Second Empire townhouses were designed by Frank Furness.

21. 2123-25 Spruce Street

Wilson Eyre designed this fine Neo-Georgian house on Spruce Street.

22. Rudolf Ellis House
2111 Spruce Street

This 1878 house is another by Frank Furness; restrained under a mansard roof.

TURN LEFT ON 22ND STREET.
TURN LEFT ON DELANCEY PLACE.

23. Rosenbach Museum and Library
2008-2010 Delancey Place

This elegant 1860s townhouse was the home of brothers Abraham Simon Wolf Rosenbach and Philip H. Rosenbach for a quarter-century beginning in 1926. Abraham was a rare book dealer and Philip was expert in fine arts in antiques. The Rosenbach Museum & Library houses one of the world's great collections of manuscripts, literature and rare books. Their rare book business was widely considered the most successful in the world and launched many a library collection.

A list of some of the treasures amassed by the Rosenbach brothers is amazing in itself – Lewis Carroll's own copy of Alice in Wonderland, a first edition of Don Quixote, James Joyce's handwritten manuscript for Ulysses, and the earliest extant letter from George Washington – but the real treat is to see them among the Egyptian statuary,

Persian rugs, 18th-century furniture and Thomas Sully paintings that graced the 1860s mansion during the Rosenbachs' lifetime.

A list of some of the treasures amassed by the Rosenbach brothers is amazing in itself – Lewis Carroll's own copy of *Alice's Adventures in Wonderland*, a first edition of *Don Quixote*, James Joyce's handwritten manuscript for *Ulysses*, and the earliest extant letter from George Washington – but the real treat is to see them among the Egyptian statuary, Persian rugs, 18th-century furniture and Thomas Sully paintings that graced the 1860s mansion during the Rosenbachs' lifetime.

In 1954, after the deaths of the Rosenbach brothers – Dr. A.S.W., a dealer in rare books and manuscripts, and Philip, a dealer of fine arts and antiques – their individual libraries and collections were organized in the Rosenbach townhouse at 2010 Delancey. The library has more than 130,000 manuscripts and 30,000 rare books; the museum boasts the largest U.S. collection of miniature portraits painted in oil on metal. In 2002, the museum expanded into the historic house next door for more research and display space.

24. Delancey Place
between 19th and 20th streets

There are a myriad of things to see in this block of Delancey Place: the caryatids (female statues) as mullions (vertical window separators) on the window of 1810, perhaps the only ones in the city; the acanthus leaves and grape design on the ironwork fence at 1823; the leaded and stained glass windows at 1821; or the small garden with the iron fence at 1835. From the vantage point of the garden we can have a fine view of 1900 Delancey Place, now the offices of the law firm. Designed by Frank Furness, it is generally considered one of the finest examples of his townhouses. The ornate decoration, the oval window above the entrance door give it a distinctive appearance in this age of austerity in architectural decoration. Be sure to observe the cherubim and seraphim on the pediments.

TURN LEFT ON 19TH STREET AND RETURN TO THE TOUR STARTING POINT IN RITTENHOUSE SQUARE.

Look Up,

Philadelphia

(Society Hill)

A Walking Tour of Society Hill...

The Free Society of Traders, a stock company that invested in William Penn's colony, set up shop on Dock Creek (later filled in and called Dock Street) in 1682 to oversee their new assets which soon included a sawmill, a glasshouse and a tannery in the the new settlement of Philadelphia. The Society barely saw the 1700s before they went bankrupt and disappeared. But their name lives on in the city.

It is this long-gone stock company for which Society Hill is named, even though the area attracted locally and internationally wealthy residents when Philadelphia was the capital and dominant city of the new Republic in the late 1700s. As the land juxtaposed the river and the seat of government, it was the most valuable in the city. From greed and speculation, lots were divided and divided again. The result: the serpentine walkways, abrupt angles, and tiny alleys that today make the area so appealingly intimate.

By the mid 1900s. Society Hill had lost its cachet and ultimately became a dilapidated slum. The city redevelopment plan called for every building built after 1840 to be torn down and everything before 1840 would be saved and rehabilitated. About 600 Georgian and Federal buildings were renovated but countless Victorian buildings that gave the neighborhood its diversity were lost forever. To insure the area retained its Colonial look all new buildings were made to blend in seamlessly with their older models.

Society Hill is loosely defined as the land between the Delaware River and Washington Square, bounded by Walnut Street to the North and Lombard Street to the South. This walking tour of Society Hill will begin on the waterfront in Penn's Landing which has been severed from Society Hill by I-95 but where parking is plentiful...

1. Penn's Landing
   at Delaware River

William Penn first sailed up the Delaware River in the fall of 1682 aboard the ship Welcome, an aptly named vessel, for in Penn's progressive vision of his colony, all religions would be welcome to pray as they pleased. Penn arrived in Philadelphia by barge from the downriver town of Chester where the Welcome had moored. He alit near a tidewater basin called the Dock fed by a creek of the same name. At the time of Penn's arrival, the area was inhabited, though sparsely, by some landowners in his "holy experiment," as well as by Swedes, Dutch, and Indians. Many of these locals gathered to welcome Penn near the Blue Anchor Tavern, an inn being built along Dock Creek.

Nineteenth-century historian John Fanning Watson, author of the nonpareil "Annals of Philadelphia and Pennsylvania," believed that the landing of Penn in Philadelphia rivaled the landing of the Pilgrims at Plymouth Rock in importance and should have been similarly canonized.

The area today known as Penn's Landing stretches along the Delaware River for about 10 blocks from Vine Street to South Street, and encompasses the spot where William Penn, Philadelphia's founder, first touched ground in his "greene country towne." After Penn's arrival, this area quickly became the center of Philly's maritime soul and the city's dominant commercial district. Starting in 1967, the city began to redevelop the area's dilapidated docks into a recreation park along the river. Walkways were put in, an amphitheater was built, a World Sculpture Garden installed — and finally, trees were planted along the river.

CROSS I-95 AT SPRUCE STREET.

2. A Man Full of Trouble Tavern
   125-127 Spruce Street

A Man Full of Trouble Tavern, built around 1760, is the only tavern from Colonial Philadelphia that stands today. Looking much like the surrounding buildings it shows there was little design difference between commercial and residential properties at that time. it was built on the banks of the Little Dock Creek that still flowed at the time and most of the patrons came from the dock area. Inside the rooms feature low ceilings and there is a cellar where the workers slept. Pipe smokers dropped a penny in an "honesty box" - so named because it was assumed the pipe smoker would extract only one pipeful of tobacco from the bowl.

3. Society Hill Towers
   2nd and Locust streets

This is the project that kicked off the renovation of Society Hill after it had become a widespread slum by the middle of the 20th century. After winning a design competition Ieoh Ming Pei designed three modern International-Style towers built with poured-in-place concrete. Pei also designed a group of three-story townhouses across Philip Place at 3rd and Locust streets. the new houses were designed to blend in with their centuries-old neighbors and utilize red brick laid in a Flemish-bond pattern (the stretcher, long side, alternate with the headers, short side).

4. Abercrombie House
   270 South 2nd Street

This house was one of the finest and tallest structures in Philadelphia when it was built in 1758 for Scottish sea captain James Abercrombie. The townhouse was rehabilitated by Leon Perelman, a philadelphia native and president of American Paper Products, in 1968 to start the Antique Toy Museum. Perelman's private collection included more than 1,000 early American tin and cast-iron toys and the world's largest collection of mechanical toy banks.

TURN RIGHT ON 3RD STREET.

5. Powel House
   244 South 3rd Street

Samuel Powel was the last colonial mayor of Philadelphia before the Revolution. He was the first mayor after the Revolution. His grandfather, also Samuel Powell, came to the colonies in 1685 and through an advantageous marriage and an extraordinary gift for carpentry and bridge-building, became the wealthy owner of dozens of Philadelphia homes houses.

Young Samuel dropped the second "l" in his surname to become Powel. He also declined to move into one of the 90 houses he now owned and instead purchased this house on 3rd Street from Charles Stedman. Stedman was the part-owner of a forge and a substantial landowner, who eventually fell upon hard times and wound up in debtors' prison in 1774.

The Powels became known as great entertainers. George and Martha Washington became good friends and when Benjamin Franklin died Samuel served as one of the pallbearers. Samuel Powel, "the Patriotic Mayor," died in the Yellow Fever epidemic that swept the city in 1793. The house was almost demolished for an open-air museum in 1931 but survives today as a museum.

TURN LEFT ON WILLINGS ALLEY.

6. **St. Joseph's Church**
   321 Willings Alley

On the north wall is a commemorative plaque that pays tribute to William Penn, who in his Charter of 1701 granted religious toleration and understanding in his colony. the plaque reads:

When in 1733 / St. Joseph's Roman Catholic Church / was founded and / Dedicated to the Guardian of the Holy Family / it was the only place / in the entire English speaking world / where public celebration of / the Holy sacrifice of the Mass / was permitted by law.

The first church was built on this site in 1733, enlarged in 1821 and rebuilt in 1838. During a period of church-burning during the Anti-Catholic Riots of 1844, this church emerged unharmed, perhaps because it is tucked away in a courtyard accessed through a narrow arch with iron gates. Today it is the oldest Roman Catholic church in Philadelphia.

TURN RIGHT ON 4TH STREET.

7. **Philadelphia Contributorship**
   212 South 4th Street

In 1730, the most disastrous fire to rage in Philadelphia's history burst from the timbers of Fishbourn's wharf, a Delaware River structure. All the stores on the wharf burned and the fire spread across the street destroying three more homes. Damage ran into several thousand pounds. Benjamin Franklin commented in his Gazette that as there was no wind that evening, if people had been provided with good engines and firefighting instruments, the fire would likely have been contained.

Franklin's recommendations ultimately led in 1736 to the forming of Philadelphia's first volunteer fire brigade, the Union Fire Company. So many men wanted to join Franklin's Union Company that he suggested it would be more beneficial to the salubrity of the city if they formed their own fire brigades. In 1751, Franklin and members of his Union Fire Company met with firefighters from other brigades to form the oldest fire insurance company in the United States.

Afterwards rival fire companies would literally fight each other at the scene of a blaze to determine who would have the opportunity to extinguish the fire and receive payment from the Contributorship. Philadelphia would not get a city fire department until 1871 but, through luck and its aggressive firefighting-for-pay system, never suffered a citywide catastrophic conflagration. The Contributorship Greek Revival building that dates to 1836 caught fire once — it was quickly extinguished. .

TURN RIGHT ON WALNUT STREET.

8. **Pennsylvania Savings Fund Society**
   306 Walnut Street

Founded in 1816, the Philadelphia Savings Fund Society was the first savings bank in the United States. This is their first headquarters, designed by Thomas Ustick Walter, who would later have a hand in the United States Capitol in Washington DC, in the Greek Revival style in 1839. Marble quarried in Chester County was used in construction; the pediment is an 1880s addition.

TURN AROUND AND WALK WEST ON WALNUT STREET, AWAY FROM THE RIVER.

9. **Curtis Center**
   northwest corner of 6th Street and
   Walnut Street

Cyrus Curtis founded what was to become the largest magazine publishing company in the the country, largely on the strength of the Saturday Evening Post and the Ladies Home Journal, in 1883. This Beaux Arts office building was designed for the company in 1910 by Edgar V. Seeler.

10. **Washington Square**
    bounded by Walnut Street on the north,
    6th Street on the east, South
    Washington Square on the south and
    West Washington Square on the west

Washington Square was one of five squares - called Southeast Square at the time - by William Penn in 1682. For most of the next 100 years this was a potter's field and among the bodies buried beneath the square are fallen Revolutionary War soldiers. Burials were generally done on the cheap: bodies bound in canvas — sans coffins.

It was in the air over Washington Square that Americans first witnessed flight. Aeronaut Jean Pierre Blanchard made the first balloon ascension in America from the Walnut Street Jail in 1793.

It picked up the name of America's first president, who served his two terms in Philadelphia, in 1825 but the statue, a bronze cast of the 1791 marble original by Jean-Antoine Houdon, dates to the 1920s.

TURN LEFT ON 6TH STREET.

11. **Penn Mutual Insurance Company**
    510 Walnut Street ; east side of
    Washington Square

At the corner of 6th and Walnut Streets, on the Square's eastern side, is an office building belonging to the Penn Mutual Insurance Company. In 1913, Edgar Seeler, architect of the Curtis Center, also designed this structure. The adjacent skyscraper also belonging to Penn Mutual is of interest. The facade of John Haviland's 1838 Egyptian Revival design for the Pennsylvania Fire Insurance Co. was retained intact and serves as a faux facade for the skyscraper.

Penn Mutual was built on the site of Robert Smith's historic Walnut Street Jail which stood from 1775 to 1835. This prison was the site of the earliest experiments in criminal rehabilitation in the United States. After serving as a brutal military prison for both sides in the Revolutionary War, it underwent change in 1790 when the Pennsylvania Assembly passed a series of prison reform bills. New prison practice included segregation of the sexes, separation of juveniles from adults, and the creation of distinct prisons for debtors and felons.

George Washington spent a good amount of time in the debtor's prison — visiting his good friend Robert Morris, the financier of the Revolution. Morris had fallen on hard times, in part due to his attempt at building a personal Xanadu on High (Market) Street which bankrupted him.

12. **Athenaeum of Philadelphia**
    219 South 6th Street; east side of
    Washington Square

Apparently drawing inspiration from English clubhouses, architect John Notham created the first Italianate building in America for the private library that began in 1818. This building is from 1845 and its reading room, the city's finest, saw the likes of Charles Dickens and Edgar Allen Poe. Notham had wanted marble for his Italian palazzo but settled for the cheaper brownstone.

13. **Lea & Febiger**
    600 South Washington Square; east side
    of Washington Square

America's oldest continuously operating book publisher, Lea & Febiger, spent about a third of its 225 years in this building they built in 1923. Mathew Carey started the company in 1785, thanks in part to a $400 loan from the Marquis de Lafayette.

TURN RIGHT ON SOUTH
WASHINGTON SQUARE.
TURN RIGHT ON 7TH STREET.

14. *Farm Journal* Building
     230 West Washington Square; west side
     of Washington Square

The *Farm Journal's* first readers in 1827 were "farmers living within a day's buggy ride" of Philadelphia. Today it is the largest farming magazine in the country. The *Farm Journal* Building, with its stone-carved horn of plenty overflowing at the entrance, was built in 1911.

15. W.B. Saunders Building
     northwest corner of 7th and Locust
     streets; west side of Washington Square

Washington Square was the center of Philadelphia's robust publishing industry that began flourishing in the 19th century. The W.B. Saunders Company dates to 1888 and moved here in 1910. Though long a leader in the field of medical publishing, specializing in technical - and typically dry - works, it is best known for the landmark Sexual Behavior in the Human Male, more popularly known as "the Kinsey Report" that was the first graphic study of human sexual behavior.

16. N.W. Ayer Building
     210 West Washington Square; west
     side of Washington Square

Francis Wayland Ayer was 21 years old when he started a business in 1869 to represent religious weekly magazines. Ayer was the first agency to hire a full-time copywriter (1892) and the first to hire an artist (1898). Over the next hundred years it grew to be Philadelphia's largest advertising agency and the country's oldest before defecting to New York City in 1973.

The building, a paean to advertising and the Age of Art Deco, was built in 1928 by Ralph Bencker. Pairs of giant deco sculptures seem to grow out of each side of the top of the 15-story building. The bronze doors of the building's entrance facing Washington Square depict advertising employees at work while all about them signs of the zodiac are presumably influencing them. Curiously, the figures are all dressed in Pharaoh-like robes while doing their office work.

17. Bible House
     701 Walnut Street; north side
     of Washington Square

This is home to the Pennsylvania Bible Society, the oldest such group in the country. The Society, formed in 1808, has distributed Bibles in 73 different languages.

TURN LEFT ON WALNUT STREET.

18. Philadelphia Savings Fund Society
     700-710 Walnut Street; west side
     of Washington Square

This marble Italianate palazzo was the second of three headquarters for the venerable Philadelphia banking house that opened its doors down Walnut Street in 1816 as a benevolent institution without stockholders. The building has seen a couple of additions but the original slice was built in 1869 at the corner opposite Washington Square. Addison Hutton won a design competition for the commission and this is considered his first major success.

TURN LEFT ON 8TH STREET.

19. Reynolds-Morris House
     225 South 8th Street

This Georgian-style house was built by physician John Reynolds in 1787. Later purchased by Luke Wistar Morris in 1817, it is one of two freestanding houses remaining in Philadelphia from the immediate post-Revolution period.

20. Pennsylvania Hospital
     8th Street between Spruce
     and Pine streets

This is the oldest hospital in America, founded to take care of the "sick poor" and the insane. Benjamin Franklin and Dr. Thomas Bond raised money to found the hospital in 1751, the first patient was admitted a year later.

The hospital's original home was the Pine Building, still a section of the hospital, which was built in three sections over 50 years. The Federal-style central section is superbly rendered from a design by David Evans, Jr in 1800. The cells in the basement were originally intended for mentally ill patients. The hospital has had fire insurance longer than any other building in the country.

RETURN TO SPRUCE STREET AND WALK TOWARDS THE DELAWARE RIVER.

21. Girard Row
326-334 Spruce Street

Built in 1831-33, these fine Greek Revival rowhouses stand apart from other middle-class houses of the period for their stone trim and marble ground floor facings that contrast with the red brick.

TURN RIGHT ON SOUTH 4TH STREET.

22. Hill-Physick House
321 South 4th Street

Henry Hill made one of America's first fortunes importing Madeira, the wine from Portugese islands that wasn't taxed by the British. Madeira was the drink of choice for Thomas Jefferson who used it to toast the Declaration of Indpendence. Hill used his money to construct one of the most magnificent houses in Philadelphia on the site of the Old City Alms House. It is one of only two freestanding Federal townhouses extant in the city. Finished in 1786, the semi-elliptical fanlight across the entrance that was imported from England is the highlight of a textbook facade.

From 1815 to 1837 Dr. Philip Syng Physick lived in the house. Physick's grandfather, the renowned silversmith Philip Syng, designed the inkstand from which both the Declaration and Constitution were written, and which is still displayed at Independence Hall. Dr. Physick, who built his reputation fighting the Yellow Fever epidemic that claimed Hill's life in 1798, is credited with being the first doctor to use a stomach pump and is often called the "Father of American Surgery."

23. St. Mary's Church
252 South 4th Street

Founded in 1763 as the city's second Roman Catholic church, the Continental Congress met here officially four times. On July 4, 1779, the first public religious commemoration of the Declaration of Independence was held here. The church has been remodeled several times, the last in 1884 when the Gothic facade was added and the entrance placed on 4th Street. The cemetery dates to 1759. Inside a crucifix was carved by renowned sculptor William Rush. The front of the church's organ was crafted by Thomas U. Walter, the man responsible for designing the Capitol in Washington, D.C.

24. Old Pine Street Church
412 Pine Street

Philadelphia's first Presbyterian church was erected in 1704. Although Philadelphia is associated with William Penn and other Quakers, in fact by 1739, Presbyterians outnumbered all other religious denominations in Philadelphia. This building dates to 1768 and is the only Presbyterian church still standing in the city from the days before the American Revolution. The British occupied the Church in 1777 and used it for a hospital and stable. Notables buried in the churchyard include William Hurry, who rang the Liberty Bell the day The Declaration of Independence was read for the first time, Philadelphia symphony conductor Eugene Ormandy and mathematician David Rittenhouse.

TURN LEFT ON PINE STREET.

25. St. Peter's Church
313 Pine Street

The church was built by members of Christ Church, who were building houses in newly settled Society Hill, in 1761. George Washington worshiped here. Four of early America's finest architects and craftsmen all contributed at various times to the building of this church that is transporting in its beauty and colonial charac ter. Robert Smith, a member of the Carpenters' Company, built the church in Palladian style. The tower and spire were added in 1842 by William Strickland and the iron staircases (which are no longer there) were installed in 1846 by Thomas U. Walter (who designed the Capitol Dome in Washington, D.C.). Two wooden angels made by William Rush were brought from Old St. Paul's Church.

26. Thaddeus Kosciuszko National Memorial
northwest corner of 3rd and Pine streets

This land has as eclectic a history as any in Philadelphia, with religious, political, military and commercial connections. The land was once owned by Jacob Duche who was the head of the Episcopal Church in the American colonies. It is believed that John Nixon, the first man to read the Declaration of Independence publicly, was born on the site, though not at this house. Edward Piszeck, the founder of Mrs. Paul's seafood donated the building to the National Park Service in the early 1970s.

But this Georgian townhouse built in 1775-1776 is on the national radar because it was briefly the home of Proceed to the northwest corner of 3rd and Pine Streets which was for a time was the home of Polish-born engineering genius, Thaddeus Kosciuszko, called by Thomas Jefferson, "as pure a son of liberty as I have ever known." As a commissioned colonel earning $6 a month, Kosciuszko first planned forts along the Delaware River during the Revolution and then masterminded defenses from West Point to Georgia.

27. Head House Square
2nd Street, between Pine and
Lombard streets

In 1745 sheds, called the Shambles. were erected to allow merchants to gather in a marketplace to sell food and wares. By the early 1800s Federal-style headhouses were added at each end, used for city meetings and local fire companies. This is the nation's oldest firehouse and, restored in 1960, marketplace.

CONTINUE TO THE END OF PINE STREET AT FRONT STREET AND TURN LEFT. MAKE THE FIRST RIGHT AT SPRUCE STREET TO CROSS BACK OVER I-95 TO PENN'S LANDING AND THE TOUR STARTING POINT.

Look Up,

Phoenixville

A Walking Tour of Phoenixville...

One of the first Europeans to arrive in what would become Phoenixville was attorney Charles Pickering who sailed to America with colony founder William Penn. While Penn sought religious freedom for his fellow Quakers, Pickering sought financial opportunity in "Penn's Woods." He obtained a large tract of land around the creek that now bears his name and began silver mining operations. His silver ore was found to be worthless by inspectors back in England. Pickering's financial affairs spiraled downward and he was eventually imprisoned for counterfeiting.

A few years later, a Moses Coates and his friend James Starr purchased a strip of land along the French Creek within the present boundaries of the borough. The entire 1000 acres of forest had been deeded to Chester County political figure David Lloyd, who called it the "Manavon Tract" after his birthplace in Great Britain. Starr cleared his portion of the land for agriculture and built a grist mill around which a little village grew.

After the Revolutionary War a small mill was built to make nails. It was to be the precursor of Phoenix Steel. The town was renamed Phoenixville, because the Foundry's molten metal reminded the manager of the fabled bird that died and rose from its ashes. During the first half of the 19th century, the iron industry expanded enormously, growing from a few small rolling and slitting mills to several larger blast furnaces and finishing mills. With the completion of the Chester County Canal in 1828 and the Philadelphia and Reading Railroad in 1837 ironmasters gained easier access to raw materials and more efficient transportation of finished products. After the mid-nineteenth century Phoenix Iron and Steel became the largest iron and steel producer in Chester County, and one of the largest in southeast Pennsylvania. By 1881 Phoenix Iron Company used 60,000 tons of ore annually in the blast furnaces to produce 30,000 tons of pig iron, and employed 1,500 men.

Our walking tour will start in Reeves Park, a greenspace donated by David Reeves, founder and president of the Phoenix Iron Works, the economic engine that drove Phoenixville through its development years...

1. **David Reeves Memorial**
   Reeves Park, center

Phoenix Iron Works arose from a small nail factory set up in 1812. It never produced more than three tons of nails per day, and was eventually sold. In the early 1820s, David Benjamin Reeves and James Joseph Whitaker provided a much-needed infusion of capital to the little foundry. In 1835, the Phoenixville enterprise was reorganized and incorporated as the Phoenix Iron Company with David Reeves, founder, as president and his son Samuel as vice president and treasurer and Phoenixville was on its way from small farming community to nationally known steel town. The monument in his namesake park was paid for by employees of Phoenix Iron Company and dedicated, two years after his death, in 1873.

2. **Street Clock**
   Reeves Park, southeast corner of 2nd
   Avenue and S Main Street

This is a four-sided replica of a Victorian Seth Thomas Street Clock, installed in 2006. Connecticut-born Seth Thomas founded America's oldest clock company in 1813 when he was 28 years of age. The famous clock in the center of Grand Central Terminal in New York City is a Seth Thomas clock.

3. **Griffen Cannon**
   Reeves Park, in corner along 3rd Avenue
   and S Main Street

In 1854 John Griffen, Superintendent of the Safe Harbor Iron Works, owned by the Phoenixville Iron Company, was hammering and rolling round iron for Government lighthouses. Griffen convinced Samuel Reeves, then President of Phoenix Iron, that the technique could be applied to guns and produced a prototype that was successful in Army trials. During the Civil War the company delivered 1,400 highly accurate rifled cannons to the Union Army. Gunnery like the one on display here were credited with laying the foundation for Northern success in many battles, including Gettysburg in 1863.

CROSS S MAIN STREET AT
3RD AVENUE.

4. **Saint Ann Roman Catholic Church**
   southwest corner of S Main Street and 3rd
   Avenue

In 1905 Archbishop Patrick Ryan established the fourth Catholic Parish in Phoenixville, named in honor of St. Ann, the grandmother of our Savior Jesus Christ, the mother of the Mother of God, and the spouse of St. Joachim. Work on the new church began in March 1905 and on Sunday, September 15, 1907, Archbishop Ryan dedicated the new Church.

WALK SOUTH ON S MAIN STREET
(REEVES PARK WILL BE ON YOUR
RIGHT).

5. **Dismant House**
   northwest corner of S Main Street and 3rd
   Avenue

The beautifully preserved Queen Anne Victorian Dismant House with a turret, several gables, and tall slender chimneys was built around 1890.

6. **Byrne Mansion**
   400 S Main Street, southwest corner of S
   Main Street and 2nd Avenue

Thomas F. Byrne was born on October 21, 1854 in the village of Carrigans in County Tyrone, Ireland. Nine days later his mother, Ann Lynch Bryne, died. Having migrated from Ireland to the United States, and with the consent of his father, the 18-year old Thomas F. Bryne entered into a three year indenture as an apprentice with the Phoenix Iron Company in order to be instructed "in the art, trade or mystery of a machinist." Byrne would develop and patent a number of inventions, and he made a fortune in the manufacture of seamless underwear. The Byrne Knitting Mill, once one of the largest such mills in the country, still stands at Lincoln and Morgan streets.

The south portion of the stone mansion house dates back to 1884. The remainder was added in 1898 by Byrne. The basement is home to the Schuylkill Valley Model Railroad Club that hosts open houses on weekends in November, December and January.

7. **Phoenixville Public Library**
   northeast corner of S Main Street and 2nd Avenue

The Public Library of Phoenixville began its existence in 1896 when a group of prominent citizens took advantage of a law passed by Pennsylvania legislators making it legal for school districts to own and operate public libraries. A small collection of books from the Young Men's Literary Union, a private subscription Library set up in the mid 1850s, formed the core collection of the new Library, which was housed in a succession of rented buildings. In 1901, the Library trustees contacted famed steel magnate and philanthropist Andrew Carnegie, who was then actively engaged in bestowing Library buildings on worthy communities in the United States and Scotland. Carnegie agreed to supply a town Library and sent architect's plans and $20,000. The school Directors purchased a lot at Second and Main Streets and the new building of Avondale stone and Indiana limestone with a high covered ceiling was opened in September 1902.

8. **215 S Main Street**

This brick Second Empire Victorian features a tell-tale mansard roof. It dates to 1890.

9. **208 S Main Street**

Somewhere along the line the owners of this 1885 Dutch Revival duplex could not agree on an exterior color.

10. **F.E. Bader House**
    northeast corner of S Main Street and Washington Avenue

The F.E. Bader House looks much as it has for over 100 years.

11. **First Presbyterian Church of Phoenixville**
    145 S Main Street

The colonnade of Doric columns are not original; the facade is a 20th century addition to the Greek Revival-styled church.

12. **Civic Center**
    123 S Main Street

The City Armory, built of bricks with battlements atop the roofline, was the gathering spot for servicemen during World War I. Today it is occupied by the Phoenixville Civic Center.

13. **Phoenixville Historical Society**
    southwest corner of S Main Street and Church Street

The English Gothic Central Lutheran Church was built in 1873; today it is home to the Phoenixville Historical Society. The Society museum, dedicated in 1980, has many Phoenix Iron and Phoenix Steel Company artifacts, including a sample of the famous Phoenix Column. It is open Wednesdays, Fridays and Sundays.

14. **Farmers & Mechanics National Bank**
    southeast corner of S Main Street and Church Street

The Neoclassical Farmers & Mechanics National Bank dates to 1925.

15. **Farmers & Mechanics National Bank**
    northeast corner of S Main Street and Church Street

The Phoenixville Trust Company building has not changed much in the past 100 years although the bank is no longer serving the community.

TURN RIGHT ON CHURCH STREET.

16. **Sacred Heart Church**
    148 Church Street

During the late 1800s many Slovaks settled in eastern Pennsylvania to work in the coal fields and steel mills, including the Phoenix Iron Company. In 1901 the local Slovak population purchased a building that was being used as the town library and renovated it in a Romanesque Revival style for a new church. Its round arch window and column facade are dominated by the large square tower and broached spire. The recessed, round arch doorways face out from vaguely Gothic peaks and buttresses.

17. Phoenixville Senior Center
153 Church Street

The Phoenixville Senior Center began life as a Greek Revival Methodist church.

18. Saint Peter's Episcopal Church
121 Church Street

The Saint Peter's Episcopal congregation goes back 170 years. The church is in the style of a typical English parish church, built entirely of stone, and enhanced by many very beautiful stained glass windows that illustrate not only the history of the church but also honors important local leaders of the congregation. St. Peter's Episcopal is the classical epitome of a stone Gothic church, complete with heavy buttresses, cinquefoil tracery and stained .glass windows, and ornate pointed arches. Designed by Philadelphia architect George Nattree, its Gothic embellishments and sprawling size are indicative of the financial support by its congregation.

AT THE END OF CHURCH STREET CROSS STARR STREET AND CLIMB THE STONE STEPS TO THE PARKING LOT ON THE HILL.

19. Whitestone
Starr Street

Whitestone was built by John Griffen, Phoenix Iron Works superintendent, in 1858. Its style is Italianate, with a central tower and large window areas.

RETURN TO STARR STREET AND TURN RIGHT. TURN RIGHT ON BRIDGE STREET.

20. Mansion House Inn
37 Bridge Street

The Mansion House was built in 1830 and put in more than 100 years of service as an inn close to, first, water traffic on the Schuylkill River and then for railroad travelers. Those travelers from a century ago would still recognize the building. The Mansion House is an imposing Federal struc-ture over three stories tall with double gable-end chimneys, gable dormers, and a two-story veranda with original spool-work railings.

21. Philadelphia & Reading Railroad Station
east end of Bridge Street at Schuylkill River

The Philadelphia & Reading Railroad was established in 1834 to haul coal from Schuylkill County. In the 1870s, it was the largest corporation in the world. This station handled passenger service while a depot on Vanderslice Street received freight trains. The Phoenixville station once sported two large spires but otherwise looks much the same as a catering business as it did when it serviced thousands of riders.

Bridge Street takes its name from the bridge that spans the Schuylkill River at this point, connecting Phoenixville with Mont Clare. That bridge at one time was one of the longest covered bridges ever built in Pennyslvania. The wooden bridge burned spectacularly in 1912 and was replaced with a concrete bridge. That in turn was replaced by the present bridge in 1997.

WALK AWAY FROM THE RIVER BACK UP BRIDGE STREET.

22. Phoenix Iron Works Office
101 Bridge Street

Only two buildings remain from the great Phoenix Iron Works complex; this brownstone Victorian-era headquarters and the foundry down the street. The building has recently been rehabilitated and put back to use as a restaurant.

23. Columbia Hotel
148 Bridge Street

Frank H. Ecock opened his hotel and restaurant on April 6, 1893. He called it the Columbia House. The cherry and mahogany bar was built in London, England in 1892. The Columbia Hotel is a brick Period Revival inn built by T. D. Grover. It is three stories with an outstanding two story spool-work veranda topped by a third story single width porch and gable roof. The window treatments are typical of the Period Revival influence—half-round and elliptical arch/ accenting plain and relieving arch styles. Today's Columbia Bar & Grille still looks much as it did then. When Steve McQueen was filming his first feature, the cult classic *The Blob*, he frequently ate at the Columbia, proclaiming it, according to legend, to serve "the best steak and apple fritters I ever had."

24. Molly Maguire's
northeast corner of Bridge and Main streets

The Irish pub is a recent inhabitant; in the 1800s this building was the home of the Dancy Drugstore.

TURN LEFT ON MAIN STREET.

25. Old Post Office
15 Main Street

When this building served as the Phoenixville Post Office for decades through the 1930s it had a cornice over the first floor that matched the roof cornice, still unchanged, on the Main Street side of the building.

WALK BACK DOWN MAIN STREET TO THE MURAL AT THE CORNER OF BRIDGE STREET.

26. Phoenixville Mural
northwest corner of Bridge and Main streets

This prime retail location was occupied by the John Smith business at the turn of the 20th century dealing in men's hats, neckwear and general haberdashery. Many other businesses followed until the building burned in 1970. Instead of rebuilding, the space was replaced with Renaissance Park and the wall mural in 1994.

CONTINUE ON N MAIN STREET.

27. Starr House
10 N Main Street

James Starr, one of the first settlers to arrive in the area, erected a grist mill and his home here,

considered now the oldest structure in Phoenixville. It wasn't nearly this large; merely a log cabin in 1732 that has been engulfed by alterations over the years. The nail factory that would evolve into the Phoenix Iron Company originated here.

28. The Foundry/Schuylkill River Heritage Center
2 North Main Street

Built in 1882 along French Creek in the Richardsonian Romanesque style the foundry of Phoenix Iron & Steel Company poured iron castings well into the 1970s. The fortunes of the Phoenix works peaked in the early twentieth century. The company moved into steel production, but sales of bridges soon declined, in part due to a string of catastrophic failures of Phoenix bridges under construction, including the 1907 collapse of a bridge being built in Quebec that killed seventy-five workmen. The Phoenix works also encountered a formidable competitor, the United States Steel Company, organized in 1901. The growing use of reinforced concrete in bridges further reduced sales of metal bridges. The two World Wars temporarily increased sales of structural steel, but did not stave off the end. In 1962 the bridge company went out of business. The parent company struggled on, but, like much of the Pennsylvania steel industry during the late 1970s and 1980s, it too died, and the Phoenix works ceased production in 1984.

Abandoned after the decline of the steel industry and the company's shuttering in 1987, the symbol of Phoenixville's industrial past has been resurrected as the home of the Schuylkill River Heritage Center. Blending old and new, a unique band of clerestory windows divide the double-tiered roof structure allowing light to pour into the column-free open space. Inside, there is a huge wooden cantilever crane still in its original location and thought to be the last and largest of its kind in the United States.

29. Phoenix Columns
The Foundry/2 N Main Street

The greatest claim to fame for the Phoenix Iron Works was the invention, fabrication, sale, and utilization of the versatile Phoenix Column. Invented by Samuel Reeves in 1862, the Phoenix

Column is hollow and circular and made up of four, six, or eight wrought-iron segments that are flanged and riveted together. Reeves had created a device that would greatly facilitate the construction of tall buildings by eliminating the need for brutally heavy and thick load-bearing walls. The column also had application in bridges, viaducts, and elevated lines. Phoenix Columns played a vital role in many noteworthy buildings in New York City and the Eiffel Tower.

STAND IN FRONT OF THE FOUNDRY AND LOOK ACROSS FRENCH CREEK TO THE TOP OF THE HILLSIDE.

30. Vanderslice Mansions
47 N 4th Street

Phoenixville has one of the largest collections of high style mansions built by mill owners and entrepreneurs in northern Chester County. Levi Oberholtzer and John Vanderslice adhered to the Second Empire style for their mansions overlooking the valley on the north side of French Creek.

WALK UP THE STEPS BEHIND THE FOUNDRY TO MILL STREET.

31. Worker Housing
1-31 Mill Street

Phoenixville has the largest collection of mid-nineteenth century worker housing in Chester County. Most of this housing is vernacular in appearance and has little ornamentation. In 1846 Reeves, Buck and Company, which was the forerunner of Phoenix Iron and Steel, erected 1-31 Mill Street for employees at their nearby nail factory. The construction helped alleviate an acute housing shortage when the mill increased it work force to 300 men and the town's population doubled during the mid-1840s.

RETURN TO BRIDGE STREET AND WALK WEST (AWAY FROM THE RIVER).

32. *Independent-News* Office
203 Bridge Street

This Italianate commercial building dates to 1856, erected for Vosburg N. Shaffer, editor and publisher of the *Independent Phoenix*, the town's first daily newspaper.. Note the well-proportioned label lintels on the two-over-two windows that compliment the elaborate cornice fenestration It wasn't always the *Independent-News* Office, but the ornate top of the building has never changed even when the lettering inside does. In the early 1900s this was the Benjamin Hardware Company and lettered as such. The original newspaper name was restored with the building.

33. Italianate Commercial Buildings
200 block of Bridge Street

Phoenixville's collection of Italianate commercial buildings constructed between 1850 and 1890 is unique in northern Chester County. For example, Vosburg Shaffer and John L. Dismant, as well as Philip, Christian and Frederick Wall popularized the Italianate style with their commercial buildings at 203 Bridge Street, 224-228 Bridge Street, and 214-216 Bridge Street.

34. Children's Plaza
Bridge Street opposite Bank Street

Children's Plaza was established on Bridge Street in 2008, built with Phoenix columns.

35. National Bank of Phoenixville
225 Bridge Street

The National Bank of Phoenixville building, with its Neoclassical facade of four fluted Ionic columns, dates to 1924. Today it houses the offices of *The Phoenix* newspaper.

36. Colonial Theatre
227 Bridge Street

The Colonial may be the only theater in the country more famous for being in the movies than for showing movies. After a fire and financial reversals in 1901 the world famous Griffin-Smith-Hill Pottery, producers of Majolica, at the bottom of Church Street went out of business, casting secretary and treasurer Harry Brownback out of work. Now free to pursue his dream of bringing top quality theatrical productions to Phoenixville he used his proceeds from the sale of the pottery plant to purchase two adjoining properties on Bridge Street and built Harry's Colonial Opera House at a total cost of $30,000.

The first stage show was held on Saturday, September 5, 1903. Internationally known actor, Fred E. Wright, starred in the musical extravaganza *The Beauty Doctor*. The first movie presentation, a series of four one-reelers lasting 40 minutes, was shown on Saturday, December 19th. Harry Houdini appeared in 1917, freeing himself from a burglar-proof safe. The last stage show appeared in 1925 and in 1928 the first talking picture, *The Jazz Singer*, was screened at the Colonial.

Meanwhile the restrained Italianate facade was modernized with marquee and colorful lights. In 1957 the theater was used as a location in the very low-budget sci-fi film, *The Blob*, with an unknown named Steve McQueen in the lead. In the movie patrons run in frenzy out of the theater after realizing a creature from outer space was among them. The marquee proudly announcing that the Colonial is "healthfully air conditioned" is clearly visible in the movie.

Years later, with McQueen a Hollywood legend and *The Blob* a cult classic, the Colonial Theatre, now restored to its former grandeur is the centerpiece for the Blobfest celebration every summer.

37. Odd Fellows Building
237 Bridge Street

The Odd Fellows Temple in the heart of the business district is a tall Italianate building with an ornate bracketed cornice and impressive inscribed fenestration frontispiece.

38. Hotel Chester
400 Bridge Street

The Queen Anne style Hotel Chester, built in 1894, had forty rooms offering both gas and electricity. The building has soldiered on into the 21st century.

DETOUR: CONTINUE THREE BLOCKS ON BRIDGE STREET TO ROUTE 23, NUTT ROAD...

The Fountain Inn, originally the William Fussell residence during Colonial times in the 1770s, was the furthest point inland reached in America by the British during the Revolutionary War. The British arrived in Manavon (Phoenixville) on September 21, 1777 with 14,000 troops. According to firsthand reports, the British camp stretched along Nutt Road from the old Bull Tavern one mile east of the borough, all the way to present-day Bridge Street. For the three days that they were here, the British and their hired military, the German Hessians, ransacked every home and business in the area. The spot is memorialized by a stone marker in the intersection.

TURN LEFT AND WALK EAST ON CHURCH STREET. IF YOU HAVE TAKEN THE DETOUR RETURN TO CHURCH STREET AND TURN RIGHT.

39. Benham Residence
northeast corner of Church and Gay streets

A square brick addition for commercial purposes has been glued to the middle of an elegant house.

40. Baptist Church
southeast corner of Church and Gay streets

This stone church with Gothic and Romanesque influences was built in 1911, replacing an earlier Baptist church located on the same site.

TURN RIGHT ON GAY STREET.

41. Phoenixville Post Office
northwest corner of Church and Gay streets

The current post office, with Neoclassical Palladian elements, was built in the 1930s.

42. Charles Bader House
Gay Street at Morgan Street

The Charles Bader residence is an example of the Second Empire, late Victorian style from the 1880s. Many grand homes were built along Gay Street and most retain much of their original appearance. Along the street you can examples of Queen Anne, Gothic, and Craftsman-style homes.

43. Gay Street School
Gay Street between Morgan Street and Washington Avenue

The Gay Street School was built in the Italianate style in 1874. Over the years it has done duty as an elementary school and a secondary school. It no longer operates as a school but the four-sided clock is still visible across Phoenixville.

TURN LEFT ON FIRST AVENUE.

44. Forge Theatre
241 First Avenue

The Forge Theatre, a community theater founded in 1962, operates in the former F.B. Neiman and Sons Funeral Home. Performances range from classic to contemporary, musical to non-musical, comedy to drama.

RETURN TO GAY STREET AND TURN LEFT TO CONTINUE WALKING SOUTH. TURN RIGHT ON 2ND AVENUE.

45. Barkley Elementary School
320 2nd Avenue

This brick building with engaged Greek columns was built in 1930 as a junior high school. In 1963 it was renamed the Samuel K. Barkley Elementary School and has been educating younger children ever since. A complete renovation in the 1990s retained the original appearance of the building.

TURN AND WALK EAST ON 2ND AVENUE TO REEVES PARK AND THE TOUR STARTING POINT.

Look Up,

Pittsburgh

(Cultural District)

A Walking Tour of Pittsburgh's Cultural District...

The Cultural District was the vision of H.J. Heinz II, grandson of Henry J. Heinz, who was Chief Executive Officer of the company his grandfather founded for 25 years. It was his belief that the arts could spearhead an urban revitalization and economic development of a city's blighted area. The turn-around started in 1971 with the restoration of Heinz Hall, once a motion-picture palace, into a home for the Pittsburgh Symphony.

In 1984 the Pittsburgh Cultural Trust was formed to transform a fourteen-square block area of downtown Pittsburgh along the Penn-Liberty corridor. Today two dozen venues attract over 2,000,000 people to the Cultural District every year in one of the City's best preserved and most nearly intact districts.

Pittsburgh's streets were laid out in 1784 by the surveyors George Woods and Thomas Vickroy, who were agents of the Penn family in Philadelphia. This has historically been a diverse mix of urban uses and by 1900 many important local architects had left their mark on the Penn-Liberty area. A rail line ran down Liberty Avenue at the district's southern edge and an elevated rail line was slated to run along the Allegheny River shore. But with the Depression of the 1930s the commercial buildings, theaters, hotels and stores began to slide into decline.

Our walking tour will explore these blocks of rebirth along the Allegheny River but first we'll start where Pittsburgh started, at the confluence of two great rivers coming together to form a third...

1. **The Point**
    101 Commonwealth Place

Point State Park is at the confluence of two rivers forming a third. The Monongahela River, which originates in Fairmont, West Virginia, flows northward over 128 miles to Pittsburgh. The Allegheny River begins 325 miles upriver near Coudersport and drains northwestern Pennsylvania and part of New York. These two rivers meet here, launching the Ohio River 981 miles to the Mississippi River and down to the Gulf of Mexico by New Orleans, Louisiana.

This was once the western terminus for the Pennsylvania Railroad, covered with railyards and warehouses. Then the heavy industry disappeared leaving behind dilapidated hulks of buildings. The National Park Service had plans to create a park here as far back as the 1930s but it wasn't until August 30, 1974 that Point State Park was formally opened when the majestic fountain at the headwaters of the Ohio River was dedicated by the Commonwealth of Pennsylvania

When the fountain is in operation, there are over 800,000 gallons of water in the system - the main column of the fountain shoots water 100 feet high. The circular basin of the fountain is 200 feet in diameter and the water, which is obtained from a 54-foot deep well within the fountain, is re-circulated.

WALK AWAY FROM THE POINT, TOWARDS DOWNTOWN AND THE GOLDEN TRIANGLE.

2. **Blockhouse**
    Point State Park

During the mid-1700s, the armies of France and England vied for control of the Ohio Valley. Four different forts were built at the forks of the Ohio within a period of five years. The British, in the form of a group of Virginians, came first. In 1754, French forces captured Fort Prince George. George Washington led British forces to recapture the fort, but he suffered his first and only surrender at Fort Necessity, 50 miles to the south.

The French then built Fort Duquesne at the Forks, which gave them control of the Ohio Valley. In 1755 General George Braddock led the British to capture the forks, but he was defeated at

the Battle of the Monongahela, eight miles from the fort. Not willing to meet defeat a third time, General John Forbes amassed an army 6,000 men strong in Carlisle and marched west. The French, realizing they were badly outnumbered, burned the fort and departed two days before the British arrived on November 25, 1758. The British then constructed Fort Pitt, named in honor of William Pitt, secretary of state of Britain, that was destined to be the most extensive fortification by the British in North America.

In 1777, the Continental Army used it for its western headquarters. The first Peace Treaty between the American Indians and the United States was signed at Fort Pitt in 1778. Fort Pitt was finally abandoned in 1792 due to its deteriorating condition. It had served to open the frontier to settlement as Pittsburgh became the "Gateway to the West."

The location of Fort Duquesne is marked by a granite tracery (outline) within the Great Lawn area; a bronze medallion depicts the fort. The locations of four of the five bastions of Fort Pitt have been delineated. Built by Colonel Henry Bouquet in 1764, the blockhouse is the oldest architectural landmark in Western Pennsylvania.

LEAVE POINT STATE PARK ON THE EAST SIDE AND TURN LEFT ON PENN AVENUE.

3. **Gateway Center**
    Commonwealth Place to Stanwix Street and Fort Duquesne Boulevard to Penn Avenue

Gateway Center, a complex of high-rise office buildings and a hotel, was one of America's first urban renewal projects when it was developed in the 1950s. Ninety industrial and warehouse buildings were demolished for the first trio of gleaming steel high-rises.

4. **Fifth Avenue**
    120 Fifth Avenue

Standing as the maître d' to downtown Pittsburgh is this 1980s skyscraper from modernist architect Hugh Stubbins. It is dominated by over-scaled windows and the glass central inset inside a granite jacket.

5. Joseph Horne Co.
   northwest corner of Penn Avenue and Stanwix Street

Joseph Horne was born in Bedford County and moved to Pittsburgh where he landed his first job in the retail trade with Christian Yeager. In 1849, at the age of 23, he bought the F.H. Eaton store and eventually renamed it the Joseph Horne Co. as it evolved into one of America's earliest department stores. In 1879, a new central location was built at the corner of Penn Avenue and Stanwix Street. The seven-story landmark was the first department store in the city's downtown district. The iconic regional department store chain operated for nearly 145 years until 1994 when it was swallowed up by the Federated Dept. Stores, Inc. The Beaux Arts building from the early 1900s has been redeveloped but the facade remains.

TURN LEFT ON SIXTH AVENUE.

6. Renaissance Pittsburgh Hotel
   107 Sixth Avenue

This was the Fulton Building when built in 1906 by Henry Phipps, the most socially minded of the U.S. Steel magnates. It is the sole survivor of a set of downtown skyscrapers he built. The Fulton's trademark was its seven-story-high arch fronting the Allegheny River that was designed by New York architect Grosvenor Atterbury to draw the moist air from the water to cool the building by pushing the hot air up. Federal funds were tapped to transform the building into a four-star hotel. Forty thousand pounds of baking soda were used to clean the copper cladding on the light well, making it the largest copper restoration project on the East Coast since the Statue of Liberty restoration in 1986. Three hundred pounds of coal dust were removed from the exterior surface of the skylight, making the lobby space within one of Pittsburgh's most spectacular.

7. Byham Theater
   101 Sixth Street

Originally built as the Gayety Theater, the Byham Theater opened on Halloween night, 1904. It ran for many years as one of the coun-try's foremost stage and vaudeville houses, with appearances from such stars as Ethel Barrymore, Gertrude Lawrence and Helen Hayes. The Gayety boasted pressed copper cherubs painted with a bronze patina, imitation gold leaf, stained glass windows, plaster columns and wainscot of scagolia, an Italian faux marble technique. In the 1930s, the theater was renamed The Fulton and became a full time movie palace. The Pittsburgh Cultural Trust purchased the theater in 1988 and following the first of four planned phases of renovation, the Fulton was reopened in May 1991. It was later renamed the Byham Theater through a naming gift from the Byham family following the second phase of renovation in 1995.

8. Allegheny River Bridges

Originally named for the streets to which they connected–– Sixth, Seventh, and Ninth––these identical self-anchored suspension bridges were long referred to as the "Three Sisters" after they were built in the 1920s. Recently, they were renamed to honor baseball legend Roberto Clemente (1934-1972), who played for the Pittsburgh Pirates from 1955 to 1972; Pittsburgh-born pop artist Andy Warhol (1928-1987); and scientist and author Rachel Carson (1907-1964), who was born in Springdale, about 15 miles up the Allegheny from the Point.

9. PNC Park
   115 Federal Street

PNC Park was built in 2001 as the home of the Pittsburgh Pirates. A classic-style baseball park, it was designed to fit in with the existing street grid and to provide terrific views of the downtown skyline. Before the stadium was built, an archaeological dig was conducted on the site. Pots, pans, dinner plates, a book, and other artifacts were unearthed from the 1830s home of General William Robinson, Jr., the first mayor of Allegheny City. Allegheny was the third largest city in Pennsylvania at the time of its forced annexation to Pittsburgh in 1907.

TURN RIGHT ON FORT DUQUESNE BOULEVARD.

10. **Haas Mural**
    east side of Fort Duquesne Boulevard,
    between Sixth and Seventh streets

Painter Richard Haas, famous for his architectural murals, created this interior of a steel mill, its furnaces pouring white-hot metal, on the Ft. Duquesne facade of the Byham Theater in 1992. The style is known as a trompe l'oeil, or "fool of the eye." Haas called the mural "one of the most complicated façades I've done." This is where the original entrance of the theater was.

TURN RIGHT ON SEVENTH AVENUE.

11. **Century Building**
    130 Seventh Street

Built in 1907 by the Century Land Company, the Century Building was designed by Frederick Russell and Frank Rutan, disciples of Henry Hobson Richardson, designer of Pittsburgh's Allegheny County Courthouse and Jail and the leading American architect of the late 19th century. The Century Building is faced in matte white or near-white materials, while the solids around the windows are in glossy bronze-green terra-cotta. The commercial office building has been adapted into 60 residential lofts, commercial, retail and amenity spaces.

12. **Agnes Katz Plaza**
    southwest corner of Penn Avenue and
    Seventh Street

This public space is adorned with linden trees and granite benches designed by legendary New York artist Louise Bourgeois. She also designed the 25-foot bronze fountain cascade, which was dark brown when installed in 1999 but is now turning green. Scattered around the plaza are pairs of eyeball benches.

TURN RIGHT ON PENN AVENUE.

13. **Theater Square**
    655 Penn Avenue

This is the first of two adjacent buildings on Penn Avenue designed by Michael Graves (the second he created, in 2003). The colorful ten-story building features a JumboTron electric message board delivering the latest information about cultural happenings in Pittsburgh. Inside is the 253-seat Cabaret at Theater Square, the newest performance venue in the Cultural District.

14. **O'Reilly Theater**
    621 Penn Avenue

Sitting on the former site of the Lyceum Theater, one of the city's many vaudeville houses demolished after the 1936 St. Patrick's Day flood, the O'Reilly is the fourth theater project of The Pittsburgh Cultural Trust. The O'Reilly is the only brand-new theater in the District and home of the Pittsburgh Public Theater.

The 650-seat theater is the only downtown performance venue that features a thrust stage, surrounded by the audience on three sides. The theater features 650 seats and state-of-the-art theater technology. The $25 million theater's namesake is Jack Heinz's successor, Anthony J.F. "Tony" O'Reilly. It opened in 1999.

TURN AND WALK NORTH ON PENN AVENUE.

15. **Benendum Center**
    northeast corner of Penn Avenue and
    Seventh Street

The Stanley Theater was built in 1927 at a cost of $3 million and opened on February 27, 1928. It was built in the Art Deco style by James Bly Clark, an early theater tycoon who helped found MGM. The Stanley was billed as "Pittsburgh's Palace of Amusement." In attendance on opening night were Governor John S. Fisher, Mayor Charles H. Kline and Adolph Zukor, president of Paramount Studios. Regular admission cost 65 cents - 25 cents if you came before noon. Notice the old "Stanley Photoplays" sign on the side of the building -- photoplays being the first word for movies.

On St. Patrick's Day in 1936, the theater flooded within two feet of the balcony. Several men were trapped for three days until police arrived in a motorboat and rescued them. After years of decline, the movie palace was remodeled to present rock and roll concerts through 1982.

The late H.J. Heinz II focused his attention on the historic restoration of the Stanley Theater, and as a result, this became The Pittsburgh Cultural Trust's first project after its founding in 1984. It took $43 million dollars and two years, to faithfully restore the glory of the Stanley, now named Benedum Center for the Performing Arts in honor of the Claude Worthington Benedum Foundation, which made the largest contribution toward the rehabilitation. The 2,880-seat Benedum now hosts performances by Pittsburgh's leading ballet, opera and musical theater companies, and is a stop for touring Broadway shows.

The signature piece of the Benedum Center is the original main chandelier which weighs 4,700 pounds, is 20 feet high and 12 feet wide and consists of 500,000 crystal pieces. There are 1,500 feet of brass rail in the theater, most of which is original.

16. 800 Block of Penn Avenue

The Irish Block, named after the family who developed the space in the early 1900s, is a gracious row of buildings, a study in pattern and color.

TURN LEFT ON NINTH STREET.

17. Pittsburgh Creative and Performing Arts (CAPA) High School
111 Ninth Street

One of ten City of Pittsburgh High Schools, CAPA is an $80 million state-of-the-art facility built largely through the generosity of The Bitz Foundation. The design of the new building plays off the design of the adjacent historic structure of 1915 by Pittsburgh architect Charles Bickel. Classrooms flow from one building into the other. Student work is displayed on a four-story exterior JumboTron on the Ft. Duquesne Boulevard façade.

RETURN TO PENN AVENUE AND TURN LEFT.

18. William G. Johnston Building
900 Penn Avenue

This is a tour-de-force of the brick-layers' craft, built in 1885 and remodeled in 1915. William G. Johnston & Co. were printers and stationers. The building now houses apartments in the upper stories and a ground-floor restaurant.

19. 905 Penn Avenue

This three-story. three-bay townhouse with ornamental window hoods is thought to be the last building constructed in downtown Pittsburgh as a single-family residence. It dates to 1870.

20. 911–13 and 915–21 Penn Avenue

The two buildings at 911–13 and 915–21 Penn Avenue came from the pen of Charles Bickel in the first decade of the 20th century. Bickel opened an architectural firm in Pittsburgh in 1885 and was, by all available records, the most frequently hired architect in the Penn-Liberty area.

21. Keech Block
931 Penn Avenue

This five-story commercial loft was built by Alfred Gilliand for Levi Wade in 1892. Architect James T. Steen designed this and a neighbor since destroyed by fire in the Richardsonian Romanesque style. A single bay hangs from below the fifth floor, with arches and applied ornamental columns at the upper two stories. Known as the Keech Block, these buildings served the W. H. Keech Co. furniture business.

22. David L. Lawrence Convention Center
1000 Fort Duquesne Boulevard

The $375 million facility, the cornerstone to western Pennsylvania's hospitality industry, opened in 2003. The Center is the first and largest "green" convention center in the world certified by the U.S. Green Building Council.

TURN RIGHT ON 10TH STREET.
TURN RIGHT ON LIBERTY STREET.

23. August Wilson Center for African American Culture
980 Liberty Avenue

With its signature four-story glass and metal "sail," the $39.5 million center is named after the late Pulitzer Prize-winning playwright, and includes a 486-seat theater and two gallery spaces.

24. Ewart Building/Maginn Building
925/915 Liberty Avenue

Here are two more creations of Charles Bickel in the Richardsonian Romanesque style: the Maginn Building at No. 915 was built in 1891 and the Ewart Building at No. 925 rose a year later. Open space is between them.

25. "Flatiron" Building
Liberty Avenue, Seventh Avenue and Smithfield Street

Pittsburgh's street grid runs parallel and perpendicular to both rivers. Eventually these two grids must crash into each other, and that place is Liberty Avenue. A series of small triangular spaces are occupied with similarly shaped buildings, known as "flatiron" buildings.

26. Federal Reserve Bank
northwest corner of Ninth Street and Liberty Avenue

This corner building was originally the Federal Reserve Bank, designed in 1911 by Alden & Harlow; the builder was Thompson Starrett of New York whose more famous contract was the Empire State Building. Frank E. Alden and Alfred B. Harlow dominated the local architectural scene from 1896 until Alden's death in 1908.

27. Harris Theater
809 Liberty Avenue

Formerly known as the Art Cinema, the Harris represented the cornerstone of the redevelopment of Liberty Avenue in 1995. The Harris Theater was the first moving picture house in Pittsburgh to commercially show "art movies" until competition from other city theaters led to its conversion to an adult, pornographic movie house in the 1960s. The Harris was named through a gift from the Buhl Foundation after John P. Harris, co-founder of the Nickelodeon — the first theater solely dedicated to the showing of motion pictures — and a Pennsylvania State Senator. Today the theater features contemporary, foreign and classic films, programmed by Pittsburgh Filmmakers.

28. Baum Building
812 Liberty Avenue

This Beaux-Arts gem was purchased, cleaned, and renovated by the Pittsburgh Cultural Trust in 2003. The terra-cotta-clad building includes "Space," a 4,000-square-foot gallery for changing exhibits, and a jewelry store that has been located on the second floor since 1925.

29. Wood Street Station/Wood Street Galleries
601 Wood Street

The one-time Monongahela Bank now houses one of downtown Pittsburgh's four "T" stations and an art gallery on the upper floors. The present building was designed in 1927 by Edward Stotz. After apprenticing with notable local architects and touring Europe, Stotz opened his own firm in 1889; it continues today as MacLachlan, Cornelius & Filoni. Notice the new metal canopy designed by Jeffrey DeNinnos, with ginkgo leaf patterns etched in the glass.

TURN LEFT ON WOOD STREET.

30. German National Bank
northwest corner of Wood Street and Sixth Avenue

The German National Bank was organized in 1864 and this eight-story Richardsonian Romanesque headquarters was constructed in 1890 on the deposits from the hard-working German immigrant community. It was national news eight years later when a run on the bank forced the German National to close.

TURN RIGHT ON SIXTH AVENUE.

31. Keenan Building
northwest corner of Seventh Street and Liberty Avenue

In 1907 Thomas Hannah modeled this building after the Spreckels Building in San Francisco. It was erected for Colonel Thomas J. Keenan, the chief owner of the Penny Press and a man with an eye for publicity. His skyscraper is decorated with portraits of 10 "worthies" from Pennsylvania and the fancy dome was once capped with the figure of an eagle in flight. The building is now used as moderate-income housing.

TURN LEFT ON LIBERTY AVENUE.

32. Heinz Hall
Sixth Street between Liberty Avenue and Penn Avenue

A motion-picture palace where live performances were also given, Loew's Penn Theatre was chosen in the late 1960s as a centrally located home—at first temporary, then permanent— for the Pittsburgh Symphony. During remodeling in 1971, the last maker of architectural terra-cotta in the United States was commissioned to match the warm off-white of the original facing, and did an almost-perfect job.

TURN LEFT ON MARKET STREET.

33. Heinz Healey's
160 Fifth Avenue at Market Street

This Arts & Crafts building, with its deep overhanging roof, wooden window framing and stucco, was designed for the Regal Shoe Company in 1908 by Alden & Harlow, the city's leading architectural firm. It is part of a restoration project on the block that retains the facades of three historic buildings and integrates their interiors to function together.

34. Buhl Building
204 Fifth Avenue at Market Street

Designed by Janssen & Abbott in 1913, this building is clad in blue and creamy-white terra-cotta and decorated in Renaissance motifs.

35. Camera Repair Service
411 Market Street

This narrow, Art Deco building in buff brick has lots of geometric ornamentation: overlapping brick piers, rows of cubes, horizontal strips of protruding-retracting brickwork, and a vertical chain of rectangles.

36. Market Square
Forbes Avenue and Market Street

Market Square, or the "Diamond," was laid out in 1784 as an open space of market stalls. The first Allegheny County Courthouse was located here; later a market house and City Hall sat in the square. In the early 1900s the Diamond Market was built, occupying all four quadrants of the square. It featured a rolling skating rink on the top floor. The Diamond Market was demolished in 1961 and in 1972 Market Square was designated by the City as its first historic district.

WALK CLOCKWISE AROUND MARKET SQUARE.

37. 1902 Landmark Tavern
24 Market Square

1902 Tavern was Dimling Brothers Bar and Restaurant, a German restaurant, when it opened on Market Square. After 1960, it had many names, including Cheshire Cat and Crazy Quilt. When Jeff Joyce took over and reopened it in 1982, it became 1902 Landmark Tavern -- for the date he saw on old pictures that still hang in the restaurant. At 23 Market Square, Nicholas Coffee has been doing business on the square since 1919.

38. Old Original Oyster House
20 Market Square

When the Oyster House first opened in 1870, oysters sold for a penny and beer was 10 cents a glass. The enormous fish sandwiches, which require a special bun, were introduced by Louis Americus, who was the proprietor from 1916 to 1970. The building, a Pittsburgh Historic Landmark, has been a favorite location for the movie industry having had 25 films shot at the location.

39. Primanti Brothers
   2 Market Square

Back in the 1930s, Joe Primanti opened a cart in the Strip District selling sandwiches to truckers on the go. It was decided that he should expand to a small restaurant on 18th Street. His brothers, Dick and Stanley, joined him along with nephew John DePriter who was the cook.

According to John, "One winter, a fella drove in with a load of potatoes. He brought a few of 'em over to the restaurant to see if they were frozen. I fried the potatoes on our grill and they looked pretty good. A few of our customers asked for them, so I put the potatoes on their sandwiches." And the rest is gustatory history. The Primanti Sandwich: a true taste of Pittsburgh.

EXIT MARKET SQUARE AND CROSS FOURTH AVENUE TO PPG PLACE.

40. PPG Place

PPG (Pittsburgh Plate Glass) Place is a majestic six-building complex sitting atop a 5.5-acre, three city block site in the heart of downtown. Completed in 1984, PPG Place is one of three downtown buildings made to show off the company product: the others being the former Alcoa Building and U.S. Steel Tower. The gleaming glass and steel structures were developed by John Burgee Architects with the internationally renowned architect Philip Johnson from New York. The 40-story tower is 680 feet high. This complex, with its thicket of 231 Neo-Gothic spires was designed to weave into the architecture of Pittsburgh and recall its great buildings, such as the Cathedral of Learning and the Allegheny County Courthouse. Nearly one million square feet of reflective glass was used, glazed in 19,750 pieces of glass, which provides a high degree of energy efficiency, unmatched in many new buildings.

TURN RIGHT ON THIRD AVENUE. TURN LEFT ON STANWIX STREET.

41. Saint Mary of Mercy Church
   202 Stanwix Street

William P. Hutchins, an important Pittsburgh Roman Catholic designer of churches, schools, and convents. used vivid red brick to complements the steely gray glass of PPG Place for this church in 1936. To the left of the church entrance, about five feet up, is a plaque indicating the 46-foot "All-time-high water mark" of the St. Patrick's Day Flood that crested on March 18, 1936. The disaster spurred flood control development on Pittsburgh's three rivers.

TURN RIGHT ON THE BOULEVARD OF THE ALLIES.

42. United Steelworkers Building
   60 Boulevard of the Allies

The welded stainless steel web of these thirteen-story truss walls is constructed of three different strengths of steel, which progressively lighten as the building rises and the load lessens. This web is dual-purpose, being both the structure and a sunscreen for the interior. With its floor, wall, and elevator loads all carried on a central core, the open interior, with spans up to fifty-four feet, enjoys the highest possible internal flexibility. When it was constructed in the 1960s it was one of the first buildings since the dawn of the skyscraper age 75 years before to feature load-bearing walls.

43. *Pittsburgh Post-Gazette*
   34 Boulevard of the Allies

On July 29, 1786, John Scull and Joseph Hall published the first newspaper west of the Allegheny Mountains, the *Pittsburgh Gazette*. This four-page weekly was produced on a wooden press, the first ever to make the precarious wagon journey over the mountains from Philadelphia. From this humble start, the *Pittsburgh* Post-Gazette, in the guise of a half-dozen names, has grown to a circulation of more than 243,000 daily and more than 424,000 on Sunday.

CROSS OVER COMMONWEALTH PLACE INTO POINT STATE PARK AND THE TOUR STARTING POINT.

Look Up,

Pittsburgh

(Financial District)

A Walking Tour of Pittsburgh's Finanical District...

The Pittsburgh streetscape is the mirror image of its fellow urban pillar of the Commonwealth, Philadelphia. In Philadelphia, city planners made the decision to knock down most of the its building stock that came after the 1840s to promote a Colonial appearance. In Pittsburgh the city planning was done by a fire that ignited on the southeast corner of Ferry and Second streets at noon on April 10, 1845. Before the windswept flames burned themselves out virtually every building in the downtown area was gone. Only one life was lost but an estimated 1,100 houses were destroyed along with cotton-factories, ironworks, glassworks, hotels and several churches. So, virtually all of Pittsburgh's buildings date to after the 1850s.

Coincidentally, this is about the time the Pennsylvania Railroad reached the Allegheny River from Philadelphia and oil was discovered north of the city near Titusville. Pittsburgh was set to explode. The city's great industrialists - Carnegie, Frick, Oliver and Phipps - were making unthinkable fortunes in steel mills and factories and finance. And soon they were itching to throw millions of dollars into building monumental skyscrapers to their legacies.

The avenue of choice for this building splurge was Grant Avenue, historically the outer limit of Pittsburgh. Grant Avenue was at one time Grant's Hill, a natural eastern boundary for the city but also an impediment to a growing metropolis. Over the decades some 60 feet of "the Hump" would be removed. And after the most famous architect of the 20th century, Henry Hobson Richardson, constructed the epic Allegheny County Courthouse in 1884 it ignited a wave of modern skyscrapers that converted the street into downtown Pittsburgh's showcase thoroughfare.

Our walking tour will begin in a small park in the shadow of Pittsburgh's tallest skyscraper and later explore the narrow 25-foot wide street that emerged as Pittsburgh's Wall Street in the late 1800s and early 1900s...

1. Mellon Green
Sixth Avenue and Grant Street

This tiny oasis of greenspace between gargantuan office towers was carved out in 2002. It provides a pedestrian link through the downtown Mellon campus of four major buildings and a tree-lined promenade of rustic terrazzo and granite pavement directs pedestrians through the park to one of four downtown "T" (transit) stations. A granite fountain, designed by Geoffrey L. Rausch to symbolize the strength and stability of Pittsburgh, serves as the focal point, while ample landscaped seating areas, including a wisteria-covered, trellised seat wall framing the lawn, invite passersby to stop and enjoy the view.

WALK NORTH ON GRANT STREET.

2. U.S. Steel Tower
600 Grant Street

At sixty-four stories and 841 feet high, the U.S. Steel Tower was the tallest building between New York and Chicago when it was completed in 1971. It has an exposed frame of Cor-Ten weathering steel (a U.S. Steel patent); the steel is self-oxidizing and is free of any further rust. The exterior features eighteen exposed vertical steel columns, each set three feet outside the curtain wall, such that columns and curtain wall connect at every third floor. The columns run the full height of the building and are filled with a mixture of water, anti-freeze, and an anti-corrosive so, should the tower ever be engulfed in flames, it would keep cool for four hours before collapsing in the heat.

3. First Lutheran Church
615 Grant Street

First English Evangelical Lutheran Church was born on January 15, 1837, as the first English-speaking Lutheran congregation west of the Allegheny Mountains. There were once four churches on Grant Street back when it still had the feel of a small-town main street in the late 1800s. This High Victorian Gothic church, built in 1888, is the only survivor of those days. The graceful dimensions of First Lutheran Church complement the massive Courthouse down the street.

4. Koppers Building
436 Seventh Avenue at southwest corner
of Grant Street

Andrew Mellon, mega-wealthy businessman who was doubling as Secretary of the Treasury in the 1920s, engineered four key public and private buildings on this once-blighted corner in the early days of the Great Depression. Here, as principle shareholder with his brother, R. B. Mellon, in Koppers and Gulf, manufacturer of construction materials, Mellon gave the city one of its most sumptuous Art Deco creations.

Designed by Chicago architects Graham, Anderson, Probst and White -- the successor firm to the father of the modern skyscraper, Daniel Burnham - the building rises 35 stories with two setbacks. The first three stories of Koppers are polished gray granite, while the tower is Indiana limestone. A chateau-style copper roof tops off the creation, spotlighted at night in a dramatic green glow. The interior, splashed with colorful marbles on the floor and walls, bronze metalwork and polychrome cornice moldings is one of Pittsburgh's most splendid. The cast-iron mailbox is the Koppers Building in miniature, roof included.

5. Federal Courthouse and Post Office
northeast corner of Grant Avenue and
Seventh Avenue

The Federal Courthouse and Post Office, filling an entire block, came from the offices of noted New York architects Trowbridge & Livingston in 1932. During a $68 million renovation in 2004-05, the exterior stonework was cleaned, six new courtrooms were added in the original building light wells, and an atrium was constructed to allow natural light to illuminate the new third-floor lobby space and historic fourth-floor courtrooms.

TURN LEFT ON SEVENTH AVENUE.

6. Gulf Tower
northwest corner of Grant Avenue and Seventh Avenue

Trowbridge & Livingston did the work on this tower as well, another project for Andrew Mellon, as the headquarters for his Gulf Oil. This 44-story tower, in two tones of grey granite, was the tallest in Pittsburgh until 1970. The architects went down 90 feet to find a proper footing for their great tower, which Gulf abandoned in 1985. The colossal doorway on Seventh Avenue features a 50-ton granite entablature. Its red-illuminated, stepped-pyramid roof is topped by a weather beacon and a strobe light that signals Pirates home runs and wins.

7. Bell Telephone Building
416 Seventh Avenue

This seven-story Romanesque Revival building is one of the oldest telecommunications facilities still in use in the country. It was erected in 1890 to serve as Bell Telephone of Pennsylvania's switching hall. Leading local architect Frederick J. Osterling delivered one of the tallest commercial buildings in downtown Pittsburgh at the time with a rusticated sandstone base supporting a three-story brick arcade and alternating Roman and segmental arches. The exterior load-bearing walls are constructed of thick masonry walls, mostly brick. The interior is wooden post-and-beam construction, as no steel was used to support the building. As the business grew. Bell Telephone expanded into several other buildings on this block, including a 1905 eleven-story tower to the south by Alden & Harlow, the successor firm to the fabled H.H. Richardson of Brookline, Massachusetts.

TURN LEFT ON WILLIAM PENN WAY.

8. Allegheny HYP Club
619 William Penn Way

Alumni of Harvard (H), Yale (Y) and Princeton (P) had been active in western Pennsylvania for many years, but no one group was large enough to maintain a clubhouse. In 1929, efforts were made to band together and procure a joint

headquarters. Small tenement buildings, constructed in 1894 as workers' row housing were given a Georgian makeover and transformed into a private club. The HYP Club is registered as a National Historic Landmark and continues to be the last remaining tenement housing from 1890s Pittsburgh.

9. Regional Enterprise Tower (ALCOA Building)
423 Sixth Avenue at William Penn Way

This 30-story office tower was the future when it was constructed in 1953. Appearing shortly after World War II, it was intended the showcase the ease of using light-weight aluminum in high-style construction. Aluminum panels could be bolted swiftly on their frames and swivel windows could be cleaned in a snap. However the headquarters for the Aluminum Corporation of America (ALCOA) did not lead a construction revolution into modern America and aluminum-clad buildings are rarely seen today. In 1998, ALCOA constructed a new building on the North Shore along the Allegheny River and donated this iconic building to serve as the headquarters for various nonprofit organizations serving the region.

10. Mellon Plaza
bounded by Sixth Avenue, William Penn Way, Oliver Avenue and Smithfield Street

This was the site of Turner Hall in the 19th century where Samuel Gompers galvanized attendees of the 1881 meeting of the National Labor Congress into what would become the world's largest labor organization, the American Federation of Labor (AFL). Ironically, several generations later, in 1949, all vestiges of the AFL's birthplace would be wiped away for a six-level underground parking garage covered up with terrazzo walks, fountain cascades, and granite benches paid for by those titans of big business - the Mellons. The plaza became a model for cities around the country looking to maximize scarce downtown space.

11. Smithfield United Church
Sixth Avenue at Smithfield Street

The congregation of this church is the descendant of the original German Protestant church that received a land grant from the Penn family ion 1787. The present building was constructed after the congregation sold or leased its land on Sixth Avenue, and the former church was demolished to make way for a commercial building. Henry Hornbostel topped off his 1925 Gothic-style building with an openwork aluminum spire, one of the world's first structural uses of aluminum.

12. Gimbel's Department Store
Sixth Avenue at Smithfield Street

The building originally housed the Kaufmann and Baer Department Store, which was purchased by Gimbel's in 1926. It is a thirteen-story structure sheathed in white terra-cotta and detailed in the Classical style. Particularly noteworthy are the two-story arcade and the heavy projecting cornice at the roofline.

13. Trinity Cathedral
328 Sixth Avenue

This slice of Pittsburgh was part of a land grant from the family of William Penn, on some of the farthest reaches of land of the Pennsylvania founder. Quakers didn't settle this land, however, it was Presbyterians and Anglicans who found their way out here. This is the third church building for Trinity Cathedral; the first Episcopalian house of worship was a block further down on the site of the Wood Street Galleries. Gordon Lloyd created this Victorian-era church building in the English Gothic style in 1870.

Trinity Cathedral is located on a terrace that was a low hill used as a burial ground by Native Americans, French, British, and American settlers; a portion of that graveyard still survives between Trinity and First Presbyterian. In 1864 a funeral was held here for composer Stephen Collins Foster, the most famous popular song composer of the 19th century. Trinity was Foster's home church, but he is not to be found in its graveyard; after the service he was buried at Allegheny Cemetery.

14. First Presbyterian Church of Pittsburgh
320 Sixth Avenue

This congregation traces its history back to 1773 when David McClure and Levi Frisbie arrived in the region to minister to Scotch-Irish settlers who were meeting in member's homes. The first church was a simple log structure erected in 1787. In 1805 a yellow brick structure was built around the log church which continued to host services inside. When the brick church was completed the logs were dismantled, passed through the windows and used in other frontier buildings. That church stood until 1853. The current twin-towered church in the English Gothic style was designed by Theophilus P. Chandler in 1905. A pair of 150-foot-high trees in Oregon were felled for the ceiling supports of the sanctuary that is distinguished by 14 memorial stained-glass windows; 13 were designed and installed by the famous Tiffany Studios.

15. Duquesne Club
325 Sixth Avenue

In 1940, *Time* magazine wrote, "For of all businessmen's clubs, the Duquesne is among the richest and most discreet. Its big, squarish, brownstone-fronted building in the centre of the Golden Triangle is the citadel of Pittsburgh tycoonery. There Mellons, Scaifes, Weirs, Benedums, McClintics, other Pittsburgh bigwigs eat, drink, relax, play poker, shoot craps, make deals. Some 35 corporations maintain suites for business purposes at the Duquesne."

Founded in 1873, the Duquesne Club is the oldest and most prestigious of Pittsburgh's private clubs. That "squarish" brownstone clubhouse was designed by one of the successor firms to H. H. Richardson, the architect of the Allegheny County Courthouse, in the Romanesque style. The original building was symmetrical, with its arched entrance located between two shallow projecting bays.

TURN AND WALK BACK A HALF-BLOCK TO SMITHFIELD STREET. TURN RIGHT.

16. Oliver Building
535 Smithfield Street

Henry W. Oliver was born in Ireland in 1840 but the family was in Pittsburgh before young Henry was talking. Oliver began working at the age of thirteen as a messenger boy for the National Telegraph Company. He served in the Civil Wa before returning in 1863 to manufacture nuts and bolts on a small scale. His brothers joined the enterprise and within 20 years the company was one of the largest manufacturers of bar iron and iron specialties in the United States. Oliver was one of the first iron barons to exploit the great Mesabi ore region in Minnesota and eventually spun off the Oliver Iron Mining Company from his other interests in a venture with the Carnegie Steel Company. Oliver passed away in 1904 and his family directed the construction of this 24-story skyscraper in 1909 as a memorial. Daniel Burnham & Company designed it in the classical base-shaft-capital form typical of early high-rise buildings with a stone base supporting a terracotta skin that rises to a graceful arcade and cornice at the roof.

17. Mellon Bank/Lord & Taylor's
514 Smithfield Street

Trowbridge & Livingston, the architectural firm of choice for the Mellon family, delivered this grand vault for the headquarters of Mellon bank in 1924. This building conforms to the classic image of the banking house: a somber gray stone exterior that greeted depositors inside with a long, subdued hall lined with colossal marble Ionic columns and a grand balcony running its length.

18. Park Building
northwest corner of Smithfield Street at 355 Fifth Avenue

Standing on the former site of the Pittsburgh Iron Foundry, which supplied artillery and projectiles to American forces in the War of 1812, architect George B. Post designed this building for steel magnates David and William Park in 1896. It is considered the oldest surviving steel-framed skyscraper in Pittsburgh. Post followed the Classical form of skyscraper design (stone base, brick shaft, and ornamental cap) with his most spectacular affectation being a row of crouching male figures (called "atlantes" or "telemones") supporting the decorative cornice at the roofline. An unfortunate remodeling during the 1960s altered the windows and their historical ornamental surrounds in the central section of the building.

19. Kaufmann's Department Store
Fifth Avenue and Smithfield Street

Kaufmann's was founded in Pittsburgh in 1871 by Jacob and Isaac Kaufmann. The flagship store on the corner of Fifth Avenue and Smithfield Street was constructed in 1887 and became known as the "Big Store." In 1913, architects Janssen and Abbott designed a larger white terracotta-sheathed section with Renaissance Classical detailing and a large ornamental public clock at the corner. This clock became a popular meeting place, and prompted the coining of the phrase "Meet me under Kaufmann's clock."

In the late 1920s, Edgar Kaufmann commissioned an Art Deco redesign of the main floor of the department store with striking black Carrara glass columns, bronze metalwork, terrazzo floors, and a million dollars' worth of new elevators. The building was the largest department store in Pittsburgh with 12 stories and 750,000 square feet of selling space and covering the entire block. Edgar Kaufmann would later make one of the most famous commissions in the history of American architecture when he hired Frank Lloyd Wright, who created the iconic "Fallingwater" in the southwestern Pennsylvania woods.

TURN RIGHT ON FORBES AVENUE.

20. Honus Wagner Store
320 Forbes Avenue

Honus Wagner, the legendary Pittsburgh Pirate shortstop and one of the five original members of the Baseball Hall of Fame, moved his sporting goods store into this building, the former Royal Restaurant (the name can still be seen on the decorative upper facade) in 1952.

21. Colonial Trust Company
314 Forbes Avenue

In 1902 prominent local architect Frederick J. Osterling designed this building for the Colonial Trust Company. It survives as the downtown's best example of Edwardian Baroque, a style characterized by the rusticated ground-floor level, the pairing of the colossal columns, and the elaborate cartouche that breaks into the crowning pediment.

Many buildings, including this one, have been assumed by Point Park University - 22 as of this counting. Today this is just an elaborate exit - to see the magnificently restored classroom, theater and library walk around the corner to the entrance at 414 Wood Street.

22. Olympic Theatre
313-317 Forbes Avenue

This building started life as the Olympic Theatre. When J.C. McCrory Company took over in 1937 a geometric Art Deco facade in buff brick was applied.

23. Courthouse Tavern
310 Forbes Avenue

This building was constructed in 1888 but the facade and interior goes back only to the 1920s when this was the Wheel Cafe, a favorite stop on the burlesque circuit.

24. 2T Jewelers
428 Wood Street at 5th Avenue

This building was constructed in 1888 but the facade and interior goes back only to the 1920s when this was the Wheel Cafe, a favorite stop on the burlesque circuit.

25. Skinny Building
241 Forbes Avenue at Wood Street

The Skinny Building is a mere five-feet, two-inches wide, built just after Forbes Avenue was widened in 1900. Officials at the Greater Pittsburgh Convention and Visitors Bureau have proposed the slim architectural curiosity as the world's skinniest building but have yet to displace the Sam Kee Building in Vancouver in the *Guinness Book of World Records*. That building has a second-floor balcony that juts out four feet and that stretches almost from one end to the other while the Skinny Building never expands in all its three stories.

Next door on Wood Street, the elegant stone building with fluted Doric columns was built in 1925 for John M. Roberts & Company, a family-owned jewelry store.

26. CVS Pharmacy
239 Forbes Avenue

Most drugstores don't come with a colonnade of massive Corinthian columns. This was once Donahoe's Market and Cafeteria, a Pittsburgh landmark for nearly a half-century starting in 1923. A tip-off to the building's heritage is the "D" above the second-floor windows, the Classical panels of fruits and vegetables, and the elegant urns in the window pediments. The third floor was once a dance hall.

27. G. C. Murphy Company Building
219 Forbes Avenue

This Art Deco building, festooned with geometric shapes and stylized ferns and flowers, was erected in 1930 by H. E. Crosby, corporate architect of the G.C. Murphy Company, at a cost of $250,000. George C. Murphy started in McKeesport in 1906. By the 1930s, there were 170 stores in 11 states. Even during the Depression 40 new stores were built.

WALK INTO MARKET SQUARE AND EXIT TO THE LEFT. TURN LEFT ON FOURTH AVENUE.

28. Burke's Building
209 Fourth Avenue

John Chislett, an English architect, constructed this spare Greek Revival building in 1836 for attorneys Andrew and Robert Burke. As a rare survivor of the Great Fire of 1845, it is the oldest office in the commercial district and just about carries the city's history of Greek Revival architecture by itself. The design is accented by a minimum of classical ornament-- a slightly projecting central bay with two pediments, double laurel wreaths and fluted columns at the entrance.

29. Benedum-Trees Building
221-225 Fourth Avenue

On commission from Haynes Allen Machesney, an attorney, Pittsburgh architect Thomas H. Scott designed this transitional skyscraper in 1905. The classical base-shaft-capital composition with a three-story Corinthian entrance and intricately molded balcony and cornice all harken back to the Victorian era but the choice of light colored granite, white brick and terra-cotta building materials demonstrate a forward-looking design. The building was purchased in 1913 by oil prospectors Michael Benedum and Joseph Trees. The elaborate interior lobby with marble, bronze, and plaster ornament is largely intact.

30. Investment Building
235-239 Fourth Avenue

This 21-story skyscraper was built as the Insurance Exchange at the tail-end of development along Fourth Avenue, in 1927. Washington, D.C. architect John M. Donn used limestone, and a dark, textured brick to give it a modern face. At the top, notice the corners chamfered with obelisk-like elements.

31. Centennial Building
241 Fourth Avenue

In a city that cherishes its architectural heritage as Pittsburgh does, it is unusual that a sophisticated building could escape design credit. But that is the case with the three-story Centennial Building, which, in fact, was completed in 1876.

32. Arrott Building
401 Wood Street at northwest corner of
Fourth Avenue

Frederick J. Osterling turned his pen loose to create this highly ornamented skyscraper in 1902. He gave the 260-foot high tower alternating bands of reddish-brown brick and white terra-cotta marching up to a palatial capital and massive cornice. On the way he added stone balconies with elegant colonnades. The lion's heads

on the exterior are a popular motif on many downtown buildings. The deep entry arch and the arcades in the upper floors are impressive, as is the small but ornate lobby.

33. Pittsburgh National Bank
northeast corner of Fourth Avenue and
Wood Street

The architects Alden and Harlow provided this early downtown skyscraper (1902) with an exuberantly rusticated base of pink granite and a highly contrasting deep red brick and terra-cotta shaft. Unfortunately, much of the terra-cotta was removed in the 1960s. The corner entrance arches are enlivened by sculptures by John Massey Rhind.

34. Union National Bank
southeast corner of Fourth Avenue and
Wood Street

Architects MacClure & Spahr calmed things down a bit on the corner of Wood Street and Fourth Avenue with their simple design of gray granite for the Union National Bank in 1906. In addition to the lack of ornamentation, the building materials are appreciably lighter than those used at the time, as well. The rounded corner with its Doric columns suggests a seriousness and power inside. The interior lobby uses green Cipollino marble columns, one of the first uses of Cipollino marble since antiquity, since the quarries were only reopened around 1905. The beginning of the former bank's second century will be as condominiums.

35. Commercial National Bank
315 Fourth Avenue

Dating to 1897 this building has long ago lost its dignity as a former bank but it retains the slender Roman bricks and unglazed terra-cotta detailing. The bull's-eye wreathes are notable survivors.

36. Colonial Trust Company
317 Fourth Avenue

This sprawling institution once had fronts on Fourth and Forbes avenues and a third entrance on Wood Street. The Classical features incorporated into this 1902 building by Frederick J. Osterling are the Corinthian columns, distinguished by capitals decorated with acanthus leaves; the cartouche, or ornamental tablet, above the entrance arch; and the triangular pediment.

37. Commonwealth Trust Company
316 Fourth Avenue

The two-story base of this high-rise is done in a Classical manner with Ionic columns supporting an entablature bearing the company name. The shaft above is a repetitive design in which pairs of windows are separated vertically by flat pilasters and horizontally by small decorative panels.

38. Keystone Bank
322 Fourth Avenue

Although this building has been altered in recent years, largely through the filling in of windows, several of the original sculptural elements remain. Keystones bearing lion's heads cap the ground floor arches, and an eagle with wings spread perches on a keystone, Pennsylvania's state symbol and the buildings namesake. J. J. Vandergrift, the famous Pittsburgh riverboat captain and oil magnate, was president of Keystone Bank and a founder of the Pittsburgh Stock Exchange.

39. *Times* Building
336 Fourth Avenue

This mid-rise office building constructed for the *Pittsburgh Times* newspaper was one of Frederick Osterling's early commissions in 1892. He followed the fashionable Richardsonian Romanesque style with rusticated masonry and a series of arches resting on short columns. The Fourth Avenue front is faced in granite; the Third Avenue front is faced in sandstone.

40. Industrial Bank
333 Fourth Avenue

Architect Charles M. Bartberger usually busied himself with private homes in the East End but in 1903 he delivered a powerful vault with an over-scaled Neoclassical arch in smooth, coursed granite for the Industrial Bank. The Pittsburgh Stock Exchange was housed here from 1962 to 1974.

41. Union Trust Company
337 Fourth Avenue

The early maestro of the skyscraper, Daniel Burnham of Chicago, made his first mark in Pittsburgh with this building in 1898. Between 1898 and 1910, the firm designed sixteen buildings in the city, including the Frick Building (1901-02), the Oliver Building (1908-10), and the Highland Building (1910) in East Liberty. Here he delivered a Grecian Doric temple for Union Trust; today the building is the headquarters of the Engineers' Society of Western Pennsylvania.

42. Fidelity Trust Company
341 Fourth Avenue

This mid-rise office building, designed by James T. Steen, has a rusticated granite facade in the Romanesque style, popularized in Pittsburgh by the contemporary Allegheny County Courthouse on Grant Street. In addition to designing the side wings for the Dollar Savings Bank, Steen was also the architect for several office and warehouse buildings in the Penn Liberty district downtown.

43. Dollar Bank
340 Fourth Avenue

This Connecticut brownstone hall housed the first mutual bank in Pittsburgh. The wildly ornamental Baroque facade for the 1870 structure came from Philadelphia architect Isaac Hobbs, who honed his trade on many picturesque houses in the region. The interior sports Pittsburgh's best-preserved banking space. For generations the life-sized lions have represented the gateway to Pittsburgh's "Wall Street" along Fourth Avenue. The two lions, each carved by Max Kohler in 1871 from a single block of Connecticut brownstone, were lifted by a crane, loaded onto a flatbed truck, and transported to Oberlin, Ohio for restoration in 2009. When they return the recumbent beasts will be displayed inside where they will no longer be damaged by weather.

44. Pittsburgh Bank for Savings
northwest corner of Smithfield Street and Fourth Avenue

Many of the early skyscrapers in American cities were inspired by Italian Renaissance palazzos with dark stonework and exuberant Classical detailing. That's what is seen here, in a work of 1903 by Alden & Harlow, the city's leading local architectural firm between 1896 and 1908. The granite and pompeiian brick facade is heavily rusticated and articulated by horizontal banding. The base of the building has been remodeled, however, the Fourth Avenue entrance remains intact.

45. Grant Building
330 Grant Street at Fourth Avenue

Henry Hornbostel designed this 40-story tower in 1930. The beacon on top of the building was the largest such beacon in the world when constructed. It spells out 'Pittsburgh' in morse code.

TURN LEFT ON GRANT STREET.

46. City-County Building
414 Grant Street

Henry Hornbostel, who had come from New York City to Pittsburgh in 1904 to design the Carnegie Technical Schools (now Carnegie Mellon University), won the design competition for the City-County Building in 1913. Rather than compete with the towers and pointed roofs of the Allegheny Courthouse next door, Hornbostel limited ornament at the City-County Building to the high triple-arched portico, the Doric colonnade above it, and the barrel-vaulted interior galleria. That ground floor interior is one of Pittsburgh's finest interior spaces - a 43-foot high by 150-foot long light-filled corridor flanked by bronze columns and framed, at either end, by great arched windows spanned by catwalks.

47. Allegheny County Courthouse & Jail
436 Grant Street from Fifth Avenue to Sixth Avenue

Henry Hobson Richardson, of Brookline, Massachusetts, was the most famous architect of the 19th century. After the city's Greek Revival courthouse burned in 1882, Richardson won a design competition to create a replacement. Richardson would die, prematurely, in 1886 at the age of 47, two years before the Courthouse was finished. On his deathbed he is reported to have said: "If they honor me for the pigmy things I have already done, what will they say when they see Pittsburgh finished."

It is indeed among America's most imitated buildings; many architectural historians regard it as the finest public building in the United States. It was no less important to the City of Pittsburgh. When Richardson came to town there were no monumental buildings in downtown Pittsburgh. In fact, there was no real downtown Pittsburgh, only street after street of sprawling industry. Richardson's courthouse was designed to tower over the city, providing an anchor for a defined streetscape. With a model of great architecture on a grand scale suddenly placed in their midst, Pittsburgh's titans of industry were eager to emulate its designs for their new commercial palaces that soon lined Grant Street.

Richardson, who had studied in Paris, was inspired by the 11th- and 12th-century castles of France and Spain. His intimidating design for Allegheny Courthouse included great, round-arched door and window openings. Some things have been compromised in its 125 years (the towering Frick Building across the street eliminated its position as centurion of the city) but most of its impact remains as awe-inspiring as the master architect intended it. A self-guided walking tour brochure for the courthouse and jail is available inside.

48. Frick Building
437 Grant Street

Funny how things work out. Magnate Henry Clay Frick was responsible for a number of Pittsburgh's most notable buildings - this one he built for himself in 1902. This specific site is thought to have been selected to dwarf the Carnegie Building, owned by Frick's long-standing business nemesis Andrew Carnegie, that stood next door to the west. The Carnegie Building is now half-a-century gone and the building that the Frick tower looms over, effectively blocking satisfying views, is Henry Hobson Richardson's masterpiece, the Allegheny County Courthouse. The Frick Building has an architectural pedigree itself; master builder Daniel Burnham contributed a classic base-shaft-capital design with a ring of columns around the base.

49. Union Trust Building
501 Grant Street

Truly, look up, Pittsburgh, for a gander at the City's most fantastical skyline. The Flemish Gothic roofline is the stuff of legend. Some say the abundance of pointed gables were demanded by the Catholic Church of Henry Clay Frick as pseudo-chapels for building on the site of the old St. Paul Cathedral. Chapels for commerce maybe. Called the Union Arcade when it opened in 1917, inside there was space for 240 shops and 700 offices. The office floors were built with a strength remarkable today, since tenants were apt to bring in massive iron safes and locate them as they pleased. Four street entrances, now as originally, meet at a dramatic interior space beneath a stained-glass dome.

50. William Penn Hotel
southwest corner of Grant Street and
Sixth Avenue

This is Pittsburgh's classic downtown 1920s hotel, distinguished by the Art Deco Urban Room on the 17th floor. Deep light courts (easily noticed from Mellon Square) allow the maximum number of guest rooms to have natural ventilation and outdoor views. The towers are clad in red brick, not a common sight in downtown Pittsburgh, a Colonial affectation that namesake William Penn would surely appreciate. During a $22 million renovation in 2004, many of the building's original elements were restored.

YOU HAVE NOW RETURNED TO THE TOUR STARTING POINT.

Look Up,

Pottstown

A Walking Tour of Pottstown...

John Potts built a Colonial-era iron empire at the confluence of the Schuylkill River and Manatawney Creek in the 1750s. In 1761 he advertised building lots for sale in a new town he was calling Pottsgrove along the Great Road that led from Philadelphia out to Reading. The village grew slowly, inhabited mainly by Pottses - John had 13 children. There were still only a few hundred inhabitants a half-century later when Pottsgrove officially became Pottstown when it was incorporated as the second borough in Montgomery County, just three years after the first, Norristown, was established.

By 1840 there were still less than a thousand people living in the rural village when the Philadelphia and Reading Railroad made a fateful decision to run its tracks on Pottstown's side of the Schuylkill River and locate much of its car building and repair facilities in the town. The population would grow 16-fold before the end of the 19th century.

Pottstown's heavy industry became known nationwide. The first iron truss bridge in the United States was built in 1845 in the Philadelphia & Reading Railroad blacksmith shop. A girder from that bridge is on display in the Smithsonian Institute in Washington, D.C. Iron and steel from Pottstown's furnaces and rolling mills were used in the George Washington Bridge, on the locks of the Panama Canal and in America's first skyscrapers. John Ellis had built a factory to produce his Ellis Champion Grain Thresher, which was being shipped to practically every grain growing country in the world.

Most of the building stock on Pottstown's present-day streets emanates from the boom days of the late 1800s through early 1900s. There are many fine examples of residential and commercial buildings from that time when Pottstown was an important iron center.

Our walking tour will explore the Old Pottstown Historic District that roughly adheres to the town laid out by John Potts in 1761 and we'll begin at the elegant Georgian home of the old ironmaster himself...

1. **Pottsgrove Manor**
   100 West King Street

John Potts and his wife Ruth (Savage) had 13 children, several of whom made the family even more prominent. Potts, a successful ironmaster and merchant was appointed Justice of the Peace and Judge on the Philadelphia County Court of Common Pleas. He was elected to the Pennsylvania General Assembly from both Berks and Philadelphia counties.

He began construction of his manor house, one of the finest homes to be built in the region, in 1752. Considered one of the finest extant examples of Georgian architecture in Pennsylvania, Pottsgrove Manor features ashlar walls, pedimented gables and classic five-part symmetry under a cedar roof. Only about four acres of the expansive Potts plantation remain today but fortunately it includes this building, the oldest structure in the borough.

LEAVE POTTSGROVE MANOR ON KING STREET AND TURN RIGHT, HEADING FOR TOWN ACROSS MANATAWNEY CREEK.

2. **36 King Street**

Various prominent Pottstown families owned this Federal-style home from the mid-19th century as a rental property. It underwent a facade restoration under the auspices of the former Old Pottstown Preservation Society. The simple decorative details and flat window trim are hallmarks of the Federal style.

3. **Weitzenkorn House**
   53 King Street

Abraham Weitzenkorn was born in Leitmar, Germany. He came to America at the age of 17, settled in Pottstown, and began his trade as a peddler. He opened his first store in 1864 at 108 South Hanover Street before moving to High Street where it has remained for over 125 years. Weitzenkorn built this Second Empire house within sight of the family business in the 1870s. It features one of Pottstown's outstanding mansard roofs with dormer windows and heavily bracketed cornices.

TURN LEFT ON HANOVER STREET.

4. **Trinity Reformed Church**
   58 Hanover Street

Trinity Reformed Church was built in the Gothic Revival style in 1865 of red sandstone. In 1926, lightning struck Trinity's spire, causing a fire which gutted the structure. It was altered during reconstruction the following year and the steeple was not replaced.

5. **Transfiguration Lutheran Church**
   79 Hanover Street at southwestern corner of Chestnut Street

The English Evangelical Church of the Transfiguration was built catercorner from Zion's in 1861 in the Romanesque Revival style. Windstorms destroyed its original steeples in 1878 and 1934, and the latter was replaced with a shorter clock tower. The abundant use of masonry and arched windows lend the building an air of solemnity.

6. **Old Brick Church**
   100 Hanover Street at northeastern corner of Chestnut Street

John Potts donated this land to German and Quaker settlers for a church in 1753. A log chapel was ready for worship in 1760. In 1796 this brick church was constructed by two congregations, the Lutherans and the Reformed, running over budget and reaching a cost of $6,000. It is said that at the dedication nearly every member gave a silver dollar when the offering was made. The "Old Brick Church" was laid in Flemish bond brickwork with alternating headers and stretchers, an extravagance rarely found in Pottstown. Now the Zion's United Church of Christ, it is the oldest church in town and the only Georgian building in the Old Pottstown Historic District.

7. **Emmanuel Lutheran Church**
   150 Hanover Street at southeastern corner of Walnut Street

This fine Romanesque Revival church was erected in 1868; a windstorm ten years later toppled its spire and it was never replaced. A memorial plaque with the names of early Pottstown residents is located between Emanuel Lutheran and the neighboring Old Brick Church.

TURN RIGHT ON WALNUT STREET.

8. 239 Walnut Street

Popularized by the Sears & Roebuck catalogs of the 1920s, this American Four-Square house provided the homeowner with the most usable space for the least amount of money.

9. 243 Walnut Street

Another housing style popularized by the Sears catalog was the bungalow; this one and one-half story example is similar to one advertised in the 1920s. Unlike its neighbor this design was considered expensive in relation to the amount of living space provided to its occupants.

10. 245 Walnut Street

This house from around 1850 is one of the rare frame Federal period structures in the Pottstown Historic District. The flat-topped windows and 6/6 configuration of the window panes are typical of the style. The porch and rear addition came along later.

RETRACE YOUR STEPS TO PENN STEET AND TURN LEFT. TURN LEFT ON CHESTNUT STREET.

11. Philadelphia Steam Engine Fire Company #1
southeast corner of Penn Street and Chestnut Street

Pottstown's first fire company takes its name from its first piece of equipment - a hand drawn pumper apparatus, from the Philadelphia Fire Company #18. The company was organized on January 3, 1871 after a series of bad fires the previous year. The "Phillies" first firehouse was located on the south side of the 100 block of King Street; this Italianate-styled building with bracketed cornices and a hose drying tower was dedicated on June 12, 1880. There have been only two renova-

tions to the firehouse over the years, one in the 1930s to change the doors for bigger equipment and in the 1940s to move the social quarters from the basement to the second level replacing the parlor that had been used for meetings.

12. 249 Chestnut Street

This is Pottstown's finest Second Empire home. The building is entirely original with trademarks of the Civil War-era style such as arched windows and doors, a heavily bracketed cornice, and a concave mansard roof with dormer windows.

13. 258 Chestnut Street

Built in the late 1860s, this late Federal-style home makes use of Italianate windows. The red brick facade features a polished marble stoop and handcrafted wooden double front doors.

TURN RIGHT ON CHARLOTTE STREET. TURN RIGHT ON KING STREET.

14. Pennsylvania National Guard Armory
261 King Street

The red-brick armory, stripped of most of its original stone ornamentation, was built in 1909 for Company A of the 6th Regiment of the National Guard.

15. Old Borough Hall
245 King Street

This one-time home to Pottstown's government services was built in the Neoclassical style in 1924. The Opera House, which stood next door at one time, was the cultural heart of the town for many years.

TURN LEFT ON HANOVER STREET.

16. Pottstown *Mercury*
24 North Hanover Street at southeast corner of King Street

In 1887, P. Elwood Baum purchased the newspaper, then the *Chronicle*, that would eventually become the present day *Mercury*. He renamed it the Pottstown *Daily News*. After Baum's death in 1892, Thomas Taylor took over the paper and in 1896, built *The News* Building at 17 North Hanover directly across the street, where the paper would remain until 1926. To expand its facilities, the paper purchased this property and built a headquarters of concrete and buffed brick, with outside trimmings of Indiana limestone. The first paper was printed here on March 22, 1926. Finally, in 1933; The Pottstown *Mercury* purchased the publication and property of the *News*.

17. St. Clair Mansion Site
   200 High Street at southeast corner of Hanover Street

The St. Clair Mansion was built by John Potts, Jr., the third son of the founder of Pottstown. A judge of the Common Pleas Court, he elected to remain loyal to England during the American Revolution and had to flee the country when his properties were confiscated. In 1782, General Arthur St. Clair purchased the property for £6,700 in Continental currency. In 1785, he was elected to the Continental Congress and in 1787 became President of the Congress, the head of the country under the Articles of Confederation that governed America at the time.

The property changed hands a number of times over the next hundred years serving as a tavern, a dry goods store, Fegely's Hardware Store, and the Victor Movie Theater and Grant Koon's cigar factory and store. In June 1924, George Bros. Confectioners purchased the corner portion and William and Charles Mills the "L-shaped" 204 High Street. By 1926 two new, similarly constructed buildings stood in their place. The opening of the St. Clair Spa was marked "by the playing of music by O'Dell's Orchestra and every adult visitor received a box of candy." A bronze tablet marking St. Clair's house was removed from the mansion and installed on the new building.

18. Security Trust Building
   152 High Street at southwest corner of Hanover Street

Across Hanover Street once stood another stone house belonging to the Potts family, constructed in 1770. In 1842, Jonas Smith purchased it from one of its subsequent owners and opened a store. In 1886, the Security and Iron Banks acquired the property and began construction of its bank on the town's most prominent intersection. A total of 700,000 bricks were used at a cost of $8.00 per thousand. The ornate brickwork features many interesting patterns. Samuel Buchanan, a relative of President James Buchanan, laid 13,000 yards of plaster. The stone came from Monocacy and all other materials were supplied locally.

Each bank occupied a side of the first floor until 1915 when the Iron Bank moved out. The Security Co. reorganized as The Security Trust and expanded to the entire first floor. Since then a parade of tenants has followed into one of Pottstown's most significant landmarks.

TURN RIGHT ON HIGH STREET.

19. Weitzenkorn's Clothiers
   145 High Street

Founded in 1864, Weitzenkorn's Clothiers is thought to be the second oldest family-owned men's clothing store in the United States. Around town several advertising murals have been restored to their original form and color; here is a painted sign for Hart Schaffner & Marx. A few doors down is a Coca-Cola advertisement at 113 High Street.

20. Reading Terminal
   High Street and York Street

When people learned of the railroad coming to Pottstown in the 1830s, the two rival hotel keepers, John Boyer and Joshua B. Missimer, vied for their business by building hotels on either side of the railroad tracks. Both lost out. In 1839, the railroad built a small depot just west of Missimer's Hotel. After a short time the depot became too small, so the railroad bought Missimer's Hotel for $10,000 and turned the small depot into a baggage and express office. This hotel, the first building on the site, served as Pottstown's passenger station for almost a century with but a few alterations.

In 1925, the Reading Railroad started buying properties on the south side of the tracks and in 1928, began demolishing the hotel to make way for the present edifice. The building was dedicated on November 6, 1929. The building is of Seasholtzville granite of a pink hue, laid in a broken range ashlar with level beds and vertical joints. The base is of New England granite, while the trim and cornice are of ornamental terra-cotta. The former passenger station and freight office were connected by a corridor. The total cost of the structure, listed on the *National Register of Historic Places*, was $250,000.

21. 71 High Street

This Gothic Revival building is a good example of the application of the tri-column pillared porch. Other notable features include bay windows and ornate wood trim. Built in 1890, this home reflects high design and quality materials found in the Victorian age.

22. Elks Home
61 High Street

Jacob Fegely constructed this striking Queen Anne mansion in 1888. Fegely began his business career in coal and later owned a hardware store across the street. He was also president of the Iron Bank and owner of the Merchant's Hotel. After his son, Calvin, died in 1913, the Elks, who had organized a decade earlier in 1902, moved in. Notable exterior features include ornamental woodwork in the flanking tower and gable, intricate balconies and a large stained glass window above the door.

23. Pottstown Brewing Company
High Street and Manatawney Street

In 1886, Joseph M. Selinger moved his brewery from a stone building about a mile from Pottstown to a three story brick building on this site. The brewery changed hands frequently in its early years and was sheriffed in 1897 due to financial problems brought on by competition with rival breweries. The new owners razed the brewery and constructed another building for The Pottstown Brewing Company was born. At its high point, the Pottstown Brewing Co. produced 40,000 barrels a year. Prohibition sounded the death knell for the brewery; and in the latter part of 1920, the machinery and equipment were sold to

investors from Cuba for a brewery there.

In 1921, the buildings and property were purchased by the Pottstown Wholesale Grocery Co. that operated from that location until 1935. The Kleen Mattress Co. occupied the buildings from 1946-50 and the Kiwi Shoe Polish Company from 1953-79. During that period, the eastern buildings were torn down for parking and in the 1980's all existing brewery buildings were erased from memory.

CONTINUE WALKING WEST ON HIGH STREET ACROSS MANATAWNEY CREEK TO THE TOUR STARTING POINT AT POTTSGROVE MANOR.

Look Up,

Pottsville

A Walking Tour of Pottsville...

Pottsville's history is tied to anthracite coal like a twisted pretzel braid. Its beginnings with the black diamond date to 1790 and the whimsical legend of a hunter named Necho Allen. Seems he fell asleep one night at the base of the Broad Mountain and woke to the sight of a large fire. His campfire had ignited an outcropping of coal. By 1795, an anthracite fired iron furnace was established on the Schuylkill River. In 1806, John Pott purchased the furnace and then founded the city of Pottsville.

Construction of the Schuylkill Canal was completed to Port Carbon by 1828 to transport the coal to larger markets. The nine counties in northeast Pennsylvania contain 97% of the country's anthracite coal reserves (the type of coal with the highest heating value, containing 86-97% carbon) and by 1854 half of all coal produced in America was Pennsylvania anthracite.

The growth of mine-related industries produced a population surge as immigrants came to work in the mines. The population doubled between 1820 and 1840. This led to the development of businesses, churches, and schools. Other industries grew up to support the mines. One was the Phillips Van Heusen company which was founded in 1881 when Moses Phillips and his wife Endel began sewing shirts by hand and selling them from pushcarts to the local coal miners.

During the 1870s, Pottsville began its greatest period of prosperity, an era that would last until the Great Depression. In the 1920s Pottsville even fielded one of the most powerful professional football teams in the country. After winning the championship of the Anthracite League comprised of Pennsylvania mining town teams in 1924, the Pottstown Maroons (supposedly named for the color of their jerseys) joined the National Football League in 1925. They won their first game against Buffalo 28-0 and finished the season 9-1-1. Then the Maroons dispatched the Chicago Cardinals in the NFL championship game, 21-7. The title was later taken away, however, when the team played a college all-star team and so the Pottsville Maroons were stripped from the NFL record books. The franchise left for Boston in 1929.

The region survived the Depression because of the demand for coal and Works Project Administration jobs constructing City Hall and the old Post Office. After World War II, however, recession in the mines struck the region hard. Hundreds moved as mines shut down and construction of a bypass routed traffic away from the downtown. Our walking tour will get off that bypass and begin at City Hall, the last major building constructed in downtown Pottsville...

1. **Pottsville City Hall**
   401 North Center Street

David Yuengling opened his Eagle brewery here in 1829 but it was completely destroyed by fire after only two years of operation. He moved up to Mahantongo Street, where operations continue today. The City Hall was a Depression-era Works Progress Administration project and the sleek Art Deco building opened in 1937. The government moved here from a cozy two-story building at 14 North Third Street.

WALK WEST ON LAUREL STREET.

2. **Schuylkill County Courthouse**
   401 North Second Street between Laurel and Sanderson Street

This is the county's third courthouse, the second on this site. The first courthouse was a two-story brick structure built at a total cost of $5,000. It was a simple building with the courtroom on the first floor, and jury rooms and public offices on the second. The first court was held there in 1816. In 1846 the ground at Second and Sanderson Streets was selected for the erection of the new courthouse. On this site stood the homestead of George Farquhar, a prominent member of the county bar. In this house his son, Guy E., who also was destined to become a prominent county attorney, was born. In 1914 Guy, while arguing a case, was suddenly stricken ill and died on the very spot of his birth.

The current courthouse is adjacent to the one it replaced, which was vacated and eventually torn down. A massive cornerstone about two cubic feet in size took more than an hour to maneuver into place when it was laid in 1889. It contains a large hollow space filled with artifacts from 1889, such as a copy of the construction contract; copy of the bond issue; copy of the rules of court; trial list for the September 1889 term; photograph of the first courthouse built in Pottsville; bottle of Catawba wine made by Court Crier Seitzinger in 1886; several old coins; and a list of County officials and their employees. The five-story Romanesque structure constructed from Ohio sandstone cost $320,000, almost $180,000 over the initial estimate.

TURN RIGHT ON NORTH SECOND STREET.

3. **Schuylkill County Prison**
   230 Sanderson Street

Napoleon LeBrun, prominent Pennsylvania architect best known for his ecclesiastical work, designed the county jail in 1851. He had previously done the Trinity Episcopal Church down the street which probably helped him win this commission. On June 21, 1877, six members of the "Molly Maguires," an alleged secret society of Irish mine-workers, were hanged here. Pinkerton detective James McParlan's testimony led to convictions for violent crimes against the coal industry, yet the facts of the labor, class and ethnic conflicts, even the existence of the organization, remain contested. Seven others were hanged on this day at the county jail at Mauch Chunk; ten more were executed in the state through 1879.

WALK BACK DOWN SECOND STREET PAST THE COURTHOUSE AND TOWARDS THE CENTER OF TOWN.

4. **Lee Building**
   southwest corner of Market Street and Second Street

Decorative quoins and cornice give the Lee Building a jeweled appearance.

TURN RIGHT ON MARKET STREET.

5. **Nicholas Building**
   209 West Market Street

This townhouse was uilt in 1858 by the noted physician John T. Nicholas as his office and residence. From 1844 Nicholas served this area, wrote scholarly papers for the Medical Society, was a member of the Miner's Lodge #20, and was one of the first in the city to light his office with gas.

6. Pottsville Free Library
215 West Market Street

The Pottsville Free Public Library opened its door for the first time November 9, 1911, in a three story building at 208 West Market Street. On the upper floors were eight small "dormitories" the fledgling library planned to sublet for $1.50 to $3.50 a week, depending on room size, and a meeting hall to be used free by townspeople. The Library was located in a first-floor area. Pottsville's present red brick library, with a facade modeled after Independence Hall in Philadelphia, opened in 1922. It was financed primarily through gifts from Arthur, Henry W. and Louise Sheafer, members of a wealthy Pottsville family whose fortune had been made in coal and iron, and the Andrew Carnegie Foundation.

7. First United Methodist Church
330 West Market Street

This beautiful stone church is Pottsville's best example of the brawny Richardsonian Romanesque style that was popular with church and civic buildings of the 1890s. The congregation had formed a half-century earlier as the First Methodist Episcopal Church.

8. Garfield Diner
402 West Market Street

The Garfield Diner was manufactured by Kullman, a leader in diner construction. The Original Kullman Diner was built in 1927 by company founder Sam Kullman. It opened here originally as the Pottsville Diner in 1953. During the 1960 presidential campaign, Senator John F. Kennedy stopped here and spoke to the crowd in front of the Art Deco diner, prior to his victory over Richard M. Nixon.

9. Garfield Square
Fifth Street and West Market Street

Garfield Square is named in honor of assassinated President James Garfield. Prominent sculptures grace this small grassy island in the street around which trolley lines once ran, including monuments to Schuylkill County veterans of the Civil War and Spanish American War. The Civil War monument, erected in 1951, was dedicated to "Nicholas Biddle of Pottsville - first man to shed blood in the Civil War - April 18, 1861." Don't shed too many tears for Biddle; he wasn't killed in the incident. At the start of the Civil War, two companies of Pottsville soldiers were among the "First Defenders," the first troops to arrive in Washington D.C. Along the way, Biddle, an African-American from Pottsville marching with the troops, was struck in the head by a brick thrown by rioting "southern sympathizers." So Biddle got the notoriety as the first to shed blood in the Civil War. Hundreds from the Pottsville area served, including men of the 48th Pennsylvania Infantry and Colonel Henry Pleasants. Pleasants led the construction of an underground mine which resulted in the disastrous "Battle of the Crater" at Petersburg, Virginia in July, 1864.

TURN LEFT ON SOUTH NINTH STREET.

10. St. John the Baptist Church
913 Mahantongo Street

In 1840 Reverend Hirslaus Steinbacher rode from Reading to Pottsville on horseback once a month to minister to German Catholics. The members of the small congregation built a church on the corner of Fourth Street and Howard Avenue the following year. It was followed in 1870 by this imposing hilltop structure at the corner of Mahantongo and Tenth streets. Noteworthy in the church are the rare Wilhelm Derrick stained glass windows, valued at over $1.5 million dollars. Also of interest are the huge hand carved wooden statues made in Germany.

TURN LEFT ON MAHANTONGO STREET.

11. Burd Patterson House
803 Mahantongo Street

In the 1830s Philadelphia capitalists staged a contest offering $5,000 to the first person who could smelt iron ore using the anthracite (hard) coal that was found in abundance in nearby northeast Pennsylvania. This was when a dollar a day was a good working wage.

Burd Patterson won. He had hired builder William Lyman and ironmaster Benjamin Perry to apply the "hot blast" method for his Pottsville Furnace, also called Pioneer Furnace. It could reach a temperature of 600 degrees for burning anthracite in ovens at its base. The furnace used a steam engine to power the blast, which reduced the raw materials to molten iron. Burd Patterson's success was an important step towards ending the country's dependence on imported iron: he had proven it possible to produce iron in America with fuel from America, and, importantly, with American businessmen's interests backing the endeavor.

It was not Patterson's first pioneering effort. A few years earlier he developed the slope method for mining below the water table. Patterson's slope method drove a gangway down along the coal vein's pitch, to several hundred feet below the surface. Slope mining became the preferred method in the 1850s, and by the 1860s it became shaft mining, driving a vertical shaft even deeper. He also pioneered residential life in Pottsville - his late Federal-style home, built between 1830 and 1835, was first of the mansions to line Mahantongo Street.

12. First Baptist Church
701 Mahantongo Street

This Italian villa-styled building serves a congregation that is more than 160 years old.

13. John O'Hara House
606 Mahantongo Street

Pottsville native John O'Hara stands squarely in the first rank of American writers. He was born January 31, 1905 five blocks down Mahantongo Street at the corner of Second Street and moved here in 1916. The move uphill on Mahantongo Street was symbolic of an upward shift in status that would appear often in O'Hara's work. He used his hometown as a template for five novels and over 50 short stories and novellas, with the fictional Gibbsville standing in for Pottsville. Mahantongo Street was called Lantenango Street and the *Pottsville Journal*, where O'Hara worked as a reporter from 1924 through 1926 became the *Gibbsville Standard*. This stately three-story townhouse was built prior to 1870 for brewmaster David Yuengling and patterned after those on New York City streets. Dr. O'Hara died in 1925 and his widow moved out in 1940.

14. Braun School of Music
607 Mahantongo Street

Robert Braun, who was born in the 1880s, was the son of a Pottsville physician. After obtaining his initial training, he served on the faculty of the Sternberg School of Music in Philadelphia, and was organist and choirmaster of the Trinity Episcopal Church of Pottsville. In 1908 he left to study in Europe, earning degrees from the Royal Conservatory of Music in Leipzig, Germany. Upon his return from Europe, Braun established a School of Pianoforte Playing at his father's home. Later he moved to ten rooms on the second and third floors of the Whitney Estate on Centre Street and renamed his enterprise the Braun School of Music. The school began occupying this building, fronted by a quartet of imposing two-story Ionic columns, in March of 1934, just before its 25th anniversary.

15. D.G. Yuengling & Son Brewery
Fifth and Mahantongo streets

In 1829 David Yuengling, a newly arrived German immigrant, opened the Eagle Brewery in the foothills of the eastern Appalachian Mountains. The new brewhouse, located on Centre Street, was not two years old before fire consumed it. In 1831 Yuengling rebuilt the brewery, like many old-time breweries, on a mountainside where tunnels gouged from the rock provided natural cold temperatures necessary for aging and fermentation. That brewery stands here today, officially recognized in the *National Register of Historic Places* as America's oldest brewery. In 1890 there were 2,156 American brewing companies. Over 100 years later Yuengling, still family-owned, is one of only 20 breweries that produce 20,000 barrels of beer annually in the same location.

16. Church of Saint Patrick
319 Mahantongo Street

The Church of St. Patrick is the third oldest church of the Roman Catholic Diocese of Allentown, founded in 1827.

17. United Presbyterian Church
214 Mahantongo Street

The Presbyterian Church was built in 1874. The most interesting aspects of this structure are the two Lewis Comfort Tiffany stained glass windows which face Third Street and the large round stained glass window facing Norwegian Street.

18. Reading Anthracite Company Historical Library and Museum
200 Mahantongo Street

This Beaux Arts office building was constructed in 1905 for the Philadelphia and Reading Coal and Iron Company that was formed in 1871 to mine anthracite coal. Today it is the headquarters for the Reading Anthracite Company.

19. John O'Hara Boyhood Home
southeast corner of Second Street and Mahantongo Street

This was the office and home of Dr. Patrick H. O'Hara from 1895 until his death on March 18, 1925. Famous author John O'Hara was born in this building in 1905.

20. Pottsville Republican Building
111 Mahantongo Street

Joseph Henry Zerbey had owned the *Weekly Schuylkill Republican* for five years when, about a week before the presidential election of 1884, he decided to go daily until the votes were cast in support of Republican candidate James Blaine. After Blaine lost narrowly to Democratic candidate Grover Cleveland, Zerbey decided to continue to publish The *Daily Republican* from his offices in the Henry Clay Building on the 100 block of Mahantongo Street. Pottsville already had two daily newspapers, the *Miners Journal* and the *Evening Chronicle*, but helped by Zerbey's fiery commentaries the paper thrived and survives today 125 years later as the *Republican-Herald*.

WALK BACK A HALF-BLOCK AND TURN LEFT ON SECOND STREET AND BEGIN WALKING UP THE HILL.

21. Cloud Home
351 South Second Street

Pottsville lawyer John Bannan, a specialist in land titles in the coal fields, built his Greek Revival mansion of fieldstone atop Sharp Mountain in 1850. His wife, Sarah, named it Cloud Home because it was "so close to the sky." The Bannans imported rare varieties of trees and shrubs for their seven-acre estate, many of which still grace the grounds. Added to the *National Register of Historic Places* in 1978, the city landmark became a Friendship House Group Home for Schuylkill County boys in 1989.

22. *Henry Clay Monument*
Clay Park, end of Second Street

When Henry Clay, the "Great Compromiser" of the United States Senate from Kentucky, died on June 29, 1852, the citizens of Pottsville decided to honor Clay for his long advocacy of protective foreign tariffs. One was a tariff placed on iron that increased production of iron products and created demand for the region's anthracite coal which was used to smelt iron. That hardly seems like an issue that would galvanize a citizenry to go build a monument.

In fact, Benjamin Bannan, the publisher and editor of the *Miners' Journal*, a Whig newspaper, was a strong supporter of Clay's policies, and was one of the first to call for a monument to the statesman. The first idea the rapidly formed Clay Committee had was to show their respect by holding a funeral procession for him. John Bannan then offered the committee land on which a monument could be erected. The idea evolved quickly, and a building committee was formed.

The funeral procession took place with 1,600 people in the parade and afterwards and the ceremonies concluded with the laying of the cornerstone. Meanwhile, work on the casting of the statue by Robert Wood was progressing in Philadelphia. But fundraising problems postponed the dedication of the $7,151.00 monument two years. Come on people - he supported a tax on foreign goods! On June 23, 1855, a team of twelve mules dragged the statue up South Second Street followed by a large crowd of onlookers.

WALK BACK DOWN THE HILL AND TURN RIGHT ON UNION STREET. TURN RIGHT ON CENTRE STREET.

23. Jerry's Classic Cars & Collectibles Museum
394 South Centre Street

The original portion of this building was constructed in 1855 as the carriage house and stables for the adjacent Atkins Mansion. Charles Atkins, an early steel baron, was considered America's second richest man for a time. In the early 1900s the building was expanded for the needs of Morgan Studebaker Automobile Sales of Pottsville. Centre Street was the avenue of choice in town for early car dealers. From the 1950s to 1970s the Scranton Electrical Company operated a repair center for industrial motors. In 1994 the building was purchased by Jerry Enders and, after an extensive renovation, now houses Jerry's Classic Cars & Collectibles Museum.

RETRACE YOUR STEPS AND WALK NORTH ON CENTRE STREET.

24. YWCA
325 South Centre Street

The YWCA of Pottsville was established in 1924 and moved to its current location in 1956.

25. Partridge House
315 South Centre Street

This early example of Gothic Revival architecture dates to 1829. The three-story brick house features vergeboards in its gables, Gothic windows, steeply pitched roofs and Gothic front doors. It has recently been renovated to serve as a bed-and-breakfast.

26. Mootz Candies
220 South Centre Street

Mootz Candies has been owned and operated by the same family for more than 80 years. The business evolved from the days when the extras from Catherine Mootz's most recent batch of homemade candies were displayed in the window of Mootz's Imported and Domestic Grocery Store. Over the next ten years, her candy became so popular that candy sales exceeded grocery sales and Mootz Candies was founded. Check out the "Black Diamonds," a black licorice flavored hard candy which looks like coal.

27. Trinity Church
200 South 2nd Street at Centre Street

The Trinity parish grew out of St. Luke's church, the first in Pottsville that had organized in 1827. William Strickland, a Philadelphia architect who was America's foremost practitioner of the Greek Revival style, did the work on St. Luke's. A larger church, based on the English Gothic designs drawn up by Napoleon LeBrun, was begun in 1847. That building, seen today, was extensively renovated by the New York architectural firm of Henry Dudley and Frederick Diaper in 1866.

28. Miners National Bank
120 South Centre Street

Miners National Bank was the first bank established in Schuylkill County, organized in 1828. The bank and its successors has stood on this site since 1830. Originally a wood structure, the current Colonial Revival building dates to the bank's centennial in 1928. It features a Georgia marble entablature and pediment, Harvard bricks and, over the three large arched windows, two marble heads of *Mercury*, god of trade and wealth, and *Pluto*, god of mineral wealth. Under the marbled portico at the entrance are the cast bronze grill doors depicting scenes typical of deep mining operations. Interior architecture includes walls of Jeanne d'Arc sandstone from France, seven colors and 14 types of marble from the United States, Italy, Greece and Africa; fine crafted wood paneling throughout, an immense door weighing 55 tons, and 55 feet above are original glass and bronze skylights. The bank is one of the finest buildings in Schuylkill County.

29. Necho Allen Hotel
southwest corner of Centre and Mahantongo streets

The Necho Allen Hotel opened in the 1920s at a cost of over a million dollars as Pottsville's fanciest hotel. There was a bar in the basement, the Coal Mine Taproom, that had anthracite walls and mining timber supports; waiters took orders with pads illuminated by the lanterns set in their miner's helmets. The Necho Allen closed in 1981 and now provides housing for the elderly.

30. Union Bank and Trust Company
25 South Centre Street at Mahantongo Street

The Union Safe Deposit Bank organized in 1896 from the financial seeds sown back in 1852 by the Pottsville Mutual and Joint Stock Life Insurance Company of Schuylkill County. The bank's capital was $100,000 and its modest offices were located in the former pay office of the Philadelphia and Reading Coal and Iron Company located a block away at the corner of Norwegian Street. Todays its assets are $125,000,000. The bank moved into its new Beaux Arts headquarters here in 1913. The fireproof institution was one of only a few that survived a ravaging fire in Pottsville on December 17, 1914. That blaze destroyed most of the block on the west side of Centre Street between Norwegian and Mahantongo Streets.

31. Schuylkill Trust Company
101 North Centre Street

This eight-story Neoclassical mini-skyscraper was erected for the Schuylkill Trust company in 1925. It conforms to the idea of the high-rise building as a classical column with base (decorated ground floor)- shaft (middle floors) and capital (decorative cornice).

32. William Boyer Building
201 North Centre Street

Boyer, an expert tobacconist, who paradoxically never smoked, came to Pottsville in 1843 as a young cabinet maker by trade and grew into one of the most prominent businessmen in the city before his death in 1898. This site includes two joined buildings, the back being built in the 1840s and the front several years later. From here William Boyer manufactured and wholesaled custom Havana cigars between 1854 and 1898. He also lived here with his family.

33. Sovereign Majestic Theater
209 North Centre Street

Built in 1910, the Majestic Theater is an eclectic style, two-and-a-half story building with a Beaux Arts-classical facade. The movie house thrived through the age of silent films but closed its doors with the coming of "talkies" in 1930. The building remained empty for nine years before being reopened as a Farmers Market in 1939, a function it served for more than 30 years. But in 1998 the Sovereign Majestic Theater Association was created in 1998 to champion the revitalization of the 1910 Majestic Theater into a state-of-the-art, all-purpose facility for theater, music, and motion picture presentations. Today the Sovereign Majestic Theater is a 224-seat venue for the presentation of professional cultural programs for children and adults.

34. Historical Society of Schuylkill County
305 North Centre Street

Incorporated in 1903, the Historical Society of Schuylkill County has been housed since early this century at the site of the first school in Pottsville, the Female Grammar School, built in 1863.

35. Joulwan Park
300 block of North Centre Street, west side

This small park honors George Alfred Joulwan, a Pottsville native who attended the United States Military Academy, served in Vietnam and eventually rose to be Supreme Allied Commander of NATO forces under President Bill Clinton.

36. Park Hotel
315 North Centre Street

The Buckwalter tavern was built in 1828, by Jacob Buckwalter, and it became a part of the Northwestern Hotel when the four-story brick addition which is now the main part of the hotel was built. The Northwestern became the Park Hotel and is now a restaurant.

YOU HAVE NOW RETURNED TO THE TOUR STARTING POINT.

Look Up,

Reading

A Walking Tour of Reading...

In 1733, the site of present day Reading was chosen. It was set at the intersection of two great valleys, the east Penn-Lebanon Valley and the Schuylkill River. This site was known as Finney's Ford until 1743 when Thomas Lawrence, a Penn Land agent, made the first attempt at the layout for Reading. In 1748, the town was laid out by Thomas and Richard Penn, the sons of William Penn. The name was chosen after Penn's own county seat, Reading, in Berkshire, England. In 1752, Reading became the county seat of Berks County.

During the French and Indian war, Reading became a military base for a chain of forts along the Blue Mountains. The local iron industry, by the time of the Revolution had a total production that exceeded that of England, a production that would help supply Washington's troops with weapons including cannons, rifles and ammunition.

The center of Reading was known as market square, with open sheds where farmers would sell their produce and hold a yearly fair. Later the square became the center of government and commerce with the County Courthouse, banks, stores and hotels located on the site. The construction of the Reading Railroad, its lines radiating in all directions from the City, was probably the greatest single factor in the development of Berks County. Established in 1833 to transport coal, its operations grew to include coal mining, iron making, canal and sea-going transportation and shipbuilding. By 1870 it was the largest corporation in the world.

Reading did not officially incorporate as a city until the 1840s, when its population had grown to 12,000 people living in rows of red brick houses. In the fifty years following the Civil War, Reading continued to grow as an industrial city, supporting one of the most diverse manufacturing bases of any city in the country. Bicycles, wagons, hats, cigars, clocks, shoes, brass, bricks, steam engines, rope, beer and pretzels, and many other items were all manufactured in the city or the surrounding area. In 1900 Charles Duryea came to Reading to make one of the earliest automobiles. Duryea Drive on Mt. Penn still carries his name and is the site of an annual car race up to the top of the mountain.

Our walking tour will begin in City Park, or Penn's Common, just east of city center...

1. Penn's Common (City Park)
11th Street at the head of Penn Street

This large parcel of land was set apart as early as 1749 by John and Richard Penn as public commons, although the land was not formally conveyed to the city until November 19, 1800. Despite the Penns' wishes that the common remain, in its totality, a place for "public recreation" the park saw numerous early uses including washing clothes in the stream that ran through the property, mustering of troops, iron-mining and even public hangings at "gallows hill," a prominent point in the Commons, located within the triangle bounded on two sides by Perkiomen Avenue and Hill Road. That hill was leveled by extensive grading in 1878.

Beginning in the 1820s recreation took a back seat to other uses deemed in the the public good. The Reading Water Company constructed a waterworks and reservoir in the Commons and later a prison and a fairground followed. Eventually an act was passed that stated that Penn's Common could never be used for any purpose other than as a public park and parade ground. Today a number of statues and memorials can be seen in Penn's Common:

Frederick Lauer

The first statue erected in Reading was that of Frederick Lauer, the pioneering Reading brewer. Lauer was born on October 14, 1810 in Gleisweiler, Germany. At the age of 12, his family immigrated to the United States, settling in nearby Womelsdorf. Under his father's tutelage he quickly learned the brewing process. By age 16, Fred was foreman and accountant of the brewery, now in Reading. In 1835, he became proprietor of the new plant on North Street, and remained there until his retirement.

In 1885, the United States Brewers' Association hired Henri Stephens to create the Lauer statue as the first monument erected in Reading because he embodied the ideals of a large part of his community. The physical structure is quite tall, and consists of two parts. The top part of the monument is a life-size likeness of Lauer, cast in bronze. He is portrayed wearing a suit which is covered by a long overcoat.

First Defenders Monument

The First Defenders Monument was dedicated in the park on July 4, 1901. Berks County had its First Defenders in two wars. When Boston was besieged by the British and the Continental Congress issued a call for troops in 1775, three companies of Penn's riflemen were summoned because they were such expert shots. One of these came from Berks and was commanded by George Nagle, of Reading. In 1861 Reading sent the Ringgold Artillery of Washington with that famous body of soldiers known as the First Defenders, the men who were the minute men of the Civil War.

William McKinley

The addition of William McKinley to "monument row" occurred shortly after the Ohioan became the third United State President to be assassinated by an anarchist in Buffalo, New York in 1901. Much of the funding came from "penny, nickel, and dime" donations from city schoolchildren.

Christopher Columbus

The monument to Christopher Columbus was donated to the city by the Italian community in 1925. The statue is on a marble pedestal with with four bronze bas relief tablets with scenes from Columbus's life. On October 11, 1992, rededication ceremonies of the newly restored statue marked the 500th anniversary of Columbus's voyage.

Firefighters' Memorial

At the entrance to City Park stands the Volunteer Firefighter Monument. The Reading Fire Department was officially organized on March 17, 1773, with the founding of the Rainbow Volunteer Fire Company. According to legend, the new company's name was being boisterously debated in the tavern where the meeting was being held, when a rainbow appeared in the eastern sky following an early spring thunderstorm, thus giving birth to the name. The Rainbow company was formed on St. Patrick's Day and a shamrock became the company's insignia.

WALK NORTH ALONG 11TH STREET.

2. Berks County Conservancy
   25 N 11th Street

This well-turned out brick Victorian was once the Reading Bureau of Water building and today serves as the headquarters for the Berks County Conservancy.

3. *USS Maine* Anchor
   City Park, just south of the intersection of 11th Street and Washington Street

An explosion that sent the battleship *Maine* to the bottom of Havana harbor in Cuba on the night of February 15, 1898 triggered the Spanish-American War. In 1914, one of the *Maine's* six anchors was taken from the Washington Navy Yard to City Park and dedicated during a ceremony presided over by Franklin D. Roosevelt, then assistant Secretary of the Navy. The ceremony commemorated those who died in the explosion.

TURN LEFT ON WASHINGTON STREET. TURN RIGHT ON 10TH STREET.

4. Bethel A.M.E. Church
   119 N 10th Street

This is Berks County's oldest Black church building. Erected in 1837 by free African Americans it became an Underground Railroad station for escaped slaves seeking freedom. The church was rebuilt in 1867 and remodeled in 1889. The congregation, dating from 1822, moved to Windsor Street in 1974.

RETURN TO WASHINGTON STREET AND TURN RIGHT (WEST).

5. Zion's United Church of Christ
   824 Washington Street

The United Church of Christ in Berks County dates to 1760 when members of the Lutheran and Reformed congregations did the uniting near Windsor Castle.

6. City Hall
   815 Washington Street

The current City Hall replaced an overwhelmed old one at Fifth and Franklin streets. In 1925 the voters by referendum decided upon a $750,000 bond issue for the purpose of securing a site and erecting a new building. For some reason no action was taken until 1928, at which time the old High School for Boys was purchased at a cost of $510,000. The 1904 Beaux Arts building was designed by the Philadelphia firm of Davis & Davis. The imposing granite facade was retained during alterations. The refurbished City Hall was dedicated in 1929.

7. Reading YMCA
   631 Washington Street

The first meetings of the Young Men's Christian Association in Reading were held in early 1858, a little more than six years after the founding of the first YMCA in the United States in Boston. The first "reading rooms" were located on the northeast corner of Sixth and Penn Streets. The first YMCA-owned building was erected at 628-630 Penn Street at a cost of $65,000 and dedicated on June 9, 1895. The present-day Central Branch YMCA was dedicated on May 24, 1914.

8. Trinity Lutheran Church
   531 Washington Street

Trinity Lutheran Church was founded in 1751 by Henry Melchoir Muhlenburg as a congregation of the "Ministerium of Pennsylvania." It is now the "mother church" of the city of Reading. Built in 1791, the Georgian Colonial church now has Greek Revival and Victorian details. The majestic steeple, towering some 203 feet in the air, at one time, was the tallest structure in the state of Pennsylvania. Dr. Bodo Otto, chief surgeon of the Valley Forge encampment during the winter of 1777-78, is buried in the churchyard.

9. The Berkshire Hotel
   501 Washington Street

The classically designed 8-story Berkshire was built in 1914. The venerable hotel was converted into multi-use office space in 1986.

10. Abraham Lincoln Hotel
100 North Fifth Street

The Abraham Lincoln Hotel opened its doors in 1930. Throughout its history, a host of distinguished visitors including John Philip Sousa patronized this grand hotel named for our 16th President. After closing in the late 1900s the building was renovated and revived in 2001.

11. Metropolitan Edison Building
412 Washington Street

This is one of the best Sullivanesque style skyscrapers in Pennsylvania based on the work of Chicago architect Louis Sullivan. The Sullivanesque style developed in response to the emergence of tall, steel-frame skyscrapers in the 1890s. Sullivan's approach was to use ornament and design to delineate a tall building into three distinct parts, an entry level with prominent window and door openings, a mid section with bands of windows with vertical piers, and a top with a highly decorative cornice, often featuring round porthole windows. The effect was to simulate a classical column.

12. Goggleworks
2nd Street and Washington Street

In 1871, during a time when the United States depended solely on Europe for optical lenses, Thomas A. Willson & Co. erected the first factory to manufacture optical glass for lenses and reading glasses at the corner of Washington and 2nd Streets. Founded by Gile J. Willson and son Thomas, their first innovation, among many that would follow, was a protective lens that blocked dangerous and blinding rays produced by metal processing equipment.

The National Safety Council was created in 1913, and T.A. Willson & Co. Inc. helped to set the bar for the establishment of uniform safety standards in industry. By 1981 the company was manufacturing more than 3,000 separate items in protective gear, and at that time became Willson Safety Products. The company did not survive into the 21st century but the GoggleWorks Center for the Arts has become a prime example of adaptive reuse in architecture.

TURN LEFT ON 2ND STREET.

13. Keystone Hook and Ladder Street
2nd Street and Penn Street

The Queen Anne-style firehouse dates to 1886. Its central tower articulated on the main building facade by piers or pilasters, and capped by a pyramidal roof, strongly marked horizontal facade stringcourses, and symmetrical compositions is typical of architectural pattern books of the day.

TURN LEFT ON PENN STREET.

14. Peanut Bar Restaurant
332 Penn Street

The Peanut Bar Restaurant traces its roots back to Wernersville in the 1920's. Founder Jimmie Kramer moved the business around a lot during Prohibition before settling on Penn Street in 1933, where it has become a local institution.

15. *Reading Eagle* Company
345 Penn Street

The first *Daily Reading Eagle* appeared on the street on January 28, 1868. It was the descendent of a handful of Reading newspapers that date to the *Adler*, a German weekly, published by the Ritter family in 1797. J. Lawrence Getz attempted to print the city's first daily newspaper, the *Reading Daily Gazette*, in 1847 but the paper lacked advertising and readers and folded in 1857. The *Reading Daily Times* quickly followed in 1858 but was sold a year later to one of its biggest advertisers, Henry A. Lantz, a bookseller, for $150. In 1861 Lantz went off to fight in the Civil War and sold the paper for a penny.

After the war the two newspaper companies stabilized and prospered for more than a century. In 1982 the staffs merged. On June 28, 2002, the last edition of the afternoon *Reading Eagle* and the last edition of the weekday daily *Reading Times* were published. The *Eagle* nameplate moved to the morning publication. In 2007 the Reading Eagle Company began construction of a 77,000-square-foot addition to its facility at 345 Penn Street.

TURN RIGHT ON 4TH STREET.

16. **Log House, Hiester House, and Market Annex**
    30 South 4th Street

Joseph Hiester was born on a Berks County farm in 1752. After leading Pennsylvania militia in the American Revolution he went into the mercantile business but did not linger long as a merchant. He served in the state legislature and the United States Congress before winning election as governor of Pennsylvania at the age of 68.

RETURN TO PENN STREET AND TURN RIGHT.

17. **Farmers National Bank**
    445 Penn Street

This was the site of the Federal Inn beginning in 1763; President George Washington was entertained here in 1794. Beginning in 1814 the building was used as a banking house. A century later, in 1925, the current Neoclassical structure, for the Farmers National Bank, was opened.

18. **Colonial Trust Company**
    northwest corner of Penn Street and 5th Street

The Colonial Trust was organized on July 2, 1900, with resources of $375,000. A series of mergers during the Great Depression allowed Colonial to not only survive but be designated as one of the two banks in Reading that was financially healthy enough to open for business after the "Bank Holiday" imposed by the Roosevelt administration in March 1933. The Colonial Trust Company building has lorded over Penn Square for more than a century.

TURN LEFT ON 5TH STREET.

19. **Christ Episcopal Church**
    435 Court Street, northwest corner of Fifth Street

The lot of ground on which Christ Church stands was number 71 in the plan of the borough to be "held in trust, for the erection of an Episcopal Church, whenever it should be found convenient, and as a place of burial, for the Epis-

copalians, within the town of Reading, and the vicinity, and of such other persons, not Episcopalians, as the said trustees shall permit to be buried therein, and for no other purpose whatsoever."

RETURN TO PENN STREET AND TURN LEFT (EAST).

20. **Reading Trust Company**
    515 Penn Street

The Reading Trust Company was organized in 1886; this headquarters building was erected in 1930.

TURN LEFT (NORTH) ON 6TH STREET.

21. **Berks County Trust Company Building**
    35-41 North 6th Street

The Berks County Trust Company was organized in 1900 and this Neoclassical building with its march of Corinthian columns dates to 1910.

TURN RIGHT (EAST) ON COURT STREET.

22. **Berks County Courthouse**
    633 Court Street

This massive and ornate 19-story Art Deco granite structure, built in 1932 to last a century, at a cost of $2,000,000 during the Depression, stands 308 feet tall, making it the tallest courthouse in the United States, and also the most expensive building in Berks County. It is also the second-tallest municipal building in the state of Pennsylvania. Only Philadelphia's City Hall is taller.

WALK BEHIND THE PARKING GARAGE AND TURN RIGHT TO REACH PENN STREET.

23. **Reading Railroad Massacre**
    7th and Penn streets

Located midway between Pennsylvania's rich anthracite coal fields and the port of Philadelphia, the small city of Reading was at the heart of America's rapidly developing coal, iron, and railroad industries. The Philadelphia and Reading Railroad, popularly called the Reading, was a corporate giant during the 1870s. The Reading's thirty-six-acre shop complex dominated the downtown area, and 1,500 of the city's estimated 40,000 residents worked for the company.

Under the iron-fisted rule of its president, Franklin Gowen, the Reading gobbled up coal mines, canals, and shipping vessels. Gowen ran roughshod over workers" attempts to unionize. Scorning his labor force, Gowen proclaimed that "a man with ordinary intelligence can become a conductor, a brakeman, or a fireman after an hour's instruction."

In July 1877, after enduring 10 percent pay cuts, railroad workers revolted across the country in the Great Strike of 1877. The strike spread rapidly, becoming the first nationwide labor action and prompting governors in several states to call out their national guard units as well as, eventually, federal troops to maintain order. In Reading, on the nights of July 22 and 23, rioters burned the Reading's Lebanon Valley Railroad wooden bridge over the Schuylkill River—severing its Harrisburg main line. Meanwhile, a mob of strikers and sympathetic citizens gathered in the center of Reading. On the evening of July 23, the National Guard's Fourth Regiment arrived from Allentown. Brigadier General Frank Reeder of Easton ordered his men—about 253 strong—to march into a thirty-foot-deep, 300-yard-long man-made "cut," or depression, where strikers had blocked a train. The surrounding mob, estimated at several thousand people, pelted the guardsmen below with rocks and bricks. In the violence and confusion that followed, panicked troops fired into a taunting crowd at the far end of the cut, killing ten people and wounding dozens more.

Unlike the rioting workers in Pittsburgh, who avenged the shootings of their fellow workers by burning the Pennsylvania Railroad's station and roundhouse, Reading strikers resisted calls to set fire to the shops and depots in the center of their town. On January 1, 1878, the city of Reading hosted the first national assembly of the Knights of Labor, which in the year that followed grew into the nation's largest industrial union, and organized national campaigns for the worker benefits and rights.

TURN LEFT (EAST) ON PENN STREET.

24. Sovereign Center
700 Penn Street

The Sovereign Center is situated on the erstwhile site of the Astor Theatre, which finally closed in the year 1975. The theater lay vacant until it was torn apart in the year 1998 and space was made for the new arena, the Sovereign Center. Built in the year 2001, its seating capacity is 7,083.

CONTINUE ON PENN STREET TO THE TOUR STARTING POINT IN PENN'S COMMON.

Look Up,

Ridgway

A Walking Tour of Ridgway...

The Ridgway name in question belonged to Jacob Ridgway, a Philadelphia shipping merchant. Ridgway never visited the town - in fact, he didn't spend much time in Philadelphia. He spent large chunks of the early 19th century abroad in London, sending back heaping quantities of money to be invested in real estate. The records are a bit murky, but it is generally accepted that Ridgway owned in excess of 100,000 acres of Western Pennsylvania woods. Into that wilderness in 1821 rode James L. Gillis, nephew of Jacob Ridgway by marriage and appointed the land agent for Ridgway's holdings. Gillis, his wife and their three children arrived by packhorse and ox-team.

Ridgway was plotted as an unincorporated village in 1833 in Jefferson County and a decade later when Elk County formed it became the county seat. Ridgway quickly evolved into an important local political hub and regional manufacturing center, home to large tanneries and, most importantly, lumber fortunes.

The most poweful of Ridgway's lumber businesses was the Hyde-Murphy Company, an internationally recognized producer of architectural millwork and art glass. Joseph Hyde was an early town pioneer and lumberman and Walter Murphy was a carpenter, contractor and mill owner before joining forces with Hyde in 1884. The company was responsible for countless projects in the north-central Pennsylvania region, including the vast majority of substantial buildings erected in the Ridgway historic district. Its long list of clients include the Pentagon, embassies in Washington, D. C., and the Tripoli Hospital in Honolulu, among many other prestigious buildings. The Hyde-Murphy operation occupied a fifteen-building campus just north of the historic district along Race Street. The company ceased operation in 1961 and in 1974 the remaining buildings of the large complex were demolished to make way for the Ridgway Community Park.

Enough trees were felled and floated down the Clarion River that by the end of the 1800s it was said that there were more millionaires per capita living in Ridgway than any other place in America. Their legacy in the "Lily of the Valley" was recognized by the National Park Service in 2002. Our walking tour will start in front of the seat of justice for Elk County and proceed to see the handiwork of some of Pennsylvania's biggest lumber barons...

1. Elk County Courthouse
250 Main Street

Two acres of land for the first Courthouse had been reserved during the Survey of 1833 as a town public square. The first courthouse was of wood frame construction and was completed in May 1845, most likely near the present courthouse. The Courthouse served as Elk County's seat of justice for thirty-four years, by which time it was severely overburdened by the region's growth. In early 1879. County representatives went on a tour of northcentral Pennsylvania and decided the recently built courthouse at Warren would suit their needs. They hired its architect and builder, J.P. Marston, to guide Elk County's new Victorian courthouse. It was finished in 1880.

In April 1879, the old courthouse was sold at an auction to Hugh McGeehin who moved it down Main Street to become part of the Bogert House, a hotel owned by McGeehin and P.F. Bogert. When a new Bogert House was built in 1906, the dining room was part of the former courtroom. Tragically the Bogert House was consumed by fire on January 28, 1990.

WALK EAST ON MAIN STREET ACROSS BROAD STREET. TURN RIGHT ON EAST AVENUE.

2. William H. Hyde Residence
344 Main Street at southwest corner of East Avenue

Joseph Smith Hyde and his son William opened a department store reputed to be the largest in Western Pennsylvania. The third floor contained the Opera House, the first opera house in Ridgway. The department store, located at the southeast corner of the Main Street and Broad Street, was later known as the Hall, Kaul & Hyde Company Store. The story goes that when J. S. Hyde arrived in frontier Ridgway in 1838 he walked into a store hoping to buy an axe on credit. After he was refused and told to come back when he could buy the axe, he replied that he would come back when he could buy the store. Joseph Hyde would go on to make a fortune in the cutting of rough timber and the production of fine woodwork at the head of the Hyde-Murphy and Company.

This massive Richardsonian Romanesque mansion was built in 1907, a few years after William Hyde's death. The interior is stuffed with examples of fine cherry, oak, curly birch and maple woodwork produced by the family business.

3. John G. Whitmore House
12 East Avenue

John Whitmore was counsel to the Pennsylvania Railroad and the Baltimore & Ohio Railroad when he was appointed to the bench of the Supreme Court of Pennsylvania in 1930. His Queen Anne house was constructed in 1898 and it is resplendent with carved lion heads, curling acanthus leaves, and cross panels finished with French-styled cartouches. The accompanying carriage house features an original carriage lift that hoisted a buggy to the second floor in order to make room for the horses.

TURN LEFT ON HYDE AVENUE.

4. Frederick Clawson House
522 Hyde Avenue

Frederick Clawson made his fortune selling chemicals to tanneries to turn animal hides into leather. The Clawson Chemical Company in Hallton eventually faced financial reversals in the 1920s and the plant was sold. Clawson built this enormous Georgian Revival house on the hill when he was still flush in 1907. the double set of leaded and beveled front doors are original.

5. William Moore House
524 Hyde Avenue

This Shingle-Style house was built in 1909 as a wedding present for the original owner and his bride by the groom's father, a lumber baron. The four reception rooms each display a different wood, carved and decorated in the famous Hyde-Murphy style. The reception hall is feudal oak, the living and dining rooms mirror each other in cherry, and the study/den is white oak. The three-story octagonal tower provided Taylor Moore and his wife Penelope a commanding view of the historic neighborhood.

6. Charles A. Kline House
   522 Hyde Avenue

Charles A. Kline's was an iconic American rags-to-riches story. A Crenshaw native, Kline came to Ridgway for a minor job with the Hyde-Murphy Company. His work ethic was quickly realized and he rose to a position of great responsibility while still a young man. He hired architect Henry C. Park to build Ridgway's finest example of English Tudor architecture in 1907 but before he was able to move in, Kline died from appendicitis at the age of 32.

TURN AND RETRACE YOUR STEPS TO SOUTH STREET AND TURN LEFT.

7. Jerome Powell House
   330 South Street

Jerome Powell was born in the borough and county of Warren in 1827, the son of a blacksmith. In 1850 he moved to Ridgway, where he established the *Elk County Advocate*, continuing its publication until 1855. He then embarked in mercantile pursuits for decades with Robert V. Kime, and later also in the manufacture of lumber, both of which created his fortune. He built this striking Italian villa in 1865, updating it steadily through the 1890s. Inside, soaring first floor ceilings are crowned with oak and cherry beams finished with egg and dart moldings and the grand staircase is flanked by imposing oak Ionic columns.

8. Edgar Powell House
   324 South Street

North-central Pennsylvania's most prominent architect of the late-nineteenth and early twentieth century was Henry C. Park, who made his home in Ridgway from the early 1890s until his death nearly thirty years later. Born in the village of Waverly, on the New York-Pennsylvania line, Park moved to Ridgway in 1894 and became the resident architect for the Hyde-Murphy Company. He was equally at ease with Queen Anne residential design and more formal Georgian Revival institutional work.

Park designed this eclectic house for Powell,

next to his father's house, in 1903. Edgar served as Mayor of Ridgway for three years before leaving with his brother Robert for California where they lost much of the family fortune.

TURN RIGHT ON BAKER ALLEY. TURN RIGHT ON CENTER STREET.

9. Ridgway Free Library
   329 Center Street

This Colonial Revival building with a two-side Ionic portico was constructed in 1905 as a residence for Madison S. Kline, a local banker and sales manager for Russell Car and Snow Plow Company. Kline was forced to sell his showcase house in 1910 to the Hall family, one of Elk County's most prominent clans. J.K.P. Hall was a state senator and two-term United States Congressman and was married to Kate Hyde, daughter of lumber baron Joseph S. Hyde. Their son James became president of the Stackpole Carbon Company and founded the Stackpole-Hall Foundation. Kate Hyde Hall was instrumental in founding the Ridgway Public Library in 1899 and when its home was marked for demolition in 1921 donated this building to the library association with the stipulation that it be used for a library for at least 25 years and it assume the $10,000 mortgage for the house. It has the home to the library for more than 75 years.

TURN AND WALK EAST ON CENTER STREET.

10. Henry S. Thayer
   330 Center Street

Henry S. Thayer operated the Laurel Mill, whose lumbering operations accounted for between twelve and fifteen million board feet annually; his spacious home at 330 Center Street was described in 1893 as being "one of the handsomest in the state." Thayer was the grandson of David Thayer, an early settler of Ridgway. The carriage house was part of the first homestead, built in 1861 by Justus C. Chapin, one of the first District Attorneys in Elk County.

TURN RIGHT ON BROAD STREET.

11. Trinity Methodist Episcopal Church
   21 South Broad Street

J. C. Fulton of Uniontown designed this Gothic-style church of rough-faced stone and terra-cotta.

RETURN TO CENTER STREET AND TURN RIGHT, HEADING WEST.

12. Burr Cartwright House
   244 Center Street at southwest corner of Broad Street

Burr E. Cartwright was born in 1850 in Buffalo, New York where he first engaged in the lumber business. He came to Ridgway in 1879 as purchasing agent for the firm of Scatchard & Son, in whose employ he remained until 1881. In that year he and W. W. Mattison formed a partnership that evolved into the Ridgway Lumber Company. In short order Cartwright owned the largest lumber operation in Pennsylvania and his empire included coal, brick and railroad operations. It all ended when the Panic of 1893 left him bankrupt and eventually Cartwright returned to Buffalo where he rebuilt some of his fortune in gold mines. Before he left he built this three-story eclectic house in the center of town that featured some of the finest cherry, maple and oak woodwork seen in these parts. The third floor featured the largest ballroom in Ridgway and retains its original gas chandelier.

13. Byron F. Ely House
   200 Center Street

Byron Ely was one of the first residents in Ridgway, arriving in 1836 at the age of 16 with his father, Lafayette. He went into lumbering and became involved in several successful ventures, the last being on Elk Creek. He was one of the town's most prominent business men when he had this grand Queen Anne home built in 1888. Ely didn't enjoy his new home long, he died within months of moving in.

14. Perry R. Smith Residence
   136 Center Street

Now a funeral home, this was the 1896 residence of Perry R. Smith. Smith made his way to Ridgway from Liberty, New York a quarter-century earlier and went to work as a tanner, eventually becoming vice-president at Elk Tanning Company. In 1898, with his brothers Flavius and Charles, he founded the Smith Brothers Department Store and moved into the Grand Central Building on Main Street in 1907. It would become one of the largest retail chains in Western Pennsylvania, lasting until 1958.

15. Beverly P. Mercer House
   122 Center Street

The original core of this house was built in 1896 for meat market owner B.P. Mercer. The second owner, Madison J. Beach, president of the Elk Tanning Company, one of the largest corporations in Pennsylvania, added the fashionable cut stone porch and updated the interior. One thing he couldn't do was soundproof the house and with the growing popularity of automobiles on Ridgway streets, the Beaches abandoned this buff brick Victorian for a quieter abode on South Street in 1920.

16. Elder Campbell House
   121 Center Street

This Queen Anne house from 1886 was first built as a clapboard home with a barn on the site of a planing mill in the 1870s. Campbell was the owner of the Eagle Valley Store and a local sawmill. Later Flavius C. Smith of the Smith Brothers Department Store chain moved here.

17. George Dixon House
   118 Center Street

This Shingle Style originated in cottages along the trendy, wealthy Northeastern coastal towns of Cape Cod, Long Island, and Newport in the late 19th century. Architectural publishers publicized it, but the style was never as popular around the country as the Queen Anne style from which it borrows wide porches and asymmetrical forms. They are also characterized by unadorned doors, windows, porches, and cornices; continuous wood shingles; a steeply pitched roof line; and large porches. This one features a sleeping porch atop the turret. George Dixon, a businessman and educator, had this home built in 1888. He was also admitted to the Bar in 1878 and served four terms as a Pennsylvania Assemblyman. The home retains its original carriage stone where horse-drawn buggies would pull up to the front stoop.

18. Homer B. Norton House
   ### 114 Center Street

Homer Norton was an engineer most noted for designing the H.B. Norton Dam that provided the water supply for the town that helped squelch an outbreak of typhoid fever. Norton applied his engineering talents to his home, which was constructed in 1916 around an older 1874 structure. On the third floor the entire weight of the roof is cantilevered to the exterior walls making one large room with no visible supporting structures.

TURN RIGHT ON ELK AVENUE.
TURN RIGHT ON MAIN STREET.

19. Bogert House
   ### 150 Main Street

When Hugh McGeehin constructed his new hotel in 1879 he incorporated a section of the original county courthouse into the brick structure. P.F. Bogert was in the hotel business for a dozen years in his native Sullivan County, New York before coming to Ridgway at the age of 36 in 1880 to establish the Bogert House. In its prime, the hotel featured a restraurant, bar, 31 rooms and 11 apartments. The building was ravaged by fire in 1990.

20. Union Hall
   ### 241 Main Street

All the buildings on Main Street, save one, between Mill and Broad streets were consumed by a fire that ignited on September 29, 1882. The buildings destroyed were of wood, unsightly in appearance and haphazardly placed. Scarcely had the ground cooled before the monied merchants of Ridgway set about creating a new block of substantial brick buildings in the popular Italianate commercial style of the day. There would be the Grand Central block, the Rhines Building and a new Ridgway bank. Here Fred Schoening and James McGinnis constructed the $20,000 Union Hall as a meeting lodge and commercial space. Today, Two Scoops offers an interior of an early 20th century soda fountain.

YOU HAVE NOW RETURNED TO THE TOUR STARTING POINT IN FRONT OF THE ELK COUNTY COURTHOUSE.

Look Up,

Scranton

A Walking Tour of Scranton...

The first European settlers in Scranton were the Abbott brothers, who founded a grist mill here in 1786. In 1800 the Slocum brothers took the mill over and began a charcoal furnace for iron manufacturing. A post office opened in 1811 and the delivery address was Slocum Hollow.

It was still an area of random small businesses in 1842 when William Henry, a native of Nazareth who had been operating a blast furnace in New Jersey, arrived with his son-in-law, Seldon T. Scranton. William Henry was a geologist and surveyor. He had previously visited the area and discovered deposits of iron ore in the hills surrounding the Roaring Brook and Lackawanna River. Soon, Seldon's brother, George W. Scranton, arrived from Connecticut; the Slocum property was purchased, and funds were secured from a number of venture capitalists for the construction of the Lackawanna Furnace. By 1846, the Lackawanna Furnace and Rolling Mills Company was producing nails for market.

Still more Scrantons began arriving. This time it was cousin Joseph, who was a successful Georgia merchant. The next year, a United States post office was established in the town then called "Scrantonia" after the Scranton family. Also, during this time period the coal boom was in full swing and the first wave of immigrants from England, Wales, Ireland, and Germany was beginning to settle in the region. Scranton, then part of Luzerne County, continued to grow until it surpassed the county seat, Wilkes-Barre, in population and importance. Residents had long agitated for their own county; Brandford and Susquehanna counties had seceded from Luzerne with little contest. But losing Scranton - and its rich industrial taxbase - was a different matter. When a new State constitution in 1874 allowed voters of a proposed breakaway county to decide their own fate, citizens of Lackawanna County voted nearly 6 to 1 in favor of creating Pennsylvania's last county, ending a nearly 40-year struggle.

Scranton earned the nickname "Anthracite Capital of the World" and coal kept the city humming through the early 1900s. The declining demand for coal after World War II forced Scranton, earlier than other industrial centers, to endeavor to find ways to diversify its economy. Its Scranton Plan, a revitalization scheme devised in 1945, has been used as a model for other cities in decline.

Our walking tour of the downtown area will encounter splashes of that rebirth while exploring the core of one of America's great mid-size cities of the industrial age...

1. Lackawanna County Courthouse
200 Washington Avenue

When Lackawanna County was formed in 1878, the city block that now houses the Lackawanna County Courthouse was known as "Lily Pond" or Tamarack Bog." The property was a dump for ashes and cinders and was used for skating in the winter. In 1879, the Lackawanna Iron and Coal Company and the Susquehanna and Wyoming Valley Railroad and Coal Company donated the land for public buildings and a park.

Isaac Perry of Binghamton, New York was awarded the commission for the new county courthouse. Perry's design called for a Victorian Chateau-style built in the warm tones of the city's native west mountain stone, trimmed in Onondaga limestone. Construction was complete in 1884. In 1896, local architect B. Taylor Lacey designed the building's third floor, adding eclectic stylistic influences such as a steeply pitched hipped tile roof, wall dormers with scrolled Flemish parapets topped by broken pediments and urns, a dentillated cornice and pyramidal-roofed towers.

The Lackawanna County Courthouse gained national attention in 1902 for its role as the meeting site for the Anthracite Coal Strike Commission's sessions in Scranton. The Commission - appointed by President Theodore Roosevelt - met in the Superior Courtroom to hear testimony in America's first non-violent federal intervention between labor and ownership. John Mitchell spoke on behalf of the mine workers and famed attorney Clarence Darrow represented management.

START AT THE 104-FOOT HIGH SOLDIERS & SAILORS MONUMENT AND WALK CLOCKWISE AROUND COURTHOUSE SQUARE.

2. *Soldiers & Sailors Monument*
Washington Avenue side of Courthouse Square

The Harrison Granite Company of Barre, Vermont directed the construction of this remembrance to Lackawanna County's Civil War heroes, dedicated on November 15, 1900. The monument is about 104 feet to the top of the 14-foot bronze statue of *Victory* brandishing a laurel wreath and sword. During a storm in 1967 the sword fell off the monument and was never replaced. The shaft bears the names of major battles and bronze plaques depict battle scenes. When the statue was first unveiled Ray Fuhrman, United States Navy, climbed a long rope - hand-over-hand, seaman style - to cut the ribbons on the draping.

3. William J. Nealon Federal Courthouse and Post Office
235 Washington Avenue

The present United States post office was constructed in 1930 and replaced an earlier federal building from 1894. Architect James Wetmore of Washington, D.C. designed the building in a Neoclassical style with Art Deco details. In 1999 the William J. Nealon Federal Building was completed on the site of the Old Park Plaza Building.

TURN RIGHT ON COURTHOUSE SQUARE ALONG LINDEN STREET.

4. Scranton Electric Building
507 Linden Street

Lansing Holden designed this Beaux Arts, eight-story building for the Scranton Board of Trade, precursor of the Chamber of Commerce, in 1896. In 1926 the building with carved stone front and copper-and-tile roof was sold to the Scranton Electric Company which erected the landmark "Electric City" rooftop sign. The designation was earned in 1886 when Scranton completed the first commercially viable, all-electric trolley system in America.

5. Ad-Lin Building
600 Linden Street, southeast corner at Adams Avenue

When the P.P. Carter Building, as the Ad-Lin (Adams & Linden streets) Building, was originally known, was constructed in 1896 it employed a Classical Revival/Commercial Style design not common among local commercial buildings of its era. Carter was selling axe and mining tools.

Since then this pivotal downtown corner has been home to a printing company, sweet shop, bank, dance studio, advertising agency, bus terminal and newsstand. Aside from some general sprucing up in 1985, no major alterations have taken place on this building that is listed on the National Register of Historic Places.

TURN RIGHT ALONG ADAMS AVENUE.

6. Grace Hope Mission
234 Adams Avenue

This is one of the earliest structures built on Courthouse Square, dating to the 1870s. It is typical of the early Italianate commercial buildings that once lined Scranton's streets.

7. Stoehr & Fister Building
200 Adams Avenue, at northeast corner of Spruce Street

This white-tile, six-story structure was erected in 1923 for Stoehr and Fister, one of the largest furniture houses in Pennsylvania. Note the detailed carvings of furniture-making elves on the band between the first and second floors. Today it houses Lackawanna County offices.

8. Bliss-Davis Building
150 Adams Avenue, at southeast corner of Spruce Street

Built by architect Lewis Hancock in 1911, this Gothic style building was designed with additional stories to match the height of nearby buildings but they were never constructed.

STAY ON ADAMS AVENUE TO LEAVE THE SQUARE, CROSSING SPRUCE STREET.

9. Medallion Garage
140 Adams Avenue

On this location in the 1920s an early parking garage was constructed for the Hotel Casey. It featured 18 terra-cotta medallions depicting roadsters from the era. When the original garage was demolished in 2005, the medallions were removed, restored and have been incorporated into the new garage facade.

RETRACE YOUR STEPS TO SPRUCE STREET AND TURN LEFT ALONG COURTHOUSE SQUARE.

10. Scranton Life Building
538 Spruce Street, at southwest corner of Adams Avenue

This eight-story Chicago Style building with Gothic accents was designed by Scranton architect Edward Langely for Scranton Life Insurance in 1916. The crenelated top with mounted eagles symbolizes the assurance of protection and strength of the firm.

11. Mears Building
150 Washington Avenue, at southeast corner of Washington Avenue

In 1896, Isaac L. Williams designed the Mears Building, Scranton's oldest 10-story office building. Its arched windows and stone facade suggest a Richardsonian Romanesque influence. The building was sold to many owners over the years and has been renovated many times.

12. Brooks Building
436 Spruce Street, at southwest corner of Washington Avenue

This building was constructed in 1891 for Judge Alfred Hand as the Commonwealth Building. It was designed by Lansing C. Holding who gave his Chicago Style building Romanesque details - a flat roof with deep projecting eaves and decorative spandrels above and below bay windows.

The large bay window at the corner of the building caused great controversy in its day. When Scranton city planner Joel Amsden laid out the city streets he included a 10-foot setback rule so buildings wouldn't take up too much sidewalk space. Judge Hand took advantage of an exception for porches and bay windows to create his massive extension to the building. Early tenants included the People's National Bank and the J.H. Brooks brokerage firm.

13. Rite-Aid Building
   201 Washington Avenue, at northwest corner of Spruce Street

Rite-Aid founder Alexander Grass was a Scranton native. The first Rite-Aid store opened in Scranton on September 12, 1962.

STAY ON SPRUCE STREET TO LEAVE COURTHOUSE SQUARE.

14. Dime Bank
   400 Spruce Street, at southwest corner of Wyoming Avenue

Built in 1891 by architect Frederick Brown, the bank was designed in the Chateauesque style with fine stone work and heavy cornice.

15. Bank Towers
   321 Spruce Street, at northeast corner of Wyoming Avenue

Constructed in 1896 as the Trader's National Bank, this Beaux Arts style structure includes a unique corner entrance. The bank underwent major renovations in the 1930s to reflect the clean lines of the International Style.

16. Hotel Jermyn
   326 Spruce Street, at northwest corner of Wyoming Avenue

Opened in 1895, the Hotel Jermyn was built by architect John Duckworth in the Neoclassical style. This hotel hosted famous performers of the Big Band era of the 1930s and 1940s, including the Dorsey Brothers and Glenn Miller. Note the carving of the Manhattan skyline surrounding the Spruce Street entrance.

TURN LEFT ON PENN AVENUE.

17. Scranton *Times*
   149 Penn Avenue, at southwest corner of Spruce Street

This restrained Greek Revival residence was constructed in 1843 and is most significant when viewed in relation to its next door neighbor...

18. Samters Building
   101 Penn Avenue, at northwest corner of Lackawanna Avenue

Built between 1923 and 1925, this upscale clothing store was constructed in the Chicago style. Samuel Samter opened his first store in Scranton shortly after arriving in town in 1872 at the age of 21. Samter Brothers, "Clothiers, Furnishers, Hatters," operated in this location beginning in 1888 and closed in 1978.

CROSS LACKAWANNA AVENUE AND WALK INTO THE MALL AT STEAMTOWN. WALK UP THE STAIRS TO THE SECOND FLOOR, THROUGH THE FOOD COURT AND OUT THE BACK DOOR ONTO THE PEDESTRIAN WALKWAY.

19. Steamtown National Historic Site

Steamtown National Historic Site occupies about 40 acres of the Scranton railroad yard of the former Delaware, Lackawanna and Western Railroad, one of the earliest rail lines in northeastern Pennsylvania. At the heart of the park is the large collection of standard-gauge steam locomotives and freight and passenger cars that New England seafood processor F. Nelson Blount assembled in the 1950s and 1960s. In 1984, 17 years after Blount's untimely death, the Steamtown Foundation for the Preservation of Steam and Railroad Americana, Inc., brought the collection to Scranton, where is occupied the former DL&W yard. When Steamtown National Historic Site was created, the yard and the collection became part of the National Park System.

The Steamtown Collection consists of locomotives, freight cars, passenger cars, and maintenance-of-way equipment from several historic railroads. The locomotives range in size from a tiny industrial switcher engine built in 1937 by the H.K. Porter Company for the Bullard Company, to a huge Union Pacific Big Boy build in 1941 by the American Locomotive Company (Alco). The oldest locomotive is a freight engine built by Alco in 1903 for the Chicago Union Transfer Railway Company.

WHEN YOU ARE READY TO
RESUME THE TOUR RETRACE
YOUR STEPS TO LACKAWANNA
AVENUE AND TURN RIGHT. TURN
LEFT ON WYOMING AVENUE.

20. Place I
117 Wyoming Avenue

The painted tiles on this facade are a fine souvenir of the Art Deco stylings of the late 1920s and 1930s.

21. Lewis & Reilly Building
114 Wyoming Avenue

Architects Edward Davis and George Lewis applied the classical base-shaft-capital structure of early American skyscrapers to this building, originally a shoe store, in the 1920s. Lewis & Reilly's was co-owned by Jennie Lewis Evans, one of the first woman business owners in Lackawanna County.

22. Third National Bank Building
120 Wyoming Avenue

This Neoclassical Greek temple was built in 1918 for the Third National Bank of Scranton, known around town as "the 3rd." The bank was founded in 1872.

23. The Globe Department Store
119 Wyoming Avenue

The Cleland Simpson Company purchased an 1870 building in 1878 to convert into a department store for owners John Simpson, John Cleland and William Taylor. It perished in a fire in 1889. The rebuilt emporium was designed in 1908 by Edward Langley and purchased by Charles P. Hancock. Hancock had worked as a clerk for Cleland, Simpson & Taylor before striking out on his own by opening the Globe Store in his hometown of Danville.

When he migrated to Scranton, the Globe Store would gain local fame. It was one of the only stores of its kind in town, often compared to the stores of New York City with its large display windows, enormous selection of the latest fashions, and its restaurant, the Charlmont. It always had elaborate outside decorations during the Christmas season. The Globe struggled to last through the 20th century but finally went the way of all downtown department stores and disappeared in 1994.

TURN AND RETRACE YOUR STEPS
TO LACKAWANNA AVENUE AND
TURN LEFT.

24. Scranton Dry Goods
409 Lackawanna Avenue, at northeast corner of Franklin Street

Jonas Long was the first retailer in this building, designed by Lansing Holden in 1897. I.E. Oppenheim purchased it in 1916 for his Scranton Dry Goods Company and soon expanded it to an eight-story Neoclassical tour de force that rivaled the finest department stores in the big cities of the Northeast. It was first to install escalators in the city. It had the first on-premises cold-storage vault for furs. It was the first store with a beauty salon, an air-conditioned tea room, a garden center, and an employees' cafeteria. In the 1960s, "Scranton Dry" was bustling with 200,000 square feet of selling space. Scranton Dry Goods became Oppenheim's but the upscale name couldn't stave off the migration of shoppers to the suburbs and the grand emporium shuttered on November 1, 1980.

25. Bosak State Bank Building
434 Lackawanna Avenue, at southwest corner of Washington Avenue

Michael Bosak was born in 1869 in Austria-Hungary and came to eastern Pennsylvania at the age of 18 to work as a breaker in a Hazleton coal mine. Bosak became a clerk for several liquor merchants, saving enough to open his own liquor store in Hazleton and in 1893 started Glinsky's Tavern in Olyphant.

By 1907, Bosak was selling wholesale and opened the Scranton branch on Lackawanna Avenue. He acquired a shipping agency and established a bank in Olyphant that was known as "The Michael Bosak Private Bank." In 1902, he was a founding partner of the First Citizens Bank of Olyphant, followed quickly by the Slavonic

Deposit Bank in Wilkes-Barre and, in 1915, this bank. The warm stone building was designed by Edward Davis in a Colonial Revival style.

His operations were such a success that he claimed the title of "richest Slovak in America." His most popular spirit was Horke Vino, a bitter, port-based wine that was claimed to be a remedy for many ills, as was common at that time. The economic crash of 1929 stripped Bosak of his fortunes and his businesses faltered and closed in 1931. He died in 1937.

26. Scranton National Bank
108 Washington Avenue, at northeast corner of Lackawanna Avenue

The skyscraper rose in 1915, designed by Edward Davis in the classic Chicago School style of making a high-rise resemble a column with base-shaft-capital. it was the second home of the bank, originally named the Union National Bank.

27. Railway Express Agency Building
600 Lackawanna Avenue

This office was built in 1908 for the Railway Express, a national firm that moved shipments of packages and freight quickly over freight lines like the ones behind its back door.

28. Lackawanna Station
700 Lackawanna Avenue

This was the original headquarters and main passenger terminal for the Delaware, Lackawanna & Western Railroad. After passenger service ended in 1970 it was adapted for use as a hotel in the 1980s. Kenneth Murchison designed the command center in the Neoclassical style in 1907-08.

CONTINUE WALKING TO YOUR LEFT AS LACKAWANNA AVENUE BENDS INTO JEFFERSON AVENUE.

29. Scranton Gas & Water Company
135 Jefferson Avenue

This Beaux Arts structure was constructed in 1920-21 as headquarters for the Scranton Gas & Water Company by the firm of Edward Davis and George Lewis. Fish and dragon carvings on the facade represent the water and fire provided by the company.

30. Leahy Hall
243 Jefferson Avenue, at southwest corner of Linden Street

Originally the Young Women's Christian Association, the structure was built in 1907 in the Colonial Revival style. The building now houses students and offices for the University of Scranton.

31. Elm Park United Methodist Church
712 Linden Street, at southeast corner of Jefferson Avenue

Elm Park United Methodist Church traces its history to 1839, when a Methodist Class was organized in Slocum Hollow, now Scranton. The church was incorporated on September 8, 1859. After outgrowing several buildings, the congregation broke ground for the new church home on September 8, 1891. The site was a triangular piece of land known as Elm Park. After two major fires and reconstruction, a dedication service was held on December 17, 1893.

32. O'Hara Hall
310 Jefferson Avenue, at northeast corner of Linden Street

This handsome building with rusticated base was built as the headquarters of the Glen Alden Coal Company in 1922 in the Neoclassical style. It is home to offices of the University of Scranton today.

33. Houlihan McLean Center
346 Jefferson Avenue, at southeast corner of Mulberry Street

This Victorian Gothic stone building was erected as the Emmanuel Baptist Church in 1910. It is now the Performing Arts Center for the University of Scranton.

TURN LEFT FOR A FEW STEPS ON MULBERRY STREET.

34. Herold Apartments
618 Mulberry Street

This is one of the first Art Deco apartment buildings constructed in the United States. Legend has it that a Mr. Herold, a Navy veteran, worked with the architect to design this 1937 building to look like a ship.

RETURN TO JEFFERSON AVENUE
AND TURN LEFT.

35. Blair House
401 Jefferson Avenue, at northwest corner of Mulberry Street

Built in the 1870s, the Victorian-style residence of Colonel Austin Blair, son of a founder of the Delaware, Lackawanna & Western Railroad, was remodeled in 1910 to add the imposing Corinthian portico and a third floor ballroom, the better to host Blair's swanky parties. The house was converted into a special events venue, catering facility and boutique hotel known as The Colonnade in 2006.

36. St. Matthew's Evangelical Lutheran Church
425 Jefferson Avenue

James C. Cady created this French Norman cottage-style church for Scranton's Presbyterian parish in 1886.

37. St. Nicholas Orthodox Church
505 Jefferson Avenue, at northwest corner of Vine Street

In 1895 a stone mansion was constructed on this corner for Judge Albert Hand, whose business interests included, among other things, canals and water rights in the New Mexico Territory. In 1939 his heirs sold the property to the Greek Orthodox congregation who dismantled the house and reassembled the stones to form the present structure.

38. Lackawanna College Fitness Center
500 Jefferson Avenue, at northeast corner of Vine Street

This corner was the domain of John Jermyn, an Englishman who came to America as a youth and was a digger in the Diamond coal mine in 1847 at the age of 17. From those humble beginnings Jermyn would become one of the leading anthracite coal operators in Pennsylvania, developing mines at Dickson City, Scranton, Old Forge and elsewhere. He sold all but the Old Forge mines and by the time of his death in 1902 his estate was valued at several million dollars. The Diocese of Scranton built a Catholic Youth Center here in 1949 and it is now owned by Lackawanna College.

39. Woolworth House
520 Jefferson Avenue

Charles Sumner Woolworth, brother of five-and-dime empire-builder Frank W. Woolworth, was brought into the business early on and helped guide it to prominence. "Sum," as he was called made Scranton his home (the Woolworth's was at 125 Penn Avenue) and base of operations for timber and railroad ventures. After Frank died, Charles followed him as president. His Neoclassical house was designed by Lansing Holden in 1909.

40. American Red Cross Building
545 Jefferson Avenue

Fenwick L. Peck, founded the successful Lackawanna Lumber Company but accumulated rare wealth when he was one of the first to envision the potential of the vast Mississippi yellow pine forests in 1896. He purchased the controlling interest in the Newman Lumber Company in Hattiesburg, Mississippi and at its peak of production, the company owned 400,000 acres of timberlands and produced 75,000,000 board feet of lumber per year.

His Colonial-style dwelling was constructed in 1901 by Lansing Holden. The Peck family donated it to the Scranton Chapter of the American Red Cross in 1942.

41. Porter House
544 Jefferson Avenue

This was the home of John T. Porter, wholesale grocer and president of the Scranton Board of Trade.

TURN LEFT ON OLIVE STREET.
TURN LEFT ON ADAMS STREET.
TURN RIGHT ON VINE STREET.

42. Lackawanna County Children's Library
520 Vine Street

The former First Church of Christ Scientist was built in 1914 by architects Snyder & Ward in a pure Greek Revival style. The Lackawanna County Library System bought the building in 1985.

43. Lackawanna College
501 Vine Street

The dramatic Central High School was built here in 1895, replacing a similarly imposing Second Empire school that had stood since 1858. This building, by Little & O'Connor, served almost a century before closing in 1991. It is now the centerpiece of Lackawanna College.

44. Albright Library
500 Vine Street, at souhteast corner of Washington Avenue

John Joseph Albright, water power pioneer and president of the Marine National Bank of Buffalo (NY) donated the land of his old family homestead and funds for this extraordinary building in 1893 to honor his parents who had recently passed away. The firm of Green and Wicks, leading Buffalo architects, modeled the library in the French Renaissance style after the chateau monastery, Musee de Cluny, to give a splendid view at the northern gateway to downtown Scranton.

The exterior of the building is composed of Indiana limestone in a warm gray color above a base of brown Medina stone, all laid in course ashlar. The building has high, steeply-pitched roofs; there are twelve dormer gables covered in black Spanish tiles. In the panels of the dormers and on other parts of the building, there are symbols of notable bookmakers elaborately carved in the stonework.

The grounds around the Library were designed by Frederick Law Olmsted, who is heralded as the father of American landscape architecture. The design itself was completed in the 1890s, but due to a lack of funding, the actual landscaping was not to be realized until August 1999.

TURN LEFT ON
WASHINGTON AVENUE.

45. Scranton School Administration Building
425 Washington Avenue

Designed and built by Lewis Hancosky, Jr. in 1911, this ornate Gothic Revival style structure is approaching 100 years of service to the Scranton School District.

46. Masonic Temple and Scottish Rite Cathedral
420 Washington Avenue

Completed in 1930 as a Masonic temple and Scottish Rite Cathedral, this magnificent building is a mix of Art Deco and Gothic styling. It came from the pen of Raymond Hood, designer of Radio City Music Hall.

47. American Legion Koch-Conley Post
415 Washingotn Avenue

Owned by Lackawanna College, the building was designed in 1937 by architect David Jones as an American Legion Post.

48. Elks Club
406 Washington Avenue

Built in 1914 in the Colonial Revival style, the former fraternal club is now part of Lackawanna College.

49. Scranton Club
404 Washington Avenue

Originally a private men's club, this Colonial Revival style building was designed by Edward Langley and opened in 1906.

TURN LEFT ON MULBERRY STREET.

50. Central Fire Department
518 Mulberry Street

Where once horse-drawn engines pulled through the broad arches onto the streets of Scranton, now, more than 100 years later, come modern fire-fighting equipment. The Victorian Gothic style firehouse was designed by Frederick Brown in 1905.

TURN AND WALK WEST ON MULBERRY STREET.

51. Scranton Municipal Building
340 Washington Avenue, at southeast corner of Mulberry Street

Constructed in 1888, Scranton's City Hall was designed by city native Edwin Walter in the Victorian Gothic style and built using local West Mountain stone.

TURN LEFT ON BUTLER LANE. TURN LEFT ON WASHINGTON STREET.

52. Chamber of Commerce
southwest corner of Washington Avenue and Mulberry Street

Edward Langley designed this structure in the Modern style with Art Deco flourishes in 1925 to house the Chamber after its move from Courthouse Square.

TURN RIGHT ON WYOMING AVENUE.

53. Finch Building
434 Wyoming Avenue

Named for the Finch Manufacturing Company, this Gothic structure was constructed in 1899 by architect W. Scott Collins. It served as the first headquarters of the International Correspondence School and later housed the offices of the Hudson Coal Company.

TURN LEFT ON VINE STREET.

54. Dickson Works
225 Vine Street, at northwest corner of Penn Avenue

This industrial structure dates to 1878 and was part of the extensive Dickson Locomotive Works, manufacturers of stationary steam engines, heavy mining equipment and locomotives. For more than 50 years the firm, organized by Thomas Dickson in 1856, ranked not only among the leading industries in Scranton but held high place in the state and country. Today it is most known for its brief starring appearance in the opening montage of the television comedy, *The Office*.

TURN LEFT ON PENN AVENUE.

55. Banshee
322 Penn Avenue

This Irish pub reflects the architectural history of Scranton's past. The wooden door was taken from the Wyoming House Hotel, and the woodwork and the bar inside were constructed from the wooden shelving from Eisner and Sons, former occupants of the building.

56. 300 Block of Penn Avenue

This commercial stretch was the hub of early 19th century industrial Scranton. Miners could purchase supplies and equipment at the Anthracite Jobbing Company and spend wages in the emporium of Eisner and Sons next door. The Lackawanna Steam Laundry provided cleaning service for hotels and households.

TURN LEFT ON LINDEN STREET.

57. GAR Building
305 Linden Street, at northeast corner of Penn Avenue

The ornate brick and terra-cotta the Grand Army of the Republic Building is one of the best and most magnificent representations of Victorian Romanesque architecture in northeastern Pennsylvania and it survives close to its original design. It was created in 1886 by John Duckworth, a Toronto native, who had a long resume behind him of buildings in New York, San Francisco and Chicago before moving to Scranton in 1884, where he practiced for 28 years - a tenure coinciding with the city's era of greatest prosperity.

The building was originally the Windsor Hotel & Saloon before it was purchased by the Civil War veterans group, the Grand Army of the Republic. The GAR Post maintained a large Civil War museum and library here.

58. St. Peter's Cathedral
northwest corner of Linden Street and Wyoming Avenue

The cathedral was built as the Church of St. Vincent de Paul in 1865 by Joel Amsden, Scranton's first civil engineer. It was originally designed in the Italianate style but received a make-over along more classical lines in 1884. The Beaux Arts building next door was the Bishop's Residence, designed in 1908 by Lewis Hancock.

TURN RIGHT ON WYOMING AVENUE.

59. Ritz Theater
222 Wyoming Avenue

This block was once the heart of Scranton's nationally renowned entertainment district. Almost all the historic theater buildings are gone now. Built by vaudeville theater magnate Sylvester Poli, the Poli Theater opened in 1907 at a then-monumental sum of $250,000. A large house, the Poli seated more than 2,000 patrons. By the late 1920s, the theater began showing movies only and was renamed Ritz Theatre. In 1930, it was remodeled and renamed again as the Comerford Theatre. The theater lasted for decades and in its last years was a dollar house struggling against a local United Artists multiplex. In the early 2000s the Ritz, with its nearly 100 years of service, closed. Most recently a blues club has continued the tradition of entertainment in this location.

TURN AND WALK BACK TOWARDS LINDEN STREET.

60. St. Luke's Episcopal Church
232 Wyoming Avenue

This Gothic Revival church was built in 1871 by architect Richard Upjohn, a leading practitioner of the form. The neighboring Parish House was built nearly 30 years later in the Victorian Gothic style by Frederick Brown.

TURN RIGHT ON LINDEN STREET AND WALK ONE BLOCK TO THE TOUR STARTING POINT IN COURTHOUSE SQUARE.

Look Up,

Sharon

A Walking Tour of Sharon...

The first settlement here was established in 1795 when Benjamin Bentley came from Washington County and explored the region along the Shenango River. The next year he brought his wife and six children to Sharon in a canoe, having erected a crude log cabin the year before. A great deal of the downtown section of the city now covers what were the farms of these early settlers that lay on a flat plain bordering the Shenango River. According to legend, the community received its name from a Bible-reading settler who likened the location to the Plain of Sharon in Israel.

Sharon grew very slowly. At the time of its incorporation as a borough in 1841 there were about 400 inhabitants; in 1850, 541; and in 1860, still only 900. But things were about to change. Coal was first discovered by accident early in 1835, cropping out of the hillside west of Sharon. Charles Meek opened the first mine on the property. This was the beginning of the famous Mercer County block coal. Because the coal possessed a peculiar structure, and because it retained its shape until it fell into ashes, it was especially fitted for the manufacture of pig iron. Pig iron made from this coal in 1876 was claimed to be the best made in America. From 1835 to 1876 more than fifty mines were opened.

Mercer County block coal did not run in veins but was deposited in "basins" or "swamps," varying in thickness from five to seven feet in the center. It tapered off into rock at the edges. The coal was removed usually from drift mines. The mine cars, of about 1200 pounds capacity, were pulled from the mines on wooden tracks by large dogs. Due to these large coal deposits, Sharon became a beehive of industrial activity, with rolling mills, boiler and machine shops, furnaces, flour mills, ordnance works, and manufactories of explosives, nails, horse collars, spokes, chains, stoves, and lumber products. By the time Sharon was incorporated as a city in 1917, the population had swelled to more than 20,000, the largest city in Mercer County.

Sharon remained a booming steel town into 1960s. The Malibu division of National Castings, Sharon Steel Corporation and Westinghouse Corporation were all major employers. Most of the plants have shuttered and industry moved on. Today, Sharon is best known to outsiders for its quirky Big Three - a trio of stores that bill themselves as the "World's Largest," selling candy, shoes and discount clothes.

Our walking tour will begin atop the Shenango River that dissects the town and we'll move from the recently rehabilitated State Street Bridge aways up those hills that cradle the town on both sides...

1. **River Walk Place**
   30 East Market Street

The most dramatic of several Art Deco era structures on State Street, this gray brick office building is constructed directly on the Shenango River.

TURN LEFT ON SHENANGO STREET. TURN RIGHT ON PITT STREET. TURN RIGHT ON RAILROAD STREET.

2. **Corinthian**
   47 Vine Street, at southwest corner of Pitt Street

Built in 1909 as a lodge for the local Masonic chapter, the building was renovated in 2002 to enter its second century as a banquet hall. The grand ballroom can accommodate 380 guests and encompasses both the second and third floors.

TURN LEFT ON EAST STATE STREET.

3. **Buhl Community Recreation Center**
   28 North Pine Avenue

After traveling down State Street in 1900 and seeing so many people standing on the street corners, industrialist Frank H. Buhl began to worry that there was no place to go to spend an evening in town and very few places that could keep a young man from "falling into devious ways." On September 19, 1903, he delivered the deed of the F. H. Buhl Club to its directors and officers.

The club flourished and by 1906 it was known as "the finest equipped club of its kind in the world." For five dollars a years members had full use of music rooms, educational classrooms, game rooms, a gymnasium, a library and a bowling alley. More than a century later the center continues to offer recreation and educational activities to the citizens of Sharon.

4. **Buhl Mansion**
   422 East State Street

Frank Buhl, a native of Detroit and graduate of Yale, came to Sharon in 1869 and became manager of the extensive Sharon Iron Works, a concern co-founded by his father. Buhl left town for ten years in 1878, returning to Michigan to take charge of the Detroit Copper and Brass Rolling Mill. He returned in 1888 to oversee the operations at Sharon Iron Works and marry the daughter of town scion Henry Forker.

Buhl Steel Co. was formed in 1896 with Frank H. Buhl as its president. Three years later, Buhl Steel was absorbed by the National Steel Co. After the merger Buhl, often referred to as "The Father of the Industrial Shenango Valley", co-founded Sharon Steel Castings and Sharon Steel. After U.S. Steel absorbed both National Steel and Sharon Steel, Buhl retired from the industry.

The Buhls were childless and devoted much of their fortune to the betterment of the community, contributing to hospitals, parks, libraries and churches. One of the stipulations in his will provided for the perpetual maintenance of a 9-hole golf course; thus, Sharon has the only free golf course in America.

Ironically, one thing his legacy did not provide for after his death in 1918 was upkeep on the magnificent castle he lived in for three decades. Charles Owsley, a Youngstown architect, designed the rough-hewn Richardsonian Romanesque building. Construction on the native ashlar sandstone mansion began in 1890 and was completed in 1896 for a total cost of $60,000 - at a time when the average worker pulled in about a dollar a day.

After Frank and Julia passed away, the property changed hands many times and was stripped of many of its spectacular architectural features including all the staircases, chandeliers, many door and window casings and all but four fireplace mantles. After years of abandonment and neglect, the house has been privately restored to serve as a guesthouse and spa.

5. Daffin's Candy Store
496 East State Street

The original family store was started in 1903 by George Daffin in Woodsfield, Ohio. The business wound through the family and across northeast Ohio until it landed in downtown Sharon in 1947. It was here that Pete and Jean Daffin created their now famous Peter Rabbit - a solid chocolate Rabbit sold during the Easter season. As demand for Daffin's candy soared, the couple moved their location to a bigger 20,000 square-foot store in Sharon. Still a family-run business - each piece of candy continues to be hand-decorated - Daffin's bills itself as the World's Largest Candy Store. Inside, the "Chocolate Kingdom" features remarkable sculptures of chocolate animals - some weighing over a quarter ton.

TURN AND WALK BACK DOWN EAST STATE STREET. TURN LEFT ON DOCK STREET.

6. Sharon *Herald*
52 Dock Street

Today's Sharon *Herald* has its roots in three local papers. R.C. and James Frey founded the *Herald*, a weekly newspaper, in 1864. It became a daily in April 12, 1909. The newspaper's office at the foot of Pitt Street in Sharon was washed into the Shenango River during a flood in March 1913. The newspaper missed only four issues and resumed publication with temporary production for about a month at the printing plant of the New Castle *News* before a new office and pressroom were set up on Chestnut Street.

The *Herald* merged with its main competitor, the Sharon *News-Telegraph*, on May 13, 1935. That paper had incorporated the old Farrell *News* (founded 1925) and Sharon *Telegraph* (a daily since 1893). The new newspaper kept the Sharon *Herald* as its name but production moved to the *News-Telegraph* building two blocks away on South Dock Street.

TURN RIGHT ON CONNELLY BOULEVARD. TURN RIGHT ON CHESTNUT STREET.

7. Quaker Steak & Lube
101 Chestnut Street

The Quaker Steak and Lube opened here in 1974 when two friends came up with the idea of preserving the culture of old gas stations by setting up a restaurant inside an abandoned one. The idea took off and the chain now boasts 38 locations throughout Ohio and Pennsylvania. A 1936 Chevy that was inside the original garage hangs from the ceiling.

TURN LEFT ON EAST STATE STREET.

8. Reyers Outlet
69 East State Street

Reyers was founded in 1886 by a German immigrant shoemaker, John A. Reyer. Six decades later, John's son Carl sold the small, 1200-square-foot family shoe store to Harry Jubelirer, himself a second generation shoeman from Pittsburgh. Harry moved his small family 60 miles north to Sharon. At the time, there were six other shoe stores in the downtown area. The main store, still family owned, is now located in an old grocery store on South Water Street and lays claim to being "The World's Largest Shoe Store." The store encompasses 36,000 square feet and has more than 100,000 pairs of shoes in its inventory. Reyers fits women sizes 4 through 14, from AAAA to EE, men's sizes 6 through 22 available in AA through EEEEEE. The remodeling of this downtown outlet store dates to the 1950s.

CROSS OVER THE SHENANGO RIVER ON THE STATE STREET BRIDGE.

9. First National Bank
7 West State Street

The First National Bank of Sharon, one of the oldest and most reliable banks of western Pennsylvania, was founded in 1868, John J. Spearman, the iron manufacturer of more than sixty years standing and one of the most influential men in this part of the state, having been one of its incorporators and its president since January, 1872.

There was but one other incumbent of that office, George Prather, the first president, who died in the latter part of 1871. In 1875 the bank erected an excellent building on State Street, which, with alterations and improvements to conform to modern requirements, is still occupied.

10. The Winner
32 West State Street

Housed in an 1888 building, The Winner, "The World's Largest Off-Price Fashion Store, opened in 1989. The Winner boasts "four floors of savings ... great customer service ... better than outlet prices ... over 100,000 square feet of merchandise ... no seconds or rejects."

11. Columbia Theatre
62 West State Street

The Columbia Theatre first opened on November 29, 1922, as part of the Columbia Amusement Company's system of company-owned vaudeville facilities. New York architect Arland W. Johnson designed the 1,732-seat performance hall with imported marble staircases to the balcony, ornate plaster medallions and grillwork, full stage, orchestra pit, and seven dressing rooms. The Columbia was hailed as the "finest theatre between Pittsburgh and Erie.

On January 29, 1981, while operating as a single-screen movie house, fire started in the adjacent Morgan Grand building that had one been a Victorian-era opera house. The Morgan Grand was destroyed and the Columbia heavily damaged, and closed. In 1984, on the 62nd anniversary of the once-majestic theater's opening, it was purchased by Sharon native Tony Butala, founding member of The Lettermen vocal group, at a tax sale for $10,500. Since then, despite volunteer efforts at restoration the Columbia, now owned by the Vocal Group Hall of Fame, co-founded by Butala, has resisted efforts at re-opening.

12. St John's Episcopal Church
226 West State Street

The formation of a community of Episcopalians in and about Sharon took place in the 1860s, and the first public service of the church was held by Reverend Thomas Corlett, on December 10, 1865. The cornerstone of the first parish church was laid some eight months later. The present church, built in a Norman Gothic style, dates to 1895.

13. Sacred Heart Church,
40 South Irvine Street at State Street

During the building of the Pittsburgh & Erie Canal a large number of Catholics were employed on that public work, and missionary priests made periodical trips along the line of the canal to hold services and minister to the spiritual wants of the members of that faith. Sharon being one of the principal points on the route, was also one of the places where mass was occasionally celebrated. It was, however, some years after this period before the town possessed any Catholic settlers and it wasn't until 1864, when the cornerstone of the Sacred Heart Church was laid, that a proper church was built for services.

14. First Baptist Church
301 West State Street

Reverend David Philips came to the Sharon community as a missionary in 1802, and after working in this vicinity about two years gathered the Baptists into a regular organization in April, 1804. William Budd donated a lot for a church and graveyard, and the first building to be erected there was a log church twenty by thirty feet in dimensions. This was in 1807.

The log church served for 36 years until it was removed and replaced with a frame church. The current brick structure, erected at a cost of $15,000, was dedicated in 1884.

15. Donald V. Sawhill Memorial Center
   #### 300 West State Street

Donald V. Sawhill arrived in Sharon in 1935 as a receiver to close out a tube mill, which had 50 employees. Instead, within a few months he had the plant making money, eventually employing 1,200 workers. His grand symmetrical Colonial Revival home, rife with Palladian windows, is now the home to the United Way.

TURN AND RETRACE YOUR STEPS DOWN THE HILL ON WEST STATE STREET BACK TO THE TOUR STARTING POINT.

Look Up,

Stroudsburg

A Walking Tour of Stroudsburg...

Stroudsburg stands on the site of Fort Hamilton, built in 1756 at the direction of Benjamin Franklin. It was one of a chain of frontier forts built to protect European settlers from Indian attacks. In 1760, Jacob Stroud, a former indentured servant, settled on land along the Pocono, McMichaels, and Brodhead Creeks, which later powered his grist and sawmills. Following the bloody Wyoming Valley Massacre in 1778, Stroud built a stockade around his house and substantial land holdings. The Stroud compound later became known as Fort Penn, which stood on what is today the 500 block of Main Street.

Stroudsburg is the oldest town in the region, founded a generation before Monroe County was created. Jacob Stroud advertised the subdivision of his property on October 17, 1799 in the *American Eagle*, a newspaper published in Easton, then the county seat for the entire area, thusly: "Looking to dispose on very reasonable terms to mechanics and others, who will build upon the lots. A condition of building within three years will be part of every contract, and therefore no person need apply for a lot unless he is determined to become an improver of the town which will hence forward be called Stroudsburg."

The streets were named for his relatives, and lots sold quickly. Stroudsburg had attracted enough people and commerce by 1815 to incorporate as a borough and it was a popular choice for a county seat when Monroe County was created in 1836. Still, real growth did not come until it rode into town on the rails of the Delaware, Lackawanna and Western Railroad that linked Stroudsburg to New York City in 1856. The population would triple over the remainder of the 19th century.

Lumber mills, tanneries, and textile mills along McMichaels Creek powered the early economy. About 1853, Ephram Culver built a grist mill, only to see it burned by Indians. Later, more mills were built. Many were destroyed by floods. The present dam, believed to be built before 1884, diverted water to mills and factories along lower Main Street via a mill race which has long since been buried. Eventually all would cede importance to the tourist trade in the Pocono Mountains.

Our walking tour will start at the house of the man who started the town...

1. Stroud Mansion
900 Main Street

The historic 1795 Stroud Mansion is acknowledged as the finest example of Georgian-style architecture in Monroe County. It features such classical details as a symmetrical facade, flat-arch window lintels with pronounced keystones, simulated stone walls and quoins that accentuate the corners, plus tooth-like dentils beneath the cornice. Built by Jacob Stroud, founder of Stroudsburg and a Revolutionary War colonel, as a home for his eldest son, John, the 12-room house was an imposing structure in its day. John lived here for only a few years before moving to another home outside of town; the property remained in the Stroud family until 1893. It did time as the town library and since 1921 has been home to the Monroe County Historical Association.

CROSS THE STREET, TURN RIGHT AND WALK UP HALF-A-BLOCK.

2. Monroe County Bar Association
913 Main Street

This building was built in the early 1900s for John Kern, a transitional house between the Queen Anne and Colonial Revival styles. Starting in 1947, the building was used for the Monroe County Public Library, and was renovated to become home to the Monroe County Bar Association. Several features in the house are original, including leaded glass windows, stained glass windows and shutters, and pocket doors.

RETRACE YOUR STEPS, WALKING EAST ON MAIN STREET, TOWARDS THE TOWN CENTER. STAY ON THE SOUTH SIDE OF THE STREET.

3. George Tillotson House
905 Main Street

This picturesque house was built around 1880 for Judge Samuel and Sallie Dreher. Dreher gained national recognition at the the time as one of the presiding judges in a series of sensational murder trials between 1875 and 1877 involving the radical group of Irish mine workers known as the Molly Maguires. The workers engaged in sporadic collective violent protest characteristic in rural areas and Dreher's rulings helped break the society. Before his election as judge, he served as president of the Stroudsburg National Bank.

It is the only survivor of three similar mansions located along Main Street in the late 1800s and is the finest example of Second Empire architecture in Monroe County. George Tillotson purchased the house in 1892 when he arrived in Stroudsburg to supervise the Ryle Silk Mill that operated in East Stroudsburg. After a century of residential service the house was converted into a restaurant in the 1980s and retains most of its stylistic features, including a patterned mansard roof, porthole dormers, decorative window hoods and brackets and a central pavilion.

4. Stroudsburg National Bank
southeast corner of Main Street and 7th Street

Until this century, a bank had occupied this prominent corner in Stroudsburg for over 140 years. In the 1850s the Stroudsburg National Bank was organized; one of its original directors was Jay Gould, then in his early 20s. Gould would soon amass one of America's great fortunes in railroads. when he died in 1892, he left $77 million to his heirs.

An appropriately somber, temple-fronted vault was built here for the bank in 1857. In 1893 this Richardsonian Romanesque-style building replaced the first bank. In the 1920s the bank expanded along both Main and Seventh streets and its first floor facade received a classical makeover with columns and smooth-faced stone. The bank is gone but the original vault remains in the rear of the retail store.

5. Dunkelberger's
585 Main Street

Dunkelberger's Sports Outfitter started as a one man shop on North 6th Street in February 1972. Since moving to Main Street, a series of expansions has united diverse buildings under a single retail banner. The eastern section was once the store and residence of Darius Dreher, dating to 1865. A four-bay Italianate addition came along a few years later, now the center section of the retail operation. Architects T.I. Lacey & Son created the corner edifice as a lodge for the Freemason Society in 1890. The Masonic Building featured a commercial storefront on the ground floor and meeting space upstairs. The building features elements of the Romanesque Revival style such as an arcaded corbel table and terracotta panels above the third-story windows.

6. First Presbyterian Church
575 Main Street

Moravian Brethren from the Bethlehem area came into the community in 1743. The Presbyterians also responded to the call of the "Great Awakening" in 1744 with the arrival of David Brainerd of Connecticut. The Brainerd Presbyterian Church in Snydersville bears his name. from these seed sprung the Presbyterian church in Monroe County.

7. Malta Temple
565 Main Street

The Malta Temple was built in 1904 for a fraternal society known as the Knights of Malta but this site is best known as the former home of the L'homemedieu Music publishing company. The storefont has been altered but the stone ornamentation and columns flanking the windows remain as evidence of its original Romanesque Revival architectural style.

8. Stroudsburg United Methodist Church
547 Main Street

Circuit riding preachers first visited Stroudsburg in 1788 and held Methodist services in private homes. The first Methodist house of worship appeared around 1830 on Eighth Street. The Main Street church was dedicated in 1854 and enlarged in 1871. This church building, with stonework imitating English Gothic Revival church architecture, dates to 1915.

CROSS THE STREET TO THE
SHERMAN THEATER.

9. Sherman Theater
524 Main Street

A proud tradition of entertainment on this site began in 1776 when Jacob Stroud had an orchestra perform for guests at his large mansion here. Later, a stockade was constructed, and the Stroud mansion became Fort Penn. The Sherman Theater opened on January 7, 1929 with Stan Laurel and Oliver Hardy headlining. Daily matinees were offered at 2:30 p.m. and evening shows at 7:00 and 9:00. The Sherman continued to offer vaudeville until touring acts disappeared from the American landscape, after which it became a movie house.

Like many of its cousins across America, the Sherman struggled in the face of suburban flight in the 1960s and 1970s. To stave off the inevitable the theater was twinned and even took to screening X-rated adult fare. The Sherman closed its doors on December 28, 1983.

The Sherman was kept alive when a small group of East Stroudsburg University students campaigned to save the theater and transform it into a performing arts center in the late 1980s. Despite non-existent maintenance and sporadic bookings the theater soldiered on until it was burglarized in November 1993. It went mostly dark for a decade before it was renovated and reopened in 2005 and is once again a premier performance venue.

WALK BACK WEST
ON MAIN STREET.

10. Wyckoff Department Store
564 Main Street

The Wyckoff Department Store began in 1875 as "The New York Store, Wyckoff, Cooke and Bell." It would remain a downtown Stroudsburg icon for more than a century. Amzi Wyckoff, the store's founder, became its sole owner in 1892. Wyckoff's closed in 1981, not long after the Stroud Mall opened north of town.

11. Hollinshead Block
636 Main Street

Although it was altered into a flat-roofed box in the 1930s, this building, known as the Hollinshead Block, has anchored one of the prime corners of downtown Stroudsburg for over 100 years. Some of the original Romanesque Revival details remain from its construction in the early 1890s such as heavy stone window arches and decorative terra-cotta panels beneath the belt course. In its early days it housed a grocery store, clothing store and law offices.

TURN RIGHT ON 7TH STREET.

12. Metzgar Buildings
west side of Courthouse Square

The Metzgar Buildings, constructed circa 1870, were once owned by local physicians Thomas and Marshall Metzgar. Note the paired, pointed arch windows in the dormers, a Gothic Revival stylistic detail.

13. Monroe County Court House
Courthouse Square

Here once stood the original brick courthouse of Monroe County, built in 1836 when it was created out of Northampton, Pike and Wayne counties. In 1890 it was demolished, the bricks carted away and a new native sandstone courthouse in the Richardsonian Romanesque style was created by T.I. Lacey, Stroudsburg's architect of choice. A 1934 addition to the rear mimics the building's original features. The courthouse is on the *National Register of Historic Places*.

STAY ON 7TH STREET, WALKING ON THE WEST SIDE OF COURT-HOUSE SQUARE (THE COURT-HOUSE IS ON YOUR RIGHT).

14. Stroudsburg Fire Department
700 Sarah Street

The Stroudsburg Chemical and Hook and Ladder Company #1 was formed in 1909 and the 40 members set about raising funds for the purchase of a truck and equipment. The first apparatus would be a hand-drawn Kanawha system chemical and hose cart, costing $1200 fully equipped. The next year arrangements were made with the borough to lease the old County House, which was completely remodeled. Also that year the borough created The Stroudsburg Fire Department, combining the Chemical Company #1 and Phoenix Fire Company #2. Phoenix had been the first fire company of Stroudsburg, organized in 1845.

TURN LEFT ON SARAH STREET.

15. Academy Hill Historic District
north of Sarah Street, between 8th Street and 5th Street

Sarah Street is the southern boundary of the Academy Hill Historic District, a residential area that reflects the tremendous growth in Stroudsburg in the latter decades f the 1800s. Most of the high-style homes were not architect-designed but were the product of big city influences filtered through pattern books and executed by the talents of local carpenter-builders. Thomas Street, one block to the north, developed into the finest residential street in town, noted for its shade trees and well-kept lawns.

This block of Sarah Street exhibits none of the picturesque attributes of the Italianate and Gothic and Queen Anne styles in the rest of the neighborhood. Instead, they represent a conservative folk-building tradition that produced boxy structures built on the end gables.

TURN LEFT ON 8TH STREET.

16. 800 Monroe Street

It was not unusual for rural dwellers to come into town to spend winters in the late 1700s and early 1800s. This early 19th-century townhouse is a good example of such a house that could have served up needed comfort and convenience. The two-story Federal townhouse is similar to those found in Philadelphia and New York City with large windows surmounted by flat lintels, a fanlight above the front door and quarter-circular windows in the gable end. The Federal style of architecture, also known as Adamesque, was the dominant American building style from 1790 to 1820.

17. Zion United Church of Christ
14 North 8th Street

In 1882, Zion's Reformed Church was founded in Stroudsburg as a mission congregation of the German Reformed Church.

TURN RIGHT ON MAIN STREET.

18. 800-804 Main Street

This row of high-design eclectic houses recall a time of prominence in Stroudsburg at the beginning of the 20th century. Joseph H. Shull, a physician and attorney, commissioned T.I. Lacey & Son of Binghamton, New York to design his house at No. 800 in 1890. The Stick Style house features a two-story front porch and terra-cotta panels on the east facade. Robert Bixler, owner of the venerable Bixler Hardware store, blended elements of the Colonial (classical columns) and Tudor (half-timbering) revival styles for his house at No. 802. Next door, the stylish tower dominates the 1910-era home. It was subdivided into apartments in the 1950s; the other two buildings found new life as law offices, a common fate of large, older Stroudsburg homes.

CONTINUE WALKING ONE-HALF BLOCK BACK TO THE TOUR STARTING POINT AT THE CORNER OF 9TH STREET AND MAIN STREET.

Look Up,

Titusville

A Walking Tour of Titusville...

There was never any first discovery of oil. Petroleum had been known for thousands of years, gurgling from oil springs or seeps bubbling to the surface. It was used as medicine and for light in its natural state despite a nasty odor. In the early 1850s a number of people began experimenting with refining crude oil to improve its burning properties and eradicate its foul smell. They were successful enough that the demand for kerosene would soon outstrip the supply of oil.

The Seneca Oil Company of New Haven, Connecticut, leased land in western Pennsylvania and skimmed petroleum off oil springs in the region. In 1858 Edwin L. Drake was sent to Titusville, a town founded in 1800 by two former surveyors for the Hoeland Land Company, Jonathan Titus and Samuel Kerr who purchased land and established residences, to find a way to increase production. At first he tried digging but soon decided to drill a well, similar to the way saltwater was excavated. Progress was slow; the soft glacial till around Oil Creek kept caving into the hole. Drake finally hit on the idea of driving a pipe down to bedrock and drilling inside it.

It was not long before Drake's ingenuity paid off. On August 27, 1859, 69 feet inside the earth, he struck pay dirt in the world's first oil well. He was lucky; had he drilled a few yards in either direction he would have had to go down another 100 feet to tap his oil reservoir. A pump was attached to his well and soon Drake was producing about 20 barrels of oil a day, double the rate of production of all existing sources at the time. Speculators soon lined Oil Creek with derricks and pumps.

The world had never seen anything like it. Boomtowns burst into existence over-night. One town, Pithole City, went from a farm to a city of 15,000 people to a ghost town all in a span of 500 days. Titusville reigned as "Queen City" of the region for little more than a decade before the action drifted away. Drake himself made no fortune from oil. The glut of oil drove the price so low by 1862 that he was out of business. He processed leases for speculators and later lost money in oil speculation. He died 30 years after his historic strike, a poor and forgotten man.

The first great development period in Titusville was lumber related and the lumber industry did not end with the oil boom. The early oil boom years only served to increase the demand for wood used in the production of shipping barrels, the construction of derricks, worker housing and other community buildings. Our walking tour will visit the Titusville Historic District built on these riches, nominated to the *National Register of Historic Places* in 1984, that is a compact representation of the town's development from the beginning of the oil industry through the turn of the 20th century...

1. **Western NY & PA Railway Station**
   west side of South Perry Street, south of
   Mechanic Street

The Western New York and Pennsylvania Railway was formed on February 14, 1883 from the consolidation of the Buffalo, New York and Philadelphia Railway, the Buffalo, Pittsburgh & Western, the Olean and Salamanca Railroad, and the Oil City and Chicago Railroad. By 1887 the line was in receivership and sold at foreclosure, eventually to be taken over by the Pennsylvania Railroad in 1900. The freight station was renovated in 1988 to serve as a short-line freight line.

TURN LEFT AND WALK NORTH ON PERRY STREET.

2. **Titusvlle Iron Works**

Once used to manufacture oil industry engines and boilers, this facility was the major supplier of big artillery guns and shells to the Navy during World War II. Today, buildings on both sides of the street house Charter Plastics Company.

3. **Scheide Park**
   bounded by Perry, Central, Washington and Spring streets

John Scheide was a Titusville businessman and world-famous book collector. He created this greenspace by demolishing all the buildings on the block except the Second National Bank. The park contains a gazebo, a fountain, a time capsule to be opened in 2096, and memorials to military veterans from George Washington to Desert Storm.

4. **Church of Christ**
   221 West Main Street, southeast corner of Perry Street and Main Street

The Universalist denomination was one of three churches in Titusville prior to the birth of the oil industry in 1859. It is a unique example of Greek Revival architecture with Italianate elements. Constructed of red brick with arched windows and door moldings, the wooden octagonal clock and bell tower were originally topped by a dome and a spire.

TURN RIGHT ON MAIN STREET.

5. **James P. Thomas House**
   224 West Main Street

James P. Thomas, born in Genesee County, New York was elected Mayor of Titusville, on the Republican ticket, on February 19, 1884. After seeing considerable service in the Civil War and being wounded both at Antietam and Gettysburg, Thomas came to Titusville in 1865 and engaged in the business of producing oil with the Roberts Torpedo Company. Thomas shot his first oil well with nitroglycerine in 1870 and was involved with many patent infringement suits brought by the company. The three-story red brick structure with dark woodwork in the Queen Anne style was built about 1890. It incorporates a gabled roof with iron balustrade and sandstone key and end stones on window heads.

6. **W.H. Abbott House**
   215 West Main Street

In December 1865 William H. Abbott acquired a part interest in the Van Syckel pipeline from Jonathan Watson, oil operator and officer of the First National Bank of Titusville. W.H. Abbott and Henry Harley formed an important company in 1866 by combining Harley's Benninghoff Run - Shaffer pipeline and Abbott's share of the Van Syckel pipeline. This was the beginning of the Abbott and Harley pipelines - America's first great pipeline company. Abbott established a market for oil in New York, invested in the Miller Farm to Pithole Railroad, and contributed to the Pithole/Titusville plank road.

His house was designed in 1870 by his son-in-law H. E. Wrigley, an oil region cartographer. Robert McKelvy, a director of the Commercial Bank of Titusville, purchased the house across from his parents in 1903 and radically altered the house, removing its Victorian cupola and refitting the house in the popular Colonial Revival style of the day. The house has a front pediment and lunette, and a large porch with fluted Ionic columns and semicircular pavilion.

7. Scheide House
214 West Main Street

This clapboard Queen Anne adaptation dates to 1884 and has a multi-gabled slate roof with iron cresting and wooden shingle trim. Oilman John H. Scheide was educated at Princeton University and by 1880 had amassed a personal library that included a Guttenberg Bible. Part of this valuable collection was given to Princeton and part of it became the foundation of the Drake Well Museum Research Library.

8. J.L. Chase Home
204 West Main Street

J.L. Chase was a lumberman and retail merchant who became a partner in the Chase and Stewart Block in 1896. His Queen Anne home is one of the oldest brick residences in Titusville. It was later owned by Byron Benson who organized the Tidewater Pipeline Company in an effort to avoid Standard Oil's transportation monopoly.

9. Isaac Shank Home
118 West High Street

Isaac Shank was a retail merchant who moved into lumbering. When he died at age 97 in 1936, he was one of Titusville's oldest citizens. His Colonial Revival-style home, built in the early 1900s, features a gabled roof and dormers, a projecting central pavilion with front columns and two-story porches. Today, it is Titusville Apartments.

TURN LEFT ON HYDE STREET AND WALK ON THE WEST (LEFT) SIDE OF THE STREET.

10. Hyde House
201 North Franklin Street

This two-story Italianate brick house, dating to the 1860s, has wide eaves lined with paired brackets, a cupola with eyebrow cornices and window heads, flat-roofed open porches, and carved panels over the doors. Built on property owned by Jonathan Titus, the home was owned by Charles Hyde, founder of the Second National Bank and stockholder in the Tidioute and Warren Oil Company. It was later purchased by oil producer John Fertig and donated to the YWCA. This house and the Chase residence are the oldest brick homes in Titusville. The white oak tree in the yard was standing before the founding of Pennsylvania.

11. Benson Memorial Library
213 North Franklin Street

This two-story red brick Colonial Revival style building is reminiscent of the carriage style library. It has a hipped roof, sandstone entablature, paired Ionic columns supporting the pediment, and a Palladian style entrance. The vestibule is made of Knox and Italian marble.

CROSS THE STREET AND TURN TO WALK SOUTH ON FRANKLIN STREET.

12. First Presbyterian Church
216 North Franklin Street

The early Scotch-Irish established a small Presbyterian congregation in 1802, the first in Titusville. They began by worshipping outdoors or in barns. By 1815 they had built a primitive log meeting house, which was soon followed by a larger structure of hewn logs. The third building of framework was placed on land donated by Jonathan Titus. He and Samuel Kerr, co-founders of the town, were original incorporators of the church.

The population continued to increase during the oil boom. A larger church featuring a "battened" style of construction was built at the corner of Franklin and Walnut streets. By 1887 plans were completed for yet a larger building. The battened church was moved southeast on the lot and continued to serve as a chapel and social hall. In 1888 the fifth, and current, church was dedicated.

13. St. James Memorial Episcopal Church
112 East Main Street at northeast corner of Franklin Street

The Bishop of Pennsylvania, deciding it was important to establish a mission in the boisterous new oil region, sent the Reverend Henry Purdon to gather a congregation. The first membership was small and, belying the objective of the mission, consisted mostly of women. The cornerstone for the church was laid on September 14, 1863 at the exact geographic center of town. The church became the town's first permanent place of worship and may also be the first permanent building of any kind in Titusville. Edwin Drake served as its first warden and treasurer. This Gothic Revival stone structure which, with improvements since made, cost about $20,000, has maintained much of its interior detail work, including the Tiffany windows in the baptistery.

14. Kingsland House
107 North Franklin Street

Nelson Kingsland owned timber land, cleared it, and sold the lumber in the early 1860s to the contractors building Titusville's houses. This building was remodeled in Greek Revival fashion as the grand Bush Hotel in 1865. Likely added at the time were the large pediment supported by full-height, fluted columns with prominent Ionic capitals that dominate the Franklin Street facade. The small window with the semicircular hood seen in the pediment is inconsistent with the rectilinear and angular nature of Greek Revival. This structure has served as Titusville's City Hall since 1872.

15. Chase and Stewart Block
west side of Franklin Street between Spring and Central streets

Built as three separate structures with Italianate treatment in the 1870s, the southernmost section became known as the Cohen Building, which housed a men's clothing and haberdashery store. The middle section, completed last, has a unique slate mansard roof containing a spacious fourth floor. The E. K. Thompson Drug Store was established in this section in 1865. The northernmost section, known as the S. S. Bryan building,

housed a hardware store until 1994. Famed oil photographer John Mather's studio was located upstairs in the buildings.

16. First National Bank Building
northeast corner of South Franklin and Diamond streets

This three-story Italianate building is the oldest brick commercial structure in Titusville, erected in 1864. It has a wide, plain entablature, dentiled ornate eyebrow windows, and segmental hood moldings. It became the Western Union Telegraph Office in 1871.

TURN RIGHT ON SPRING STREET.

17. Reuting Block
122-126 West Spring Street

This eclectic style building from 1891 has a corbelled parapet and projecting second floor bay windows. The second story housed the Midland Oil Company of J. L. and J. C. McKinney. J. C. McKinney was one of three businessmen who established the Titusville Trust Company.

18. Titusville Trust Company
127 West Spring Street

This Beaux Arts adaptation is characterized by massive stone construction, a parapet with central statuary, and segmental moldings around the windows. "There are few bank buildings in America which equal this in permanence and quality of construction...," remarked architect Arthur Zimm. The *Titusville Herald* reported that "...few were prepared for the beauties revealed when its doors were thrown open..."

The building featured specially selected types of marble, cork floors for the tellers, broad windows to "provide the best of ventilation," and a vault "equipped with every known burglar proof and safety device." Alfred Valiant painted the ceiling mural showing oil industry history around his memorial portrait of Edwin Drake. The basement housed a barber shop, locker rooms, ice-making plant, fur storage room, elaborate chandeliers, manicure and hair dressing rooms and public bath parlors.

19. **site of the world's first oil exchange**
    north side of Spring Street, northwest
    corner of Exchange Place

The Titusville Oil Exchange was formed in 1871 by independent oil producers, to strategize and stabilize a growing and highly competitive industry, sell shares of stock, establish prices, and enter into refining agreements. Before a formal exchange was formed, producers often discussed industry business along Centre Street and in nearby business establishments. A rail car was even outfitted - complete with cigars and whiskey - for such purposes.

As the industry matured a new venue emerged and the Exchange was formally housed in the American Hotel that stood on this spot. It moved to other sites before returning here in a new three-story brick building in 1881. Eventually John D. Rockefeller's South Improvement Company and its dominance of Pennsylvania's oil industry negated the need for the exchange. It dissolved in 1897. The building was razed in 1956.

20. **Algrunix Building**
    northeast corner of South Washington
    and West Spring streets

This two-story Victorian Gothic building with ornate brick work is distinguished by oriels, various corbel tables, niches, arches, and is unique for its distinctive corner turret with wooden shingles. Built in 1894, it was named from the last names of three owners: prominent building contractor Edward Allen, Samuel Grumbine, an attorney who trained himself well enough to be admitted to the bar in 1875; and wife of a local building contractor Hattie Nixon.

21. **Second National Bank**
    northwest corner of South Washington
    and West Spring streets

This eclectic style brick-and-sandstone bank with Gothic overtones from 1865 was originally four stories high with a mansard roof. The roof was eliminated in 1918 and replaced with its present remodeled parapet. Charles Hyde's Second National Bank, is now known as the Park Building, but its former name remains elegantly engraved across the façade.

22. **Titusville *Herald***
    208 North Wsahington Street

This is the fifth site for The Titusville *Morning Herald* that published its first issue on June 14, 1865, the area's first daily newspaper. Owner Joseph M. Bloss changed the name to simply *The Titusville Herald* in 1913 prior to its purchase in 1922 by E. T. Stevenson. Throughout most of its history, the paper was owned by those two local families. The first home of *The Herald* was a three-story structure on South Franklin Street in the Millers Block which burned in December of 1865. Its fourth home was the first in its own building, on the corner of Franklin and Arch streets. That move took place in 1873; operations in this building began in 1956.

WALK ONE-HALF BLOCK TO PERRY STREET AND TURN LEFT TO RETURN TO THE TOUR STARTNG POINT.

Look Up,

Uniontown

A Walking Tour of Uniontown...

Uniontown is unusual for Western Pennsylvania towns in that it did not grow on a navigable river and it is also unique for having not one boom, but two. The first great growth spurt took place from 1811 to the 1850s with the construction of the National Road from Cumberland, Maryland to Wheeling, West Virginia and eventually into Illinois. Uniontown became an important stop on the road, with stagecoach factories, stage and wagon yards, stables and blacksmith shops and at least a dozen taverns to serve weary travelers. After the railroad reached Wheeling in 1852 the National Road gradually diminished in importance and devolved into a local market road. How quiet did it become in Uniontown? Only eight buildings extant in the historic district were built between 1860 and 1880.

Then came the coal and coke boom and Uniontown bubbled with activity for the next 50 years, until the Great Depression. The existence of soft, bituminous coal in the region had been known since Henry Beeson settled here and built a mill on Redstone Creek in 1768. But when the hungry mills in Pittsburgh demanded coke distilled from coal to make steel they turned to the coal fields in their back yard, which just happened to possess immense deposits of the best metallurgical coal in the world. Uniontown had three major mines and tens of thousands of beehive coke ovens nearby but its principal contribution was as the operational and financial center of the coal and coke industry. These new coal barons liked to build - in 1912 Uniontown counted in its downtown nine banks, 13 theaters and 14 hotels.

That's not the Uniontown you will experience today. Our walking tour of the quieter streets of the 21st century will begin at the site of the boyhood home of one of the 20th century's most accomplished men, a place that has been transformed into Uniontown's Gateway...

1. **George C. Marshall Memorial Plaza**
   Fayette Street, Mt. Vernon Avenue, and
   Main Street

The George C. Marshall Memorial Plaza is located in the birthplace and boyhood home of the General of the Army, Secretary of State and 1953 Nobel Peace Prize winner as architect of the Marshall Plan that rebuilt Europe following World War II. George Catlett Marshall was born the son of a a prosperous coke and coal merchant in 1880 and lived here until leaving for the Virginia Military Institute. Marshall, who was twice named *Time* magazine's "Man of the Year," returned to Uniontown three times, the last in 1954, five years before his death, to dedicate the restoration of George Washington's Fort Necessity.

The plaza, sited at the locally known "Five Corners," includes narrative plaques, rare historical photographs, a statue of the General, the Flags of Nations and an arched bridge over Coal Lick Run where Marshall played as a boy. It also contains statues of everyday soldiers - a World War I "doughboy" and a World War II "GI."

WALK EAST ON MAIN STREET.

2. **White Swan Apartments**
   117 West Main Street

There has been a White Swan on this site since 1805 when a tavern of that name operated here. A six-story brick building was constructed in 1925 as the White Swan Hotel. There is a projecting circular ballroom in the rear. The White Swan of the 21st century is an apartment house for the elderly.

3. **Titlow Tavern**
   92 West Main Street

George Flavius Titlow bought the Frost House, built in 1890, in 1905 and acquired its first liquor license for the enterprise. He solicited some of the town's millionaires to invest in the Titlow Hotel. George also bought the Lingo Block adjacent to the Frost House on the west side. He extended the building upward four floors and back to Peter Street. His grand opening on May 16, 1906 brought 1500 guests. It was the most luxurious hotel in the region. Titlow sold the hotel in 1923 during Prohibition saying that he could not run a hotel without spirits.

4. **Knights of Pythius Building**
   84 West Main Street

This three-story brick Victorian Gothic building was constructed as a meeting hall for the Knights of Pythius in 1885. Next door the Strickler-Hess Renaissance Revival commercial building dates to 1903.

5. **Thompson-Ruby Building**
   southwest corner of Main Street and
   Morgantown Street

The most ornate presence in downtown Uniontown, with a distinctive rounded corner and topped by a gilded dome, the Renaissance Revival building was constructed as a bank in 1900. It is built of the finest materials of the day - brick, stone and terra-cotta.

6. **Fayette Bank Building**
   50 West Main Street, at northwest corner
   of Pittsburgh Street

This was the First National Bank Building when it was built in 1902 for coal baron Josiah Van Kirk Thompson. J.V. Thompson's fortune was second to none in the late 1800s but he did not own coal mines nor manufacture any products from coal - he was a speculator buying and selling coal lands. Thompson hired renowned skyscraper architect Daniel Burnham of Chicago to create the 11-story monument to his success. In 1915 the First National Bank failed triggering a downward spiral in Thompson's life that included a public and expensive divorce and a collapse in the coal industry. He died bankrupt in 1933.

Noted for its rounded corner overlooking Main and Morgantown streets, the renamed Fayette Bank Building was listed on the *National Register of Historic Places* in 1989. It now houses professional offices and apartments with a panoramic view of the surrounding city. The ornate main bank lobby remains intact, featuring a rounded corner of windows, a service counter, floors of terrazzo marble, and the original crown moldings.

7. **Federal Building**
    northwest corner of Pittsburgh Street and
    Peter Street

Now operating as a federal government office building, this was a high-style, low-slung Neoclassical post office from 1930, when it was constructed, until 1966. An unusual feature of this building is the row of gargoyles projecting from the facade above the Romanesque arched windows.

TURN AROUND AND WALK BACK
TO MAIN STREET. TURN LEFT AND
CONTINUE TRAVELING EAST.

8. **Heritage Plaza**
    northeast corner of Pittsburgh Street and
    Main Street

Another tribute to favorite son, George C. Marshall, here located at the junction of the roadways that unite Uniontown to both Pittsburgh and Morgantown. General Marshall is portrayed in a bronze statue sitting atop his horse "Apple Jack" with dog "Fleet" by his side.

9. **Gallatin National Bank**
    northwest corner of Main Street and
    Beeson Boulevard

The Gallatin National Bank was the only Uniontown bank to survive the Depression, perhaps aided by the imposing appearance of it headquarters with three-story tall Ionic columns across its front and fluted pilasters marching down its side. The eight-story granite building was constructed in 1924.

10. **Penn Theatre**
    5-9 East Main Street

The Penn Theatre was Uniontown's largest theater, built in 1913. It screened movies and hosted touring vaudeville shows. The theater closed in 1952 to accommodate a retail expansion on the block.

11. **Storey Square**
    11 East Main Street

Named in honor of local historian-journalist, Walter "Buzz" Storey, the square received a makeover in 2005. It features a canopied stage, a hand-painted 1,500-square foot mural on its east wall and hosts a variety of events throughout the year.

12. **State Theatre Center for the Arts**
    27 East Main Street

The State Theatre was hailed as "...the largest, finest and most beautiful playhouse in Western Pennsylvania" when it opened in 1922. It was designed by one of America's foremost theater architects, Thomas Lamb, celebrated for his fine acoustical planning in classically appointed Federal-style buildings. Seating 1,605 patrons, the interior was created by Ingstrip-Burke Company of Chicago, also in the Federal style of Robert Adam. On the bill were the finest vaudeville acts of the day and the latest silent movies. The State Symphony Orchestra held forth in the pit with a $40,000 Pleubet Master Organ. As music trends shifted and the Big Band sound emerged, the State hosted many of the country's greatest musical attractions including Paul Whiteman, Glen Gray and the Dorsey Brothers. When "talkies" arrived, the State was the third theater in the nation to employ projected sound films.

But even the the State Theatre was not exempt to the suburban flight of the 1960s and 1970s that led to the mass extinction of America's downtown movie palaces. It closed in June of 1973. A reincarnation as The State Music Hall didn't take but in 1988 the Greater Uniontown Heritage Consortium purchased the theatre, restored its name and, in 1989, began presenting a series of professional programs ranging from Broadway musicals to big bands, symphonies to country music superstars. Today, the Grand Old Lady of Main Street continues as a vibrant performing arts center.

13. **Alonzo Hagan Building**
    30 East Main Street

Alonzo Hagan, a Uniontown lawyer, built this elegant Renaissance Revival building in 1906. The ground floor formerly housed a theater, once a jewelry store and currently a restaurant.

14. **Union Trust Building**
    37-39 East Main Street at northwest corner of Gallatin Street

This five-story Renaissance Revival building was fitted into a narrow lot in 1905 as the Gallatin Hotel. Later it did duty as a bank.

15. **Gallatin Apartments**
    41 East Main Street

This sleek eight-story brick building was designed in the Moderne style in 1929 for a furniture store. It has since been converted into apartments for the elderly.

16. **Blackstone Building**
    50 East Main Street

This three-story stone building was constructed as law offices in 1897. With its arched doors and windows it was meant to complement the Richardsonian Romanesque styling of the courthouse nearby.

17. **Dawson Law Building**
    57 East Main Street

This wonderfully preserved Federal-style, two-story brick building has remained remarkably unaltered since its construction in 1832. It was built for use as law offices and has been used for that purpose for its entire history.

18. **Fayette County Courthouse**
    61 East Main Street

Built in 1847, Fayette County purchased the property where the courthouse stands from Uniontown's founder Henry Beeson for six pence which is the equivalent of about six cents today. The Richardson Romanesque structure was built out of local materials and features a clock tower along with a statue of the county's namesake Marquis de Lafayette in its lobby. The eight-foot wooden statue was carved in 1847 by David Blythe, who became one of the outstanding native-scenes artists of his century. Larger than life, the poplar planks are pinned together and his high hat is fashioned from tin. The statue periodically goes traveling to museums and art exhibits.

TURN LEFT DOWN COURT STREET IN FRONT OF THE COURTHOUSE (ON THE WEST SIDE).

19. **Fayette County Prison**
    northeast corner of Court Street and Peter Street

The county prison was constructed in the same Richardsonian Romanesque style with the same sandstone face as the adjoining courthouse, to which it is joined by a "Bridge of Sighs."

RETURN TO MAIN STREET AND TURN LEFT, CONTINUING TO TRAVEL EAST.

20. **County Building**
    61 East Main Street

The County Building was added to the government complex in 1927, built in a Spanish Colonial style. It is connected to its older siblings.

21. **Barnes Mansion**
    97 East Main Street

This beautifully symmetrical Georgian Revival mansion was erected in 1900 for coal baron James R. Barnes. Born in July, 1860, Barnes attended public school at Uniontown and then followed his father into the mines. He was able to transition into management and became one of the area's largest operators. The mansion has since been converted into law offices, as have two carriage houses to the rear.

TURN RIGHT ON CHURCH STREET.

22. **Central School**
    23 East Church Street

This large brick school building was constructed in the Collegiate Gothic style in 1916. The Central School was once called the Ella Peach School after a one-time educator. It was an elementary school for many years and is now used for administrative offices.

TURN LEFT ON BEESON STREET
AND CROSS FAYETTE STREET.

23. Asbury United Methodist Church
20 Dunbar Street at Beeson Street

Dedicated in 1919, built of Hummelstown brownstone, the church features Tiffany stained glass windows. It is the fourth building in town for this congregation that descends from the first Methodist church in Uniontown, founded in 1785.

RETURN TO BEESON STREET AND
TURN LEFT.

24. Great Bethel Baptist Church
47 West Fayette Street

Built in 1902, the entire complex is a uniform example of Gothic Revival architecture. This congregation descends from the first organized church of any denomination west of the Allegheny Mountains, founded in 1770. It succeeds a small log church and a simple, steepled building.

25. Trinity United Presbyterian Church
79 West Fayette Street at southwest corner of Morgantown Street

This traffic-stopping church was built in 1896 on designs by Pittsburgh architect William Kauffman in the French Gothic style, closely resembling Henry Hobson Richardson's landmark Trinity Church in Boston's Copley Square. It is built of Peninsula blue sandstone and roofed with deep red corrugated tile. The massive square lantern tower, soars 150 feet above the ground, dominating the downtown skyline. This is the congregation's third church; the first was erected in 1827 after Uniontown had been a stop on the Presbyterian church preaching circuit since 1799.

TURN LEFT ON
MORGANTOWN STREET.

26. St. Peter's Episcopal Church
60 Morgantown Street

Built in 1884 in the 14th Century English Gothic, the church features a Norman tower without a spire, an intricate patterned slate roof, and one Tiffany window. This was the home church of General George C. Marshall.

TURN AND WALK NORTH ON
MORGANTOWN STREET,
ACROSS FAYETTE STREET.

27. Robinson Building
26 Morgantown Street at South Street

This Queen Anne building was constructed in 1899, actually pre-dating the rounded corners that would distinguish its more illustrious neighbors on the next intersection at Main Street.

28. Whylel Building
43 Morgantown Street

This much-altered building began life as a Methodist church in 1878. The church moved to a new location in 1919. The steeple was removed and the building converted into a ground-level storeroom and apartments above.

TURN LEFT ON SOUTH STREET.

29. Old West School
75 West South Street

Enos West purchased a lot on South Street around 1820 on which stood a log building. He tore away the logs and erected several frames, one of which he made his home. He also built this log school house, perhaps crafted from the logs taken from the original house. It stands today as an example of a frontier one-room school.

CONTINUE TO FAYETTE STREET
AND TURN RIGHT TO RETURN TO
THE TOUR STARTING POINT.

Look Up,

Washington

A Walking Tour of Washington...

The French began staking claims to this land in 1669. In 1748, Virginia planters formed the Ohio Company to affect settlement in southwestern Pennsylvania and carry on Indian trade on a large scale. It took a decade - and a loss on the field at Fort Necessity by George Washington - before the British could expel the French and settlements began in the area of present Washington County. One of those clusters of log structures was "Bassett, alias Dandridge Town," laid out by John and William Hoge. Later named Washington, a log courthouse was constructed in 1787 to serve as the county seat of Washington County, the first county in the United States to be named in honor of General George Washington. Washington County was formed to allow "the inhabitants of the area west of the Monongahela River to have more convenient courts and public offices, rather than the inconvenience and hardship of being so far remote from the seat of justice."

A school was holding classes as early as 1781 and a newspaper and post office were in place by 1800. George Washington's early years as a surveyor enabled him to see the need for a "national" road through the Allegheny Mountains connecting the eastern seaboard centers with the Ohio Valley and the western frontier. Completed in 1818 and still in use today, the National Pike (Route 40) runs through Washington on Maiden Street. The town's influence and prestige grew steadily through the 1800s as one of the gateways for immigration to the West and its bustling commerce.

The region was built on the pillars of coal, steel, oil and glass and the town of "Little Washington" provided the support for these industries. At the height of its prosperity, in 1900, a magnificent, muscular county courthouse was constructed in the center of town and that is where our walking tour will get under way...

1. **Washington County Courthouse**
   southwest corner of Beau Street and Main Street

The Italian Renaissance Washington County Courthouse, from the pen of leading Pittsburgh architect Frederick Osterling, stands as one of Pennsylvania's most magnificent temples of justice. Completed in 1900 at the total cost of $1,000,000, this is the county's fourth courthouse. A log structure built in 1787 served as the first county courthouse when the town was still called Basset. Still in use today, the courthouse is constructed of Columbia sandstone from Cleveland, South Carolina granite, iron and steel, brick and cement - all rising 150 feet to a huge, classical dome supporting a larger than life statue of George Washington.

2. **Washington Trust Building**
   southwest corner of Beau Street and Main Street

Commerce came to this key corner in 1790 when John Purviance opened a tavern. Later operators added a log hotel and after that burned, the three-story brick American House was built here. That building and many of its neighbors burned in the early morning hours of January 6, 1899.

The replacement was another creation of Pittsburgh's leading architect of the age, Frederick J. Osterling. The major tenant of the six-story Washington Trust Building, was the city's first savings bank, the Dime Savings Institution. Said to be fireproof, it quickly became home to the offices of almost all of Washington's doctors and lawyers. The Elks Club occupied the entire sixth floor, and the main retail space on Main Street was taken by Woolworth's Five and Ten.

In 1922, the 10-story addition was added to the building by architect Jay W. Percowper, who also designed the George Washington Hotel, the Observer Publishing Co. building and Washington Hospital. Topping the 186-foot addition is a Neoclassical temple; the first level contains communication equipment, and the upper level houses the machinery that runs the elevators - all original and immaculately maintained.

WALK SOUTH ON MAIN STREET.

3. **Caldwell's Building**
   26 South Main Street

This is Washington's oldest commercial block; the ground floor of this hundred-year old building has been severely altered but the upper floors retain their decorative pilasters and balustraded cornice.

4. **Citizens Bank**
   40 South Main Street

This powerful Neoclassical vault with fluted Ionic columns became a Citizens Bank branch in 1948.

5. **George Washington Hotel**
   60 South Main Street

Lou Gehrig signed the guest book. So did Henry Ford. John F. Kennedy gave a speech to supporters from the marble steps of the Oval Room when he was on the campaign trail. Even the Beatles - John, Paul, George and Ringo - stayed here when they played the Civic Arena in Pittsburgh in 1964.

The 200-room George Washington Hotel was built in 1927, designed by renowned architect William Lee Stoddard to resemble the legendary Willard Hotel in Washington, D.C. The 10-story building boasted a two-story, balconied grand ballroom with hardwood floors and crystal chandeliers and a grand entrance on West Cherry Avenue that delivered guests into an exquisite marbled lobby. The walls of an elegant dining room told the story of the Whiskey Rebellion in the early 1790s via a series of murals by Washington artist Malcolm Parcell .

By the 1980s the George Washington had been converted into apartments. A series of negligent owners left it near condemnation in the early 2000s but a recent multi-million dollar restoration has brought the downtown landmark back to its former glory.

TURN RIGHT ON
WHEELING STREET.

6. Masonic Temple
   44 West Wheeling Street

Freemasonry is the world's oldest and largest fraternity. Many of our nation's early patriots were Freemasons, as well as 13 signers of the Constitution and 14 Presidents of the United States, including town namesake George Washington. Sunset Lodge No. 623 Free and Accepted Masons of Pennsylvania, constituted in 1901, is one of 95 chapters in the Commonwealth. This Federal-style building was given a Victorian update with a decorative cornice and a pair of prominent oriel windows.

7. Dr. Joseph Mauer House
   97 West Wheeling Street

Listed on the *National Register of Historic Places*, this corner house with Second Empire mansard roof and Italianate detailing was the home of Joseph Mauet, an early practitioner of homeopathic medicine in the late 1800s.

TURN LEFT ON FRANKLIN STREET. TURN LEFT ON MAIDEN STREET.

8. City Hall
   55 West Maiden Street

The current City Hall began life as a Neoclassical post office; you can still see the drive-in on the east side of the building where pick-ups were made.

TURN LEFT ON MAIN STREET.

9. Bradford House
   175 South Main Street

David Bradford was a successful lawyer, businessman, and Deputy Attorney General of Washington County. When this house was completed in 1788 it was said to be the finest house west of the Allegheny Mountains. Part of the inside woodwork was brought from England; the stone for the exterior was quarried near Washington and the house made quite an impression in a village of small, rustic, log buildings.

David Bradford and his family lived in this house until 1794 when his involvement as the leader of the "Whiskey Rebellion" led to a warrant for his arrest and he fled south to Spanish West Florida (which is present-day Louisiana). In that year the new federal government, which isolated settlers on the frontier scarcely recognized, imposed a high excise tax on whiskey. This tax was particularly onerous because local farmers typically converted their grain to whiskey to lessen the shipping expense. When federal tax collectors appeared in the area to collect these taxes, local mobs drove them off and President George Washington decided it was critical for the new government to enforce its laws. A militia of more than 12,000 men was assembled and George Washington took command to march from Harrisburg. It was one of only two times a sitting President personally commanded the military in the field. The rebellion was squashed without opposition and signaled to the new American people that changes to the law would have to take place through Constitutional means or the government would meet such treats to disturb the peace with force. Eventually, David Bradford received a pardon for his role in the Whiskey Rebellion. The house was converted into a furniture and coffin store in the early 1900s. In 1959, the Pennsylvania Historical and Museum Commission assumed control of the house and supervised a restoration back to its original 18th-century design.

WALK BACK DOWN TO MAIDEN STREET AND TURN LEFT.

10. LeMoyne House
   49 East Maiden Street

John Julius LeMoyne, a physician, built this stone block house in 1812. His son Francis Julius LeMoyne also became a successful doctor and builder of the first crematory in the western hemisphere. But he is best remembered as a social reformer who, despite the strict Fugitive Slave Law of 1850, risked his personal freedom and fortune to open his home as a stop along the Underground Railroad, a series of safe houses that harbored runaway slaves. The LeMoyne House is Pennsylvania's first National Historic Landmark of the Underground Railroad. Only about six or seven other such sites exist in the entire United States.

TURN LEFT ON COLLEGE STREET.

11. First Baptist Church
southwest corner of South College Street and East Wheeling Street

First Baptist Church was regularly constituted October 14, 1814, with eleven charter members, after having been in existence as a Mission since 1811. Seven of the members were from North Ten Mile Baptist Church, the oldest congregation in Washington County that traces its roots back to 1773. The first meeting house was built on Lot 77 of the original town plat on West Wheeling Street.

The congregation sputtered around the time of the Civil War but the town Baptists reorganized in the 1890s and built a new church on this site. It was replaced with this Colonial Revival building in 1931. To help defray the $176,000 price tag the ladies of the Church served luncheons during the Depression.

12. First Presbyterian Church
100 East Wheeling Street

The First Presbyterian Church of Washington was officially founded in 1793 and met in a stone academy, that presently houses administrative offices for Washington & Jefferson college. Dr. Matthew Brown, school president, was the first minister. The congregation later met in a local tavern and the courthouse, before building a church on Strawberry Avenue. In 1851, that building was sold to the Hays Carriage Company and a new Greek Revival church was built on the present site in 1851. The land was originally deeded to George and Martha Washington, but reverted back to the original owners, the Hough family. In the spring of 1868, building deficiencies required that the structure be taken down to the foundation and a third church built.

TURN RIGHT ON
EAST WHEELING STREET.

13. Old Main
northeast corner of East Wheeling Street and South College Street

At the time of its construction in 1836, "Old Main" was a simple, three-story brick building that served as the chapel and classrooms for Washington College that had not yet merged with Jefferson College. A decade later two wings and a dome were added in a Colonial make-over. With the dawn of the Victorian age Old Main took on its present appearance with a fourth floor and the two dominant towers that symbolize the union of Washington College and Jefferson College on March 4, 1865. To maintain the face of the school the building has undergone two sandblastings and new roofs in 1998.

14. Washington & Jefferson College Admissions House
60 South Lincoln Street at East Wheeling Street

This three-story Victorian mansion of 28 rooms was built in 1894 as the residence of Andrew Happer. The exterior of Missouri sandstone and frame features ornate trimmings and stained glass windows typical of the high-Victorian style of architecture. Happer enrolled in Washington College in 1859. His studies were interrupted by the Civil War, however, and he never received a degree from the College which now owns his home. The original parquet floors, massive carved staircase and brass trimmings are still intact.

15. Thompson Memorial Library
East Wheeling Street

Thompson Memorial Library opened in 1905, a gift to the Washington & Jefferson College from William R. Thompson as a memorial to his mother. The elegant Beaux Arts building was designed by Rutan & Russell of Pittsburgh with hand-laid mosaic tile floors and skylights.

16. President's House
33-41 South Sixth Street

Built in 1892 by the Duncan family, this Victorian mansion, a superior example of Queen Anne Victorian style, was presented to the college in

1944 by Walter Hudson Baker, class of 1907, in memory of his wife, Amy Duncan Baker. Trademarks of the style shown here include exterior "gingerbread" ornamentation, the stained, leaded, and beveled glass, and the recessed doors and windows with louvered wooden shutters. The house consists of seventeen rooms with a central hallway plan. The mansion has been the home to the college's presidents since its donation.

CONTINUE ON EAST WHEELING STREET AND ENTER THE EAST WASHINGTON HISTORIC DISTRICT.

This late Victorian residential neighborhood is awash in examples of Shingle Style, Queen Anne and Colonial Revival houses. Several large houses on elevated, panoramic lots can be found at the eastern edge of the Washington and Jefferson campus, some of which have become student housing. Streets ringing the campus are more tightly packed but no less picturesque with imaginative rooflines, turrets and fanciful porches. In a region where simple, vernacular residences ruled the streets, the East Washington Historic District marked a dramatic shift in fortunes and today represents one of the richest and most intact collections of fashionable turn-of-the-19th-century housing in southwestern Pennsylvania.

TURN LEFT ON SOUTH WADE AVENUE.

18. Church of the Covenant
267 East Beau Street

The Church of the Covenant had its beginnings when the First Presbyterian Church of Washington outgrew its facilities in 1860. The Second Presbyterian Church leased a building on Beau Street for 14 years and then built its first church building in 1887 at 65 East Beau Street. The present Gothic structure was erected in 1929. In 1959 the Third Presbyterian Church was forced out of its building by a redevelopment project and voted to merge with the Second Presbyterian Church to establish the Church of the Covenant.

19. Washington and Jefferson College
southwest corner of Lincoln Street and
Beau Street

Founded in 1781 by three Presbyterian ministers on the American frontier, this is the oldest college west of the Alleghenies. In September 1787, a charter was granted for an academy to be situated in Washington and on April 10, 1789, Washington Academy opened. The McMillan Building behind Old Main was built in 1793 and is the eighth oldest college structure still in use in the United States.

In 1794 the Canonsburg Academy and Library Company was established in nearby Canonsburg. In 1802, this school was chartered by the Pennsylvania legislature as Jefferson College. Four years later, Washington Academy received its charter as Washington College. Rivalry between the two small colleges, located only ten miles apart in a sparsely populated region, served to block the progress of both. When the Civil War drained enrollment dramatically, the schools were left on the verge of extinction.

In March 1865, the Pennsylvania legislature granted a charter for a united college, but with the provision that some classes be taught in Canonsburg and others in Washington. This arrangement proved impractical, and in 1869, the legislature authorized reorganization of the College. Two months later, the trustees voted that all departments be located in Washington. The bronze statue was unveiled in 2007.

20. First United Methodist Church
29 College Street, at Beau Street

The Methodist Society organized in 1784 in the cabin of Thomas Lackey, who lived southeast of the current town. His home was a preaching point on the Redstone Circuit, which was laid out by Francis Asbury, the first bishop of Methodism. A log church, the first church building in Washington, was erected in 1801. By 1816, to accommodate a growing congregation, a brick church was erected. President-elect Andrew Jackson attended service there in 1829 on his way to Washington, D.C. for his inauguration. In 1848, a third church building, also make of brick, was built on West Wheeling Street. President Ulysses S. Grant attended service in this church in 1871.

The current brick structure was completed in 1876. Many of the stained glass windows, including the majestic windows at the rear of the sanctuary, are original.

TURN RIGHT ON COLLEGE STREET. TURN LEFT ON CHESTNUT STREET.

21. Basle Theater
100 North Main Street, at northeast corner of Chestnut Street

The Art Deco Basle Theater opened on September 15, 1939 and was hailed as "The Theater of Tomorrow". It later became the Midtown, and survived until 1985, when it closed. A limited liability group purchased the theater in 2002 and now offers live performances. The theater is also used as a church. It helps anchor the town's blossoming art scene.

TURN LEFT ON MAIN STREET.

22. Davis Block
50 North Main Street

Although the ground floor of this 1883 building has been greatly altered the upper floors retain the tall, slender windows and decorative cornice of the Italianate commercial style that typified this block.

23. 3 North Main Street

This exuberant Beaux Arts, three-story commercial structure demonstrates a flourish of rounded arched windows under an elaborate cornice. Its face looks down on Main Street with paired Corinthian columns on the second and third floors.

YOU HAVE NOW REACHED THE TOUR STARTING POINT.

Look Up,

Wellsboro

A Walking Tour of Wellsboro...

Wellsboro was founded in 1806 by Quaker settlers from Delaware, Maryland and Philadelphia; it was incorporated in 1830. Tradition has long held that the little settlement was named in honor of Mary Wells, wife of one of the original settlers, Benjamin Wister Morris. It is her life-size bronze statue that stands at the Tioga County Historical Society but some historians have argued that the credit may belong to William Wells, Mary's brother.

This section of the state was part of the Connecticut Grant that extended the north and south boundaries of the colony of Connecticut all the way to the Great Lakes; consequently it was settled by many of the early New England colonists. The large houses set well back from the streets on spacious well-kept lawns are truly indicative of the planning of New England towns. Noted for beautiful elms, maple trees and wide boulevards with gas lights, Wellsboro has long been a favorite of travelers. The 50-mile long Grand Canyon of Pennsylvania is a scant ten miles from town.

Wellsboro's earliest period of growth, between the 1830s and the turn of the twentieth century, was at first of an agricultural character and later associated with the lumber industry. Commercial development in the downtown occurred in the wake of two major fires in the 1870s which destroyed much of the downtown. As rebuilding occurred, brick became the favored construction material and the extant character of the commercial portion of the historic district reflects this era of reconstruction. In 1872 the Lawrenceville and Wellsboro Railroad laid the first line into the community, followed in 1881 by the Jersey Shore, Pine Creek, & Buffalo. As the lumber industry waned it was followed by coal extraction and, most importantly, in the early 1900s, by the glass industry - light bulbs and then Christmas lights.

The Wellsboro Historic District was listed on the *National Register of Historic Places* in 2005. The architecture of the district reflects the level of maturity in Wellsboro at the turn of the twentieth century, by which time many of the resources in the district were in place. High-style houses were built for civic and industrial leaders, primarily along Main Street and West Avenue. A feature which adds considerably to the visual character of the district is found along portions of both Main Street and Central Avenue, which have boulevards with trees, grass, and Wellsboro's signature gas street lights mounted on cast iron poles.

Our walking tour will begin in the center of town around the New England-style Green and explore first the residential area along Main Street to the west and then come back and see the business district to the east...

1. **The Green**
   Main Street, west side of Central Avenue
   to Charles Street

Wellsboro's community park occupies a serene square in the heart of the community, dissected by walkways and sprinkled with mature trees. The centerpiece fountain is a bronze of children's literature characters Wynken, Blynken and Nod from Eugene Field's *The Dutch Lullaby*, penned in 1889. It was erected in 1938 and was dedicated to the memory of Elizabeth Bailey, the wife of community leader Fred Bailey. Of the other memorials and markers, the earliest is the *Soldiers and Sailors Memorial* which was dedicated on November 18,1886 and honors Tioga County's Civil War veterans. Among the other objects on the Green are a statue of a sailor honoring veterans of all wars, a commemorative stone remembering long-time newspaper editor and publisher Edwin Van Valkenberg and the 1886 John Magee statue which honors the founder of the locally-prominent Fall Brook Coal Company.

CROSS OVER TO THE NORTH SIDE OF MAIN STREET AND TURN LEFT, WALKING WEST.

2. **Sheriff's House and Jail / Wellsboro**
   Chamber of Commerce
   114 Main Street

This sturdy Italianate red brick structure was built in 1860 to serve as the Sheriff's House and Jail, which it did all the way until 1985 - a fine return on its $10,000 construction price tag. Of equal interest is the historic elm tree in the front yard that has been growing for over 200 years. In July, 2009 it lost a massive limb and the health of the tree that pre-dates the town is in question going forward.

3. **Tioga County Courthouse**
   118 Main Street

Tioga County was formed on March 26, 1804 from parts of Lycoming County. The name, derived from an Indian word meaning "the forks of a stream," honors the Tioga River. The county seat got this Colonial Courthouse, with cupola, in 1835. It is constructed of native sandstone and conglomerate, which was hauled on ox sleds for several miles over poor roads; high on the southwest wall is carved the outline of an eagle, insignia of one of the stonecutters from the neighboring Welsh settlement.

4. **Robinson House**
   120 Main Street

This building was originally a tavern and the proprietor was the first Sheriff of Tioga County, Alpherus Cheney. In the 1830s four rooms, two upstairs and two downstairs, were added by Samuel Dickinson. It was later purchased by John L. Robinson, a founder of the First National Bank of Wellsborough. Unlike some wealthy homeowners who might make expensive additions or renovations, banker Robinson took a different tack - he built a replica of his bank in the back yard. The house today is the home of the Tioga County Historical Society.

5. **Williams House**
   126 Main Street

This brick house with Stick Style woodworking in the gables, lintels and porch supports was built in 1885 for Henry W. Williams, then President Judge of Tioga County. Two years later he was appointed to the Supreme Court of Pennsylvania.

6. **First Presbyterian Church**
   130 Main Street

When this Presbyterian church appeared on the Wellsboro streetscape in 1894 it was hailed as "the finest church of its size in Northern Pennsylvania."

7. **Green Free Library**
   134 Main Street

The borough of Wellsboro was already more than 100 years old when the first effort was made to establish a free public library. In 1911, a local philanthropist, Charles Green of Roaring Branch, left a $50,000 trust with instructions to create the Green Free Library. Several years passed until Mary B. Robinson bequeathed Chester Place, the family home built in 1855 by her father, Chester

Robinson. After extensive renovations to Chester Place, swapping its Victorian original for Colonial Revival, the new Green Free Library officially opened on January 26, 1917.

8. "Lincoln Door House"
140 Main Street

This 1850 Italianate-style residence is locally known as the "Lincoln Door House." When the Shearers purchased the house in 1858, the front door was given to Mrs. Shearer by Mary Todd Lincoln, a close friend from the time that they both lived in Springfield, Illinois. The door had come from an unidentified Springfield home.

9. West End Market
152 Main Street

This is the oldest grocery store in Wellsboro; it opened its doors in 1902. For more than 100 years it has operated as a convenience market, a fish market and a bulk food store.

KEEP WALKING PAST MAIN STREET AND TAKE THE BEND IN THE ROAD AS IT BECOMES WEST AVENUE, TO THE RIGHT.

10. Harrison House/Carleton Nursing Home
10 West Avenue

This substantial Italian Villa style, capped with a belvedere, was the home of banker and philanthropist Leonard Harrison. He owned and developed 121 acres of land bordering Pine Creek, then known as "The Lookout" that he operated as public picnic ground. He donated the land to the Commonwealth in 1922 that became Leonard Harrison State Park.

TURN AND WALK THE SHORT DISTANCE BACK TO MAIN STREET AND CROSS TO THE SOUTH SIDE OF THE STREET.

11. Jesse Robinson House
141 Main Street

Wellsboro's outstanding example of Queen Anne architecture was designed by Joseph Pierce and Otis Dockstader, a leading firm in south-central New York and northern Pennsylvania. The client was Jesse Robinson, a son of banker John L. Robinson. After beginning his own career as a cashier in 1876, Jesse took the reins of the bank after his father's death in 1893. He died suddenly three years later and in his will stated that his wife Hattie could live in the house until her death but if she chose to re-marry or move from Wellsboro, all would transfer to their children. Hattie successfully broke the will and sold the house two years later.

The 1888 mansion features asymmetrical massing over three stories under a steeply pitched roof with a beautiful wrap-around, lattice-trimmed porch. The exterior is primarily of red brick with specially cut wood shingle siding in the dormer areas. No major alterations have taken place since the house was built in the midst of Wellsboro's flourishing lumber years.

12. Waldo Miller House
139 Main Street

Comparable in size and style to the Robinson House across King Street, the Miller house actually predates it by almost a decade. This early Queen Anne-style house was built in 1879. It stands today as a funeral home.

TURN RIGHT ON CHARLES STREET.

13. Old Lutheran Church
2 Charles Street

This 1860 former Lutheran Church is of Greek Revival design; after being a house of worship it served as the home of the Wellsboro School District until 2008.

TURN LEFT ON PEARL STREET.

14. **St. Paul's Episcopal Church**
    south side of The Green at the corner of
    Charles and Pearl streets

Benjamin Morris, a Quaker who built a meetinghouse for fellow worshippers, founded Wellsboro in 1806. After the Quaker group disbanded, James Lowery and Joshua Sweet headed a group interested in forming a new church. In 1838, the church leaders hired an Episcopal priest, Charles Breck, for $250 to minister to the town's first organized church. After services at the courthouse and, later, in an old school building on the corner of Charles and Walnut Streets, the present Romanesque structure was completed at a cost of just over $30,000 with regular services beginning on Easter Sunday, April 2, 1899.

15. **Bingham Estate**
    33 Pearl Street

This Second Empire building with mansard roof was erected prior to the Civil War as the office of the Bingham Estate, a land company. It was moved from its original site in 1897 when St. Paul's Episcopal Church was built.

TURN LEFT ON CENTRAL AVENUE.

16. **Lawyers Row**
    Central Avenue between Main and Pearl
    streets

Towns designated as county seats often developed a row of law offices near the County courthouse. In Wellsboro this block of brick offices housed law firms and insurance companies. Many have living quarters upstairs. The Queen Anne-style residence at 19 Central Avenue was built by judge Mortimer F. Elliot, who served as congressman-at-large in the 48th Congress.

TURN RIGHT ON MAIN STREET AND WALK DOWN THE SOUTH SIDE OF THE BUSINESS DISTRICT.

17. **Garrisons Mens Store**
    85 Main Street

This red brick storefront is typical of the Italianate-style commercial buildings that populated Wellsboro's business district in the latter half of the 19th century. Garrisons has been in business since 1955.

18. **Dunham's Department Store**
    45 Main Street

Roy and Fannie Dunham opened their first store in Wellsboro in 1905. After it was severely damaged by fire in 1913 the emporium was rebuilt and expanded in the same location. During the Depression, when a lot of rural residents had no way of getting to town, the Dunhams created the "Rolling Store," a modified truck that carried dry goods, hardware and candy to residents in outlying areas. The truck traveled around the county until World War II when gasoline and tire rationing put the brakes on the rolling store. The current three-story Art Deco style building of Dunham's, still family-owned after 100 years, dates to 1932 and is of poured concrete.

19. **Wellsboro Diner**
    19 Main Street

The Moderne style Wellsboro Diner opened in 1939 and has been in continuous operation as a diner ever since, still in its original location.

CROSS OVER TO THE NORTH SIDE OF THE STREET AND TURN LEFT, WALKING WEST ON MAIN STREET.

20. **United Methodist Church**
    northwest corner of Main Street and
    Queen Street

Methodism in Tioga County can be traced back to the circuit riding preachers of the Genesee Conference, organized in 1810. The nascent village of Wellsboro landed on the circuit in 1822. The first church building was located at 7 Main Street and was a simple, neat church finished very plainly inside. It was dedicated on May 21, 1842 being the second church building in the borough at the time. By 1867 the church needed repairs and improvements, which were completed in November. The evening of the first Sunday service held after the work was done, the church was discovered in flames and it burned to the ground.

The people worshiped in the Courthouse for the next two years while a new brick church was built until a substantial Gothic structure was dedicated on this site on November 17, 1869, exactly two years to the day after the fire. Due to construction defects the church was determined to be unsafe for use in 1900. It was torn down in 1904 and a new Gothic Revival church of yellow brick and Hummelstown sandstone was begun. The present church building, now into its second century, was dedicated on October 1, 1905.

21. Arcadia Theatre
50 Main Street

Irvin Focht and Leon Klock opened the Arcadia Theatre on December 12, 1921, showing *The Old Nest* to patrons paying 15 and 25 cents. The theater housed one screen and seated 900 people. To accompany the silent movies, the theater was equipped with an organ, piano, and room for an orchestra. In 1926, William Woodin, the owner of the Towanda theatre, along with W.H. Seigel, purchased the Arcadia and three years later some of the first "talkies" in Pennsylvania were screened here.

In 1949, the Arcadia held its first premiere, *Top O' the Morning* starring Bing Crosby. The theater remained a vital part of Wellsboro's downtown through the 1970s but it gasped through the 1980s and early 1990s until it was completely renovated in 1996. In celebration of its 75th year, the Arcadia Theatre reopened on March 21, 1997 as a state-of-the-art four-screen facility, yet preserving the classic look of an old-time movie house.

22. Penn-Wells Hotel
62 Main Street

Wellsboro's first tavern/inn was built here in 1816 and the site has always been occupied by a tavern, inn or hotel. In 1869 A.P. Cone erected a four-story brick hotel. The building was purchased in 1885 by J.S. Coles and renamed the "Cole House." A fire in 1906 damaged the fourth floor so badly that it had to removed. The largest building in the historic district and a significant anchor within the central business district, it was purchased by a group of local residents in 1925, closed for extensive remodeling and the addition of a fourth floor. At that time, the entire hotel was fire protected by a sprinkler system. It re-opened in 1926 as the Penn-Wells Hotel.

23. First National Bank
90-92 Main Street

The First National Bank of Wellsboro was organized February 27,1864, chartered March 21,1864, and commenced business May 17,1864. William Bache was chosen president in order to enable John L. Robinson, the founder, to act as cashier and get the bank well under way. After a service of about two years, Mr. Bache retired and Mr. Robinson was elected president. The building first occupied by the bank was an old two-story frame store purchased by Robinson back in 1834. It was used until 1876 when it was removed to the northeast corner of Crafton and Pearl streets. But before it moved it was involved in one of the notorious incidents in Wellsboro's history.

On the night of September 16, 1874 the bank was robbed by a band of skilled burglars in one of the most boldly-planned and successfully-executed robberies in the history of Pennsylvania. The old-fashioned frame store with wooden shutters and doors could be entered easily by any expert thief but the vault was a very strong one fitted with the best combination locks. So the gang of seven men captured First National's president Robinson and his family at their house and ordered the son to accompany a few of them to the bank and open the vault. News of the robbery along the local telegraph line was delayed, and the bandits fled with more than $30,000 in cash. Eventually, two of the robbers were captured, but the rest escaped and criminals supposedly tied to the heist were being arrested as far away as San Francisco for years to come.

The new two-story brick bank building was built on this site in 1876 and replaced with the Neoclassical vault now on Main Street in the early 1900s. Today the bank is owned by the Citizens and Northern Bank.

WALK ONE MORE BLOCK TO THE TOUR STARTING POINT AT THE GREEN.

Look Up,

West Chester

A Walking Tour of West Chester...

West Chester grew up at the intersection of two Colonial wagon roads, one that went from Philadelphia to Lancaster and one that went from Wilmington to Reading. The crossroads was roughly a day's ride for teamsters from each of the four cities and was an ideal location for a tavern. That tavern appeared in the 1760s and became known as Turk's Head Tavern.

By the 1780s the name "West Chester" was being used by petitioners trying to pry the Chester County seat off the Delaware River at Chester where it had been since since the county's creation in 1720 as Pennsylvania's first jurisdiction outside Philadelphia. In 1788 West Chester became that more centrally located seat and was incorporated as a borough in 1799.

But there was no industry here, no water to power it, no marketplace. For the better part of 50 years there was no development beyond shouting distance of the little courthouse. The first to take a gamble on West Chester was William Everhart who set up shop on Gay Street in 1824 to sell ceramics imported from England. Everhart's reputation was made when he survived a shipwreck off the Irish coast, losing $10,000 in the tragedy. Afterwards he declined to accept any of the money found in the wreckage because he couldn't vouch that it was his.

In 1829 Everhart paid $16,000 for 102 acres of farmland on the western edge of town. Confounding skeptics who had witnessed no growth in West Chester for decades, he divvied the land up into building lots and listed them for sale. On the very first day he sold fifty lots and recouped his original investment. He would continue to hold land auctions into the 1840s and built over 100 brick homes on his lots along the streets he laid out and named after his friends - Miner, Barnard, Darlington, Wayne.

Like its fellow suburban county seats Doylestown and Media, West Chester never became an industrial town despite its new residential appeal. It developed as the governmental, legal, cultural and commercial focal point of its county. Much of the downtown remains intact and the entire district is listed on the *National Register of Historic Places*.

In 2001 an exuberant *Philadelphia Inquirer* article declared West Chester "the perfect town" and borough promoters have taken the compliment and run with it. Our walking tour to see for ourselves will begin, appropriately enough, at the highest point in town...

1. **Marshall Square Park**
    northeast corner of North Matlack Street
    and East Biddle Street

The borough's oldest park was acquired from Anthony and Adelaide Bolmer in 1841. The five-acre park, initially used as a water basin, was named after Humphrey Marshall, a noted local botanist. Rare trees, some of which can still be found in the park, would be planted here over the years. In 1886 surviving members of the 97th Regiment raised $5,000 to erect a monument to their service in the Civil War. The granite soldier at parade rest was dedicated on October 29, 1887; a brief history of the unit is inscribed on its base. The monument is sited at the highest point in West Chester.

LEAVE THE PARK ON THE
NORTHEAST CORNER AND
TURN LEFT, WALKING WEST ON
MARSHALL STREET. TURN RIGHT
ON HIGH STREET. TURN LEFT
ON WEST VIRGINIA AVENUE.

2. **Four Sisters**
    100 and 200 blocks of West Virginia
    Avenue, north side

Much of the land in West Chester from the northern edge of the business district along Chestnut Street to the current West Chester Country Club was farmland and orchards belonging to John Rutter. Rutter was a Delaware County farmer who migrated to West Chester in the 1820s to become a lawyer and businessman. The four lots that came to be known as the "Four Sisters" were all sold by Rutter in 1872 and each contains a home designed by Addison Hutton, one of the busiest architects of the age along the East Coast. Hutton's design for Main Hall, the first structure of the West Chester State Normal School won him these commissions. The four houses he designed feature Gothic and French Second Empire detailing and, most dramatically, all are created with green Chester County serpentine stone. A notoriously fragile building materials, the Four Sisters are weathering impressively towards their 150th birthdays.

The house closest to High Street (101 West Virginia) graces a corner estate owned by Thomas Marshall, president of the National Bank of Chester County). Moving west is a more modest home (121 West Virginia) built for dry goods merchant Samuel Parker and two houses (205 and 221 West Virginia) constructed for lawyers, Robert T. Cornwell and William B. Waddell.

RETURN TO CHURCH STREET
AND TURN RIGHT, HEADING FOR
DOWNTOWN.

3. **Rothrock Manor**
    428 North Church Street

Joseph T. Rothrock, an influential 19th century conservationist and "Father of the Pennsylvania State Forest," lived in this house from 1876 until his death in 1922. He pioneered the development of forest fire control, reforestation and methods of scientific forestry. The brick house was built in the late 1850s for noted Chester County attorney Addison May and is one of the earliest Gothic houses to be built in West Chester.

4. **West Chester Public Library**
    415 North Church Street

The West Chester Public Library was established in 1872 and moved into its current Queen Anne building in 1888. Note the festive "Library" inscribed in the corner tower.

5. **Swedenborg Foundation**
    320 North Church Street

This handsome Georgian brick building houses the offices of the Swedenborg Foundation, founded in 1849 to propagate the words of eighteenth-century Swedish scientist, nobleman, civil engineer, and religious visionary Emanuel Swedenborg. His work covers such areas as the afterlife, heaven and hell, dream imagery, angels, and a new understanding of Christianity.

6. **Washington Square**
   21 West Washington Street at
   Church Street

Schools came early to West Chester, in 1837. The first public school was built on Barnard Street four years later. West Chester High School graduated its first class in 1866; bricks from that building, demolished during World War I, were used in building this Biddle Street School in 1917. The Colonial Revival-style elementary school has since been adapted for residential living.

TURN RIGHT ON GAY STREET.

7. **Taylor's Music Store**
   116 West Gay Street

The family-owned music store has been in operation since 1929, although not in the family of founder John Taylor, who sold the business decades ago. In addition to being a full-line music store, Taylor's offers 25 studios. Its distinctive "keyboard awning" is a creative use of the distinctive Pennsylvania pent roof form.

8. **St. Agnes Church**
   233 West Gay Street

This is the third Catholic church to stand on this site, the first being the first church in West Chester, erected in 1793. It was a one story brick structure containing three windows on each side with a front door facing west. It accommodated 150 people.

RETRACE YOUR STEPS ON GAY STREET TO CHURCH STREET AND TURN RIGHT.

9. **First West Chester Fire Company**
   14 North Church Street

The First West Chester Fire Company dates its service to the community back to 1799. This station house, one of West Chester's most picturesque buildings, was designed in the Queen Anne style with red brick and terra-cotta by architect T. Roney Williamson in 1887. The side tower was used for drying fire hoses.

10. **Judge Bell House**
    101 South Church Street

This highly refined Federal Style residence, the home of Judge Thomas Bell, is attributed to celebrated architect Thomas U. Walter. Note also the marble stoop and brass handrail.

11. **Samuel Barber home**
    107 South Church Street

This was the boyhood home of orchestral and vocal works composer Samuel Barber, who twice won the Pulitzer Prize in music, in 1958 and 1963. Among his least important, though no less beloved pieces, is West Chester High School's Alma Mater song.

TURN RIGHT ON MINER STREET.

12. **First Presbyterian Church**
    130 West Miner Street

This is the oldest extant church in West Chester and one of the first commissions for Thomas U. Walter, who would later become the Architect of the United States Capitol. The 27-year old old Walter gave the new Presbyterian congregation a Greek Revival temple entered through a pair of impressive Ionic columns. The first service was held on January 7, 1834 with 52 original members.

RETRACE YOUR STEPS ON MINER STREET, CROSS CHURCH STREET AND GO TO HIGH STREET. TURN LEFT.

13. **Old Borough Hall**
    15 South High Street

This Colonial Revival building was built as the borough hall in 1912 but it has been a dining establishment nearly as long.

14. Buckwalter Building
11-13 South High Street

Henry Brinton, the leading bank and real estate developer in town, constructed this building in 1893. It is listed on the *National Register of Historic Places*.

15. Farmers and Mechanics Building
southwest corner of Market Street and High Street

This became West Chester's first "skyscraper" when it was constructed on the most prominent intersection in town in 1907. The roof of the building was used in World War II as a lookout station for enemy planes.

TURN LEFT ON MARKET STREET.

16. Lincoln Biography Building
28 West Market Street

The first published biography of Abraham Lincoln was printed in this building on February 11, 1860. It was prepared from Lincoln's own notes, and served to introduce him to the public as a potential presidential candidate.

CROSS OVER TO THE NORTH SIDE OF MARKET STREET AND TURN RIGHT, HEADING BACK FOR HIGH STREET.

17. Court House Annex
northwest corner of Market Street and High Street

In 1891 T. Roney Williamson designed the Court House Annex. Built of Indiana limestone, it is an interpretation of the Italian Renaissance style and was erected contiguous to the Greek Revival Court House. The interior was embellished with Italian marble wainscoting; stained art glass; and decorative wood garlands, diamonds, and pilasters.

TURN LEFT ON HIGH STREET.

18. Town Drinking Fountain
northwest corner of Market Street and High Street

The Town Drinking Fountain "for people, horses, and dogs" was donated in 1869 by John and Mary Hickman. This was its original location but it must have wandered off for a time because it was restored here in 1987.

19. Chester County Courthouse
2 North High Street

In 1682 William Penn established Chester County as one of three original counties in the Pennsylvania Colony and a Court House was constructed in 1724 in Chester near the Delaware River. Population density and immigrant migration necessitated moving the facility inland. Between 1784 and 1786 a Court House was built in the village of West Chester on High Street. The current Chester County Courthouse, the architectural centerpiece of West Chester, was designed by Philadelphia architect Thomas U. Walter in the Greek Revival Style and opened officially on Washington's Birthday, 1848. In 1859 the stone-and-brick Court House facades were faced with Pictou stone.

20. First National Bank of Chester County
9 North High Street

Founded in 1863, First National is the eighth oldest bank in the country, operating for nearly 150 years as an independent wholly owned financial institution. The current Neoclassical headquarters building was constructed in 1912.

21. Smith-Sharpless House
15 North High Street

This early Federal Style building was built in 1789 and includes most of the elements of the style: side-gable form, central front door with elongated sidelights, simple porch with classical elements, planar walls, simple exterior woodwork, and dormers. It is one of a handful of buildings that survive from West Chester's nascent days; another is across the street, a 1793 residence that was converted to a drugstore in 1866 and remains commercial to this day.

22. First Bank of Chester County
17 North High Street

The First Bank of Chester County was designed by Thomas U. Walter and completed in 1837, eleven years before the completion of the Courthouse and 13 years before he was chosen to re-configure the dome on the U.S. Capitol in Washington. The First Bank of Chester County was designed in the Greek Revival Style.

TURN RIGHT ON GAY STREET.

23. Chester County Trust Building
15 East Gay Street

This small mid-block bank vault was built in the newly popular Beaux-Arts style in 1905 for the Chester County Trust Company.

24. Post Office
northeast corner of Gay Street and Walnut Street

This Colonial Revival post office was built at a time when the post office was the federal government to most people and it was intended to be an impressive bit of local architecture.

RETRACE YOUR STEPS ON GAY STREET TO HIGH STREET AND TURN RIGHT.

25. Green Tree Building
northeast corner of Gay Street and High Street

Art Deco is not a common architectural style on the West Chester streetscape but there are some decorative touches of the style on the Green Tree Building, including the namesake symbols. The current building that houses luxury apartments remembers the Green Tree Hotel and Tavern that was built on this corner in 1787.

26. Iron Hill Brewery
3 West Gay Street at northwest corner of High Street

This building, an excellent form of early 1900s commercial architecture once housed the town's Woolworth Store. It was built in 1928.

27. Warner Theatre
120 North High Street

Opened in 1930, the Warner Theatre was designed by the firm of Rapp & Rapp in flamboyant Art Deco style. The vertical sign and facade of the West Chester Warner was very similar in appearance to the Rapp's famous Warner Theatre in Erie, which opened a year after this theater. After its movie days ended in the 1970s, the Warner Theatre was renovated and live entertainment was presented for a few years, until the theater closed in the early 1980s. The Warner Theatre was listed on the *National Register of Historic Places* in 1979 but couldn't stave off demolition. Surviving are the lobby and one-story stores.

28. Major John C. Groff Memorial Armory
226 North High Street

The town National Guard armory is named for John Groff. Groff entered World War I as a captain and rose to the rank of major in action in Europe. When he ran for the office of Register of Wills in 1919 the *Daily Local News* wrote, "He is of Chester County stock, upon which there isn't a single stain, and so it happens in recognition of his merits in civil and military life his many friends are backing him for the count office he now seeks." He won the election.

29. Horticultural Hall
225 North High Street

When Thomas U. Walter designed this unassuming serpentine stone building with a round-arched Romanesque Revival entrance in 1848 it was only the second building in the United States built for horticultural exhibitions. Over the next 160 years it would be home to four different organizations. Besides the Chester County Horticultural Society, founded in 1846, the West Chester Opera House, the McCall Post of the Grand

Army of the Republic and the Chester County Historical Society would all set up shop here. In 1852 women's rights activist Hannah Darlington convened the first Pennsylvania Women's Rights Convention in the building. This convention passed resolutions promoting women's legal, educational, and vocational rights.

TURN RIGHT ON EAST WASHINGTON STREET.

30. Simon Barnard Row
104-116 East Washington Street

Simon Barnard was a farmer until the age of 50 when he moved to West Chester and went into the lumber business and began building houses. The Barnard family was active in the antislavery movement in the southern section of Chester County as well as in the Underground Railroad. Many of the Federal-style houses on East Washington Street were Barnard's. Wild West show promoter Buffalo Bill Cody rented a house on East Washington for a winter in the 1870s.

31. Sharples Works
300 Evans Street at Franklin Street

Sharples Works was originally built in the 1890s to house the dairy industry's first tubular cream separator. At the time, it was considered one of the country's most significant industrial production plants as it efficiently churned out cream products for countless Chester County dairy farmers. Obsolete by the Second World War the complex of redeveloped brick buildings has been re-adapted as residential apartments.

TURN LEFT ON FRANKLIN STREET TO RETURN TO THE TOUR STARTING POINT IN MARSHALL SQUARE PARK.

Look Up,

Wilkes-Barre

A Walking Tour of Wilkes-Barre...

In *A History of Luzerne County*, published in 1893, Wilkes-Barre was described thusly: "The important city and the first settlement in Luzerne county is the one descriptive phrase applicable to this city. A beautiful city, queen of the Susquehanna north of Harrisburg to its source: a crown-jewel on the east bank of the river and in the center of the far-famed Wyoming valley; the county seat of Luzerne county, the center and hub from where flows out in every direction by electric and steam railroads, her rich trade, and the daily and hourly ever swelling stream of visitors for business and pleasure; where is elegance, refinement and culture; where there are more families of great wealth, comparatively to numbers, than can be found in any other city in the United States. A city that never had a 'boom' but that now is forging ahead at a marvelous step, and on every hand are suburban boroughs that are progressing rapidly. Here is the capital of a county that is of itself a rich and distinct empire."

A town like that is worth fighting over, and that is what happened in its early days. The first Europeans to settle the area arrived in 1769, from Connecticut, a colony which had a land grant from the British crown that extended all way to the Great Lakes. The settlement was named after John Wilkes and Isaac Barré, two members of Parliament who supported colonial America. Armed men loyal to Pennsylvania, wielding a claim to the land by virtue of William Penn's grant, twice attempted to evict the residents of Wilkes-Barre in what came to be known as the Pennamite Wars. The conflict was not put to rest until after the American Revolution when the settlers were allowed to retain title to their lands but had to transfer their allegiance to Pennsylvania.

Wilkes-Barre's population exploded due to the discovery of anthracite coal in the 1800s, which gave the city the nickname of "The Diamond City." The wealth that flowed into the city from the world's largest coal field began showing up on the Wilke-Barre streetscape in the form of fancy hotels, massive mansions and imposing churches.

Wilkes-Barre took a major blow from Tropical Storm Agnes in 1972 when rainwaters swelled the Susquehanna River to a height of nearly 41 feet, four feet above the city's levees, flooding downtown with nine feet of water. While no lives were lost, 25,000 homes and businesses were either damaged or destroyed, and damages were estimated to be $1 billion.

Much remains, however, and our walking tour will begin the investigation in the Public Square, a diamond set in the center of the "Diamond City"...

1. **Public Square**
   intersection of Main Street and Market Street

Over the centuries Public Square has held a fort, a church, a school, and the Luzerne County courthouse and jail. In 1909, the old courthouse was demolished and the Square became a park. Today, the park has a potpourri of public displays including a church bell, fountains and remembrances to Christopher Columbus and the two British members of Parliament who championed the American Colonies' desire for independence: John Wilkes and Colonel Isaac Barre, the city's namesakes. An amphitheater hosts ceremonies and celebrations; in May you'll find the Fine Arts Fiesta, Pennsylvania's oldest arts fair staged here. Thursdays in summer and autumn you can partake in the long tradition of the Farmers Market.

TAKE YOUR TOUR AROUND PUBLIC SQUARE IN A COUNTER-CLOCKWISE DIRECTION STARTING WITH THE BUILDING ACROSS THE STREET FROM THE MONUMENT TO WILKES AND BARRE.

2. **Chamber Building**
   2 Public Square

Public Square was set diagonally into the city grid, and the prominent lots that resulted at the points of the diamonds have challenged the creativity of generations of architects. Here New York architect P. J. Lauritzen, designed this five-story landmark for the Jonas Long's Sons Department Store. He dealt with the oddly shaped site by creating a dramatic three-story entrance arch to mark the corner and draw in shoppers. The store was home to Pomeroy's for generations of Wilkes Barre shoppers. In 1994, 99 years after its creation, the Greater Wilkes-Barre Chamber renovated the building for office and retail use.

3. **First National Bank**
   59-63 Public Square

Wilkes-Barre architect Albert H. Kipp created this Neoclassical vault in 1906 with formidable pediment and Corinthian columns. The bank was organized in Hazleton in 1888; today it is owned by the city.

4. **Luzerne Bank Building**
   69 Public Square

New York architect Bertram Cunynham designed this fourteen-story building in 1928, rising from a Romanesque base to an airy penthouse that calls to mind an Italian villa. The foyer ceiling has fine decorative reliefs in the Art Deco.

5. **F. M. Kirby Center for the Performing Arts**
   71 Public Square

M. E. Comerford opened Wilkes-Barre's largest, best-equipped, and most modern movie palace in 1938. Designed in a Deco-Moderne stylized ziggurat composition the theater is faced with terra-cotta tile and green marble. Interior spaces are covered in walnut, translucent marble panels, ornamental plasters and bronze throughout. The Comerford Theater is the only survivor of the city's three movie palaces. The theater was rehabilitated after being damaged in Hurricane Agnes and is now a performing arts center.

LEAVE THE PUBLIC SQUARE ON WEST MARKET STREET, WALKING TOWARDS THE SUSQUEHANNA RIVER (THE CHAMBER BUILDING WILL BE ON YOUR RIGHT).

6. **PNC Bank Building**
   11 West Market Street

Historically, the intersection of Market and Franklin Streets has been the financial center of Wilkes-Barre. The three large banks at this corner date from the era of the City Beautiful Movement in the early 1900s. Local architects McCormick and French designed this bank like other early "skyscrapers" as an abstracted classical column, with a base (the banking hall), shaft (the office floors), and capital (the top floor).

7. Citizens Bank
8 West Market Street

Daniel H. Burnham of Chicago designed the Citizens Bank Center, a landmark on Wilkes-Barre's skyline since 1911. Burnham had been chief architect of Chicago's 1893 Columbian Exposition– the event that spawned the City Beautiful Movement. The coffered polychrome ceiling of its banking hall is especially handsome.

8. Wyoming National Bank
26-28 West Market Street

Wyoming National Bank was organized November 16, 1829 and moved to this corner in 1861. Another creation of McCormick and French, this marble Neoclassical vault was constructed in 1914.

9. Hotel Sterling
47-65 West Market Street at northeast corner of River Street

Architect J.H.W. Hawkins had planned a brick Victorian castle, but developer Walter Sterling convinced him to change the design midway and Wilkes-Barre got its first Neoclassical Revival building in 1897. The result – modeled after a flat-roofed Renaissance palazzo, and clad in rough-faced limestone –marked the end of the Victorian era in Wilkes-Barre's architecture. At one time, the Sterling was the city's largest and most luxurious hotel, and its guests included movie stars and nationally-known politicians. By the 1970s it was being used as apartments, then condemned by the city in 1998. The Sterling is now undergoing a complete rehabilitation.

10. Market Street Bridge
Market Street at Susquehanna River

This stunning gateway into the central city was also inspired by the City Beautiful Movement; Carrere and Hastings, architects of the New York Public Library and many of the classical buildings in Washington, D.C., designed it. The beauty of the Market Street Bridge and the proud eagles that guard its entrance towers have made it a well-loved landmark; this has been the site of several spans across the Susquehanna, and as early as 1912, Frederick C. Olds had plans for a riverside park on the west side and a monumental bridge to link Wilkes-Barre with still rural Kingston. In 1922, F. M. Kirby, a partner in the F. W. Woolworth Company, hired the renowned Olmsted Brothers to design a park, which he then donated to the city of Wilkes-Barre. A quick walk across the Market Street Bridge will bring you to Kirby Park and its neighbor, Nesbitt Park.

TURN LEFT ON RIVER STREET (THE RIVER WILL BE ON YOUR RIGHT).

11. Guard Center
16 South River Street

The Guard Center building was constructed in just ninety days during the winter of 1908 to house the Lehigh and Wilkes-Barre Coal Company, one of eight major coal operators dominating the industry at the turn of the century. Its imposing granite columns signify the important role that the coal companies once played in the life of the city. Wilkes-Barre architects Welsh, Sturdevant and Poggi designed this Neoclassical Revival structure.

12. Chapman Hall
24 South River Street

Lehigh and Wilkes-Barre Coal Company president Frederick Huber commissioned Welsh, Sturdevant and Poggi to design his home next door to his office building in 1911. The Craftsman Style detailing of the three-story mansion hints at the influence of contemporary Prairie School architects like Frank Lloyd Wright.

In the early 1800s, River Street was Wilkes-Barre's commercial hub: its gateway, via the Susquehanna, to the world. The street was dotted with taverns and shops as well as houses; there were boat landings and warehouses on the River Common. After the construction of the canal to the rear of the town, commerce shifted away from the river, and the neighborhood became the preserve of the great family houses of the nineteenth century – residences made possible by the tons of coal moving on the canals to market. Wilkes University, founded in 1933, owns most of the remaining mansions on South River Street and uses them for residence halls, offices, and classrooms.

13. McClintock Law Office
34 South River Street

Attorney Andrew McClintock's small Italianate law office from the middle of the 19th century, now the Baltimore Company, is a quaint survivor from Wilkes-Barre's days as a sleepy county seat.

14. McClintock House
44 South River Street

Andrew McClintock's house has borne witness to both phases of River Street's existence. Originally, the house was designed in the Greek Revival style. In 1863, McClintock, made wealthy by the growth of the mining industry, engaged New York architects Calvert Vaux and F. C. Withers to remodel his house. The spare structure was soon transformed into the first High Victorian Gothic house in Wilkes-Barre, boasting a polychrome brick arcade which made the house as fashionable as any of its neighbors.

15. Sterling Hall
72 South River Street

The elaborate cast-iron ornament of this house, reminiscent of New Orleans, was made possible by the mass production of the Industrial Revolution; forged in an anthracite-fueled foundry. Philadelphia architect Samuel Sloan designed this cubical Italian villa for banker Walter Sterling.

16. Rifkin Hall
80-84 South River Street

This High Victorian Gothic mansion was designed by architect Bruce Price for the Murray Reynolds family. Price married into a prominent local family, and he enjoyed a steady business from Wilkes-Barre society. He would eventually leave for New York City, becoming one of the most prominent turn-of-the-century architects in America. This was once the home of Colonel Robert B. Ricketts, a Battle of Gettysburg hero, lumber baron, and early conservationist, who donated fabulous Ricketts' Glen State Park to the people of Pennsylvania.

17. Catlin Hall
92 South River Street

This restrained Greek Revival residence was constructed in 1843 and is most significant when viewed in relation to its next door neighbor...

18. Weiss Hall
98 South River Street

At one time this was an almost identical Greek Revival neighbor to Caitlin Hall. In 1886, new owner E. L. Brown had architect Albert Kipp remodel his house, now known as Weiss Hall, into a turreted, richly textured Queen Anne showpiece. The transformation led to new commissions for Kipp throughout the neighborhood, including the rowhouses on the other side of Northampton Street.

19. Conyngham Student Center
130 South River Street

The Chateauesque-style structure was designed in 1897, by original owner William Hillard Conyngham's friend, Charles Gifford. William and his first wife lived in the home for only a few years before her death. The house was then left vacant until 1918, when Mr. Conyngham and his new wife, Mrs. Jessie Guthrie Conyngham, and their three sons called it home. When Jessie passed away in 1974, Conyngham was left to Wilkes.

The first floor was severely damaged by four and a half feet of Hurricane Agnes flood waters in 1972. Only a few months later, fire scorched several walls. More than $350,000 was spent to reconstruct the building to make it livable in 1979.

20. Chase Hall
184 South River Street

Chase Hall was built from 1917-1918, for Frederick Chase, who was president and manager of the Lehigh Valley Coal Company. The building is a two-and-one-half story Tudor Revival stuccoed brick house. It has a gable roof with cross gables, segmented arch windows, and double-hung windows. Chase Hall was donated by Admiral Harold Stark as a memorial to Mrs.

Frederick Chase, Stark's sister, and her husband. Included on the property was a garage, which was used by Wilkes as a theater -- the Chase Theater. Until 1965, numerous one-act plays were presented in the 90-seat theater. The building was demolished in 1975.

21. Kirby Hall
202 South River Street at northeast corner of South Street

This regal corner mansion was built for Reuben Flick by architect F.C. Withers in 1872. In 1905 Fred M. Kirby, Woolworth & Company executive and philanthropist on a grand scale, purchased the mansion for $55,000.

22. Bedford Hall
96 West South Street

The former residence of attorney George Bedford was given to Wilkes College in November 1967, after his death. Bedford, who had attended Harry Hillman Academy, graduated from Princeton University, and received a law degree from the University of Pennsylvania, became a member of the Board of Trustees at Princeton University. The brick building was designed in High Victorian Gothic style in 1878 by Bruce Price, considered one of his finest early works.

23. Temple Israel
236 South River Street

This is the home of the Wyoming Valley's Conservative Jewish congregation, which was first established in 1922. The Byzantine Revival copper-domed exterior, typical of many synagogues of the period, is faced with buff tapestry brick and trimmed with granite and polychrome terracotta; the interior is remarkable for its woodwork and domed stained glass ceiling. Ralph M. Herr was the architect.

TURN LEFT ON ROSS STREET.

24. Stegmaier Mansion
304 South Franklin Street at southeast corner of Franklin Street

The Stegmaier mansion was built in 1870 by locally renowned Victorian architect Missouria B. Houpt as his private residence. Frederick Stegmaier, president of the Stegmaier Brewery, purchased the mansion in 1906 and it remained in the Stegmaier family until the late 1940s. In 2001 the mansion was meticulously restored to its former opulence and operates today as a bed and breakfast.

TURN LEFT ON FRANKLIN STREET.

25. Congregation Ohav Zedek
242 South Franklin Street

During the nineteenth and early twentieth centuries, American architects struggled to find an architectural language appropriate to the synagogue: the Moorish Revival style, with its "Middle Eastern" overtones, was one common design response. Local architect Austin Reilly designed this colorful synagogue for Wilkes-Barre's largest Orthodox Jewish congregation, founded by a group of Hungarian Jews. Moorish Revival horseshoe arches, rendered in terra-cotta tile, highlight the façade, which is crowned by a large curved gable.

26. Max Roth Center
215 South Franklin Street

In designing this elegant townhouse for a dentist, local architect J. H. W. Hawkins was influenced by two of America's greatest architects. The intricate naturalistic ornament in the window frieze is an echo of Chicago architect Louis Sullivan's designs, while Boston architect H. H. Richardson inspired the rusticated walls and stubby Syrian arches.

27. Weckesser Hall
170 South Franklin Street

This house was built between 1914 and 1916 as a residence for Frederick J. Weckesser, who moved to the Wilkes-Barre area at the turn of the nineteenth century. He became associated with

F.M. Kirby and orchestrated the merger of the local five-and-dime Kirby empire with the famous Woolworth Company. Weckesser would later become director of the F.W. Woolworth Company. This grand Chateauesque home, built by Charles H.P. Gilbert of New York -- the architect of Frank W. Woolworth's Fifth Avenue home, is actually the second Wilkes building to carry the Weckesser name. The first was located at 78 West Northampton Street

28. Mary Stegmaier House
156 South Franklin Street

Wilkes-Barre architects Knapp and Bosworth delivered this Colonial Revival mansion in 1911 for Mrs. George Stegmaier, descendent of the Wilkes-Barre brewing family. The house is dominated by a grand Ionic portico.

29. Luzerne County Medical Society
126 South Franklin Street (rear of building)

Wilkes-Barre's own Pantheon is tucked away behind a Second Empire house on Franklin Street. In 1914, architect Brice Hayden Long designed this Colonial Revival building, modeled loosely on Rome's great round temple, for the county's doctors. The first floor contains a medical library, while a circular auditorium, lit from above by a skylight, occupies the second floor. The Medical Society still calls this home, and visitors are welcome during business hours.

30. Moses and Gelso Law Offices
120 Franklin Street

Wilkes-Barre architects Olds and Puckey designed this urbane 1907 Beaux Arts mansion –reminiscent of a Parisian townhouse – for department store magnate Henry Lazarus. The prim brick façade, garlanded in limestone, rises to a balustrade below a steep mansard roof.

31. YMCA
40 West Northampton Street at southeast corner of Washington Street

This fortress of a building is really the welcoming home of the Wilkes-Barre YMCA. Wilkes-

Barre architect Thomas Foster modeled the exterior after the palaces of medieval Florence. Foster, a versatile architect, also designed the Collegiate Gothic First Baptist Church on South River Street.

32. First Presbyterian Church
97 South Franklin Street

This massive edifice for the Wyoming Valley's oldest congregation (founded 1779) is clad in Laurel Run redstone, a popular local building material. Look around downtown, and you will see the distinctive purple stone everywhere. With this rugged Romanesque exterior, New York City architect James Cleveland Cady introduced large-scale steel frame construction to the region. Cady also designed the American Museum of Natural History in New York.

33. Osterhout Free Library
71 South Franklin Street

Wilkes-Barre's unusual Gothic Revival public library was originally built as the First Presbyterian Church. In 1889, when Isaac S. Osterhout, a local merchant, left his estate "to establish and maintain in the city of Wilkes-Barre a free library," famed librarian Melville Dewey, inventor of the Dewey Decimal System, recommended that the old church building be utilized as a "temporary" library until a permanent replacement could be built." Still waiting for that building to come, the library added a children's wing in 1981.

34. Luzerne County Historical Society Museum
69 South Franklin Street

The Historical Society, founded in 1858, currently occupies two buildings on South Franklin Street, as well as the Swetland Homestead across the Susquehanna River in Wyoming. In its museum behind the Osterhout Free Library, three floors of exhibits highlight the history of the Wyoming Valley.

35. Bishop Memorial Library
49 South Franklin Street

This house, a late example of the Italian Villa style with Queen Anne revisions, is a reminder of quieter times on South Franklin Street. Designed by architect Willis Hale, it now houses the research library and administrative offices of the Historical Society. It is open to the public, as is the restored Victorian garden in the back.

36. WBRE-V and WYOU-TV
62 South Franklin Street

Samuel Moskowitz, a pioneer of contemporary architecture in the Wyoming Valley, designed the studios for Wilkes-Barre's first television station. Inspired by the International Style, this is an elegant combination of aluminum, glass, limestone, and marble. Moskowitz also designed the Jewish Community Center on South River Street.

37. St. Stephen's Episcopal Pro-Cathedral
35-41 South Franklin Street

This landmark church, built of locally-quarried yellow stone, was modeled after the colorful Gothic churches of Northern Italy. It was the second church that Philadelphia architect Charles M. Burns designed for the site: the first, built in 1885, burned in a spectacular Christmas Day fire in 1896, leaving only the tower standing.

38. Spring Brook Water Supply Company Building
30 North Franklin Street

Rows of intricately carved dolphins seem to spew water from the top of this Neoclassical Revival office building. They playfully declare the purpose of the structure over which they stand guard, for it was designed for the Spring Brook Water Supply Company by architects Welsh, Sturdevant, and Poggi.

39. Irem Temple
52 North Franklin Street

With four crescent-topped minarets piercing the skyline, this exotic fantasy on North Franklin Street probably provokes more comments than any building in the downtown since its erection in 1907. Wilkes-Barre's Shriners constructed the Moorish Revival style auditorium for their activities. For many years, Irem Temple was the city's premiere cultural venue. Architect F. Willard Puckey patterned its design after the Mosque of Omar on the outside and after the Court of Lions of the Alhambra Palace on the inside.

40. First United Methodist Church
45-53 North Franklin Street

The front of this imposing building rises like a mountain range from the sidewalk, reflecting architect Bruce Price's interest in evolving from his earlier, more spindly Victorian designs to something more simplified and modern in 1883. Price combined stylistic elements of French Gothic and Romanesque to compose the rugged façade of this building.

41. Kirby Health Center Annex
63 North Franklin Street

This house, which was publicized nationally in *American Architect and Building News*, began a phase of architect Bruce Price's career which greatly influenced the early work of Frank Lloyd Wright. Price designed it for his aunt in 1883 at the same time that he was working on the very different Methodist Church next door. The architect started with a simple gabled form, which he pushed and pulled, using different materials and textures to express the varied spaces of the interior. With this residence, Wilkes-Barre was introduced to the Queen Anne style, which had a wide influence on domestic architecture in the area.

42. Pennsylvania Millers Mutual Insurance Company
72 North Franklin Street

Though Wilkes-Barre's days as a farming town are long gone, this building, the headquarters of an insurance company founded for the purpose of insuring gristmills against fire, serves as a reminder of that time. The company recently demonstrated how the past and present can work together when it rehabilitated its original building, with its elegant combination of Art Moderne and

Colonial Revival motifs, joining it to a new office wing in the back.

43. Kirby Memorial Health Center
71 North Franklin Street

Designed by Thomas Atherton, the Kirby Health Center is a magnificent example of simplified Classical style. Its interiors exhibit a fabulous use of the tiles and colors that were favored in the 1920s and 1930s. The Center, another gift to the community from the generous Kirby family, is dedicated to Angeline Elizabeth Kirby; its purpose is "to promote the health of the people and the control and elimination of diseases." Many health services and organizations are housed in the Center and its annexes; visitors are welcome. The intricate tile work on the underside of the front portico is only a hint of what awaits you inside.

44. Stickney Block
108-118 North Franklin Street at northwest corner of Union Street

With its striking front bays and Gothic Palladian windows, the Stickney Block is an urbane example of the rowhouses built throughout the city's fashionable neighborhoods during the last quarter of the nineteenth century. This handsome reminder of things Victorian was designed by William W. Neuer, a local contractor turned architect.

TURN LEFT ON UNION STREET.

45. Beaumont Block/Dickson Row
54-64 Union Street

The prolific architect Albert Kipp designed two adjacent sets of rowhouses here. The Beaumont Block, which now houses Luzerne County offices, is a solid work rendered in brick and Laurel Run redstone. A decade later, the architect drew upon more playful influences for the Dickson Row, constructed toward the end of his career. Steep "Dutch" step-end gables crown three of the houses, while the fourth wears a mansard roof and features French doors opening onto a front terrace.

TURN RIGHT ON NORTH RIVER STREET.

46. King's College Administration Building
133 North River Street

King's College is a liberal arts school founded in 1946 by the Congregation of the Holy Cross, who also established the University of Notre Dame. The administration building was built in 1913 as the headquarters of the Lehigh Valley Coal Company. It was designed by Daniel H. Burnham of Chicago, also architect of the Citizens Bank Center. Nearby, at the corner of Franklin and Jackson Streets, the college's Chapel of Christ the King houses a moving tribute to the tempestuous relationship between coal and the Wyoming Valley – a 4,200-pound anthracite altar, created for King's in 1954 by the great coal sculptor C. Edgar Patience, a Wilkes-Barre resident.

47. Luzerne County Court House
North River Street and West North Street

Throughout its planning and construction in the first decade of the 20th century, controversy and scandal swirled around the Beaux Arts courthouse. Pittsburgh architect F. J. Osterling originally designed it to be placed on Public Square. It was finally completed by architects McCormick and French, who designed the lavish interior with its stunning rotunda. Step inside to see the history of the county illustrated in mosaics and murals.

Built during the period of Wilkes-Barre's greatest prosperity, the Court House is now a treasured local landmark. The site of the Court House was once the Public Basin of the Wyoming Division of the North Branch Canal. From 1834 to 1881, when the last canal boat left Wilkes-Barre, the canal was a major means of transporting coal and other commodities in and out of the Wyoming Valley.

On the courthouse lawn are memorials to the county's war dead and the anchor of the *USS Wilkes-Barre*, a World War II cruiser. The nearby cast-iron deer is a relic of the 1850s, when the courthouse sat on Public Square. Local wags would commonly cite the deer as a source of courthouse gossip in newspaper columns.

48. Memorial Presbyterian Church
   29 West North Street

This beautiful church, built in 1872 by a grieving father as a memorial to the three children he lost to a scarlet fever epidemic, was designed by Edward Kendall of New York. Three gorgeous Tiffany windows in the baptistry depict the children so that they, "being dead, might yet speak." Another large window, above the front entrance, symbolically illustrates the twelve Apostles. Built of Campbell's Ledge sandstone laid up in elaborate rubblework, with a rare stone spire and exceptionally well-detailed porches, dormers, and cast iron cresting, Memorial Presbyterian is a Gothic Revival gem.

TURN RIGHT ON MAIN STREET.

49. Polish Union Building
   53 North Main Street

The surface of the streamlined classical Polish Union Building is embellished with Art Deco bas-relief carvings; note particularly the eagle – a symbol of Poland – over its central entrance. Joseph E. Fronczak of Buffalo was the architect for this, the headquarters of a national Polish fraternal organization. The Polish Union is only one of the many ethnic institutions founded by the immigrants who came to call Wyoming Valley home; two blocks away, at the corner of North Main and North Streets, inscriptions on another building proclaim its former role as the home of the Pennsylvania Slovak Roman & Greek Catholic Union.

50. Blue Cross Operations Center
   30 North Main Street

The streamlined Operations Center, built as the Wyoming Valley Veterans Building, was the first major structure to be built here in a truly modern idiom, in 1946. The horizontal bands of windows and rounded corners of this nine-story building are marks of the International Style. The architects were L. Vern Lacy and Thomas Atherton, founders of a local firm.

51. Wilkes Barre *Times-Leader*
   15 North Main Street

In what can safely be described as a lively town for newspapers, the *Times-Leader* has been operating since 1879.

TURN LEFT ON BUTLER LANE. TURN LEFT ON WASHINGTON STREET.

52. James M. Coughlin High School
   80 North Washington Street

When it was opened in 1912, Coughlin High School was the city's only public high school. Within a decade, however, Wilkes-Barre's population growth necessitated the construction of two more high schools in other parts of the city. Wilkes-Barre architect Owen McGlynn won an architectural competition organized to select a design for the high school; years later, McGlynn's florid Beaux Arts building continues to serve its original purpose.

TURN AND WALK SOUTH ON WASHINGTON STREET.

53. Fraternal Order of Eagles Lodge
   39 North Washington Street

The eagle perched atop the offices of Quad Three Group testifies to the building's past life as the Fraternal Order of Eagles Lodge. Wilkes-Barre architects Schmitt and Schroeder designed it in 1925. The intriguing little Classical Revival building next door, built as the offices of Wilkes-Barre's first electric utility, later served as the home of the Wilkes-Barre Press Club, a one-time haunt of local newspapermen. President William Howard Taft and Admiral Robert Peary, among others, enjoyed the hospitality within these walls during their visits to Wilkes-Barre. Quad Three Group, a local architectural and engineering firm, rehabilitated both buildings for its use in the 1980's.

TURN LEFT ON EAST MARKET STREET.

54. Wilkes Barre City Hall
40 East Market Street at northeast corner of Washington Street

When it appeared on the Wilkes-Barre streetscape in 1893, City Hall presented a dramatic blend of architectural styles: a redstone Romanesque base; Victorian banded brick and terra-cotta upper floors with gargoyles and balconies; and Queen Anne towers and gables at the roofline. William W. Neuer and Benjamin Davey, Jr designed Wilkes-Barre's first municipal building. The towers and gables are gone and the only High Victorian souvenir remaining from that time is a stained glass window of the city seal over the front door. The honeybees illustrated in the seal are emblematic of the city's nineteenth-century boast that it was "busy as a beehive."

55. Stegmaier Brewing Company
northeast corner of East Market Street and Wilkes-Barre Boulevard

In 1948, 27-year old Charles Stegmaier, already with a resume featuring stints as brewmaster at several large local breweries, sailed from Germany to America. He quickly found employment at the small Corporation Brewery in Philadelphia. By 1851 he was in Wilkes-Barre brewing the first lager beer in the region. Success was elusive over the following decades and Stegmaier even left the brewing business for a time to run a hotel. He eventually formed a partnership with his son, Christian and successfully increased business to the extent that C. Stegmaier & Son could build a new brewhouse and storage facility in 1894 with an annual capacity to 300,000 barrels.

Between 1910 and 1913 Stegmaier won eight gold medals at expositions in Paris, Brussels and Rome. After Prohibition it became one of the largest independent breweries in North America, reaching an output of a half million barrels in 1940. Using a 60-truck fleet and rail services, the distribution areas eventually covered the East Coast from Maine to Florida - a considerable evolution from the days of 1857 when Charles Stegmaier personally delivered each barrel of beer with an express wagon drawn by a husky goat. The Company remained a family-run business for four generations until the Stegmaier label was sold to Lion, Inc. of Wilkes-Barre in 1974. At the

time, Stegmaier was the third largest brewery in Pennsylvania, producing 800,000 barrels of beer annually. Stegmaier beer is still produced by Lion and remains one of the firm's best-selling products.

A.C. Wagner, a brewery design specialist, built the Stegmaier Brewery. This cupola-topped brewhouse became the city's last great Victorian red brick pile and an impressive reminder of one of the region's major industries. Today it serves as a Federal office building – the result of an epic 20-year preservation battle.

56. Lehigh and Susquehanna Passenger Station
33 South Wilkes-Barre Boulevard at East Market Street

The Lehigh and Susquehanna Division was established by Philadelphia investors who conquered the mountains and tapped the Wyoming coal fields as the Lehigh Coal and Navigation Co. It was leased in 1871 to the Central Railroad of New Jersey. This Italianate railroad station served Wilkes-Barre for a century before it closed in 1972.

RETRACE YOUR STEPS ON EAST MARKET STREET TWO BLOCKS TO WASHINGTON STREET AND TURN LEFT.

57. Pennsylvania Labor & Industry Building
37 South Washington Street

The heroic terra-cotta garment workers flanking the entrance were salvaged from the International Ladies' Garment Workers Union Health Center that once stood here. Enormous mills built for silk and lace manufacture still dominate many Wyoming Valley neighborhoods, testimony to an industry drawn here by the massive supply of female labor. During the collapse of the anthracite industry after World War II, jobs in the dress factories kept many mining families from financial ruin.

415

58. St. Mary's Roman Catholic Church
134 South Washington Street

This is the oldest Roman Catholic parish in Luzerne County, founded in 1842 by Irish emigrants. Designed by E.F. Durang, a Philadelphia architect who specialized in Catholic churches, it has a stately Baroque façade and a grand interior boasting a frescoed ceiling and gilded columns. Its tower, however, is no more, having been toppled by a tornado in 1890.

59. St. Nicholas German Catholic Church
240 South Washington Street

This church is one of the greatest High Victorian Gothic structures in northeastern Pennsylvania. German-born architect William Schickel gave the church its German flair in the form of the single central tower and triple-entried frontispiece. For decades, people set their watches, went to lunch, and closed shop by the clock on its steeple. The interior woodcarvings and stained glass windows particularly breathtaking.

WALK BACK TO SOUTH STREET AND TURN LEFT. TURN LEFT ON SOUTH MAIN STREET.

60. Good Shepherd Lutheran Church
190 South Main Street

This is the oldest church in Wilkes-Barre. The simple Greek Revival structure, built by German immigrants, is one of the traditional focal points of what was once a largely German neighborhood.

TURN AND WALK WEST ON GOLDSBOROUGH STREET.

61. Max Rosenn U.S. Courthouse
197 South Main Street

The original 75,000 square foot building, constructed in the early 1930's, has a classical limestone facade.

TURN RIGHT ON MAIN STREET AND WALK TWO BLOCKS TO THE TOUR STARTING POINT AT PUBLIC SQUARE.

Look Up,

Williamsport

A Walking Tour of Williamsport...

Williamsport for decades was an unremarkable crossroads community of less than 2,000 people, a stop along the Pennsylvania Canal and a marketing destination for the numerous small farms of the area. In 1847, the potential for the logging business took a great leap forward with the establishment of the first "Log Boom" in the Susquehanna River. The west branch of the river from Linden to Halls Station was referred to as the "Long Reach," which was an area of almost no fall in the elevation of the riverbed. This provided an ideal point to locate a log boom, which was a series of river piers with heavy chains strung between them used to catch the slow moving logs as they came down the river. This fostered the development of an entire series of related lumber processing sites in Williamsport that included log cribs and ponds, sawmills, storage and rail yards.

The impact on the town was dynamic; between 1860 and 1870, six major railroad lines arrived and the population tripled. By 1886, there were 28,000 inhabitants of the city. Williamsport, with 29 sawmills, became known as the lumber capital of the world. Its great mills, strategically located on the Susquehanna River, were supplied by the log boom that stretched seven miles along the river front and was credited with a holding capacity of over 250 million board feet of lumber or nearly two million logs.

It was on this wooden foundation that fortunes were made. Williamsport was said to have had more millionaires than any place in America for a time. The lumber barons built spectacular homes, first along East Third Street and then migrating to West Fourth Street, which remained a fashionable neighborhood well into the 1900s before numerous demolitions and commercial development nearly erased all vestiges of its one-time splendor.

In 1889, the Susquehanna River swelled over its banks and caused considerable damage to the lumber facilities located in the city. This, coupled with the declining timber resources, signaled an end to the traditional economic base, although the lumber business remained until the early 1900s.

Our walking tour will begin just east of Millionaires Row, as West Fourth Street came to be know, and explore the downtown area before reversing course and seeing what traces remain of some of Pennsylvania's greatest fortunes...

1. **City Hall**
   245 West Fourth Street

Originally built as a U.S. Post Office and Federal Building, construction began in 1888 according to the design by William A. Ferret in the Richardsonian Romanesque style with semicircular windows and entryways, squat stone columns, and gargoyles. Ferret also designed at least two other public buildings now on the *National Register of Historic Places.*

2. *Sun* **Building**
   252 West Fourth Street

Originally built for the Williamsport *Sun*, an afternoon daily established in 1870 by Levi Tate, the corner building was erected in the early 1900s and the old press building at the rear in 1926. Another paper, started by William F. Buyers in 1801, was the Lycoming *Gazette*. In the 1860s, the *Gazette* merged with the West Branch *Bulletin* to become the *Gazette and Bulletin*, an afternoon daily. In 1955 the Sun merged with the *Gazette and Bulletin*, creating the *Sun-Gazette*. Based on this lineage, the *Sun-Gazette* is the twelfth oldest newspaper in the nation and the fourth oldest in Pennsylvania. Art Deco terra-cotta sculptures add color and interest to the façade.

3. **Williamsport Municipal Water Authority**
   Business Office
   253 West Fourth Street

This is one of several flatiron buildings built in the city to make full use of wedge-shaped tracts of land, all squat emulations of New York City's iconic twenty-story Flatiron Building. The blocked-off garage doors and plate-glass windows betray the building's origins as an auto dealership.

WALK SOUTH DOWN WEST STREET ALONG THE MUNICIPAL WATER BUILDING. TURN LEFT ON WEST THIRD STREET.

4. **The** *Grit* **Building**
   200-222 West Third Street

The *Grit* began in 1882 as a Saturday afternoon supplement to the *Daily Sun and Banner*. Printer Dietrick Lamade bought out his partner in 1884 and turned the *Grit* into an independent Sunday newspaper that grew to become known as "American's greatest family newspaper." Avoiding the "yellow journalism" of post-Civil War newspapers and instead, catering to the rising Victorian middle class, the newspaper focused on the goals and values of a family-oriented audience. The paper remained in the Lamade family until it was sold and relocated to Topeka, Kansas, in 1992. The original building from 1892 on the corner was renovated for re-use. With its rounded arches, deep window and door reveals, and contrasting bands of colors, the building's façade reflects the uniquely American Romanesque Revival style of architect H.H. Richardson.

5. **The Old Jail**
   154 West Third Street

On the northeast corner stands the second Lycoming County Jail, built after fire destroyed the original structure that had served the county since 1799. Impressive for its day, the 1868 jail, designed by York architect Edward Haviland, could, if need be, hold as many as 138 prisoners. Hangings took place in the courtyard until 1914 when the gallows were removed and burned. The Old Jail shows the 19th century fondness for medieval architectural styles, though its original Norman-inspired battlements and tower have been removed. In 2001, the Old Jail was converted into The Cell Block, a club with live music in "The Gallows."

6. **A.H. Heilman Company Building**
   101 West Third Street

In the 1990s, the removal of corrugated siding covering the front of this building, including the windows, revealed this attractive building designed by T.J. Litzelman in 1912. Heilman specialized in fine rugs and carpets and, before its 1929 closing, outfitted some of the grandest homes and hotels in the Northeast. The building subsequently housed a furniture company, then a dry goods firm, and then the Carroll House, a department store, which closed in 1977, following the movement of many downtown businesses to suburban malls.

7. First National Bank Building
21-25 West Third Street

This was Williamsport's tallest commercial building when it was erected in honor of the bank's fiftieth anniversary. On opening day of Williamsport's first "skyscraper" in 1913 citizens had an opportunity to ride up the elevator for their first aerial views of the city.

8. The Hart Building
26-30 West Third Street

The Hart Brothers ran a successful men's clothing store on this spot in the late 19th century. They hired Amos Wagner (an architect who designed two homes and Annunciation Church on Millionaires' Row) in 1895 to design this existing Hart Building for commercial trade. The building was added to the *National Register of Historic Places* in 1984.

9. The Charles C. Mussina Building
18 West Third Street

Jacob Mussina, a 23-year old trained watchmaker, opened a jewelry store in 1830. He was responsible for keeping the courthouse clock in working order. Mussina became adept with new technologies, becoming Williamsport's first telegraph operator in 1851 with machinery he installed in his store. In 1858, he built a new store on the northeast corner of Market Square. After he retired in the 1870s, his son Sylvester took over the store and another son, Charles C. Mussina, built his own store on the northwest corner of the square. The exterior of the Charles C. Mussina building was restored in 2003. The Mussina family has remained in the area over the generations; today the best-known member of the family, Mike Mussina, was a star pitcher for the Baltimore Orioles and New York Yankees before retiring in 2008.

10. The Ulman Opera House
2 East Third Street

This 1867 cultural landmark was built in the imposing Second Empire style popular during the second half of the nineteenth century. On New Year's Eve of 1869, Samuel Clemens (Mark Twain) appeared here to promote his most recent book, *The Innocents Abroad*. Among other popular entertainments presented here was Buffalo Bill's Wild West Show. Still-life artist Severin Roesen had a studio in this building, and artist George Luks, one of the Ashcan Eight, was born in a building across the street.

11. Moose Lodge
33 East Third Street

The first Moose Lodge on this site was a former doctor's office purchased by the group in 1917 and destroyed by fire in 1939. After the Moose Lodge moved to South Williamsport in the 1990s three partners purchased the building, renovated it to emphasize its Art Deco features, and turned it into an upscale restaurant. The "33" medallion on the façade covers the original bas-relief sculpture of a moose.

12. First Presbyterian Church
102 East Third Street

The First Presbyterian Church houses what may be one of the unluckiest congregations in the area. The original structure, built in 1842 on the northwest corner of Market and Willow Streets, was destroyed by fire in 1849. A second church, built in 1849, burned down in 1859 and was replaced by a third structure that parishioners used until 1884 when the congregation decided to build the present church, which has remained intact at this location. Built for a congregation of prominent Victorians, the church's polychromatic exterior and pointed arches show their taste for Victorian Gothic.

TURN LEFT AND WALK NORTH ON MULBERRY STREET.

13. The Gamble-Reighard Residence
330 Mulberry Street

This 1875 house was the first of Mary White's wedding-gift houses; when she remarried after the death of her first husband, her new spouse built her a home on Millionaires' Row (835 W. 4th St.). Mary's first husband was Judge Gamble's son, James M. Gamble, Jr. During his short life – he died at age 44 – he served as president of the Williamsport Water Company, director of the Bald Eagle Valley Railroad Co., and director of the Lycoming National Bank. In 1889, another one of Judge Gamble's children, Elizabeth, moved into the house with her husband, Oliver H. Reighard, a Williamsport native and lawyer. With its slender proportions and flat, gently pitched roof with wide eaves and brackets, the house presents trademarks of the Italian Villa style. The porches and cupola of the original house have been removed, and the house has undergone many changes since its "unwrapping" as a young bride's wedding gift.

14. Judge James Gamble House
106 East Fourth Street; southeast corner of Mulberry Street

This 1869 Greek Revival residence built by prominent Williamsport resident Judge Gamble displays later additions of Victorian trim. Born on a homestead farm near Jersey Shore, Judge Gamble enjoyed a successful career as a Congressman and as an attorney, moving to Williamsport in 1868 to serve as president judge of Lycoming County. Judge Gamble presided over the controversial "Sawdust War" trial that followed a 22-day lumber mill strike during the summer of 1872. Striking workers hoped to reduce their workday from more than twelve hours to ten for the same amount of pay. Twenty-seven men were arrested during strike-related riots. Judge Gamble convicted 21 men to terms in the county jail and four leaders to one-year terms in the federal penitentiary. In response to a petition signed by community citizens, the Governor pardoned the men two days later and none served time.

15. Christ Episcopal Church
426 Mulberry Street

Founded in 1840, the Christ Church congregation held its first service in this building in 1869. Both the interior and the exterior are excellently crafted with hand-carved woodwork and stained glass windows by Tiffany and Lamb. The church's Reverend Dr. John Henry Hopkins, Jr., who served as rector from 1876 to 1887, penned the words and music of the famous Christmas carol, "We Three Kings of Orient Are." The stumpy – but interesting – church steeple may not be a peaked European-style Gothic steeple, but the polychromatic details mark this magnificent edifice as a fine example of Victorian Gothic architecture.

TURN LEFT AND WALK WEST ON EAST FOURTH STREET.

16. Elks Lodge
36 East Fourth Street

The Williamsport Chapter of the Elks moved from their Victorian home on West Third Street to this building, which they occupied until 1971. Finished in 1927, it seems to have been Williamsport's last major building project to be completed before the beginning of the Great Depression. With the conversion or destruction of the major theaters in town, the Elks auditorium provided the city's largest space dedicated to live performances in the 1930s.

17. The William Howard Memorial Masonic Temple and Acacia Club
southeast corner of East Fourth Street and Market Street

This group of interconnected structures extends across a quarter of a block south of the Brown Library. The Masonic Temple, which faces Market Street, was built in 1898. A prominent Mason, William Howard, born in Yorkshire, England moved to Williamsport in 1854 and became a successful lumberman. His will provided for the Howard Memorial Cathedral, facing East Fourth Street, which was built in 1901. The Acacia Club, built in 1910, is frequently booked for weddings and other receptions.

18. James V. Brown Library
19 East Fourth Street

The James V. Brown Library was a bequest to the city from lumber baron and philanthropist James Van Duzee Brown who died on December 8, 1904, at age 78. Already a widower with no children, Brown had dreamt for years of giving Williamsport a free, public library.

James V. Brown came from a large family in New York state, and was a descendant of the family that founded Brown University in Providence, Rhode Island. Arriving in Williamsport in 1859, he worked in the printing and flour mill trades, then went into lumbering where he made his fortune as a partner in the Brown, Early & Company Lumber Mill. As president of the Williamsport Water Company he masterminded the development of the city's water system. He was also president of the Citizen Gas Company, an original stockholder of the Market Street Bridge (it was a privately owned toll bridge), a controlling stockholder of the *Gazette Bulletin* newspaper, the Central PA Telephone Company, and organizer of First National Bank.

Designed by architect Edgar V. Seeler and built on the site of James' brother Henry's residence, the library opened its doors to the public on June 17, 1907. Seeler studied at the Ecole des Beaux-Arts in Paris, bringing the classical detail of the popular style to the library.

TURN RIGHT ON MARKET STREET.

19. 433-445 Market Street

These structures may have been among the earliest brick buildings to be built in downtown. Their symmetrical design, with matching chimneys at either end, smooth brick facades, and lintel-type window heads are typical features of the Federal style. These sites have been occupied at least since 1866, when the first city directories were published. In the 1880s several doctors had their offices here, including one of the region's first women physicians, Dr. Phoebe H.F. Hagenbuch. Number 445, which has modern brick facing, housed a German-owned bakery from about 1910 into the 1930s. After a hiatus when it served as a real estate office and barber shop, it became Joanna's Italian Bakery.

TURN LEFT ON EDWIN STREET. TURN LEFT ON PINE STREET.

20. Rialto Theatre
470 Pine Street

The Rialto was the most expensive movie theater in town and boasted the city's largest outdoor sign on its southern side when it opened in 1927. The architecture is a pastiche of Neoclassical Revival early Art Deco styles. In the late nineteenth century Miss Wilson's Private School for Young Ladies and children stood on the site.

21. Old City Hall
454 Pine Street

A signature piece of architect Eber Culver, the Old City Hall is located on the former site of the Ross Park Cemetery that was sadly neglected on the northwestern edge of the Victorian business district. During a tour promoting his new book, Mark Twain spotted it, and, disgusted by its neglect, wrote a newspaper article entitled, "Remarkable Dream," which records the thoughts of a disgruntled resident of the cemetery, though Twain omitted Williamsport's name. The remains in the cemetery were later moved. This beautiful Victorian Romanesque building is a fine example of 19th century taste. The statue in front is the *Sailors and Soldiers Monument* erected as a tribute to the men who served in the Civil War.

22. Updegraff Hotel
southeast corner of West Fourth Street and Pine Street

Daniel Updegraff (brother of abolitionist Abraham) built this hotel in 1892, the largest of its day in the city, on the site of the old Hepburn Inn, where abolitionist Fredrick Douglass spoke in the 1870s. The old structure may have provided temporary shelter to runaway slaves before the Civil War. The Updegraff family eventually sold the building which became the Ross Hotel. The hotel is now the Center City Building, but its distinctively Second Empire-style façade and gabled roof remain.

TURN RIGHT AND WALK WEST ON WEST FOURTH STREET.

23. West Branch Bank Building
102 West Fourth Street

With its Corinthian columns, monumental arched windows and entrances, and marble façade, this 1917 building is a fine local example of Beaux-Arts classicism. The building's original dome is gone, and the demolition of the J.C. Penney store to make room for a parking lot left the brick wall exposed on the western side of the building. The bank's president, Abraham Updegraff, was a prominent abolitionist active in the Underground Railroad.

24. The Genetti Hotel
200 West Fourth Street

The Lycoming Hotel, as it was originally known, held an opening ball for invited dignitaries, including a Pullman car full of guests from New York City, on June 21, 1922, just one of a three-day slate of activities to celebrate the completion of the most modern hotel in Pennsylvania. The hotel was built as a community project through the efforts of the Williamsport Board of Trade, which hired New York architect William Lee Stoddart, who went on to design hotels in North Carolina and Virginia that are on the *National Register of Historic Places*.

25. Community Arts Center
220 West Fourth Street

The Capitol Theatre, the grandest movie theater of its day, was built on the site of the historic Sterling Hotel, damaged by a 1924 fire. The first local theater to be equipped for "talkies," it opened with *The Singing Fool* starring Al Jolson, accompanied by a visiting organist. It went through several owners and closings for the next few decades and finally closed for good as a movie theater in 1990. After restoration efforts, a new five-story structure replaced the outer lobby. The post-modern, two-toned brick façade blends in with the older buildings on the street, while the bold marquee is a modern interpretation of the streamlined Art Deco style of the theater's original era.

CONTINUE WALKING PAST THE TOUR START ONTO MILLIONAIRES' ROW THAT BEGINS ON WEST FOURTH STREET ACROSS HEPBURN STREET.

26. A.D. Hermance House
405 West Fourth Street

The Hermance House, designed in a Romanesque style, is constructed of gray limestone with a red slate roof. It was built in 1885 for industrialist Albert Hermance, who made his fortune on manufacturing woodworking machinery at the Rowley and Hermance Machine Company.

27. Peter Herdic House
407 West Fourth Street

Peter Herdic's classic Italianate home is constructed of brick and covered with stucco. The highly unique porch columns are executed with Lotus Petal motifs. This is the earliest surviving residence from the lumber era, built in 1855. Herdic himself was one of the premier influences on West Fourth Street and Williamsport in general. Along with his architect, Eber Culver, Herdic was responsible for such structures as the A. D. Hermance House, the Weightman Block, and the "Herdic House" located at the intersection of Campbell and Fourth Streets, which is considered the center of the district. The Herdic House (now known as the Park Home) was a four-story, brick, Italianate Hotel that served the well-to-do guests of Williamsport. Directly behind the hotel was the Pennsylvania Railroad Station, which Herdic was able to locate there in order to service his hotel and restaurant.

28. Lemuel Ulman House/Peter Herdic Inn
411 West Fourth Street

Moses Ulman's Sons was a clothier and hatter operating on West Third Street. This was the home of Lemuel, who worked in the family business. Now a bed and breakfast, the house contains many original gas light fixtures.

29. Church of the Covenant
436 West Fourth Street

Originally Church of the Covenant when it was built in 1893 and more recently St. Paul's Lutheran Church, this limestone structure has a center spire, bell tower, and steeply pitched roof with stone finials. The windows are pointed and arched. It has the largest expanse of Tiffany stained glass in northcentral Pennsylvania. Note the arched entryway with decorative insets.

30. Lewis Jameson House
508 West Fourth Street

Built for lumberman Lewis Jameson in 1875, this rambling clapboard house is in the Stick Style with Gothic and Queen Anne influences. Look for multiple window shapes - arched, flat and round. It once sported a cupola and tower extension; both have been removed.

31. J.N. Kline House
519 West Fourth Street

This Neoclassical home with prominent two-story portico fronted by fluted Ionic columns was built for hardware dealer J.N. Kline in 1910. There are pilasters at the entry, door sidelights and an overhead transom.

32. Hiram Rhoads House
522 West Fourth Street

The Queen Anne-style mansion of Hiram Rhoads is one of the best preserved homes in the district. Eber Culver designed it in 1888 with bejeweled windows, gilded bronze door hardware and magnificent woods of cherry, pecan and mahogany. Among the many features are front doors with unusual stained glass design, hallway and staircase of hand-carved mahogany, five fireplaces, upstairs bathtub encased in mahogany, solid pecan floor in the living room, and the most magnificent chandeliers in Williamsport. In 1878 Rhoads led a team of investors to bring the first telephone exchange to Williamsport and only the second in the Commonwealth (behind Erie). He made a fortune in the telephone and transportation industries but died only six years after this house was built.

33. Dubois House
525 West Fourth Street

This vibrant Italianate Victorian was designed in 1870 by Eber Culver. Features of the style include a low-pitched roof with overhanging eaves, large brackets, corner quoins, a central tower and decorative panels on the cornice.

34. Emery Cottage
535 West Fourth Street

Another Eber Culver design, this time a Queen Anne built in 1888. The corner turret is covered in fish-scale siding. The hefty red stone lentils over the doors and windows and a similar stone belt course stand out. William V. Emery was a lumberman who started out in the mercantile grocery trade.

35. Walter Bowman House
619 West Fourth Street

This Queen Anne style house has a wrap-around porch, columns and pedimented front. Notable in the 1894 house is a multi-gabled roof with soaring chimneys and dormers highlighted by fish-scale trim. The gables are stucco and wood. the protruding bay on the northeast is topped with a battlement. There is a carriage porch on the east side and a carriage house in the rear. Bowman was an influential lumber mill owner and champion of professional baseball in Williamsport; Bowman Field, the second oldest field in the minor leagues, is named for him.

36. Smith/Ulman House
634 West Fourth Street

The largest Second Empire home in the district is from Philadelphia architect Isaac Hobbs. Look for the large brackets, heavy detail, and flared mansard roof. Henry B. Smith was a Maine native who made his Williamsport fortune in lumber; later it was home to the Moses Ulman family.

37. Annunciation Church
700 West Fourth Street

Built in 1886, this church has 43 arched stained-glass windows. The center tower was capped and construction of a planned spire stopped when three builders fell to their deaths. The interior has marble altars and Tiffany windows. Designed in the Romanesque style by Amos Wagner on land donated by Peter Herdic, the local Irish community used Ralston Quarry sandstone to build this church.

38. Rowley House
707 West Fourth Street

This spectacular 1888 Queen Anne house of E. A. Rowley still sports its original design and the interior has had its marble fireplaces, stained glass and woodwork well maintained. Architect Eber Culver used carved wood gables, protruding corner bay, projecting dormer and massive turned porch posts. The roof has patterned slates, metal ridge caps, tall, decorative chimneys and large overhanging eaves. Opened to the public as a Victorian House Museum in 2007, the cherry and oak woodwork is in excellent condition, and the electric light fixtures are extremely rare.

39. Elias Deemer House
711 West Fourth Street

Another Eber Culver creation in the Queen Anne style, this 1880 home displays large wraparound porches, delicate spindlework, a gabled roof with a bay and wood panels and roof dormer. The brick contains subtle patterns and chimneys are tall and decorative.

40. Addison Candor House
741 West Fourth Street

There is a clipped roof gable on the west side of this 1888 brick home built for lawyer Addison Candor. The roof dormers have contrasting gable styles: Gothic, Stick and Italianate. The patterned brick heads feature a dark belt in the wall courses.

41. Herdic/Weightman Opera Block
754-770 West Fourth Street

In 1871 Peter Herdic hired Eber Culver to design this commercial block in the Italian style with arched window heads, bracketed cornice roof, patterned brick between floors and decorative stone on the first floor. Each floor has a different style window lentil. Built without steel beams, it has 16-inch thick plaster walls and 18-foot high ceilings. After Herdic went bankrupt the project was taken over by Weightman.

42. Heredic House Hotel
800 West Fourth Street

This brick Italianate Railroad Hotel once had four stories and rooms for 700 guests. The top two stories have been removed since its salad days. The hotel has massive paired brackets supporting the eaves, decorative carved, arched lentils and brick quoins. The Eber Culver creation was saved from demolition in 2001.

43. Covenant Central Church
807 West Fourth Street

This stone building with red tile roof was designed in the Richardsonian Romanesque style in 1906. The many arched, stained glass windows are accompanied by thick window lentils. The large, semicircular arched entries and three doors are topped with stained glass fanlights.

44. Parsons House
829 West Fourth Street

In the 1880s a 20-year old house was reborn in the Queen Anne style with large porch and multi-gabled slate roof. The hand-carved cherry front door has leaded sidelights. The roof dormers have fish-scale siding and mullioned windows.

45. Emery House
835 West Fourth Street

This house was an 1889 wedding gift for Mary White Gamble Emery. The exterior walls are rock-faced course Ashlar. The building has a tower and deep-set windows. Look for stained glass fanlights, arched windows with stone lentils and gabled roof with a stepped front.

46. Trinity Episcopal Church
844 West Fourth Street

Built in 1875 with stone from the Bald Eagle Mountain at Muncy and brownstone from Hum-

425

melstown, it has the first nine bell Westminster chimes in America and a mural by Westly Little. The church was paid for by Peter Herdic and given to Trinity Parish for one dollar as long as the pews remain "forever free." Note the pointed arches and windows, steeply pitched colored slate roof and 265-foot spire.

47. Hinckley House
870 West Fourth Street

Many building materials are used at this home; brick on the first floor, tile on the second and wooden fish scales on the gables. It has a multi-gabled slate roof, ornamented chimneys and a protruding bay on the southeast corner. The porch on the 1880 house was pulled off and the current one is not original.

48. LeVan House
878 West Fourth Street

This stylish Second Empire house was built in 1865 by Peter Herdic and sold to his accountant. Mr. LeVan was the 3rd owner. Elements of the Second Empire style include deep cove moldings and center medallions in the interior with double front doors with etched glass It retains the original stucco.

49. Johnson-Lamade House
901 West Fourth Street

Designed in 1890 by Amos Wagner and built for Henry Johnson, a state legislator from Muncy. Johnson moved to the city to help his six daughters find suitable husbands among the wealthy men of Williamsport. This home represents the Queen Anne style of architecture. The Johnsons were so pleased with Wagner's work they had him build a similar home next door on Maynard Street for one of their daughters.

50. Foresman House
912 West Fourth Street

This Colonial Revival mansion is one of the last built on Millionaires Row, having been erected in 1907. The brick is laid in Flemish bond. The four imposing Ionic columns are 74 inches at the base and 18 feet high. The 15-foot entrance has

sidelights and a transom. The Dutch-inspired gambrel roof has slate with wood shingle roof dormers and a protruding two-story bay on the west side.

51. Harrar House
915 West Fourth Street

This house was another wedding gift. Eber Culver got the commission from the parents of Lucy Eutermarks in the early 1870s and delivered this Italianate design. The house was originally assigned 913 West Fourth Street, but the bride's parents, thinking this was unlucky, had the house number changed to 915. The brick mansion has been pared down over the years, surrendering a cupola and an extensive porch.

52. Foresman-Cleveden Mansion
949/951 West Fourth Street

When built in 1865 this 50-room brick mansion was designed in the French Second Empire style with a mansard roof. A third story and a Queen Anne roof were added after a fire in 1885. It has arched windows with Italianate lentils, multiple gables with red tile cresting and decorative wood, dormers and a second floor cornice. The stained glass windows feature portraits of Mozart and Milton.

53. Herdic Double
942-944 West Fourth Street

To attract families to West Fourth Street, Peter Herdic built many double houses; this is from 1875. The double houses typically had a mansard roof and protruding central bay with a cupola on top. This home has stone corner quoins and decorative chimneys. The west side has arched windows, the east side has rectangular windows. The front porch trims differ now but once were mirror images of one another.

TURN AROUND AND WALK BACK DOWN WEST FOURTH STREET TO THE TOUR STARTING POINT.

Look Up,

York

A Walking Tour of York...

York was the first town laid out west of the Susquehanna River. In 1741, Thomas Cookson, a surveyor for the Penn family, plotted a town site of 446 acres in the heart of the family's Springettsbury Manor. This tract had been laid out for Springett Penn, a grandson of William Penn, in 1722.

Cookson staked out straight streets, a generous 80 feet in width on each side of the junction of the Monocacy Road and the Codorus Creek. Squares measured 480 feet by 500 feet and provision was made for the location of public buildings in the very center of the town on a tract 110 feet square, now known as Continental Square. York can be considered one of the first instances of thoughtful city planning. The streets were assigned the English names of High (now Market, "High" was the traditional English moniker for a town's main street), King, George, Duke, Queen, and Princess. The town itself was called York, after York, England. Along with the name, the town founders adopted the symbol of the English city, the white rose, while the neighboring city of Lancaster similarly adopted the red rose.

The town of York did not fill up rapidly; although its framing was English, most of the first settlers were Germans. York was originally governed as a part of Lancaster County but the distance from judge and jail encouraged thieves to operate with impugnity. A petition of the citizens for a separate county was granted in 1749 and York became the first county west of the Susquehanna River, and the fifth in Pennsylvania. A colonial courthouse was ready by 1756 and next door was a market house.

During the American Revolution, when British General Howe's armies occupied Philadelphia in September, 1777, the members of Continental Congress fled to Lancaster, where they remained but one day. Then, feeling that they would be safer with the Susquehanna between them and the British, they crossed at Wrights' Ferry and resumed sessions in the Colonial Courthouse in the tiny frontier town of York. They stayed nine months and when the Articles of Confederation, a provisional plan of government in which the term "United States of America" was first used, were adopted here York laid claim to being the nation's first capital. In 1789, Congressman Thomas Hartley, speaking before Congress, took a swing at making York the permanent capital of the United States but the honor was ticketed further south, along the Potomac River.

Our walking tour will begin amidst the historical relics of the 18th century and transition through the impressive York architecture that reflects the prosperous 19th century industrial community it became...

1. **Colonial Courthouse Replica**
   201 West Market Street, at northwest corner of Pershing Avenue

With the British capture of Philadelphia in 1777 the Continental Congress took refuge in York. It served as the nation's capital from September 30, 1777, to June 27, 1778, although never more than half the 64 delegates were in residence at any one time. On November 15, 1777, the Congress adopted the Articles of Confederation here, giving York the foundation to claim itself as "the first capital of the United States." It was also in York that Congress learned that France was to throw its support to the colonies, and they also took time to issue the first National Thanksgiving Proclamation, giving thanks not so much for a bumper harvest but for news that the Continental Army had dealt the British a critical setback in Saratoga, New York.

The original York County Courthouse was constructed in 1756 and stood in what is now known as Continental Square (then called "Centre Square"). It was renovated in 1815 and torn down in 1841. A replica of the symmetrical Georgian brick building was erected beside the Codorus Creek for America's Bicentennial celebration in 1976. Sitting atop the cupola is a silhouette weathervane made in honor of Polish Count Casimir Pulaski that topped the original courthouse. Pulaski came to York as a general in the American Revolution, enlisting troops from a recruiting station on George Street. Leaving York, he marched his new recruits to Georgia where he was fatally wounded in Savannah leading a cavalry charge.

WALK OVER TO THE CODORUS CREEK AND LOOK AT THE HOTEL CODORUS ON THE SOUTH SIDE OF MARKET STREET.

2. **Hotel Codorus**
   226 West Market Street

This 1904 hotel with a mansard roof was dilapidated, ravaged by time and raging flood waters in 1933. Today you can admire an award-winning restoration job.

TURN AND WALK EAST ON MARKET STREET.

3. **Golden Plough Tavern**
   157 West Market Street, at northeast corner of Pershing Avenue

The oldest standing building in York, it was built in 1741 by Martin Eichelberger, a native of the German Black Forest. Its massive hewn half-timbers reflect a style almost unknown today, of medieval architecture. Roman numerals carved in each wood section helped carpenters assemble timbers after cutting. The Golden Plough served as a meeting place, hotel and tavern for travelers well into the 1800s.

4. **Gates House**
   157 West Market Street

Although carrying the name of General Horatio Gates, president of the Board of War during the American Revolution, he was only a boarder. It was built in 1751 in the Georgian style using stone and brick. Tradition holds that the Marquis de Lafayette attending dinner in this house, toasted the health of General George Washington and disrupted a plot to overthrow Washington known as the Conway Cabal. The "toast" is more myth than fact, and most historians today dispute that the Cabal was anything more than a letter-writing campaign of several disgruntled officers and Congressional delegates. Noteworthy architectural features include the balanced front façade, pent roof, end chimneys, and central hall floor plan.

5. **York Gas Company**
   127 West Market Street

This Beaux Arts building is distinguished by a decorative façade with wreath festoons, a modillion course and a dentil course, and foliate brackets with cartouche.

6. Bon-Ton Department Store
100 West Market Street, at southwest corner of Beaver Street

The Bon-Ton was started in 1898, when Max Grumbacher and his father, Samuel, opened S. Grumbacher & Son, a one-room millinery and dry goods store on Market Street. It has since grown into a retailing empire of nearly 300 stores in 23 states. This location was the site of the first printing press west of the Susquehanna River, the Hall & Sellers Press. It was used to print Continental currency while Congress met in York.

John A. Dempwolf, a popular local architect, adapted the Chicago-style for this department store in 1911. The style was popular for department stores allowing large quantities of natural lighting from expansive windows. A restoration in 1992 by the York county government returned the building to its original grandeur.

7. National House
53 West Market Street

The original section of this landmark hotel building dates to 1828 when it operated as the White Hall Hotel. Martin Van Buren, one of only two people to serve as Secretary of State, Vice President and President, stayed here two years after he left office in 1839 and Charles Dickens was a guest in 1842. The hotel was expanded and given an Italianate makeover in 1863. After a century of tinkering and alterations it was restored to its Civil War appearance in 1985.

8. Rosenmiller Building
37 West Market Street

John A. Dempwolf did most of the design work on this block and here his Rosenmiller Building, constructed in 1909, contains window keystones, modillions, and a classical entrance. Dressing up the commercial building are Beaux Arts elements along the roofline - a balustrade and sculptured centerpiece.

9. York Traction Company
27 West Market Street

This Art Noveau building was constructed in 1904 to house the operations of the York Traction Company that included street railways, electric companies, and York Steam Heating. After many decades in the stylistic wilderness the building has regained much of its decorative appearance.

10. Wall of History/Cherry Lane
21-23 West Market Street

The building adjacent to 27 West Market was razed in 1979 for the construction of Cherry Lane Park. Outlines of that building and earlier structures on the site are still visible on the neighboring brick facade. These structural ghosts, since dubbed "The Wall of History," display the architectural evolution of the city.

York County's cherries, both the sweet and the sour pie varieties, have been famous for generations. After more than fifteen years of research John A. C. Ziegler, Jr., and Horace B. Faber developed the first self-pollenating sweet cherry tree. The new hybrid was named the York Imperial Sweet Cherry.

11. Trinity United Church of Christ
32 West Market Street

York's first congressmen, Colonel Thomas Hartley lived on this site. The Trinity congregation dates to 1743, this church dates to 1865. 100 years later its solid cast iron cross was sent toppling to the ground by a bolt of lightning. The 700-pound cross was too heavy to be properly reinstalled so it has since been replaced with a light weight replica.

12. Fluhrer Building
17 West Market Street

John A. Dempwolf delivered this rare example of a Florentine Revival commercial building for Fluhrer Jewelers. The glazed terra-cotta building sparkles like the wares on display inside. The arches above the fourth-story windows mark the date the business was founded (1884) and the year the building was constructed (1911).

13. Rupp-Schmidt Building
   2 West Market Street

The Rupps became merchants in York in 1848. becoming successful enough to retain John Dempwolf in 1892 to design a six-story building for the family business. Dempwolf's Romanesque Revival design features a tower with pyramidal roof and rounded windows. Look for a brownstone bear on the facade that contains the date of construction and the name D.A. Rupp. H.S. Schmidt, purveyor of mens wear and president of the York Athletic Association, bought the building in 1919 and it remained in the Schmidt family until 1974. This was the site of the former Globe Inn, a hotel that played host to such notable guests as Marquis de Lafayette.

TURN RIGHT ON GEORGE STREET.

14. Colonial Hotel
   18 South George Street

There is little that is "colonial" in the Colonial Hotel. It was built in the late 1800s, not 1700s and architect John A. Demwolf created a French chateau-influenced hotel with 186 rooms and a top floor dining room for the York Hotel Company. The building once boasted a mansard roof with conical turrets but they were destroyed in a 1947 fire. The old hotel was renovated in the early 1980s to house professional offices and condominiums.

15. Christ Lutheran Church
   29 South George Street

The congregation of the Christ Lutheran Church, organized in 1733, is one of the oldest Lutheran congregations west of the Susquehanna River. This house of worship dates to 1812-14 and reflects the influence of Christopher Wren's English churches from the mid-1600s with Federal-style windows and tiered steeple.

16. Reineberg Shoes
   59 South George Street

The original Reineberg Shoe store opened down the street at 7 South George in 1890. The family moved the business to this location in the 1940s, into this smart Art Deco building. Reineberg is no longer fitting Florsheims here but the business is still providing personal shoe service in York.

17. Washington Hall
   100 South George Street

Also known as the Odd Fellows Hall, the Washington Hall was constructed in 1850. For many years it housed a theater on the second floor. The Greek Revival structure takes the form of an ancient temple with full-height Corinthian pilasters flanking the front façade.

RETRACE YOUR STEPS TO MARKET STREET AND TURN RIGHT.

18. Golden Swan Tavern
   2 East Market Street

This location served as a depository for flint lock muskets and rifles during the American Revolution. Benjamin Hersch constructed the brick building here as the Golden Swan Tavern around 1800. The tavern proprietor sold the business to Samuel Weiser in 1808 for use as a dry goods store.

19. Trolley Kiosk
   **Continental Square, northeast corner of
   George Street and Market Street**

This kiosk was used as a trolley dispatcher's office in Continental Square, near the end of the trolleys' run, which started in 1887. With its copper roof, it was known as the "Teapot Dome." After trolley service ended in 1939 the little building left Continental Square and began an epic journey. It was moved to a car barn and then purchased and moved to a parking lot on South George Street. Attorney J. Eugene Stumpf bought it and planted it in his back yard as a playhouse at 1465 Whiteford Road. Eventually the city reclaimed it and, with a broken base, rotting sides and a water-damaged roof, turned it over to the Kinsley Education Center for refurbishing.

The trolley kiosk was returned to its former location on Continental Square in 2009. And the best thing about it is that it won't be used as anything - just a reminder of days gone by.

20. First National Bank
1 North George Street, at northeast corner of Market Street

Dominating the northeast quadrant of Continental Square is the First National Bank Building, constructed in 1924. The bank was organized in 1864, as the cornerstone attests. The Beaux Arts styling incorporates classical features - double fluted Corinthian pilasters, roof balustrade - and a touch of Egyptian Revival symbolism in its prominent eagle overlooking Market Street. This building is located on the site of the National Treasury from 1777-1778, when the Continental Congress located in York.

21. York Trust Company
21 East Market Street

Reinhardt Dempwolf teamed with his brother John to design this beautiful Beaux Arts vault in 1910. The York Trust Company had been in business for twenty years at the time it moved into its new home behind colossal Ionic columns and a rusticated façade.

22. York County Courthouse
28 East Market Street

This is courthouse number three for York County. A replica of the first one was where the tour started; its replacement rose here in 1840. The ever-busy John Dempwolf was called in for a redesign in 1898 and he incorporated the Ionic columns you see today from that courthouse into his design. He topped the building with three distinctive domes inspired by the Florence (Italy) Cathedral. The classical domes feature both Corinthian and rectangular pilasters, sculptured leaf roof elements, window pediments, dentil course, and—in the main cupola—a bell. The new courthouse was initially covered in yellow brick, including the central portion of the 1840 building. The courthouse expanded in 1957, receiving east and west wings and a facade replacement in red brick.

23. Lafayette Club
53 East Market Street, at northwest corner of Duke Street

This Greek Revival home was built in 1839 for local businessman Philip A. Small. His company sold retail and wholesale dry goods and hardware. The house was purchased for an exclusive York club, founded in 1891, and named in honor of the Marquis de Lafayette.

24. Yorktowne Hotel
48 East Market Street, at southwest corner of Duke Street

York's grand hotel is truly an architectural treasure that belongs to the community. Knowing that the city needed a high quality, modern hotel in the 1920s, funds for the Yorktowne were raised through the sale of stock to the community. The Georgian Revival structure opened the doors to its 198 rooms on October 5, 1925. The building's red brick exterior is trimmed with ornamental terra-cotta. Design-wise, this building incorporates many features of the Renaissance Revival Style, including formal design, rusticated ground level, round arched windows with keystones, and roof balustrade. With the exceptions of the first floor and marquee, visitors today see the same visage that greeted excited guests in 1925.

TURN RIGHT ON DUKE STREET.

25. Rex and Laurel Fire Company
49 South Duke Street

First organized as the Sun Fire Company in 1770 and then as the Laurel Fire Company in 1790, this is one of the oldest continuously operating fire companies in the United States. This striking Italianate firehouse with Gothic highlights dates to 1878. Architectural features include high mansard roof, round and pointed arches, corner quoins, a heavy bracketed cornice, pediments over the garage doors, hood molds above the windows, paired arched windows, and modillions.

26. Motor Rose Motor Club
118 East Market Street

The White Rose Motor Club built their Art Moderne headquarters along the lines of the streamlined automobiles of the day in 1949. With rounded shapes and sleek stainless steel and smooth stone the building practically appears as if it is ready to pull out of its parking spot.

27. York Water Company
130 East Market Street

The York Water Company traces its origins to 1816 when water was carried from nearby streams in hollow logs. This Neoclassical temple use Egyptian-inspired columns inscribed with symbolic fountain and water scenes. The interior ceiling, executed by the Philadelphia Decorating Company n 1929, was restored to its original magnificence in 1995.

28. Bonham House
152 East Market Street

Horace Bonham was admitted to the bar and worked as a newspaper editor and a congressional aide before, at the age of 34, he went to Europe in February 1869 to study painting. He visited the great museums, met artists and sketched scenes wherever he traveled. He bought this house in 1875, remodeling and enlarging it over the years. Bonham is best remembered today as a genre painter who captured routine events with his brush; his work was unusual for its inclusion of diverse people in his scenes. Elizabeth Bonham, his oldest daughter, left the property to the Historical Society of York County in 1865.

29. The Brownstone
153 East Market Street

David E. Small, a railway car manufacturer, built this Italianate-style brownstone with corner quoins and arched windows with keystones in 1866. The interior parlor features elaborately painted wall and ceiling frescoes by Italian artist Philipo Costagini, famous for his work in the United States Capitol. In the 1940s a restaurant operated here, one of the first structures in York to be fully air-conditioned. Look for lighter colored patches on the facade, attempts to repair the notoriously fragile brownstone.

30. Martin Library
159 East Market Street

Built in 1935, the Martin Library is a beautiful design of Colonial Revival architecture by Frederick Dempwolf, continuing in his father John's architectural practice. The brick façade is highlighted by an Indiana limestone entrance. A graceful octagonal cupola, complete with weathervane, tops his creation.

31. First Presbyterian Church
201 East Market Street

This land was a gift of the Penn family to the English Presbyterian Congregation of Yorktown in 1785; the original church was holding services by 1793. This Gothic Revival expression in brick was constructed in 1860. A small chapel was added in 1931. Colonel James Smith, York's signer of the Declaration of Independence is buried in the church graveyard.

32. Charles Billmeyer House
225 East Market Street

Charles Billmeyer was a partner in the Billmeyer and Small Co., pioneer and leading builder of narrow gauge railroad cars in the United States, with David Small who built the Brownstone. Billmeyer constructed this exuberant Italian villa the same year as his partner's, 1866. It also features interior frescoes by U.S. Capitol painter Philipo Costagini. The building features prominent quoins, cast stone trim around the door, arched windows with hood mold and foliate keystone, multiple chimneys, and an oriel on the east side. The entire confection is topped with a cupola on the hipped roof. Now on the *National Register of Historic Places*, the Billmeyer house was slated for demolition in the 1970s before it underwent restoration for use as offices for the First Presbyterian Church.

33. Historical Society of York County Museum
250 East Market Street

This Colonial Revival building that houses the York County Heritage Trust was built in 1921 as the J. W. Richley Auto Company and you can still see the original checkered showroom floor when you walk in to explore the exhibits of the Historical Society's museum.

TURN LEFT ON PINE STREET. TURN LEFT ON PHILADELPHIA STREET.

34. William Goodridge House
123 East Philadelphia Street

William Goodridge, a former slave, became a prosperous merchant. He reportedly hid runaway slaves in a secret room in the cellar of this house and in straw-filled pits in what was then the backyard. Architect Reinhardt Dempwolf purchased the house in 1897 and gave it the Colonial Revival style seen today.

35. York *Dispatch* Newsroom Building
15 East Philadelphia Street

In the 1870s it became popular in large cities to use pre-fabricated cast iron as building facades. Often molded in Italianate style with ornate cornices and pilasters, cast iron cut the time of construction from months to weeks. The Variety Iron Works Plant in York provided many buildings with iron used just for that purpose. York's most outstanding example of a cast iron building is the York *Dispatch* Building, built in 1887. It resides on the *National Register of Historic Places*.

TURN LEFT ON GEORGE STREET.

36. Strand-Capitol Performing Arts Center
50 North George Street

The pulse of the cultural center of York beat through these two theaters which, although similar in appearance, were two distinct structures, both executed by Reinhardt Dempwolf. The Capitol, designed in the formal Renaissance Revival Style with rusticated ground level, distinct horizontal divisions, and roof balustrade, was built first, in 1917. The Strand followed in 1925, created in the Beaux Arts style. On both structures Dempwolf employed the concept of "piano nobile," placing visual emphasis on the second story.

Beginning with vaudeville and silent films, the Strand-Capitol was the destination for entertainment for Yorkers until the 1970s. Like downtown theaters everywhere, competition from suburban multiplexes killed the duo and a date with the wrecking ball loomed. But after a large capital fund drive, the previously deteriorated Strand-Capitol reopened in all its splendor on April 12, 1980.

TURN AROUND AND WALK NORTH ON GEORGE STREET, CROSSING PHILADELPHIA STREET.

37. Valencia Ballroom
142 North George Street

Opened in 1911 as The Coliseum Ballroom, the building is better known as The Valencia. In the 1930s it was recognized far and wide as one of the best ballrooms in the region, playing host to crowds of up to 2,000 people listening to the likes of Duke Ellington, Tommy Dorsey, Benny Goodman, and Frank Sinatra. The Valencia even had its own band, the Blue Moon Orchestra. The original façade was torn down in the early 1930s, replaced with an Art Deco influenced exterior. The grand ballroom was restored and reopened in the late 1980s.

RETURN TO PHILADELPHIA STREET AND TURN RIGHT.

38. Central Market
34 West Philadelphia Street

Intended as the heart of the city when it was built in 1887, the Central Market House remains so today. Its five towers with pyramidal roofs unite this Romanesque Revival Structure, which was designed by John A. Dempwolf.

39. Heidelberg United Church of Christ
47 West Philadelphia Street

This Neo-Gothic church was constructed in 1901 and is awash in pointed arches, pinnacles and battlements along the roofline.

40. Old York Post Office
55 West Philadelphia Street, at northeast corner of Beaver Street

This impressive Richardsonian Romanesque structure was built as a post office in 1895 but served less than two decades before a new downtown post office was erected on South George Street as a memorial to the Continental Congress in 1912. The heavy brownstone entrance arch is a defining trademark of the style. It has since been used as a Masonic hall and youth center.

TURN RIGHT ON NORTH BEAVER STREET.

41. Gethsemane Hall
115 North Beaver Street

After purchasing the old York post office next door the Masons built this unique stone Neo-Norman castle, complete with towers and battlement, as a Masonic temple in 1918.

42. The Episcopal Church of St. John the Baptist
140 North Beaver Street

The congregation first worshiped on this site in 1771. Portions of the walls of that original church are buried deep within this structure that has been enlarged several times - in 1839, 1865 and 1882. There is no resemblance between today's Gothic Victorian structure and its 18th century ancestor. York's Liberty Bell is housed in the church. Originally hung in the Colonial Courthouse, the bell was rung to signify the signing of the Declaration of Independence.

RETURN TO PHILADELPHIA STREET AND TURN RIGHT.

43. Friends Meeting House
135 West Philadelphia Street

The Willis family settled in York County in 1754 after a deed by Thomas Penn and Richard Penn granted 480 acres to fellow Quakers John Wright and James Wright and William Willis. The Wrights operated a ferry across the Susquehanna River and Willis farmed and made bricks. He won the contract to make the bricks for the York County courthouse. He completed the masonry work on the Meeting House in 1766 and was appointed overseer of the York meeting in 1768.

The meeting house has been in continuous use ever since and is associated in local histories with the underground railroad. John Elgar, who built the *Codorus*, America's first iron steamboat, is also buried in the churchyard. The *Codorus* was launched on the Susquehanna River in 1825.

TURN LEFT ON PERSHING AVENUE.

44. Barnett Bobb House
behind 157 West Market Street, east side of Pershing Avenue

Unlike many buildings in Lancaster and York counties influenced by Pennsylvania German architecture, the Barnett Bobb house is an English-style, squared-timber log home. Constructed in 1812, its distinctly English features include a symmetrical exterior façade, a central hall and corner fireplaces. Preservationists moved this structure to its present site from three blocks away to spare it from demolition.

YOU HAVE NOW RETURNED TO THE TOUR STARTING POINT.

IDENTIFYING AMERICAN ARCHITECTURE

Recognizing Early American Architecture (1600-1840):

POST-MEDIEVAL ENGLISH COLONIAL (1600-1700)

* steeply pitched, side-gabled roof
* small casement windows with many small panes (restored often)
* massive chimney
* vertical board (batten) door
* little or no eave overhang, no cornice detailing
* one room deep

DUTCH COLONIAL (1625-1840)

* side-gambreled roof
* usually one story
* batten door, most divided into upper and lower halves
* little or no eave overhang

FRENCH COLONIAL (1700-1830)

* steeply pitched roof, either hipped (four-sided) or side-gabled (two-sided)
* one story
* tall, narrow door and window openings
* doors and windows typically divided vertically into pairs
* walls of stucco (over half-timbered frame)

SPANISH COLONIAL (1660-1850)

* low-pitched or flat roof
* normally one story
* few small windows
* multiple external doors
* walls very thick in stucco over adobe brick or rubble stone
* long, narrow porches opening to courtyards

GEORGIAN (1700-1780)

* windows with double-hung sashes, typically nine or twelve small panes per sash; windows are never in adjacent pairs
* paneled door, normally with decorative crown (most often pedimented but at times broken-pedimented) and supported by decorative pilasters
* row of small rectangular panes beneath door crown
* cornice usually emphasized with tooth-like dentils or other decorative molding
* windows typically five-ranked and symmetrically balanced with center door; less commonly three-ranked or seven-ranked

ADAMESQUE (FEDERAL) (1780-1820)

* windows with double-hung sashes, typically six small panes per sash; windows are never in adjacent pairs
* semi-circular or elliptical fanlight over paneled door, typically accompanied by sidelights, elaborated crown and surround, and/or extended as small entry porch
* cornice usually emphasized with tooth-like dentils or other decorative molding
* windows typically five-ranked and symmetrically balanced with center door; less commonly three-ranked or seven-ranked
* while similar to Georgian, features are often "lighter"

GREEK REVIVAL (1825-1860)

* gabled or hipped roof of low pitch
* entry porch or full-width porch supported by square or round, prominent columns
  - *Doric*: plain capitals
  - *Ionic*: capitals with scroll-like spirals
  - *Corinthian*: capitals shaped like inverted bells decorated with leaves
* narrow line of transom and sidelights around door, usually incorporated into elaborate door surround
* cornice lines emphasized with wide, divided band of trim

Recognizing Victorian Architecture (1840-1910)

* roof ornaments
* bay (protruding) windows
* three-part Palladian (rounded in middle) windows
* gingerbread porch trim

GOTHIC REVIVAL STYLE (1835-1875)

* high-pitched center gables
* pointed arch windows and doors
* pendants and finials extending from roof

ITALIANATE STYLE (1840-1885)

* brackets under roof cornices
* cupolas on the roof
* narrow, square porch posts with chamfered corners
* tall, slender windows

SECOND EMPIRE STYLE (1855-1885)

* mansard roof, concave or convex, with dormer windows on steep lower slope
* molded cornices bound lower roof slope above and below
* eaves normally with decorative brackets below

Stick Style (1860-1890)

* stick-like bracketing on porches, often diagonal or curving
* stick-like grid on wall surfaces
* Jerkin-Head (cut-off triangular) roofs and dormers
* pent (or shed) roofs on dormers, porches and bays
* decorative trusses in gables; often steeply pitched gross gables
* wooden wall cladding (boards or shingles)

Queen Anne (Eastlake) Style (1880-1910)

* asymmetrical facade
* patterned shingles
* turned porch posts and trim
* corner towers and turrets
* wraparound porch
* steeply pitched, irregular roofline

Shingle Style (1880-1900)

* shingled walls without interruption at corners
* multi-level eaves above asymmetrical facade
* extensive porches
* walls and roofs covered with continuous wood shingles

Richardsonian Romanesque (1880-1900)

* based on the innovative designs of Boston architect Henry Hobson Richardson
* round topped arches over windows, porch supports or entrance
* most have towers, usually round with conical roofs
* always masonry walls, usually with rough-faced, squared stonework
* facade usually asymmetrical

Recognizing 20th century Architecture:

Colonial Revival (1885 and beyond)

* accentuated front door with fanlights and sidelights
* symmetrical facade around centered entrance
* windows with double-hung sashes
* large dormers
* round, smooth porch columns, often clustered

Neoclassical (1895-1950)

* facade dominated by full-length porch supported by classical columns, typically Ionic or Corinthian
* facade shows symmetrically balanced windows and center door
* revivals may have curved porticos, two-story entrances, paired or tripled windows and/or bays not seen on originals
* often very large

Tudor (1890 -1940)

* massive chimneys, commonly crowned by decorative chimney pots
* facade dominated by one or more prominent cross gables, usually steeply perched
* decorative half-timbering often present
* steeply pitched roof, usually side-gabled
* tall, narrow windows, commonly in multiple groups with multi-pane glazing
* walls of brick, stone, wood, stucco or in combination

French Chateauesque (1890-1930)

* busy roof line with many vertical elements (spires, pinnacles, turrets, gables, shaped chimneys)
* steeply pitched hipped roof
* multiple dormers, usually wall dormers extending through cornice line
* walls of masonry, usually stone

Beaux Arts (1890-1930)

* wall surfaces with decorative garlands, floral patterns or shields
* masonry walls, usually of light-colored stone
* facade with corner quoins and columns, often paired with Ionic or Corinthian capitals
* first story typically rusticated (stonework) with exaggerated joints
* facade symmetrical

Spanish Mission Style (1890-1930)

* shaped Mission dormer or roof parapet
* porch roofs supported by large square piers, commonly arched above
* commonly with red tile roof covering
* widely overhanging eaves, usually open
* wall surface usually smooth stucco

Pueblo Revival (1910-present)

* flat roof with parapeted wall above
* stucco wall surface, usually earth-toned
* projecting wooden roof beams (vigas)
* wall and roof parapet with irregular, rounded edges
* unpainted wood porch columns - maybe just tree trunks
* tile or brick floors

Prairie Style (1900-1920)

* low-pitched roof with widely overhanging eaves
* two stories with one-story porches or wings
* massive square porch supports
* detail emphasizing horizontal lines
* hipped roofs are more common than end or side gables
* one of few indigenous American styles developed by Chicago architects Louis Sullivan and Frank Lloyd Wright and built only during first two decades of century

CRAFTSMAN (1905-1930)

* low-pitched gabled roof with wide, unenclosed eave overhang
* roof rafters usually exposed
* porches supported by square columns
* decorative braces or false beams under gables
* columns frequently continue to ground level without a break at porch level
* generally one or one-and-a-half stories

ART DECO (1920-1940)

* zigzags and other geometric and stylized motifs
* towers and other vertical projections
* smooth stucco wall surface
* decorative motifs: geometric floral; chevron with lozenge; reeding and fluting, often around doors and windows; sunrise pattern

ART MODERNE (1920-1940)

* streamline, curved corners
* smooth stucco wall surface
* asymmetrical facade
* flat roof, usually with ledge at roof line
* horizontal grooves, lines, balustrades
* windows can turn corners and can be roundly shaped
* glass-block windows or sections of the wall

INTERNATIONAL (1925-PRESENT)

* no decorative detailing at doors or windows
* smooth, unornamental wall surface
* asymmetrical facade
* flat roof, usually without ledge at roof line
* windows usually metal casements set flush with outer walls

Made in the USA
Middletown, DE
09 May 2015